THE PRACTICE OF COMPUTING USING

PYTHON

WILLIAM PUNCH

RICHARD ENBODY

Michigan State University

Addison-Wesley

Boston   Columbus   Indianapolis   New York   San Francisco   Upper Saddle River
Amsterdam   Cape Town   Dubai   London   Madrid   Milan   Munich   Paris   Montreal   Toronto
Delhi   Mexico City   Sao Paulo   Sydney   Hong Kong   Seoul   Singapore   Taipei   Tokyo

Editor-in-Chief: Michael Hirsch
Acquisitions Editor: Matt Goldstein
Editorial Assistant: Chelsea Bell
Marketing Coordinator: Kathryn Ferranti
Managing Editor: Jeffrey Holcomb
Production Project Manager: Heather McNally
Senior Manufacturing Buyer: Carol Melville

Image Interior Permission Coordinator:
  Silvana Attanasio
Art Director: Linda Knowles
Cover Designer: Elena Sidorova
Cover Art: John Lund/Getty Images
Full-Service Project Management: Kelly Ricci,
  Aptara® Corporation
Composition: Aptara® Corporation

Credits and acknowledgments borrowed from other sources and reproduced, with permission, in this textbook appear on appropriate page within text.

Microsoft® and Windows® are registered trademarks of the Microsoft Corporation in the U.S.A. and other countries. Screen shots and icons reprinted with permission from the Microsoft Corporation. This book is not sponsored or endorsed by or affiliated with the Microsoft Corporation.

The programs and applications presented in this book have been included for their instructional value. They have been tested with care but are not guaranteed for any particular purpose. The publisher does not offer any warranty or representation, nor does it accept any liabilities with respect to the programs or applications.

Many of the designations by manufacturers and sellers to distinguish their products are claimed as trademarks. Where those designations appear in this book, and the publisher was aware of a trademark claim, the designations have been printed in initial caps or all caps.

Library of Congress Cataloging-in-Publication Data

Punch, W. F. (William F.)
  The practice of computing using Python / W.F. Punch and R.J. Enbody.
      p. cm.
  Includes bibliographical references and index.
  ISBN-13: 978-0-13-611067-5 (alk. paper)
  ISBN-10: 0-13-611067-3 (alk. paper)
  1. Python (Computer program language)   2. Computer programming.   I. Enbody, Richard J.
II. Title.
  QA76.73.P98P92 2010
  005.13'3–dc22

                                                        2009051074

1 2 3 4 5 6 7 8 9 10—EB—14 13 12 11 10

Addison-Wesley
is an imprint of

PEARSON

www.pearsonhighered.com

ISBN 10: 0-13-611067-3
ISBN 13: 978-0-13-611067-5

To our long suffering spouses Laurie and Wendy,
our kids Zach, Alex, Abby, Carina and Erik,
and our parents.
We love you and couldn't have done this
without your love and support.

BRIEF CONTENTS

CONTENTS

PREFACE

A FIRST COURSE IN COMPUTER SCIENCE IS ABOUT A NEW WAY OF SOLVING PROBLEMS: computationally. As a result, the focus of a first course in computation should be on problem solving. Practically speaking, however, the teaching of problem solving is inexorably intertwined with the computer language used. Thus, the choice of language for this first course is very important.

We have chosen Python as the introductory language for beginning programming students—majors and nonmajors alike—based on our combined 30 years of experience teaching undergraduate introductory computer science at Michigan State University. Having taught the course in Pascal, C/C++, and now Python, we know that an introductory programming language should have two characteristics. First, it should be relatively simple to learn. Since a first course in programming is mostly about problem solving and learning to be more rigorous in applying problem solving to new problems, the programming language should get in the way as little as possible. Python's simplicity, powerful built-in data structures, and advanced control constructs allow students to focus more on problem solving and less on language issues. Second, it should be practical. Students should see that they might use what they are learning while they are learning it. Python supports learning not only fundamental programming issues such as typical programming constructs, a fundamental object-oriented approach, common data structures, and so on, but also more complex computing issues such as threads and regular expressions. Python can also be used to address practical problems such as Web access, database manipulation, and thousands of others from nearly any discipline imaginable using tools provided by an active and generous Python community (see http://pypi.python.org). From having taken *one* course in programming, a student—any student (major or not)—should walk away from a CS1 course and somewhere later in his or her career address a problem by thinking, "Hey, I'll just write a program to solve that." For us, that defines computational thinking. We have seen many examples of this kind of success every semester since the move to Python—in particular, students returning to tell us how useful Python has been to them in their studies and jobs.

We emphasize both the fundamental issues of programming and practicality by focusing on data manipulation and analysis as a theme—allowing students to work on real problems using either publicly available data sets from various Internet sources or self-generated data sets from their own work and interests. We also emphasize the development of programs, providing multiple, worked out, examples and three entire chapters for detailed design and implementation of programs. As part of this one-semester course, our students have analyzed breast cancer data, catalogued movie actor relationships, predicted disruptions of satellites from solar storms, and completed many other data analysis problems. We have also found that concepts learned in a Python CS1 course transitioned to a CS2 C++ course with little or no impact on either the class material or the students.

Our goals for the book are as follows:

1. Teach problem solving within the context of CS1 to both majors and nonmajors using Python as a vehicle.
2. Provide examples of *developing* programs focusing on the kinds of data analysis problems students might ultimately face.
3. Give students who take no programming course other than this CS1 course a practical foundation in programming, enabling them to produce useful, meaningful results in their respective fields of study.

BOOK ORGANIZATION

At the highest level our text follows a fairly traditional CS1 order, though there are some differences. For example, we cover strings rather early (before functions) so that we can do more data manipulation early on. We also include elementary file I/O early for the same reason, leaving detailed coverage for a later chapter. Given our theme of data manipulation, we feel this is appropriate. We also "sprinkle" topics like plotting and drawing throughout the text in service of the data manipulation theme.

We use an "object-use-first" approach where we use built-in Python objects and their methods early in the book, leaving the design and implementation of user-designed objects for later. We have found that students are more receptive to building their own classes once they have experienced the usefulness of Python's existing objects. In other words, we motivate the need for writing classes. Functions are split into two parts because of how Python handles mutable objects such as lists as parameters; discussion of those issues can only come after there is an understanding of lists as mutable objects.

Three of the chapters (3, 10, and 13) are primarily program design chapters, providing an opportunity to "tie things together," as well as showing how to design a solution. A few chapters are intended as supplemental reading material for the students though lecturers may choose to cover these topics as well. For background, we provide a Chapter 0 that introduces some general concepts of a computer as a device and some computer terminology. We feel such an introduction is important—everyone should understand a little about a computer, but this material can be left for reading. The last chapters in the text may not be reached in some courses.

BOOK FEATURES

Data Manipulation

Data manipulation is a theme. The examples range from text analysis to breast cancer classification. Along the way, we provide some analysis examples using simple graphing. To incorporate drawing and graphing, we use established packages instead of developing our own: one is built in (Turtle graphics); the other is widely used (matplotlib with numpy).

We have tried to focus on non-numeric examples in the book, but some numeric examples are classics for a good reason. For example, we use a rational numbers example for creating classes that overload operators. Our goal is always to use the best examples.

Problem Solving and Case Studies

Throughout the text, we emphasize problem solving, especially a divide-and-conquer approach to developing a solution. Three chapters (3, 10, and 13) are devoted almost exclusively to program development. Here we walk students through the solution of larger examples. In addition to design, we show mistakes and how to recover from them. That is, we don't simply show a solution, but show a *process of developing* a solution.

Code examples

There are over 180 code examples in the text—many are brief, but others illustrate piecemeal development of larger problems.

Interactive Sessions

The Python interpreter provides a wonderful mechanism for briefly illustrating programming and problem-solving concepts. We provide almost 250 interactive sessions for illustration.

Exercises and Programming Projects

Practice, practice, and more practice. We provide over 275 short exercises for students and nearly 30 longer programming projects (many with multiple parts).

Self-Test Exercises

Embedded within the chapters are 24 self-check exercises, each with 5 or more associated questions.

Programming Tips

We provide over 40 special notes to students on useful tips and things to watch out for. These tips are boxed for emphasis.

SUPPLEMENTARY MATERIAL ONLINE

- For students
  - All example source code
  - Data sets used in examples

The above material is freely available at www.pearsonhighered.com/cssupport.

- For instructors
  - PowerPoint slides
  - Laboratory exercises
  - Figures (PDF) for use in your own slides
  - Exercise solutions

Qualified instructors may obtain supplementary material by visiting www.pearsonhighered.com/irc. Register at the site for access. You may also contact your local Pearson Education representative or send e-mail to computing@aw.com.

Python 2.x versus 3.x

The text is based on Python 2.x (for x > = 6) rather than Python 3.x since the latter is not backward compatible with standard Python packages at this time. In an appendix we outline the differences. For what we cover in the text, the differences are trivial, but the support of current Python packages is critical to our approach, and we will not be able to move to 3.x until standard packages are more widely available in that release.

ACKNOWLEDGEMENTS

We are particularly appreciative of the reviewers who provided valuable feedback at multiple stages of this endeavor: Claude Anderson (Rose-Hulman Institute of Technology), Chris Brooks (University of San Francisco), Judy Franklin (Smith College), Alan Garvey (Truman State University), Ronald I. Greenberg (Loyola University), Andrew Harrington (Loyola College), Steve Harrison (Virginia Tech), Christopher Haynes (Indiana University), Cinda Heeren (University of Illinois/Urbana-Champaign), Brian Howard (DePauw University) Janardhan Iyengar (Franklin & Marshall College), Andree Jacobson (University of New Mexico), John Lasseter (Willamette University), Jim Mahoney (Marlboro College), Joe Oldham (Centre College), Holly Patterson-McNeill (Lewis Clark State College), John

Rabung (Randolph-Macon College), Ben Schafer (University of Northern Iowa), David G. Sullivan (Boston University), David A. Sykes (Wofford Colllege). Here at Michigan State University, Erik Eid (now of Bowling Green State University) provided valuable feedback on the first draft. Laurie Dillon provided feedback when she taught from a draft. C. Titus Brown read a draft from a Pythonic perspective and provided encouragement. As a high school student, Angus Burton provided valuable feedback from a novice's perspective. Srikanth Vudayagiri provided many excellent exercises. Scott Buffa made corrections to an early draft. The summer CSE 231 class provided many exercises. Members of the class were: Mohammed Alwahibi, Younsuk Dong, Michael Ford, Gabriel Friedman, Adam Hamilton, Meagan Houang, Ruba Jiddou, and Adam Palmer. The organization of our course was established by Mark McCullen, who is always available for advice. Larry Nyhoff (Calvin College) shared valuable insights over a dinner that started it all.

W. F. PUNCH
R. J. ENBODY

PART 1

Thinking About Computing

Chapter 0   The Study of Computer Science

CHAPTER 0

The Study of Computer Science

0.1 WHY COMPUTER SCIENCE?

It is a fair question to ask. Why should anyone bother to study computer science? Furthermore, what is "computer science"? Isn't this all just about programming? All good questions. We think it is worth discussing them before you forge ahead with the rest of the book.

Importance of Computer Science

Let's be honest. We wouldn't be writing the book and asking you to spend your valuable time if we didn't think that studying computer science is important. There are a couple of ways to look at why this is true.

First, we all know that computers are everywhere, millions upon millions of them. What were once rare, expensive items are as common place as, well, any commodity you can imagine (we were going to say the proverbial toaster, but there are many times more computers than toasters. In fact, there is likely a small computer *in* your toaster!). However, that isn't enough of a reason. There are millions and millions of cars and universities don't require auto mechanics as an area of study.

A second aspect is that computers are not only common, but they are also more universally applicable than any other commodity in history. A car is good for transportation, but a computer can be used in so many situations. In fact, there is almost no area one can imagine where a computer would *not* be useful. That is a key element. No matter what your area of interest, a computer could be useful there as a *tool*. The computer's universal utility is unique, and learning how to use such a tool is important.

Computer "Science"

> Any field that has the word science in its name is guaranteed thereby not to be a science.
>
> Frank Harary

A popular view of the term "computer science" is that it is a glorified way to say "computer programming." It is true that computer programming is often the way that people are introduced to computing in general, and that computer programming is the primary reason many take computing courses. However, there is indeed more to computing than programming, hence the term "computer science." Here are a few examples.

Theory of Computation

Before there were the vast numbers of computers that are available today, scientists were thinking about what it means to do computing and what the limits might be. They would ask questions, such as whether there exist problems that we can conceive of but cannot compute. It turns out there are. One of these problems, called the "Halting Problem,"[1] cannot be solved by a program running on any computer. Knowing what you can and cannot solve on a computer is an important issue and a subject of study among computer scientists that focus on the theory of computation.

Computational Efficiency

The fact that a problem is computable does not mean it is easily computed. Knowing roughly how difficult a problem is to solve is also very important. Determining a meaningful measure of difficulty is, in itself, an interesting issue, but imagine we are concerned only with time. Consider designing a solution to a problem that, as part of the solution, required you to sort 100,000 items (say cancer patient records, or asteroid names, or movie episodes, etc.). A slow algorithm, such as the sorting algorithm called the Bubble Sort, might take approximately 800 seconds (about 13 minutes); another sorting algorithm called Quick Sort might take approximately 0.3 seconds. That is a difference of around 2400 times! That large a difference might determine whether it is worth doing. If you are creating a solution, it would be good to know what makes your solution slow or what makes it fast.

Algorithms and Data Structures

Algorithms and data structures are the currency of the computer scientist. Discussed more in Chapter 3, algorithms are the methods used to solve problems, and data structures are the organizations of data that the algorithms use. These two concepts are distinct: a general approach to solving a problem (such as searching for a particular value, sorting a

---

[1] http://en.wikipedia.org/wiki/Halting_problem

list of objects, encrypting a message, etc.) differs from the organization of the data that is being processed (as a list of objects, as a dictionary of key-value pairs, as a "tree" of records). However, they are also tightly coupled. Furthermore, both algorithms and data structures can be examined independently of how they might be programmed. That is, one designs algorithms and data structures and then actually implements them in a particular computer program. Understanding abstractly how to design both algorithms and data structures independent of the programming language is critical for writing correct and efficient code.

Parallel Processing

It may seem odd to include what many consider an advanced topic, but parallel processing, using multiple computers to solve a problem, is an issue for everyone these days. Why? As it turns out, most computers come with at least two processors or CPUs (see Section 0.6), and many come with four or more. The present day PlayStation3™ uses a special IBM chip that has eight processors, and Intel has recently announced prototypes of chips that have eighty processors! What does this mean to us, as both consumers and new computer scientists?

The answer is that new algorithms, data structures, and programming paradigms will be needed to take advantage of this new processing environment. Orchestrating many processors to solve a problem is an exciting and challenging task.

Software Engineering

Even the process of writing programs itself has developed its own sub discipline within computer science. Dubbed "software engineering," it concerns the process of creating programs: from designing the algorithms they use, to supporting testing and maintenance of the program once created. There is even a discipline interested in representing a developed program as a mathematical entity so that one can *prove* what a program will do once written.

Many Others

We have provided but a taste of the many fields that make computer science such a wonderfully rich area to explore. Every area that uses computation brings its own problems to be explored.

Computer Science Through Computer Programming

We have tried to make the point that computer science is not just programming. However, it is also true that for much of the book we will focus on just that aspect of computer science: programming. Beginning with "problem solving through programming" allows one to explore pieces of the computer science landscape as they naturally arise.

0.2 THE DIFFICULTY AND PROMISE OF PROGRAMMING

If computer science, particularly computer programming, is so interesting, why doesn't everybody do it? The truth is that it can be hard. We are often asked by beginning students, "Why is programming so hard?" Even grizzled programming veterans, when honestly looking back at their first experience, remember how difficult that first programming course was. Why? Understanding why it might be hard gives you an edge on what you can do to control the difficulty.

Difficulty 1: Two Things at Once

Let's consider an example. Let us say that, when you walk into that first day of Programming 101, you discover the course is not about programming but French poetry. French poetry? Yes, French poetry. Imagine that you come in and the professor posts the following excerpt from a poem on the board.

A une Damoyselle malade

Ma mignonne,
Je vous donne
Le bon jour;
Le séjour
C'est prison.

Clément Marot

Your assigned task is to translate this poetry into English (or German, or Russian, whatever language is your native tongue). Let us also assume, for the moment, that:

(a) You do not know French.
(b) You have never studied poetry.

You have two problems on your hands. First, you have to gain a better understanding of the syntax and semantics (the form and substance) of the French language. Second, you need to learn more about the "rules" of poetry and what constitutes a good poem.

Lest you think that this is a trivial matter, an entire book has been written by Douglas Hofstadter on the very subject of the difficulty of translating this one poem ("Le Ton beau de Marot").

So what's your first move? Most people would break out a dictionary and, line by line, try to translate the poem. Hofstadter, in his book, does exactly that, producing the crude translation in Figure 0.1.

My Sweet/Cute
[One] (Feminine)

My sweet/cute [one] (feminine)	
I [to] you (respectful) give/bid/convey	**A une Damoyselle malade**
The good day (i.e., a hello, i.e., greetings).	Ma mignonne,
The stay/sojourn/	Je vous donne
visit (i.e., quarantine)	Le bon jour;
{It} is prison.	Le séjour
	C'est prison.

FIGURE 0.1 Crude translation of excerpt.

The result is hardly a testament to beautiful poetry. This translation does capture the syntax and semantics, but not the poetry, of the original. If we take a closer look at the poem, we can discern some features that a good translation should incorporate. For example:

- Each line consists of three syllables.
- Each line's main stress falls on its final syllable.
- The poem is a string of rhyming couplets: *AA, BB, CC, . . .*
- The semantic couplets are out of phase with the rhyming couplets: *A, AB, BC, . . .*

Taking some of these ideas (and many more besides) into account, Hofstadter comes up with the translation in Figure 0.2.

Not only does this version sound far more like poetry, but it also matches the original poem, following the rules and conveying the intent. It is a pretty good translation!

Poetry to Programming?

How does this poetry example help? Actually, the analogy is pretty strong. In coming to programming for the first time, you face exactly the same issues:

- You are not yet familiar with the syntax and semantics of the language you are working with—in this case, of the programming language Python and perhaps not of *any* programming language.
- You do not know how to solve problems using a computer—similar to not knowing how to write poetry.

Just like the French poetry neophyte, you are trying to solve two problems simultaneously. On one level, you are just trying to get familiar with the syntax and semantics of the language. At the same time, you are tackling a second, very difficult task: creating poetry in the previous example, and solving problems using a computer in this course.

My Sweet Dear	**A une Damoyselle malade**
My sweet dear,	Ma mignonne,
I send cheer –	Je vous donne
All the best!	Le bon jour;
Your forced rest	Le séjour
Is like jail.	C'est prison.

FIGURE 0.2 Improved translation of excerpt.

Working at two levels, the meaning of the programming words and then the intent of the program (what the program is trying to solve) are the two problems the beginning programmer has to face. Just like the French poetry neophyte, your first programs will be a bit clumsy as you learn both the programming language and how to use that language to solve problems. For example, to a practiced eye, many first programs look similar in nature to the literal translation of Hofstadter's in Figure 0.1. Trying to do two things simultaneously is difficult for anyone, so be gentle on yourself as you go forward with the process.

You might ask whether there is a better way. Perhaps, but we have not found it yet. The way to learn programming is to program, just like swinging a baseball bat, playing the piano, and winning at bridge; you can hear the rules and talk about the strategies, but learning is best done by doing.

Difficulty 2: What is a Good Program?

Having mastered some of the syntax and semantics of a programming language, how do we write a good program? That is, how do we create a program that is more like poetry than like the mess arrived at through literal translation?

It is difficult to discuss a good program when, at this point, you know so little, but there are a couple of points that are worth noting even before we get started.

It's All About Problem Solving

If the rules of poetry are what guides writing good poetry, what are the guidelines for writing good programs? That is, what is it we have to learn in order to transition from a literal translation to a good poem?

For programming, it is *problem solving*. When you write a program, you are creating, in some detail, how it is that *you* think a particular problem or some class of problems, should be solved. Thus, the program represents, in a very accessible way, your thoughts on problem solving. Your thoughts! That means, before you write the program you must *have* some thoughts.

It is a common practice, even among veteran programmers, to get a problem and immediately sit down and start writing a program. Typically that approach results in a mess, and, for the beginning programmer, it results in an unsolved problem. Figuring out how to solve a problem requires some initial thought. If you think before you program, you better understand what the problem requires as well as the best strategies you might use to solve that problem.

Remember the two-level problem? Writing a program as you figure out how to solve a problem means that you are working at two levels at once: the problem-solving level and the programming level. That is more difficult than doing things sequentially. You should sit down and think about the problem and how you want to solve it *before* you start writing the program. We will talk more about this later, but the rule is:

> | **Rule 1:** Think before you program!

A Program as an Essay

When students are asked "What is the most important feature a program should have?" many answer, "It should run." By "run," they mean that the program executes and actually does something.

Wrong. As with any new endeavor, it is important to get the fundamentals correct right at the beginning. So **RULE 2** is

> | **Rule 2:** A program is a human-readable essay on problem solving that also happens to execute on a computer.

A program is an object to be read by another person, just as any other essay. Although it is true that a program is written in such a way that a computer can execute it, it is still a human-readable essay. If your program is written so that it runs, and even runs correctly (notice we have not discussed "correctly" yet!), but is unreadable, then it is really fairly worthless.

The question is why? Why should it be that people must read it? Why isn't running good enough? Who's going to read it anyway? Let's answer the last question first. The person who is going to read it the most is you! That's correct, *you* have to read the programs you are writing all the time. Every time you put your program away for some period of time and come back to it, you have to re-read what you wrote and understand what you were thinking. Your program is a record of your thoughts on solving the problem and you have to be able to read your program in order to work with it, update it, add to it, and so on.

Furthermore, once you get out of the academic environment where you write programs solely for yourself, you will be writing programs with other people as a group. Your mates have to be able to read what you wrote! Think of the process as developing a newspaper edition. Everyone has to be able to read each others' content so that the edition, as a whole, makes sense. Just writing words on paper isn't enough—they have to fit together.

Our goal is to write programs that other people can read, as well as be run.

The Promise of a Computer Program

A program is an essay on problem solving and that will be our major focus. However, it is still interesting that programs do indeed run on a computer. That is, in fact, one of the unique, and most impressive parts about a program. Consider that idea for a moment. You can think of a way to solve a problem, write that thought down in detail as a program, and (assuming you did it correctly) that problem gets solved. More importantly, the problem can be solved again and again because the program can be used *independent of you*. That is, your thoughts not only live on as words (because of the essay-like nature of the program), but also as an entity that actually implements those thoughts. How amazing is that! Do you have some thoughts about how to make a robot dance? Write the program, and the robot dances. Do you have some ideas on how to create music? Write the program, and music is written automatically. Do you have an idea of how to solve a Sudoku puzzle? Write the program, and every puzzle is solved.

So a computer program (and the computer it runs on) offers a huge leap forward, perhaps the biggest since Gutenberg in the mid 1400's. Gutenberg invented moveable type, so that the written word of an individual—i.e., their thoughts—could be reproduced independently of the writer. Now, not only can those thoughts be copied, but also implemented to be *used* over and over again.

Programming is as open, as universally applicable, as the thoughts of the people who do the programming, because a program is the manifest thought of the programmer.

0.3 CHOOSING A COMPUTER LANGUAGE

We have selected a particular programming language, the language called Python, for this introductory text. You should know that there are lots of programming languages out there. Wikipedia lists more than 500 such languages.[2] Why so many languages, and why Python for this text?

Different Computer Languages

If a program is a concrete, runnable realization of a person's thoughts, then it makes sense that different people would create languages that allow them to better reflect those thoughts. In fact, computer scientists are crazy about languages, which is why there are so many. Whatever the reason that some language was created, and there can be many reasons, they all reflect some part of the creator's view of how to best express solving problems on a computer. In fact, computer scientists are specifically trained to write their own language to suit their needs—a talent few other disciplines support so fully!

So given all these languages, why did we pick Python?

---

[2] http://en.wikipedia.org/wiki/Alphabetical_list_of_programming_languages

Why Python?

> I set out to come up with a language that made programmers more productive.
>
> Guido van Rossum, author of Python

There are three features that we think are important for an introductory programming language:

- The language should provide a low "cognitive load" on the student. That is, it should be as easy as possible to express your problem-solving thoughts in the mechanisms provided by the programming language.
- Having spent all your time learning this language, it should be easy to apply it to problems you will encounter. In other words, having learned a language, you should be able to write short programs to solve problems that pop up in your life (sort your music, find a file on your computer, find the average temperature for the month, etc.).
- The programming language you use should have broad support across many disciplines. That is, the language should be embraced by practitioners from many fields (arts to sciences, as they say) and useful packages, collections of support programs, should be available to many different types of users.

So how does Python match up against these criteria?

Python Philosophy

Python offers a philosophy: *There should be one—and preferably only one—obvious way to do it.* The language should offer, as much as possible, a one-to-one mapping between the problem-solving need and the language support for that need. This is not necessarily the case with all programming languages. Given the two-level problem the introductory programmer already faces, reducing the programming language load as much as possible is important. Though Python does have its short cuts, they are far fewer than many other languages, and there is less "language" one has to remember to accomplish your task. In fact, the Python developers are working to create new versions of the language (Python 3.0, Appendix D) that brings the language even more in line with this philosophy.

A "Best Practices" Language

One of our favorite descriptions of Python is that it is a "best practices" language. This means that Python provides many of the best parts of other languages directly to the user. Important data structures are provided as part of the standard language; iteration (described later) is introduced early and is available on standard data structures; packages for files, file paths, the Web, and so on are part of the standard language. Python is often described as a "batteries included" language in which many commonly needed aspects are provided by default. This characteristic means that you can use Python to solve problems you will encounter.

Python Is Open Source

One of Python's most powerful features is its support from the various communities and the breadth of that support. One reason is that Python is developed under the *Open Source* model. Open Source is both a way to think about software and a culture or viewpoint used by those who develop software. Open Source for software is a way to make software freely available and to guarantee that free availability to those who develop new software based on Open Source software. Linux, a type of operating system, is such a project, as are a number of other projects, such as Firefox (web browser), Thunderbird (mail client), Apache (web server), and, of course, Python. As a culture, Open Source adherents want to make software as available and useful as possible. They want to share the fruits of their labor and, as a group, move software forward, including the application areas where software is used. This perspective can be summarized as follows:

A rising tide lifts all boats.

Each person is working explicitly (or implicitly) as part of a larger group towards a larger goal, making software available and useful. As a result of Python's Open Source development, there are free, specialized packages for almost any area of endeavor including: music, games, genetics, physics, chemistry, natural language, geography, and others. If you know Python and can do rudimentary programming, there are packages available that will support almost any area you care to choose.

Is Python the Best Language?

The answer to that question is that there is no "best" language. All computer programming languages are a compromise to some degree. After all, wouldn't it be easiest to describe the program in your own words and just have it run? Unfortunately, that isn't possible. Our present natural language (English, German, Hindi, whatever) is too difficult to turn into the precise directions a computer needs to execute a program. Each programming language has its own strengths and weaknesses. New programmers, having mastered their first programming language, are better equipped to examine other languages and what they offer. For now, we think Python is a good compromise for the beginning programmer.

0.4 WHAT IS COMPUTATION?

It can be difficult to find a good definition for a broadly used word like "computation." If you look, you will find definitions that include terms like "information processing," "sequence of operations," "numbers," "symbols," and "mathematical methods." Computer scientists interested in the theory of computation formally define what a computation is, and what its limits are. It is a fascinating topic, but it is a bit beyond our scope.

We will use an English language definition that suits our needs. In this book we will define a computation as:

| *Computation* is the manipulation of data by either humans or machines.

The data that is manipulated may be numbers, characters, or other symbols.

0.5 WHAT IS A COMPUTER?

The definition of a computer then is

| A *computer* is something that does computation.

That definition is purposefully vague on *how* a computer accomplishes computation, only that it does so. This imprecision exists because what counts as a computer is surprisingly diverse. However, there are some features that almost any system that does computation should have.

- A computer should be able to *accept input*. What counts as input might vary among computers, but data must be able to enter the computer for processing.
- If a computer is defined by its ability to *do computation*, then any object that is a computer must be able to manipulate data.
- A computer must be able to *output data*.

Another characteristic of many computers is their ability to perform computation using an assembly of only simple parts. Such computers are composed of huge numbers of simple parts assembled in complex ways. As a result, the complexity of many computers is the organization of their parts, not the parts themselves.

Computation in Nature

There are a number of natural systems that perform computation. These are areas of current, intense investigation in computer science as researchers try to learn more from existing natural systems.

The Human Brain

When electronic computers were first brought to the public's attention in the 1950's and even into the 1960's, they were often referred to as "electronic brains." The reason for this was obvious. The only computing object we had known up to that time was the human brain.

The human brain is in fact a powerful computing engine, though it is not often thought of in quite that way. It constantly takes in a torrent of input data—sensory data from the five senses—manipulates that data in a variety of ways, and provides output in the form of both physical action (both voluntary and involuntary) as well as mental action.

The amazing thing about the human brain is that the functional element of the brain is a very simple cell called the *neuron*, Figure 0.3.

Structure of a Typical Neuron

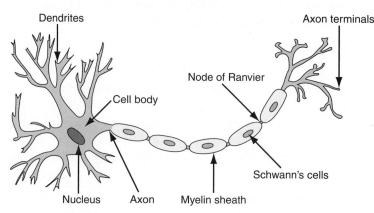

FIGURE 0.3 An annotated neuron. [SEER Training Modules, U.S. National Institutes of Health, National Cancer Institute.]

Though a fully functional cell, a neuron also acts as a kind of small switch. When a sufficient signal reaches the *dendrites* of a neuron, the neuron "fires" and a signal is transmitted down the *axon* of the neuron to the *axon terminals*. Neurons are not directly connected to one another; rather, the dendrites of one neuron are located very close to the axon terminals of another neuron, separated by a space known as the *synapse*. When the signal reaches the axon terminal, chemicals called *neurotransmitters* are secreted across the synapse. It is the transmission of a signal, from neurotransmitters secreted by the axon terminals of one neuron to the dendrites of a connecting neuron that constitutes a basic computation in the brain.

Here are a few interesting facts about neuronal activity:

- The signal within a neuron is not transmitted by electricity (as in a wire), but by rapid chemical changes that propagate down the axon. The result is that the signal is very much slower than an electrical transmission down a wire—about a million times slower.
- Because the signal is chemical, a neuron must typically recover for a millisecond (one-thousandth of a second) before it can fire again. Therefore, there is a built-in time delay to neuronal firing.
- A neuron is "fired" in response to some combination of the number of signals that are received at its dendrite (how many other neurons are firing in proximity) and the

strength of the signal received (how much neurotransmitter is being dumped into the synapse).

One thing to note is how *slow* the neuron is as a switch. As you will see in Section 0.6, electronic switches can act many millions of times faster. However, what the brain lacks in terms of speedy switches, it makes up for in sheer size and complexity of organization. By some estimates, the human brain consists of of 100 billion (10^{11}) neurons and 100 trillion (10^{14}) synapses. Furthermore, the organization of the brain is incredibly complicated. Scientists have spent hundreds of years identifying specific areas of the brain that are responsible for various functions, and how those areas are interconnected. Yet for all this complexity, the main operational unit is a tiny, slow switch.

Scientists have been fascinated by the brain, so much so that there is a branch of computer science that works with simulations of *neural networks*, networks consisting of simple switches such as those found in the brain. Neural networks have been used to solve many difficult problems.

Evolutionary Computation

The evolution of biological species can be viewed as a computation process. In this view, the inputs of the computational process are the environmental variables the biological entity is subjected to; the computational process is the adaptation of the genetic code and the output is the adaptation results from the genetic code modification.

This point of view has been incorporated into approaches known as *genetic algorithms*. These techniques take the concepts of simple genetics, as proposed by Gregor Mendel, and the processes of evolution as described by Charles Darwin, and use them to compute.

The basic parts of a genetic algorithm, shown in Figure 0.4, are:

- A way to *encode* a solution in a linear sequence, much like the sequence of information contained in a chromosome. This encoding depends on the problem, but it typically consists of parameters (struts for a bridge, components for a circuit, jobs for a schedule, etc.) that are required to constitute a solution.

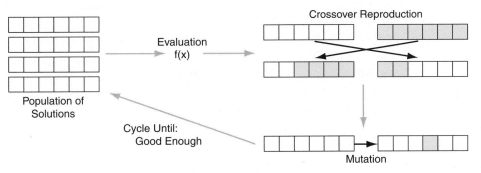

FIGURE 0.4 A genetic algorithm.

- A method to *evaluate* the "goodness" of a particular solution, called the *evaluation function* and represented as f(x) in the diagram.
- A *population* of solutions, often initially created by random selection of the solution components, from which new solutions can be created.
- Some genetic *modification* methods to create new solutions from old solutions. In particular, there is *mutation*, which is a modification of one aspect of an existing solution and *crossover*, which combines aspects of two parent solutions into a new solution.

The process proceeds as follows. Each solution in the population is evaluated to determine how fit it is. Based on the fitness of the existing solutions, new solutions are created using the genetic modification methods. Those solutions that are more fit are given more opportunity to create new solutions; less fit solutions are given less opportunity. This process incorporates a "survival of the fittest" notion. Over time, better and better solutions are evolved that solve the existing problem.

Genetic algorithms and other similar approaches have been used to solve many complex problems such as scheduling, circuit design, and others.

The Human Computer

The common use of the word "computer" from around the seventeenth century to about World War II referred to *people*. To compute difficult, laborious values for mathematical constants (such as π or e), fission reactions (for the Manhattan Project), and gun trajectory tables, people were used (Figure 0.5). However, using people had problems.

A classic example of such a problem was created by William Shanks, an English amateur mathematician, who in 1873 published π calculated to 707 decimal places. The calculation by hand took 28 years. Unfortunately, he made a calculation error at the 528th digit that made the last two years of calculation a waste of time. His error wasn't found until 70 years later using a mechanical calculator.

The U.S. Army's Ballistics Research Laboratory was responsible for the creation of gun trajectory tables. Each new artillery piece required a table for the gunner to use to calculate where the round would land. However, it took a lot of human effort to make these tables. Kay Mauchly Antonelli, a mathematician from the University of Pennsylvania and one of the six original programmers of the ENIAC, the first general-purpose electronic digital computer, said, "To do just one trajectory, at one particular angle, usually took between 30 to 40 hours of calculation on this [mechanical] desk calculator." These tables exceeded 1800 entries and required up to four years to produce by hand.[3]

It was obvious that something had to be done. People were neither accurate enough, nor fast enough, to do this kind of calculation. A more modern, faster, and accurate approach was needed.

---

[3] http://www.comphist.org/pdfs/Video-Giant%20Brains-MachineChangedWorld-Summary.pdf.

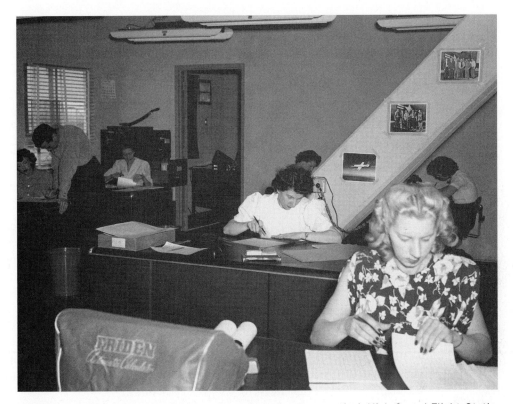

FIGURE 0.5 NACA (National Advisory Committee for Aeronautics) High-Speed-Flight Station Computer Room. [NASA/Courtesy of nasaimages.org]

0.6 THE MODERN, ELECTRONIC COMPUTER

Although there may be many notions of a computer, we all know what a modern computer is. We read email on it, text message each other, listen to music, play videos, and play games on them. The design of these computers was first conceived around World War II to solve those tedious calculation problems that humans did so slowly, especially the Army's ballistics tables. How do electronic computers work? What makes them so special?

It's the Switch!

Modern digital computers use, as their base component, nothing more complicated than a simple switch. Very early computers used mechanical switches or relays; later versions used vacuum tubes, and finally, modern computers use transistors (see Figure 0.6).

A switch's function is pretty obvious. It is either on or off. When turned on, electricity flows through the switch and when turned off, no electrical flow can occur. Using a switch

FIGURE 0.6 Vacuum tube, single transistor, and chip transistor (the dot). [Reprint Courtesy of International Business Machines Corporation, copyright ©International Business Machines Corporation].

and its on/off nature, you can construct some simple logic circuits. In logic, we have only two states: True and False. In our logic circuit, we translate True and False to the physical process of a switch. The True condition is represented by a current flowing through the circuit and False is represented by lack of current flow. Though we will cover Boolean logic in more detail in Chapter 2, there are two simple combinations of switches we can show: the **and** and **or** circuits.

For the Boolean **and**, a True value results *only* if both of the two input values are True. All other combinations of input have a False output. In the **and** circuit, we connect two switches together in series as shown in Figure 0.7. Electricity can flow, that is, the circuit represents a True value, only if *both* switches are turned on. If either switch is turned off, no electricity flows and the circuit represents a False value.

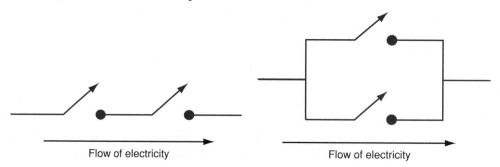

Flow of electricity   Flow of electricity

FIGURE 0.7 Switches implementing an "and" gate (left) and an "or" gate (right).

We can do the same for the Boolean **or**. An **or** is True if *either one or both* of its inputs are True; otherwise, it is False. In the **or** circuit of Figure 0.7, we connect two switches together in parallel. Electricity can flow if *either* switch is turned on, representing a True value. Only when both switches are turned off does the circuit represent a False value.

Similar Boolean logic elements, usually called logic *gates*, can be constructed from simple circuits. The amazing thing is that using only simple logic circuits, we can assemble an entire computer. For example, an **and** and **or** gate can be combined to make a simple circuit to add two values, called an *adder*. Once we can add, we can use the adder circuit to build a subtraction circuit. Further, once we have an adder circuit we can do multiplication (by repeated addition), and then division, and so on. Just providing some simple elements like logic gates allows us to build more complicated circuits until we have a complete computer.

The Transistor

Although any switch will do, the "switch" that made the electronic computer what it is today is called a *transistor*. The transistor is an electronic device invented in 1947 by William Shockley, John Bardeen and Walter Brattain at Bell Labs (for which they eventually won the Nobel Prize in Physics in 1956). It utilized a new technology, a material called a semiconductor, that allowed transistors to supersede the use of other components such as vacuum tubes. Though a transistor has a number of uses, the one we care most about for computer use is as a switch. A transistor has three wires with the names Source, Sink and Gate. Electricity flows from the Source to the Sink. If there is a signal, a voltage or current, on the Gate then electricity flows—the switch is "on." If there is no signal on the Gate, no electricity flows—the switch is "off." See Figure 0.8.

FIGURE 0.8 A diagram of a transistor and its equivalent "faucet" view.

In the switch examples given, we can use transistors as switches, e.g., as in Figure 0.7. In that way, transistors are used to construct logic gates, then larger circuits, and so on, eventually constructing the higher-level components that become the parts of a modern electronic computer.

What makes the transistor so remarkable is how it has evolved in the 60 years since its first creation. It is this remarkable evolution that has made the modern computer what it is today.

Smaller Size

The size of a transistor has changed dramatically since its inception. The first Shockley transistor was very large, on the order of inches (see Figure 0.9). By 1954, Texas Instruments was selling the first commercial transistor, and had shrunk the transistor size to that of a postage stamp.

However, even the small size of individual transistor components was proving to be a limitation. More transistors were needed in a smaller area if better components were to be designed. The solution was the *integrated circuit*, invented by Jack Kilby of Texas Instruments

FIGURE 0.9 The Shockley transistor—the first transistor. [Reprinted with permission of Alcatel-Lucent USA Inc.]

FIGURE 0.10 Kilby's first integrated circuit (left) and the Intel 4004 microprocessor (right). [Image courtesy of Texas Instruments (left). Image courtesy of Intel Museum (right).]

in 1958-1959 (for which he won the 2000 Nobel Prize in Physics); see Figure 0.10. The integrated circuit was a contiguous piece of semiconductor material upon which multiple transistors could be manufactured. The integrated circuit allowed many transistors to be embedded in a single piece of material, allowing a more complex functional circuit on a very small area. By 1971, Intel managed to manufacture the first complete computer processing unit (or CPU) on a single chip, a microprocessor named the Intel 4004 (see Figure 0.10). It was approximately the size of a human fingernail (1/8 × 1/6 of an inch) with 2300 transistors. By this time, the size of the transistor on this microprocessor had shrunk to 10 microns, the width of the a single fiber of cotton or silk.

The shrinkage of the transistor has continued. Today, the size of a transistor has reached amazingly small levels. Figure 0.11 shows an electron microscope picture of a gate recently developed by IBM. The size of the gate is 50 nanometers, 50×10^{-9} meters, a thousand times smaller than transistors in the Intel 4004. That is more than 10 times smaller than a single wavelength of visible light. It is approximately the thickness of a cell membrane, and only 10 times larger than a single turn of a DNA helix.

FIGURE 0.11 A photomicrograph of a single 50nm IBM transistor (left) and a scale small items (right). [Reprint Courtesy of International Business Machines Corporation, copyright © International Business Machines Corporation (left) Sebastian Kaulitzki/Shutterstock (right)].

Year	Transistor Count	Model
1971	2,300	4004
1978	29,000	8086
1982	134,000	80286
1986	275,000	80386
1989	1,200,000	80486
1993	3,100,000	Pentium
1999	9,500,000	Pentium III
2001	42,000,000	Pentium 4
2007	582,000,000	Core 2 Quad
2008	2,100,000,000	Itanium Quad

TABLE 0.1 Transistor counts in Intel microprocessors, by year.

Quantity and Function

As the size of a transistor shrank, the number of transistors that could be put on a single chip increased. This increase has been quite dramatic. In fact, there is a famous statement made by the founder of Intel, Gordon Moore, that predicts this amazing trend. In 1965, Moore predicted that the number of transistors that can be placed inexpensively on a single chip would double about every two years.[4] This trend has proven to be remarkably accurate and continues to hold to this day. Named in the popular press as "Moore's Law," it's demise has been predicted for many years, yet it continues to hold true. A summary of this trend is shown in the Table 0.1.

---

[4] The original estimate was one year, but was later revised upward.

By increasing the number of transistors in a CPU, more functionality can be introduced on each CPU chip. In fact, recently the *number* of CPUs on a single chip has also increased. A common chip in production at the writing of this book is the quad-core processor (see Figure 0.12) which contains four complete CPUs.

FIGURE 0.12 Intel Nehalem Quad Core Processor.[Courtesy of Intel Corporation.]

Faster

Smaller transistors are also faster transistors, so smaller transistors provide a doubling factor: more and faster. But how does one measure speed?

When you buy a computer, the salesman is more than happy to tell you how fast it is, usually in terms of how many "gigahertz" the computer will run. The value the salesman mentions is really a measure of a special feature of every computer called its *clock*. The clock of a computer is not much like a wall clock, however. Rather, it is more like a drummer in a band. The drummer's job in the band is to keep the beat, coordinating the rhythm of all the other members of the band. The faster the drummer beasts, the faster the band plays. The components on a CPU chip are like the band—they need something to help them coordinate their efforts. That is the role of the clock. The clock regularly emits a signal indicating that the next operation is to occur. Upon every "beat" of the clock, another "cycle" occurs on the chip, meaning another set of operations can occur.

Therefore, the faster the clock runs, the faster the chip runs and, potentially, the more instructions that can be executed. But how fast is a gigahertz (GHz)? Literally, 1 gigahertz means that the clock emits a signal every nanosecond, that is, every billionth of a second (10^{-9}). Thus, your 1 GHz computer executes instructions once every nanosecond. That is a very fast clock indeed!

Consider that the "universal speed limit" is the speed of light, roughly 186,282 miles/second (299,792,458 meters/second) in a vacuum. Given that an electrical signal (data) is carried at this speed, how far can an electric signal travel in a nanosecond? If we do the math, it turns out that an electric signal can only travel about 11.8 inches. Only 11.8 inches! At 2 GHz, it can only travel 5.9 inches; at 4GHz, only 2.95 inches. Consider that 5.9 inches is not even the width of a typical computer board! In fact, at the writing of this book a further doubling of speed of present computers is limited by the distance electricity can travel.

Given a measure of the speed of a computer, how does that translate to actual work done by the computer? The process of measuring computing operations, known as "benchmarking," can be a difficult task. Different computing systems are better or worse, depending on how you measure the benchmark. However, manufacturers do list a measure called *instructions per second* or *IPS*. That is, it's a measure of how many instructions, such as an addition, can be done every second. In Table 0.2, we can see how the measure of increased clock rate affects the IPS (MIPS is millions of IPS). One interesting note is that, since about 2000, the clock speed has not increased dramatically for the reasons mentioned previously. However, the existence of multiple CPUs on a chip still allows for increases in IPS of a CPU.

Year	CPU	Instructions/second	Clock Speed
1971	Intel 4004	1 MIPS	740 kHz
1972	IBM System/370	1 MIPS	?
1977	Motorola 68000	1 MIPS	8 MHz
1982	Intel 286	3 MIPS	12 MHz
1984	Motorola 68020	4 MIPS	20 MHz
1992	Intel 486DX	54 MIPS	66 MHz
1994	PowerPC 600s (G2)	35 MIPS	33 MHz
1996	Intel Pentium Pro	541 MIPS	200 MHz
1997	PowerPC G3	525 MIPS	233 MHz
2002	AMD Athlon XP 2400+	5,935 MIPS	2.0 GHz
2003	Pentium 4	9,726 MIPS	3.2 GHz
2005	Xbox360	19,200 MIPS	3.2 GHz
2006	PS3 Cell BE	10,240 MIPS	3.2 GHz
2006	AMD Athlon FX-60	18,938 MIPS	2.6 GHz
2007	Intel Core 2 QX9770	59,455 MIPS	3.2 GHz

TABLE 0.2 Speed (in millions of IPS or MIPS) and clock rates of microprocessors, by year.

0.7 A HIGH-LEVEL LOOK AT A MODERN COMPUTER

Now that you know something about the low-level functional elements of a computer, it is useful to step up to a higher-level view of the elements of a computer, often termed the computer's *architecture*. The architecture is used to describe the various parts of the computer and how they interact. The standard architecture, named after the stored program model of John von Neumann, looks something like the following (see Figure 0.13):

- **Processor:** As we have mentioned, the processor is the computational heart of a computer. Often called the CPU (Central Processing Unit), it can itself consist of a number of parts including the ALU (Arithmetic and Logic Unit), where logical calculations are done; local fast storage, called the cache; connections among components, called the bus, as well as other elements.
- **Main Memory:** A processor needs data to process and main memory is where data is stored. Main memory is traditionally volatile; i.e., when power is turned off, data is lost. It is also called RAM = Random Access Memory, i.e., retrievable in any order. Use of non-volatile memory is increasing, especially in portable devices.
- **Disk:** The disk is for permanent (non-volatile) storage of data. The disk is also known as the "hard drive." Data must be moved from the disk to main memory before it can be used by the processor. Disks are relatively slow, mechanical devices that are being replaced by non-mechanical memory cards in some portable devices.
- **Input/Output:** These devices convert external data into digital data and vice versa for use and storage in the computer.
- **Network:** A network is needed to communicate with other computers. From the viewpoint of the processor the network is simply another input/output device.

Consider a simple operation theSum = num1 + num2. The theSum, num1, and num2 terms are called *variables*, readable names that contain values to be used in a program. The statement adds the two numbers stored in num1 and num2 to produce a result which is stored in theSum. Assume that num1 and num2 represent numbers that are stored on the disk and that the result theSum will also be stored on the disk. Assume that the instruction itself, theSum = num1 + num2, also resides on the disk. Here is how it works:

1 **Fetch Instruction:** When the processor is ready to process an instruction, it fetches the instruction from memory. If the instruction is not in memory but on the disk, the memory must first fetch it from the disk. In this way, the instruction theSum = num1 + num2 will move from the disk through memory to the processor.
2 **Decode Instruction:** The processor examines the instruction ("decodes" it) and sees that operands num1 and num2 are needed, so it fetches them from memory. If num1 and num2 are not in memory, but on the disk, the memory must first fetch them from the disk.
3 **Execute Operation:** Once the processor has both the instruction and the operands, it can perform the operation, addition in this case.
4 **Store Result:** After calculating the sum, the processor will store the resulting sum in memory. At some point before power is turned off, the data in memory will be stored on the disk.
5 **Repeat:** Go back to Fetch Instruction to fetch the next instruction in a program.

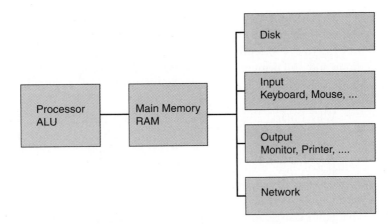

FIGURE 0.13 A typical computer architecture.

The Fetch-Decode-Execute-Store cycle is fundamental for all computers. This simple, sequential process is the basis for all modern computers. These four steps are done in lockstep to the beat of a clock, as we described previously.

How complex is each operation? Not very. The ALU of a processor can add, subtract, multiply, and divide. It can also compare values and choose which instruction to do next based on that comparison. That's it. In reality, it is slightly more complex than that, but not much.

Also, the processor can handle only two types of operands: integers and floating points. For our purposes, you can think of floating-point values as fractional values represented in decimal notation, e.g., 37.842. There will be a separate ALU for integers and a separate one for floating-point numbers, called the FPU = Floating Point Unit.

The important concept is that everything a computer does boils down to a few simple operations, but at billions of operations per second, the result is significant computational power.

0.8 REPRESENTING DATA

The underlying element of a computer is typically a switch, usually a transistor. Given that, what is the most obvious way to represent data values? The obvious choice is binary. Binary values can only be either 1 or 0, which corresponds to the physical nature of a switch, which is on or off. What is interesting is that we can represent not only numbers in binary, but music, video, images, characters, and many other kinds of data also in binary.

Binary Data

By definition, a digital computer is binary, which is base 2. Our normal number system is decimal, base 10, probably because we have 10 fingers for counting. People haven't always worked in base 10. For example, the ancient Babylonians (2000 BC) used base 60 (sexagesimal) for the most advanced mathematics of that time. As a result, they are the source of modern time-keeping and angle measurement: 60 seconds in a minute, 60 minutes in an hour, and 360 degrees in a circle. For decimals we use ten digits: 0, 1, 2, 3, 4, 5, 6, 7, 8, 9. For sexagesimal the Babylonians used sixty digits: 0, 1, 2, 3, . . . , 58, 59. For binary there are only two digits: 0, 1.

Why binary? Two reasons, really. As we have said, the first reason is the hardware being used. Electronic transistors lend themselves very naturally to base two. A transistor is either on or off, which can be directly translated to 1 or 0. However, the second reason is that two digits are easy to store and easy to operate on. Storage devices in binary need a medium that has two states: a state called "one" and another state "zero." Anything with two states can become digital storage. Examples include: high/low voltage, right/left magnetism, charge/no-charge, on/off, and so on. For example, main memory has small capacitors that hold a charge (1) or not (0). Disks are magnetized one way (1) or the other (0). CDs and DVDs reflect light one way (1) or the other (0).

Manipulations of the underlying data can also be done simply using electronic gates that we discussed previously, that is, the Boolean logic: and, or, not. Because such logical circuits can be extremely small and fast, they can be implemented to do calculations quickly and efficiently. For example, the adder circuit we discussed previously that adds two binary digits or *bits* (bit = BInary digiT) can be done with logical circuits: sum = (A and (not B)) or ((not A) and B)). From such simple logic all arithmetic operations can be built. For example, subtraction is the addition of a negative value, multiplication is repeated addition, and division can be done using the other three operations. A choice can be made based on the value of a bit: choose one thing or another. That choice bit can be calculated using any arbitrary logical expression using the logical operators: and, or, not. Therefore, the entire ALU (and the rest of the computer) can be built from the logical operators: and, or, not.

Working with Binary

A brief look at the binary representation of numbers and characters provides useful background for understanding binary computation. Because our world is a world of decimal numbers, let's look at representing decimals in binary. We begin with a review of place holding in decimals, by taking you back to elementary school. For example, consider the number 735 in base 10 (written as 735_{10}). Notice in the last line how the exponents start at 2 and work down to 0 as you move from left to right.

$$735_{10} = 7\ hundreds + 3\ tens + 5\ ones$$
$$735_{10} = 7 * 100 + 3 * 10 + 5 * 1$$
$$735_{10} = 7 * 10^2 + 3 * 10^1 + 5 * 10^0$$

In binary we only have two digits: 0, 1. Also, our base is 2 rather than 10. Therefore, our rightmost three places are: fours, twos, ones. As with base 10, the exponents will decrease as we move from left to right—in this case: 2, 1, then 0. Using the previous notation, but working backwards from the last line to the first line, let us determine what 101 in binary (101_2) is in base 10 (decimal).

$$101_2 = 1 * 2^2 + 0 * 2^1 + 1 * 2^0$$
$$101_2 = 1 * 4 + 0 * 2 + 1 * 1$$
$$101_2 = 4 + 0 + 1$$
$$101_2 = 5_{10}$$

In a similar way, any decimal integer can be represented in binary. For example,

$$1052_{10} = 10000011100_2$$

Fractions can be represented using integers in the scientific notation that you learned in science classes:

$$1/8 = 0.125 = 125 * 10^{-3}$$

The mantissa (125) and exponent (−3) are integers that can be expressed and stored in binary. The actual implementation of binary fractions is different because the starting point is binary, but the principle is the same: binary fractions are stored using binary mantissas and binary exponents. How many bits are allocated to mantissa and how many to exponents varies from computer to computer, but the two numbers are stored together.

There are four important concepts that you need to know about representation:

- All numbers in a computer are represented in binary.
- Because of fixed, hardware limits on number storage, there is a limit to how big an integer can be stored in one unit of computer memory (usually 32 or 64 bits of storage).
- Fractions are represented in scientific notation and are approximations.
- Everything is converted to binary for manipulation and storage: letters, music, pictures, and so on.

Limits

We have covered the representation of numbers in binary. Let's look at limits. Most computers organize their data into *words* that are usually 32 bits in size (though 64-bit words are growing in use). There are an infinite number of integers, but with only 32 bits available in a word, there is a limited number of integers that can fit. If one considers only positive integers, one can represent 2^{32} integers with a 32-bit word, or a little over 4 billion integers. To represent positive and negative integers evenly, the represented integers range from negative 2 billion to positive 2 billion. That is a lot of numbers, but there is a limit and it is not hard to exceed it. For example, most U.S. state budgets will not fit in that size number

(4 billion). On the other hand, a 64-bit computer could represent 2^{64} integers using a 64-bit word, which in base 10 is 1.8×10^{19}: a huge number—over 4 billion times more than can be stored in a 32-bit word.

Fractional values present a different problem. We know from mathematics that between every pair of Real numbers there are an infinite number of Real numbers. To see that, choose any two Real numbers A and B, and (A + B)/2 is a Real number in between. That operation can be repeated an infinite number of times to find more Real numbers between A and B. No matter how we choose to represent Real numbers in binary, the representation will always be an approximation. For example, if you enter 19/5.0 into Python, it will be calculated as 3.7999999999999998 instead of the expected 3.8 (try it!). The approximation is a feature of storage in binary rather than a feature of Python.

Bits, Bytes and Words

Computer words (as opposed to English words) are built from *bytes*, which contain 8 bits so one 32-bit word is made of 4 bytes. Storage is usually counted in bytes, e.g., 2 GB of RAM is approximately 2 billion bytes of memory (actually, it is 2^{31} bytes, which is 2,147,483,648 bytes). Bytes are the unit of measurement for size mainly for historical reasons.

Representing Letters

So far we've dealt with numbers. What about letters (characters): how are characters stored in a computer? Not surprisingly, everything is still stored in binary, which means that it is still a number. Early developers created ways to map characters to numbers.

First, what is a character? Characters are what we see on a printed page and are mostly made from letters (a, b, c, . . .), digits (0, 1, 2, . . .), and punctuation (period, comma, semicolon, . . .). However, there are also characters that are not printable such as "carriage return" or "tab" as well as characters that existed at the dawn of computing to control printers such as "form feed." The first standardized set of computer characters was the ASCII (American Standard Code for Information Interchange) set, shown in part in Table 0.3, developed in 1963 (full table is in Appendix F).

The ASCII table is a mapping between numbers and characters. Each character has an associated number, that is "A" is 65 while "a" is 97. Knowing this relationship, we can interpret a set of numbers as characters and then manipulate those characters just as we would numbers.

Note that the ASCII set of characters was developed by English speakers. As computing has spread across the globe a richer character set was developed to represent the different characters in languages such as Russian, Japanese, and Chinese. Unicode was developed to provide more room to represent the many characters in all languages, especially languages such as Chinese, which can have more than a thousand characters. Python can handle both ASCII and Unicode, but for most of our purposes, ASCII is sufficient and much simpler, so we discuss ASCII here. We'll talk more about this topic in Chapter 4.

Char	Dec	Char	Dec	Char	Dec	Char	Dec
NUL	0	SP	32	@	64	`	96
SOH	1	!	33	A	65	a	97
STX	2	"	34	B	66	b	98
ETX	3	#	35	C	67	c	99
EOT	4	$	36	D	68	d	100
ENQ	5	%	37	E	69	e	101
ACK	6	&	38	F	70	f	102
BEL	7	'	39	G	71	g	103
BS	8	(	40	H	72	h	104

TABLE 0.3 Table of ASCII characters (first few rows—see Appendix E).

Representing Other Data

You must get the idea by now: what computers can represent is numbers. If you want to represent other data, you must find a way to turn that data into numbers.

Images

How to store an image? If the image is discrete—that is, built of many individual parts—we can represent those individual parts as numbers. Take a close look at your monitor or TV screen (with a magnifying glass, if you can). The image is made up of thousands of very small dots. These dots, called *pixels* (short for picture elements), are used to create an image. Each pixel has an associated color. If you put a lot of these pixels together in a small area, they start to look like an image (see Figure 0.14).

FIGURE 0.14 A computer display picture with a close-up of the individual pixels. [Juliengrondin/Shutterstock]

Each pixel can be represented as a location (in a two-dimensional grid) and as a color. The location is two numbers (which row and which column the pixel occupies), and the color is also represented as a number. Although there are a variety of ways to represent color, a common way is to break each color into its contribution from the three basic colors: red, green, and blue. The color number represents how much of each basic color is contributed to the final color. An 8-bit color scheme means that each color can contribute 8 bits, or

2^8 = 256 possible shades of that color. Thus, a 24-bit color system can represent 2^{24} different colors, or 16,777,216.

The quantity of pixels is important. Standard analog television (extinct as of the writing of this book) used 525 lines of pixels, with each line containing 480 pixels, a total of 252,000 pixels. High-definition television has 1920 × 1080 pixels for a total of 2,073,600, a much higher resolution and a much better image.

Music

How to represent music as numbers? There are two types of musical sound that we might want to capture: recorded sound and generated sound. First, let's look at recording sound. A sound "wave" is a complex wave of air pressure that we detect with our ears. If we look at the shape of this sound wave (say with an oscilloscope), we can see how complex the wave can be. However, if we record the height of that wave at a very high rate—say, at a rate of 44,100 times/second (or 44kHz, the sampling rate on most MP3s)—then we can record that height as a number for that time in the sound wave. Therefore, we record two numbers: the height of the recorded sound and the time when that height was recorded. When we play sound back, we can reproduce the sound wave's shape by creating a new sound wave that has the same height at the selected times as the recorded sound at each point in time. The more often we "sample" the sound wave, the better our ability to reproduce it accurately. See Figure 0.15 for an example.

FIGURE 0.15 A sound wave and the samples of that sound wave (green bar height) over time

To generate our own new sound, we can write computer programs that generate the same data, a wave height at some point in time, and then that data can be played just like recorded sound.

What Does a Number Represent?

We've shown that all the data we record for use by a computer is represented as a number, whether the data is numeric, text, image, audio, or any other kind of data. So how can you tell what a particular recorded data value represents? You cannot by simply looking at the bits. Any particular data value can be interpreted as an integer, a character, a sound sample, and so on. It depends on the use for which that data value was recorded. That is, it depends on the *type* of the data. We will talk more of types in Chapter 1, but the type of the data indicates for what use the data values are to be used. If the type is characters, then the numbers represent ASCII values. If the type is floating-point, then the numbers represent the mantissa and exponent of a value. If the type is an image, then the number would represent the color of a particular pixel. Knowing the type of the data lets you know what the data values represent.

How to Talk About Quantities of Data

How much data can a computer hold, and what constitutes "a lot" of data? The answer to that question varies, mostly depending on when you ask it. Very much like Moore's law and processing speed, the amount of data that a commercial disk can hold has grown dramatically over the years.

Again, there are some terms in common usage in the commercial world. In the context of data amounts, we talk about values like "kilobytes" (abbreviated KB) or "megabytes" (abbreviate MB) or "gigabytes" (abbreviated GB), but the meaning is a bit odd. "Kilo" typically refers to 10^3 or 1 thousand of something, "mega" 10^6 or 1 million of something, and "giga" usually to 10^9 or 1 billion of something, but its meaning here is a little off. This is because of the fact that 10^3 or 1000 is *pretty close* to 2^{10} or 1024.

So in discussing powers of 2 and powers of 10, most people use the following rule of thumb. Any time you talk about multiplying by 2^{10}, that's pretty close to multiplying 10^3, so we will just use the power of 10 prefixes we are used to. Another way to say it is that every 3 powers of 10 is "roughly equivalent" to 10 powers of 2. Thus a kilobyte is not really 1000 (10^3) bytes, but 1024 (2^{10}) bytes. A megabyte is not 1 million bytes (10^6), but 1,048,576 (2^{20}) bytes. A gigabyte is not 1 billion bytes (10^9), but 1,073,741,824 (2^{30}).

How Much Data is That?

At the writing of this book, the largest standard size commercial disk is 1 terabyte, 1 trillion bytes (10^{12}). On the horizon is the possibility of a 1 petabyte, 1 quadrillion (10^{15}) bytes. Again, the growth in disk sizes is dramatic. The first disk was introduced by IBM in 1956 and held only 4 megabytes. It took 35 years before a 1 gigabyte disk was made, but only 14 more years until we had 500 gigabyte disks, and only two more years until a 1 terabyte (1,000 gigabyte) disk was available. A petabyte disk (1,000,000 gigabytes) is predicted for 2010.

So, how big is a petabyte? Let's try to put it into terms you can relate to:

- A book is roughly a megabyte of data. If you read one book a day every day of your life, say 80 years, that will be less than 30 gigabytes of data. Because a petabyte is 1 million gigabytes, you will still have 999,970 gigabytes left over.

- How many pictures can a person look at in a lifetime? If we assume 4 megabytes per picture and 100 images a day, after 80 years that collection of pictures would add up to 30 terabytes. So your petabyte disk will have 970,000 gigabytes left after a lifetime of photos and books.
- What about music? MP3 audio files run about a megabyte a minute. At that rate, a lifetime of listening—all day and all night for 80 years—would consume 42 terabytes of space. So with a lifetime of music, pictures and books, you will have 928,000 gigabytes free on your disk. That is, almost 93% of your disk is still empty.
- The one kind of content that might overflow a petabyte disk is video. For DVDs the data rate is about two gigabytes per hour. Therefore, the petabyte disk will hold about 500,000 hours worth of video. If you want to record 24 hours a day, 7 days a week, the video will fill up your petabyte drive after about 57 years.

Of course, why stop there? More prefixes have been defined:

- exa is 2^{60} = 1,152,921,504,606,846,976
- zeta is 2^{70} = 1,180,591,620,717,411,303,424
- yotta is 2^{80} = 1,208,925,819,614,629,174,706,176

Does anything get measured in exabytes or even zetabytes? By 2006, the total Internet traffic in the U.S. was estimated to be roughly 8.4 exabytes for the year. However, video is increasing Internet traffic dramatically. By the end of 2007, YouTube was estimated to be generating 600 petabytes per year all by itself. If YouTube were in high definition, it would have generated 12 exabytes by itself that year. Amateur video is estimated to capture 10 exabytes of video per year, but much of that does not show up on the Internet. Netflix currently distributes movies by sending DVDs through the U.S. mail. If they distributed through the Internet, that would consume 5.8 exabytes of Internet bandwidth per year. If the movies were high definition, they would consume 100 exabytes per year. Video conferencing and Internet gaming are also increasing dramatically. Taken together, these applications have the potential to create what has been termed the "Exaflood" of the Internet. The most extreme estimates put the demand on the Internet of potentially 1000 exabytes in 2015—that is, a zetabyte!

0.9 OVERVIEW OF COMING CHAPTERS

This text is divided into five parts. The first gets you started on Python, computing, and problem solving. With that in hand, we get down into details in the next part where we develop both the Python language and problem-solving skills sufficient to solve interesting problems. The third part provides more tools in the form of Python built-in data structures, algorithm and problem solving development, and functions. Part 4 shows you how to build classes—your own data structures. The final part includes more on Python.

Summary

In this chapter, we considered ways that data can be represented and manipulated—at the hardware level. In subsequent chapters, we will introduce ways in which you, as a programmer, can control the representation and manipulation of data.

PART 2

Starting to Program

CHAPTER **1**

Beginnings

OUR FIRST STEPS IN PROGRAMMING ARE TO LEARN THE DETAILS, SYNTAX, AND semantics, of the Python programming language. This necessarily involves getting into some of the language details, focusing on level 1 (language) issues as opposed to level 2 (problem solving) issues. Don't worry: we haven't forgotten that the goal is to do effective problem solving, but we have to worry about both aspects, moving between levels as required. A little proficiency with Python will allow us to write effective, problem-solving programs.

Here are our first two **RULES** of programming:

> **Rule 1:** Think before you program!
> **Rule 2:** A program is a human-readable essay on problem solving that also happens to execute on a computer.

1.1 PRACTICE, PRACTICE, PRACTICE

Let's start experimenting with Python. Before we get too far along, we want to emphasize something important. One of the best reasons to start learning programming using Python is that you can easily experiment with Python. That is, Python makes it easy to try something out and see the result. Anytime you have a question, simply try it out.

Learning to experiment with a programming language is a very important skill, and one that seems hard for introductory students to pick up. So let's add a new **RULE**.

> **Rule 3:** The best way to improve your programming and problem skills is to practice!

Problem solving—and problem solving using programming to record your solution—requires practice. The title of this section is the answer to the age-old joke:

> **Student:** How do you get to Carnegie Hall?
> **Teacher:** Practice, practice, practice!

Learning to program for the first time is not all that different from learning to kick a soccer ball or play a musical instrument. It is important to learn about fundamentals by reading and talking about them, but the best way to *really* learn them is to practice. We will encourage you throughout the book to type something in and see what happens. If it doesn't work, who cares? Try again; see if you can fix it. If you don't get it right the first time, you will eventually. *Experimenting* is an important skill in problem solving and this is one place where you can develop it!

We begin with our first QUICKSTART. A QUICKSTART shows the development of a working program followed by a more detailed explanation of the details of that program. A QUICKSTART gets us started, using the principal of "doing" before "explaining." Note that we ask you to try some things in the Python shell as we go along. Do it! Remember **RULE 3**. (To get Python see Appendix A.)

1.2 QUICKSTART, THE CIRCUMFERENCE PROGRAM

Let's start with a simple task. We want to calculate the circumference and area of a circle, given its radius. The relevant mathematical formulas are:

- circumference = $2 * \pi * radius$
- area = $\pi * radius^2$

To create the program, we need to do a couple of things:

1. We need to prompt the user for a radius.
2. We need to apply the mathematical formulas listed previously using the acquired radius to find the circumference and area.
3. We need to print out our results.

Here is that program. Let's name it `circumference.py`. The ".py" is a file *suffix*.

PROGRAMMING TIP

Each suffix indicates the type of file. Python files usually have a ".py" suffix. IDLE, Python's default editor (see Appendix A) is fairly picky about this. If you save your program without the ".py" suffix, you will know it right away, as all the colors in the editor window disappear. Add the suffix, resave, and the colors come back. Those colors are useful in that each color indicates a type of thing (yellow for strings, blue for keywords) in the program, making it more readable.

Code Listing 1.1

```python
# calculate the area and circumference of a circle from its radius
# Step 1: prompt for a radius
# Step 2: apply the area formula
# Step 3: Print out the results

import math

radiusString = raw_input("Enter the radius of your circle: ")
radiusInteger = int(radiusString)

circumference = 2 * math.pi * radiusInteger
area = math.pi * (radiusInteger ** 2)

print "The cirumference is:",circumference,  \
      ", and the area is:",area
```

Important: The line numbers shown in the program are *not* part of the program. We list them here only for the reader's convenience.

Before we examine the code, let's illustrate how the program runs with two different input radii to confirm that it works properly.

The easiest way to run a program is to open that program in the IDLE editor, then select Run → Run Module (F5). This *imports* the file into the shell and runs it. Note that every time you run the program, the Python shell prints the "====== RESTART ======" line, indicating that the shell is restarting and running your program.

You can choose some "obvious" values to see if you get expected results. For example, a radius value of 1 results in the area having the recognizable value of $\pi = 3.14159...$. Although not a complete test of the code, it does allow us to identify any gross errors quickly. The other case has a radius of 2 that can be easily checked with a calculator:

```
IDLE 2.6.2
>>> ============================== RESTART ==============================
>>>
Enter the radius of your circle: 1
The cirumference is: 6.28318530718 , and the area is: 3.14159265359
>>> ============================== RESTART ==============================
>>>
Enter the radius of your circle: 2
The cirumference is: 12.5663706144 , and the area is: 12.5663706144
>>>
```

Examining the code

Let's examine the circumference.py code line-by-line. In this first example, there are many topics that will be explained in detail in subsequent chapters. Note that we number only every fifth line in the code listing. Here is a walk through of this code.

Lines 1–4: Anything that follows a pound sign (#) is a comment for the human reader. The Python interpreter ignores it. However, it does provide us as readers some more information on the intent of the program (more on this later). Remember **RULE 2**. Comments help make your document easier to understand for humans.

Line 6: This line imports special Python code from the math *module*. A module is a Python file containing programs to solve particular problems; in this case, the goal is solving common math problems. Modules are described in more detail in Section 1.4. Python has many such modules to make common tasks easier. In this case we are interested in the value π provided by the math module. The value is named `math.pi`; that is, it is the value named "pi" in the "math" module that is written as `math.pi` (more on that naming convention later).

Line 8: This line really has two parts: the Python code to the right of the = sign and the Python code on the left:

- On the right, `raw_input` is a small Python program called a *function*. Functions (see Chapter 5) are often-used, small program utilities that do a particular task. The `raw_input` function prints the characters in quotes "Enter the radius of your circle:" to the Python shell and waits for the user to type a response. Whatever the user types in the shell before pressing the Enter key at the end is *returned*, provided as input to program.
- On the left side of the = is a *variable*. For now, consider a variable to be a name that is associated with a value. In this case, the value returned from `raw_input` will be associated with the name `radiusString`.

  Think of the = as a kind of glue, linking the values on the right side with the variable on the left. The = is called an *assignment statement*; we will have more to say about assignment in Section 1.5.

Line 9: The user's response returned by `raw_input` is stored as a sequence of characters, referred to in computer science as a *string* (see Chapter 4). Python differentiates a sequence of characters, such as those that constitute this sentence, from from numbers that it can perform operations on, such as add, subtract, and so on. Strings are differentiated from numbers using quotes, single or double quotes are acceptable ("hi mom" or 'monty'). For this program we want to work with numbers, not characters, so we must convert the user's response. The `int` function takes the value associated with the variable `radiusString` and returns the integer value of `radiusString`. In other words, it converts the string to an integer. As in the previous line, the value returned by `int` is associated with a variable using the assignment statement. For example, if `radiusString` holds the string of characters '27' the `int` function will convert those characters to the integer 27 and then associate that value the new variable name `radiusInteger`.

The difference between the characters "27" and the number 27 will likely seem strange at first. It is our first example of value *types*. Types will be described in more detail in Section 1.6, but for now, let's us say that a type indicates the kinds of things we can do to a value and the results we obtain.

Line 11: Here we calculate the circumference using the following formula:

$$\texttt{circumference = 2*}\pi\texttt{*radius}$$

In Python, as in most programming languages, the multiplication symbol is * to avoid confusion between the standard math symbols ($\cdot$ and $\times$) and the period and letter "x". The integer 2, the value associated with the variable `math.pi`, and the value associated with the `radiusInteger` are multiplied together, and then the result is associated with the variable named `circumference`. As you will later see, the ordering is important: the mathematical expression on the right-hand side of the equal sign is evaluated, and then the result is associated with the variable on the left-hand side of the equal sign.

Line 12: Similarly, we calculate the area using the formula listed previously. There isn't a way to type in an exponent (superscript) from a keyboard, but Python has an exponentiation operator `**` by which the value on the left is raised to the power on the right. Thus `radiusInteger ** 2` is the same as $\texttt{radiusInteger}^2$. Note that we use parentheses to group the operation. As in normal math, expressions in parentheses are evaluated first, so the expression `math.pi * (radiusInteger ** 2)` means: square the value of `radiusInteger`, then take that result and multiply it by *pi*.

Lines 14 and 15: We print the results using the Python *print* statement. The print statement can print both strings bracketed by quotes (either single or double quotes) and the value associated with a variable. Quoted expressions are printed exactly; variables have their associated *values* printed. Each object (string, variable, value, etc.) that is to be printed is separated from other objects by commas. In this case, the *print* statement outputs: a string, a variable value, another string, and finally a variable value. The backslash character (\) indicates that the statement continues onto the next line—in this case, the two-line *print* statement behaves as if it were one long line. Stretching a statement across two lines can enhance readability—particularly on a narrow screen or page. See Section 1.4.

1.3 AN INTERACTIVE SESSION

An important feature of Python, particularly when learning the language, is that it is an *interpreted* language. By interpreted we mean that there is a program within Python called the interpreter that takes each line of Python code, one line at a time, and executes that code. This feature means that we can try out lines of code one at a time by typing into the Python shell. The ability to experiment with pieces of code in the Python shell is something that really helps while you're learning the language—you can easily try something out and see what happens. That is what is so great about Python—you can easily explore and learn as you go.

Consider our circumference program. The following code shows a session in a Python shell in which a user types each line of the program we listed previously, to see what happens. We also show a few other features, just to experiment. *Open up a Python shell and follow along by trying it yourself.* The comments (text after #, the pound sign), are there to help walk you through the process. There is no need to type them into the Python shell.

```
>>> import math
>>> radiusString = raw_input("Enter the radius of your circle: ")
Enter the radius of your circle: 20
>>> radiusString        # what is the value associated with radiusString
'20'
>>> radiusInteger = int(radiusString)   # convert the string to an integer
>>> radiusInteger       # check the value of the integer
20                      # look, no quotes because it is a number
>>> int(radiusString)   # what does int() return without assignment (=)
20
>>> radiusString        # int() does not modify radiusString!!
'20'
>>> math.pi             # let's see what value is associated with math.pi
3.1415926535897931
>>> circumference = 2 * math.pi * radiusInteger   # try our formula
>>> circumference
125.66370614359172
>>> area = math.pi * radiusInteger ** 2    # area using exponentiation
>>> area
1256.6370614359173
>>> math.pi * radiusInteger ** 2     # area calculation without assignment
1256.6370614359173

>>> print "Circumference: ", circumference, ", area: ", area
Circumference:  125.663706144 , area:  1256.63706144   # output from the print
statement
>>>
```

Within the Python shell, you can find out the value associated with any variable name by typing its name followed by the Enter key. For example, when we type `radiusString` in the shell shown in the example, '20' is output. The quotes indicate that it is a string of characters, '20', rather than the integer 20.

Interestingly, Python treats single quotes ('20') the same as double quotes ("20"). You can choose to designate strings with single or double quotes. It's your choice!

We can see that after the conversion of the string to an integer using the `int` function, simply typing `radiusInteger` results in the integer 20 being printed (no quotes).

We can also try the expression `int(radiusString)` without assigning the result to `radiusInteger`. Note that `radiusString` is unchanged; its value is simply provided to the function. We then check the value of π in the `math` module named `math.pi`. Next we try out the circumference and area formulas. The area calculation is next using the exponentiation operator (`**`), raising `radiusInteger` to the second power. Finally, we try the ***print*** statement. Remember **RULE 3.**

An advantage of Python over other languages such as C, C++, and Java is the Python shell. Take advantage of this feature, because it can greatly enhance learning what the Python language can do. If you wonder about how something might or might not work, try it in the Python shell!

1.4 PARTS OF A PROGRAM

RULE 2 describes a program as an essay on problem solving that is also executable. A program consists of a set of *instructions* that are executed sequentially, one after the other in the order in which they were typed. We save the instructions together in a *module* for storage on our file system. Later, the module can be imported into the Python interpreter, which runs programs by executing the instructions contained in the module.

Modules

- A *module* contains a set of Python commands.
- A module can be stored as a file and *imported* into the Python shell.
- Usage:
  import module *# load the module*

More than 200 modules come with the standard Python distribution—the math module and many more can be found and imported. You can even write your own modules and use them as tools in your own programming work!

Statements and Expressions

Python differentiates code into one of two categories: *expressions* or *statements*. The concept of an expression is consistent with the mathematical definition, so it may be familiar to you.

Expression: a combination of values and operations that creates a new value, a *return value*. If you enter an expression into the Python shell, a value will be returned and displayed; that is, the expression x + 5 will display 7 if the value of x is 2. Note that the value associated with x is not changed as a result of this operation!

Statement: does not *return a value*, but does perform some task. Some statements may control the flow of the program, and others might ask for resources; statements perform a wide variety of tasks. As a result of their operation, a statement may have a *side effect*. A side effect is some change that results from executing the statement. Take the example of the *assignment statement* myInt = 5 (shown in the following example). This statement does not have a *return value*, but it does set the value associated with the variable myInt to 5, a *side effect*. When we type such an assignment into the Python shell, no value is returned, as you can see here:

```
>>> myInt = 5  # statement, no return value but myInt now has value 5
>>> myInt
5
>>> myInt + 5  # expression, value associated with myInt added to 5
10
>>> myInt      # no side effect of expression, myInt is unchanged
5
>>>
```

However, after we type the assignment statement, if we type the variable myInt, we see that it does indeed now have the value of 5 (see the example session). A statement never returns a value, but some statements (not all) may have a side effect. You will see more of this behavior as we explore the many Python statements.

☞ PROGRAMMING TIP

Knowing that an expression has a value, but a statement does not, is useful. For example, you can print the value generated by an expression, e.g. **print** x + 5 (as long as x has a value). However, if you try to print a statement, Python generates an error. If no value is returned from a statement, then what will the print output? Python avoids this by not allowing a statement to be printed. That is, it is not allowable syntax.

```
>>> print x + 5        # printing an expression
7
>>> print y = x + 5    # trying to print a statement
SyntaxError: invalid syntax
```

There are a number of instances of entering expressions and statements into the Python shell in the previous examples. Whenever an expression was entered, its return value was printed on the following line of the console. Whenever a statement was entered, nothing was printed: if we wanted to see what a statement changed (side effect), we had to inquire about the change.

Whitespace

When we type, we usually separate words with what is typically called *whitespace*. Python counts as whitespace the following characters: space, tab, return, linefeed, formfeed and vertical tab and has the following rules about how whitespace is used in a program:

- Whitespace is *ignored* within both expressions and statements.
  For example, Y=X+5 has exactly the same meaning as Y = X + 5.
- *Leading* whitespace, whitespace at the beginning of a line, defines *indentation*. Indentation plays a special role in Python (see the following section).
- Blank lines can also be considered to be whitespace, and the rule for blank lines is trivial: blank lines are allowed anywhere.

Indentation

Indentation is used by all programmers to make code more readable. However, indentation is treated uniquely in Python. Python requires it for *grouping*. When a set of statements or expressions needs to be grouped together, Python does so by a consistent indentation. Grouping of statements will be important when we get to control statements in Chapter 2.

Python requires consistency in whitespace indentation. If previous statements use an indentation of four spaces to group elements, then that must be done consistently throughout the program.

The benefit of indentation is *readability* so Python's whitespace indentation forces readability. The disadvantage is that maintaining consistency with the number of spaces versus tabs can be frustrating, especially when cutting and pasting. Fortunately, Python-aware editors such as IDLE automatically indent and can repair indentation.

PROGRAMMING TIP

IDLE provides commands under the Format menu to help change indentation. If you are having problems with indentation, or if Python is complaining about irregular indentation, use these commands to repair the problem.

Continuation

Long lines of code, those wider than the width of a reasonably sized editing window, can make reading code difficult. Because readability is very important (remember **RULE 2**), Python provides ways to make long lines more readable by splitting them. Such splitting is called a *continuation*. If a statement needs to run onto extra lines to help with readability, you can indicate that continuation by placing a backslash character (\) at the end of a line. Multiple-line expressions can be continued similarly. In this way, a long line that may be difficult to read can be split in some meaningful and readable way across multiple lines. The first program in this chapter, circumference.py, used such a backslash character in the print statement.

Comments

> Let us change our traditional attitude to the construction of programs: Instead of imagining that our main task is to instruct a computer what to do, let us concentrate rather on explaining to human beings what we want a computer to do.
>
> Donald Knuth[1]

We will say many times, in different ways, that a program is more than "just some code that does something." A program is a document that describes the thought process of its writer. Messy code implies messy thinking, and is both difficult to work with and understand. Code also happens to be something that can run, but just because it can run does not make it a good program. Good programs can be read, just like any other essay. Comments are one important way to improve *readability*. Comments contribute nothing to the running of the program, because Python ignores them. In Python, anything following a pound character (#) is ignored on that line. However, they are critical to the readability of the program.

There are no universally agreed upon rules for the right style and number of comments, but there is near-universal agreement that they can enhance readability. Here are some useful guidelines:

- The *why* philosophy: "Good comments don't repeat the code or explain it. They clarify its intent. Comments should explain, at a higher level of abstraction than the code, what you're trying to do." (*Code Complete* by McConnell)
- The *how* philosophy: If your code contains a novel or noteworthy solution, add comments to explain the methodology.

Of course, as a student, readability is important because your grader needs to understand your program in order to give you an appropriate grade.

Special Python Elements: Tokens

As when learning any language, there are some details that are good to know before you can fully understand how they are used. Here we show you the special keywords, symbols, and characters that can be used in a Python program. These language elements are known generically as *tokens*. We don't explain in detail what each one does, but it is important to

---

[1] "Literate Programming," *Computer Journal* 27(2), 1984

note that Python has special uses for all of them. You will become more familiar with them as we proceed through the book.

Keywords

Keywords are special words in Python that cannot be used by you to name things. They indicate commands to the Python interpreter. The complete list is in Table 1.1. We will introduce commands throughout the text, but, for now, know that you cannot use these words as names (of variables, of functions, of classes, etc.) in your programs. Python has already taken them for other uses.

and	del	from	not	while
as	elif	global	or	with
assert	else	if	pass	yield
break	except	import	print	class
exec	in	raise	continue	finally
is	return	def	for	lambda
try				

TABLE 1.1 Python Keywords

Operators

Operators are special tokens (sequences of characters) that have meaning to the Python interpreter. Using them implies some operation, such as addition, subtraction, or something similar. We will introduce operators throughout the text. The complete list is in Table 1.2. You can probably guess many of them, but some of them will not be familiar.

+	-	*	**	/	//	%
<<	>>	&	|	^	~	
<	>	<=	>=	==	!=	<>
+=	-=	*=	/=	//=	%=	
&=	|=	^=	>>=	<<=	**=	

TABLE 1.2 Python Operators

Punctuators and Delimiters

Punctuators, a.k.a. delimiters, separate different elements in Python statements and expressions. Some you will recognize from mathematics; others you will recognize from English. We will introduce them throughout the text. The complete list is in Table 1.3.

(	)	[	]	{	}
,	:	.	`	=	;
'	"	#	\	@	

TABLE 1.3 Python Punctuators

Literals

In computer science, a *literal* is a notation for representing a fixed value, a value that cannot be changed in the program. Almost all programming languages have notations for atomic values such as: integers, floating-point numbers, strings, and booleans. For example, 123 is a literal; it has a fixed value and cannot be modified. In contrast to literals, variables are symbols that can be assigned a value and that value can be modified during the execution of the code.

Naming Objects

> The practitioner of . . . programming can be regarded as an essayist, whose main concern is with exposition and excellence of style. Such an author, with thesaurus in hand, chooses the names of variables carefully and explains what each variable means. He or she strives for a program that is comprehensible because its concepts have been introduced in an order that is best for human understanding, using a mixture of formal and informal methods that reinforce each other.
>
> Donald Knuth[2]

If writing a program is like writing an essay, then you might guess that the names you use in the program, such as the names of your variables, would help greatly in making the program more readable. Therefore, it is important to choose names well. Later we will provide you with some procedures to choose readable names, but here we can talk about the rules that Python imposes on name selection.

1. Every name must begin with a letter or the underscore character (_):
   - A numeral is not allowed as the first character.[3]
   - Multiple-word names can be linked together using the underscore character (_), i.e., `monty_python`, `holy_grail`. A name *starting* with an underscore is often used by Python and Python programmers to denote a variable with special characteristics. You will see these as we go along, but for now it is best to *not* start variable names with an underscore until you understand what that implies.

---

[2] *ibid*

[3] This is so that Python can easily distinguish variable names from numbers.

2. After the first letter, the name may contain any combination of letters, numbers, and underscores:
   - The name cannot be a *keyword* as listed in Table 1.1.
   - You cannot have any delimiters, punctuation, or operators (as listed in Tables 1.2 and 1.3) in a name.
3. A name can be of any length.
4. UPPERCASE is different from lowercase:
   - `myName` is different than `MyName` or `myname` or `Myname`.

1.5 VARIABLES

A *variable* is a name you create in your program to represent "something" in your program. That "something" can be one of many types of entities: a value, another program to run, a set of data, a file. For starters, we will talk about a variable as something that represents a value: an integer, a string, a floating-point number, an so on. We create variables with meaningful names, because the purpose of a good variable name is to make your code more readable. The variable name *pi* is a name most would recognize, and it is easier to both read and write than 3.1415926536. Once a variable is created, you can store, retrieve, or modify the data associated with that variable. Every time you use your variable in a program, its value is retrieved by Python and used in that variable's place. Thus, a variable is really a way to make it easier to read the program you are writing.

☞ PROGRAMMING TIP

Because Python is case sensitive, another way to connect multiple words in a name is called *camelCase*. The style camelCase is the popular practice of writing compound words or phrases such that the words are joined without spaces but every new word begins with a capital letter, such as `myVariableName`, `ThisIsAnInteger`. We use this style extensively in our code examples. Underlines vs. camelCase is mostly personal preference, though Python officially prefers underlines to indicate separate words in names.

How does Python associate the value of the variable with its name? In essence, Python makes a list of names (variables, but other names as well) that are being used right now in the Python interpreter. The interpreter maintains a special structure called a *namespace* to keep this list of names and associated values (see Figure 1.1). Each name in that list is associated with a value, and the Python interpreter updates both names and values during the course of its operation. The name associated with a value is an *alias* for the value, i.e., another name for it. Whenever a new variable is created, it is placed in the list along with an association to a value. If a variable name already exists in the table, its association is updated.

FIGURE 1.1 Namespace containing variable names and associated values.

Variable Creation and Assignment

How is a variable created? In Python, when a variable is first used (assigned a value, defined as a function name, etc.) is when the variable is created. Python updates the namespace list with the new name and its associated value.

Assignment is one way to create a variable. The purpose of assignment is to associate a name with a value. The symbol of assignment for Python is the equal (=) sign. A simple example follows:

```
myInt = math.pi + 5
```

In this case, 5 is added to the value of variable associated with `math.pi` and the result of that expression is associated with the variable `myInt` in the Python namespace. It is important to note that the value `math.pi` is **not** modified by this operation. In fact, assignment does not change any values on the right-hand side. Only a new association is created by assignment—the association with the name on the left-hand side.

The general form of the assignment statement is the same as in mathematics:

left-hand side = right-hand side

Although we use the familiar equal sign (=) from mathematics, its meaning in programming languages is different! In math, the equal (=) indicates equality: what is on the left-hand-side of equal sign (=) has the same value as what is on the right-hand-side. In Python, the equal sign (=) represents *assignment*. Assignment is the operation to associate a value with a variable. The left-hand side represents the variable name and the right-hand-side represents the value. If the variable does not yet exist, then the variable is created and placed in the namespace table; otherwise, the variable's value is updated to the value on the right-hand side. This notation can lead to some odd expressions that would not make much sense mathematically, but make good sense from Python's point of view, such as:

```
myVar = myVar + 1
```

We interpret the previous statement as follows: get the value referred to by myVar, add 1 to it, and then associate the resulting sum with the variable myVar. That is, if myVar's value was 4, then after assignment, its value will be updated to be 5. More generally, evaluate everything in the expression on the right-hand side first, get the value of that expression, and associate that value with the name on the left-hand side.

Evaluation of an assignment statement is a two-step process:

1. Evaluate the expression on the right-hand side.
2. Take the resulting value from the right-hand expression and associate it with the variable on the left-hand side (create the variable if it doesn't exist: otherwise update it)

For example:

```
myVar = 2 + 3 * 5
```

First evaluate the expression on the right-hand side, resulting in the value 17 (remember, multiplication before addition), then associate 17 with myVar, that is, update the namespace so that myVar is an alias for 17 in the namespace. Notice how Python uses the standard mathematical rules for the order of operations: multiplication and division before addition or subtraction.

In the earlier assignment statement:

```
myVar = myVar + 1
```

notice that myVar has two roles. On the right-hand side, it represents a value: "get this value." On the left-hand side, it represents a name that we will associate with value: "what we do with the value."

With that in mind, we can examine some assignment statements that do not make sense and are thus not allowed in Python:

- 7 = myVar + 1 is illegal because 7, like any other integer, is a literal, not a legal variable name, and cannot be changed (you wouldn't want the value 7 to somehow become 125).
- myVar + 7 = 14 is illegal because "myVar + 7" is an expression, not a legal variable name in the namespace.

- Assignment cannot be used in a statement or expression where a value is expected. This is because assignment is a statement; it does not return a value. The statement "***print*** myVar = 7" is illegal, because print requires a value to print, but the assignment statement does not return a value.

Check Yourself: Variables and Assignment

1. Which of the following are acceptable variable names for Python?
   (a) xyzzy
   (b) 1stvar
   (c) rich&bill
   (d) long_name
   (e) good2go

2. Which of the following statement(s) best describe a Python namespace?
   (a) A list of acceptable names to use with Python
   (b) A place where objects are stored in Python
   (c) A list of Python names and the values with which they are associated
   (d) All of the above
   (e) None of the above

3. Give the values printed by the following program for each of the labeled lines.

```
intA = 27
intB = 5
intA = 6
intC = 010 + 2
print intA        # Line 1
print intB + 5    # Line 2
print intB        # Line 3
```

   (a) What is printed by Line 1?
   (b) What is printed by Line 2?
   (c) What is printed by Line 3?

1.6 OBJECTS AND TYPES

In assignment, we associate a value with a variable. But what exactly is that value? What information is important and useful to know about that value?

In Python, every "thing" in the system is considered to be an *object*. In Python, though, the word "object" has a very particular meaning. An object in Python has:

- An *identity*.
- Some *attributes*.
- Zero or more names.

Whenever an object is created by Python, it receives an identification number. If you are ever interested in the number of any object, you can use the id function to discover its ID number. In general, the ID number isn't very interesting to us, but that number is used by Python to distinguish one object from another. We will take a brief look at the ID here because it helps explain how Python manages objects.

Notice that in addition to the ID number, an object can also have a name, or even multiple names. This name is not part of the object's ID, but is used by us, the programmers, to make the code more readable. Python uses the namespace to associate a name (such as a variable name) with an object. Interestingly, multiple namespaces may associate different names with the same object!

Finally, every object has a set of attributes associated with it. Attributes are essentially information about the object. We will offer more insight into object attributes later, but the one that we are most interested in right now is an object's type.

In Python, and in many other languages, each object is considered an example of a *type*. For example, 1, 27, and 365 are objects, each of the same type, called int (integer). Also, 3.1415926, 6.022141×10^{23}, 6.67428×10^{-11} are all objects that are examples of the type called floating-point numbers (Real numbers), which is the type called float in Python. Finally, "spam", 'ham', "'fred'" are objects of the type called strings (more in Chapter 4).

Knowing the type of an object informs Python (and us, the programmers) of two things:

- *Attributes* of the object. For example, there are no decimal points in an integer object, and there are no letters in either an integer object or a float object.
- *Operations* we can perform on the object and the results they return. For example, we can divide two integer objects or two float objects, but the division operation makes no sense on a string object.

If you are unsure of the type of an object in Python, you can ask Python to tell you its type. The function type returns the type of any object. The following session shows some interaction with Python and its objects:

```
>>> aInt = 7
>>> id(aInt)
16790848
>>> type(aInt)      # because 7 is an integer, aInt is of type int
<type 'int'>
>>> bFloat = 2.5
```

```
>>> id(bFloat)      # note that bFloat's ID is different than aInt's ID
17397652
>>> type(bFloat)    # because 2.5 is Real, bFloat is of type float
<type 'float'>
>>> aInt = bFloat   # associate aInt with bFloat's object
>>> type(aInt)
<type 'float'>      # aInt is now of type float
>>> id(aInt)        # aInt's now has the same ID as bFloat
17397652
```

Notice a few interesting things in the example session:

- When we ask for the ID (using `id`), we get a system dependent ID number. That number will be different from session to session or machine to machine. To us, the ID number is hard to remember (though not for Python). That is the point! We create variable names so that we can remember an object we have created so we don't *have* to remember weird ID numbers. We show the ID here to help explain Figure 1.2.
- The information returned by a call to the `type` function indicates the type of the value. An integer returns `<type 'int'>`, a floating-point object returns `<type 'float'>`, etc.
- Most important, the type of an object has *nothing* to do with the variable name; instead it specifies only the *object* with which it is associated. In the previous Python session, an int object (`aInt = 7`) and a floating point object (`bFloat = 2.5`) associated (respectively) with `aInt` and `bFloat`. We then assign the floating point object to the variable named `aInt`, `aInt = bFloat`. The type of object associated with `aInt` is now float.

  The name of the variable has nothing to do with the type of object with which it is associated. However, it can be useful if the name *does* say something about the associated object for those who must read the code. In any case, Python does not enforce this naming convention. We, as good programmers, must enforce it. Note that the ID of the object associated with `aInt` is now the same as the ID of the variable `bFloat`. Both names are now associated with the same object.

Figure 1.2 shows the namespace before and after the last assignment of the previous Python session.

Python (and therefore we) must pay particular attention to an object's type, because that type determines what is "reasonable" or "permissible" to do to that object, and if the operation can be done, what results. As you progress in Python, you will learn more about predefined types in Python, as well as how we can define our own types (or, said in a different way, our own *class*— see Chapter 11).

The following sections describe a few of the basic types in Python.

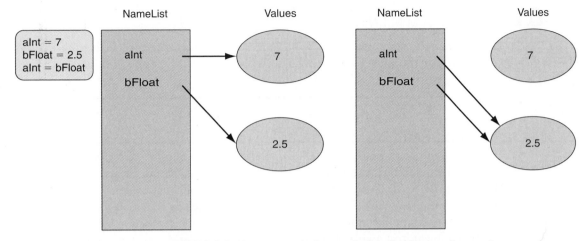

FIGURE 1.2 Namespace before and after the final assignment.

Numbers

Python provides several numeric types. We will use these types for the early chapters, because they relate to numeric concepts that we are familiar with. You will add more types as we move through the book.

Integers

The integer type is designated in Python as type *int*. The integer type corresponds to our mathematical notion of integer. The operations we can perform are those that we would expect: + (addition), - (subtraction), * (multiplication), and / (division, though there is a catch with /—see Section 1.7) as well as a few others. In Python, integers can grow to be as large as needed to store a value and that value will be exact. What is the result of 123456789 * 987654321? Why 121932631112635269L of course (try it in Python). The "L" at the end indicates that it is a long integer, a different type than *int*. The difference between a regular and long integer is an implementation detail. Essentially, integers can grow to be as large as you need, but really big integers can be slower to operate on.

How big an integer can you make? Give it a try.

Integers can be written in normal base 10 form or in other base formats, in particular base 8 (called *octal*) and base 16 (called *hexadecimal*). We note this because of an oddity you might run into with integers. There is a difference to Python between the number 12 and the number 012. The first is your typical, base 10 integer representing the value 12. The second, because of the leading 0, is actually 12_8 (12 base 8) whose decimal value is actually 10!

Python assumes that, if you precede a number with a leading 0, you mean to encode it as an octal, base 8, number. Also, a number written in the form 0x10 is a hexadecimal value (the decimal value 16). The prefix 0x designates hexadecimal.

☞ PROGRAMMING TIP

If you are getting strange results with your integer values, check to make sure that you didn't precede the integer with a leading 0. That means octal, not decimal, and can be very confusing at first!

Floating Point Numbers

Floating point or real numbers are designated in Python as type *float*. The floating-point type refers to non-integer numbers, numbers with decimal points. Floats are created either by typing the value, such as 25.678 or by using exponential notation, with the exponent represented by an "e". Thus, 2.99×10^8 is written as 2.99e8; 9.109×10^{-31} as 9.109e-31. The operators are, like integers, +, −, * and / (see Section 1.7 for more detail). Floats represent Real numbers, but only approximately. For example, what is the exact decimal representation of the operation 2.0/3.0? As you know, there *is* no exact decimal equivalent as the result is an infinite series, that is 2.0/3.0 = 0.666 . . .. Because a computer has a finite amount of memory, Real numbers must be represented with approximations of their actual value. For example, if you type the previous expression into the Python interpreter, you will get:

```
>>> 2.0/3.0
0.66666666666666663
>>>
```

In fact, sometimes you get what looks like odd results when you do floating point operations. If you were to do the calculations yourself, you would find that 12345.6/2.0 is equal to 6172.8. However, if you type the same expression into the Python interpreter, you get:

```
>>> 12345.6/2.0
6172.8000000000002
>>>
```

The result is close; it is a good approximation, but not exact. It is important to remember that floating point values are approximate values, not exact, and that operations using floating point values yield approximate values. Integers are exact and operations on integers yield exact values.

Finally, unlike integers in Python, a leading 0 on a floating point number carries no significance: 012.3 is equivalent to 12.3.

Complex Numbers

Python also provides the type *complex* for complex numbers. Complex numbers consist of two parts: the real and imaginary parts. Complex numbers are written in the form `realPart + imaginPartJ` such as 2 + 3j. That is, the J (either upper- or lower-case) at the end indicates that it is a complex number.

Other Built-In Types

Python has more types that we will introduce in the coming chapters. We mention them briefly here as a preview.

Boolean

A Boolean value has a Python type *bool*. The Boolean type refers to the values `True` or `False` (note the capitalization). If an object is of type Boolean, it can be only one of those two values. In fact, the two Boolean objects are represented as integers: 0 is `False` and 1 is `True`. There are a number of Boolean operators, which we will examine in Chapter 2.

String

A string in Python has the type *str*. A string is our first *collection* type. A collection type contains multiple objects organized as a single object type. The string type is a *sequence*. It consists of a collection of characters in a sequence (order matters), delimited by single quotes (' ') or double quotes (" "). For example, "This is a string!" or 'here is another string' or even a very short string as "x". Some languages such as C and its derivatives consider single characters and strings as different types, but Python only has strings. Operations on strings are described in Chapter 4.

List

A list in Python is of type *list*. A list is also sequence type, like a string, though it can have elements other than characters in the sequence. Because sequences are collections, a list is also a collection. Lists are indicated with square brackets ([and]) and its contents are separated by commas. Lists will be covered in Chapter 6. Here is a list:

[4, 3.57, 'abc']

Dictionary

A dictionary in Python is of type *dict*. A dictionary is a *map* type, a collection though not a sequence. A map type consists of a set of element pairs. The first element in the pair is the *key* and the second is the *value*. The key can be used to search for a value, much like a dictionary or phone book. If you want to look up the phone number (the value) or a person (the key), you can efficiently search for the name and find the number. Curly braces, ({ and }), indicate dictionaries; a colon separates the key and value pair. Dictionaries will be covered in Chapter 8. Here is a dictionary:

{ "Jones":3471124, "Larson":3472289, "Smith":3471288 }

Set

A set in Python is of type *set*. A set is a collection of unique elements—similar to a set in mathematics. A set supports the mathematical set operations such as *union* and *intersection*. Sets will be covered in Chapter 8. Here is a set:

$$\text{set}([1,3,5])$$

Object types: not variable types

As noted earlier, every object has a type in Python. Variables can freely change object association during a program. A Python variable can refer to any object, and the value and type can change over time, for example, holding a string one time and be reassigned to an integer later on. Consider this Python session:

```
>>> myVar
Traceback (most recent call last):
  File "<stdin>", line 1, in <module>
NameError: name 'myVar' is not defined
>>> myVar = 7              # create myVar as type int (integer)
>>> myVar
7
>>> myVar = 7.77           # now associate myVar with a float (floating point)
>>> myVar
7.7699999999999996
>>> myVar = True           # now type is bool (Boolean)
>>> myVar
True
>>> myVar = "7.77"         # now type is str (string)
>>> myVar
'7.77'
>>> myVar = float(myVar)   # convert string myVar to float (floating point)
>>> myVar
7.7699999999999996
>>>
```

Initially, myVar is undefined so the Python interpreter complains when you ask for its associated object. Remember that to create a variable name in the namespace, we must assign (or otherwise define) the variable. Subsequently in the example, we assign an integer value (type int) to myVar, the integer 7. Next, we assign a floating point value to myVar, so it is now associated with an object of type float. The value 7.6999... is the closest approximation that the hardware can store for the desired 7.77. Next we assign a Boolean value to myVar, so it becomes associated with a type bool (Boolean) value. Finally, we assign a string to myVar (type str). For illustration purposes, the characters we chose for the string are the same ones used for the floating-point example. However, note the quotes! Because we put the characters in quotes, the Python interpreter considers the characters to be a string (a sequence of printable characters) rather than a number. To further illustrate that point, we then used the *float* function to convert the string value in myVar to a floating point object and then assigned that floating point object value back to myVar. Python's *float* could create the new floating point object from the string object, because the string consisted of only numbers and a decimal point. If we had tried to convert a string of letters, *float* would have generated an error: *float* ("*fred*") is an error.

Because the computer has separate hardware for integers and floating point arithmetic, the Python interpreter keeps careful track of types for use in expressions. Also, operators may perform different operations depending on the type of the operands. For example, with the plus (+) operator, if the operands are integers or floating points, addition will be performed, but if the operands are strings, concatenation will be performed. Here is an example showing the two interpretations of plus (+):

```
>>> myVar = 2
>>> myVar + myVar
4
>>> myVar = "Ni"
>>> myVar + myVar
'NiNi'
```

PROGRAMMING TIP

Because the type information is not part of the variable, it is often helpful to help keep track of types by affixing the type name to their variables, such as intVar, myInt, phoneBookDict. This style of naming is sometimes called "Hungarian notation." Invented by Charles Simonyi, a programmer who worked at Xerox PARC, Hungarian notation puts the type of the value associated with the variable in front of the name (much as Hungarian puts the family name before the surname).

Constructing New Values

We noted earlier that every object has a type, and that the type determines both what is stored in the object and the kinds of operations that can be performed on that object.

There are also some operations associated with the type itself. One of the most useful of those operations is the *constructor*. A constructor is a special operation that is used to *make* a particular object of that type. For example, the operation *int* will create a new object that is of type integer.

Each type has an associated constructor: the constructor's name is the name of the type (int, float, str, ...). If no value is provided within the parentheses, then a default value of that type is provided (for int it is 0; for float it is 0.0, for str it is ''). If a value *is* provided in the parentheses, then the constructor will *convert* that value to a new object of the specified type if it can. Thus, constructors can be used to convert one object to a new object of a different type. You have already seen conversion in examples:

- *int*(myVar) returns an integer representation of the object associated with myVar.
  - Note myVar itself is unaffected. The associated object is provided, converted, and then a new, converted object is returned.
  - If the object associated with myVar cannot be converted to an integer (say, the value 'a'), then an error will occur.
- *float*(myVar) returns a floating-point representation of the object associated with myVar. As with *int*, if the object cannot be converted to a floating-point number, then an error will occur.
- *str*(myVar) returns a string representation of the object associated with myVar.

  It is again important to note that 1 and "1" are very different.

- 1 is the integer 1.
- "1" is the character digit that gets typed on a keyboard.

  Next is an example Python session that illustrates using constructors for conversion. The comments explain what is happening:

```
>>> int("1")           # convert string to integer
1
>>> int(1.7)           # convert floating point to integer; note the truncation
1
>>> int(True)          # convert Boolean to integer
1
>>> int('1.1')         # can't go from a string, to a float, to an int. Too far!
Traceback (most recent call last):
  File "<stdin>", line 1, in <module>
ValueError: invalid literal for int() with base 10: '1.1'
>>> float("3.33")      # convert string to floating point; note the approximation
3.3300000000000001
>>> float(42)          # convert integer to floating point; note the .0
42.0
>>> str(9.99)          # convert floating point to string; note the quotes
'9.99'
>>> myVar = "2"        # create a string
>>> myVar
'2'
>>> int(myVar)         # show that conversion does not change myVar
2
>>> myVar
'2'
>>> myVar = int(myVar) # need assignment to change myVar
```

```
>>> myVar
2
>>>
```

Note what happens when you convert a floating-point value like 1.7 into an integer. No error occurs: the decimal portion is simply removed and the integer portion used as the value. When an integer is converted to a float, a decimal portion is added (that is, .0 is appended).

1.7 OPERATORS

As we noted in Section 1.6, for every type there is a set of operations that can be performed on that type. Given the limited number of symbols available, some symbols are used for different purposes for different types. This is called *operator overloading*, a term that indicates that a symbol might have multiple meanings depending on the types of the values. For example, we saw earlier that the plus sign (+) performs different operations depending on whether the operands are integers or strings.

Integer Operators

Most of the operators for integers work exactly as you learned in elementary arithmetic class. The plus sign (+) is used for addition, the minus (−) is for subtraction, and the asterisk (*) is for multiplication.

However, division is different, because—unlike the other operators—the integers are not closed with respect to division. By closure, we mean that if you add two integers, the sum is an integer. The same is true for subtraction and multiplication. However, if you divide two integers, the result is not necessarily an integer; it is a rational number (fraction) and we cannot exactly represent a fraction as an int. Consider how you did division in elementary school. For example, consider 5 divided by 3, as shown in Figure 1.3.

```
   1  R2
3 ⌐ 5
   3
  ───
   2
```

FIGURE 1.3 Long division example.

The *quotient* is 1 and the *remainder* is 2. Observe that both the quotient and remainder are integers, so the integers are closed under the quotient and remainder operations. Therefore, in Python (and many other programming languages), the integers have separate operators for quotient (/) and remainder (%).[4] We can see these two operators in action by showing

---

[4] The remainder operation is known in mathematics as the *modulo* operation.

the same 5 divided by 3 equation from Figure 1.3 expressed with the two expressions for quotient and remainder:

```
>>> 5/3    # integer quotient
1
>>> 5%3    # integer remainder
2
```

Therefore, the full set of operators for integers is:

- +   addition
- -   subtraction
- *   multiplication
- /   quotient
- %   remainder
- ** exponentiation

In all cases, the result is an integer.

Floating Point Operators

Floating point operators work as expected, including division:

- +   addition
- -   subtraction
- *   multiplication
- /   division
- ** exponentiation

As with integers, addition, subtraction, and multiplication perform as expected. Unlike integers, floating-point numbers represent Real numbers and the Reals are closed with respect to division: divide two Reals and the result is a Real. Therefore, division of floating point numbers works as expected. For example, 5.0/3.0:

```
>>> 5.0/3.0
1.6666666666666667
```

Mixed Operations

What is the difference between the number 42 and 42.0?[5] The answer is that they are different types. Same value, but different types! Therefore, when you perform operations with them, you might get different answers.

---

[5] The answer to Life, the Universe, and Everything is 42 according to Douglas Adams's *The Hitchhiker's Guide to the Galaxy.*

What happens when you mix types? For example, how does the computer handle dividing an integer by a floating-point number? The answer is, "it depends." In general, operations provided by each type dictate the rules of what can and cannot be mixed. For numbers, a computer has separate hardware for integer and floating-point arithmetic. Because of that hardware, the operation is best done in one type or the other, so the numbers must be of the same type. Those that are not of the same type must be converted. Given that, what is the correct conversion to perform: integer-to-float or float-to-integer?

Clearly no information is lost when converting an integer to a float, but conversion of a float to an integer would lose the fractional information in the float. Therefore, most programming languages, including Python, will "promote" an integer to be a floating point so that both operands are floats and the operation can be performed as floats:

```
>>> intVar = 42
>>> floatVar = 42.0
>>> intVar/5          # integer quotient
8
>>> floatVar/5.0      # floating-point division
8.4000000000000004
>>> intVar/5.0        # floating-point division
8.4000000000000004
>>> floatVar/5        # floating-point division
8.4000000000000004
```

PROGRAMMING TIP

One would normally expect 2/3 to yield 0.666... but in fact it yields 0. This is one of the most common errors introductory programmers make. The integer result of 2/3 is 0 (quotient), and the floating point result of 2.0/3.0 is 0.666.... Note that 2.0/3 is 0.666..., as the 3 is converted to float. Be careful of this.

Order of Operations and Parentheses

The order of arithmetic operations in Python and most common programming languages is the same as you learned in arithmetic: multiplication and division before addition or subtraction. The term used to describe the ordering is *precedence*. In this case, we say that multiplication and division have greater precedence than addition or subtraction, so they are done first. Further, exponents have greater precedence than multiplication and division, also as in arithmetic. If operations have the same precedence—that is, multiplication and division—they are done left to right. Finally, as in arithmetic, parentheses can be used to override the precedence order and force some operations to be done before others, regardless of precedence. The precedence of arithmetic operations is shown in Table 1.4; the order in the table is from highest precedence (performed first) to lowest.

Operator	Description
( )	Parenthesis (grouping)
**	Exponentiation
+x, -x	Positive, Negative
*, /, %	Multiplication, Division, Remainder
+, -	Addition, Subtraction

TABLE 1.4 Precedence (order) of arithmetic operations: highest to lowest.

Here is a session to illustrate precedence and parentheses:

```
>>> 2+3-4        # same precedence: left to right
1
>>> 4/2*5        # same precedence: left to right
10
>>> 2+3*5        # multiplication before addition
17
>>> (2+3)*5      # parentheses force addition before multiplication
25
>>> 2+3*5**2     # exponents before multiplication before addition
77
>>> 2+3*5**2-1
76
>>> -4+2         # negation before addition and subtraction
-2
```

In Chapter 2, you will learn about Boolean operators and their precedence with respect to the arithmetic operators. The full table of all Python operator precedence is in Appendix F.

Augmented Assignment Operators: A Shortcut!

Operations—especially groups of operations—that are used repeatedly are often provided with a *shortcut*, a simpler way of typing. Python, like other languages, has such shortcuts. They are not required, but they do make typing easier and, at some point, make the code shorter and easier to read.

Our first short cut is the combination of an integer operation and the assignment (=) sign. Though you might not have noticed, they were listed in Table 1.2. They are a combination of one of the arithmetic operators such as +, -, *, / along with the assignment sign = . Some examples would be +=, -=, /=, *=. Note that the operation comes before the assignment sign, not after!

What does += mean? You can add 2 to a variable myInt using either expression myInt += 2 or myInt = myInt + 2. The first is a shortcut, the second the "long" way. Table 1.5 lists the most commonly used shortcuts. However, incrementing myInt += 1 is by far the most commonly used shortcut.

Shortcut	Equivalence
myInt += 2	myInt = myInt + 2
myInt -= 2	myInt = myInt - 2
myInt /= 2	myInt = myInt / 2
myInt *= 2	myInt = myInt * 2

TABLE 1.5 Augmented Assignment

Check Yourself: Types and Operators

1. Give the values printed by the following program for each of the labeled lines and answer the associated questions.

```
floatA = 2.5
intA = 7
intB = 6
print intA/intB        # Line 1
print intA/floatA      # Line 2
print intA% intB       # Line 3
print int(floatA)      # Line 4
print float(intA)      # Line 5
```

(a) Line 1: what is the resulting value's type?
(b) Line 2: what is the resulting value's type?
(c) Line 3: what is the resulting value's type?
(d) Line 4: what is the resulting value's type?
(e) Line 5: what is the resulting value's type?

2. Give the values printed by the following program for each of the labeled lines.

```
intA = 10
intB = 3
intC =
print intA + intB * intC      # Line 1
print (intA + intB) * intC    # Line 2
print intB ** intC            # Line 3
print 010 + intC              # Line 4
```

(a) What is printed by Line 1?
(b) What is printed by Line 2?
(c) What is printed by Line 3?
(d) What is printed by Line 4?

☞ PROGRAMMING TIP

You must be a careful with an augmented assignment statement. What can show up on the left-hand side is a variable *that is associated with a value.* You cannot define a variable using augmented assignment. What would it mean to say
`myInt = myInt - 2` if `myInt` doesn't have a value?

1.8 YOUR FIRST MODULE, MATH

Python has many strengths, but one of its best is the availability of the many *modules* for various tasks. If you take a look at the Python Package Index (`http://pypi.python.org/pypi`) you will see that there are more than 6500 packages provided as modules for you to use in Python—all for free! The Python community, part of the Open Source community, created those modules for everyone to use. As we described earlier, a module is a collection of instructions saved together as a whole. Those instructions can be loaded into our program using the ***import*** command. We did just that—we used the ***import*** command to import the math module in the program to determine the circumference of a circle in Section 1.1. Let's take a deeper look at the math module.

When we import that math module, all the code contained in the math module is made available to our program. The contents of the math module can be found in a couple of ways. The best way is to look online in the Python documentation. Go to the Python docs and take a look: `http://docs.python.org/library/math.html`. You could also import the math module in IDLE, and do the following:

- Type ***import*** math
- Type math.<TAB>

When you type the tab character after "math.", a list will be created of all the code that was brought in during the import.

What is typically brought in is either a function (a piece of code we can call to perform some operation) or a variable. Either way, the *name* of the imported code is always preceded with `math.`. Thus, in Section 1.1, we used the variable `math.pi`. The "math." indicates that the variable "pi" is the variable in the math module. All the code imported from the math module is referenced in this way. Although there are other ways to import a module, this is the preferred way.

Functions will be properly introduced in Chapter 5. A function has two parts: the *name* of the function, which hopefully indicates what operation it performs, and an *argument* list, which is a parenthetical list of values to be sent into the function as part of its operation. When the function completes its operation, a *return value* is returned from the function. A typical function is the `math.sin(aFloatValue)` function. The name of the function is `math.sin` and the argument list follows: a parenthetical list of one value, which must be a floating point number. When `math.sin(aFloatValue)` completes, the sine of `aFloatValue` (which would also be a float) is returned. The returned value can be captured with an assignment, printed, or otherwise used elsewhere in the program.

Some useful functions in the math module include:

`math.sin` Takes one numeric argument, and returns the sine of that argument as a float.

`math.cos` Takes one numeric argument, and returns the cosine of that argument as a float.

`math.pow` Takes two numeric arguments, x and y, and returns x^y (x raised to the power y) as a float.

`math.sqrt` Takes one numeric argument, and returns the square root of that argument as a float.

`math.hypot` Takes two numeric arguments, x and y, and returns $\sqrt{x^2 + y^2}$, the Euclidean distance.

`math.fabs` Takes one numeric argument, and returns the absolute value of the argument.

At any time, you can type help(object) and Python will provide help on that object. For example:

```
>>> import math
>>> help(math.pow)

Help on built-in function pow in module math:

pow(...)
    pow(x,y)

    Return x**y (x to the power of y).
(END)
>>>
```

1.9 DEVELOPING AN ALGORITHM

You know a lot more than when we started this chapter about how to write programs, especially with numbers. Let's take a look at solving a simple problem to see how well you can do. Here's a question:

> If one inch of rain falls on an acre of land, how many gallons of water have accumulated on that acre?

This problem really has to do with the weather and how it is reported. When the weather person on television tells you that "one inch of rain" has fallen, what does that really mean? In case you didn't know, "one inch of rain" means pretty much what it says. Rain has accumulated to a depth of one inch over a certain area.

How do we attack this problem? Our goal is to develop an *algorithm* from which we can derive our program. What is an algorithm? It is one of those common words that can be hard to define precisely. One definition that works for what we need to do in this book is:

> **algorithm:** A method—a sequence of steps—that describes how to solve a problem or class of problems.

When we describe an algorithm, we are describing what we—as human problem solvers—need to do to solve a problem. We can provide a description in a variety of ways: English language, diagrams, flow charts, whatever works for us. Having worked out a solution to a problem in our own best way, we can translate that algorithm into the code that realizes that algorithm.

For our rainfall problem, how can we develop our algorithm? First, we observe that the problem statement (the "if" part) is a combination of linear measurement (one inch) and square measurement (one acre), but the desired result is in volume (gallons). We must find some intermediate unit for the conversion process. Representing volume in cubic feet is one way; metric units would work as well.

Our algorithm starts with these steps:

1. Find the volume (in cubic feet) of water (where volume = depth * area).
2. Convert the volume (in cubic feet) to gallons.

The Internet can provide the conversion formulas:

> 1 acre = 43,560 square feet
> 1 cubic foot = 7.48051945 gallons

With this information, we can fill in our algorithm:

1. Find the volume in cubic feet of water of one inch over one acre
   1 inch = 1/12 foot
   volume = depth * area = (1/12)*43560 cubic feet
2. Convert the volume in cubic feet to gallons
   gallons = volume * 7.48051945

Now let's try this in Python. We can begin in the Python shell and try out the volume formula:

```
>>> volume = (1/12) * 43560
>>> volume
0
```

Well, 0 cubic feet looks wrong. What happened? Because we are in the Python shell, we can experiment. Let's try each part individually to see if we can find the problem. So, let's try 1/12 and see what we get. One way that we can develop algorithms is to test ideas we wish to use and see how well they work:

```
>>> 1/12
0
```

Arithmetic tells us that $1/12 = 0.08333\ldots$, so we have found our problem. The question is: why?

Remember that in Python when you use the slash (/) operator with integers, it finds the *integer* quotient. It does not result in a floating point number as we would expect from arithmetic. If we want a decimal (fractional) result, we must use floating point (approximations of Reals). There are many ways to make that happen, but an easy way is to make one of the operands a floating-point value. We can make either one or both operands floating point, because if at least one is floating point, the whole operation will be done in the floating-point hardware unit, so the result will be a floating point.

Let's try it.

```
>>> 1/12        # integer quotient
0
>>> 1.0/12      # floating-point division
0.083333333333333329
>>> 1/12.0
0.083333333333333329
>>> 1.0/12.0
0.083333333333333329
```

That's better, so let's try the volume formula again:

```
>>> volume = (1.0/12) * 43560
>>> volume
3630.0
```

That is much better. Note that the type of `volume` is now floating point because the right-hand side of the assignment statement was a floating-point expression, because of the one floating point value: 1.0.

Let's include the conversion to gallons:

```
>>> volume = (1.0/12) * 43560
>>> volume
3630.0
>>> gallons = volume * 7.48051945
>>> gallons
27154.2856035
```

That looks reasonable. Now let's put it together in a program (in IDLE) and call it rain.py. See Code Listing 1.2

Code Listing 1.2

```
# Calculate rainfall in gallons for 1 inch on 1 acre
volume = (1.0/12)*43560
gallons = volume * 7.48051945
print "1 in. rain on 1 acre is", gallons, "gallons"

>>>
1 in. rain on 1 acre is 27154.2856035 gallons
>>>
```

The result is fine, but the output isn't very pretty. Take a look ahead at Section 4.4 for ways to make the output prettier.

1.10 CONCLUSION

In this chapter, we introduced a simple, but complete program followed by a description of expressions vs. assignments, whitespace and indentation, and finally operators. Most importantly, we showed how to use the Python shell to practice.

VISUAL VIGNETTE

1.11 TURTLE GRAPHICS

Python version 2.6 introduced a simple drawing tool known as Turtle Graphics. Appendix B provides an introduction and describes a few of the many commands that are available. The concept is that there is a turtle that you command to move forward, right, and, left combined with the ability to have the turtle's pen move up or down.

Let's draw a simple five-pointed star. We begin by importing the turtle module. By default, the turtle begins in the middle of the window pointing right with the pen down. We then have the turtle repeatedly turn and draw a line.

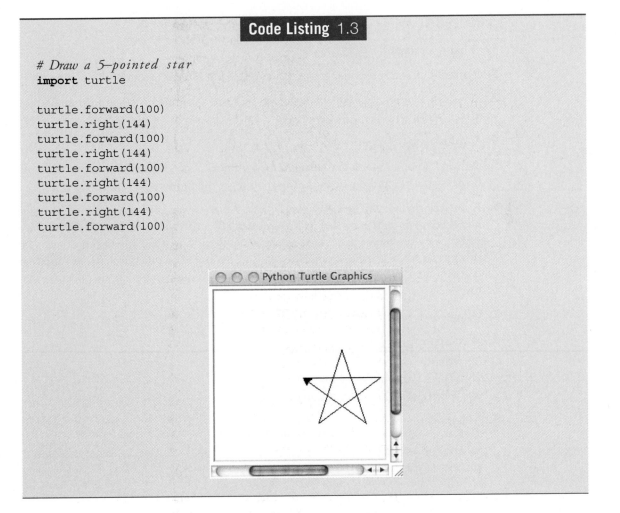

```
Code Listing 1.3

# Draw a 5-pointed star
import turtle

turtle.forward(100)
turtle.right(144)
turtle.forward(100)
turtle.right(144)
turtle.forward(100)
turtle.right(144)
turtle.forward(100)
turtle.right(144)
turtle.forward(100)
```

As with any problem, the hard part is the thinking that goes into figuring out the details. In this case, what are the angles that we need on each turn? Notice that the center of the star is a regular pentagon. A quick Internet check reveals that each internal angle is 108°. One can view the star as five (isosceles) triangles attached to the pentagon. Because a side of the pentagon extends into a side of a triangle, supplementary angles are formed so the base angle of each triangle is 72° (supplementary angles: 180° − 108°). The two base angles of an isosceles triangle are equal and combine to be 144° so the third angle must be 36° (a triangle has 180°: 180° − 144°). To make the sharp turn, at each point of the star we need to make a 144° turn (180° − 36°). That is why we have turtle.right(144) for each point.

Exercises

1. What is a program?

2. Python is an interpreted language. What does "interpreted" mean in this context?

3. What is a Python *comment*? How do you indicate a comment? What purpose do they serve?

4. What is a *namespace* in Python?

5. Write a Python program that prompts for a number. Take that number, add 2, multiply by 3, subtract 6, and divide by 3. You should get the number you started with.

6. A nursery rhyme: *As I was going to St. Ives, I met a man with seven wives. Every wife had seven sacks, and every sack had seven cats, every cat had seven kittens. Kittens, cats, sacks, and wives, how many were going to St. Ives?* There are interesting aspects to this puzzle, such as who is actually going to St. Ives. For our purposes, assume that everyone and everything are headed to St. Ives. Write a program to calculate that total.

7. Using Turtle Graphics draw a *six* pointed star.

8. Whitespace:
   (a) What is whitespace in Python?
   (b) When does whitespace matter?
   (c) When does whitespace not matter?

9. Assignment:
```
myInt = 5
myInt = myInt + 3
print myInt
```

   (a) If you execute the three lines of code, what will be printed? Explain your answer using the rules of assignment.
   (b) Rewrite `myInt = myInt + 3` using the += symbol.

10. Assignment:
```
myVar1 = 7.0
myVar2 = 5
print myVar1 % myVar2
```

    If you execute these three lines of code, what will be printed?

11. Explain the difference between a statement and an expression. Give an example of both, and explain what is meant by a statement having a *side effect*.

12. Try to predict what will be printed by the following:

```
x = 4
y = 5
print x/y
```

13. Given the expression: 30 - 3 ** 2 + 8 / 3 ** 2 * 10

(a) What is the output of the expression? (You can check your answer in the Python shell.)

(b) Based on precedence and associativity of the operators in Python, correctly parenthesize the expression such that you get the same output as above.

14. Predict the output (check your answer in the Python shell):

(a) 2**2**3

(b) 2**(2**3)

(c) (2**2)**3

Why do two of the expressions have the same output?

Rewrite expression (c) with one exponention operator (**) and one multiplication operator (*).

15. Mixed operations:

(a) What type results when you divide an integer by a float? A float by an integer?

(b) Explain what that resulting type makes sense (as opposed to some other type).

16. Prompt for input and then print the input as a string, an integer and a float point value. What values can you input and print without errors being generated?

17. (Integer operators) One way to determine whether an integer is even is to divide the number by two and check the remainder. Write a three-line program that prompts for a number, converts the input to an integer, and prints a zero if the number is even and a one if the number is odd.

18. (Order of operations) One example expression was 2 + 3 * 5, the value of which was 17. Using the same expression, include parentheses to arrive at a different value for the expression.

19. Write a program to calculate the volume of water in liters when one centimeter of water falls on one hectare.

20. (Illegal expressions) In a Python shell, try some of the illegal expressions mentioned in the chapter and observe the error messages. For example, try assigning a value to a keyword, such as: **and** = 4. Each error message begins with the name of the error and that name is useful in checking for errors. Generate at least five different error messages.

21. Table 1.2 lists Python operators, some of which may have been unfamiliar to you. Open up the Python shell and experiment with unfamiliar operators and see how many you can define.

22. We know from mathematics that parenthesis can change the order of operations. For example, consider a + b * c, (a + b) * c, and a + (b*c). In general, two of those expressions will be the same and one will be different. Through trial and error, find one set of integer values for a, b, and c so that all three expressions have the same value and a != b != c.

23. Consider integer values of a, b, and c, and the expression (a + b) * c. In mathematics, we can substitute square brackets, [ ], or curly braces, { }, for parentheses, ( ). Is that same substitution valid in Python? Try it.

24. Consider the expression (a + b) * c, but with string values for a, b, and c. Enter that into the Python shell. What happens? Why?

25. A day has 86,400 secs (24*60*60). Given a number in the range 1 to 86,400, output the current time as hours, minutes, and seconds with a 24-hour clock. For example: 70,000 sec is 19 hours, 26 minutes, and 40 seconds.

26. A telephone directory has N lines on each page and each page has exactly C columns. An entry in any column has a name with the corresponding telephone number. On which page, column, and line is the Xth entry (name and number) present? (Assume that page, line, column numbers and X all start from 1.)

27. If the lengths of the two parallel sides of a trapezoid are X meters and Y meters, respectively, and the height is H meters, what is the area of the trapezoid? Write Python code to output the area.

28. Simple interest is calculated by the product of the principal, number of years, and interest, all divided by 100. Write code to calculate the simple interest on a principal amount of $10,000 for a duration of 5 years with the rate of interest equal to 12.5%.

29. The radius and mass of the Earth are $r = 6378 \times 10^3$ meters and $m1 = 5.9742 \times 10^{24}$ kg, respectively. Mr. Jones has a mass of X kg. Prompt the user to input X and then calculate the gravitational force (F) and acceleration due to gravity (g) caused by the gravitational force exerted on him by the Earth. Remember, $F = G(m1)(m2)/(r^2)$ and $F = mg$. Let the universal gravitational constant $G = 6.67300 \times 10^{-11}$ (in units of $m^3 kg^{-1} s^{-2}$ assuming the MKS [Meter-Kilogram-Second] system). Check that the resulting value of g is close to $9.8 m/s^2$.

30. (Using modules) Python comes with hundreds of modules. Here is a challenge for you: find a module that you can import that will generate today's date so you can print it.

Use your favorite search engine for help in finding which module you need and how to use it. In the end, your task is to do the following:

```
>>> print "Today's date is:", X
Today's date is: 2009-05-22
```

31. Consider a triangle with sides of length 3, 7, and 9. The law of cosines states that given three sides of a triangle (a, b, and c) and the angle C between sides a and b: $c^2 = a^2 + b^2 - 2 \star a \star b \star cos(C)$. Write Python code to calculate the three angles in the triangle.

32. In football, there is a statistic for quarterbacks called the *passer rating*. To calculate the passer rating, you need four inputs: pass completions, pass attempts, total passing yards, and interceptions. There are five steps in the algorithm. Write a program that asks for the five inputs and then prints the pass rating:

(a) C is the "completions per attempt" times 100 − 30 all divided by 20
(b) Y is the "yards per attempt" −3 all divided by 4
(c) T is the "touchdowns per attempt" times 20
(d) I is 2.375 minus ("interceptions minus attempts" times 35)
(e) The pass rating is the sum of C, Y, T, and I all divided by 6 and then multiplied by 100

33. Checking the user input for errors is a vital part of programming. The following simple program below attempts to take a string input and convert it into an integer. What will happen if the user enters "Hello World" at the prompt rather than a number? Can you think of a way that the program can be altered to handle this input (hint: think about adjusting how the program handles different types of input)?

```
Raw1 = raw_input ('Please enter a number:')
Int1 = int (Raw1)
```

34. Body Mass Index (BMI) is a number calculated from a person's weight and height. According to the Centers for Disease Control, the BMI is a fairly reliable indicator of body fatness for most people. BMI does not measure body fat directly, but research has shown that BMI correlates to direct measures of body fat, such as underwater weighing and dual energy X-ray absorptiometry. The formula for BMI is:

$$weight/height^2$$

where *weight* is in kilograms and *height* is in meters.

(a) Write a program that prompts for metric weight and height and outputs the BMI.
(b) Write a program that prompts for weight in pounds and height in inches, converts the values to metric, and then calculates the BMI.

Programming Projects

1. **The Great Lakes are how big?**

   The Great Lakes in the United States contain roughly 22% of the world's fresh surface water (22,810 km^3). It is hard to conceive how much water that is. Write a program to calculate how deep it would be if all the water in the Great Lakes was spread evenly across the 48 contiguous U.S. states. You will need to do some Internet research to determine the area of that region.

2. **Where is Voyager 1?**

   The Voyager 1 spacecraft, launched September 15, 1977, is the farthest traveling earth-made object. It is presently on the outer edges of our solar system. The NASA update page on September 25, 2009, reported it as being a distance of approximately 16,637,000,000 miles from the Sun, traveling away from the Sun at 38,241 miles/hour.

   Write a program that will prompt the user for an integer number that indicates the number of days after 9/25/09. You will calculate the distance of Voyager from the Sun using the numbers from 9/25/09 (assume that velocity is constant) plus the entered number of days and report:

   - Distance in miles
   - Distance in kilometers (1.609344 kilometers/mile)
   - Distance in Astronomical Units (AU, 92,955,887.6 miles/AU)
   - Round trip time for radio communication in hours. Radio waves travel at the speed of light, listed at 299,792,458 meters/second.

3. **Oil conversions and calculations.**

   Write a program that will prompt the user for a floating point number that stands for gallons of gasoline. You will reprint that value along with other information about gasoline and gasoline usage:

   - Number of liters
   - Number of barrels of oil required to make this amount of gasoline
   - Number of pounds of CO_2 produced
   - Equivalent energy amount of ethanol gallons
   - Price in U.S. dollars

   Here are some approximate conversion values:

   - 1 barrel of oil produces 19.5 gallons of gasoline.
   - 1 gallon of gasoline produces 20 pounds of CO_2 gas when burned.
   - 1 gallon of gasoline contains 115,000 BTU (British Thermal Units) of energy.
   - 1 gallon of ethanol contains 75,700 BTU of energy.
   - 1 gallon of gasoline costs $3.00/gallon.

   Look on the Internet for some interesting values for input such as the average number of gallons consumed per person per year, or consumed by the country per day, or consumed per year.

4. Population estimation.

The U.S. Census provides information on its web page (`http://www.census.gov`) about the current U.S. population as well as approximate rates of change.

Three rates of change are provided:

- a birth every 7 seconds.
- a death every 13 seconds.
- a new immigrant every 35 seconds.

These are obviously approximations of birth, death, and immigration rates, but they can assist in providing population estimates in the near term.

Write a program that takes years as input (as an integer) and prints out an estimated population (as an integer). Assume that the current population is 307,357,870, and assume that there are exactly 365 days in a year.

Hint: note that the rate units are in seconds.

CHAPTER 2

Control

If you come to a fork in the road, take it.

Yogi Berra

The ability to make billions of decisions per second and make them repeatedly is the source of computing's power. In this chapter, we introduce control in the form of selection (making decisions) and repetition (doing the same thing over and over). With such control in hand, you will have the ability to create any program.

Our plan is to begin this chapter with a QUICKSTART introduction to selection and repetition along with a couple of examples so that you can get a feel for the power of control constructs. The second half of the chapter will cover control in detail. Up to this point, all we have been able to do is write code that is executed one statement after another, as shown in Figure 2.1.

We have not yet shown a way to incorporate either decisions or repetition into our programs. So let's get into that now.

2.1 THE SELECTION STATEMENT FOR DECISIONS: *IF*

The simplest decision presents a choice of doing one of two things: of executing one statement or another. Such a simple choice fits nicely with computer hardware, because the choice itself can be represented as a zero (*False*) or not-zero (*True*). More complex decisions can be built from combinations of simple ones.

Consider executing instructions one after another until a decision point is reached. It is like a fork in the road: you must choose to go one way or the other. After evaluating the decision criteria, a result is returned. If the result is *True*, we take one fork and execute one set of statements; if it is *False*, we take the other fork and execute a different set of

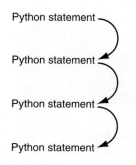

FIGURE 2.1 Sequential program flow.

statements. Afterwards, we continue on with the rest of the program, executing statements in sequence one at a time. This flow is shown in Figure 2.2.

Booleans for Decisions

The choices in the Yogi Berra quote above are binary: go one way or the other. Python provides a type of value known as a *Boolean* for this purpose. A Boolean expression can yield only a value of *True* or *False*. Such a result can be used for making programming

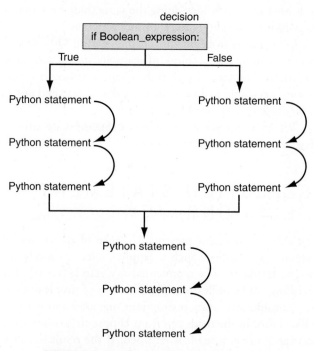

FIGURE 2.2 Decision making flow of control.

decisions. If an expression evaluates to *True*, execute one statement (or set of statements); if the expression is *False*, execute a different statement (or set of statements). As a result, any expression that evaluates to *True* or *False* can be used for a decision.

An expression such as "x greater than 5" is a Boolean expression. It is a Boolean because, once evaluated, it returns either *True* or *False*. In Python we write that expression in a familiar way: x > 5. If we want to express "x greater than or equal to 5," we use a *pair* of characters (>=), x >= 5, because there is no single "greater-than-or-equal-to" key on our keyboards. Expressing equality in a Boolean expression is a bit of a challenge. We are used to using the = sign for equality, but as you have seen, the = represents assignment, not equality, in Python. To deal with this problem, Python uses a *pair* of equal signs, ==, to represent equality. For example, x == 5 is a measure of equality: is the value represented by x equal to 5? Based on the previous information, it is fairly easily to guess the remaining Boolean operators, but Table 2.1 lists them for you.

<	less than
>	greater than
<=	less than or equal to
>=	greater than or equal to
==	equal to
!=	not equal to

TABLE 2.1 Boolean Operators.

The *if* Statement

The **if** statement expresses selective execution in Python. It is our first control statement and, simple as it is, it is quite powerful. Selective execution is one of the primary control mechanisms in general programming. It is a critical part of enabling computers to perform complex tasks.

The Basic *if* Statement

We begin with a basic **if** statement. It has a Boolean expression that is evaluated, and the result of that Boolean expression dictates what happens next.

Code Listing 2.1

```
if booleanExpression:
    # suite of Python statements
# rest of the Python program
```

The basic **if** statement does the following:

1. Evaluate booleanExpression, yielding either *True* or *False*.
2. If booleanExpression yields *True*,
    (a) Execute the Python code *indented* under the **if**.
    (b) Once the indented code is executed, continue with any Python code *after* the indented code (that is, any code following the **if** at the same indentation as the **if** itself).
3. If booleanExpression yields *False*,
    (a) Ignore any code indented under the **if**, (that is, do not execute it).
    (b) Continue with any Python code *after* the indented code (that is, any code following the **if** at the same indentation as the **if** itself).

Indentation and a Suite of Python Code

As mentioned earlier (Section 1), indentation in Python matters. Indentation is Python's method for associating or grouping statements. Indentation gets used in many Python statements, including the **if** statement. For **if**, the indentation indicates that the statement(s) following the **if** is associated with that **if**. This group is called a *compound statement*, where the **if** is the *header* and the indented statement(s) the *suite*. A compound statement is considered to be one logical statement.

A suite of statements is a set of statements that has the same indentation and these statements are executed as a group. Other languages use explicit characters to mark compound statements, but because indentation makes compound statements easier to read, Python settles for the indentation alone. Therefore, indentation has a dual purpose: to indicate compound statements and to make compound statements easier to read.

Let's take a look at a short example. The **if** statement checks to see whether a number is negative, and if so, it changes the number to zero:

```
>>> points = -5
>>> if points < 0:
        points = 0

>>> print points
0
>>>
```

In this example, the value of the variable points is -5. We begin by evaluating the Boolean expression points < 0. The "less-than" operator works on these two integer values just like in mathematics, comparing the two values and returning a value, a Boolean. In this case, the Boolean expression evaluates to *True*. As a result, the **if** suite points = 0 is executed. Note the indentation on the second line of the **if** statement (done automatically after typing the colon (:) in IDLE). Once execution finishes with the compound **if** statement, the next statement after the **if** (the **print** statement, in this case) is executed, and we see that the value of `points` is indeed 0.

The *if-else* Statement

A variation on the basic **if** statement adds the ability to do something only if the Boolean expression is *False*.

Code Listing 2.2

```
if booleanExpression:
    # suite executed for a True boolean result
else:
    # suite executed for a False boolean result
# rest of the Python program
```

The **if-else** statement operation does the following:

1. Evaluate `booleanExpression` to yield *True* or *False*.
2. If `booleanExpression` yields *True*,
   (a) Execute the **if** suite, indented under the **if**.
   (b) Continue with the rest of the Python program.
3. If `booleanExpression` yields *False*,
   (a) Execute the **else** suite, indented under the **else**.
   (b) Continue with the rest of the Python program.

Let's see a short example. In this example, if the `points` variable is greater than the `seconds` variable, the program prints "Lead is safe."; if not, the program prints "Lead is not safe."

```
>>> points = 10
>>> seconds = 20
>>> if points > seconds:
        print "Lead is safe."
    else:
        print "Lead is not safe."


Lead is not safe.
>>>
```

In this example, the Boolean expression `points > seconds` evaluates to *False*, so the program skips to the **else** clause and executes the **print** "*Lead is not safe.*" statement. That output is shown at the bottom of the example.

Example: What Lead is Safe in Basketball?

Basketball is a high-scoring game in which a lead can evaporate quickly. As a spectator, it would be nice to be able to figure out when a lead is insurmountable near the end of a game. Fans of the leading team would like to know when they can relax and be comfortable in the knowledge that victory is almost certain. Sports writer Bill James of the online magazine www.slate.com has pondered that problem and developed an algorithm for determining when a lead in basketball is insurmountable.[1]

James's algorithm, developed after many years of watching basketball, determines whether a lead is insurmountable: "safe" in his terminology. Of course, this algorithm does not guarantee that a lead is safe—anything can happen. Here is his algorithm, exactly as he wrote it:

1. Take the number of points one team is ahead.
2. Subtract three.
3. Add a half-point if the team that is ahead has the ball, and subtract a half-point if the other team has the ball. (Numbers less than zero become zero.)
4. Square that result.
5. If the result is greater than the number of seconds left in the game, the lead is safe.

It took years of observation to come up with the algorithm, but with the algorithm in hand, we can easily convert it to a Python program. You will learn that the coming up with the algorithm is the hardest part of programming.

Let's take these steps one at a time.

1. *Take the number of points one team is ahead.*
   We can ask a user to input the number of points using the *raw_input* command. We remind ourselves that *raw_input* yields a string by using an appropriate variable name. We then convert the input to an integer. See Code Listing 2.3.

Code Listing 2.3

```
# 1. Take the number of points one team is ahead.
pointsStr = raw_input("Enter the lead in points: ")
points = int(pointsStr)
```

2. *Subtract three.*
   That's simple arithmetic—we can do that. Remember that we use an assignment statement to capture the result of the arithmetic in a variable. See Code Listing 2.4.

---

[1] "The Lead Is Safe," by Bill James, March 17, 2008, http://www.slate.com/id/2185975/

Code Listing 2.4

```
# 2. Subtract three.
points = points - 3
```

---

3. *Add a half-point* **if** the team that is ahead has the ball, and subtract a half-point **if** the other team has the ball. (Numbers less than zero become zero.)

Here it gets interesting. Notice the two **if**s that we highlighted. That English statement needs to be converted to a Python *if-else* statement. However, first we need to know whether the leading team "has the ball" so we have to ask the user using `raw_input`. In Code Listing 2.5, note the use of the double-equal sign in the Boolean expression to check for equality: ==. Further, note that if the user enters "No," the Boolean expression will be *False*, resulting in the **else** statement (`points = points - 0.5`) being executed. Notice that we are are comparing strings. That is, we are comparing whether two sequences of characters, the string "Yes" and the user response, to see whether they are the same (more of that in Chapter 4).

Code Listing 2.5

```
# 3. Add a half-point if the team that is ahead has the ball,
#    and subtract a half-point if the other team has the ball.

has_ball = raw_input("Does the lead team have the ball (Yes or No): ")

if has_ball == 'Yes':
    points = points + 0.5
else:
    points = points - 0.5
```

We overlooked the statement in parentheses: numbers less than zero become zero. Actually, that was our first **if** example. Let's add it in to complete this step (Code Listing 2.6):

Code Listing 2.6

```
# 3. Add a half-point if the team that is ahead has the ball,
#    and subtract a half-point if the other team has the ball.
```

```
has_ball = raw_input("Does the lead team have the ball (Yes or No): ")

if has_ball == 'Yes':
    points = points + 0.5
else:
    points = points - 0.5

# (Numbers less than zero become zero)
if points < 0:
    points = 0
```

4. *Square that.*
   Simple arithmetic—remember the exponentiation operator (**) (Section 1.2) and assignment (Code Listing 2.7):

Code Listing 2.7

```
# 4. Square that.
points = points ** 2
```

5. **If** *the result is greater than the number of seconds left in the game, the lead is safe.*
   Here we have another **if** statement, nicely phrased by James. We'll expand his algorithm to also inform the user when the lead is *not* safe. That expansion requires an **else** clause, and is the example we used earlier. Also, we need to ask the user to input the seconds remaining, and convert the input to an integer. Notice that we used the `raw_input` *as an argument* to the `int` function. As discussed earlier (Section 1.7), we execute code *inside* the parentheses first, the `raw_input`, and then that result is used by `int`. Combining these two lines of code may make it more readable (Code Listing 2.8).

Code Listing 2.8

```
# 5. If the result is greater than the number of seconds left in the game,
#    the lead is safe.
seconds = int(raw_input("Enter the number of seconds remaining: "))

if points > seconds:
    print "Lead is safe."
```

```
else:
    print "Lead is not safe."
```

Let's take a look at the whole program (Code Listing 2.9). Notice how we used comments to include James's original algorithm. The next time you watch a basketball game, try it out and see how well James did with his algorithm.

Code Listing 2.9

```
# Bill James' Safe Lead Calculator
# From http://www.slate.com/id/2185975/

# 1. Take the number of points one team is ahead.
pointsStr = raw_input("Enter the lead in points: ")
points = int(pointsStr)

# 2. Subtract three.
points = points - 3

# 3. Add a half-point if the team that is ahead has the ball,
#    and subtract a half-point if the other team has the ball.
has_ball = raw_input("Does the lead team have the ball (Yes or No): ")

if has_ball == 'Yes':
    points = points + 0.5
else:
    points = points - 0.5

# (Numbers less than zero become zero)
if points < 0:
    points = 0

# 4. Square that.
points = points ** 2

# 5. If the result is greater than the number of seconds left in the game,
#    the lead is safe.
seconds = int(raw_input("Enter the number of seconds remaining: "))

if points > seconds:
    print "Lead is safe."
```

```
else:
    print "Lead is not safe."
```

With a working program in hand, it is useful to look back over it for refinements. For example, what if the user answers "YES" or "yes" instead of exactly "Yes" to the question of whether the leading team has the ball? It would be reasonable to accept all three. How can we do that? It will take some work on your part to manipulate the strings, something you will see more of in Chapter 4.

Repetition

The *if* statement provided selection as a way to make decisions. Next we consider ways to *repeat* statements. The ability to execute instructions—especially decisions—over and over is the source of considerable power in programming. That is, repeatedly making billions of simple (True/False) decisions per second allows the computer to make complex decisions to complete complex tasks.

Python offers two different styles of repetition: *while* and *for*. In this chapter, we introduce the two main repetition commands: the *while* loop and the *for* iterator, to be described in more detail in Section 2.2.

The *while* statement introduces the concept of *repetition*. The *while* statement allows us to repeat a suite of Python code as long as some condition is *True*. When the condition becomes *False*, we move on with the rest of the program. The *for* statement implements *iteration*. Iteration is the process of examining all elements of a collection, one at a time, allowing us to perform some operations on each element. One characteristic of Python is that it provides powerful iterators so one frequently uses *for* in Python programs.

Finally, programmers often refer to the any repeating construct as a "loop," because a diagram of the construct looks like a loop.

Basic *While*

We want to execute a set of instructions repeatedly and, most importantly, to control the condition that allows us to keep repeating those instructions. Each time we consider executing the set of instructions, we make a decision that can be expressed as a Boolean: Repeat? Yes/No (or *True*/*False*). That is, we will repeat the instructions if the Boolean expression is *True* and stop if its value is *False*. A consequence of designing repetition this way is that the Boolean expression may be *False* the first time it is evaluated, in which case the set of instructions would never be executed at all.

The *while* loop contains a Boolean decision and can be expressed in English as:

"While the Boolean expression is *True*, keep looping—executing the suite."

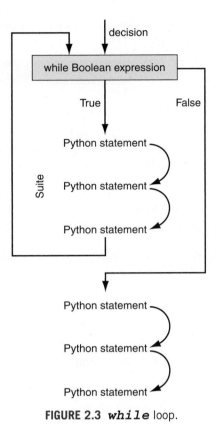

FIGURE 2.3 *while* loop.

Figure 2.3 is a diagram that shows the control flow of a **while** loop.

The Python syntax is:

```
while booleanExpression:
    # while suite
```

A **while** loop works as follows:

1. The program enters the **while** construct and evaluates the Boolean decision expression.
2. If the Boolean expression is *True*, then the associated **while** suite is executed.
3. At the end of the suite, control flows back to the top of the **while** where the Boolean expression is re-evaluated.
4. If the Boolean expression yields *True*, the loop executes again. If the Boolean yields *False*, then the **while** suite is skipped and the code following the **while** loop is executed.

Let's take a look at a simple example that prints out the numbers zero through nine. See Code Listing 2.10.

Code Listing 2.10

```
# simple while

x_int = 0      # initialize loop-control variable

5  # test loop-control variable at beginning of loop
while x_int < 10:
    print x_int,  # print the value of x_int each time through the while loop
    x_int = x_int + 1 # change loop-control variable

10 print
print "Final value of x_int: ", x_int  # bigger than value printed in loop!
```

```
>>>
0 1 2 3 4 5 6 7 8 9
Final value of x_int:  10
```

Let's take a look at Code Listing 2.10 line by line:

Line 3: Begin with loop-control variable initialization: x_int = 0. The variable x_int in the Boolean decision expression at the beginning of the *while* loop needs a value.

Line 6: Test the loop-control variable in the Boolean decision expression: *while* x_int < 10:. Because we initialized x_int to be zero, this Boolean expression will be *True* for x_init values of 0, 1, 2, 3, 4, 5, 6, 7, 8, and 9, but will be *False* for any values 10 or greater. Alternatively, we could achieve the same result with *while* x_int <= 9:.

Line 7: The *print* x_int, simply prints the value of the variable. The "extra" comma at the end of the statement indicates to the *print* statement to not "skip to the beginning of the next line" when the *print* statement ends. This means that the output from multiple calls to *print* will occur on the same output line.

Line 8: In the final instruction of the suite, we change the value associated with the loop-control variable. In this case, we increase its present value by 1 and reassign it (re-associate it) with the variable. If we forget to change the loop-control variable, the value of the *while* Boolean decision expression will never change, the value yielded by the Boolean will always be *True*, and the loop will never stop.

Line 10: After the *while* suite, the code prints the value of x_int. This shows the conditions under which the *while* loop ended. The value printed is 10, meaning that when the loop ended, x_int == 10. This made the Boolean expression *False*, which is why the *while* loop ended.

Iteration: The Basic *for* Statement

An iterator is an object associated with all the collection types in Python. As we briefly mentioned (Section 1.6), a *collection* in Python is a single object that contains multiple elements that are associated with the collection object. For example, a string is such a collection. It is a single object that has a group of individual characters, each associated with the string. In fact, a string is a particular kind of collection, called a *sequence*. A sequence is a collection where there is an order associated with the elements. A string is a sequence because the order of the characters is important. A *set* is a collection that is not a sequence, as membership, not order, is important for a set. However, for both a string and a set—in fact, for any Python collection— an iterator allows us to examine each individual element in that collection, one at a time. For a sequence, the access is ordered. When we iterate through a sequence, we iterate through each element in the sequence in order, from first to last. The **for** loop uses the collection's associated iterator to give us programmatic access to the individual elements of a collection.

The generic pattern of the **for** loop is shown in Code Listing 2.11. The variable anElement is a variable associated with the **for** loop that is assigned the value of an element in the collection. The variable anElement is assigned a different element during each pass of the **for** loop. Eventually, anElement will have been assigned to each element in the collection. The variable object is a collection that has an associated iterator that acts as the source of elements being iterated through. The keyword **in** precedes the object collection. Like the **if** and **while** statement, the **for** statement has an associated suite.

Code Listing 2.11

```
for anElement in object:
    # for suite
```

A simple example of a **for** loop and its output is shown here:

```
>>> for theChar in 'hi mom':
...     print theChar
...
h
i

m
o
m
>>>
```

Because the collection in this case is a string, the variable theChar is assigned, one at a time, to each character in the string. Since a string is also a sequence (i.e., an ordered collection) the variable theChar is assigned *in order* from the first character, "h", to

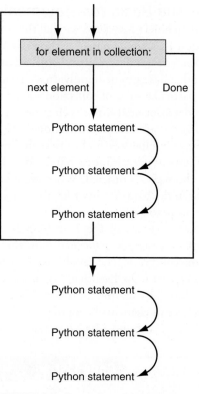

FIGURE 2.4 Operation of a *for* loop.

the last, "m". All the code in the **for** suite is evaluated during each pass of the loop. One can therefore perform operations on each of the elements of the sequence in a very straightforward way. In this particular case, we print only the value of theChar each time the **for** loop iterates. The **for** loop completes when the last of the elements has been assigned to theChar. The result in this case will be a printout with six lines, each line printing out one character (including the blank space at the third position).

In general a **for** statement operates as shown in Figure 2.4.

Example: Finding Perfect Numbers

Numbers and number theory are an area of study that dates back to antiquity. Our ancestors were interested in what numbers were and how they behaved, to the extent that some ancient philosophers, such as Pythagoras, attributed mystical properties to numbers.

One class of integers created by the ancients is the *perfect number*. It dates back at least to Euclid and his *Elements* from around 300 B.C. A perfect number is an integer whose sum of integer divisors (excluding the number itself) add up to the number. Following are the first four perfect numbers:

$$
\begin{aligned}
6 &= 1 + 2 + 3 \\
28 &= 1 + 2 + 4 + 7 + 14 \\
496 &= 1 + 2 + 4 + 8 + 16 + 31 + 62 + 124 + 248 \\
8128 &= 1 + 2 + 4 + 8 + 16 + 32 + 64 + 127 + 254 + 508 + 1016 + 2032 + 4064
\end{aligned}
$$

Numbers whose sum of divisors is larger than the number are called *abundant numbers*. Those whose sum is less than the number are called *deficient numbers*. Perfect numbers have other interesting properties[2], but for this project we are interested only in writing a program that sorts integers into one of three categories: perfect, abundant, or deficient.

Program to Evaluate Whether a Number is Perfect

Now that you understand what perfect, deficient, and abundant numbers are, how can you write a program that takes in a single number and properly classifies it?

A useful strategy is to develop our solution a little at a time. In this case, let's begin with an approach that sums up the integer divisors of a number. Furthermore, let's express our ideas in English first—not Python code yet.

1. Get the number we are going to evaluate. Let us call it `theNum`.
2. Find all the integer divisors of `theNum`.
3. For each of those integer divisors, add that divisor to a `sumOfDivisors` value. `sumOfDivisors` should start at 0.
4. Based on the value associated with `sumOfDivisors` and the number itself, we need to decide whether the number is perfect (and evaluate deficient or abundant later).

Having broken our problem down into simpler pieces, let us attack each one individually. It's always good to do the easy ones first, so let's start with steps 1 and 4.

Step 1, Get a Number: We need an initial number to check. We saw the Python function `raw_input` in Section 1.2. It allows the programmer (that's us!) to write a prompt to the user and then assign the result to a variable. Remember: the returned result is a string (a sequence of characters), not an integer, so we have to convert it. How about:

Code Listing 2.12

```
theNum = raw_input("Please enter a number to check:")
theNum = int(theNum)
```

---

[2] See http://en.wikipedia.org/wiki/Perfect_number

Step 4, Check Perfection: We need to see whether `sumOfDivisors` is equal to `theNum`. How about:

```
Code Listing 2.13

if theNum == sumOfDivisors:
    print theNum,"is perfect"
else:
    print theNum,"is not perfect"
```

Finally, we can attack steps 2 and 3.

Step 2, Find the Divisors What is a divisor? For a number N, a divisor is a number that divides into N evenly. What does "divide evenly" mean? It means that the remainder is zero. That is, for a potential divisor D, we need to determine whether the remainder of the integer division N/D is 0. Expressed as Python, we need to determine if **if** N % D == 0. If so, then D is a divisor of N.

Let's construct a trial piece of code to print the divisors of some number N. We'll have our potential divisors start at 1 (why is it bad in this case to start with zero?) and try each one (up to N). Because we listed the divisors of 28 earlier, we have those values to check against, so let's use $N = 28$:

```
>>> N = 28
>>> divisor = 1
>>> while divisor < N:
        if N % divisor == 0:    # found a divisor
                print divisor,
        divisor = divisor + 1  # get next divisor candidate

1 2 4 7 14
```

Step 3, Sum the Divisors Now that we have a loop that generates divisors, we need to find the sum of those divisors. We can initialize `sumOfDivisors` to zero, and then every time we find a new divisor (we printed divisors earlier), we can add it to `sumOfDivisors`. Here is our code:

```
Code Listing 2.14

divisor = 1
sumOfDivisors = 0
while divisor < theNum:
    if theNum % divisor==0:           # divisor evenly divides theNum
        sumOfDivisors = sumOfDivisors + divisor
    divisor = divisor + 1
```

Note a few things about this piece of code:

- We initialize divisor = 1 and sumOfDivisors = 0 before the loop begins.
- The decision condition of the loop is the Boolean expression: divisor < theNum.
- We increment divisor each time through the loop, so the Boolean expression changes (hopefully, eventually becoming *False* so the loop will halt).

Putting It All Together

We have all the pieces now; we just need to put it all together. The details of doing that are still important—we could get it wrong, but we have solved some of the subproblems. We just need to assemble them in a reasonable way. Remember what the parts were:

1. Prompt for the number to check.
2. Find all the integer divisors of that number, from 1 up to but not including the number.
3. Sum all those divisors.
4. Classify the number based on the sum.

Code Listing 2.15 assembles all the pieces together.

Code Listing 2.15

```
# perfect number checker

# get a number to check
theNum = raw_input("Please enter a number to check:")
theNum = int(theNum)

# find and sum up the divisors
divisor = 1
sumOfDivisors = 0
while divisor < theNum:
    if theNum % divisor==0:
        sumOfDivisors = sumOfDivisors + divisor
    divisor = divisor + 1

#classify the result
if theNum == sumOfDivisors:
    print theNum,"is perfect"
else:
    print theNum,"is not perfect"
```

If we run that code, we get the following results:

```
>>>
Please enter a number to check:100
```

```
100 is not perfect
>>> ============================= RESTART ================================
>>>
Please enter a number to check:128
128 is not perfect
>>> ============================= RESTART ================================
>>>
Please enter a number to check:496
496 is perfect
```

Example: Classifying Numbers

We can now take a particular number and classify it as to whether it is perfect or not. However, it would be more satisfying if we could check a whole range of numbers and decide what each number is: abundant, deficient or perfect. Then we could look for more perfect numbers!

The Process of Changing a Program

As we have said before, a program is an object to be read and understood as well as an object that performs some function. This is especially true when we want to *extend* a program, add functionality that was not there previously. Our last version does much of what we want, but not all. If we were to describe what we would like to do *now*, it would be:

1. Check all numbers in a range of numbers for their classification. Previously, we checked only one number.
2. For each number, determine the sum of its divisors. This task is largely complete.
3. Classify the number based on the sum of the divisors. We only checked for perfect numbers in the previous version.

Therefore, we do have to change the first part and the last part of the previous program, but the main part, the summation of divisors, remains roughly the same. Because we wrote the program in a readable, understandable way, it is much easier to see what was done and what must be changed to extend the program.

Looking at a Range of Numbers

How can we check a whole range of numbers? A loop is a likely candidate. Instead of prompting for each number individually, it would be helpful to the user if they were only required to enter the last number in a range of numbers. Thus, we will ask the user to enter the highest number in a range of integers, and our program will then check every number up to that number for its classification. We start with the number 2, because by definition, the number 1 cannot be perfect. Code Listing 2.16 reflects this.

Code Listing 2.16

```
topNumStr = raw_input("What is the upper number for the range:")
topNum = int(topNumStr)
theNum=2
while theNum <= topNum:
    # sum the divisors of theNum
    # classify the number based on its divisor sum
    theNum += 1
```

Notice that we use the increment shortcut to add 1 to theNum. Remember that that statement is equivalent to theNum = theNum + 1.

We prompt for the upper range number, convert it to an int, then count from 2 to that number. For each number in the range, we get the sum of divisors for the number and classify that number. Note that those last two parts are left unspecified in the code provided, but we used comments as markers, pieces of the code that we must fill in. We often call such a piece of incomplete code a *skeleton* of a program. We indicate what must be done, but not necessarily at the level of Python code. We add "meat" to the skeleton, the details of the code, as we go along, but we clearly see what must be added. Thus, the organization of our solution is clear, even though it will not run as a program—at least not yet!

Summing Divisors

Good news here. We can just take the entire section of code for divisor summing derived previously and stick it in at the comment of our skeleton code. Code Listing 2.17 shows the next version.

Code Listing 2.17

```
topNum = raw_input("What is the upper number for the range:")
topNum = int(topNum)
theNum=2
while theNum < topNum:
    # sum up the divisors
    divisor = 1
    sumOfDivisors = 0
    while divisor < theNum:
        if theNum % divisor==0:
            sumOfDivisors = sumOfDivisors + divisor
```

```
    divisor = divisor + 1
# classify the number based on its divisor sum
theNum += 1
```

We must be careful with the indentation. The entire section of code that does the divisor summing is now within a **while** loop, as indicated by the indentation.

Classify the Numbers

Now we have three categories to check for. If sumOfDivisors is greater than theNum, theNum is abundant. If sumOfDivisors is less than theNum, theNum is deficient. Otherwise, it must be perfect. We can extend the previous code to account for the three conditions as shown in Code Listing 2.18.

Code Listing 2.18

```
topNum = raw_input("What is the upper number for the range:")
topNum = int(topNum)
theNum=2
while theNum <= topNum:
    # sum up the divisors
    divisor = 1
    sumOfDivisors = 0
    while divisor < theNum:
        if theNum % divisor==0:
            sumOfDivisors = sumOfDivisors + divisor
        divisor = divisor + 1
    # classify the number based on its divisor sum
    if theNum == sumOfDivisors:
        print theNum,"is perfect"
    if theNum < sumOfDivisors:
        print theNum,"is abundant"
    if theNum > sumOfDivisors:
        print theNum,"is deficient"
    theNum += 1
```

Finish the Loop

The last thing the loop does is increase the value associated with theNum by 1. Failure to do so will mean we have an infinite loop—a loop that will end only when we manually stop it.

Check Yourself: Basic Control Check

1. What output occurs for the following program on the given inputs?

```
userVal = raw_input("Please enter a positive integer:")
# Line 1
myInt = int(userVal)
count = 0

while myInt > 0:
    if myInt % 2 == 1:
        myInt = myInt/2
    else:
        myInt = myInt - 1
    count = count + 1                # Line 2

print count                          # Line 3
print myInt                          # Line 4
```

(a) Given user input of 11, what value is output by Line 3 of the program?

(b) Given user input of 12, what value is output by Line 4 of the program

(c) What type is referenced by (associated with) `userVal` in Line 1 of the program?

(d) What is the purpose of the = (equal sign) on Line 2 of the program?

(e) What is the purpose of the : (colon) at the end of the **while** statement?

2.2 IN-DEPTH CONTROL

The intelligence that computers appear to have comes from their ability to make billions of tiny decisions every second. Each of those decisions is based on a choice between the truth or falsity of statements. In this section, we begin with a closer look into the variables that can hold the logical values of *True* and *False*. Then we examine how to use them for control.

To consider truth and falsity we begin with a nineteenth century school teacher: George Boole.

True and False: Booleans

George Boole was a mid-nineteenth century school teacher who wrote a few articles that established an important branch of mathematics upon which the logic of computers is based. The title of one of his articles tells of his topic's importance: "An Investigation of the Laws of Thought, on Which are Founded the Mathematical Theories of Logic and

Probabilities."[3] The importance of his work was not realized until a century later (1940) when Claude Shannon learned of Boole's work in a philosophy class and demonstrated that electrical circuits could perform Boolean algebra to do arithmetic. Shannon's master's thesis[4] is considered a seminal work for computing.

Boolean Variables

Python and most other computing languages explicitly represent the values of *True* and *False*, and call that type a *Boolean*. In Python, the values of *True* and *False* are capitalized.

> The type Boolean has a value of *True* or *False* (note capitalization).

Because computer hardware can store only ones and zeros, the Boolean value *True* is stored as 1 and *False* as 0. More generally, an object with value zero is considered to be *False* and any nonzero value is considered to be *True*. In addition, any empty object such as an empty string (' ') is considered to be *False*.

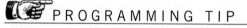PROGRAMMING TIP

An *empty* object (0 for int, 0.0 for float, '' for string) is considered to be *False*; all *non-empty* objects are considered to be *True*.

Relational Operators

As you saw earlier, Boolean expressions are composed of relational operators that yield results that are evaluated as *True* or *False*. The relational operators are well known: less than, equal to, etc. Remember the unusual "equal to" sign: it has a *pair* of equal signs so that it can be differentiated from an assignment operator.

These operators are common across many currently popular programming languages. Remember the Table 2.1, which lists the relational operators.

We will next explain these in detail with some examples.

```
>>> 3 > 2
True
>>> 5+3 < 3-2   # expressions evaluated first then comparison
False
```

---

[3] Boole, George. "An investigation of the laws of thought, on which are founded the mathematical theories of logic and probabilities." London: Walton and Maberly and Cambridge: Macmillan and Co, 1854.

[4] C. E. Shannon, "A Symbolic Analysis of Relay and Switching Circuits," Massachusetts Institute of Technology, Department of Electrical Engineering, 1940

```
>>> '1' < 2      # weird mixture of string and int; avoid them!
False
>>> 5 == 6       # equality test
False
```

 PROGRAMMING TIP

What happens when you forget to use "==" and use "=" instead? For example, what happens when you try to compare two numbers and accidentally use the "=" sign **print** `'0 and 0.0 are:'`, 0 = 0.0 Python generates an error. Do you remember why? The "=" is the assignment statement and it has a side-effect (assign the right-hand-side to the left-hand-side), but it *doesn't return a value*. Python helps you avoid such an error.

Explanation:

- 3 > 2: is 3 greater than 2? True
- 5 + 3 < 3 − 2
  - Boolean operators have low precedence. That is, other operations are completed first before the Boolean operators are applied.
  - Here, we complete the addition and subtraction before we apply the Boolean relation '<'
    - 5 + 3 < 3 − 2
    - 8 < 1
    - False
- '1' < 2   # avoid expressions like this!
  - False
  - This result may not be what you expect. When you compare two different types, a string and a number for example, Python has a set of rules to deal with the situation. Python arbitrarily designates different types as "smaller" than others. For example, a string, no matter its contents, is always larger than any number, no matter the number. However, this arbitrary rule is controversial, and will change in the next version of Python (see Appendix D). *Most importantly*, you should avoid comparisons between incompatible types. It is not always obvious what the result will be!
  - Be careful to compare what you want. Did you mean to convert the string to a number?:
    - int('1') < 2
    - True

- Did you mean to convert the number to a string?
   - '1' < str(2)
   - True

What Does It Mean to be Equal?

Equality presents a special problem on a computer, especially in Python. There are really two different kinds of equality:

- Two different names are associated with objects that have the *same value*.
- Two different names are associated with the *same object* (i.e., objects with the same ID).

Do you remember our diagram on namespace in Section 1.5, Figure 1.1, that showed the relationship between names and their associated objects? Consider the three lines of code and the namespace of Figure 2.5.

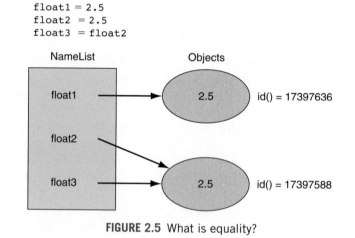

```
float1 = 2.5
float2 = 2.5
float3 = float2
```

FIGURE 2.5 What is equality?

Both names `float3` and `float2` have been associated with the same object (because of the `float3 = float2` assignment) so they also are both equal in value. The `float1` name is associated with a different object whose value happens to be the same as the other object. Python provides a way to check each kind of equality:

`==` to check whether two names refer to objects that have the *same value*

is to check whether two names refer the *same object* (have same ID)

Here is the example of Figure 2.5 in the Python shell:

```
>>> float1 = 2.5     # float1 and float2 are associated with different objects
>>> float2 = 2.5
>>> float3 = float2  # float3 and float2 are associated with the same object
>>> float1 == float2 # values are the same
True
>>> float3 == float2
True
>>> float1 is float2 # objects are different
False
>>> float3 is float2 # objects are the same (so values are, too)
True
>>> id(float1)       # look at id to understand "is"
17397636
>>> id(float2)
17397588
>>> id(float3)
17397588
```

When you assign the same object in the separate assignments, you create separate objects that happen to have the same value. Therefore, the equality check (= =) returns *True*, but the sharing check (*is*) returns *False*.[5]

While we are on the subject of equality, let's discuss equality of floating point values. Remember that floating points are approximations of Real numbers because of the problem of storing infinitely large Real value in the finite number of bits in a computer word. If one executes a series of computations, especially with floating-point values, some round off is likely to occur. For example, in mathematics, the associative property of addition says that $(u + v) + w$ is the same as $u + (v + w)$. However, with a computer, rounding-off may give you a different result. Using the two previous expressions and the values $u = 11111113$, $v = -11111111$, and $w = 7.51111111$, one would expect both to yield the same value. It's close, but not exactly the same:

```
>>> u = 11111113
>>> v = -11111111
>>> w = 7.51111111
>>> (u + v) + w
9.5111111099999999
>>> u + (v + w)
9.511111104488373
>>> (u + v) + w == u + (v + w)
False
```

---

[5] For efficiency, small integers work in an implementation dependent way. That is, it works differently on different systems. There is little value in applying "is" to system-defined objects such as integers.

How can we handle the rounding off of floating-point calculations? Check to see if the difference is very small—you decide what "small" is. For example, let's take the previous example one step further.

```
>>> u = 11111113
>>> v = -11111111
>>> w = 7.51111111
>>> x = (u + v) + w
>>> y = u + (v + w)
>>> x == y
False
>>> (x - y) < 0.0000001
True
```

In the case of x == y, we are checking to see if x and y have *identical values*. In the case of (x - y) < 0.0000001, we are checking to see if x and y are "close enough." When comparing for floating point equality, the latter is the correct way to do it. The former will often result in incorrect results with floating-point values.

PROGRAMMING TIP

Instead of performing a strict equality test of two floating point numbers

$$if \quad x \quad == \quad y:$$

test whether they are close. Furthermore, use the absolute value of the difference (using math.fabs) to get signs correct. That is, for some small delta of your choice, such as delta = 0.0000001,

$$if \quad math.fabs(x \quad - \quad y) \quad < \quad delta:$$

Chained Relational Operators

Chained relational expressions work just like they do in mathematics (which is not true for many programming languages):

```
>>> aInt = 5
>>> 0 <= aInt <= 5
True
>>> 0 <= aInt <= 2
False
```

The two expressions represent:
- is aInt greater than or equal to 0 and less than or equal to 5
- is aInt greater than or equal to 0 and less than or equal to 2.

The first expression yields *True*, the second *False*.

Boolean Operators

The basic Boolean operators are: and, or, not[6]. Many students learn the Boolean operators as part of a high-school geometry course, but they are worth reviewing in the context of Python. A common way to describe Boolean operators is to list all the possible operands in combination in a table. Along with the combinations are listed the result of the operation. Traditionally, p and q are the names of the operands that represent a Boolean expression.

- **not** p
  - The **not** operator flips the value of the operand. That is, it converts *True* to *False*, and *False* to *True*.

p	**not** p
True	*False*
False	*True*

- p **and** q
  - The **and** operator requires both p and q to be *True* for the whole expression to be *True*. Otherwise, the value of the expression is *False*. Observe that the four rows in the p and q columns represent all the possible values that p and q can have. You should take a moment and convince yourself of that observation.

p	q	p **and** q
True	*True*	*True*
True	*False*	*False*
False	*True*	*False*
False	*False*	*False*

- p **or** q
  - The **or** operator only requires one of p or q to be *True* for the whole expression to be *True*. Therefore, the expression is *False* only when neither p nor q is *True*.

p	q	p **or** q
True	*True*	*True*
True	*False*	*True*
False	*True*	*True*
False	*False*	*False*

---

[6] There are other operators, such as "exclusive or," which is also known as XOR. Students who go on to build circuits as electrical and computer engineers will study them.

With Boolean operators in hand, we can revisit the chained expression mentioned previously:

```
aInt = 5
0 <= aInt <= 5
```

The chained expression is the equivalent of a Boolean expression for evaluation. First the expression is converted into two relations (<=), which are **and**'ed together. That is, the expression 0 <= aInt <= 5 means that you are checking that 0 <= aInt *and* aInt <= 5. You can then evaluate each relational expression and combine the results referring to the **and** table. In the table, you can see that if p == *True* and q == *True*, then the value of the whole expression is *True*.

```
(0 <= aInt) and (aInt <= 5)
  (0 <= 5) and (5 <= 5)
    True and True
         True
```

Examples:

- X = 3

```
(X > 2) or (X > 5)
 (3>2) or (3>5)
  True or False
      True
```

- Order of operations: **and** before **or**

```
True and False or True and False
(True and False) or (True and False)
      False or False
            False
```

Precedence

In Chapter 1 you learned the that precedence of arithmetic Python operators was the same as in arithmetic. In this chapter, we have introduced a number of new operators. Where do they fit in precedence with respect to the arithmetic operators? Table 2.2 shows the combined precedence. The full table of all Python operator precedence is in Appendix F.

Boolean Operators Example

Although the description of the Boolean operators might seem complicated, most of us use these operators nearly every day. Where? Why, search engines of course!

Operator	Description
()	Parenthesis (grouping)
**	Exponentiation
+x, -x	Positive, Negative
*,/,%	Multiplication, Division, Remainder
+,-	Addition, Subtraction
<, <=, >, >=,! =, ==	Comparisons
not x	Boolean NOT
and	Boolean AND
or	Boolean OR

TABLE 2.2 Precedence of relational and arithmetic operators: highest to lowest.

The interaction most users have with search engines is to provide a list of keywords. The search engine uses those keywords to find online documents that contain those words. However, we all know that finding the right combination of words can be quite difficult. To aid in writing a better search, most engines provide an interface that uses Boolean operators to improve the search. Google's advanced search interface is shown in Figure 2.6.

FIGURE 2.6 The Google advanced search page.

The "all these words" text field is really an ***and*** of all the words: all the words listed should be in the document found. The "one or more of these words" text field is clearly an ***or*** of the words: one or more of the words should occur. Finally, the "any of these unwanted words" text field is a ***not*** condition: those words should not occur in the document. In this way, we see the three Boolean operators (and, or, not) incorporated into the Google advanced search.

The standard Google search assumes an ***and*** of all the words listed. However, you can construct Boolean expressions in the Google search field. As mentioned, the default situation for a list of words is ***and***, to indicate ***or*** the phrase OR in all caps is required, and ***not*** is indicated by the minus (-) sign.

Let's do a little egosearch on Google (see Figure 2.7). The search expression for one of the authors is:

"Punch Bill OR William"
which translates to a normal Boolean expression as:
'*Punch*' ***and*** ('*Bill*' ***or*** '*William*')

FIGURE 2.7 The Google advanced search page after our egosearch.

This expression generates some undesired search results, in particular some nasty pages about punching a certain Microsoft executive. We clean it up by changing the search expression to:

"Punch Bill OR William -gates"
which translates to a normal Boolean expression as:
'Punch' **and** *('Bill'* **or** *'William')* **and not** *'gates'*

Check Yourself: Boolean Value Check

1. What output occurs for the following program on the given inputs?

```
intStr = raw_input("Please give me an integer:")
intFirst = int(intStr)
intStr = raw_input("Please give me a second integer:")
intSecond = int(intStr)
tensCount = 0
loopCount = 0

while intFirst > 10 and intSecond < 20:
    if intFirst == 10 or intSecond == 10:
        tensCount += 1
    intFirst -= 5
    intSecond += 5
    loopCount += 1

print tensCount        # Line 1
print loopCount        # Line 2
print intFirst         # Line 3
print intSecond        # Line 4
```

   (a) Given user input of 20 followed by an input of 10, what value is output by:
      1. Line 1 of the program?
      2. Line 2 of the program?
      3. Line 3 of the program?
      4. Line 4 of the program?
   (b) Given user input of 20 followed by an input of 20, what value is output by:
      1. Line 1 of the program?
      2. Line 2 of the program?
      3. Line 3 of the program?
      4. Line 4 of the program?
   (c) Under what conditions will both `intFirst` and `intSecond` both be equal to 10?

If we do the search and then go to the Advanced Search page after the search is completed, we see that the text fields were filled in as we described.

Another Word on Assignments

Remember how assignment works:

LHS = RHS

Step 1: Evaluate the RHS (Right Hand Side) to get a value.
Step 2: Associate that value with the variable named on the LHS (Left Hand Side).

Multiple Assignment

In Python, we can do multiple assignments on the same line by separating corresponding LHS and RHS by commas. That is,

```
aInt, bInt, cInt = 15, 10, 17
```

is equivalent to

```
aInt = 15
bInt = 10
cInt = 17
```

The multiple assignments work in a natural way. The first name on the LHS gets the first value on the RHS, the second name on the LHS gets the second value on the RHS, and so on.

 PROGRAMMING TIP

When doing multiple assignments, make sure that the number of variables on the LHS is the same as the number of values being returned by the RHS. If there is a mismatch, you will get errors like the following:

```
>>> aInt, bInt = 1,2      # exactly two objects on each side of "="
>>> print aInt, bInt
1 2
>>> aInt, bInt = 1, 2, 3  # different number of objects: Error

Traceback (most recent call last):
  File "<pyshell#10>", line 1, in <module>
    aInt, bInt = 1, 2, 3
```

```
ValueError: too many values to unpack
>>> aInt, bInt, cInt = 1, 2   # different number of objects: Error

Traceback (most recent call last):
  File "<pyshell#11>", line 1, in <module>
    aInt, bInt, cInt = 1, 2
ValueError: need more than 2 values to unpack
```

Swap

Swapping the values of two variables can be confusing when done on a computer. For example, suppose that aInt = 2 and bInt = 3 and that we would like to swap values so aInt = 3 and bInt = 2. Consider the naïve way of doing it:

```
>>> aInt = 2
>>> bInt = 3
>>> aInt = bInt
>>> bInt = aInt
>>> aInt
3
>>> bInt
3
>>> aInt is bInt
True
```

What happened? The problem came with the statement aInt = bInt. The last line illustrates the problem: that assignment associated the names aInt and bInt with the same object. A key point is that when the assignment was done, the value of aInt was lost. Therefore, we need to keep aInt's value somewhere, if we are to swap correctly. We will introduce a third variable tempInt to temporarily store aInt's value, which can later be assigned to bInt. Here is it again, but with tempInt:

```
>>> aInt = 2
>>> bInt = 3
>>> tempInt = aInt    # remember the original aInt
>>> aInt = bInt
>>> bInt = tempInt
>>> aInt
3
>>> bInt
2
```

Python's multiple assignment lets us perform a swap in one line:

```
>>> aInt = 2
>>> bInt = 3
>>> aInt, bInt = bInt, aInt
>>> aInt
3
>>> bInt
2
```

How is this done in one line in Python? Consider the way we described the assignment process, as having two steps: get the value(s) of the RHS and then assign the value(s) to the LHS. The "get the value(s)" on the RHS stores those values in temporary memory locations so implicitly it is as if we were using `tempInt`—actually two `tempInt`'s in the case of swap—one temporary storage for each of the two values on the RHS of swap.

The Selection Statement for Decisions

We have shown *if* and *if-else* statements as a way to make decisions. Let's take a look at what constructs Python offers for selection. The simplest decision presents a choice of doing one thing or another—of executing one statement or another. Such a simple choice fits nicely with computer hardware, as mentioned, because the choice itself can be represented as a zero (*False*) or not-zero (*True*). We saw this behavior implemented as the *if-else* statement. More complex decisions can be built from combinations of simple ones.

Booleans for Decisions

As we have noted, if the choices are binary, as in the prevous examples (that is, they can go one way or the other), then it is natural to use Booleans to represent choices. In fact, that is the primary use of Booleans in programming languages.

Remember, What Counts as True *and* False. As we discussed previously, Booleans represent *True* and *False* with values other than just *True* and *False*. In Python, we define values equivalent to *False* to be "empty" things. For example, 0 is equivalent to *False*; " (the empty string) is equivalent to *False*. If a value isn't *False* (as we just defined), then it is automatically equivalent to *True*. By tradition we tend to use 1 for *True*, but the hardware actually returns *True* for everything that is not zero. We will make more use of this fact later.

Compound Statements and Suites

When a selection statement such as an *if-else* causes our code to branch, there is no limit to the number of lines of code on either path. You may have one line of code or thousands of lines of code. Also, you might well have other decisions within one of those paths so that you can create more complex decisions. That is, we will frequently make decisions within decisions.

We need a way to group statements together to capture the notion of these sequential lines of code being executed together. Generally, programming languages call such a grouping a *compound statement*. If a compound statement is executed, all the statements within the group are executed in order. Python calls the first part of the statement the *header* and the group under the header a *suite*, as shown in Figure 2.8. Grouping is done by indentation of the suite under the header.

PROGRAMMING TIP

Pay *attention* to indenting in Python, because the indentation indicates the structure of the code. Be *consistent* with indentation: four spaces is common. More importantly, do not mix tabs and spaces! Use spaces. That is the Python way.

Using suites in statements

How do we select a compound statement to execute? A compound statement header starts with a keyword such as *if* or *while* and ends with a colon, as shown in Figure 2.8. All the statements following the colon that have the same indentation underneath the header statement (are indented more than the header statement) are considered to be part of the same suite (group) of the compound statement. Of course, one can have compound statements within compound statements, and the indentation indicates how they relate to each other.

FIGURE 2.8 Control expression.

More on Python Decision Statements

The *if* statement is a header for a compound statement. The *if* statement expresses selective execution in Python, but it comes in a number of variations. We examine these in this section.

You have seen the basic *if* and *if-else* statements in Section 2.1. Let's briefly restate them, and then move on to the variations. First the basic *if*:

```
if booleanExpression:
    # suite executed when True
```

The *if-else* statement has a suite for each choice of a decision: one when the decision results in *True* and one when the decision results in *False*:

```
if booleanExpression:
    # suite executed when True
else:
    # suite executed when False
```

Pay particular attention to the indentation: the **else** and the **if** part of the expression are at the same indentation (they are part of the same overall statement). Furthermore, both can have an associated suite of statements to be executed. The **if** has an associated Boolean expression; the **else** does not. Take a moment and convince yourself why **else** alone does not need its own Boolean expression.

The *if-else* statement operation is as follows:

1. Evaluate booleanExpression to yield the value *True* or *False*.
2. If booleanExpression yields *True*,
   (a) Execute the true suite.
   (b) Continue with the next statement after the entire *if-else* statement.
3. If booleanExpression yields *False*:
   (a) Skip the true suite.
   (b) Execute the false suite.
   (c) Continue with the next statement after the *if-else* statement.

The *if-elif-else* Statement

We can add any number of **else** clauses with a corresponding **if** statements using the **elif** statement. The **elif** is simply shorthand for "else if"—a shorthand that also exists in some other languages. Again, note the indentation: the keywords (if, elif, else) are indented the same amount as they are part of the overall **if** statement. Further, each of the **if**, **elif**, and **else** statements can have an associated suite. Finally, any **else** is not required; it is fine to have simply *if-elif* with no last **else**:

```
if booleanExpression1:
    # suite1
elif booleanExpression2:
    # suite2
elif booleanExpression3:
    # suite3
# as many elif statements as you like
else:
    # suiteLast
```

The *if-elif-else* statement operation is as follows

1. Evaluate booleanExpression1 to yield *True* or *False*.

2. If booleanExpression1 yields *True*,
   (a) Execute suite1.
   (b) Continue with the next statement after suiteLast.
3. If booleanExpression1 yields *False*, then evaluate boolean Expression2.
   If booleanExpression2 yields *True*,
   (a) Execute suite2.
   (b) Continue with the next statement after suiteLast.
4. If all preceding booleanExpressions yield *False*, evaluate boolean Expression3.
   If booleanExpression3 yields *True*,
   (a) Execute suite3.
   (b) Continue with the next statement after suiteLast.
5. If all preceding booleanExpressions yield *False*,
   (a) Execute the **else** part and suiteLast.
   (b) Continue with the next statement after suiteLast.

For each **elif** statement the associated suite will be executed if all preceding booleanExpressions are *False* and its booleanExpression is *True*.

Updating Our Perfect Number Example

If we write our code so that we can read and understand what we have written, we are better able to update that code to take advantage of new constructs, more efficient approaches, improved algorithms and so on. The process of taking existing code and modifying it such that its structure is somehow improved but the functionality of the code remains the same is called *refactoring*. Let's take a look at our perfect number example from Section 2.15 and see if we can improve it by refactoring.

The area of interest is the classification part of the code. Let's take a look at that part.

Code Listing 2.19

```
# classify the number based on its divisor sum
if theNum == sumOfDivisors:
    print theNum,"is perfect"
if theNum < sumOfDivisors:
    print theNum,"is abundant"
if theNum > sumOfDivisors:
    print theNum,"is deficient"
theNum += 1
```

In this part of the solution, we observe that we checked for conditions that we know are not going to be *True*. For example, if the number is indeed perfect, it cannot be abundant or deficient, but we checked those conditions anyway. A better approach would be to rewrite this code so that as soon as a condition is found to be *True*, the associated suite is run and the statement ends. Using an ***if-elif-else*** statement seems like a good choice. We can rewrite this part of the code, without changing its functionality for the rest of the solution, as shown in Code Listing 2.20.

Code Listing 2.20

```
# classify the number based on its divisor sum
if theNum == sumOfDivisors:
    print theNum,"is perfect"
elif theNum < sumOfDivisors:
    print theNum,"is abundant"
else:
    print theNum,"is deficient"
theNum += 1
```

Notice that the final Boolean expression theNum > sumOfDivisors is no longer, needed because if a number is neither perfect nor abundant it must be deficient.

There are two more things to note here. First, because the solution was written in a readable, logical way, it was relatively easy to modify. Second, the modification we made does not affect the answers provided by the solution, but it does make better sense, and is less wasteful, by using a more appropriate construct.

Repetition: the *while* Statement

Earlier we introduced the ***for*** iteration statement and the ***while*** repetition statement. The ***for*** statement makes use of iterators to move through a collection, one element at a time, allowing us to perform an operation on each element using the suite of the ***for*** statement. The ***while*** executes its suite of statements as long as its Boolean expression is *True*. When working with collections, which is very common in Python, the ***for*** statement is the first choice for looping. However, the ***while*** statement is a general expression of repetition, and is also very useful.

Basic Repetition and the *while* Loop

The ***while*** loop is sometimes called a "top-tested loop," because there is a Boolean expression to be evaluated at the top of the loop. Some programming languages also provide a "bottom-tested loop" in which the Boolean expression is evaluated at the bottom of the loop. Such a loop construct will always execute the suite of instructions at least once before testing the Boolean expression. Python does not have a bottom-tested loop, so to get that behavior, a Boolean expression must be crafted so that it will be `True` at least once.

Loop Control and Initialization

The Boolean decision expression controls the loop, so care must be taken in designing it. Often, especially for novice programmers, there is one variable in the expression, so we'll consider that case. That variable is often called the *loop control variable*. Our comments generalize naturally to more complex expressions.

Initialization is critical and requires some thought. Fortunately, Python requires some initial value when a variable is created. The most common initial values are 1 and 0 though the initial value for *your* program depends on the problem. As you will see in the following example, the fact that 0 and 1 are respectively the additive and multiplicative identities is the reason they are the most common initial value[7]. That is, if the initial value is 0, the first value you add to the initial value becomes the value of the variable. Multiplication works similarly when you start with 1.

Typically, somewhere in the **while** loop suite, the loop control variable is modified so that eventually the Boolean expression of the **while** becomes *False* and the loop ends. The loop control variable gets initialized before the loop, and then modified within the loop. As a result, the loop control variable will have a different value in the suite for each iteration of the loop. Because it has a different value in each iteration, the loop control variable is frequently (but not always) used in expressions within the loop suite.

There are two consequences of the Boolean decision expression on the **while** loop construct. For novice programmers they are often undesirable:

Loop never starts: Because the first action of a **while** loop is to evaluate the Boolean expression, if that expression yields *False*, the suite of instructions will not be executed.
Loop never stops: If the Boolean expression yields *True*, the loop will stop only if some instruction within the suite of instructions changes the loop control variable so that the Boolean expression evaluates to *False* at some point. If the Boolean expression is always *True*, this situation is called an *infinite loop*.

PROGRAMMING TIP

Generic While Structure:

> Set an initial value for loop-control variable.
> **while** some Boolean tests the loop-control variable :
>   Perform tasks as part of the loop.
>   At the loop's end, update the loop-control variable.

---

[7] Additive identity: $0 + x = x$; Multiplicative identity: $1 * x = x$.

Check Yourself: More Control Check

1.
```
numStr = raw_input("Give me an int:")
num = int(numStr)
cnt = 0

while num > 0:
    if num % 2 == 0:
        num = num / 2
    elif num % 3 == 0:
        num = num / 3
    else:                   # Line 1
        num = num - 1       # Line 2
    cnt = cnt + 1

print "Count is: ",cnt      # Line 3
print "Num is: ",num        # Line 4
```

(a) Given user input of 9, what value does Line 3 of the program print?

(b) Given user input of 9, what value does Line 4 of the program print?

(c) Given user input of 7, what value does Line 3 of the program print?

(d) Given user input of 1, what value does Line 3 of the program print?

(e) If the else clause on Line 1 and Line 2 were removed, what effect would that have on the program with the input value 1?

    i. No effect, program would give the same results.

    ii. cnt would be larger.

    iii. cnt would be smaller.

    iv. The **while** loop would not end.

    v. None of the above.

Else and Break

Similar to the *if-else* statement, you can have an *else* clause at the end of a *while* loop.

```
while booleanExpression:
    # suite1
# else:
    # suite2
```

The *else* clause is entered when the *while* loop's Boolean expression becomes *False*. See Figure 2.9. This entry occurs even if the expression is initially *False* and the

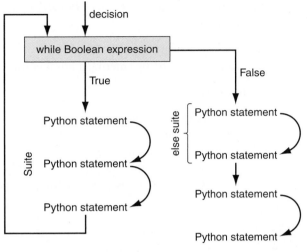

FIGURE 2.9 while-else.

while loop never ran (its suite was never executed). Again, the **else** part of the **while** loop can have its own associated suite of statements. Think of the **else** statement on the **while** loop as "clean up" for the action performed as the loop ends normally.

The **else** clause is a handy way to perform some final task when the loop ends normally. Figure 2.9 shows how the **else** works.

Break statement and non-normal exit

The **else** clause is often used in conjunction with the **break** statement. The **break** statement can be used to exit the execution of the loop and skip past all the remaining parts of the loop suite, including the **else** suite. The **break** statement is useful for stopping computation when the "answer" has been found or when continuing the computation is otherwise useless.

We like the clarity of the **while** and **if** statements. They make it clear to the reader how the program might enter and exit the various suites and, as we have said repeatedly, readability is important for correctness. However, sometimes we need to take a non-normal exit, and that is what we consider next. We choose a non-normal exit sparingly, because it can detract from readability, but sometimes it is the "lesser of two evils" and will provide the best readability, and, on occasion, better performance. A non-normal exit is sometimes called an *early exit*.

To illustrate **while-else**, Code Listing 2.21 is a short program that plays a number guessing game. The program starts by generating a random number hidden from the user that is between 0 and 100. The user then attempts to guess the number, getting hints as to which direction (bigger or smaller, higher or lower) to go on the next guess. The game can end in one of two ways:

- The user can correctly guess the number.
- The user can quit playing by entering a number out of the range of 0–100.

Here is an algorithm for the game:

Choose a random number.
Prompt for a guess.
while guess is in range:
    Check whether the guess is correct; print a win message and exit if so.
    Otherwise, provide a hint and prompt for a new guess.

Code Listing 2.21

```
# while-else
# Simple guessing game: start with a random number and
# guess with hints until:
#     guess is  correct
5 #     the guess is out of range indicating the user is quitting

import random  # get the random number module
number = random.randint(0,100) # get a random number
                              # between 0 and 100 inclusive
10 print "Hi-Lo Number Guessing Game: between 0 and 100 inclusive."
print

# get an initial guess
guessString = raw_input("Guess a number: ")
15 guess = int(guessString)  # convert string to number

# while guess is range, keep asking
while 0 <= guess <= 100:
    if guess > number:
20        print "Guessed Too High."
    elif guess < number:
        print "Guessed Too Low."
    else:                    # correct guess, exit with break
        print "You guessed it. The number was:",number
25        break
    # keep going, get the next guess
```

```
        guessString = raw_input("Guess a number: ")
        guess = int(guessString)
    else:
30      print "You quit early, the number was:",number
```

Here is a line-by-line look at the program in Code Listing 2.21:

Lines 7–8: To get a random number we first import the `random` module. The random module provides a number of useful functions, including functions to generate random numbers. One such function is named `randint` (read as "random integers"); it generates and returns a random integer. The full name, `random.randint`, indicates that the `randint` name is to be found in the `random` module (which we imported in the preceding line). The function takes two arguments: an integer lower value and the upper value. The function will then generate a random number within the range. For example, `random.randint(0,100)` will generate a random number between 0 and 100 (including both 0 and 100).

Lines 14–15: You have seen *raw_input* before. In this case, the string "Guess a number:" will be printed as a prompt to the user. The variable `guessString` will be the string returned that needs to be converted to a number (integer) for further processing. At this point, we have a randomly chosen number to try to guess and a first guess. Notice how we need to get an initial guess for the Boolean expression in the *while* loop. What would happen if that were not true? Try it!

Line 18: This is the "normal" exit condition for the loop. As long as the guess is in the range 0–100 *inclusive*, the loop will continue. As soon as the expression becomes *False*, the loop will end and the associated *else* suite will be run.

Lines 19–22: If the guess is incorrect (either too high or too low), we provide a hint to the user so that they might improve their next guess.

Lines 23–25: If it wasn't high and it wasn't low, it must be the answer. Is that true—or could it have been a number not in the range we were looking for (0–100)? No, we checked that in the *while* Boolean expression. It must be the correct number. We print a winner message and then use the *break* statement to exit the loop. Remember, a *break* will skip the *else* suite of the *while* loop!

Lines 27–28: We prompt for another guess at the bottom of the *while* suite. Note the pattern:

> Prompt for a guess.
> *while* guess is not correct:
>   Do something (e.g. provide a hint).
>   Prompt for a new guess.

This is a common pattern: you prompt before the *while* starts so the loop may begin, and then prompt again at the end of the *while* suite so we may change the value associated with guess. This is the pattern noted earlier in the "Programming Tip." You need to have some information for the Boolean expression before you encounter it the first time, and then at the bottom of the suite you need to again get information for the Boolean expression before you encounter it again.

Lines 29–30: You get to this print statement only if the *while* loop terminated normally so that you know without further checking that 0 <= guess <=0 is no longer *True* and the user quit. Note that the *break* statement skips this suite.

A sample interaction is shown in the following session:

```
> python hiLoGame.py
Hi-Lo Number Guessing Game: between 0 and 100 inclusive.

Guess a number: 50
Guessed Too Low.
Guess a number: 75
Guessed Too Low.
Guess a number: 82
Guessed Too High.
Guess a number: 78
Guessed Too High.
Guess a number: 77
Guessed Too High.
Guess a number: 76
You guessed it. The number was: 76

>python hiLoGame.py
Hi-Lo Number Guessing Game: between 0 and 100 inclusive.

Guess a number: 50
Guessed Too High.
Guess a number: 25
Guessed Too High.
Guess a number: 10
Guessed Too Low.
Guess a number: -100
You quit early, the number was: 23
```

More Control Inside of a *while* Loop

Continue

Sometimes we might want to simply skip the rest of the *while* suite we are executing and go back to the beginning of the *while* loop. That is, exit early from this *iteration* of the loop (not the loop itself), and keep executing the *while* loop. In this way, the *continue* statement is less drastic than the *break*. Similar to the *break*, it can make the flow of control harder to follow, but there are times when it yields the more readable code.

Consider writing a program that continuously prompts a user for a series of integers that the program will sum together. If the user makes an error and enters a non-integer, the program should indicate an error, ignore that input, and continue with the process. Finally, we need a way to end the loop. Let's choose a special character to stop the looping. In our case, if the special character "." is entered, the program will print the final sum and end.

The basic algorithm will be:

1. Prompt the user for a number.
2. If the input (now a string) is a numeric, something that can be converted by the *int* function, add it to the running sum.
3. If the input is not numeric, print an error message—don't add it into the sum, just continue on.
4. If the input is the special character ".", end and print the final sum.

Checking user input for errors

Remember, when we prompt the user for a value using *raw_input*, we get a string back, not a number. We must convert that string to an integer to be able to process it. However, if we try to apply *int* to a non-numeric string like "abc", Python will give an error (what is the integer value of abc?). To avoid this problem, we can use the string *method*[8] isdigit. The isdigit method checks whether a string contains only numbers, returning a Boolean value: *True* or *False*. If it does, we can convert it to an integer. If not, then we should not try to convert it to avoid a Python error.

Briefly, a method is a function that is called on a particular object. The way to indicate what object is used for the function is to use the "dot call" notation. That is, we join the object with the method using a period. In general, the dot call notation looks like someObject.aMethod(arguments). This form means to call the method aMethod on the object someObject. For example, if we use the form '23'.isdigit(), this calls isdigit on the string object '23'. Such a call asks the question "does the object '23' consist only of digits"? If yes, the method returns *True*, otherwise *False*. Methods are a powerful part of the object-oriented paradigm that Python represents and we will see much more of them.

Code Listing 2.22 shows a solution to the problem.

Code Listing 2.22

```
# sum up a series of numbers
# make sure user input is only numbers

print "Allow the user to enter a series of integers. Sum the integers"
print "Ignore non-numeric input. End input with a '.'"
```

---

[8] Methods will be explained later.

```
     # initialize the input number and the sum
     theNumStr = raw_input("Number:")
     theSum = 0

10   # Stop if a period (.) is entered
     # remember, theNum is a string  until we convert it
     while theNumStr != "." :
         if not theNumStr.isdigit():          # not a number, an error
             print "Error, only numbers please"
15           theNumStr = raw_input("Number:")
             continue       # if the number is bad, ignore it
         theSum += int(theNumStr)
         theNumStr = raw_input("Number:")

20   print "The sum is:",theSum
```

Details:

Lines 7–8: Initialize the variables. theNumStr is set to the result of a *raw_input* request to the user. Note that if the user enters a "." the loop will end without running. We append "Str" to the variable name so we may keep straight that it in fact is a string, not a number. theSum is initially set to 0.

Line 12: The period (.) is our special indicator that indicates the loop should end, so we loop until a period is input.

Lines 13–16: Here we check whether theNumStr contains only numbers using the isdigit string method. If it is indeed not convertible to an integer, we print the error message and then re-prompt the user. We ***continue*** which means that we go to the top of the ***while*** loop and evaluate its Boolean expression, skipping over the *int* function below.

Lines 17–18: Remembering the rules of assignment, we first perform the operations on the right-hand-side, convert theNum to an integer, then add that integer to what is presently in theSum, storing the new value back into theSum. We then prompt the user for a new number.

Line 20: After the loop ends, print the sum of the integers accumulated in the variable theSum.

You might have noticed a few things about the example solution. In particular, it has two places in the loop for prompting the user. Can we do it more effectively, using only one? Let us try and refactor using ***if-else***. A solution without continue is shown Code Listing 2.23.

Code Listing 2.23

```
# sum up a series of numbers
# make sure user input is only numbers

print "Allow the user to enter a series of integers. Sum the integers"
5  print "Ignore non-numeric input. End input with a '.'"

# initialize the input number and the sum

theSum = 0
10
# Stop if a period (.) is entered
# remember, theNum is a string   until we convert it
theNum = raw_input("Number:")
while theNum != "." :
15     if  not theNum.isdigit(): # not a number, an error
           print "Error, only numbers please"
       else:
           theSum += int(theNum)
       theNum = raw_input("Number:")
20
print "The sum is:",theSum
```

The new example is improved in three ways:

1. **continue** is replaced with **if-else**. No non-normal control flow is required.
2. The oneChar input line appears before the loop and at the end of the loop, in keeping with our pattern described previously.
3. Only one prompt of the user is required.

If you think you need a **continue** statement, consider adjusting your algorithm to eliminate it, because you'll often find the resulting code is more readable.

Sentinel Loop

A *sentinel loop* is a loop that is controled by a sentinal—a guard. That is, a particular value is used to terminate the loop. The Boolean expression will be in the form: **while not** sentinelValue:.

```
value = someValue
while value != sentinelValue:
    # process value
    # get another value
```

An example of a sentinel loop is the preceeding example, where we stopped if a period was entered:

```
while theNum != ".":
```

Summary of Repetition

We can put all the variations of **while** into one generic pattern:

```
while booleanExpression1:
    # statementSuite1

    if booleanExpression2:
        break # Exit loop now; skip else.
    if booleanExpression3:
        continue # Go to top of loop now.

else:
    # statementSuite2
```

More on the *for* Statement

Code Listing 2.24

```
for anElement in object:
    # for suite
```

The **for** statement was introduced in an earlier section. Just like the **while** statement, the **for** statement can support a terminal **else** suite, as well as the control modifiers **continue** and **break**. Their roles are as previously described, that is:

1. The **else** suite is executed after the **for** loop exits normally.
2. The **break** statement provides an abnormal exit of the **for** loop, skipping the **else** clause.
3. The **continue** statement abnormally halts the present iteration of the loop, continuing with the rest of the iterations.

Its more general form is shown here:

```
for target in object:
    # statementSuite1
```

```
if booleanExpression1:
    break # Exit loop now; skip else.
if booleanExpression2:
    continue # Go to top of loop now.


else:
    # statementSuite2
```

Using *range* to Generate a Number Sequence

As we have mentioned, Python provides a number of collection data types that can be examined by iterating through the collection's elements using a *for* loop. However, it turns out that we can easily generate a collection—in fact, a sequence—of numbers using a special function provided by Python: the *range* function.

Let's look at *range*. Its operation generates a sequence of integers, in which the size and values in the range are dictated by its arguments. It takes up to three arguments: the start value, the end value, and the step or separation between each value. The range function generates what is termed a *half open* range. Such a range does *not* include the end value in the sequence generated. Python, when it works with ranges, usually assumes that the range will be half-open.

The start value is the first value included in the sequence and, if not provided, defaults to 0. The stop value is used to determine the final value of the sequence. Again, the stop value itself is *never* included in the sequence. The stop value is a required argument. The step value is the difference between each element generated in the sequence, and, if not provided, defaults to 1. If only one argument is provided, it is used as the stop value. In the case of one argument, constituting the stop value, the start value is assumed to be 0 and the step value assumed to be 1. If two arguments are provided, the first is the start and the second is the stop. There is a step argument only if three arguments are used.

Here are some examples using *range*. Try some examples yourself in the Python shell to gain an understanding of how *range* works.

```
>>> range(5)
[0, 1, 2, 3, 4]
>>> range(3,10)
[3, 4, 5, 6, 7, 8, 9]
>>> range(1,20,3)
[1, 3, 5, 7, 9, 11, 13, 15, 17, 19]
>>> range(1,20,4)
[1, 5, 9, 13, 17]
```

Such a sequence can be iterated through using a *for* loop. Code Listing 2.25 is a simple example of such use. This famous example is reputed to have been solved by the noted mathematician Gauss in primary school: the problem is to find the sum of the first

100 whole numbers. The teacher assigned it to keep the students busy, but Gauss solved it immediately.

Code Listing 2.25

```
# simple for
# find the sum of the numbers from 1 to 100

theSum = 0

for number in range(1,101):
    theSum = theSum + number

print "Sum is:", theSum
```

The details are as follows:

Line 4: Initialize variable theSum to 0 to provide a starting point for the addition in the *for* loop.

Line 6: The expression range(1,101) returns a sequence of numbers from 1 to 100. It is used by the *for* loop to associate the variable number with each value of the sequence, one value at a time.

Line 7: The suite of the *for* loop. It adds the present value associated with number to the value associated with theSum, then assigning the sum back to theSum.

Line 9: After the loop ends, print the value associated with theSum

The code shown prints the value 5050. Gauss is noted for taking a short cut and figuring out the formula: $n(n + 1)/2$.

PROGRAMMING TIP

One might be tempted to use the variable name sum in the code above. As it turns out, sum is a function predefined by Python! When you use IDLE or any other editor, it usually colorizes in some way pre-defined Python variables.

Interestingly, if you assign a value to sum anyway, Python will happily comply, though now sum will no longer operate as a function! However, the change is not permanent. If you make such a mistake, simply restart Python and all default Python values will be returned to their normal values.

Equivalence of *while* and *for*

It is possible to write a **while** loop that behaves exactly like a **for** loop. However, not every **while** loop can be expressed as a **for** loop.

Consider this simple **for** loop using the sequence generated by $range(5)$:

```
for i in range(5):
    print i
```

We can write an equivalent **while** loop as:

```
i = 0
while i < 5:
    print i
    i += 1
```

The **for** loop is easier to read and understand, but it is useful only for moving through the elements of objects with iterators. Fortunately, in Python you will find so many objects with iterators that you will frequently use a **for** loop.

Nesting

We have mentioned nesting and have used it multiple times in examples, but it is worth a little more discussion. Within the suite of any control construct (**if, while, for**) we can insert another control construct (**if, while, for**). Within the inserted control construct, we can insert yet another one. We can nest one within another with no limit (in reality there usually is a limit, but if you reach it, your code is unreadable and should be restructured). Each time we insert another control construct, its suite will be indented. The indentation aids readability, but if the code is nested too much, the indentation will be difficult to read. In that case, the code should be rewritten so that it can again be readable. One tool, which we will cover in Chapter 5, is a *function*, which will allows us to improve readability by encapsulating some of the indentation within a function.

If you look back to the perfect-number code, you can see the following nested control structure:

```
while ...
    while ...
        if ...
```

Hailstone Sequence Example

The Collatz conjecture is an unsolved mathematical conjecture from 1937 that makes for an interesting programming example. The conjecture is that the given the following formula and an initial positive integer, the generated sequence *always* ends in 1. Although this has

Check Yourself: *for* and *range* Check

1. What output occurs for the following program with the given inputs?

```
theMax = int(raw_input("Give me the upper limit:"))
sum = 0
extra = 0

for num in range(1,theMax):
    if num%2 and not num%3:
        sum = sum + num
    else:
        extra = extra + 1      # Line 1
print sum                      # Line 2
print extra                    # Line 3
```

(a) Given the input 10, what output is produced by Line 2 of the program?

(b) Given the input 11, what output is produced by Line 3 of the program?

(c) Which of the following is a reasonable replacement for Line 1 of the program?
   i. extra++
   ii. ++extra
   iii. extra =+ 1
   iv. extra += 1
   v. None of the above

(d) If Line 1 were removed from the program, which of the following statements would be true?
   i. No runtime errors.
   ii. Extra would always print 1.
   iii. Error, would run past the end of the range.
   iv. All of the above.
   v. None of the above.

been shown to be true for large initial integers (approximately 2.7×10^{16}) it has not yet been proven true for all. The sequence is also called the *hailstone sequence* because the numbers bounce up and down like hail until they converge to 1. Our task is to write a program to generate the hailstone sequence.

The hailstone formula is as follows:

- If the number is even, divide it by 2.
- If the number is odd, multiply by 3 and add 1.
- When the number reaches 1, quit.

The sequence is formed by applying the formula to the initial number and then repeatedly to each number generated by the formula. The result is a sequence of integers ending at 1 (if you don't stop at 1, what will happen?). For example, if you start with 5, you get the following sequence: 5, 16, 8, 4, 2, 1.

We will create a program so you can try your hand at it. We will also output the length of the sequence.

Determining whether a number is even or odd integer can be done using the remainder operator (%). If we divide a number by 2 and the remainder is 0, the number is even. Otherwise it is odd. In particular:

```
if number % 2 == 1:
    print number, "is odd"
else:
    print number, "is even"
```

Because 1 is considered to be *True* for a Boolean expression, the Boolean expression `number % 2 == 1` is often shortened to simply `number % 2` as in:

```
if number % 2:
    print number, "is odd"
else:
    print number, "is even"
```

With that notation in hand, let's apply the hailstone formula repeatedly to generate a sequence (Code Listing 2.26).

Code Listing 2.26

```
# Generate a Hailstone sequence
numString = raw_input("Enter a positive integer:")
num = int(numString)
count = 0

print "Starting with number:",num
print "Sequence is: ",

while num > 1:    # stop when the sequence reaches 1

    if num%2:             # num is odd
        num = num*3 + 1
    else:                 # num is even
        num = num/2
```

```
15      print num,",",     # add num to sequence

        count +=1          # add to the count
   else:
20      print              # blank line for nicer output
        print "Sequence is ",count," numbers long"
```

Copy this code and run it to try your hand at generating hailstone sequences; observe how they all end in 1. If you find one that does not end in 1, either there is an error in your program or you have made a fantastic discovery.

Some other interesting notes. Are there common subsequences for different initial numbers? What is the longest common subsequence? What is the longest sequence in some range of initial numbers? What does a plot of initial number and sequence length look like?

VISUAL VIGNETTE

2.3 PLOTTING DATA WITH PYLAB

In addition to drawing explicitly using tools like the `turtle` module, Python provides tools to plot data in both two and three dimensions. One of the most useful of those tools is the module pylab, which includes the plotting package matplotlib. Matplotlib is a plotting library, created in the image of the Matlab plotting library, for making publication-quality figures. Their motto is "matplotlib makes easy things easy and hard things possible." Matplotlib and pylab are described in more detail in Appendix C (including how to get and install them), but we can provide a simple introductions here. More complicated examples will be provided throughout the book.

One thing to note. As described in more detail in the appendix, matplotlib and Python's IDLE do not necessarily "play well together." You may find that, if you write a piece of code in IDLE and run it there, there are delays in the plotting window coming up. It is especially true if you are plotting interactively. Read the Appendix C for ways around this problem.

First Plot and Using a List

As with many things in Python, plotting requires that you use one of the collection data structures called the *list* data structure. Lists are covered in detail in Chapter 6, but we can teach you enough about lists here to do some simple plotting.

A list is just a sequence of objects. Lists are denoted with square brackets, and individual elements in a list are separated by commas. Thus [1,2,3,4] is a list of four integer values. The empty list is designated by [], and a very useful method used in conjunction with lists is the append method. A useful function is len. A typical use is demonstrated in Code Listing 2.27.

Code Listing 2.27

```
listOfInts = []
for counter in range(10):
    listOfInts.append(counter*2)

5 print listOfInts
  print len(listOfInts)
```

```
>>>
[0, 2, 4, 6, 8, 10, 12, 14, 16, 18]
10
```

The variable listOfInts starts out empty, as designated by a pair of brackets ([]), and we append ten integers to the list. At the end, the length of the list is 10.

To plot the list we just created, all we need to do is import pylab, and add two lines to the program.

Code Listing 2.28

```
import pylab
listOfInts = []
for counter in range(10):
    listOfInts.append(counter*2)

print listOfInts
print len(listOfInts)

# now plot the list
pylab.plot(listOfInts)
pylab.show()
```

A new window is exposed, as shown in Figure 2.10. The values in listOfInts provide the values for the y-axis of the plot. The pylab.plot method provides the x-axis

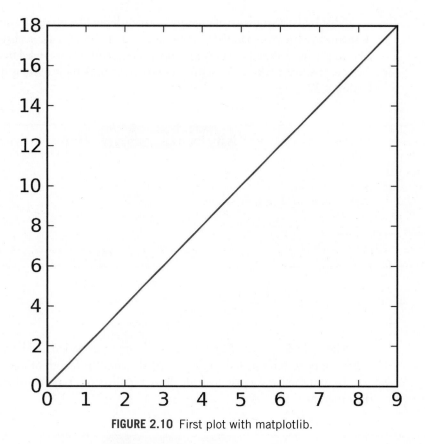

FIGURE 2.10 First plot with matplotlib.

values as the sequence indices of the list. The first value in the list gets x-value 0, the second value gets x-value 1, and so on.

More Interesting Plot: a Sine Wave

As their motto indicates, matplotlib can do complicated things, but allows you to add complexity as necessary. There are an enormous number of options that you can use, but here are a couple of immediately useful ones.

Plotting Elements and Their Colors

You can plot using all kinds of "markers" for each point in the graph. Each "formatting string" consists of a two-character string:

Color: The first is a lowercase letter for the color. The mappings are fairly obvious: 'r' is red, 'b' is blue, 'g' is green. The only odd one is that 'k' is black.

Marker The second element is a single character indicating the type of marker. These are rather obscure—you simply have to learn them. For example: 'o' is for circles, '.' is for dots, 'x' is for an x marker, and '+' is for a plus marker. Look in Appendix C and the plot documentation for more details.

Putting them together, the formatting string 'ro' will print red circles, and 'bx' will print blue x's.

More detailed call of plot

Using that information on markers, we can pass more than just a single list to `plot`. A more detailed invocation would be: `pylab.plot(xValues,yValues,format String)`. Using this form, Code Listing 2.29 below plots a sine wave from 0 to $4 * \pi$ in increments of 0.1 with red circles. We provide both the x and y values.

Code Listing 2.29

```
# plot a sine wave from 0 to 4pi

import math
import pylab

#initialize the two lists and the counting variable num. Note is a float
y_values = []
x_values = []
num = 0.0

#collect both num and the sine of num in a list
while num < math.pi * 4:
    y_values.append(math.sin(num))
    x_values.append(num)
    num += 0.1

#plot the x and y values as red circles
pylab.plot(x_values,y_values,'ro')
pylab.show()
```

The resulting plot is shown Figure 2.11.

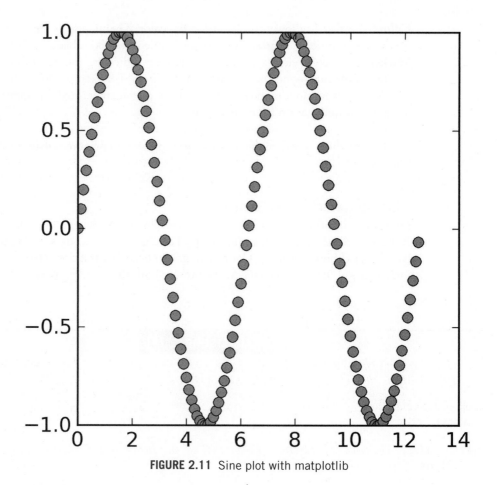

FIGURE 2.11 Sine plot with matplotlib

2.4 COMPUTER SCIENCE PERSPECTIVES: MINIMAL UNIVERSAL COMPUTING

Minimal Universal Computing

An interesting question is:

How much language power do we need to be able to write any computer program?

Rephrased:

What is the minimal set of instructions that we need to compute any result that can be computed?

In the early days of computing, there was quite a competition to figure out the minimum. It turns out that theoretically, you do not need much. The answer is useful for us, because it indicates how little is needed to write all programs, and it shows the importance of control.

The results are usually presented in assembly language. Assembly language is the somewhat English-like description of the ones and zeros of the computer's actual machine language. That is, assembly language is specifically matched to the CPU it runs on to generate commands for that CPU. The basic instructions involve manipulating memory—either an actual location or an "accumulator" register on the processor—and jumping to a specific instruction in a program. (You can think of the accumulator as what stores the result of your calculations when you use a calculator.) Accumulators were common on the first computers when hardware was expensive.

Here is a minimal instruction set[9]:

LOAD A	; load contents at RAM address A into accumulator
STORE A	; store accumulator contents into address A in RAM
CLR	; clear accumulator
INC	; increment accumulator
BRZ X	; branch to address X in RAM if accumulator is zero

All computer programs can be written using just those five instructions. *All* programs, ever! That is a very significant result! Such a program might be nearly impossible to make sense of (i.e., not readable), but it can be done in theory.

Notice that a "branch" instruction is one of the necessary instructions. That branch instruction is the most primitive type of control, and it is closely related to the simple *if* statement introduced earlier. This branch instruction, the "BRZ" instruction, tests the accumulator value to see whether it is all zeros, and if it is, the next instruction to execute is at address X in memory. Otherwise, it executes the instruction that follows, i.e., the instruction at the address immediately following this BRZ instruction. There are more powerful and more readable styles of control instruction, but the BRZ is the simplest.

This simple branch instruction allows us to repeatedly do the INC instruction so we can perform addition: if you want to add 5 to something, increment it 5 times. Once you can do addition, you can do all the other arithmetic. It will be messy to read, but it is possible.

What is the point? After all, assembly language is very different from a high-level language such as Python. The point is that a simple combination of *if*, the BRZ instruction, and the ability to repeat, in this case by branching back to the beginning of the program if one so chooses, is enough to write any program. Selection and repetition are two core parts of programming!

---

[9] R. Rojas, "Conditional Branching is not Necessary for Universal Computation in von Neumann Computers", *Journal of Universal Computer Science*, Vol. 2, No. 11, 1996, pp. 756–767

Summary

In this chapter, we have introduced two control constructs: decision and repetition. With these in hand, you now have sufficient programming power to write any program. Everything after this point makes programs easier to read and easier to write—powerful concepts in their own right.

Exercises

1. How many three-digit numbers are divisible by 17? Write a program to print them.

2. Sum of consecutive integers

   (a) Write a program that prompts for an integer—let's call it X—and then finds the sum of X consecutive integers starting at 1. That is, if X = 5, you will find the sum of 1 + 2 + 3 + 4 + 5 = 15.

   (b) Modify your program by enclosing your loop in another loop so that you can find consecutive sums. For example, if 5 is entered, you will find five sums of consecutive numbers:

   ```
   1             =   1
   1+2           =   3
   1+2+3         =   6
   1+2+3+4       =   10
   1+2+3+4+5     =   15
   ```

   Print only each sum, not the arithmetic expression.

   (c) Modify your program again to only print sums if the sum is divisible by the number of operands. For example, with the sum 1 + 2 + 3 + 4 + 5 = 15, there are five operands and the sum, 15, is divisble by 5 so that sum will be printed. (Do you notice a pattern?)

3. In this exercise you will convert knuts to sickles and galleons (the currency of the Harry Potter novels). Perform the calculation, and print only non-zero values. That is, if there are not enough knuts for there to be one sickle, then "0 sickle" should not be printed. (There are 29 knuts in one sickle and 17 sickles in one galleon.)

4. (Perfect numbers). In this chapter is a program that checks for *perfect* numbers. If you wanted to check many numbers (a large range of numbers), to see if any were perfect, then the program we wrote might not be the best. What could we do to improve it? For example, how would we output only perfect numbers, but just keep count of the deficient and abundant numbers? Do we need to check every number from 2 to `theNum-1`?

5. In an earlier set of exercises, you were asked to calculate one's BMI. Augment that program by printing out where that BMI fits in the CDC standard weight status categories:

BMI	Weight Status
Below 18.5	Underweight
18.5 - 24.9	Normal
25.0-29.9	Overweight
30.0 and above	Obese

6. Write a program that prompts for an integer and prints the integer, but if something other than an integer is input, the program keeps asking for an integer. Here is a sample session:

```
Input an integer: abc
Error: try again. Input an integer: 4a
Error: try again. Input an integer: 2.5
Error: try again. Input an integer: 123
The integer is : 123
```

Hint: the string `isdigit` method will be useful.

7. Write a program to generate the following arithmetic examples.
Hints:
(1) Divide-and-conquer: what simpler problem do you need to solve?
(2) Consider using strings to build numbers and then convert.
(3) The `range` iterator may be helpful.

```
1 * 8 + 1 = 9
12 * 8 + 2 = 98
123 * 8 + 3 = 987
1234 * 8 + 4 = 9876
12345 * 8 + 5 = 98765
123456 * 8 + 6 = 987654
1234567 * 8 + 7 = 9876543
12345678 * 8 + 8 = 98765432
123456789 * 8 + 9 = 987654321

1 * 9 + 2 = 11
12 * 9 + 3 = 111
123 * 9 + 4 = 1111
1234 * 9 + 5 = 11111
12345 * 9 + 6 = 111111
123456 * 9 + 7 = 1111111
1234567 * 9 + 8 = 11111111
12345678 * 9 + 9 = 111111111
123456789 * 9 + 10 = 1111111111
```

```
9 * 9 + 7 = 88
98 * 9 + 6 = 888
987 * 9 + 5 = 8888
9876 * 9 + 4 = 88888
98765 * 9 + 3 = 888888
987654 * 9 + 2 = 8888888
9876543 * 9 + 1 = 88888888
98765432 * 9 + 0 = 888888888

1 * 1 = 1
11 * 11 = 121
111 * 111 = 12321
1111 * 1111 = 1234321
11111 * 11111 = 123454321
111111 * 111111 = 12345654321
1111111 * 1111111 = 1234567654321
11111111 * 11111111 = 123456787654321
111111111 * 111111111 = 12345678987654321
```

8. Write a program that checks to see if a number N is prime. A simple approach checks all numbers from 2 up to N, but after some point numbers are checked that need not be checked. For example, numbers greater than $\sqrt{N}$ need not be checked. Write a program that checks for primality and avoids those unnecessary checks. Remember to import the `math` module.

9. The perfect number example in this chapter uses two **while** loops. Rewrite the program replacing the two **while** loops with two **for** loops and *range*.

10. (Quadratic formula) The forumla that calculates roots for a quadratic equation $ax^2 + bx + c$ is the quadratic formula $x = -b \pm \sqrt{b^2 - 4ac}/2a$. Because the square root of a negative is imaginary, one can use the expression under the square root (known as the *discriminant*) to check for the type of root. If the discriminant is negative, the roots are imaginary. If the discriminant is zero, there is only one root. If the discriminant is positive, there are two roots.

    (a) Write a program that uses the quadratic formula to generate real roots, i.e., ignores the imaginary roots. Use the discriminant to determine whether there is one root or two roots and then prints the appropriate answer.

    (b) Python uses the letter 'j' to represent the mathematical imaginary number 'i' (a convention used in electrical engineering). However, the Python 'j' must always be preceeded by a number. That is, '1j' is eqivalent to the mathematical 'i'. Add the ability to handle imaginary roots to your program.

11. Control:

```
if myVar % 2:
    if myVar**3 != 27:
        myVar = myVar + 4    # Assignment 1
    else:
        myVar /= 1.5         # Assignment 2
else:
    if myVar <= 10:
        myVar *= 2           # Assignment 3
    else:
        myVar -= 2           # Assignment 4
print myVar
```

   (a) Find four values of myVar so each of the four assignment statements will be executed: each value should cause one assignment statement to be executed.
   (b) Find four ranges of myVar values that will cause each of the four assignment statements to be executed.

12. Write a "for" loop that will print 'pbil' when 'alphebetical' is the input.

13. Write a short program that will:
   • prompt the user for a number
   • print out whether the number is a perfect square
   • prompt the user for another number if the input was not a perfect square

14. Explain the difference between "is" and "==". Give an example (different than that used in the chapter) that illustrates items that return False for "is" and True for "==".

15. Here is an example of a **while** loop. There is an error; can you find the error in the **while** loop? Try to figure out what could be wrong by thinking through the **while** loop. Referring to the flow-chart figures in the chapter should help. Check to see if you are right by using Python!

```
sentence= "that car was really fast"
i=1
while i>0:
    for character in sentence:
        if character == "t":
            print "found a 't' in sentence"
        else:
            print "maybe the next character?"
```

16. If your **while** loop is controlled by "while True:", it will loop forever. How do you control your loop so that it will stop? Provide a brief example in Python code.

17. Create a program that prompts for a positive number greater than 2 (check this condition), then keeps taking the square root of this number until the square root is less than 2. Print the value each time the square root is taken, along with the number of times the operation has been completed. For example:

```
Enter an integer greater than 2: 20
1: 4.472
2: 2.115
3: 1.454
```

Extra: Look ahead to string formatting (Section 4.41) to print the values to only 3 decimal places as shown.

18. In the exercises for Chapter 1, an algorithm was given for calculating the pass rating for football quarterbacks. One can use the pass rating to determine whether a quarterback had a mediocre, good, or great year. A rating is poor if it is 85 or below, mediocre if above 85, good if above 90 and great if above 95. Add to the pass rating program to output "poor', "mediocre", "good", or "great".

To test your program, you can look up actual data on www.nfl.com or use the following information from 2007:

	Completions	Attempts	Yards	Touchdowns	Interceptions
Donovan McNabb	180	316	2647	18	6
Tom Brady	319	516	3529	24	12
Peyton Manning	362	557	4397	31	9

19. In order to understand what a program tries to accomplish, it is essential to be able to follow the flow of control. In the following example, what happens when x = 4?

```
while True:
    for x in range (6):
        y = 2*x+1
        print y
        if y > 9:
            break
```

(a) The program breaks out of the **while** loop and stops running.
(b) The program breaks out of the **for** loop, but the **while** condition continues to be *True*, resulting in an infinite loop.
(c) The program does not break, but simply continues processing the **for** loop.

20. Fill in the following table with values *True* or *False*—one value in each empty box.

p	q	(not p) or q	(p and q) or q	(p or q) and p	(p or q) and (p and q)
True	True				
True	False				
False	True				
False	False				

21. Consider the Python function *range(a,b)*. Label these statements as True or False.
  - Value "a" is included in the range.
  - Value "b" is included in the range.

22. What is an *iterator*? Give two examples of iterators.

23. In your own words, describe what the statements **continue** and **break** do in loops.

24. The NPR radio show "Car Talk" always offers a puzzle to solve. Occasionally, one can be solved with a program. Try this one: My car's odometer measures distance traveled in whole numbers—no tenths of miles—up to 999,999. Last week I was driving along on the freeway and noticed that the last four digits, but not the last five digits, formed a palindrome; that is, it read the same backwards as forwards (e.g., 1221). After one mile went by, though, the last five digits did form a palindrome; and, after one more mile, the middle four digits formed a palindrome. Finally, when the third mile rolled over, all six digits formed a palindrome. What was my mileage at the time I first noticed all these palindromes?

25. Find the two-digit number such that when you square it, the resulting three-digit number has its rightmost two digits the same as the original two-digit number. That is, for a number in the form AB, AB*AB = CAB for some C.

26. A famous puzzle follows.

SEND
+MORE
———
MONEY

What interger values can be substituted to make the addition correct? Write a program to solve this puzzle. Hint: Bute force works well—try all possibilities.

Programming Projects

1. **What is the invention of chess worth?**

   There is a popular myth about the man who invented chess. The local ruler was so pleased with the invention that he offered the inventor a great reward in gold. The inventor suggested an alternative reward: he would get one grain of wheat on the first square of the chess board, two grains on the second square, four on the third, eight on the fourth, etc., doubling the number of grains each time. The ruler saw that this must be a much better deal for him, and accepted. The board has 64 squares. Write a program to determine the following:

   (a) How many total grains of wheat did the ruler have to pay the inventor?
   (b) A wheat grain weighs approximately 50 mg. How much did the wheat weigh?
   (c) Pick a region (state, country, etc.) and determine how deeply that region would be covered with that quantity of wheat. Prompt for the area of the region and then output the depth including the units you use.

2. **How thick does paper folding get?**

   Take one sheet out of your newspaper, and fold it in half, then fold it in half again, and again, and again. Can you fold it 30 times? Pretending that you can (you probably can't fold it more than eight times), how thick would it be after 30 times? Assume the paper is 1/200 cm. thick. Write a program to solve this puzzle. Prompt for the number of folds and output the thickness in meters.

3. **Turtle polygons**

   Prompt for the desired number of sides for your polygon. Given that the interior angle of a regular polygon is $(sides - 2) \times 180^o)/sides$, draw the polygon. Optional: prompt for a color and color the interior of your polygon.

4. **Weird multiplication**

   For this assignment, you will be implementing the so-called "Russian Peasant" or "Ancient Egyptian" method for multiplication. It looks a little odd, but just think of it as an algorithm, a recipe for doing multiplication in a way other than what you learned in grade school.

   The algorithm is as follows. If A and B are the 2 integers (only integers) to be multiplied, we repeatedly multiply A by 2 and divide B by 2, until B cannot be divided any further, that is until its value becomes 0 (remember, this is integer division). During each step, whenever B is an odd number, we add the corresponding A value to the product we are generating. In the end, the sum of the A values that had corresponding odd B values is the product. Get it?

   Here is an example:

If the two integers to be multiplied are 34 and 19, the operations would be:

A	B	Comment
34	19	add A to the product, B is odd
68	9	add A to the product, B is odd
136	4	ignore this A value, B is even
272	2	ignore this A value, B is even
544	1	add A to the product, B is odd

Sum up all the A values that had odd B values and you get: 34 + 68 + 544 = 646 => Final product.

(a) Part 1: Write a program to find the product of two integers.

(b) Part 2: Modify your program so that it repeatedly asks whether you want to find another product.

CHAPTER 3

Algorithms and Program Development

PROBLEM SOLVING USING COMPUTATIONAL METHODS IS BASED ON ALGORITHMS AND the programs that implement them. We briefly introduced the concept of an algorithm earlier. In this chapter, we further develop the concept of an algorithm, and show its role in creating programs to solve problems.

3.1 WHAT IS AN ALGORITHM?

You will hear the word *algorithm* frequently in computer science (as well as in the closely related fields of computer engineering and mathematics). What is an algorithm?

The formal definition of an algorithm from a dictionary is (Dictionary.app, Mac OS X):

algorithm: a process or a set of rules to be followed in calculations
or other problem-solving operations.

Informally, an algorithm is sometimes described as

algorithm: a recipe for solving a problem.

The word algorithm, like the word algebra, has Arabian roots. In the Middle Ages much of the mathematical knowledge in Europe was derived from Latin translations of earlier Arabian mathematicians. In the case of algorithm the word is derived from the name of Mohamed al-Khowarizmi (äl-khō-wär-ēzmē), a mathematician of the court of Mamun in Baghdad.

147

Example Algorithms

Let's consider a couple of simple algorithms that you might find familiar. First, consider making a chocolate cake from scratch—a slightly more complicated process than making it from a box. Algorithms for preparing food are better known as recipes, and have two components: objects (ingredients) and actions on those objects. If the ingredients are fresh and we follow the steps correctly, the result is a cake to eat. Here is the recipe.[1]

Chocolate Cake Recipe
 $1\frac{1}{2}$ c. flour
 1 c. sugar
 1/2 tsp. salt
 1 tsp. baking soda
 2 tbsp. cocoa
 1 tbsp. vinegar
 6 tbsp. oil
 1 tsp. vanilla
 1 c. water

1. Sift first five ingredients together.
2. Add remaining ingredients and mix.
3. Pour into an 9-inch greased and floured square pan.
4. Bake at 350 degrees for 30 minutes.
5. Let cool and frost with your favorite frosting.
6. Eat!!!

Recipes are not just for food, but for calculations as well. Consider a mathematical algorithm to calculate the square root of a number: the Babylonian square root algorithm. It is an ancient algorithm attributed to the Babylonians[2] and first described by the Greek mathematician Heron of Alexandria in the first century. It is a surprisingly fast and accurate way to find a square root using pencil and paper that also happens to work well on a computer. The algorithm is sometimes called Newton's Method, from Newton's generalization of the algorithm. It is:

Babylonian Square Root Algorithm

1. Guess the square root of the number.
2. Divide the number by the guess.
3. Average the quotient (from step 2) and the guess.
4. Make the new guess the average from step 3.
5. If the new guess is different than the old guess, go back to step 2; otherwise, stop.

---

[1] World Famous Cake (Chocolate) http://www.cooks.com/rec/view/0,196,139177-233206,00.html
[2] Whether the Babylonians knew this algorithm is disputed, nonetheless it is known as the "Babylonian method".

The Babylonian Square Root Algorithm has a characteristic in common with many algorithms you will encounter: the devil is in the details. For example, what do we mean by "different" in step 5? Maybe if the guesses differ by a few thousandths, we will be satisfied with the answer (and worn out, if calculating with pencil and paper).

3.2 ALGORITHM FEATURES

Calling an algorithm a recipe works as a first description of an algorithm, but from a computer science point of view, it is insufficient. In particular, computer scientists are interested in what makes a *good* algorithm. There are a number of characteristics that good algorithms share. However, before we examine those characteristics, let's try to clarify the difference between an algorithm and a program.

Algorithm versus Program

Algorithms and their associated programs are so tightly coupled that sometimes one is confused with the other, especially when first learning how to program.

There is a difference, and here it is. In the simplest terms:

- An *algorithm* is a description of how a problem can be solved.
- A *program* is an implementation of an algorithm in a particular language to run on a particular kind of computer.

Consider our algorithms for chocolate cake and square roots. The cake recipe leaves out necessary details for particular kitchens. For example, it doesn't say where to find a bowl for mixing. Also, the recipe doesn't tell us how to set the oven temperature on a particular stove: do we spin a dial or punch buttons? The square root algorithm will be implemented differently when using pencil and paper than using a computer or even an abacus. In both cases, the missing details are particular to the circumstances of implementing the algorithm. To a cook working in his or her own kitchen, the implementation details missing from the recipe are not a problem, because the cook knows where the bowls are and knows how to operate the oven. In a similar way, a programmer familiar with a particular programming language, operating system, and computer will implement an algorithm as a program using those details.

Separating what we *want to do* from how we *actually did it* provides us with a couple of advantages:

- We have the opportunity to analyze the algorithm itself, independent of how it was implemented. This analysis is the "science" in the discipline of computer science. Separating the algorithm from the implementation allows us to focus on the properties of the algorithm. For example, analysis of the algorithm may suggest improvements that improve all implementations.

- We have the opportunity to see how well a programming language allows us to realize an implementation of the algorithm. Every language has strengths and weaknesses that make different aspects of an algorithm easier or harder to implement. The design of computer languages partly focuses on this idea.
- We have the opportunity to analyze the impact of a particular computer and language on the implementation. For example, there may be cost or power constraints on a particular problem, so development time may be important or hardware costs may be a constraint. A programming language choice would affect the former; a processor choice would affect the latter.

We have emphasized the difference between the algorithm and implementation, and when first learning, it is best to think of them in that way. However, they are not always as independent as we have implied. Often there are multiple algorithms that provide correct solutions for a particular problem. For example, if we want to solve a problem on a particular computer, we may want to use an algorithm that is well suited to that style of computing. Two examples come to mind. One involves the multi-core processor that can run multiple pieces of a program at the same time. Some algorithms are more suitable for such an environment than others. Another example is an embedded processor, such as one that controls brakes on an automobile. That processor may have little computing power and memory, so an algorithm with low power and memory demands may be more appropriate.

Detailed

An algorithm has to be detailed enough to specify all that must be done to accomplish the goal. However, "detailed enough" is tricky to define precisely. An algorithm needs to have sufficient detail so that by following it exactly (be it on paper or in a program), the desired result is achieved. Consider the chocolate cake algorithm (recipe). Obviously, "mix some ingredients and cook" would be insufficient, but describing how to stir with a spoon ("pick up spoon in right hand, hold bowl with left, stick spoon in mixture, . . . ") would be too much detail. Common sense and experience defines what "detailed enough" is for recipes, and even with recipes, the detail varies with the audience. A recipe for an inexperienced cook contains more detail than needed for an experienced chef. Similarly, common sense, experience, and the audience also define "detailed enough" for computer algorithms. The practice of learning about algorithms and encoding them in programs is necessary to develop an understanding of the level of detail needed in an algorithm.

Effective

Every algorithm should effectively compute its result. That's obvious, but what does that really mean in the context of computing? By effectively computing its result, we mean:

- The algorithm should halt. That is, it should stop and deliver an answer.
- The algorithm should not merely halt; it should halt in a "reasonable" amount of time.

It is interesting to note the ambiguities in those statements:

- What is "reasonable"?
- How do you measure a reasonable time without actually implementing an algorithm as a program and running it?

Be aware that an algorithm can be impossibly slow, even if implemented efficiently in a programming language, and even if it runs on the fastest computer available. Some seemingly simple problems have algorithms that take an unreasonably long time to solve. For example, there are hundreds of millions of mailing addresses in the United States: in what order should mail be delivered to use the least energy? Finding a good solution can be done in a reasonable amount of time, but finding the *best* solution could take multiple lifetimes on the fastest computers. Most people would agree that finding the best solution in that case would not be a "reasonable" amount of time. In addition, the solution time is so long that the problem itself would have changed before the best solution for the original problem was found—many addresses would have changed!

Finally, to achieve completion in a reasonable time, the behavior of the algorithm may not be exact. That is, it gets an answer all the time, but it may not be the "best" answer every time. Sometimes we must be willing to accept "close answers" as a trade-off for getting results in a reasonable time. There are many problems with this characteristic. For example, to understand how proteins work, analysis of their folding may not be perfect—yet it can yield interesting and useful results. Weather prediction is not perfect, but if it takes longer than 24 hours to get a better 24-hour forecast, it is not effective.

Specify Behavior

An algorithm must specify its behavior, that is, what it is supposed to do. An important part of behavior is the input and output. In fact, the algorithm provides a description that *relates* the input to the output. That is, given this input, we produce this output. The algorithm should indicate what inputs are required (including no inputs). The importance of specifying output is self-evident, as the output is the most visible part of the algorithm's behavior, and that of its associated program.

The "correct behavior" of the algorithm should be made clear. For example, if the algorithm is addition, then the input of two integers should result in the output of a single integer that is the sum of the two input integers.

Specifying input is also critically important for security, because most security breaches are related to incorrect input handling. Knowing what input is required and expected is necessary for correct handling of it.

General-Purpose Algorithms

Most algorithms are, at least to some extent, general-purpose. For example, a bread recipe should result in bread: different ingredients will result in different-flavored breads, but the basic recipe is the same. Similarly, a sort algorithm should sort regardless of whether the items being sorted are words or numbers. The basic steps of the algorithm are the same, but the ingredients are different.

Algorithms are general-purpose by design, because an algorithm is an idealized computational module. The implementation details (how to compare types, how to iterate through types) are the problems of the implementation, not the general approach. Although any solution you might devise to solve a problem might be deemed an algorithm by you, a really good algorithm that stands the test of time should be written in a way that can apply to any instance of the problem.

Remember: a program is an implementation of an algorithm! You formulated an algorithm in order to create the program, but the algorithm is not the program. The sharing of algorithms with others for analysis is important for both correctness and robustness.

Can We Really Do All That?

Our list of features is good to have. We would like to have all of them in every algorithm we create, but that may not be possible in every case. In particular, achieving all of them when writing one's first algorithms is particularly difficult. However, striving for detail, effectiveness, specification of behavior, and generality is a worthy goal.

In practice, especially at the beginning, you will find your algorithms to be very specific to a particular problem. Your first algorithms will not be efficient. Also, if the problem is challenging, your algorithm may not lead to an exact result. All of those characteristics are the reality for novice algorithm writers, so they are acceptable in a first course. Nonetheless, we encourage you to strive for good algorithms.

3.3 WHAT IS A PROGRAM?

If an algorithm is an idealized computational process, then a program is an actual implementation of that ideal. It exists in a particular language to be run on a specific computer. In the sense that an algorithm is an abstraction of a solution to a problem, the program is the actual solution. As such, it has a number of features that differ from an algorithm. Again, let's consider those features.

Readability

> *Programs must be written for people to read,*
> *and only incidentally for machines to execute.*

Abelson & Sussman[3]

---

[3] Abelson, H., and Sussman, G., *Structure and Interpretation of Computer Programs*, 2nd ed. (Cambridge MA: MIT Press, 1996), ISBN-13 978-0-2620-1153-2.

When students are asked, "What is the most important feature of a program?" we often get the answer "It runs and solves a problem." It is true that a program should *do* something, but that may not be its most important feature. To most novices' surprise, one of the most important features of a program is that it be *readable*—it is a document that describes to a reader how the writer is solving a problem. As an implementation of an algorithm, a program is a piece of your thoughts made concrete. That is a powerful statement and worth emphasizing. A program is your thoughts on a problem, made concrete so that not only can they be read, but implemented, and realized. This is one of the promises, and the hopes of computer programming, and it is a lofty one at that.

As such, for anyone else to understand what you were thinking, the code should be written clearly. Note that there are really two audiences for your document: the computer and the reader. Good enough to "run" need not be good enough to be understandable to a human.

Programs need to be read, and understood, to be useful. A successful program will be used more than once and possibly maintained or modified by others. In fact, a poorly written program will be incomprehensible even to the author after some time. As a test, six months after completing this course, come back and see whether you can make sense of all your code. Some of it will be incomprehensible, even to you. Imagine how it looks to others!

Someone who writes difficult-to-read programs will not be able to get effective help or advice from others. Also, such code is unlikely to be secure, and the brief history of computing has reinforced the idea that code that is examined by many eyes is more likely to do what it was supposed to do with fewer errors.

Consider the Obfuscated C Code Contest.[4] This contests challenges programmers to write code that accomplishes a specific goal while being as unreadable and obfuscated as possible. In so doing, the contest provides examples of what you can do to make the code "just run," ignoring and even defying readability. Take a look at some of the examples online and see what you think.

The Simplest Thing: Good Names

There are a variety of good rules for readable programs, but the first and most common is *good naming*. Good names help with readability, and good naming is easy. Basically, be descriptive in your naming. Descriptive names can be aided by using the camelCase style mentioned earlier, in which you stick multiple words together using capital letters, such as circleRadius.

- For variables, names should reflect their role is and, potentially, information about what they can hold, such as a type.
- For operations, names should reflect what they do and, potentially, what they return.

---

[4] Copyright © 2004–2009, Landon Curt Noll, Simon Cooper, Peter Seebach, and Leonid A. Broukhis. www.ioccc.org.

As an example, consider the following code. What does this code do?

Code Listing 3.1

```
a = raw_input("give a number: ")
b,c=1,0
while b<=a:
    c = c + b
    b = b + 1
print a,b,c
print "Result: ",float(c)/b-1
```

First, it is hard to tell what the program does. Part of the problem is that the variable names are not descriptive. We will see that there is a time and a place for single-character variables, but a readable program will have few. Second, there are two subtle errors in this program, and its lack of readability makes them difficult to find. If you run the code, one error causes it to run forever no matter what you enter as input. In addition, if that error is fixed, the wrong result will still be printed.

Here is a cleaned-up and easier-to-read version. Is it easier to understand? Can you find the changes that fix the errors in the previous example?

Code Listing 3.2

```
# Calculate the average of a sum of consecutive integers in a given range.

limit_str=raw_input("Range is from 1 to your input:")

limit_int = int(limit_str)
count_int = 1
sum_int = 0
while count_int <= limit_int:
        sum_int = sum_int + count_int
        count_int = count_int + 1
average = float(sum_int)/(count_int - 1)
print "Average of sum of integers from 1 to",limit_int,"is", average
```

What were the errors?

- We didn't convert the string input to an integer (infinite loop).
- The order of operations for the calculating the average did the division first, followed by the subtraction (wrong answer).

You need to be able to read what was written to find problems like this; otherwise, the errors (your errors!) can be very difficult to find.

Comments

Comments are essential for readability. Even though code is precise, programming languages are not the best language for human understanding—even for experienced programmers. The necessity of comments, even for the author of the code, is something that novice programmers find hard to accept. It is not uncommon for experienced programmers to go back at some time to read their own old code and find it incomprehensible. Such experience helps them appreciate the importance of comments.

Like other aspects of readability, there are no well-defined rules for how much commenting is necessary. Too many comments can make the program hard to read; too few make parts of the code difficult to understand. Finding a balance comes with experience. However, over time, some guidelines have surfaced.

Place comments to indicate:

- The overall goal of the code. This is usually placed at the top as a summary.
- The purpose of objects such as variables.
- The purpose of other functions that are provided by the system, or, as you will learn, written by us. This includes the input required and the output expected.
- Where something "tricky" or "unusual" is going on: if it required thought on your part, it should be commented.

The last guideline is particularly important. As a rule of thumb, if you experience some difficulty in writing some piece of code, either because of the problem being solved or the code needed to solve the problem, it likely deserves a comment. If it was hard to write, it will likely be hard to read unless it is explained.

An experience you will have: you write some code and provide a silly comment like "good luck here" or similar. You come back in a month after you have forgotten what you were doing, and find yourself angry at the callousness of the idiot who wrote that comment (which, as you recall, was you)!

You are enhancing readability not only for others, but also for yourself!

Indenting Code

Indenting is an important ingredient of readability. Getting indentation correct to show what code belongs to what control statement is crucial for readability. Thankfully, you *must* get this correct, because Python makes you do so. This is one of the nice aspects of Python: enforcing readability right from the start.

Robust

Programs should be *robust* in the face of unpredictability. Programs should be able to recover from inputs that are unanticipated. For example, if a program does division, and a zero divisor is provided (remember that division by zero is undefined in mathematics), the program should not halt unexpectedly. The program should be designed to deal with such erroneous input.

In an ideal world, all input should be predictable, but the reality is different—something unexpected will happen if a program is sufficiently popular, especially if it's used in situations not imagined by the designer. A program by design should know what input it expects, but be sufficiently robust to handle everything else—especially inputs the designer couldn't imagine. Most security errors in software come from mishandling of unanticipated input. Often the unanticipated input comes from the software being used in ways not imagined by the designers.

Achieving robustness requires two actions:

- The program designer should account for error situations in the design of a program. In particular, the designer should know what input is expected, and design in a way to handle situations if anything else occurs.
- The designer should devise tests to determine whether the program not only satisfies the original design, but also, as it evolves, continues to deal with all cases (including error cases), no matter how the program is changed.

It is not obvious, but it can be very difficult to "fully test" a program. The number of cases can be very large—too large to test all cases in a reasonable amount of time. It may not even be obvious how many cases there are. Although the error manifested itself in hardware, the first Intel Pentium processor had a bug in its division unit that caused *only* 1 in 9 billion floating-point divides to be incorrect. The rarity of this error evaded testing, but showed up quickly after the processor was in the public's hands. The error is even more interesting, because it turned out that a software error in loading a table for manufacturing was the root of the problem—a small part of the table came out as all zeros.[5] Testing before manufacturing showed the division to be correct, but testing after manufacturing didn't find the newly introduced error.

We talk more about testing later in Chapter 15.

Correctness

Obviously, correctness is essential. It seems equally obvious that if we design an algorithm and then implement that algorithm as a program, the program should be correct—that it does what it was supposed to do. If the program is supposed to sum two numbers, then it should produce correct sums. It seems so simple, doesn't it?

In fact, determining correctness is extremely difficult. For any program of even moderate size, it is very difficult to determine from the design of the program alone (that is, without running it on test cases) that it is correct. Combine that fact with the knowledge that

---

[5] http://en.wikipedia.org/wiki/Pentium_bug

sometimes it is not possible to test all cases, and you find that *proving* correctness is often not feasible.

Proving correctness is a vital and growing area in computer science, but designing provably-correct programs is a task for the future. For now, the best we can do is design well, and to test as best as we can. When done with care, testing early in program development can help produce more correct programs.

3.4 STRATEGIES FOR PROGRAM DESIGN

If you can't solve a problem, then there is an easier problem you can solve: find it.

Pólya

There are many strategies for solving problems in general, and these strategies also work for solving problems with a computer. Different strategies work for different problems, and some people find that some strategies fit their style of thinking better than other strategies. In the end, you need to look at various approaches and find the one that works for you for the problem at hand. There isn't a one-size-fits-all method for solving problems, but we can provide some general guidelines.

If you want reference on problem solving, consider the classic *How to Solve It* by Pólya.[6] It was written in the first half of the twentieth century, but it is still one of the best, and most libraries have a copy.

Engage and Commit

You need to be ready to work on the problem. Problem solving is an activity that requires a commitment of mental resources. Persistence helps, so don't give up easily. Put some time in, even if it seems difficult. Multitasking can be particularly distracting. For example, Dr. Thomas Jackson of Loughborough University, England, found that it takes an average of 64 seconds to recover your train of thought after interruption by email.[7] So people who check their email every five minutes waste $8\frac{1}{2}$ hours a week figuring out what they were doing moments before.

It is particularly important to find some uninterrupted quality time to do the work. Remember that time is not effort. Putting 10 hours into a program does not (necessarily) mean that you were actually programming for 10 hours. If you are wasting time, change strategies or take a break and come back to it. Of course, if you have left the problem to the last minute, these last options are not available—even though they are frequently the most valuable.

---

[6] Pólya, George, *How to Solve It*, (Princeton: Princeton University Press, 1945), ISBN 0-691-08097-6.
[7] "Breaking the Email Compulsion," Suw Charman-Anderson, 28 August 2008. Copyright Guardian News and Media Ltd 2008.

To engage with the problem, set the mood—whatever that means for you. For most people, setting the mood involves removing distractions. Music may do the trick, or possibly the right environment. Find what works for you and use it.

Understand, Then Visualize

Now that you are in problem-solving mode, you have to get a handle on the problem. You cannot solve it until you understand it.

What is the Actual Problem?

Often a problem starts as a simple statement: we want to create a "horseless carriage"—a mode of transportation that does not require a horse to get around. Designing an automobile (which is what a horseless carriage is) for the first time is difficult. No one has ever seen one before! We use strategies therefore to address the problem. For example, is our problem similar to other, hopefully solved, problems? That is, are there any similar problems that you can relate this problem to? Is the process of designing a "horsed" carriage helpful? We could use carriage wheels and perhaps a carriage body, but there are problems not yet addressed, such as the engine and transmission.

With computational problems, ask yourself whether there any similar problems with known solutions (in software design those are called "patterns"). In a course, you may find example problems or earlier homework that are sufficiently similar to use as a starting point toward understanding the problem at hand.

If the problem is something *you* have posed, finding a way to phrase the problem exactly can help. With a computational problem, that means:

- What inputs are required?
- What tests on the input are needed?
- For each input, what is the expected or required output?
- What tests on the output are appropriate?
- As mentioned earlier, do you know a similar problem?

If the problem is given to you as in a homework assignment, there may be many parts to the description. Do you understand each one? Did you get all the requirements? As with the formulation any problem you need to consider the inputs and outputs, how they relate, and how they are tested.

If you have a problem to solve and are expected to write a program to solve it, you have to understand just what is required to a level of detail that you rarely do for other problems.

Making the Problem Real

Now that you have some understanding of the problem, can you make it "real" somehow? What that means is up to you, but the result is that you can "play around" with your understanding and see better what is entailed. For example, if the problem is to write a program that plays a card game, now is the time to pull out a deck of cards and give it a try.

Other options for other problems include:

- Work some simple examples using pencil and paper.
- Work some examples using objects such as playing cards or toy cars.
- Draw some graphs.
- Create diagrams of the interaction.
- Do something!

Can you visualize the problem in some way to make it more real to you? If so, it may give you better insight into the problem. By making the problem real in some way, you can play with the problem, and get a better grasp on what you have to do to solve the problem. This activity can also help you later on, if you get stuck part way through the solution.

Think Before You Program

It is easier said than done, but it is still important that you understand the problem before you program. Often, programming while you are simultaneously trying to solve the problem leads to a condition known as "dung ball" programming. Remember the lowly dung beetle, a creature that slaps pieces of dung onto a growing ball into which it places its eggs. Programming before you "get" the problem leads to a similar approach. Pieces of program are "slapped on" to the overall solution without much view towards the overall goal. How could this approach work, if you don't fully understand the problem? Sadly, the result is the same—a ball of dung.

Experiment

Now you know the problem and you've played with it a bit. What's next?

Instead of trying to write the whole program from beginning to end, try out some strategies. Python allows you to type code directly in the interpreter. Using Python in this mode allows you to try some of your ideas without coding a whole program.

Can you translate some of your ideas into code? Even something small can give you something concrete to work with. If nothing comes immediately to mind, can you look around (help, books, Internet) and get some ideas on how to write something small as a start? That is, simplify!

It is most important to try some things to see what happens. Experiment with code. Try something—it will be wrong at first, but as Edison famously observed: you now know one more thing that doesn't work. Novice programmers especially seem very reluctant to try things. They want to just solve the problem and move on. It is better to try a few ideas out and get rid of the bad ones before they become part of your solution.

Simplify

Of all the approaches, this is the best strategy! As observed by Pólya: if you cannot solve a problem, an easier one exists, so find it!

Think of your problem as a puzzle with multiple pieces, each its own smaller problem to solve. The smaller problems will be more manageable and hence more easily solved by you. In fact, you may find the whole problem totally unsolvable, yet find each piece easy to solve. Having solved the smaller pieces, the assembly of those pieces into an overall solution is much easier than tackling the whole problem. Another name for this strategy comes from the military: divide and conquer.

To be successful with simplification, you must:

- Find the pieces. Can you find the subtasks in your problem?
- Solve each of the pieces.
- Put all the solved pieces back together as an overall solution.

The hardest part is the first step: find the pieces. The ability to find the smaller parts develops with experience, but there are few computational problems that cannot be broken down into smaller pieces. Try very hard to find the pieces.

By breaking the problem down into simpler problems, you accomplish two things. Psychologically, you make the overall problem more tractable. Rather than staring at the larger problem and lamenting that you don't know how to start, you can start by solving smaller, simpler pieces and moving on. Success breeds further success. Also, smaller pieces usually are simpler to approach. By solving the smaller problems in isolation, you can solve them better and more completely. Not only will you have broken down the problem into easier pieces, but you will also have better solutions to each piece when it comes time to put it all back together.

Persistence is important. Expect to be able to divide and conquer the problem.

Some of our longer examples illustrate the divide-and-conquer strategy. For example, look back at the Perfect number example in Section 2.1 and observe how we broke the problem into smaller and simpler pieces to solve the larger problem.

The "Onion" Approach

One useful way to divide and conquer a problem is to write the larger solution as if the solutions to the pieces already exist. For example, if you were writing a program to control a robot to go someplace, you might start with "turn in the right direction." You likely don't know how to program the robot to do exactly that, but you can simply assume that you can figure it out later and concentrate now on the next task. When you come back to that problem piece, you will need to consider only "turn in the right direction" rather than the whole problem.

In this way, you will find it easier write programs that are essentially skeletons of what you think the final program will look like. Once the skeleton is created, you can go back and begin to slowly fill in pieces. You imagine tasks and, though you may not be able to solve them immediately, you can position the task in the code, perhaps only with comments about what the task does. Work through the problem with tasks that you imagine can be done. In this way, you bring the program to "life." With the pieces identified, you can now tackle them in isolation.

In this way, you tackle the problem layer by layer, adding more to the onion until you are satisfied. The example at the end of the chapter illustrates this approach.

Stop and Think

At some point in the middle of this process, you need to stop and look at what you have done so far and evaluate your results. It might be that your skeleton is not coming to life as you had hoped. You might have started down a problem-solving path that, now that you are further along, seems like a poor approach. You need to be willing to throw something out if it isn't working. Avoid the dung-beetle approach to programming: rolling a bigger ball of dung by adding more bad code onto existing bad code. Be brave and be willing to throw the bad part away and do it right. Don't be "stiff," and don't bang your head against the wall trying force a solution you thought was correct in the beginning and isn't working anymore.

That is, stop and think.

Relax: Give Yourself a Break

If you work long enough at a difficult problem, you are likely to get stuck at some point. What do you do now? How do you unstick yourself? One of the best approaches is to walk away, let it go for a while, take a breather, and come back when you are fresh. Letting a problem sit is a way to relax and look at it with fresh eyes later on. Having broken down the problem into smaller pieces makes this step easier—reconnecting with a smaller problem is easier than with a larger problem. Also, you may be able to work for a while on a different piece of the puzzle.

However, if you have left your problem to the last minute, you do not have this step available. Use your time well. Starting late on a program makes everything harder.

3.5 A SIMPLE EXAMPLE

Let's implement the Babylonian square-root algorithm to illustrate how to apply some of the ideas presented so far.

First, note the subtle difference in this version when compared to the earlier version. Earlier, we observed that equality between two floating-point values was not precisely defined. In fact, we discussed that a "small enough" difference was good enough. Here we have addressed that issue by introducing "tolerance." That is, "different" means that the two values differ by less than some tolerance that we define as "good enough" for our algorithm. We begin with the requirements:

1. The user provides three inputs: an integer number to find the square of, an integer initial guess, and a floating-point tolerance are all required. If at some point the difference between the previous and present answer differ by a value less than the provided tolerance, the algorithm finishes.
2. Babylonian square-root algorithm:
   (a) Guess the square root of the number.
   (b) Divide the number by the guess.
   (c) Average the quotient (from step b) and the guess.
   (d) Make the new guess the average from step c.
   (e) If the new guess differs from the old guess by more than the specified tolerance, go back to step b; otherwise, stop.
3. Output the original conditions (number, guess, tolerance), its square root and the number of iterations (guesses) required to reach that result.

Build the Skeleton

Let's now try to put together an outline of the program in the form of a skeleton program. There are three parts to the description, so let's start with three parts of the skeleton. We express this skeleton first as comments in English:

```
# get three inputs from the user (two ints, 1 float)

# do the algorithm steps described above

# output the three original values, the number of
# iterations and the square root
```

See, that wasn't too hard. In fact, it was trivial, but that is the point. Start with something you can do. We now have three pieces that can be considered separately.

Output

Which piece should we solve first? Go for the easiest. Let's pick output.

```
print "Square root of",number," is:",guess
print "Took ",count," reps to get it to tolerance: ",tolerance
print "Starting from a guess of:", originalGuess
```

Some of the variables we need are defined based on the output statements. Of course, our program piece won't run yet, because those variables have not yet been assigned values. Here is what our program looks like so far:

```
# get three inputs from the user (two ints, 1 float)

# do the algorithm steps described above

# output the three original values, the number of
# iterations and the square root
print "Square root of",number," is: ",guess
print "Took ",count," reps to get it to tolerance: ",tolerance
print "Starting from a guess of: ", originalGuess
```

Input

The input looks like the next easiest task. It also will provide some values for the variables we have defined so far. Properly doing input will require checking whether we are getting the input we want, but we can begin by assuming all input is good initially. That assumption lets us get going, and allows us to come back later and solve the input problems more fully. Filling in details later makes solving the problem easier now, and allows us to focus better later when only details remain.

For our *first cut*, let's just work with one of the inputs, the number to find the square root of. We'll need to do something similar for the other two numbers, so let's keep it simple by doing one first. That is, simplify first, and then once we get that working, repeat it for the remaining numbers. What we have to do is:

- prompt the user
- turn the resulting string into the appropriate type (here, an integer)

```
numStr = raw_input("Find the square root of integer: ")
number = int(numStr)
```

Is that good enough? Yes and no. As long as you expect the user to type only integers in response to the prompt, then it is good enough. However, what if the user mistypes, an "a" instead of a "1"? What will happen? (Try it.) Whatever happens it isn't desirable, so how do we build in some robustness to guard our input? We could reprompt on an error, and ask the user to try again until they get it right. How can we know that the user mistyped a response? We can check the string to see whether it is correct. String objects have an isdigit method to see if the input is an integer; that is, is it all digits? So we could check the string before the conversion.

Here is our *second cut*:

```
numStr = raw_input("Find the square root of integer: ")
if numStr.isdigit():
    number = int(numStr)
else:
        # else what?
```

If they get it right, great. If not, what should we do? We could reprompt (repeat the first line), but what if they screw up again (and again)? It seems like we might want to keep prompting until they get it right. How do we do that? Re-prompting sounds like prompting until some condition. That suggests a loop: a "while" loop.

Here is our *third cut*: as long as they get it wrong (as long as the result of the prompt is *not* a digit), reprompt and give them a stern warning!

```
numStr = raw_input("Find the square root of integer: ")
while not numStr.isdigit():
    print "Pay attention"
    numStr = raw_input("Find the square root of integer: ")
number = int(numStr)
```

At this point, we should have a valid integer. The loop will run until we get one. Try it out by typing the code into the shell and confirm that it works.

Note the security implications of validating the input. Our program does not proceed past this point until we get the expected input. Anything else gets rejected. If done correctly, security attacks based on faulty input are removed, making our program safer for use by others.

With robust input working for one input, we can repeat the process for the other integer input. See Code Listing 3.3.

Code Listing 3.3

```
# Newton's Method to calculate square root

# get three inputs from the user (two ints, 1 float)
num_str = raw_input("Find the square root of integer: ")
while not num_str.isdigit():
        print "Pay attention"
        num_str = raw_input("Find the square root integer: ")
num_int = int(num_str)
```

```
guess_str = raw_input("Initial guess: ")
while not guess_str.isdigit():
        print "Pay attention"
        guess_str = raw_input("Initial guess: ")
guess_int = int(guess_str)

originalGuess_int = guess_int    # hang onto the original guess
count_int = 0                    # count the number of guesses

# get the float tolerance, no checking of input!
tolerance_float = float(raw_input("What tolerance :"))

# do the algorithm steps as described above

# output the three original values, the num_int of
# iterations and the square root
print "Square root of",num_int," is: ",guess_int
print "Took ",count_int," reps to get it to tolerance: ",tolerance_float
print "Starting from a guess of: ", originalGuess_int
```

Floating-Point Input

Unfortunately, there is no `isfloat` method for confirming that a string is a floating-point number. In Chapter 14, which explains exception handling, you will learn the proper way to check for input, including floating-point input. For now, we will leave the floating-point input unchecked.

Testing the Input Routine

Now we have an input process. Let's make sure that it works with the other parts of the existing program, the output. At this point, we can run the code but, as it turns out, it doesn't actually give an answer. However, it is good enough to confirm that the two provided parts work as required. If it works, we can move on to the next step:

```
Find the square root of integer: a
Pay attention
Find the square root integer: 3.5
Pay attention
Find the square root integer: 2
Initial guess: a
Pay attention
Initial guess: 1
What tolerance: 0.0001
```

```
Square root of 2 is: 1
Took  0  reps to get it to tolerance:   0.0001
Starting from a guess of:  1
>>>
```

Even though our testing is not complete, it looks good.

Doing the Calculation

Now we have two simple parts working: the input and output. Next we need to do the real work: the calculation. Here is the basic algorithm again:

Babylonian square-root algorithm:

1. Guess the square root of the number.
2. Divide the number by the guess.
3. Average the quotient (from step 2) and the guess.
4. Make the new guess the average from step 3.
5. If the new guess differs from the old guess by more than the specified tolerance, go back to step 2; otherwise, stop.

We already have the initial guess, so let's focus next on steps 2, 3, and 4. Those steps are simple enough to write directly from the English in the algorithm. Observe how steps 3 and 4 are combined into one Python statement. Step 3 is on the right-hand side and step 4 is the left-hand side of the statement.

```
quotient = number/guess
guess = (quotient+guess)/2
```

Step 5 tells us to repeat our steps, but how often? Step 5 tells us to keep going if the new guess differs from the old guess by a tolerance. Rephrased, step 5 tells us that while the difference is greater than the tolerance, we keep going. What difference? We calculate the difference between the previous guess and the current guess. The result is:

```
while previous - guess > tolerance:
    quotient = number/guess
    guess = (quotient+guess)/2
```

We now have a slight problem because the variable named `previous` does not have a value. We need to get the previous value of the variable named `guess`. A good time to do that is before `guess` gets its new value:

```
while previous - guess > tolerance:
    quotient = number/guess
    guess = (quotient+guess)/2
```

We still have a small issue with `previous` because it needs an initial value before we perform the difference the first time. An initial value of zero works fine, as there is no previous value.

```
previous = 0
while previous - guess > tolerance:
    previous = guess
    quotient = number/guess
    guess = (quotient+guess)/2
```

Now let's stick that piece of code into the rest of the program. See Code Listing 3.4.

Code Listing 3.4

```
# Newton's Method to calculate square root

# get three inputs from the user (two ints, 1 float)
num_str = raw_input("Find the square root of integer: ")
while not num_str.isdigit():
        print "Pay attention"
        num_str = raw_input("Find the square root integer: ")
number_int = int(num_str)

guess_str = raw_input("Initial guess: ")
while not guess_str.isdigit():
        print "Pay attention"
        guess_str = raw_input("Initial guess: ")
guess_int= int(guess_str)

originalGuess_int = guess_int # hang onto the original guess
count_int = 0                 # count the number_int of guesses

# get the float tolerance
tolerance_str = float(raw_input("What tolerance: "))

# do the algorithm steps as described above
previous_int = 0
count_int = 0
while previous_int - guess_int > tolerance_float:
        previous_int = guess_int
        quotient = number_int/guess_int
        guess_int= (quotient+guess_int)/2
        count_int = count_int + 1

# output the three original values, the num_int of
```

```
# iterations and the square root
print "Square root of",number_int," is: ",guess_int
print "Took ",count_int," reps to get it to tolerance: ",tolerance_float
print "Starting from a guess of: ", originalGuess_int
```

Two output variables that we didn't discuss are handled in the previous code. The first is that we needed a value for the variable `originalGuess`. It needs to go right after the conversion of `guess_str` to `guess_int` so it holds the original value of the guess. We also included `count`, which is a count of the number of times through the loop.

Now the program appears to have all the pieces, but does it give us the answers we want? Let's test it:

```
>>>
Find the square root of integer: 100
Initial guess: 5
What tolerance: 0.0000001
Square root of 100 is:  5
Took  0  reps to get it to tolerance:  1e-07
Starting from a guess of:  5
```

Hmmm, that isn't very good, is it. What's wrong?

We need to step through what we have done to find the problem. Where did we go wrong?

Scanning the output for anomalies is a good start. "Took 0 reps to get it to tolerance" sticks out. That means that the main **while** loop was never entered. Hmmm.

Let's reason our way through the code one step at a time:

- The input used means that `number` = 100, `guess` = 5 and `tolerance` = 0.0000001. There are three reasons to believe that the input part is okay. First, it is simple; second, we output the input as a check; and third, it was tested.
- We can verify by reading that `previous` correctly gets set to 0.
- When the loop is entered, the difference `previous - guess` is -5. Is -5 > .0000001? No, so the Boolean expression is *False* and we never entered our **while** loop.
- We found a problem.

The negative value in the Boolean expression is causing us a problem. The variables `previous_int` and `guess_int` are 5 apart, but the difference is -5, which, as it turns out, is less than our tolerance. It would be better for the difference to always be positive. How can a difference always be positive? How about an absolute value function? Such a function would always yield a positive number. We could write one ourselves, but at this point, we can rely on Python's modules. The math module provides a number of useful functions, including one for absolute value: `fabs`. How does one know that? At some point, you begin to trust that Python has a number of tools available and that, before you write a solution to some problem yourself, you will look to see whether it has been already done for you. The documentation and the web help with this, but you must remember to use them! We must also import the math package in our code. We will add **import** `math` at the beginning. Remember that the full name of the function is `math.fabs`. Also, the "f" stands for "float," so this function returns a floating-point value. Note that this issue is essentially the same as the Programming Tip on floating-point equality in Section 2.2.

The revised **while** loop is now:

```
while math.fabs(previous_int - guess_float) >
             tolerance_float:
```

Let's test it to see how we are doing.

```
>>>
Find the square root of integer: 100
Initial guess: 5
What tolerance: 0.0000001
Square root of 100  is:   10
Took  3  reps to get it to tolerance:  1e-07
Starting from a guess of:  5
```

That result looks promising. Let's try another:

```
>>>
Find the square root of integer: 2
Initial guess: 1
What tolerance :0.0000001
Square root of 2  is:   1
Took  1  reps to get it to tolerance:  1e-07
Starting from a guess of:  1
```

That's not right. We still have a problem, because the square root of 2 is not 1. What happened? In this case, we expected the decimal 1.4142 for an answer, but we got an integer.

Oops. The variable `guess_int` is an int, but we require a float for the answer. If we make `guess_int` a float from the beginning, then the other variables derived from it (`originalGuess_int` and `previous_int`) will also be floats. They should be renamed to be `originalGuess_float` and `previous_float`.

Now the program is:

Code Listing 3.5

```python
# Newton's Method to calculate square root

import math
# get three inputs from the user (two ints, 1 float)
num_str = raw_input("Find the square root of integer: ")
while not num_str.isdigit():
        print "Pay attention"
        num_str = raw_input("Find the square root integer: ")
number_int = int(num_str)

guess_str = raw_input("Initial guess: ")
while not guess_str.isdigit():
        print "Pay attention"
        guess_str = raw_input("Initial guess: ")
guess_float= float(guess_str)

originalGuess_float = guess_float # hang onto the original guess
count_int = 0                     # count the number_int of guesses

# get the float tolerance, no checking of input!
tolerance_float = float(raw_input("What tolerance :"))

# do the algorithm steps as described above
previous_float = 0
count_int = 0
while math.fabs(previous_float - guess_float) > tolerance_float:
        previous_float = guess_float
        quotient = number_int/guess_float
        guess_float= (quotient+guess_float)/2
        count_int = count_int + 1

# output the three original values, the num_int of
# iterations and the square root
print "Square root of",number_int," is: ",guess_float
print "Took ",count_int," reps to get it to tolerance: ",tolerance_float
print "Starting from a guess of: ", originalGuess_float
```

Let's test:

```
>>>
Find the square root of integer: 100
Initial guess: 5
```

```
What tolerance :0.0000001
Square root of 100  is:  10.0
Took  6  reps to get it to tolerance:  1e-07
Starting from a guess of:  5.0
>>> ============================== RESTART ==================================
>>>
Find the square root of integer: 2
Initial guess: 1
What tolerance :0.0000001
Square root of 2  is:  1.41421356237
Took  5  reps to get it to tolerance:  1e-07
Starting from a guess of:  1.0
```

That's much better. Of course, more testing is needed, but we'll leave that as an exercise.

Summary

In this chapter, we introduced the concept of an algorithm, especially with respect to the implementation of algorithms in programs. We also discussed some problem-solving techniques. With these two concepts in hand, we can tackle more complex problems.

Exercises

1. Write an algorithm for frying an egg. Test it out with a friend: in a kitchen, read the algorithm and have the friend do *exactly* what you say. How did you do?

2. (Algorithms vs. programs)

   (a) Define algorithm and program.
   (b) In what ways are they the same?
   (c) In what ways are they different?

3. Write an algorithm that determines whether a number is between 2 and 20, and is divisible by 3.

4. When you are stuck on creating a program, it helps to stop and think. Can you see what is wrong with the following program? Why is it generating an error?

```
intA = raw_input('Enter an integer greater than 10: ')
    while intA > 10:
    intA = intA - 1
    print intA
```

PART 3

Organizing: Data Structures and Functions

CHAPTER 4

Working with Strings

MUCH OF THE TIME SPENT ON COMPUTERS INVOLVES WORKING WITH WORDS. WE write emails and essays, we send text messages and instant messages, we post to blogs, we create Facebook pages, we Google for information, and we read web pages. In programming languages, any sequence of printable characters is referred to as a *string*. The origin of the word is unclear, but Dr. Don Weinshank notes:

> The 1971 OED (p. 3097) quotes an 1891 Century Dictionary on a source in the *Milwaukee Sentinel* of 11 Jan. 1898 (section 3, p. 1) to the effect that this is a compositor's term. Printers would paste up the text that they had generated in a long strip of characters. (Presumably, they were paid by the foot, not by the word!) The quote says that it was not unusual for compositors to create more than 1500 (characters?) per hour.[1]

A sequence of characters is not necessarily a word as we know it, that is, something that we might find in a dictionary. This distinction is particularly useful with computers, because a short-cut such as `'brb'` used in instant messaging is a perfectly fine string, but does not appear in most dictionaries. Also, strings are independent of language so `'Gesundheit'` is a legal string. In fact, something nonsensical such as `'xyz'` also counts as a string. A sequence of characters requires no underlying meaning; it is only a sequence. For us, that is all a string need be.

4.1 THE STRING TYPE

The string type is one of the many collection types provided by Python. As first discussed in Section 2.1, a collection is a group of Python objects that are collected together as a single object. In particular, a string type is a special kind of collection called a *sequence*. A

---

[1] Humanist Discussion Group, Vol. 5, No. 0883 (May 4, 1992).

sequence type has its collection of objects organized in some order—a sequence of objects. A Python string is an object that has, as an attribute, a sequence of characters. A Python string object can be constructed either by using the string constructor `str` or, as a short cut, by encompassing a group of characters in either two single quotes (') or two double quotes (").

Examples of string objects are: `'a'`, `"brb"`, `'What is your name?'`. The only requirement is that the kinds of quotes match. That is, `'bad string"` is not a good string in Python because it uses a mixture of single and double quotes. Otherwise, any sequence of characters can constitute a string.

 PROGRAMMING TIP

It is good to decide how you want to delimit strings, and then stick with it. If you like double quotes, stick with that. In general, double quotes are a little less trouble, as you can encode possessives and contractions more easily, such as `"bill's"` or `"can't"`. If you try that with single quotes, you need to use the escape character ("\") in front of the apostrophe, such as `'bill\'s'`.

The Triple Quote String

There is a special kind of string denoted by triple quotes, as in `'''Hello World'''`. This too is a string, but it has one special property. This string preserves all the format information of the string. If the string spans multiple lines, those carriage returns between lines are preserved. If there are quotes, tabs, any information at all, it is preserved. In this way, you can capture a whole paragraph as a single string. Here is an example from the "Bright Side of Life" song from the Monty Python movie, *Life of Brian*:

```
songLyricsString = '''When you're chewing on life's gristle
                      Don't grumble, give a whistle
                      And this'll help things turn out for the best...

                      And...always look on the bright side of life...
                      Always look on the light side of life...'''
```

The variable `songLyricsString` is now associated with a string object with all the formatting of the paragraph preserved.

 PROGRAMMING TIP

If you have a long, multiline comment that you want to insert, consider using a triple-quoted string. You need provide only the quotes at the beginning and the end of the comment, unlike using the #, which must appear at the beginning of every line.

Non Printing Characters

Some characters perform necessary operations but show up as "whitespace" in the output. The two most common examples are the tab and the carriage return. We need to represent them, so the backslash character is combined with another character for that purpose. See Table 4.1. Here is a session illustrating the use of \n when printing a string.

```
>>> print " first line \n second line"
 first line
 second line
```

carriage return	\n
tab	\t

TABLE 4.1 Common non printing characters.

String Representation

What is the difference between a string character and other Python types? For example, what is the difference between the integer 1 and the string '1'? One answer is obvious: they are different types! As we have discussed previously, the type of an object determines both the attributes of an object and the kinds of operations that can be performed on the object. A string is a collection type that has multiple parts: an integer is the representation of a number. Integers are created with the constructor *int* or with a number (without decimal points); strings are created with the constructor *str* or by enclosing characters with a pair of quotes. The type of an object determines much of what you can do with that object.

Characters, like all other data, are represented in a computer as a number. When you type on your keyboard, the individual characters are stored in a special computer representation know as ASCII (see Appendix E for a full list of ASCII characters). The ASCII representation is also organized to preserve the alphabetical ordering of characters. In fact, ASCII maps each character to an integer! That integer is what gets stored in a computer, and Python labels its type as string. Python provides two special functions, ord and chr, to capture the relationship between ASCII and a character. The ord() function shows the ASCII integer associated with a character. For example, ord('a') yields a value 97, because 'a' is associated with 97 in the ASCII table. Similarly, the chr function takes an integer and yields the character associated with that integer in the ASCII table. Thus chr(97) yields the value 'a' because 'a' is associated with the integer 97 in the ASCII table. Although this may appear to be an unnecessary detail, the order of characters in the ASCII table will be useful to us later when we are using comparison operators (see Section 4.2).

Strings as a Sequence

We defined string objects as a sequence of characters. Therefore, `'Hello World'` is a sequence of 11 characters—remember that a space is a character. Because a sequence has an order, we can number the characters by their position in the sequence, as shown in Figure 4.1.

FIGURE 4.1 The index values for the string 'Hello World'.

This position is called the *index* of the character within the string. In Python, and other languages as well, the first index (the first position) in a sequence is index *0*. Starting the counting at zero feels strange at first, but you will get used to it.

Python lets us look at the individual characters in the string sequence using the [ ] *indexing* operator. An example of its use is `'Hello World'[0]`. The integer in between the square brackets is the index of a character in the associated string; in this case the character `'H'`, the character at index 0.

It is important to remember that indices start at 0. Thus `'Hello World'[4]` is the character at index position 4, which is the fifth element in the sequence: character `'o'`.

Python also allows indexing from the back *end* of the sequence. Thus, if you want to index from the back, you begin with −1 and count down. Looking again at Figure 4.1 notice that −1 is the last character in the string, −2 is the second to last, and so forth.

The following session illustrates indexing. This session also shows how an index that is out of the range for the string generates an error:

```
>>> helloString = "Hello World"
>>> helloString
'Hello World'
>>> helloString[0]      # counting starts at zero
'H'
>>> helloString[5]
' '
>>> helloString[-1]     # negative index works back from the end
'd'
>>> helloString[10]
'd'
>>> helloString[11]
```

```
Traceback (most recent call last):
  File "<pyshell#19>", line 1, in <module>
    helloString[11]
IndexError: string index out of range
```

More Indexing and Slicing

Indexing in Python is more powerful than in many languages. Not only can you index a character at a single position, you can also select sub-sequences of the string when you index. For example, `helloString[6:10]` selects the sub-sequence of the original string `'Worl'`, as shown in Figure 4.2. This sub-sequence selection is called *slicing* because you are selecting a "slice" —a subsequence from the original sequence. Note that this process does not change the original string!

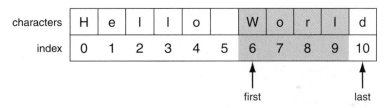

FIGURE 4.2 Indexing subsequences with slicing.

The colon (:) within the index operator brackets indicates that, instead of a single position being selected, a range of indices is being selected. Python uses a *half-open* range—as introduced in Section 2.2. A half-open range designates the beginning of the sequence that *is* included in the result along with an end of the sequence that *is not* included. For example, when we specified `helloString[6:10]` we selected the sub-sequence consisting of the characters at indices 6, 7, 8, and 9. The character at index 10 is *not* included, as shown in the following session:

```
>>> helloString[6:10]
'Worl'
>>>
```

Every sequence can be specified with two values: the beginning index of the sequence and end index of the sequence, separated by a colon (:). If a value on either side of the colon is missing, a *default* is used in place of the missing value. If the first index is missing, the index before the colon (:), Python assumes the start index is the beginning of the string, i.e. index 0. If the last index is missing, the value after the colon (:), Python assumes the end of the sequence *including* the last element.

helloString[6:]

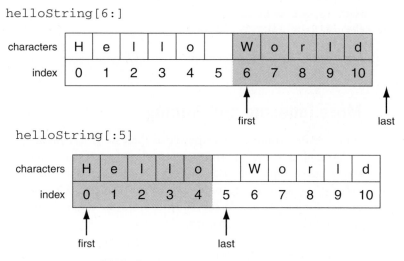

helloString[:5]

FIGURE 4.3 Two default slice examples.

Look at the examples in Figure 4.3. The helloString[6:] expression specifies a sub-sequence beginning at index 6 and continuing through the end of the string. In this case, the result is 'World'. The same result can be achieved using helloString[6:11]. The 11 is acceptable to specify the end of the sequence, as the second number indicates the index *after* the last element.

Similarly, in Figure 4.4, helloString[:5] is the subsequence from the beginning of the string up to, but not including, the character at index 5. The same result is obtained with the expression helloString[0:5]. Either way results in the subsequence 'Hello'.

Knowing that the end of a sequence is specified as one *after* the end of the desired sequence helps make sense of the negative index. The negative index means that, if the end marker is one more than the last index, the −1 (to the left) of that end marker is the last index, −2 the second to last, and so forth. Figure 4.4 shows the negative indices.

helloString[-1]

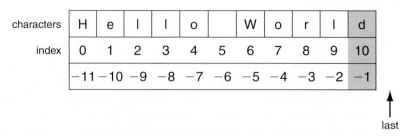

FIGURE 4.4 Negative indices.

helloString[3:-2]

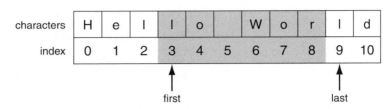

FIGURE 4.5 Another slice example.

Let's put this all together. Consider helloString[3:-2] which specifies the sequence starting at index 3 and ends three characters from the end resulting in the subsequence 'lo Wor'. See Figure 4.5.

In summary, here are the slicing operations from Figure 4.5 as they appear in the Python shell:

```
>>> helloString = "Hello World"
>>> helloString[6:11]
'World'
>>> helloString[6:]      # no ending value defaults to the end of string
'World'
>>> helloString[:5]      # no start value defaults to beginning of string
'Hello'
>>> helloString[0:5]
'Hello'
>>> helloString[-1]      # negative index works back from the end
'd'
>>> helloString[3:-2]
'lo Wor'
```

Extended Slicing

Slicing allows a third parameter that specifies the *step* in the slice. This means that you can have as many as three numbers in the index operator brackets separated by two colon characters: the first number is the beginning of the sequence, the second number specifies the end of the sequence, and the third is the step to take *along* the sequence. As with the first two arguments, the step number has a default if not indicated: a step of 1. The step value indicates how much to add to the present index to get the next element of the subsequence. For example, in the expression 'Hello World'[::2], we are indicating a subsequence from the beginning to the end of the sequence but, given a step size of 2, only every other letter is specified. The expression would yield a new string 'HloWrd'. Similarly, a step of 3 yields every third letter. Figure 4.6 shows how a step of 2 works.

helloString[::2]

FIGURE 4.6 Slicing with a step.

One odd variation that is not immediately obvious is to use a step of −1. Python interprets a *negative* step number as stepping backwards. The following session demonstrates the use of a step:

```
>>> helloString = "Hello World"
>>> helloString[::2]      # every other letter in the slice
'HloWrd'
>>> helloString[::3]      # every third letter
'HlWl'
>>> helloString[::-1]     # step backwards from the end to the beginning
'dlroW olleH'
>>> helloString[::-2]     # backwards, every other letter
'drWolH'
```

An interesting application of the step can be seen by using a string of digits. Different steps and different starting points yield even, odd, or reversed digits, as shown in this session:

```
>>> digits = "0123456789"
>>> digits[::2]      # even digits (default start at 0; skip every other)
'02468'
>>> digits[1::2]     # odd digits (start at 1; skip every other)
'13579'
>>> digits[::-1]     # reverse digits
'9876543210'
>>> digits[::-2]     # reverse odds
'97531'
>>> digits[-2::-2]   # reverse evens (start with 2nd last letter)
'86420'
```

Copy Slice

The final piece of slicing is the copy slice. If the programmer provides neither a beginning nor an end—that is, there is only a colon character in the square brackets—a copy of the string is made. If you think about this, it is clear why. The `[:]` slice takes both defaults, from the beginning through the end of the string. This feature is illustrated in the following session:

```
>>> nameOne = 'Monty'
>>> nameTwo = nameOne[:]
>>> nameTwo
'Monty'
>>>
```

Check Yourself: Slicing Check

1. Answer the questions for the following program.

```
userString = "aabbcc"
subStr1 = userString[2:]
subStr2 = userString[1:4]
subStr3 = userString[1: :2]
subStr4 = userString[:-2]
print subStr1                              # Line 1
print subStr2                              # Line 2
print subStr3                              # Line 3
print subStr4                              # Line 4
indxInt = 0
print userString[indxInt],userString[indxInt+2]   # Line 5
```

(a) What output is produced by Line 1 ?
(b) What output is produced by Line 2 ?
(c) What output is produced by Line 3 ?
(d) What output is produced by Line 4 ?
(e) What output is produced by Line 5 ?

4.2 STRING OPERATIONS

Strings can utilize some of the same binary operators that integers and floating point numbers use, though there are some interesting differences.

Concatenation (+) and Repetition (*)

The + and the * operators can be used with string objects. However, their meanings are not what you are used to with integers and floats:

+ : concatenate. The + requires two string objects and creates a new string object. The new string object is formed by joining the two string objects together: the first string joined at its end to the beginning of the second string.

* : repeat. The * takes a string object and an integer and creates a new string object. The new string object has as many copies of the string as is indicated by the integer.

The following session shows some examples.

```
>>> myString = "Hello"
>>> yourString = "World"
>>> myString + yourString        # concatenation
'HelloWorld'
>>> yourString + myString        # order does matter in concatenation
>>> 'WorldHello'
>>> myString + ' ' + yourString  # add a space
'Hello World'
>>> myString * 3                 # replication
'HelloHelloHello'
>>> 3 * myString                 # order does not matter in replication
'HelloHelloHello'
>>> (myString + ' ')*3           # parentheses force ordering
'Hello Hello Hello '
>>> myString + ' ' * 3           # without parentheses: repeats 3 spaces
'Hello   '
>>> myString
'Hello'
>>> yourString                   # neither string is changed by these operations
'World'
>>> 'hello' + 3        # wrong types for concatenation, requires two strings
Traceback (most recent call last):
  File "<stdin>", line 1, in <module>
TypeError: cannot concatenate 'str' and 'int' objects
>>> 'hello' * 'hello'  # wrong types for replication: requires string and int
Traceback (most recent call last):
  File "<stdin>", line 1, in <module>
TypeError: can't multiply sequence by non-int of type 'str'
>>>
```

A couple of points of interest:

• Both the + and * create new string objects and do not affect any string in the expression. That is, aStr + 'a' does not change the contents of aStr. Neither does aStr * 3.

- In concatenation, there is no space introduced between the end of the first and the beginning of the second string, unless you include it explicitly.
- The order of the two string objects *does* matter in concatenation. The first string shows up at the beginning of the new string object; the second string at the end. Changing the order changes the order the strings occur in the new string object.
- The order of the string and integer in replication *does not* matter.
- The types needed for each operator are very specific. For concatenation, you need two string objects. For replication, you need one string and one integer. No other combinations of types will do for each operator.

Determining When + Indicates Addition or Concatenation?

How can Python know whether to do concatenation versus addition when it sees a + operator? The answer is that the *types* of the operands indicate the operation to be performed.

In general, the fact that a single operator can perform multiple tasks is called *operator overloading*. By overloading, we mean that a single operator, such as +, will perform different operations depending on the types of its operands.

When the Python interpreter sees a + operator, it examines the types of the operands. If the operands are numbers (integers or floating-point numbers), the interpreter will perform addition. If the operands are strings, the interpreter will perform concatenation. If the operands are a mixture of numbers and strings, the Python interpreter will generate an error. Python can dynamically (as it runs) examine the types of objects associated with variables. In this way, it knows the types of operands, and so it can determine which operation to perform. As a result, it also knows what operations it can and cannot perform! If you give a Python operator a combination of types it does not have an operation for, it generates an error.

The `type` Function

In Python, you can check the type of any object. If you have named your variable poorly and can no longer remember what type of object it is associated with, you can use the `type` function. The `type` function returns the type associated with any object. The following session shows some examples:

```
>>> myString = 'Hello'
>>> type(myString)        # what type of object is associated with myString
<type 'str'>
>>> myString = 245        # bad variable name
>>> type(myString)
<type 'int'>
>>> type(3.14159)
<type 'float'>
>>>
```

We can help the reader of a program keep track of types by including the type in the objects name, e.g. `myString`. By using that protocol, a human reader who sees `myString + yourString` knows that + is supposed to mean concatenation.

Comparison Operators

As with +, you can use the common comparison operators we use with numbers to compare strings. However, the meaning of the comparison operators are, again, a little different than with integers.

Single-Character String Compares

Let's start easy and work with only single-character strings. You can compare two, single-character strings using the equality operator ==, as in `'a' == 'a'`. If the two single characters are the same, the expression returns *True*. Note that the expression `'a' == 'A'` returns *False* as those are indeed two different characters.

What about greater than (>) or less than (<) operators? The easy example would be `'a' > 'a'`, which is obviously *False*. What is the result of `'a' > 'A'`? If you type it into the shell, you will get the result *True*. Why? We introduced the functions `ord` and `chr` in Section 4.1. These two functions help us relate a character and its integer representation in the ASCII table (see Appendix E). All comparisons between two single characters are done on the basis of their ASCII number. When we compare `'a' > 'A'`, Python fetches the associated ASCII number for both characters and compares those two numbers. Because `ord('a')` is 97 and `ord('A')` is 65, the question becomes whether `97 > 65`, which yields *True*. Conveniently, the lower case letters are all sequentially ordered so that `'a' < 'b'`, `'b' < 'c'`, and so on. Similarly, the capital letters are sequentially ordered so that `'A' < 'B'`, `'B' < 'C'`, and so on. Finally, the numeric characters are also ordered so that `'0' < '1'`, `'1' < '2'`, and so on. If you wonder about character ordering, the ASCII table or the associated functions `ord` and `chr` should resolve the question.

Comparing Strings with More Than One Character

When strings with more than one character are compared, the process is slightly more complicated, though still based on the concept of a character's ASCII number.

String comparison—in fact, any sequence comparison—works as follows. The basic idea is to, in parallel, examine both string characters at some index and then walk through both strings until a difference in characters is found.

1. Start at index 0, the beginning of both strings.
2. Compare the two, single characters at the present index of each each string.
   - If the two characters are equal, increase the present index of both strings by 1 and go back to the beginning of step 2.

- If the two characters are not equal, return the result of comparing those two characters as the result of the string comparison.

3. If both strings are equal up to this point but one is shorter than the other, then the longer string is always greater. For example, `'ab' < 'abc'` returns `True`.

The following session shows some examples:

```
>>> 'abc' < 'cde'     # different at index 0, 'a' < 'c'
True
>>> 'abc' < 'abd'     # different at index 2, 'c' < 'd'
True
>>> 'abc' < 'abcd'    # 'abc' equal up to 'd' but shorter than 'abcd'
True
>>> '' < 'a'          # the empty string's length is 0
True
```

The empty string ('') is always less than any other string, because it is the only string of length 0.

It is an interesting challenge to write a string comparison algorithm using only single-character compares. See the exercises.

The in Operator

The *in* operator is useful for checking membership in a collection. An example of its use is: `'a' in 'abcd'`. The operator takes two arguments: the string we are testing and the string in which we are looking for the test string. As it is a membership check, it returns a Boolean value to indicate whether the test string showed up in the second argument. For the previous example, the return value is `True`. The test string sequence must be found *exactly*. For example in `'ab' in 'acbd'`, the question being asked is whether the exact sequence `'ab'` occurs anywhere in the string. For this example, the return value is `False`. Like other operators, *in* can be used with other collections, in which the interpretation of membership depends on the collection type. Here is a session showing some ways to use the *in* operator:

```
>>> vowels = 'aeiou'
>>> 'a' in vowels
True
>>> 'x' in vowels
False
>>> if 'e' in vowels:
        print "is a vowel"

is a vowel
```

String Collections are Immutable

Given that a string is a collection—a sequence in fact—it is tempting to try the following kind of operation: create a string and then try to change a particular character in that string to a new character. In Python, that would look something like the following session:

```
>>> myString = 'Hello'
>>> myString[0] = 'J'    # change it to the string 'Jello'
Traceback (most recent call last):
  File "<stdin>", line 1, in <module>
TypeError: 'str' object does not support item assignment
>>>
```

What is wrong? The problem is a special characteristic of some collections in Python. The string type, as well as some other types, are *immutable*. This means that, once the object is created, usually by assignment, its contents cannot be modified. Having an index expression on the left side of an assignment statement is an attempt to do exactly that—change one of the letters of the string. Such a modification is not allowed with the string type.

Check Yourself: String Comparison Check

1. Answer the questions for the following program:

```
myStr = raw_input("Input a string: ")
indxInt = 0
resultStr = ''  # empty string
while indxInt < (len(myStr) - 1):                    # Line 1
    if myStr[indxInt] > myStr[indxInt + 1]:
        resultStr = resultStr + myStr[indxInt]
    else:
        resultStr = resultStr * 2
    indxInt += 1              # Line 2

print resultStr              # Line 3
```

(a) What output is produced by Line 3 on the input 'abc' using the example program?
(b) What output is produce by Line 3 on the input 'cba' using the example program?
(c) What output is produce by Line 3 on the input 'cab' using the example program?
(d) What happens if Line 2 is removed?
(e) What happens if Line 1 is modified to **while** indxInt < len(myStr) :?

There are some efficiency reasons for this restriction. By making strings immutable, the Python interpreter is faster. However, immutable strings are an advantage for the programmer as well. No matter what you do to a string, you are guaranteed that the original string is *not* changed. By definition, it cannot be changed; it is immutable. To avoid this problem, Python string methods generate a *new* string. The strings you create are never changed.

How then to solve the problem of "changing" a string? For example, how can I change the string 'Hello' into the string 'Jello'? The approach is that we have to create a new string 'Jello' from the existing string myString (associated with the string object 'Hello'). We do so by concatenating 'J' to the front of a slice from myString. The slice myString[:1] is a new string object 'ello'. If we concatenate the two strings, we get the desired result 'Jello'.

For example, consider the following session:

```
>>> myString = 'Hello'
>>> myString = 'J' + myString[1:]   # create new string with 'J' and a slice
>>> myString                        # myString is now associated with the new string
'Jello'
```

4.3 A PREVIEW OF FUNCTIONS AND METHODS

We have seen some examples of methods and functions without really explaining how they work. Here we take a brief look at how methods and functions work—in particular, how they work with strings. We will revisit this topic in more detail later (Chapter 5).

First Cut: What is a Function?

Think of a function as a small program that performs a specific task. That program is packaged up, or *encapsulated*, and made available for use. The function can take some input values, perform some task by executing statements and evaluating expressions, and, when finished, potentially return a value. Functions are useful, because we use them to perform commonly needed tasks. Instead of writing the same code over and over again, we encapsulate that code in a function, making it easier to use.

Functions should not be a completely new concept for you, as we use functions frequently in mathematics. One example is the square-root function. It takes a real number as an argument and then returns a number that is the square root. *How* the square root is calculated is not important to us. We care only that works and that it works correctly. In this way, the square-root operation is encapsulated; the details of its operation are hidden from you.

There are many good reasons to use functions in your programs, but for now it is sufficient to know that many of the types we use in Python come with pre-defined functions that allow us to perform common tasks for that type. In Chapter 7, you will learn about how to write your own functions.

Strings come with a set of functions as well as a special kind of function called a *method*. For example, you can find out the length of a string, generate a new string that has all the letters of the original string converted to capital letters, find the position of a substring in a string, and so on. There are currently more than 35 such tasks that you can do with strings.

A String Function

Consider the `len` function. The `len` function is used to find a string's length, the number of individual characters in a string. You use a function just like any other command in Python. The function is *invoked*, or *called*, when the interpreter reaches the function name in a program. A function name is always followed by a set of parentheses, indicating that the name represents a function. Within the parentheses are zero or more *arguments*. Arguments are values that are passed to the function so the function can accomplish its task. If the function requires multiple arguments, a comma is placed between each object in the argument list. After the function completes its processing, it may return some value that can be saved by an assignment or other operation.

The `len` function requires only a single argument in its parentheses, the string whose length we are trying to find. The function returns a single integer, the length of the string. If the correct number of arguments is not given to the function, the interpreter shows an error to that effect. More generally, the function `len` can be used with any collection. Like the operator +, it is overloaded, in that it returns the length of different collections depending on what is appropriate for each collection. For strings, it is the number of individual characters in the string.

A sample session illustrating the `len` function is shown here:

```
>>> myStr = 'Hello World'
>>> len(myStr)
11
>>> strLength = len(myStr)
>>> print strLength
11
>>> len()

Traceback (most recent call last):
  File "<pyshell#48>", line 1, in <module>
    len()
TypeError: len() takes exactly one argument (0 given)
```

Again, a function invocation is a function name, followed by a parenthetical list of zero or more arguments, with multiple arguments separated by commas in the list.

A String Method

A *method* is a variation on a function. It looks very similar. It has a name and it has a list of arguments in parentheses. It differs, however, in the way it is invoked. Every method is called in conjunction with a particular object. The kinds of methods that can be used in conjunction with an object depends on the object's type. String objects have particular methods suited for strings, as do integer and integer methods, and float and float methods. The invocation is done using what is called the *dot notation*. An example would be the string type `upper` method. An example invocation would be `'A String'.upper`. In this case, the object, the string `'A String'` is calling the associated method `upper()`. This method takes the associated object and creates a new string where all the letters are converted to upper case, in this case the string object `'A STRING'`. The interpretation of this invocation, in plain English, would be something like: The object `'A String'` is calling the method `upper` on itself to create a new string, an upper-case version of the calling object. An example session for the method `upper` is shown here:

```
>>> myString = 'Python rules!'
>>> myString.upper()
'PYTHON RULES!'
>>>
```

The calling object may be just an object, such as `'A STRING'` above, or a variable associated with an object such as `myString`. There are reasons to have methods as separate from functions—concepts that we will cover in Chapter 11. In general, a method is invoked using "dot notation".

An example string method with arguments would be the `find` method. The `find` method's task is to locate a substring within the calling string (the object that invoked the method using the dot notation). The `find` method returns the index of the substring in the string where the substring *first* occurs (if there are multiple occurrences), but returns -1 if the substring is not found. As an example, let us try to find the character `'m'` in the string `'mellow yellow'`. We could do so by invoking the find method: `'mellow yellow'.find('m')`. In this method call, the object `'mellow yellow'` is invoking the `find` method, passing a single argument `'m'` as the search target. Note that the string object `'mellow yellow'` is the string to be searched by `find`, and is part of the invocation, the left part of the dot notation. The `'m'` character first found is at index 0, which is the value returned by `find` (remember that indexing starts at zero). A search for `'ll'` returns 2, which is the position of the first (leftmost) substring `find` discovered (another is at index 9). When find searches for 'z', that substring will not be found and find will return −1.

```
>>> myStr = 'mellow yellow'
>>> myStr.find('m')
0
>>> myStr.find('ll')
2
>>> myStr.find('z')
-1
```

It is interesting to think about why the find method returns a -1 in the case of not finding the substring argument in the calling object. Why wouldn't it just return 0, which is synonymous with the value *False*? Look at the example above. A successful search *might* return a 0 as the location of a successful search, the first character of the calling object! For this reason, one must be careful when using find in a Boolean expression.

Chaining of Methods

A powerful feature of the Python language is that methods and functions can be *chained*, meaning there are a series of "dot notation" invocations such as 'A string'.upper() .find('S'). The calls are chained in the sense that an object returned from one method can be used as the calling object in another method. The rule for the order of invocation is to proceed from left to right, using the resulting object of the previous method as the calling object in the next method. In our example, we first call the method 'A string'. upper() which produces the new string object 'A STRING'. That new object now becomes the calling object for the next method, the invocation 'A STRING'.find('S'). This expression yields the value 2, the index of the 'S'. Another example is shown in the session below.

```
>>> myString = 'Python rules!'
>>> myString.upper()
'PYTHON RULES!'
>>> myString.upper().find('O')  # convert to uppercase and then 'find'
4
```

Optional Arguments

Some methods have optional arguments. If the argument is not provided, a *default* for that argument is assumed. The default value depends on the method. However, you can choose to provide that argument and override the default. The find method is one with default arguments. You can start the find process from an index other than zero, the leftmost index. By default, find starts at index 0, but if you provide a second argument, that is the index where the find process begins.

Consider the assignment aString = 'He had the bat.' in which you want to find 't'. The call aString.find('t') will return 7, the index of the leftmost 't'. If you provide 8 as the second argument, you will start your search at index 8 and find the next 't'—that is, aString.find('t',8) returns 13. The find method also has a third, optional argument, the index where searching stops. The default is the end of the string, but if you provide the third argument, find will stop its search at that index. Thus aString.find('t',1,6) finds no 't', as there is no 't' in the range 1–6.

Nesting of Methods

You can also use method and function invocations as arguments to another method call. This kind of "method in a method" is called *nesting*. The rule for nested calls is that all invocations *inside* parentheses, such as those found in a function invocation, are done first. For example, how could you find the second occurrence of a substring. You do so by nesting one call of find as an argument of a find invocation in the following way. Suppose you wish to find the *second* 't'. The first step is to find the first 't'. The second step begins with a search (a second invocation of find starting from one past the location where the first 't' is found. That is, find the index of the first 't', add 1 to that index, and use that value as the starting point for a search for the second 't'. That is,

```
aString.find('t', aString.find('t')+1)
```

The nested method invocation is called first, yielding 7 + 1 = 8. The outer invocation then begins by searching for 't' starting at position 8. A session illustrating this process follows:

```
>>> aString = 'He had the bat.'
>>> aString.find('t')  # look for 't' starting at beginning
7
>>> aString.find('t',8) # start at index 8 = 7 + 1
13
>>> aString.find('t',aString.find('t')+1) # start at one after the first 't'
13
```

Determining Method Names and Method Arguments

How can you determine the methods associated with a type, and once you find the name, how can you determine the arguments?

IDLE to the rescue!

You can ask IDLE to show you all the potential methods for an object. IDLE will show all the methods available for an object of that type if you type the object (or a variable

FIGURE 4.7 In IDLE, tab lists potential methods.

of that type), the dot (.), and then a tab character. IDLE will respond by providing a list of all the potential methods that can be invoked with an object of that type, as shown in Figure 4.7.

Because the variable myString is associated with a string object, all the string methods are listed in alphabetical order. Note that find method is listed, as well as a number of other methods. If one provides the leading letter, for example 'i', before the tab is typed, then the list begins with the first method that begins with 'i', as shown Figure 4.8.

Once the object.methodName is typed, if you type the first parenthesis and wait just a moment, the list of arguments is also provided. The find function is shown in Figure 4.9.

The wording in the pop-up can sometimes be confusing, so you might have to think about the meanings. Knowing what we know about find, the pop-up indicates that there are three arguments. The first is called sub, which stands for "substring." It is a required argument. The remaining two arguments are bracketed in square brackets, indicating that they are optional. The first optional argument is start, where the search starts, and end, where the search ends. When find finishes, it returns (the →) an integer.

Of course, you can also look up the methods in the provided documentation. Select the help window in IDLE and that documentation will be brought up in your local browser.

FIGURE 4.8 In IDLE, tab lists potential methods, with leading letter.

FIGURE 4.9 IDLE pop-up provides help with function arguments and return types.

String Methods

Like many of Python's built-in types, strings have a number of powerful and useful methods. Table 4.2 lists a number of them. Remember: square brackets indicate optional arguments. Because the names are carefully chosen, you can guess what most of them do from their name. Take a moment and open a Python shell to try some string methods. Experiment!

capitalize( )	lstrip([*chars*])
center(*width* [, *fillchar*])	partition(*sep*)
count(*sub* [, *start* [, *end*]])	replace(*old, new* [, *count*])
decode([*encoding* [, *errors*]])	rfind(*sub* [,*start* [,*end*]])
encode([*encoding* [,*errors*]])	rindex(*sub* [, *start* [, *end*]])
endswith(*suffix* [, *start* [, *end*]])	rjust(*width* [, *fillchar*])
expandtabs([*tabsize*])	rpartition(*sep*)
find(*sub* [, *start* [, *end*]])	rsplit([*sep* [,*maxsplit*]])
index(*sub* [, *start* [, *end*]])	rstrip([*chars*])
isalnum( )	split([*sep* [,*maxsplit*]])
isalpha( )	splitlines([*keepends*])
isdigit( )	startswith(*prefix* [, *start* [, *end*]])
islower( )	strip([*chars*])
isspace( )	swapcase( )
istitle( )	title( )
isupper( )	translate(*table* [, *deletechars*])
join(*seq*)	upper( )
lower( )	zfill(*width*)
ljust(*width* [, *fillchar*])	

TABLE 4.2 Python string methods.

String Functions

The set of functions available for strings is smaller than the set of methods, and those functions are generally common to other sequence types. You have seen only `len` so far, but you will see others later.

4.4 FORMATTED OUTPUT FOR STRINGS

Using the default ***print*** function is easy, but it provides no control of what is called the *format* of the output. By format, we mean the way in which the characters are written to the screen. Python provides a finer level of control that gives us, the programmer, the option to provide "prettier," more readable, output. The basic approach is shown here:

> ***print*** "format string" % (data1, data2, ...)

The information in the format string is printed just like any other string, with one exception. Special character sequences that begin with a percent sign (%) indicate that a

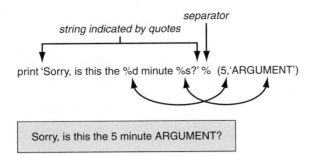

FIGURE 4.10 String formatting example.

substitution will take place at that position in the string. The substitution will be with data that comes at the end of the command in parentheses. Data will be placed in the format string, with some control provided as to *how* it will be placed in the string at that position. Surrounding text and formatting are unaffected by the substitution. After substituting the data into the formatting string, the new string is provided. An example is shown in Figure 4.10.

The data is separated from the format string by a percent sign (%), and enclosed within parentheses separated by commas (known in Python as a tuple).[2] Here is a simple example that substitutes both a string into the format string with the command "%s" and a number with the command "%d" ("d" for decimal integer). Formatting commands are matched with data items in order from left to right, so the first formatting command corresponds to the first data item, and so on:

```
>>> print "%s is %d years old." % ("Bill",25)
Bill is 25 years old.
```

Each format command can also indicate more information about how that particular data object is to be printed. The general structure of a format command is:

$$\texttt{\%[name][flags][width][.precision]code}$$

where the square brackets, [ ], indicate optional arguments. The different optional arguments are described in Table 4.3.

Descriptor Codes

Table 4.3 shows the most commonly used descriptor codes. The descriptor can control how an individual object of that type is printed to the screen. For example, float descriptors can

---

[2] The parentheses are optional, if there is only one data item.

%s	string
%d	decimal integer
%f	floating-point decimal
%e	floating-point exponential

TABLE 4.3 Most commonly used descriptor codes.

control the number of decimal points printed, and string descriptors can control leading or following spaces. However, each descriptor works only with its associated type. Associating an object of the wrong type with a descriptor will lead to a Python error. There are many more descriptor codes, but this will suffice for most work. See the Python manual if you need others.

Width Descriptor

A field width can be specified for each data item. It specifies a printing-field width, counted as the number of spaces the data occupies. If the specification is a negative value, the data is placed left-justified within the indicated width; otherwise, by default, it is right-justified within that width. In the following example, the string "Bill" is right-justified in a width of 10 spaces, and the number 25 is left-justified in a space of 10 spaces. Figure 4.11 displays an example.

FIGURE 4.11 String formatting with width descriptors.

The following session illustrates printing both without a specified field width and with field width specified. Pay attention to how both spacing and justification is done.

```
>>> print "%s is %d years old." % ("Bill",25)
Bill is 25 years old.
>>> print "%10s is %-10d years old." % ("Bill",25)
      Bill is 25         years old.
```

Floating-Point Precision Descriptor

When printing floating-point values, it is desirable to control the number of digits to the right of the decimal point—that is, the precision. Precision is specified in the format descriptor using a decimal point followed by an integer to specify the precision. For example, "%.4f" specifies that the printed value will have only four digits to the right of the decimal point. Let's illustrate using the constant pi from the math module. We show unformatted printing, precision specified, and then both precision and width specified. Notice that rounding occurred.

```
>>> import math
>>> print math.pi                  # unformatted printing
3.14159265359
>>> print "Pi is %.4f" % (math.pi) # floating-point precision 4
Pi is 3.1416
>>> print "Pi is %8.4f" % (math.pi) # specify both precision and width
Pi is   3.1416
>>> print "Pi is %8.2f" % (math.pi)
Pi is       3.14
```

 ## Check Yourself: More String Manipulation Check

1. What is the output of each *print* statement?

```
print "The word %s has %d letters." % ("Mississippi",11)
print "One number is %d; the other is %f." % (4,3.5)
month = "June"
day = 5
year = 2011
print "The date is %s %d, %d." % (month, day, year)
print "The interest rate is %.2f for you." % (2.7)
print "%-15s:%8.1f" % ("Length",23.875)
```

4.5 CONTROL AND STRINGS

Let's write some code that manipulates strings. In particular, let's look at how the find method might be implemented. Let's begin with a string:

$$river \ = \ "Mississippi"$$

We can find the first letter 'p' using the find method:

```
>>> river = "Mississippi"
>>> river.find("p")
8
```

How does the find method actually find a character and return its index? Let us see how we could reproduce the operation of that method using what we know about control and strings. Let's begin by experimenting with some features in the Python shell. First, let's find the length of the string using the len function:

```
>>> river = "Mississippi"
>>> len(river)
11
```

Let's combine the length of the string with the *range* function to print out all the indices, one for each character in the word. Remember that the last argument to *range* is one more than the last value in the range. This is actually convenient. The length of the string is 11, but the active indices in the string are from 0–10. If we want a list of indices of the string, *range*(len(river)) does nicely as a nested call. The len(river) yields the value 11, which is used by *range* to generate the numbers 0–10. Very nice!

```
>>> river = "Mississippi"
>>> len(river)
11
>>> for index in range(len(river)):   # values of 0 upto, but not including 11
        print index,                   # the comma suppresses carriage return

0 1 2 3 4 5 6 7 8 9 10
```

Now that we can print each index, we can use the same structure to print out each character in the word. Note that the unformatted **print** puts a space between each character and that a comma at the end of the **print** statement prevents a new line from being generated.

```
>>> for index in range(len(river)):
        print river[index],

M i s s i s s i p p i
```

We now have the ability to print each index, and each character associated with that index, in the string. We can now examine each character to see if it matches with the target character '*p*'. If it does, we print the index and ***break*** out of the loop, as we are only looking for the first match. If we do not find a match, the loop ends normally and any ***else*** clause of the ***for*** loop prints a failure message. The code and a session is shown in Code Listing 4.1.

Code Listing 4.1

```
# Our implementation of the find function. Prints the index where
# the target is found; a failure message, if it isn't found.
# This version only searches for a single character.

5  river = 'Mississippi'
   target = raw_input('Input a character to find: ')
   for index in range(len(river)):          # for each index
       if river[index] == target:        # check if the target is found
           print "Letter found at index: ", index  # if so, print the index
10         break                         # stop searching
   else:
       print 'Letter',target,'not found in',river
```

```
>>> =============================== RESTART ===============================
>>>
Input a character to find: s
Letter found at index:  2
>>> =============================== RESTART ===============================
>>>
Input a character to find: a
Letter a not found in Mississippi
>>>
```

We frequently look for both an index and the character, so Python provides the enumerate iterator, which provides *both* the index of the character and the character itself as it steps through the string. Let's try it:

```
>>> for index, letter in enumerate(river):
        print index,letter

0 M
1 i
2 s
3 s
4 i
5 s
```

```
6 s
7 i
8 p
9 p
10 i
```

Interestingly, notice that the **for** statement has *two* variables. This is because the enumerate statement yields two values each time: the index and the character. As in double assignment, we can capture both of those values by providing those two iterator variables. If we provided only one variable, what would we get? Let's see:

```
>>> for value in enumerate(river):
        print index,letter
```

```
(0, 'M')
(1, 'i')
(2, 's')
(3, 's')
(4, 'i')
(5, 's')
(6, 's')
(7, 'i')
(8, 'p')
(9, 'p')
(10,'i')
```

Since two values are yielded at each iteration, the two values are placed together in a *tuple*, a group of values. You'll see more about tuples in Chapter 6.

Now that you've seen how enumerate works, let's refactor our code (Section 2.2). You may find it to be more readable.

Code Listing 4.2

```python
# Our implementation of the find function. Prints the index where
# the target is found; a failure message, if it isn't found.
# This version only searches for a single character.

river = 'Mississippi'
target = raw_input('Input a character to find: ')
for index,letter in enumerate(river):           # for each index
    if letter == target:          # check if the target is found
        print "Letter found at index: ", index  # if so, print the index
        break                    # stop searching
else:
    print 'Letter',target,'not found in',river
```

Finally, what if we want to list *all* the occurrences of a letter? We can try by removing the **break** statement, and see if we can find all occurrences of the target. See Code Listing 4.3.

Code Listing 4.3

```
# Our implementation of the find function. Prints the index where
# the target is found; a failure message, if it isn't found.
# This version only searches for a single character.

river = 'Mississippi'
target = raw_input('Input a character to find: ')
for index,letter in enumerate(river):          # for each index
    if letter == target:         # check if the target is found
        print "Letter found at index: ", index # if so, print the index
        # break
else:
    print 'Letter',target,'not found in',river
```

```
>>>
Input a character to find: s
Letter found at index:   2
Letter found at index:   3
Letter found at index:   5
Letter found at index:   6
Letter s not found in Mississippi
```

Something is not quite right. Our program found all the examples of the `'s'` string but then *also* printed the failure message. What went wrong? In our previous two examples, we used the **break** statement to exit the loop which bypasses the **else**. We would execute the **else** only when the search failed. However, in this case, we did not break, meaning we *always* entered the **else** clause. What to do?

We leave fixing this problem as an exercise.

4.6 WORKING WITH STRINGS

Here are some short examples that show how to work with some of the common string methods to solve some simple problems.

Example: Reordering a Person's Name

Let's use a few string methods and try to do something useful. Here is our problem:

Transform a name from the order of `'First Middle Last'` to the order of `'Last, First Middle'`

For example, if the name provided is `'John M. Cleese'` it would be transformed into `'Cleese, John M.'`

The `split` method is very useful for this problem. The `split` method takes the calling string and creates substrings of that string, pieces of the string 'split off' at a specified character. The invocation to split on spaces is `.split(' ')`; at every comma is `.split (',')`. For example, the invocation `'The Spanish Inquisition'.split (' ')` would produce three strings: `'The'`,`'Spanish'`, and `'Inquisition'` using a split character of space (`' '`). The default is to split on whitespace, so commonly we simply use `split` with no arguments.

Remember, strings are immutable, so we do not literally remove any part of the original string. Instead, `split` makes copies of parts of it.

How could we use this to solve our problem? First, we can use the `split` method to break the string object associated with `name` into parts, where the split character is any white space character. We can then combine those results with Python's ability to do multiple assignments in the same line. For example,

```
>>> name = 'John Marwood Cleese'
>>> first, middle, last = name.split()
>>> transformed = last + ', ' + first + ' ' + middle
>>> print transformed
Cleese, John Marwood
```

The `split` method returns the three substrings from `name` when splitting at whitespace. We know this because our name is formatted as three, space-separated strings. The multiple assignment assigns the first substring to `first`, the second substring to `middle`, and the final substring to `last`. The next line assigns a rearrangement via concatenation to `transformed`, which is then printed.

Two things should be noted. This multiple-assignment approach has a problem if `split` does not return exactly three items to match the three variables on the left-hand side. You will learn later how to handle that problem using lists. Second, notice that the original string associated with `name` is not changed by the `split` method.

Here is a session that illustrates this transformation. The session also shows the error if the number of objects returned by the `split` method does not match the number of variables on the left-hand side. It also shows that `name` is not changed by these operations.

```
>>> name = 'John Marwood Cleese'
>>> first, middle, last = name.split()
>>> transformed = last + ', ' + first + ' ' + middle
>>> print transformed
Cleese, John Marwood
>>> print name
John Marwood Cleese
>>> print first
John
```

```
>>> print middle
Marwood
>>> print last
Cleese
>>> first, middle = name.split()    # error: not enough pieces

Traceback (most recent call last):
  File "<pyshell#71>", line 1, in <module>
    first, middle = name.split()
ValueError: too many values to unpack
>>> first, middle, last = name.split(' ')    # split on space ' '
>>> print first, middle, last
John Marwood Cleese
```

The `split` method can be useful for comma-separated data such as those generated by spreadsheets and databases. The following example shows a string split based on a comma. You can `split` using any string, so `'+'` can be used to separate operands from operators as shown in the following code. We also illustrate how methods can be used with string literals rather than only variables. Finally, if a split character is not specified, splitting will be done with whitespace; that is, with spaces, tabs, or returns.

```
>>> line = 'bob,carol,ted,alice'
>>> first, second, third, fourth = line.split(',')
>>> print first, second, third, fourth
bob carol ted alice
>>> op1, op2 = "A+B".split('+')
>>> print op1, op2
A B
```

Palindromes

Let's try to do something a little more complicated: determining whether a string is a palindrome. A palindrome is a string that reads the same forwards as backwards. Classic examples of a palindrome string are: "Madam, I'm Adam" or "A man, a plan, a canal, Panama".

If you look carefully though, those strings are not exactly the same forwards and backwards. We can easily show this with Python's help. We can print the string forwards and then, backwards, by simply reversing the string. Remember, string reversal is a slice from beginning to end with a -1 step. The following session shows both of the examples:

```
>>> pal1 = "Madam, I'm Adam"
>>> pal2 = "A man, a plan, a canal, Panama"
>>> print 'Forward: %s \nBackward: %s' % (pal1, pal1[::-1])
Forward:  Madam, I'm Adam
```

```
Backward: madA m'I ,madaM
>>> print 'Forward:  %s \nBackward: %s' % (pal2, pal2[::-1])
Forward:  A man, a plan, a canal, Panama
Backward: amanaP ,lanac a ,nalp a ,nam A
>>>
```

We did a few things in that session. We had to use double quotes for the first palindrome so we could capture the apostrophe in the phrase I'm, and we did a little string formatting so that we could easily compare the two strings.

These palindromes are, in fact, not exactly the same forward and backward: for example, `pal1[0] != pal1[-1]` because of case issues and and `pal1[4] != pal1[-5]` as they aren't even the same character! Why are these called palindromes again?

In fact, the rules are relaxed in terms of character comparisons when talking about palindromes. Typically, we ignore the case of the individual characters, so that the first instance we noted previously is handled, and we completely discount non alphabetic and non digit characters, which takes care of the second instance. So to evaluate for palindromes, we really have two tasks:

1. Modify the input string so that:
   • The case of all the characters is the same.
   • Only letters and digits are in the string.
2. Once modified, compare the string forward and backward to see whether it is the same string.

The second task is easy, so let's concentrate on the first.

Changing Case

You have already seen the solution for this, but here is a quick reminder. Python provides a number of string methods that create a new string, in particular to modify case. In the table in Section 4.3, there are two methods that look helpful: `lower` and `upper`. It doesn't matter which one we choose, as long as we apply it to the string and make all the characters in the string of one case. Let's use `lower`.

Only Letters and Digits

To accomplish the second sub-goal of having the string contain only alphabetic and digit characters, there are a couple of options. However, there are two string concepts that are helpful no matter the approach.

The first is the **in** operator that we introduced in Section 4.2 for checking membership in a collection. We can use the **in** operator to query whether certain characters are in the string. Conveniently, Python provides another module that stores various groups of characters as a string for exactly this purpose. If we import the `string module`, you will see that it contains a number of predefined strings, including:

string.punctuation: `'!"#  $%&\'()*+,-./:;<=>?@[\\]^_`\{\}~' |`
string.digits: `'0123456789'`
string.lowercase: `'abcdefghijklmnopqrstuvwxyz'`
string.whitespace: `'\t\n\x0b\x0c\r '`

The last looks a bit odd, but it contains the escape characters for the control characters, such as: tab, carriage return and space. We can use these predefined strings to do membership tests. For our palindrome, we want to test only lowercase letters or digits and exclude punctuation and whitespace. Once we find a character we do not want, what can we do?

Python provides another very useful method, `replace`. The `replace` method takes two arguments: the first is the string we are looking for, the second is the replacement string if the first string is found. For example, `'abbc'.replace('b','z')` would search through the string `'abbc'` looking for any `'b'` and, if found, replacing the `'b'` with a `'z'`. It would return the new string `'azzc'` (leaving `'abbc'` unchanged).

Putting It All Together
Here's a full solution. Examine it and then we'll discuss the parts.

Code Listing 4.4

```python
# Palindrome tester
import string

originalString = raw_input('Input a string:')
modifiedStr = originalString.lower()

badChars = string.whitespace + string.punctuation

for char in modifiedStr:
    if char in badChars:   # remove bad characters
        modifiedStr = modifiedStr.replace(char,'')

if modifiedStr == modifiedStr[::-1]: # it is a palindrome
    print\
'The original string is:   %s\n\
the modified string is: %s\n\
the reversal is:        %s\n\
String is a palindrome' % (originalString, modifiedStr, modifiedStr[::-1])
else:
    print\
'The original string is:   %s\n\
the modified string is: %s\n\
```

```
the reversal is:          %s\n\
String is not a palindrome' % (originalString,modifiedStr,modifiedStr[::-1])
```

Line 2: We import the string module to get the pre-defined Python strings.

Line 4: We prompt for a string to test.

Line 5: We lower case the original string to get the case uniform throughout the string. We hold onto the original string.

Line 7: We create a new string, `badChars`, which is a concatenation of all the characters we *don't* want in our modified string, namely the punctuation and whitespace characters.

Lines 9–11: The *for* loop is short and simple. We iterate through each character in the modified string. If the character is in the string of unwanted characters, we remove it. We do so by replacing all occurrences of that bad character with an empty string, `' '`, effectively deleting that character.

Line 13: This is the reversal test: is it or is it not a palindrome? That is, are the modified string and the reversal of it the same?

Lines 14–18: This is a pretty-printed line broken into multiple continuations—the back-slash (\) at the end of the lines—to get the strings to line up and produce a nicely formatted output. The backslash (\) characters force carriage returns in the output.

Most of the work we had to do was in modifying the original string so that we could do our simple reversal test. Using `replace` to remove the bad characters is not the only way to do the palindrome. We leave as an exercise how to do palindromes without using `replace`.

4.7 EXAMPLE: COUNTING POKER HANDS

The game of poker is a card game that emerged in its current form from New Orleans in the mid-nineteenth century. In its simplest form, a hand of five cards is dealt from a 52-card English deck, and the combinations within those five cards determine the value of the hand. Poker is a gambling game, so knowing the probabilities of the various combinations of hands is important. Using the mathematics of combinatorics, it is possible to calculate the probabilities, but with the computer we can also simply count the possibilities to determine probabilities.

In the 52-card English deck, each card has a rank (a.k.a. value), e.g. 9, as well as one of four suits (hearts, spades, diamonds, clubs). Therefore, a card's value is represented by a pair value:suit, e.g. nine of clubs. In poker, card values proceed from ace (the highest), to king, then queen, all the way down to 2, the lowest. For poker, players receive five cards, which constitutes a hand, and it is the score of the hand that is used to determine winners in a game. Both card value and card suit can figure in ranking overall card hands. For example, a *flush* is a hand in which all five cards have the same suit. The rankings of hands (in contrast to ranking of individual cards) are shown in a tabular form in Table 4.4 and in pictorial examples in Figure 4.12.[3] Within the same hand rank, the hand with higher ranked card values wins, e.g. a pair of tens wins over a pair of twos.

Rank	Name	Description
9	Royal flush	{Ace, king, queen, jack, ten} + flush
8	Straight flush	Straight + flush
7	Four of a kind	Four equal ranks within five cards
6	Full house	Pair + different rank three of a kind
5	Flush	Five cards with the same suit
4	Straight	Five cards, sequentially ranked with no gaps
3	Three of a kind	Three equal ranks within five cards
2	Two pairs	Two pairs of equal ranks within five cards
1	One pair	One pair of equal ranks within five cards
0	Nothing in hand	

TABLE 4.4 Poker hand rankings.

What are the chances of getting any particular hand? One way to determine the chances is to make a list of all 311,875,200 possibilities, count each type of hand, and divide each count by 311,875,200. One could approximate the exact probabilities by doing the same calculation with a smaller sample of 1,000,000 possibilities. If the smaller sample is representative, you will get a good approximation. Generating a good list of one million possibilities is an interesting problem in itself that is beyond your abilities at this point, but should be possible by the end of the book.

Fortunately, a good list of possible poker hands exists on the Internet.[4] The data file has one million lines, each containing the rank and suit of each of five cards along with the hand ranking, using the ranks in Table 4.4. The format is described in Table 4.5 with seven lines shown in Figure 4.13.[5] Each pair of values on each line represents a card. For example, the first three cards in the first line are the ten of diamonds, the seven of hearts, and the queen of spades. The number in the last (rightmost) column is the hand rank as specified in Table 4.4. Therefore, the first two hands have rank 0 which means that they have nothing of value. The third line represents a hand with rank 3 which is "three-of-a-kind"—there are three cards of rank 2 in the hand: two of diamonds, two of spades, and two of clubs. The next three hands each have one pair (hand rank 1): sevens, eights, and then sevens again. The final hand has two pairs (hand rank 2): fours and tens.

---

[3] The picture has one fewer hand because the "royal flush" is simply a special case of a "straight flush."

[4] It is available at the Machine Learning Repository at the University of California, Irvine, http://archive.ics.uci.edu/ml/datasets/ Poker+Hand

[5] This seven-line slice was formatted into more readable columns—the original has no spaces.

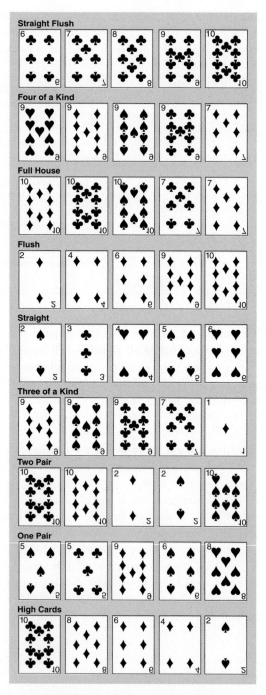

FIGURE 4.12 Poker hand rankings.

3, 10, 1, 7, 2, 12, 4, 2 , 2, 1, 0
4, 9, 4, 12, 4, 13, 2, 6 , 3, 4, 0
3, 2, 2, 2, 3, 12, 3, 1 , 4, 2, 3
4, 11, 2, 8, 1, 13, 4, 7 , 1, 7, 1
4, 8, 3, 8, 1, 3, 1, 4 , 3, 7, 1
2, 7, 2, 5, 3, 10, 4, 13 , 3, 7, 1
1, 4, 3, 4, 3, 5, 4, 10 , 2, 10, 2

FIGURE 4.13 Poker file—seven lines out of one million.

C1-suit, C1-rank, C2-suit, C2-rank, C3-suit, C3-rank, C4-suit, C4-rank, C5-suit, C5-rank, Hand Rank

TABLE 4.5 Poker file format.

Program to Count Poker Hands

Now that we understand the file format, how will we count hands? First, observe that all we care about is the last column of the file, which indicates the hand rank. Someone has already determined hand rank for us (something you will be able to do yourself by the end of the book). Also, remember that the eleventh column is column number 10, as we start counting columns at zero.

Program to Count the Total Hands in the File

As always, a useful strategy is to develop a program a little at a time. In this case, let's begin with a program that counts the number of hands in the file. We know that there should be one million—let's see if we get that. Here is our algorithm:

1. Open the file for reading.
2. Create a variable to hold our count and initialize it to zero.
3. Loop through the file, adding one to our counter each time we get a line.
4. Print the value of the counter.

Let's name the variable to hold our count `totalCount`. We create a file handle `pokerFile` by using the *open* function, giving a file name as an argument.[6] The **for** statement in conjunction with a file handle object assigns one line of the file as a *string* to the **for** target until all the lines of the file have been examined. In this example, we don't

---

[6] We will explain the term "file handle" in more detail in Chapter 9.

use the file line itself; we simply add 1 to our count. In the output, we see that we indeed have one million hands.

Code Listing 4.5

```
# count poker hands

# 1. open the poker data file for reading
pokerFile = open("poker-hand-testing.data",'rU')

totalCount = 0  # 2. create variable to hold the count — initialized it

# 3. step through each line of the file
for line in pokerFile:
    totalCount = totalCount + 1  # at each line increment the counter

print "Total hands in file:", totalCount
```

```
>>>
Total hands in file: 1000000
>>>
```

Program to Count the Hands with One Pair

Now that we can loop through the file examining every line, let's take another step toward our goal. Each line read in is a string, so the variable `line` will be associated with a string, and each time through the loop `line` will get assigned the next line of the file. Let's count the number of hands with exactly one pair. Such a hand has a rank 1, so we need to examine the last (rightmost) item in each line where the rank is. Therefore, we need to access the last element of each line. The file is in the common *comma-separated value* (CSV) format, so we will split each line on commas, and then examine the last item. We can use an index of −1 to reference the last item. Remember, the value in `line` is a string until we convert it! We also need a variable to hold our count of pairs, `pairCount`, and remember to initialize it to zero.

Let's update our algorithm with these changes highlighted in italics:

1. Open the file for reading.
2. Create *variables* to hold our *counts* and initialize *them* to zero.
3. Loop through the file one line at a time,
   (a) adding 1 to our total counter each time we get a line.
   (b) *get the hand rank: split on comma and get the last item (index −1).*
   (c) *if handRank is 1, then add one to our pair counter.*
4. Print the *values* of the counter.

Code Listing 4.6

```
# count poker hands

# 1. open the poker data file for reading
pokerFile = open("poker-hand-testing.data",'rU')

totalCount = 0   # 2. create and initialize variable to hold the total count
pairCount = 0    #    create and initialize variable to hold pair count

# 3. Loop through each line of the file
for line in pokerFile:
    totalCount = totalCount + 1      #(a) at each line increment the counter

    handRank = line.split(',')[-1] #(b) rank: split on comma, get last item
    handRank = int(handRank)         #    convert string input into an integer

    if handRank == 1:                #(c) if handRank is 1 (it is a pair)
        pairCount = pairCount + 1   #    add one to pair count

print "Total hands in file: ", totalCount
print "Count of pair hands: ", pairCount
```

```
>>>
Total hands in file:  1000000
Count of pair hands:  422498
```

The *for* loop assigns the next line from the file to the line variable. The line is a long string of values separated by commas. We use the split function, line.split(','), to split the line at the commas, and then we grab the last item, line.split(',')[-1], which is the hand rank. However, the handRank is still a string so we must convert it to an integer using int(handRank). We can now check to see whether handRank has a value of 1—remember that checking equality in Python uses a double-equal sign (==). If its value is 1, that is, *if* handRank == 1:, the hand contains one pair, so we increment the pair count: pairCount = pairCount + 1.

If we wish, we can combine the conversion into an integer with the line where we extract the hand rank: handRank = int(line.split(',')[-1]). Alternatively, we could have left handRank as a string and changed our Boolean expression in the "if" statement to: *if* handRank == '1'. However, if the string had some extra spaces before or after the '1', we might not get a match. The string method strip strips off white space (default argument), so we can clean up those values.

Finally, we use the index −1 to grab the last item of each line. We could have used an index of 10.

Program to Calculate Probability of One Pair

An astute reader will have noticed that we wanted a probability, but only did a count. The probability is simple: count of pairs divided by the total number of hands in the file. Remember that we want that division to be floating point; otherwise, the result will be 0. Simply including the expression `pairCount/`*`float`*`(totalCount)` provides the probability. That is a floating-point number which we will want to convert to a percent by multiplying by 100. Finally, we will care about only two points of precision.

We'll illustrate how we can try out these calculations in a session. After running the program, the values for `pairCount` and `totalCount` are still available, so we can play with them in the Python shell. Here is a session showing how the Python shell can be used to develop expressions to put into the program:

```
>>> =============================== RESTART ===================================
>>>
Total hands in file:  1000000
Count of pair hands:   422498
>>> pairCount/totalCount
0
>>> pairCount/float(totalCount)
0.42249799999999998
>>> print "%5.2f" % (pairCount/float(totalCount))
 0.42
# to print a percent sign use a second one, e.g. %%
>>> print "Probability is %5.2f %%." % (pairCount/float(totalCount))
Probability is  0.42 %.
>>> print "Probability is %5.2f %%." % (100 * pairCount/float(totalCount))
Probability is 42.25 %.
```

We can now put that expression into our code and try it out:

Code Listing 4.7

```
# count poker hands

# 1. open the poker data file for reading
pokerFile = open("poker-hand-testing.data",'rU')

totalCount = 0  # 2. create and initialize variable to hold the total count
pairCount = 0   #    create and initialize variable to hold pair count
```

```
# 3. Loop through each line of the file
for line in pokerFile:
    totalCount = totalCount + 1  # (a) at each line increment the counter

    handRank = int(line.split(',')[-1]) # (b) get hand rank: split on comma,
                                        #       get last item as int

    if handRank == 1:                   # (c) if handRank is 1 (it is a pair)
        pairCount = pairCount + 1       #     add one to pair count

print "Total hands in file: ", totalCount
print "Count of pair hands: ", pairCount
print "Probability of pair: %5.2f %%." % (100 * pairCount/float(totalCount))
```

```
>>>
Total hands in file:  1000000
Count of pair hands:  422498
Probability of pair: 42.25 %.
```

The Rest of the Program

We now have a partial program that calculates the probability of getting a poker hand with just one pair. To complete the program, we must include a counter for each type of hand. We need a counter for each type of hand, and we need to increment that counter each time that type of hand is encountered. The resulting program is quite a bit longer, but if you examine it carefully, you will see that we simply duplicated the counter initialization and increment statements. (Later, you will learn how to write a more compact program with one compound counter as a list to accommodate all 10 types of hands.)

Also, some details need to be decided upon—a common issue in problem solving: the devil is in the details. In this case, when we count the number of flush-type hands, do we include straight flushes, or is the flush count really "flushes that are not straight flushes?" For simplicity, we have chosen the latter, but either would be reasonable.

Code Listing 4.8

```
# count poker hands

pokerFile = open("poker-hand-testing.data",'rU') # 1. open file for reading
```

```python
# 2. create and initialize variables to hold the counts
totalCount          = 0
nothingCount        = 0
pairCount           = 0
twoPairCount        = 0
threeOfaKindCount   = 0
straightCount       = 0
flushCount          = 0
fullHouseCount      = 0
fourOfaKindCount    = 0
straightFlushCount  = 0
royalFlushCount     = 0

# 3. Loop through each line of the file
for line in pokerFile:
    totalCount = totalCount + 1  # at each line increment the counter

    # get hand rank: split on comma, get last item as int
    handRank = int(line.split(',')[-1])

    # for each type of hand, increment the appropriate counter
    if handRank == 0:
        nothingCount =          nothingCount + 1
    if handRank == 1:
        pairCount =             pairCount + 1
    if handRank == 2:
        twoPairCount =          twoPairCount + 1
    if handRank == 3:
        threeOfaKindCount =     threeOfaKindCount + 1
    if handRank == 4:
        straightCount =         straightCount + 1
    if handRank == 5:
        flushCount =            flushCount + 1
    if handRank == 6:
        fullHouseCount =        fullHouseCount + 1
    if handRank == 7:
        fourOfaKindCount =      fourOfaKindCount + 1
    if handRank == 8:
        straightFlushCount = straightFlushCount + 1
    if handRank == 9:
        royalFlushCount =       royalFlushCount + 1

print "Total hands in file: ", totalCount
print "Counts of hands: ", nothingCount, pairCount, twoPairCount, \
      threeOfaKindCount, straightCount, flushCount, fullHouseCount, \
```

```
        fourOfaKindCount, straightFlushCount,  royalFlushCount
totalCountFP = float(totalCount)  # float to force floating—point division
print "Probability:"
print " of nothing:         %5.2f %%" % (100*        nothingCount/totalCountFP)
print " of one pair:        %5.2f %%" % (100*          pairCount/totalCountFP)
print " of two pairs:       %5.2f %%" % (100*       twoPairCount/totalCountFP)
print " of three of a kind: %5.2f %%" % (100* threeOfaKindCount/totalCountFP)
print " of a straight:      %5.2f %%" % (100*      straightCount/totalCountFP)
print " of a flush:         %5.2f %%" % (100*         flushCount/totalCountFP)
print " of a full house:    %5.2f %%" % (100*     fullHouseCount/totalCountFP)
print " of four of a kind:  %5.2f %%" % (100*  fourOfaKindCount/totalCountFP)
print " of a straight flush:%5.2f %%" % (100*straightFlushCount/totalCountFP)
print " of a royal flush:   %5.2f %%" % (100*    royalFlushCount/totalCountFP)
```

```
>>>
Total hands in file:  1000000
Counts of hands:  501209 422498 47622 21121 3885 1996 1424 230 12 3
Probability:
of nothing:          50.12 %
of one pair:         42.25 %
of two pairs:         4.76 %
of three of a kind:   2.11 %
of a straight:        0.39 %
of a flush:           0.20 %
of a full house:      0.14 %
of four of a kind:    0.02 %
of a straight flush:  0.00 %
of a royal flush:     0.00 %
```

Notice how spacing was used to make both the program and the output more readable. Also, in the statement that prints the counts, notice a backslash (\). Remember, the backslash indicates that the statement continues onto the next line—usually a newline or carriage return indicates the end of a statement. This improves the readability of the code, which is important, but does not affect running the code.

Observations on the Output

The final output is interesting. Notice that slightly more than half the possible hands have no value, and that a hand with only one pair makes up almost all the remaining possibilities. Finally, notice that two types of hands have zero probability. That is clearly not right (we have the counts to see that). We need another significant digit using 5.3f in the formatting to see them.

Summary

In this chapter, we introduced the string type and the variety of methods and functions that work on them. In isolation, these tools may not yet appear to be very useful or powerful. However, when combined with the ability to make decisions and repeat instructions, these tools will be heavily used.

Exercises

1. Given the string "Monty Python":

   (a) Write an expression to print the first character
   (b) Write an expression to print the last character
   (c) Write an expression inculding `len` to print the last character
   (d) Write an expression that prints "Monty"

2. Given the string "homebody":

   (a) Write an expression using slicing to print "home".
   (b) Write an expression using slicing to print "body".

3. Given a string S with even length:

   (a) Write an expression to print out the first half of the string.
   (b) Write an expression to print out the second half of the string.

4. Given a string S with odd length:

   (a) Write an expression to print the middle character.
   (b) Write an expression to print the string up to but not including the middle character (i.e., the first half of the string).
   (c) Write an expression to print the string from the middle character to the end (not including the middle character).

5. Given the string S = "What is your name?":

   (a) What is returned by X[::2]?
   (b) What is returned by X[2:8:-1]?

6. Given the string x = 'acegikmoqsuwy' and y = '+bdfhjlnprtvxz', use indexing to create a string z that is the lower-case English alphabet.

7. The plus sign (+) is *overloaded* in Python. Explain why 5+4 equals 9, '5' + '4' equals '54' and 5+4.0 equals 9.0.

8. What will be printed by the following?

   ```
   x = 'This is a test.'
   print x * 3
   ```

9. (String operators) The Monty Python comedy troupe has a famous skit set in a restaurant whose menu is predominately Spam®—a canned meat mixture of ham and pork. One menu entry was "Spam, Spam, Spam, Spam, Spam, baked beans, Spam, Spam, Spam, and Spam." Write a Python string expression using both the concatenation (+) and repetition (*) string operators to form that menu entry.

10. We know that writing the following code:

```
print "I like writing in Python."
print "It is so much fun."
```

will result in:

```
I like writing in Python.
It is so much fun.
```

when executed. However, can you manage to do this same task with only one line of code?

11. Five string methods manipulate case: `capitalize`, `title`, `swapcase`, `upper`, and `lower`. Consider the strings: `s1 = "concord"`, `s2 = "souix city"`, `s3 = "HONOLULU"`, and `s4 = "TopHat"`.

    (a) Describe what `capitalize` does.
    (b) Describe what `swapcase` does.
    (c) Describe what `upper` does.
    (d) Describe what `lower` does.
    (e) Describe what `title` does.

12. It is possible to combine string methods in one expression. Given the expression `s="CAT"`, what is `s.upper.lower`?

13. Two string methods left- and right-justify strings within a specified width. In addition, they default by filling in with spaces, but can be specified to fill in with a character. Consider `s = "Topkapi"` and `s.rjust(20,".")` or `s.ljust(15)`. Experiment with right and left justification. Describe the rules for what `ljust` and `rjust` do.

14. Two string methods find where a character is in a string: `find` and `index`.

    (a) Both work the same if a character is found, but behave differently if the character is not found. Describe the difference in how they behave when the character is not found.
    (b) The `find` and `index` methods are not limited to finding single characters. They can search for substrings. Given `s = "Topkapi"`, what does `s.find("kap")` print? Describe the rule for what `find` prints.

15. Using the `raw_input` command prompt for input and then convert the input to lowercase.

16. Convert a string that is all capitals into a string where only the first letters are capitals. For example, convert `"NEW YORK"` to `"New York"`.

17. Experiment with the `count` method. What does it count?
For example,

```
someStr = "Hello world!"
someStr.count("o")
```

18. Experiment with the `strip` method. What does it do?
For example,

```
someStr = "Hi!......"
someStr.strip(".!")
```

19. The string methods that start with "is" all return either "True" or "False". Experiment with them to figure out how they work, i.e. what causes them to return "True" and what causes them to return "False".

20. (String operators)

(a) Suppose you want to print a line full of `'#'` characters. For simplicity, let's say that a line can have only 80 characters. One way is to create a long string to be printed. How would you do it more elegantly in Python using the plus operation (+) of strings?

(b) Suppose you want to print a column full of `'#'` characters. For simplicity, let's say that a column could have only 30 characters. Similar to (a), how would you do it more elegantly in Python using the mulitplye operation (*) of strings? Hint: Use the newline character ('\n').

21. Let, nameStr = 'Albert Einstein'. How would you extract the first name and last name from nameStr using string operator ':'?

22. In British English, there is a word 'flavour'. The American spelling is 'flavor'. Suppose you have a string in Python called brit_word = 'flavour' and you want to convert it into the American variant and store it in a string called amer_word. How would you do it?

23. Which of the following works without any error?

(a) `var = 'xyz' * 10.5`
(b) `var = 'xyz' * '5'`
(c) `var = 'xyz' * 5`
(d) `var = 'xyz' * 5.0`

24. (Reversing a string) Given a string, say X = 'Alan Turing', write an expression to reverse it to get a string, Y = 'gniruT nalA'.

25. Suppose you have a string ab_string = 'abababababababab'. Write an expression to remove all the 'b's and create a string, a_string = 'aaaaaaaa'.

26. Given the string 'abcdefghij', write a single line of code that will print the following (hint: slicing is your friend):

 (a) 'jihgfedcba'.
 (b) 'adgj'.
 (c) 'igeca'.

27. Using the `find` method, write a short program that will print out the index of both 'o's when given the input "Who's on first?".

28. Write a program that given a name in the form of "Chapman, Graham Arthur" will convert it to the form "Graham Arthur Chapman".

29. The expression 'dog' + 's' will return 'dogs'. What is returned by the expression 'dog' − 'g' ? Explain.

30. Similar to .lower: write a program that prompts for a string and prints the string in lower case without using the string.lower method.

31. In the palindrome example we used `replace` to remove bad characters. Refactor that program to **keep** the good characters rather than remove the bad characters.

32. Given the following code:

```
x=raw_input('Enter a string: ')
y=0
for i in x:
        print y,i
        y+=1
```

 (a) What will be printed, if "hello" is entered?
 (b) Refactor the code using enumerate.

33. Although Python's formtted printing can be cumbersome, it can often drastically improve the readability of output. Try creating a table of strings out of the following values:

Melting and Boiling Points of Alkanes		
Name	Melting Point (deg C)	Boiling Point (deg C)
Methane	-162	-183
Ethane	-89	-172
Propane	-42	-188
Butane	-0.5	-135

34. Given x = 'water', what is returned by x.replace('w','c',1)?

35. The following Python statement generates this error: "ValueError: too many values to unpack". Why?

```
first,second = raw_input('two space-separated numbers:')
```

36. Consider the following code:

```
myList = []
for i in range(0,6,2):
    for k in range(4):
        myList.append(i+k)

print i          # Line 1
print k          # Line 2
print myList     # Line 3
```

    (a) What is printed by Line 1?
    (b) What is printed by Line 2?
    (c) What is printed by Line 3?

37. Write a program that prompts for two strings and then compares them, printing the smaller string. The challenege of this exercise is to use only single-character comparision.

38. Write a program that plays the game of hangman. Use characters to print the hangman's status. Triple-quoted strings will be useful. Hint: draw the entire hangman status as a string picture with a full picture for each partial hangman status.

Programming Projects

1. Mastermind

Mastermind is a code-breaking game for two players; play can be simulated in text on a computer. Online versions exist and are useful for understanding how the game is played, but if you can get a hold of the actual board game, that is even better. The game is played using the following:

- A decoding board, with a shield at one end covering a row of four large holes, and twelve additional rows containing four large holes next to a set of four small holes;
- Code pegs of six different colors (we'll use "colors" ABCDEF), with round heads, which will be placed in the large holes on the board; and
- Scoring pegs, some black, some white, that are flat-headed and smaller than the code pegs; they will be placed in the small holes on the board. Only the quantity of black and white scoring pegs in each row matter in the game.

One player, the codemaker, selects four colors that are shielded from the other player, the codebreaker. In our version, colors cannot repeat, i.e., AABB is illegal. The goal of the game is for the codebreaker to correctly determine both the four colors selected by the codemaker and their position in the code.

The codebreaker tries to guess the pattern, in both order and color, within 12 turns. Each guess is made by placing a row of code pegs on the decoding board. Once placed, the codemaker provides feedback by placing from zero to four scoring pegs in the small holes of the row with the guess. A black scoring peg is placed for each code peg from the guess that is correct in both color and position. A white peg indicates the existence of a correct color peg placed in the wrong position.

Once feedback is provided, another guess is made; guesses and feedback continue to alternate until either the codebreaker guesses correctly, or 12 incorrect guesses are made.

Write a program that simulates the game by providing the feedback. The codebreaker will input each guess by entering a string of 'colors'. Your simulation will ensure that guessing rules are followed: the guess consists of exacly four colors from 'ABCDEF'. Feedback will be a count of black pegs and a count of white pegs. Your program will determine the feedback and print it. The program will declare a win if the guess is correct, or a loss after twelve incorrect guesses. In addition, the program should print the complete board state so the codebreaker can more easily view the history of guesses made.

Hints:

- Play the game using paper and pencil to understand how the game is played before designing your game playing algorithm.
- Use strings for the code and guesses.
- Use a string 'ABCDEF' for the set of allowable colors so you can check membership using "in".
- The isalpha string method is useful for checking input.
- The history can be built as a long string using concatenation. The end-of-line character '\n' will be useful for readable output.

(a) The first version of the program should prompt for the codemaker's code. Such a game program isn't much fun to play, but it is easier to test.

(b) The final version should use the random module to create the codemaker's code so it can be kept shielded from the codebreaker.

    i. Use the index = random.randint(start,end) function (from Section 2.2) to generate random indices, *start* $\leq$ *index* $\leq$ *end*, to select code characters from 'ABCDEF'.

    ii. Or, use random.sample(population,k) that returns a sample of length k from a specified population. The join expression (that we will learn the meaning of later in Chapter 6) converts to a string what is returned by the sample function:

```
code = ''.join(random.sample('ABCDEF',4))
```

2. Mad Libs

Mad Libs (madlibs.com) is an old word game for children. (If you have never played Mad Libs, try it at eduplace.com/tales/) You are prompted for categories of words (color, girl's name, place, etc.) and then those words are inserted into a predefined story. The predefined story has place holders for those words which get replaced by the values prompted for. For example: Suppose you are prompted for a verb and a noun, and respond with "giggle" and "spark". If the predefined string was the first line of Hamlet in this form:

> To VERB or not to VERB: that is the NOUN:

The revised version will be:

> To giggle or not to giggle: that is the spark:

Create your own predefined story with parts of speech replaced with their description in all capitals: VERB, NOUN, ADJECTIVE, etc. Your story will be more interesting if you augment your words to be replaced with others appropriate for your story: BOYS_NAME, COLOR, ACTIVE_VERB, etc. Be creative. If you are at a loss for ideas, begin with a fairy tale. For example, here is the beginning of "Little Red Riding Hood" (Note the backslash continuation character \\):

```
story = "Once upon a time in the middle of a ADJECTIVE_ONE NOUN_ONE stood a
    ADJECTIVE_TWO NOUN_TWO, the home of a ADJECTIVE_ONE ADJECTIVE_THREE
    NOUN_THREE known to everyone as GIRLS_NAME."
```

Prompt the user for strings to replace the various parts of speech that you have specified. Print out the revised story.

Hint: the string method `replace(old, new)` will be helpful.

3. Pig Latin

Pig Latin is a game of alterations played on words. To make the Pig Latin form of an English word the initial consonant sound is transposed to the end of the word and an "ay" is affixed. Specifically there are two rules:

(a) If a word begins with a vowel, append "yay" to the end of the word.

(b) If a word begins with a consonant, remove all the consonants from the beginning up to the first vowel and append them to the end of the word. Finally, append "ay" to the end of the word.

For example:

- dog ⇒ ogday
- scratch ⇒ atchscray
- is ⇒ isyay
- apple ⇒ appleyay

Write a program that repeatedly prompts for an English word to translate into Pig Latin, and prints the translated word. If the user enters a period, halt the program.

Hints:

- Slicing is your friend: it can pick off the first character for checking, and you can slice off pieces and concatenate to yield the new word.
- Making a string of vowels allows use of the "in" operator: `vowels = 'aeiou'`.

CHAPTER 5

Functions—QuickStart

YOU HAVE HAVE SEEN MANY EXAMPLES OF USING PYTHON BUILT-IN FUNCTIONS AND methods. In Section 4.3, we took at look at how functions work and how we could use them to manipulate string objects. In this chapter, you'll learn how to create your own functions.

The concept of a function should be familiar from its use in mathematics. Functions in programming languages share many of the characteristics of mathematical functions, but add some unique features as well that make them more useful for programming.

One of the main advantages for using functions is that they support divide-and-conquer problem solving. Remember divide-and-conquer from Section 3.4? This technique encourages you to break a problem down into simpler sub problems, solve those sub problems, and then assemble the smaller solutions into the overall solutions. Functions are a way to directly encode the "smaller subproblem" solution. You'll see more about this as we go through this chapter.

5.1 WHAT IS A FUNCTION?

In mathematics, a function defines the relationship between values. Consider the function $f(x) \Rightarrow \sqrt{x}$. If you provide a particular value of x, e.g. $x = 4$, the function will perform a calculation (here the square root operation) and return the associated value, e.g. 2. Mathematicians termed x the *argument* to the function and say that the function *returns* the value 2.

It is possible for a function to have multiple arguments, for example a function that calculates multiplication requires two arguments: $f(x, y) \Rightarrow x * y$. Mathematical functions return one object, but that object can be a *compound* object; an object with multiple parts. For example, when working with graph paper, each point is an ordered pair (x, y). A function that provides a point as a return value does indeed only return one value, but it is a value with multiple parts. An example of such a function would be the *mirror* function. The *mirror* function swaps the x and y values within the point: $f(x, y) \Rightarrow (y, x)$. Only one object is returned—a point—but that point had two values: an x and a y. The notion that the object a function returns can be a compound object is very useful, including in Python.

Python functions share many of the characteristics of mathematical functions. In particular, a Python function:

- represents a single operation to be performed
- takes zero or more arguments as input
- returns one value (potentially a compound object) as output

A function is also important because it represents an *encapsulation*. By encapsulation, we mean that the details of an operation can be hidden, providing coarser operations that we as programmers can use without having to understand the function's internal details. A function can represent the performance of an operation without making the reader plow through the details of *how* the operation is actually performed.

Consider the `sqrt` function with respect to encapsulation. There are many ways to calculate a square root that vary in accuracy and speed. However, each implementation, each method, represents the "square root" operation. Each method takes in an argument and returns that object's square root. As long as the result is correct, we need not be concerned with the details of how the operation is performed. That is encapsulation.

Why Have Functions?

As you progress in learning to program, you'll move from essential programming elements to important programming elements. Selection ("if") and repetition ("while") are essential programming constructs. It is difficult to write any program without using these two essential features. Functions, on the other hand, allow us to write *better* code in the sense that it is more readable. Also, because functions allow us to divide programs into smaller pieces, they assist in divide-and-conquer problem solving. In that way, functions make programs easier to write. Finally, once a function is written, it can be shared and used by other programmers (including ourselves). Thus, functions provide a powerful construct that we can use to make our programs easier to read, write, and maintain.

From this point on, many of the programming elements we introduce will make some tasks easier, and will subsequently make writing and understanding (that is, reading) the program easier. You could write programs without them, but those programs would be more difficult to read.

In more detail, functions provide the following features which help in programming:

- **Divide-and-Conquer Problem Solving**: As we have already mentioned, functions divide programs into smaller pieces, an approach that corresponds nicely to a divide-and-conquer approach to problem solving (introduced in Chapter 3).

- **Abstraction**: Functions provide a higher-level, more abstract interface to parts of a program. By encapsulating details, functions provide a programmer with a high-level view of program elements whose details can be filled in later—possibly by someone else. By analogy, consider how you drive a car. It has a simple interface that hides considerable complexity. Do you understand how fuel injection provides better performance for your car than a carburetor does? Do you care? You don't have to know the difference: you simply drive the car (turn the wheel, hit the gas, press the brake).
- **Reuse**: Once a function has been created, it can be re-used. If you write a function that calculates the match of two DNA strands, then anywhere in your program where such functionality is needed, you need only invoke your function.
- **Sharing**: Once your function is well tested, you can distribute it for use by other people. Those people can further test the function, refine its capabilities, and through improvement provide a service to everyone in the field. Useful functions can be collected into modules for sharing. Sharing of modules is one of Python's strengths, as programmers generously share modules in many diverse areas.
- **Security**: Small pieces of code can be carefully vetted, and sometimes proven to be correct. Functions provide an opportunity to construct secure components that can greatly aid the construction of larger, secure code.
- **Simplification/Readability** (duplication removal): Because a function provides an encapsulation, it can be used to simplify a program and make it more readable. Anywhere that multiple lines of code might be needed to address a problem, a function can replace those lines. If the replacement can be done in multiple places, the result is simpler code.

5.2 PYTHON FUNCTIONS

There are two parts to a Python function, and they correspond to the two parts found in mathematical functions[1]: the *definition* and the *invocation*. The definition defines (creates) the function; the invocation is the application of the function in a program. A function definition is the *second* way we have seen to create a name associated with an object in Python, the first being an assignment statement.

Consider an example function to convert Celsius temperatures to Fahrenheit.

- First we need a conversion formula: $C * 1.8 + 32$
- Mathematics has a function *invocation*:

$$fahrenheit = f(C)$$

where the *definition* of the function is:

$$f(C) = C * 1.8 + 32$$

---

[1] Some languages, such as those derived from C (C++, Java, C#), have a third part—the declaration.

- Python has a function *invocation* that looks very much like the mathematical one:

```
fahrenheit = f(C)
```

but the Python *definition* looks quite different:

```
def f(celsius_float):
    return celsius_float*1.8 + 32
```

As in mathematics, C is called an *argument* of the function. The `celsius_float` variable is termed a *parameter* of the function. Upon invoking the function, the argument C's value is passed to the parameter value `celsius_float` for use in the calculation.[2] More detail on the passing of values between arguments and parameters can be found in Section 7.2.

A function definition begins with the keyword **def**. The Python definition works similarly to an assignment statement. By executing a **def** statement, a new name is created in the namespace and a new object, a function object, is associated with that name. As we have observed elsewhere in Python, everything is an object, and functions are no exception.

The **def** is a compound statement, meaning that it provides a suite of other Python statements and expressions that are part of the function. The suite of statements are what will constitute the calculation done by the function object. One of the special keywords that can be used in functions is the **return** statement. The **return** indicates a value that is returned as output from the function invocation. A function ends after a **return** statement is executed. A function may have more than one **return** statement, but the first one that is executed will end the function. (We have used the phrase "to *invoke* a function," but an equivalent and frequently used phrase is "to *call* a function.") The general form of a function is shown in Figure 5.1.

Let's create a function to do our temperature conversion and use it in a session. Note the parts of the function: the **def** and **return** keywords as well as the parameter (`celsius`). Finally, notice the indentation for the suite of statements, part of the function definition. We will discuss the special comment with triple quotes (`"""`) later. In essence, it is a brief description of the function, and is called a *docstring*.

Code Listing 5.1

```python
# Temperature conversion

def celsius2fahrenheit(celsius):
    """ Convert Celsius to Fahrenheit. """
    return celsius*1.8 + 32
```

---

[2] Note that to adhere to our naming convention, the argument C should have been named better such as `CFloat` or `celsius_float`, but we left it as plain C so that it looked more like the mathematical function.

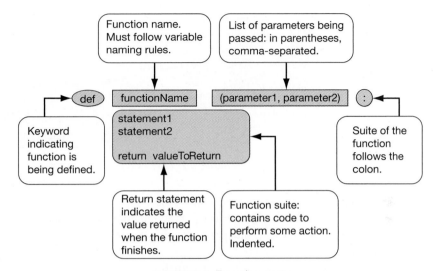

FIGURE 5.1 Function parts.

```
>>> =============================== RESTART ================================
>>>
>>> celsius2fahrenheit
<function celsius2fahrenheit at 0xcc22f0>
>>> celsius2fahrenheit(100)
212.0
>>> celsius2fahrenheit(0)
32.0
>>>
```

Notice that Code Listing 5.1 contains only the function definition—no invocation. When the file is run (we press the F5 key in IDLE), the **def** statement is executed, the name of the function is added to the namespace, and a function object is created. That function object is associated with the name in the namespace. We can type the name of the function and see that it is associated with a function object. We can then invoke (call) the function and see what results are returned. In the session, we converted 100°C to 212°F and 0°C to 32°F.

5.3 FLOW OF CONTROL WITH FUNCTIONS

Functions introduce a new flow of control model. Up to this point, a program has essentially been a series of statements and expressions that are executed in the order they appear in the

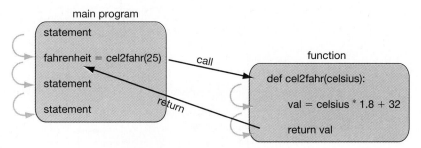

FIGURE 5.2 Function flow of control.

file. Some of the statements introduced local control paths within those statements, such as with selection or repetition, but the flow remained sequential in the file. With functions, we create a set of small, independent sub-programs that can be used to construct a larger program.

In short, the flow of control with functions is to flow from the invocation (call) in the calling program, to the function itself, and then back to the calling program with the function's return value being made available to the calling program. Control *within* a function remains sequential: one statement after another along with local control statements such as **if** and **while**.

For every program, there is usually one "main" part where execution begins. After that, the flow of control is based on the order of both statements and functions. In particular for functions, control flow is determined by the order of function invocation, not function definition. Functions can be defined anywhere in the program file, as long as they are defined *before* they are invoked. The function name must be placed in the namespace before it can be called.

Figure 5.2 shows an example of function control flow.

Function Flow in Detail

Consider two programs: the *caller,* the program presently executing, and the function. For now, a caller will be the main program. A caller executes its statements until it encounters a function invocation, `cel2fahr(25)` in Figure 5.2. At that point, the caller temporarily halts, and the function begins. Thus, one program is suspended (the caller) waiting for a result from the now executing function. When the function finishes execution, the suspended caller receives the return value from the function and continues from that point.

Because the function is essentially a new program, the function gets its own namespace when it begins execution. Any object that gets created and given a name (by assignment, by a **def**, etc.) *within* the function is placed in the function's separate namespace, not the program's namespace. If a new name is created in the function that is the same as a name that existed in the caller's namespace, the newly created association is used in the function. This protocol has some interesting consequences, which we will cover in Section 7.2.

Parameter passing is done just before the calling program suspends. The caller associates its argument values to the corresponding function *parameter* in the function object. In Figure 5.2, the argument value 25 is associated with the parameter `celsius`. In more detail, the parameter is defined in the function's namespace and associated with the value of its corresponding argument.

Argument values are typically passed to parameter names in the order they are listed.[3] The names of the corresponding argument and parameter need not match. Only the order matters: the first argument value is passed to the first parameter, second argument value to the second parameter, and so on. The number of arguments and parameters must match.[4] After values are passed, the function then begins execution.

During function execution, if a **return** statement is executed, the function ends and the return value value is provided to the caller ("return" arrow in Figure 5.2). For example, `fahrenheit = cel2fahr(25)` assigns the returned value to the main program variable `fahrenheit` as shown in Figure 5.2. After the function ends, the caller continues.

Code listing 5.2 is a sample program with a function that takes in a Celsius temperature to convert to Fahrenheit.

Code Listing 5.2

```python
# Conversion program

def celsius2Fahrenheit(celsius):
    """ Convert Celsius to Fahrenheit. """
    return celsius*1.8 + 32

# main part of the program
print "Convert Celsius to Fahrenheit."
celsiusTemp = float(raw_input("Enter a Celsius temp: "))
# call the conversion function
fahrTemp = celsius2Fahrenheit(celsiusTemp)
# print the returned value
print celsiusTemp," converts to ",fahrTemp," Fahrenheit"
```

[3] Python also has other ways to pass argument values to parameters. See Chapter 7.
[4] In Chapter 7 you will learn about *default* values, which allow fewer arguments than parameters.

```
>>> =============================== RESTART ================================
>>>
Convert Celsius to Fahrenheit.
Enter a Celsius temp: 100
100.0  converts to  212.0  Fahrenheit
>>> =============================== RESTART ================================
>>>
Convert Celsius to Fahrenheit.
Enter a Celsius temp: 0
0.0  converts to  32.0  Fahrenheit
```

Lines 3–5 define the function. Notice **_def_** beginning the compound statement, the parameter (`celsius`), and the **_return_** with its associated expression within the function suite. To repeat, the **_def_** statement is executed by Python and creates the function. Once created, it can be called (invoked) by another program. Remember, a function must be defined (the **_def_** statement must be executed) before a program can call the function.

Lines 7–13 are the "main" program:

Line 9 prompts the user for input.

Line 11 invokes (calls) the function. The value in the argument `celsiusTemp` is passed to the parameter `celsius`. Then control passes to the function. When the function ends, it returns a value that the main program assigns to `fahrTemp`.

Line 13. The main program continues with Line 13 and prints the results.

Check Yourself: Simple Functions

1. Give the output of these calls to the following function:

   ```
   def makeOdd(n):
       return 2*n + 1

   print makeOdd(2)
   print makeOdd('2')
   n = 3
   print makeOdd(n)
   print 1 + makeOdd(3)
   ```

2. Write a function `makeEven(n)`.
   What happens if you use a string as an argument?
   Why is the behavior different then with `makeOdd(n)`?

Another Function Example

You have used the `len` function to find the length of a string. Let's write our own function that does the same thing so we can see how the actual `len` might work. We will name our function `length` to avoid confusion with the Python built-in `len`.

Here is an algorithm to find the length of a string, S.

- Initialize a counter: `count = 0`
- Walk through the string: *for* s *in* S:
- For each character in the string, add 1 to the counter: `count += 1`

Let's put the algorithm in a function by adding the word *def* and a *return* statement. Then we can "run" the function (F5 in IDLE) so it is loaded into the Python shell where we can invoke it.

Code Listing 5.3

```
def length(S):
    """Return the length of S."""
    count = 0
    for s in S:
        count += 1
    return count
```

```
>>> ============================== RESTART ==============================
>>>
>>> question = "What is your quest?"
>>> length(question)    # our function
19
>>> len(question)       # the Python built-in function
19
```

With a `length` function in hand, let's modify it. Suppose that instead of the length of the string, we wanted a count of only the letters in the string. That is, we will add to our count only if we encounter a letter. Our algorithm is similar:

- Initialize a counter.
- Walk through the string.
- For each character in the string, if the character is a letter, add 1 to the counter.

The change in the algorithm is small, but the implementation takes a little more thought. How do we check "if the character is a letter"? One way to do that is to make a variable with a string consisting of the lower case letters and then check whether the character is in the string. However, we could also use the `string` module as discussed in Section 4.6 and check to see whether the character is in `string.lowercase`. Finally, we must consider upper- and lowercase. We can handle that by making the character lower case before checking to see whether it is in the string of letters. We will call our modified function `letterCount`.

Code Listing 5.4

```
import string

def letterCount(S):
    """Return the count of letters in S."""
    count = 0
    for s in S:
        if s.lower() in string.lowercase:
            count += 1
    return count
```

```
>>> ============================== RESTART ==============================
>>>
>>> question = "What is your quest?"
>>> len(question)
19
>>> letterCount(question)
15
```

Of course, there are many different algorithms to solve our letter counting problem. For example, we could have made a new string object resulting from the concatenation of `string.lowercase` and `string.uppercase` and check for membership in that string.

Function Example: Word Puzzle

Let's use strings and functions to solve a word puzzle.

> Find a word that contains the vowels `'a'`, `'e'`, `'i'`, `'o'`, and `'u'` in that order.

To do a solve a word puzzle we need a list of words.

Reading a File of Words

Many word lists can be found on the Internet by searching for either "word lists" or "dictionary", usually with one word per line. We can download a dictionary and save it in a file; let's name the file "dictionary.txt." We have worked briefly with files in Section 4.7 and will do so in more detail in Chapter 9, but let's review how to read the contents of a file.

To read through the file, one word at a time, we can do the following:

- open the file for reading
- read through the file one word (line) at a time

A Python program that reads through the whole file `dictionary.txt`, and simply prints each line of the file is Code Listing 5.5:

Code Listing 5.5

```
# Print all words in a dictionary file with one word per line

# open file named "dictionary.txt" for reading ('r')
dataFile = open("dictionary.txt", 'r')

# walk through file one line at a time
for line in dataFile:
    print line
```

The *open* function takes two string arguments: the first is a string that is the name of a file, and the second is single character `'r'` that indicates that the file is for reading (as opposed to `'w'` for writing) and creates a file handle. The file handle is an object now associated with the contents of the file, here named `dataFile`, which we can use to iterate through the contents of the file. The **for** statement iterates through the contents of the file by fetching from the file a line of the file, one line at a time. Each line is provided as a string. When the last line is fetched, the **for** loop ends.

Searching a File of Words

Now that you know how to read through a file of words, let's try to solve our puzzle.

First, we need to handle a common feature of files strings: there are often some characters that we don't want to deal with. In this case, the dictionary file contains a carriage-return character at the end of each line, and it may contain stray characters such as spaces or tabs. We can eliminate such characters using the `strip` string method, one of the methods listed in Section 4.3. If no arguments are provided to `strip`, then whitespace is removed from the ends of the string. If a string argument is provided, only those characters in the argument are removed. An example of its use is `aString.strip('.,')`, which strips commas, periods, and the space character from the beginning and end of the string `aString`. In particular, `', this.'.strip('.,')` and `' this,,.'.strip('.,')` both produce the string object `'this'`.

PROGRAMMING TIP

The strip method works only on the beginning and end of a string. For example, 'this string'.strip() produces the string 'this string'. Because no arguments are provided, the default behavior is to remove whitespace (tabs, carriage returns, space characters, etc.), but the space in the *middle* of the string is unaffected. Note that *all* the whitespace characters are removed from the beginning and the end.

For every line we fetch from the file, we strip that line to remove whitespace at the beginning or end of the line. In addition, word puzzles are often easier if all characters are known to be only lower case (or only upper case). The string method lower is useful for that. Let's create a function that strips out whitespace characters and makes all of them lowercase.

Code Listing 5.6

```
def cleanWord(word):
    """Return word in lower case stripped of whitespace."""
    return word.strip().lower()
```

Notice the use of chained method invocation in the function as described in Section 4.3.

As our word puzzle wants a word with all five vowels, the word must be at least six characters long, so there is no reason to consider shorter words. We can add that check and the cleanWord function to our file-reading program.

Code Listing 5.7

```
# Find a word with a single example of the vowels a, e, i, o, u in that order

dataFile = open("dictionary.txt", "r")

def cleanWord(word):
    """Return word in lower case stripped of whitespace."""
    return word.strip().lower()

# main program
for word in dataFile:          # for each word in the file
    word = cleanWord(word)     # clean the word
    if len(word) <= 6:         # skip word if too small to have all vowels
        continue
    print word
```

Our program still does nothing to solve our puzzle, but we now have a framework to work in: a program that reads a file of words and cleans them up.

Solving the Puzzle

To solve this puzzle, we want to determine the vowels in a word—in order. Let's write a function that returns the vowels in a word in order. A function lets us consider each word in isolation. For any word, we can check each character to see whether it is a vowel, and collect the vowels into a string. Of course, we need to create an empty string to add vowels to. Our algorithm is:

* create an empty string, let's call it vowelsInWord
* for each character char in the word
  - if char is a vowel, add it to the string vowelsInWord

How do we check whether a character is a vowel? We can create a string of vowels vowelsStr and associate it with 'aeiou' and check to see whether each character in the dictionary entry word is in vowelsStr.

Here is our algorithm implemented as a function.

Code Listing 5.8

```
def getVowelsInWord(word):
    """Return vowels in string word—include repeats."""
    vowelStr = "aeiou"
    vowelsInWord = ""
    for char in word:
        if char in vowelStr:
            vowelsInWord += char
    return vowelsInWord
```

Let's try the function out in a session to find the vowels in the word 'create'. The vowels in 'create' in order are 'eae'.

```
>>> word = "create"
>>> getVowelsInWord(word)
'eae'
```

Our function appears to be working. Of course, we need to check it more thoroughly, but we will leave that as an exercise for you to try on your own.

Now that we have a function that extracts the vowels in a word, we can consider our puzzle again. The puzzle wants a word with the five vowels in order. That is, if our getVowelsInWord function returns `'aeiou'`, we have found our puzzle answer. Our refined algorithm to solve the puzzle is:

- open the file
- for each word in the file
  - clean the word
  - if the word is too small, skip it
  - get the vowels in the word
  - if the vowels returned equals `'aeiou'`, print the word

Using that algorithm as the main part of our program, let's put it all together.

Code Listing 5.9

```
# Find a word with a single example of the vowels a, e, i, o, u in that order

dataFile = open("dictionary.txt", "r")

5  def cleanWord(word):
       """Return word in lower case stripped of whitespace."""
       return word.strip().lower()

   def getVowelsInWord(word):
10     """Return vowels in string word—include repeats."""
       vowelStr = "aeiou"
       vowelsInWord = ""
       for char in word:
           if char in vowelStr:
15             vowelsInWord += char
       return vowelsInWord

   # main program
   print "Find words containing vowels 'aeiou' in that order:"
20 for word in dataFile:          # for each word in the file
       word = cleanWord(word)     # clean the word
       if len(word) <= 6:         # if word is too small, skip it
           continue
       vowelStr = getVowelsInWord(word)   # get vowels in word
25     if vowelStr == "aeiou":            # check if you have all vowels in order
           print word
```

```
>>>
Find words containing vowels 'aeiou' in that order:
facetious
>>>
```

The dictionary.txt file we used for the example contained almost 40,000 words, and our puzzle-solving program found only one that satisfied the criteria of having the vowels 'aeiou' in that order: facetious. A larger dictionary would return a longer list.

There are a couple of points that are worth noting about the example.

- The use of functions made our problem-solving task easier. The functions allowed us to consider the problem in smaller pieces—the divide-and-conquer technique introduced in Chapter 3.
- In the main program is readable. Even if we did not know the definition of the functions cleanWord and getVowelsInWord we could guess what they (likely) did and understand what the program was trying to do.

Check Yourself: Function Practice with Strings

1. Give the output provided by the following program on the indicated input values.

```
def func1 (str1, str2):
    if str1 > str2:
        resultStr = str1[1:]
    else:
        resultStr = str2[:-1]
    return resultStr

# main program
response1Str = raw_input("Give me a string:")
response2Str = raw_input("Give me a second string:")
print func1(response1Str, response2Str)    # Line 1
print func1(response2Str, response1Str)    # Line 2
```

(a) Given the two input values (in order), abc123 and then bcd456, what output is produced by Line 1?

(b) Given the two input values (in order), abc123 and then bcd456, what output is produced by Line 2?

(c) Given the two input values (in order), aaabbc and then aaabbcd, what output is produced by Line 1?

(d) Given the two input values (in order), aaabbc and then aaabbcd, what output is produced by Line 2?

- Note the reuse of the identifier `vowelStr` in the main and in the function `getVowelsInWord`. Because the function gets its own namespace, these identifiers reference different objects. More on this in Section 7.2.

Functions Calling Functions

There is no limitation to when a function can be called (except that it must be after its `def`). It is often the case that a function will call another function. This extension does not change the process described previously, though it does make the flow of control slightly more complicated for us to follow. More on this in Chapter 7. In fact, a function can call itself—a complicated control flow to which we devote Chapter 16.

When to Use a Function

There are no hard or fast rules about when to write something as a function or when to leave code as part of a larger program. However, here are some guidelines that may prove helpful.

Do One Thing: A function should be the encapsulation of a single, identifiable operation. A function should do one thing, and of course, do it well. Functions that try to do too many things are candidates to be broken into multiple functions (i.e., refactored).

Readable: A function should be readable. As we've said frequently, *all* code should be readable. Note that this is not just a question of length, but of naming, of structure, and of other good programming style aspects.

Not Too Long: A function shouldn't be too long. What is "too long" depends on many things, but the idea is that if a function does one thing, a person should be able to read it easily and understand its purpose. If the function is too long, difficult to follow somehow, it might need to be broken into multiple functions.

Reusable: A function should be reusable in contexts other than the program it was written for originally. If possible, the function should be self-contained and not dependent on some nuance of the main program. If it has dependencies then those dependencies should be made clear so that others can use it more easily.

Complete: A function should be complete, in that it works in all potential situations. If you write a function to perform one thing, you should make sure that *all the cases* where it might be used taken into account. It is often the case that the core of the function is very straightforward, but handling all the cases it might encounter requires supporting code.

Refactoring: We first mentioned the term refactoring in Section 2.2. Again, refactoring is the process of taking existing code and modifying it such that its structure is somehow improved but the functionality of the code remains the same. Functions can play a prominent role in this process, as they allow you to take long, difficult-to-follow code and break it into smaller, more manageable, pieces. If you need to "fix" some code, consider refactoring it into functions.

☞ PROGRAMMING TIP

A useful rule of thumb for novices is to keep each function small enough to fit on the screen. Like all rules of thumb, there are many reasons to break the rule, but you should ask yourself if there is a good reason to make a function longer than that.

What If There is No Return Statement?

Sometimes we write functions without a return statement. Functions that do not return a value are often called *procedures*.

In that case, what, if anything, is returned? The answer is that a special Python value None is returned by default if the programmer does not provide a **return** statement. None is a kind of odd Python value—a value to represent nothing. Kind of cosmic!

There are some good reasons to use a procedure. One that often comes up is specially formatted output. Formatting output to look "pretty" can be laborious and potentially complicated. A print procedure is therefore a good place to do such output. The procedure isolates all the printing format but does not return a value. Other instances might require a change of state to the program, something like turning a graphics mode on or off, or changing the network connection to a different mode. Each of these elements is best isolated as a process, but as a function they do not need to return a value.

To see this process in action, let's write a trivial function that simply prints its parameter. We will then assign the result of the function to a variable. When we print the value of the variable, we see that None was printed.

```
>>> def formattedOutput(myString, myInt):
      print 'The result of the processing for %s was %d'%(myString,myInt)
      # no return statement
...
>>> formattedOutput('Bill',100)
The result of the processing for Bill was 100
>>> result = formattedOutput('Fred',75)     # capture the implicit return
The result of the processing for Fred was 75
>>> print result
None                                          # return value was None
>>>
```

What If There Are Multiple Return Statements?

If there are multiple return statements, the first return encountered ends the function at that point. Consider the following example function, which returns "positive," "negative," or "zero," depending on the value of the argument.

```
>>> def positiveNegativeZero(number):
        if number > 0:
                return "positive"
        if number < 0:
                return "negative"
        else:  # number == 0
                return "zero"
```

```
>>> positiveNegativeZero(5)  # test all three possible cases
'positive'
>>> positiveNegativeZero(-2)
'negative'
>>> positiveNegativeZero(0)
'zero'
```

Multiple return values can make following the flow of control in the function difficult. If possible, it is best to have as few returns as possible so the reader can more clearly follow the function.

VISUAL VIGNETTE

5.4 TURTLE FLAG

The first official United States flag was established by the Continental Congress on June 14, 1777, with first Flag Act: "Resolved, That the flag of the United States be made of thirteen stripes, alternate red and white; that the union be thirteen stars, white in a blue field, representing a new Constellation." The arrangement of the stars was not specified: Betsy Ross used a circle, others used rows.

Drawing a flag is an excellent illustration of the practicality of functions. In abstraction, the United States flag is a composition of two shapes: stars and stripes (rectangles). It is impractical to draw the 13 (or 50!) stars individually when a function can encapsulate the multiple steps required for each star. The same can be said for drawing the 13 stripes—they are simply rectangles. Even the blue field behind the stars is a rectangle, as is the overall shape. Therefore, to draw the flag using Python's Turtle graphics, one will want at least two functions: `drawStar` and `drawRectangle`. The program is left as an exercise.

Summary

In this chapter, we introduced the concept of functions in a programming language and showed how functions work in Python. Of particular importance, is that functions aid us in the divide-and-conquer approach to problem solving. After covering the list data structure in the next chapter, we will revisit functions to examine the complexities of passing mutable objects to functions.

Exercises

1. Draw the parts of a function and label the parts. Write a brief definition for each part.

2. Menu Writing:
   (a) A common task while writing any software is to display a menu and ask the user for a choice. One such example is the menu on your cellphone. It has messaging, contacts, games, settings, media and web (and possibly others) as options. Write a function called `displayMenu` that displays the menu to the user and allows the user to make a choice (using *raw_input*).
   (b) Write a function that takes the choice of the user and makes calls to the other functions that correspond to the operation to be performed. (Give meaningful names to the functions. You *don't* have to write the other function definitions.)

3. Write a function that takes in the final scores of two soccer teams as arguments and prints either who won the game or whether the game was tied. Refer to the teams as "Team1" or "Team2." The function returns nothing.

4. Write a function that takes as input an English sentence (a string) and prints the total number of vowels and the total number of consonants in the sentence. The function returns nothing. Note that the sentence could have special characters like dots, dashes, and so on.

5. The Fibonacci sequence is: 1, 1, 2, 3, 5, 8, 13 . . . You can see that the first and second numbers are both 1. Thereafter, each number is the sum of the previous two numbers.
   (a) Write a function to print the first N numbers of the Fibonacci sequence.
   (b) Write a function to print the Nth number of the sequence.

6. Suppose you are purchasing something online on the Internet. At the website, you get a 10% discount if you are a member. Additionally, you are also getting a discount of 5% on the item because its Father's Day.

   Write a function that takes as input the cost of the item that you are purchasing and a Boolean variable indicating whether you are a member (or not), applies the discounts appropriately, and returns the final discounted value of the item.
   Note: The cost of the item need not be an integer.

7. A leap year in the Gregorian calendar system is a year that's divisible by 4 but not by 100, unless it is also divisible by 400. For example, 1896, 1904, and 2000 were leap years but 1900 was not. Write a function that takes in a year as input and prints whether it's a leap year (or not).

8. What does this function do? What does it return for num = 5?

```
def Func(num):
    total = 0
    while num > 0:
        total = total + num*(num-1)
        num = num - 1
    return total
```

9. What does this function do? What does it return if x = 5?

```
def Func(x):
    total = 0
    for i in range(x):
        total += i * (i-1)
    return total
```

10. What does this function do? What number is returned by this function?

```
def Func():
    num = 1.0
    total = 0

    while num < 100:
        total = 1/num
        num+=1

    return total
```

11. Error checking with meaningful error messages is an important part of programming. Consider the following scenario: A customer has to pay his monthly credit card bill. The credit limit on the card is $1000. The minimum payment due is always $20. Let the payment on the credit card be $P. Write a function called makePayment(P) that takes as an argument the total payment on the credit card ($P) and prints "Success" or "Retry". Try to think of all the errors that should be taken care of and implement those in the function. One example would be that if the payment is less than $20, the program should remind the user that it's less than the minimum payment due.

12. You buy an international calling card to India. The calling card company has some special offers.

    (a) If you charge your card with $5 or $10, you don't get anything extra.
    (b) For a $25 charge, you get $3 of extra phone time.
    (c) For a $50 charge, you get $8 of extra phone time.
    (d) For a $100 charge, you get $20 of extra phone time.

    Write a function that asks the user for the amount he/she wants on the card, and returns the total charge that the user gets. Note: Values other than those mentioned above are not allowed.

13. Write a function that takes mass as input and returns its energy equivalent. ($E = mc^2$). The units should be in the meter-kilogram-second system.

14. Chat:

    (a) In certain chat programs or messaging applications, there is a limit on the number of characters that you can send in a message. Write a function that takes as input the message (a string) and checks whether the number of characters is less than 160 (or not). If the length of the message is less than 160, the message should be returned. If the length of the message is greater than 160, a string consisting of only the first 160 characters should be returned.
    (b) How would you check if the restriction is on number of words rather than characters? Write a function that allows a message with only 20 words.

15. Write a function to print all the common multiples of 6 and 10, less than 100. In general, the function should take three input parameters: two numbers (X and Y) whose common mutiples have to be found, and the upper limit Z.

16. What are three guidelines used to determine whether creating a separate function is the sensible thing to do?

17. (Refactoring) In Chapters 1 and 2, there were exercises to calculate football quarterback pass ratings and then to output the quality of the quarterback.

    (a) Write the pass rating as a function. Have the main program prompt for the five inputs and then use those inputs as arguments to the function.
    (b) Write the quality rating as a function and add it to the existing program.

18. In an exercise in Chapter 2, we presented an odometer puzzle from the "Car Talk" radio program that involved numerical palindromes. Refactor your solution by writing a palindome function and using that in your solution.

19. Write a function that takes as input a string that stores date and time (24-hour clock) in the following format:
"MM/DD/YYYY HR:MIN:SEC" and prints the following:

- DD/MM/YYYY
- HR:MIN:SEC
- MM/YYYY
- Whether the time is "AM" or "PM".

Validation of the input in the function is necessary. For example, if the user gives an input of "122/04/1990 13:12:12", the given string is invalid, as there can be only 12 months in a year. Think of all possible erroneous inputs and write code to handle them. The function doesn't return anything.

20. Write a function that takes as input a string that stores date and time in the format, "MM/DD/YYYY HR:MIN:SEC" and prints the number of seconds elapsed since "01/01/YYYY 00:00:00".

21. Write a function that prints all numbers in the range A to B (inclusive) that have all digits belonging to the set {1,3,4,8,9}. Check whether A is less than or equal to B; otherwise, swap them before proceeding. The function takes two integer arguments: A and B.

22. Given a string of length three representing a set (i.e., surrounded by curly braces) such as "{ABC}", write a function that takes the string as an argument and returns a string of its permutations in comma separated form, such as "{ABC, ACB, BAC, BCA, CAB, CBA}". Hint: use multiple *for* loops.

23. Implement a textual progress bar in Python. In any progress bar, the space occupied by it is finite. Let's say, the textual progress bar could show only 10 Xs. So, you have to divide the total time by 10, and after those many seconds, you have to print an X on the output.

For example, if the time is 100 seconds:

At 0 secs :
At 10 secs : X
At 20 secs : XX

. . .

At 100 secs : XXXXXXXXXX

Write a function that takes the number of seconds as input and implements the progress bar. This task is easier if you look up Python's time module either in the documentation or online.

Programming Projects

1. **U.S. Flag in Turtle Graphics:**
Draw the United States flag using at least four functions. The regular polygons in the US flag are natural candidates for functions.

   (a) Draw the flag shown earlier in the chapter with 13 stars arranged in rows. Add color for maximum effect.

   (b) Draw the flag with the 13 stars arranged in a circle. (Hint: is it really a circle, or is it some other *regular* figure?)

   (c) Rewrite your program so it takes as input one positive Real number that specifies a scale factor. That is, 0.5 will cause a half-size flag to be drawn and 2.8 will draw a flag that is 2.8 times larger.

2. **DNA Sequencing:**
The term *DNA sequencing* refers to methods for determining the order of the nucleotide bases, adenine, thymine, cytosine, and guanine, in a molecule of DNA. The standard representation of the bases is to use their first letters, ATCG, so that DNA is represented as a string using only those four characters. However, DNA strings are millions of bases (characters) long.

   Substring matching is the process of determining whether a shorter string (the substring) is contained within a longer string. Substring matching plays important roles in the re-construction of an unknown DNA string from pieces, and in searching for interesting substrings within a known DNA string.

   Python provides a `find(substring, start, end)` string method that returns the lowest index (integer) where the *substring* is found in the index range `start` $\leq$ `index` < `end`. The `start` and `end` arguments are optional, but for this exercise we will make them required (you will learn later how to handle optional arguments). If the substring is not found, -1 is returned.

   (a) Without using the `find` string method, write a function that behaves exactly like the `find` string method. As your function is not a string method, the string to search must be an argument—let's make it the first one. The resulting format of your function will be:

   ```
   find(someString, substring, start, end)
   ```

   (b) Biology researchers frequently want to find *all* the locations where a substring is found, not simply the first one. Write a function named `multiFind(someString, substring, start, end)` that, instead of returning one integer index, returns a string that contains zero or more indices separated by commas. In this case, the string will contain digits representing the integer indices. If the substring is not found, an empty string is returned. You may use the `find` method that you wrote earlier.

(c) A nice feature of our `multiFind` function is that if the substring is not found, an empty string is returned. In particular, if the substring is not found, the returned empty string resolves to be *False* in a Boolean expression. The returned value will be *True* otherwise. That feature allows one to use `multiFind` in an *if* statement such as: *if* `multiFind(S,substring,0,20):` the Python `find` string method does not share that characteristic (why?). Write a program that exercises both your `find` and your `multiFind` functions including their use in Boolean expressions. Create some strings using only the base letters, ATCG, and search for substrings within them.

3. **Heap of Beans:**

We are going to play a game called *the heap of beans*. You start with a heap of beans (we will start with 16 beans) and two players. Each player can remove 1, 2, or 3 beans from the pile of 16. Each player is required to take some number of beans from the pile during each turn. The players take turns removing beans, and the player who takes the last bean from the pile is the loser. You can try this game with a partner using 16 pieces of paper as beans.

Each player is to be represented by a function, so we will have two functions. Each function takes a single argument, representing the present number of beans, and returns the number of beans remaining after the player function takes its turn. During the operation of the player function, the function reports (prints) how many beans were removed. Note that the function decides how many beans to remove. It takes no input from the user.

You also need a main program. The main program initializes the heap of beans to 16, and then alternately calls the first player function and the second player function until one of them gets the last bean. The main then reports who the loser is and exits.

(a) Write a simple player function such as one that always takes exactly one bean. It isn't very interesting, but it lets you test your program.

(b) Now for the fun part. Write a "smart player" function and test it against other students' functions in your class. A class tournament would be best—who has the best strategy?

CHAPTER 6

Lists and Tuples

6.1 WHAT IS A LIST?

Python's built-in *list* type is also a collection type. In fact, like strings, lists are a sequence type and therefore share some of the characteristics of strings. However, a list differs from a string in two fundamental ways:

- A list can contain elements other than characters. In fact, a list can contain a sequence of elements of *any* type, even different typed elements mixed together in the same list.
- A list is a *mutable* type. This means that, unlike a string object, a list object can be changed after it is initially created. It can be changed in many ways; we will explore a number of those ways in this chapter.

If we keep these differences in mind, we can use our knowledge of the string type to work with lists.

Making Python Lists

Lists can be created with the `list` constructor or with square brackets ([ ]). This capability can be a little confusing, as the same square brackets are also used as the index operator. One way to tell the difference is the existence of the comma character. Each element of a list is separated by a comma. Thus, if you see square brackets with multiple elements separated by commas, you know it is a list.

Here are a few examples of making a list in a Python session:

```
>>> aList = [1,2,'a',3.14159]
>>> weekDays = ['Monday', 'Tuesday', 'Wednesday', 'Thursday', 'Friday']
>>> listOfLists = [ [1,2,3], ['a','b','c']]
>>> listFromCollection = list('Hello')
>>> aList
[1, 2, 'a', 3.1415899999999999]
```

251

```
>>> weekDays
['Monday', 'Tuesday', 'Wednesday', 'Thursday', 'Friday']
>>> listOfLists
[[1, 2, 3], ['a', 'b', 'c']]
>>> listFromCollection
['H', 'e', 'l', 'l', 'o']
>>> []
[]
>>>
```

Here are a couple of things to notice about these lists.

- `aList` is a sequence of four elements (two integers, a character, and a floating-point number). Any Python type can be a list element and different types can be in the same list. Again, this differs from a string, which *requires* its elements to all be characters.
- As previously noted, each element of the list is separated from the next by a comma. The comma marks it as a sequence, and the square brackets mark that sequence as a list.
- The `listOfLists` is a list of only two elements. The first element is a list, as is the second. Again, a list can be a sequence of any typed element—even another list!
- The `listFromCollection` is a list built using the constructor *list*. The resulting list looks like `['H', 'e', 'l', 'l', 'o']`, containing five elements, each a string with a single character. This constructor takes a single argument and that argument must be another collection. Each element of the argument collection is added as an element to the list. Non-collections (integers, floats, Booleans, etc.) cannot be used as an argument to the *list* constructor.
- The special list with no elements, designated as `[]`, is called the empty list. Like other "empty" elements, it is equivalent to a *False* value in Python.

List of Lists

We frequently use lists of lists, such as `listOfLists` in the previous session. A two-dimensional object such as a spreadsheet, the Cartesian plane, or a matrix can be represented as list of lists—conceptually as a list of rows, where each row is a list. To index an individual element, we use two pairs of brackets: the first one selects a list, the second one selects within the list. Here is a session to illustrate that concept:

```
>>> listOfLists = [ [1,3,5], ['x','a','n'], [2,'b',3.5]]
>>> listOfLists[1]
['x', 'a', 'n']
>>> listOfLists[1][2]
'n'
>>> listOfLists[0][-1]
5
```

Some observations:

- `listOfLists[1]` selects element 1 of the list—the second list.
- `listOfLists[1][2]` first selects list 1 and then selects element 2 within that list.
- `listOfLists[0][-1]` first selects list 0 and then selects the last element within that list.

This concept generalizes to any level of nesting of lists. That is, one can have lists of lists of lists, and so on.

6.2 WHAT YOU ALREADY KNOW HOW TO DO WITH LISTS

Because lists are also sequences, many things that you learned to do with strings also work for lists. Let's take a look and refresh your memory.

Indexing and Slicing

Indexing and slicing work *exactly* the same with lists and strings. To remind yourself, look at Figure 6.1.

- Each element of the list has an associated index. The index values begin at 0 on the left and get larger, or they can begin with −1 on the right and get smaller.
- The index operator is a set of square brackets with a single integer or a slice. If it contains a single integer, that integer is the index of the element within the list.
- Accessing an element at an index that does not exist in the list is an error.
- The slice operation is the same as with strings. Within square brackets, you may have one or two colons (:). The number before the first colon is the start index, the number after the first colon is the end index, and the number after the second colon is the step.

```
myList = [1, 'a', 3.14159, True]
```

myList

1	'a'	3.14159	True	
0	1	2	3	Index Forward
−4	−3	−2	−1	Index Backward

```
myList[1]  →  'a'
myList[:3]  →  [1, 'a', 3.14159]
```

FIGURE 6.1 The structure of a list.

The defaults for all three are (in order): the beginning of the list, the end of the list, and a step of 1.

• A slice uses a half-open range, meaning that the end index is not included in the slice.

The following session shows these operations:

```
>>> myList = [1,'a',3.14159,True]
>>> myList[1]
'a'
>>> myList[-1]
True
>>> myList[:]
[1, 'a', 3.1415899999999999, True]
>>> myList[:3:2]
[1, 3.1415899999999999]
>>> myList[::2]
[1, 3.1415899999999999]
>>> myList[2:]
[3.1415899999999999, True]
>>> myList[:3]
[1, 'a', 3.1415899999999999]
>>> myList[10]
Traceback (most recent call last):
  File "<stdin>", line 1, in <module>
IndexError: list index out of range
>>> [1,2,3,4,5][2]   # ugly: first [] indicates a list, the second an index
3
>>>
```

There is nothing here that is new to you except the very last expression. It is a little ugly to have both a list creation operation and a index operation together, but if you can understand what it means, you are well on your way to understanding lists. We read the expression left to right, noting that the first [ ] is creating a list (see the commas) and then, having made the list, we are indexing into that list.

Operators

You can use both the addition (+) and multiplication (*) operators with list with results similar to strings. The addition operator takes two lists as operands and concatenates the two lists together, making a new list whose contents are the first list joined at its end to the beginning of the second list. The multiplication operator takes a list and an integer as operands and replicates the list the size of the integer number of times.

As with strings, the types are fixed for this operation. You can concatenate only two lists (not a list and a string, not a list and an integer, etc.). You can replicate a list only in combination with an integer. No other combination of types will do. This is again an example of both operators being overloaded. When the addition operator (+) has two string operands, it makes a string. When it has two list operands, it makes a list. Two different types, two different operations, one symbol.

Comparison works as it did with strings, so you can use the >,<,==,<=,>=, and != signs as operators between two list operands. As with strings, comparison begins by comparing the first element of each list. If the first elements are equal, the comparison process moves to the second element of each list. It continues in this way, comparing list corresponding elements, until the two elements are different. At that point, the comparison between the two different elements determines the result of the operation. If one list is equal to but shorter than the other list, the longer list is considered greater.

Finally, the *in* operator for membership testing works as it did in strings. The expression `'a' in ['a','b','c']` is a query, testing whether the first operand exists in the second operand. In this case it does, returning *True*.

The following session demonstrates these operations on lists:

```
>>> myList = [1,2,3]
>>> yourList = ['a','b','c']
>>> concatList = myList + yourList    # concat 2 lists , operand lists unchanged
>>> concatList
[1, 2, 3, 'a', 'b', 'c']
>>> myList
[1, 2, 3]
>>> yourList
['a', 'b', 'c']
>>> repList = myList * 3               # replicate myList, myList is unchanged
>>> repList
[1, 2, 3, 1, 2, 3, 1, 2, 3]
>>> myList
[1, 2, 3]
>>> [1,2,3,4] < [1,2,3,0]              # first difference at index 3, is 4< 0?
False
>>> [1,2,3,4] < [1,2,3,4,0]            # second list longer, always greater
True
>>> 1 in myList                        # membership operation in
True
>>> 1 in yourList
False
```

Because lists are containers that can hold anything, you will sometimes find that in comparing lists that you are comparing elements of different types—effectively comparing something such as `'a' > 1`. As we mentioned in Chapter 1, we do not have a natural concept of what that result should be. Python will return a Boolean result, but you should avoid such comparisons (Python 3.X will generate an error).

Finally, comparisons underly other operations that depend on order, such as the sorting, maximizing, and minimizing operations discussed later in this chapter.

Functions

There are a number of functions that work with any collection. In particular, you have seen the `len` function. With strings, the `len` function returns the number of characters in a string. With lists, the `len` function returns the number of elements, the number of comma-separated elements, in the list. Again, remember that a list can have as an element another list. That list counts as only one element. Thus the result of `len([1, [1,2,3],3])` is 3. The second element, the element at index 1, is another list `[1,2,3]`. Here are some functions that work on collections, including lists—one only works on lists:

len(C) Return the length of collection C, i.e., the number of elements.

min(C) Return the minimum element in collection C. If the argument is a list of lists, only the first element in each list is considered.

max(C) Return the maximum element in collection C. If the argument is a list of lists, only the first element in each list is considered.

sum(L) Return the sum of elements in list L. Elements must be numbers.

List Iteration

We can iterate through all the elements of a list, in order, using the *for* operator. This action is similar to what we saw for strings.

```
>>> myList = [1,3,4,8]
>>> for n in myList: # walk through list
        print n,      # the trailing comma prints on one line

1 3 4 8
>>>
```

In this example, the variable n is assigned the values 1, 3, 4, and 8, one at a time, and then the statement(s) in the suite are executed using that value for n. In this trivial example, the print statement will execute with each value of n and print it.

6.3 NEW THINGS IN LISTS

We've seen what's the same about lists and strings, so let's look at bit more at what's different.

Lists are Mutable

When we covered strings, we emphasized that they are immutable. In particular, we noted that you could not have a string and index operator on the left-hand side of the assignment statement. In other words, you could not change a character of the string at some index into a different character. Once created, the string cannot be changed.

Lists, on the other hand, are mutable, so they can be changed. You can make a list and then change the element at an index in the list to be something else. You can even change an entire *slice* of the list to be different! This is one of the powers, and one of the dangers, of lists. They are very flexible and, as a result, are very useful. However, you must take care in using them, because you can accidentally change a list value when you do not really want to.

Let's see how mutability works in a session:

```
>>> myList = [1, 2, 'a', 'z']
>>> myList[0]
1
>>> myList[0] = True       # change the first element
>>> myList
[True, 2, 'a', 'z']
>>> myList[-1] = 7         # change the last element
>>> myList
[True, 2, 'a', 7]
>>> myList[:2] = [27]      # change the first two elements to one element
>>> myList
[27, 'a', 7]
>>> myList[:] = [1,2,3,4]  # change the whole list
>>> myList
[1, 2, 3, 4]
>>> myList[2:] = 'abc'     # change the last two elements
>>> myList
[1, 2, 'a', 'b', 'c']
>>> myList[:2]=15          # only an iterable
Traceback (most recent call last):
  File "<stdin>", line 1, in <module>
TypeError: can only assign an iterable
```

Let's note a few things about this session:

- A list in combination with the index operator can occur on the left side of the assignment statement. This means that, after the assignment occurs, the value at that index is changed to be the value of the right-hand side of the assignment statement.
- As a result of *every* operation in that session, the list is changed. This means that every time we perform one of these operations, the changed list is carried forward to the line in the session. In other words, the list elements associated with myList at the end of the session are the cumulative result of all the operations that came before, in the order they were performed.
- Because the assignment operator does not return a value, we have to type the name of the variable associated with the list to see what was changed as a result. This is not new,

but it is useful to note that the change occurred and we were not "notified" in anyway what the change was until we actively looked.

- You can change not only a single element, but also an entire slice of the list (multiple elements) at a single time. The only caveat is that the values being added must be a collection. Each individual element of that collection is added as an element to the list. You cannot change a slice to an individual value. This makes some sense if you consider it for a moment. A slice is in fact a collection (a subsequence of the original), so to replace it implies that we need another collection. The collection replacing the slice can be bigger, smaller, or the same size.

List Methods

As we mentioned previously, a method is a function that works with a particular type of Python object. The string type had a large number of methods that could be applied to strings, but those methods can be applied *only* to strings. Lists have their own associated methods that work only with lists. The number of list methods is quite a bit smaller—only nine. They come in two different categories:

- Those that change the list.
- Those that do **not** change the list.

It is important that we keep those two categories straight, so we know whether our list is changed as a result of using the method.

Non-modifying methods
These methods do *not* change the list, but they return a value as a result of their processing. They are:

index(x) Return the index of the first element in the list whose value is equal to x. Python throws an error, if there is no such value in the list.

count(x) Return the number of times x appears in the list. Returns 0, if x does not appear in the list.

Methods That Modify the List
There are two things to note about these methods. First, the list that calls the method will be modified as a result of the call. Second, none but the `pop` methods returns a value. This fact may seem odd, but taking a closer look may help. In our previous experience, every string method returned a value: a new string object. Remember, though, that strings are immutable. They *had* to return a value so that we could capture the new string object created. These list methods do not need to return a list object for the change, as the list itself is changed.

append(x) Append an element to the *end* of the list. The length of the list is increased by 1. The element is appended exactly, so a collection is added as a single element.

pop() Remove the element at the end of the list and return that element. The list is shortened by one element. If an index is specified, a.pop(anIndex) removes the element at that position and returns that item.

extend(C) Requires a collection as an argument. The list is extended by adding each element of the argument collection to the end of the list.

insert(i, x) Insert an element at a given position. The first argument is the index of the element and it indicates the index *before* which to insert, so a.insert(1, 'a') inserts the 'a' into position 1, sliding all the rest of the list elements down one (the element at index 1 moves to index 2, the element at index 2 moves to index 3, and so on).

remove(x) Remove the first element from the list whose value is x. An error results, if there is no such item.

sort() Sort the elements of the list, in place. Contrast this list method with the function sorted that returns a sorted list while leaving the original unchanged. If sorting a list of lists, only the first element in each list is considered.

reverse() Reverse the elements of the list, in place.

Let's open a Python shell and demonstrate each method. Remember the *dot* format for methods, in which you provide a list object (an object of type list), followed by a dot (.), followed by the method name:

```
>>> aList = [1, 12, 5, 8]
>>> aList
[1, 12, 5, 8]
>>> aList.append(17)            # append to the end
>>> aList
[1, 12, 5, 8, 17]
>>> aList.append([40,50,60])    # append a list rather than simply one item
>>> aList
[20, 17, 12, 5, 4, 1, [40, 50, 60]]
>>> anotherList = [20, 2]
>>> aList.extend(anotherList)   # append anotherList's elements to end of aList
>>> aList
[1, 12, 5, 8, 17, 20, 2]
>>> aList.insert(3,'a')         # insert 'a' at position 3
>>> aList
[1, 12, 5, 'a', 8, 17, 20, 2]
>>> aList.remove(8)
>>> aList
[1, 12, 5, 'a', 17, 20, 2]
>>> aList.pop()                 # pop last element off aList, and return it
```

```
2
>>> aList
[1, 12, 5, 'a', 17, 20]
>>> aList.index(17)          # find index (remember counting starts at 0)
4
>>> aList.count(5)
1
>>> aList.sort()             # sort the list
>>> aList
[1, 5, 12, 17, 20, 'a']
>>> aList.reverse()          # reverse the list
>>> aList
['a', 20, 17, 12, 5, 1]
```

The append and insert are similar: append adds to the end of the list; insert puts an element into an existing list at a particular position that must be provided. If you append or insert a list as an argument, the list (including brackets) will be added as a single element to the list. One example in the previous session shows an entire list being appended. The entire contents is appended as a single element. If you want to add the *contents* of another collection to the end, use extend. The extend method adds the contents of its argument collection (a list, a string) to the end of the list. The remove method removes an element, but only removes the first one. Because there will be an error if you try to remove something that is not there, its use is usually preceded by a check for that element's existence using the *in* operator. Because of a similar error condition for index, an "if" check is usually used in conjunction with it. The naming of pop will certainly seem strange, but it turns out to be important because of its use with the classic "queue" and "stack" data structures. The sort method is something you will likely use frequently, but it works best with homogeneous lists—those containing all elements of the same type due to difficulties in the comparison of different types that we have discussed. The closely related sorted function is frequently a better choice, as it works with any collection, whereas the sort method works only with lists. However, sorted returns a list no matter the type of the argument.

PROGRAMMING TIP

Ordering: when dealing with functions, methods or operations depend on ordering (such as sort, sorted, reverse, min, max, <, >, ==) use only homogeneous elements, e.g., all numbers or all strings. Mixed elements do not have a natural ordering, so results may seem odd.

Check Yourself: Basic Lists Check

1. Answer the following questions using the example program.

```
strLst = ['hi','mom','dad']
numLst = [1,57,15]

numLst[-1] = 25
print strLst + numLst             # Line 1
print [strLst[0],numLst[-1]]      # Line 2
print strLst.append(numLst)       # Line 3
print strLst                      # Line 4
print numLst.sort()               # Line 5
print numLst                      # Line 6
print numLst.extend([127,256])    # Line 7
print numLst                      # Line 8
print numLst.pop()                # Line 9
print numLst                      # Line 10
```

(a) What output is produced by Line 1 when the program is executed?
(b) What output is produced by Line 2 when the program is executed?
(c) What output is produced by Line 3 when the program is executed?
(d) What output is produced by Line 4 when the program is executed?
(e) What output is produced by Line 5 when the program is executed?
(f) What output is produced by Line 6 when the program is executed?
(g) What output is produced by Line 7 when the program is executed?
(h) What output is produced by Line 8 when the program is executed?
(i) What output is produced by Line 9 when the program is executed?
(j) What output is produced by Line 10 when the program is executed?

6.4 OLD AND NEW FRIENDS: RANGE, SPLIT, AND OTHER FUNCTIONS AND METHODS

Range, Split, and Multiple Assignment

We have used both the *range* function and the string method split, but we have done so without talking about how they utilize lists. Both of these operations return lists. We have avoided talking about this characteristic by using either iteration or multiple assignment from the returned lists, but now that we know about lists, you can see how these operations work.

When a string calls `split`, it uses the argument of the method (or any whitespace if no argument is provided) to create a list of the elements of the string "split" by the argument. When *range* is invoked, it creates a list of the integers indicated in the argument. If we *know* the number of elements in a list (as we did in the name reversal example in Section 4.6), we can assign every element of a list to a variable using multiple assignment.

The following session shows some of this behavior:

```
>>> result = 'this is a test'.split()              # split on whitespace
>>> result
['this', 'is', 'a', 'test']
>>> result = 'field1,field2,field3,field4'.split(',') # split on commas
>>> result
['field1', 'field2', 'field3', 'field4']
>>> rangeList = range(-5,5)                         # generate a range
>>> rangeList
[-5, -4, -3, -2, -1, 0, 1, 2, 3, 4]
>>> element1,element2,element3=[1,2,3] # multiple assignment from a list
>>> element1
1
>>> element2
2
>>> element3
3
# multiple assignment from returned list
>>> field1,field2,field3 = 'Python is great'.split()
>>> field1
'Python'
>>> field2
'is'
>>> field3
'great'
```

List to String and Back Again, Using `join`

It is sometimes very helpful to move back and forth between a list and a string. You'll often need to take a string apart with a `split`, processing the elements of the split, then putting the result back together again. One useful method for this is the string `join` method. The `join` method takes a list of strings as an argument and places each of those elements into a new string using the calling object as the separator character. For example, the call `':'.join(['a','b','c'])` concatenates all the elements of the list together using a colon (:) as a separator, generating the string `'a:b:c'`.

The following session takes a string, splits it on whitespace, reverses each string element, then recreates the string of reversed elements.

```
>>> myStr = 'This is a test'
>>> strElements = myStr.split()              # split on whitespace
>>> strElements
['This', 'is', 'a', 'test']
>>> reversedElements = []
>>> for element in strElements:              # for each element
...     reversedElements.append(element[::-1]) # reverse string and append
...
>>> reversedElements
['sihT', 'si', 'a', 'tset']
>>> newStr = ' '.join(reversedElements)  # join using blank between elements
>>> newStr
'sihT si a tset'                         # each substring reversed
>>>
```

When we do the final join, we use a space (a two quotes with a space between) to join the elements back together.

The Sorted Function

Unfortunately, the sort method works only with lists. What if we want to sort a string? We could:

- Turn a string into a list of individual characters using the *list* constructor.
- Sort the list.
- Use the join method of strings to put the string back together.

The sorted function (not a method, a function) will sort any collection, doing in one step what was done in the first two steps earlier.

The following session demonstrates the sorted function:

```
>>> myLst = [27,56,4,18]
>>> sorted(myLst)
[4, 18, 27, 56]
>>> myStr = 'Hi mom'
>>> sorted(myStr)
[' ', 'H', 'i', 'm', 'm', 'o']
>>>
```

Check Yourself: Lists and Strings Check

1. Answer the following questions using this program.

```
myList = [1.6, 2.7, 3.8, 4.9]
newList = []
aList = []

for val in myList:
    temp = str(val)
    aList.append(temp.split('.'))

for val in aList:
    newList.append(int(val[0]))

myStr = ':'.join(val)

print myList          # Line 1
print aList           # Line 2
print newList         # Line 3
print val             # Line 4
print myStr           # Line 5
```

(a) What output is produced by Line 1 when the program is executed?
(b) What output is produced by Line 2 when the program is executed?
(c) What output is produced by Line 3 when the program is executed?
(d) What output is produced by Line 4 when the program is executed?
(e) What output is produced by Line 5 when the program is executed?

6.5 WORKING WITH SOME EXAMPLES

You know a lot about lists now, so let's see if you can use them to solve a few problems.

Anagrams

An anagram is a word or phrase formed by rearranging the letters of another. For example, transform *cinema* into a different English word such as *iceman*. In this example, we will design a program that tests two words to check whether they are anagrams. How to do this? Our approach is to find some common representation that only two anagram words would share. One canonical representation would be the sorted letters of a word. Consider our example. If we take the two anagrams, *cinema* and *iceman*, and sort the letters of each word, they both form the string *aceimn*. Think about what this means. The sorted list is just one other rearrangement of the letters used to form *cinema* and *iceman* where the two words themselves are two other arrangements. Sorting the letters gives us a common representation that two anagrams words would share.

Here are the main steps for our algorithm:

1. input the two words
2. sort the words
3. compare the sorted words

The first step is "input the two words," so let's prompt the user for two space-separated words. The *raw_input* command will return the two words in one string, e.g., '*cinema iceman*'. Therefore, we use split to obtain the individual words in a list. Once we have a list of words, we need to extract the two words. We can do that extraction using indexing—remembering that indexing starts at zero. Let's try it out in a Python shell:

```
>>> twoWords = raw_input("Input two space-separated words: ")
Input two words: cinema iceman
>>> twoWords                    # check the string that was input
'cinema iceman'
>>> twoWords.split()            # split the string into a list of words
['cinema', 'iceman']
>>> twoWordsList = twoWords.split() # give the list a name
>>> twoWordsList
['cinema', 'iceman']
>>> word1 = twoWordsList[0] # extract first word (indexing starts at 0)
>>> word2 = twoWordsList[1]
>>> word1                       # check on values of words
'cinema'
>>> word2
'iceman'
>>>
```

Now that we have two words, word1 and word2, we can move on to sort the words. We use the sorted function to make a list of the characters sorted in order. In our example, word1, which is '*cinema*' gets sorted into ['a', 'c', 'e', 'i', 'm', 'n'].

```
>>> word1
'cinema'
>>> word2
'iceman'
>>> word1_sorted = sorted(word1) # sorted returns a sorted list
>>> word2_sorted = sorted(word2)
```

```
>>> word1_sorted
['a', 'c', 'e', 'i', 'm', 'n']
>>> word2_sorted
['a', 'c', 'e', 'i', 'm', 'n']
```

The words are sorted; now we need to check to see whether they are identical.

```
>>> if word1_sorted == word2_sorted:
        print "The words are anagrams."
    else:
        print "The words are not anagrams."

The words are anagrams.
>>>
```

We've developed our ideas within the Python shell. Let's put them together into a program. First, let's create a function that checks if two words are anagrams, returning *True* if they are anagrams and *False* if not. Within that function, we will sort the words and then compare the sorted lists of characters. See Code Listing 6.1.

Code Listing 6.1

```
   def areAnagrams(word1, word2):
       """Return true, if words are anagrams."""
       #2. Sort the words.
       word1_sorted = sorted(word1)        # sorted returns a sorted list
 5     word2_sorted = sorted(word2)

       #3. Check that the sorted words are identical.
       if word1_sorted == word2_sorted:  # compare sorted lists
           return True
10     else:
           return False
```

```
>>> ============================ RESTART ================================
>>>
>>> areAnagrams('cinema','iceman')
True
>>> areAnagrams('soap','soup')
False
```

With the `areAnagrams` function in hand, we can take two words as input, send them to the function, and then print an appropriate message based on whether the function returns *True* or *False*. See Code Listing 6.2.

Code Listing 6.2

```
# Anagram test

def areAnagrams(word1, word2):
    """Return true, if words are anagrams."""
    #2. Sort the words.
    word1_sorted = sorted(word1)        # sorted returns a sorted list
    word2_sorted = sorted(word2)

    #3. Check that the sorted words are identical.
    if word1_sorted == word2_sorted:   # compare sorted lists
        return True
    else:
        return False

print "Anagram Test"

# 1. Input two words.
twoWords = raw_input("Enter two words: ")
twoWordList = twoWords.split()      # split the input string into a list of words
word1 = twoWordList[0]              # extract first word
word2 = twoWordList[1]              # extract second word

if areAnagrams(word1, word2):       # function returned True or False
    print "The words are anagrams."
else:
    print "The words are not anagrams."
```

```
>>>
Anagram Test
Enter two words: cinema iceman
The words are anagrams.
```

With a working program in hand, we should refactor it. That is, we should examine it to see if we can improve it. Two modifications are worth considering simply to illustrate alternatives.

First, the **return** statement in the function can simply be to return the value of the comparison. The comparison will have a value of *True* or *False*, so let's simply return that. That is, instead of the **if** statement in the function, use the following:

```
return word1_sorted == word2_sorted
```

A second alternative code sequence is to use multiple assignment when we split `twoWords` into `word1` and `word2`. By using multiple assignment, we can skip the `twoWordList` entirely:

```
word1, word2 = twoWords.split()
```

Let's incorporate those alternatives into our code. The result (Code Listing 6.3) is more terse, and possibly more readable. See Code Listing 6.3.

Code Listing 6.3

```
# Anagram test

def areAnagrams(word1, word2):
    """Return true, if words are anagrams."""
    #2. Sort the words.
    word1_sorted = sorted(word1)      # sorted returns a sorted list
    word2_sorted = sorted(word2)

    #3. Check that the sorted words are identical.
    return word1_sorted == word2_sorted:

print "Anagram Test"

# 1. Input two words.
twoWords = raw_input("Enter two words: ")
word1,word2 = twoWords.split()   # split the input string into a list of words

if areAnagrams(word1, word2):   # function returned True or False
    print "The words are anagrams."
else:
    print "The words are not anagrams."
```

Example: File Analysis

Programmers are often required to take a file of text and analyze it in various ways. Let's use our knowledge of lists to analyze a file. Specifically, we will:

- Analyze a file's length, in words.
- Track how many unique words were in the file.

We will use as sample input President Abraham Lincoln's Gettysburg Address (1863). This address is famous for many reasons, but in particular, it is very short. Let's use Python to do some simple analysis of the address.

Length of Gettysburg Address

You have seen the `len` function that returns the length of a list, so let's put all the words of the address into a list and find the length. A good way to do that is to begin with an empty list and add words one at a time to the list using the `append` method. We downloaded the address from the Internet, put it in a file we named "gettysburg.txt," and put that file in the same folder (directory) as our program. We'll begin by opening the file and then reading the file line by line. Each line gets read as one long string, so we will use the `split` method to extract words from the string and put them in a list. We can then extend our speech list with each line's list (using `extend`).

Our algorithm:

1. open file for reading
2. initialize speech list to be empty
3. for each line in the file:
   (a) extract words from the line into a list
   (b) add that list of words onto the speech list
4. find the length of the speech list

We observe that steps 2 and 3 work nicely in a function to create a list of words from the speech. Let's call that function `makeWordList`, and incorporate it into a program that opens a file, calls our function, and then prints the result. See Code Listing 6.4.

Code Listing 6.4

```python
# gettysburg address analysis
# count words, unique words, common words

def makeWordList(gFile):
    """Create a list of words from the file."""
    speech = []         # 2. list of speech words: initialized to be empty

    for lineString in gFile:             # 3. read file line by line
        lineList= lineString.split()     # 3a. split each line to a list of words
        speech.extend(lineList)          # 3b. add words to list of speech words
    return speech

###############################

gFile = open("gettysburg.txt", "rU")     # 1. open file for reading
speech = makeWordList(gFile)

# 4. print the speech and its lengths
print speech
print "Length: ", len(speech)
```

```
['Four', 'score', 'and', 'seven', 'years', 'ago', 'our', 'fathers',
'brought', 'forth', 'on', 'this', 'continent', 'a', 'new', 'nation,'
# many lines deleted
'freedom', '--', 'and', 'that', 'government', 'of', 'the', 'people,', 'by',
'the', 'people,', 'for', 'the', 'people,', 'shall', 'not', 'perish', 'from',
'the', 'earth.']
Length:  278
```

The output is quite long, so in the session, we cut out the middle, so you can see what the speech list looks like.

In the speech list we see some nonwords: '--' in particular. We should eliminate that non-word before adding to the speech list. However, that means that we need to examine words one at a time before adding them to the speech list. Rather than using extend to add to the speech list, lets walk through the lineList one word at a time and use append to add words one at a time to the speech list. The construct **for** word **in** lineList: takes words one at a time from lineList and assigns them to word. Then we can append each word to the speech list one at a time. Before appending a word, we can check whether it is '--'. If not, append it. Code Listing 6.5 shows the program with the modified function:

Code Listing 6.5

```python
# gettysburg address analysis
# count words, unique words, common words

def makeWordList(gFile):
    """Create a list of words from the file."""
    speech = []           # list of speech words: initialized to be empty

    for lineString in gFile:            # read file line by line
        lineList = lineString.split()   # split each line into a list of words
        for word in lineList:           # get words one at a time from list
            if word != "--":            # if the word is not "--"
                speech.append(word)     # add the word to the speech list
    return speech

################################

gFile = open("gettysburg.txt", "rU")
speech = makeWordList(gFile)

# print the speech and its lengths
```

```
print speech
print "Speech Length: ", len(speech)
```

```
['Four', 'score', 'and', 'seven', 'years', 'ago', 'our', 'fathers',
'brought', 'forth', 'on', 'this', 'continent', 'a', 'new', 'nation,',
# many lines deleted
'freedom', 'and', 'that', 'government', 'of', 'the', 'people,', 'by',
'the', 'people,', 'for', 'the', 'people,', 'shall', 'not', 'perish', 'from',
'the', 'earth.']
Length:  271
```

Now when we examine the output (again with many lines deleted), we see that the `'--'` non-word is gone, and we have a more accurate count: 271 words.

Unique Words in Gettysburg Address

The address is short, which leads to the question: how many unique words are in it? How might we determine that? Let's make a list of unique words and then find the length of that list. We can start with an empty list of unique words (notice the pattern here!). We will walk through the `speech` list one word at a time, and before we add a word to the unique list, we check whether it is already in the unique list using the *in* operator. If it is not there, we add it. Here is an algorithm:

1. initialize unique list to empty
2. for each word in the speech
   (a) if word is not already in unique list,
   (b) add word to unique list

Let's make a function for that algorithm and name it `makeUnique`. See Code Listing 6.6.

Code Listing 6.6

```
def makeUnique(speech):
    """Create a list of unique words."""
    unique = []    # list of unique words: initialized to be empty

    for word in speech:          # get words one at a time from speech
        if word not in unique:   # if word is not already in unique list,
            unique.append(word)  # add word to unique list

    return unique
```

There are two slight adjustments we need to make:

- capitalized words cause duplicates, e.g., "we" and "We";
- punctuation causes duplicates, e.g., "here.", "here,", and "here".

We previously described the string method `strip`, which strips specified characters from the beginning and end of strings, as well as the `lower` method, which converts a string to lower case. The appropriate place for these adjustments are in the `makeWordList` function, where we are already doing some filtering. By filtering words through those functions, we reduce the unique count from 153 to an accurate 138. Here is the program with both functions. We removed printing of the original speech, and added printing of the list of unique words. See Code Listing 6.7.

Code Listing 6.7

```python
# gettysburg address analysis
# count words, unique words, common words

def makeWordList(gFile):
    """Create a list of words from the file."""
    speech = []          # list of speech words: initialized to be empty

    for lineString in gFile:                # read file line by line
        lineList = lineString.split()       # split each line into a list of words
        for word in lineList:               # get words one at a time from list
            word = word.lower()             # make words lower case
            word = word.strip('.,')         # strip off commas and periods
            if word != "--":                # if the word is not "--"
                speech.append(word)         # add the word to the speech list
    return speech

def makeUnique(speech):
    """Create a list of unique words."""
    unique = []   # list of unique words: initialized to be empty

    for word in speech:             # get words one at a time from speech
        if word not in unique:      # if word is not already in unique list,
            unique.append(word)     # add word to unique list

    return unique

###############################

gFile = open("gettysburg.txt", "rU")
```

```
    # 1. put words into a list
    speech = makeWordList(gFile)

    # print the speech length
35  print "Speech Length: ", len(speech)

    # 2. make a list of unique words in speech
    unique = makeUnique(speech)
    print unique
40  print "Unique Length: ", len(unique)
```

```
Speech Length:  271
['four', 'score', 'and', 'seven', 'years', 'ago', 'our', 'fathers',
# many lines deleted
'highly', 'resolve', 'shall', 'died', 'vain', 'under', 'god', 'birth',
'freedom', 'government', 'people', 'by', 'perish', 'earth']
Unique Length:  138
```

As before, we removed some of the output to save space. Now we have an accurate count of the length of the speech (271 words) and the unique words in the speech (138 unique words).

What an accomplishment to create such a noteworthy speech from only 138 different words!

6.6 MUTABLE OBJECTS AND REFERENCES

Lists are mutable—they can be changed. We briefly considered mutability earlier, but it is worth closer examination. To understand what mutable means in the context of Python, we need to review how variables and their values are structured. In Chapter 1 we discussed how variables work in Python. Let's review a few facts:

- A variable name comes into existence when it is associated with a value, e.g., $x = 5$.
- A variable name has no specific type associated with it.
- Once made, a variable is associated with a particular Python object (and that object has a type).
- Python maintains a namespace to associate variable names with objects.

Computer scientists often refer to this association as a *reference*. That is, a variable name "references" an object. Programming languages handle referencing in different ways. In Python, references are maintained in the namespace. A namespace maintains the association or reference between a variable name and an object.

```
myInt = 27
yourInt = myInt
```

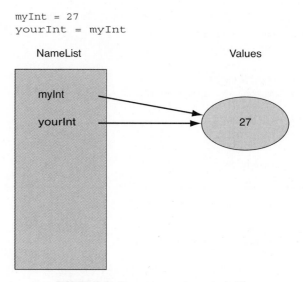

FIGURE 6.2 Namespace snapshot #1.

We will diagram some examples to review those concepts and then examine mutability in detail. The code in Figure 6.2 creates an initial set of associations.

Let's modify one of the variables, yourInt. Notice how the association changes. Figure 6.3 shows the effect.

```
myInt = 27
yourInt = myInt
yourInt = yourInt + 5
```

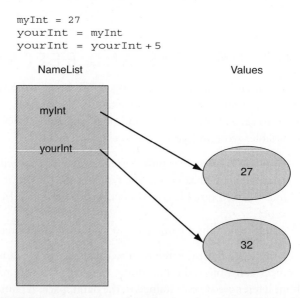

FIGURE 6.3 Modification of a reference to an immutable object.

Every operation on an immutable object creates a reference to a new object as shown in Figure 6.3. Let's now consider how mutable objects are handled differently. We'll begin with an initial association as shown in Figure 6.4.

```
list1 = [1,2,3]
list2 = list1
```

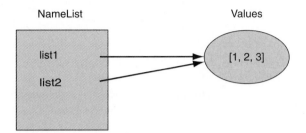

FIGURE 6.4 Namespace snapshot after assigning mutable objects.

When two names reference the same mutable object, there are some interesting consequences. With mutable objects we introduce the possibility of modifying the existing object (because they are mutable!). These consequences are easy to grasp as long as you remember that the same object is being referenced. Let's look at it in a Python session:

```
>>> list1 = [1,2,3]
>>> list1
[1, 2, 3]
>>> list2 = list1
>>> list2            # list2 is the same list as list1
[1, 2, 3]
>>> list1 is list2   # both names reference the same object? True.
True
>>> list1.append(27) # append to list1
>>> list1
[1, 2, 3, 27]
>>> list2            # the append to list1 also changed list2
[1, 2, 3, 27]
```

Changes made to `list1` affect `list2`! The reason for this behavior is reflected in Figure 6.5—both names reference the same object. In the previous session, the *is* operator is *True*, if the names reference the same object. Because these are mutable objects, Python does not maintain copies unless you ask it to. It "saves space" by reusing the existing object.

If you want to copy a list, there is the copy slice ([:]) (from beginning to end) that we introduced with strings in Section 4.1. We illustrate its use in lists in the following session. The copy slice makes a copy of the list. Explicitly, making a copy means that Python creates

```
list1 = [1,2,3]
list2 = list1
list1.append(27)
```

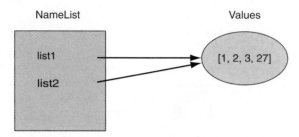

FIGURE 6.5 Modification of shared, mutable objects.

a new copy of the object, so modifying one no longer affects the other. Again, the *is* operator shows that the names do not reference the same object: result is *False*.

```
>>> list1 = [1,2,3]
>>> list1
[1, 2, 3]
>>> list2 = list1[:]    # explicitly make a distinct copy
>>> list1 is list2      # Both names reference same object? False.
False
>>> list2
[1, 2, 3]
>>> list1.append(27)    # append now only modifies list1
>>> list1
[1, 2, 3, 27]
>>> list2               # list2 is unchanged
[1, 2, 3]
```

Figure 6.6 illustrates the creation of a distinct copy of a mutable object using slicing. What happens when you do the following?

```
>>> list1 = [1,2,3]
>>> list1.append(list1)
>>> list1
[1, 2, 3, [...]]
```

When a list has itself appended as an element, an infinite regress occurs. Because the list is mutable, a reference to itself is placed at the end of the list. This means that the list refers to itself repeatedly, infinitely, as shown. Python notes this infinite regression with "..." as shown in Figure 6.7.

```
list1 = [1,2,3]
list2 = list1[:]  #explicitly make a distinct copy
list1.append(27)
```

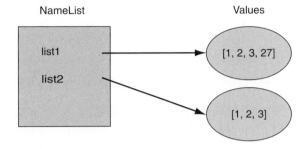

FIGURE 6.6 Making a distinct copy of a mutable object.

```
list1 = [1,2,3]
list1.append(list1)
```

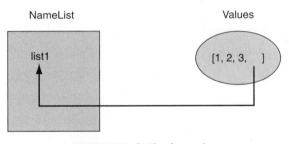

FIGURE 6.7 Self referencing.

Shallow vs. Deep Copy

What does it mean to make a copy? In Python, copying simply adds a new name to an object. To see how this works, consider this session:

```
>>> list1 = [1,2,3]
>>> list2 = [5,6,7]
>>> list1.append(list2)
>>> list1              # append stuck list2 into list1 as expected
[1, 2, 3, [5, 6, 7]]
>>> list3 = list2      # we just gave the object another name
>>> list3              # list3 looks like list2: different names for same object
[5, 6, 7]
>>> list2 is list3     # Both names reference same object? True.
```

```
True
>>> list3[2] = 88
>>> list3            # as expected: we changed the item at index 2 to 88
[5, 6, 88]
>>> list2            # list2 changed: list3 and list2 name the same object
[5, 6, 88]
>>> list1            # whoa! what happened here? we didn't touch list1!
[1, 2, 3, [5, 6, 88]]
```

To aid in understanding what is going on let's draw some pictures. Figure 6.8 shows the layout after we create `list1` and `list2`.

Figure 6.9 illustrates the namespace after the `list1.append(list2)` call. Notice how `list1` now has a reference to the object that `list2` named. Therefore, if we change

```
list1 = [1,2,3]
list2 = [5,6,7]
```

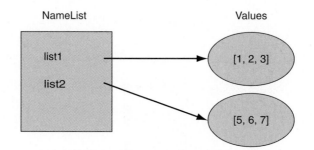

FIGURE 6.8 Simple lists before append.

```
list1 = [1,2,3]
list2 = [5,6,7]
list1.append(list2)
```

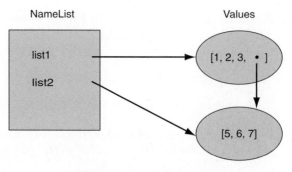

FIGURE 6.9 Lists after append.

list2, we expect to see the change reflected in list1. To make it more interesting, we introduce list3 = list2 so that list3 is another name for the object that list2 names. Finally, we change list3, which by reference also changes list2 and list1.

Figure 6.10 shows the effect of list3[2] = 88.

```
list1 = [1,2,3]
list2 = [5,6,7]
list1.append(list2)
list3 = list2
list3[2] = 88
```

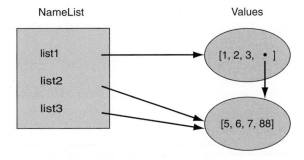

FIGURE 6.10 Final state of copying example.

A final example illustrates this copying concept further. In this Python session we show how list addition works. In the first case, we add the lists themselves; in the second case, we encapsulate the lists before adding them. The first addition creates a new list that contains the elements of list1 and list2. The second addition combines the references to list1 and list2. The modification of list1 using list1[0] = 100 has an impact only on the second addition, because it has references to the original list1.

```
>>> list1 = [1,2,3]
>>> list2 = ['a','b','c']
>>> listJoin1 = list1 + list2        # one new list from list1 and list2
>>> listJoin1
[1, 2, 3, 'a', 'b', 'c']
>>> listJoin2 = [list1] + [list2]    # a list of lists
>>> listJoin2
[[1, 2, 3], ['a', 'b', 'c']]
>>> list1[0] = 100                   # modify list1
>>> listJoin1
[1, 2, 3, 'a', 'b', 'c']             # unchanged
>>> listJoin2
[[100, 2, 3], ['a', 'b', 'c']]       # list of lists changes
```

The case in which only the references, not the objects themselves, are copied is called a *shallow copy*. Copying the contents rather than simply the reference is called a *deep copy*. There is a copy module that has a deepcopy function, forcing a deep copy if desired.

Mutable versus Immutable

It is worth taking a moment to revisit the consequences of working with mutable objects. When a variable references an immutable object, any operation that uses that variable (concatenation, replace, strip, and so on) creates a new object; it does not change the referenced object. In contrast, a variable that references a mutable object can either create a new object *or* change the referenced object itself, depending upon the operation. For example, with L = [1,2,3], L = L + [9] and L.append(9) both result in the list [1,2,3,9]. However, the former creates a new object; the latter does not.

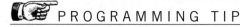

PROGRAMMING TIP

Operations on variables which reference mutable objects may change the object itself or create a new object. Operations on variables which reference immutable objects generate new objects.

Check Yourself: Mutable List Check

1. Show the output for the following program. To make it easier, draw a diagram similar to the ones above to keep straight the connections between the three lists.

```
strLst = ['hi','mom','dad',['grandma','grandpa']]
newLst = strLst
copyLst = strLst[:]

strLst[0] = 'bye'
newLst[1] = 'mother'
copyLst[2] = 'father'
copyLst[-1][0] = 'nanna'

print strLst       # Line 1
print newLst       # Line 2
print copyLst      # Line 3
```

(a) What output is produced by Line 1 when the program is executed?
(b) What output is produced by Line 2 when the program is executed?
(c) What output is produced by Line 3 when the program is executed?

6.7 TUPLES

Tuples are essentially immutable lists. A tuple shares all the characteristics of a list except those that violate immutability. That is, any function or method that can change a list is not available for tuples.

Because it is immutable, a tuple has some similarity to a string, except that it can contain elements of any type. Tuples are delimited by parentheses, and elements are separated by commas. To make a tuple, use this syntax:

```
myTuple = (1,2,3)
```

It is important to note that the *comma*, not the parentheses, is the operator that creates the tuple. The expression 1,2,3, with no parentheses, yields the tuple (1,2,3). To create a single-element tuple one, *cannot* create it with the expression (1), which simply yields 1 in the interpreter. The expression (1,) *does* create a single-element tuple. The confusion is due to the overloaded nature of the parentheses. In most situations, it indicates grouping and Python interprets it as such. The inclusion of the comma indicates that the parentheses are being used as part of tuple creation, not grouping. The bottom line is that commas are the operators that make a tuple. The following session emphasizes these facts:

```
>>> 10,12          # Python creats a tuple
(10, 12)
>>> x,y = 2,3      # a tuple on each side with items assigned by position
>>> x
2
>>> y
3
>>> x,y
(2, 3)
>>> tup = x,y      # assigning a tuple: equivalent to tup = (x,y)
>>> tup
(2, 3)
>>> (1)            # not a tuple, a grouping
1
>>> (1,)           # comma makes it a tuple
(1,)
```

The operations familiar from other sequences (lists and strings) are available, except, of course, those list operators which violate immutability.

- Operators like + (concatenate) and * (repeat) work as before.
- Slicing also works as before.
- Membership (*in*) and *for* iteration also work on tuples.
- Length (len), minimum (min), and maximum (max) work the same.

However, none of the operations that change lists are available for tuples. For example, append, extend, insert, remove, pop, reverse, and sort do not work on tuples. Here is a session demonstrating tuples:

```
>>> myTuple = (1,2,3,4,5)      # parentheses!
>>> myTuple
(1, 2, 3, 4, 5)
>>> myTuple + myTuple          # concatenation (addition)
(1, 2, 3, 4, 5, 1, 2, 3, 4, 5)
>>> myTuple * 3                # multiplication
(1, 2, 3, 4, 5, 1, 2, 3, 4, 5, 1, 2, 3, 4, 5)
>>> myTuple[1]                 # indexing
2
>>> myTuple[:3]                # slicing
(1, 2, 3)
>>> myTuple[1:3]
(2, 3)
>>> myTuple[-1]
5
>>> 2 in myTuple               # membership (in)
True
>>> 10 in myTuple
False
>>> for x in myTuple:          # for
        print x,

1 2 3 4 5
>>> len(myTuple)               # length
5
>>> min(myTuple)               # min and max
1
>>> max(myTuple)
5
```

Tuples from Lists

Converting between tuples and lists is common, and the respective constructors provide the mechanism for conversion. In the following session, we convert a list to a tuple and then illustrate how the sort method that is allowable for mutable objects such as list does not work for a tuple. Remember that sort changes the object itself, so it is allowed only for mutable objects such as a list. However, the function sorted can sort an immutable object, because it returns a sorted object rather than changing the object itself. What is the type of the object returned from sorted? It is a list.

Here is a session that illustrates these points:

```
>>> list1 = [6,1,3,4]
>>> tuple1 = tuple(list1)    # convert from list to tuple
>>> tuple1
(6, 1, 3, 4)                 # note the parentheses: indicates a tuple
>>> tuple1.sort()            # cannot sort an immutable object

Traceback (most recent call last):
  File "<pyshell#37>", line 1, in <module>
    tuple1.sort()
AttributeError: 'tuple' object has no attribute 'sort'
>>> something = sorted(tuple1)   # but sorted accepts an immutable object
>>> type(something)              # sorted returns a list
<type 'list'>
>>> something                    # note the square brackets: indicates a list
[1, 3, 4, 6]
>>> list2 = list(tuple1)     # converting a tuple to a list
>>> list2
[6, 1, 3, 4]
>>>
```

Why Tuples?

The question is, why have an immutable list, a tuple, as a separate type? The reason is that an immutable list provides a data structure with some integrity and some persistence. It is not possible to accidentally change a tuple.

Also, because tuples are immutable, they can be used in a few places where mutable objects are not allowed. When you later learn about dictionaries you will see that dictionary keys must be immutable, so a tuple can be a key, but a list cannot.

6.8 LISTS: THE DATA STRUCTURE

Python comes with a number of built-in data structures. So far we have looked at *strings*, *lists* and *tuples*.

What is a data structure? In Section 1.6, we covered the type of an object and what that entailed. We observed that a type described what was stored in an object of that type and the operations we can perform on an object of that type. More generally, we consider the concept of a *data structure*. A data structure is related to a data type, in that a data type is the realization (implementation) of a data structure in a program. Thus, a data structure is a more abstract concept, indicating what a programmer would like to be done as opposed to how the programmer actually implements the concept in code (the data type).

In particular, a data structure focuses on the *organization of data* and the operations that can act on the data—often with an emphasis on *efficiency*. For example, a Google search potentially examines the content of the whole Internet. How must one organize this vast amount of data so that searches can be both accurate and fast? Part of the answer is in how the data is organized and manipulated, i.e., what data structures are used. The company founders, Larry Page and Sergey Brin, became very rich by coming up with a more efficient data structure and algorithm for Internet data search (they named it MapReduce).

When we speak of efficiency we could mean one of a few things:

1. **Efficient with respect to an *algorithm*.** Data structures are tightly linked with the algorithms that work on them. Thus, it might be efficient to perform some operation (sorting, storing, inserting) on a particular organization of the data. However, making one operation efficient might make another operation inefficient on the same data structure.
2. **Efficient with respect to *space*.** One way to organize the data is to be efficient in memory usage. If the data being stored is very large (say, all the text in the Library of Congress), storage efficiency might be very important. Again, how data gets stored might well affect what we can efficiently do with the data.
3. **Efficient with respect to *time*.** Another important consideration is time. If you are controlling flaps on an airplane, then determining proper settings quickly is crucial. Many variables come to play in that decision and data organization (the data structure) is critical.

Not surprisingly, those three meanings of efficiency are not necessarily independent. For example, Google's data organization is tightly tied to their algorithm, storage is critical because of the immense amount of data, and time is important because a slow search is not useful to people. Entire courses are devoted to the theory of data structures and the algorithms that work well with them.

We have seen that algorithms can be described abstractly, and the same is true for data structures. The abstract data structure is an abstraction of the data organization and that organization's implications towards efficiency, however defined. When we define a data structure, we will also define a set of operations that can be done on the data structure. Various trade-offs will result: some algorithms may run slowly, certain data examples will occupy too much space, and so on. We design the data structure to solve the main problems at hand. For example, Google provides a search operation to search the Internet, but it would be silly to provide a print operation that printed the Internet.

Example Data Structure

You have already seen three Python data types: strings, lists, and tuples. Let's consider a string as a data structure. We first learned that a string was a sequence of characters. A sequence is a way of organizing data—characters, in the case of strings; anything, in the case of lists. One of the properties of a sequence is that it has an order. Other data structures do not share such a property; for example, a *set* is a data structure that is an unordered collection of items (covered in Chapter 8). We chose a sequence for strings because the order of characters is important. It wouldn't be useful if the characters were kept in some arbitrary order.

As a data structure, we saw that strings had a set of operations. For example, there was a long list of associated methods and some operators as well as the ability to do slicing.

As an abstraction, there are implementation details that are hidden from you, the user. We conceive of the string as a sequence, but don't really know (or care) about its implementation details, e.g., how it is stored and manipulated in memory. We manipulate a string using the methods and operations provided. The details don't matter as long as the methods and operators work correctly (and efficiently).

Like most data structures, a string data structure does some things efficiently and other things inefficiently (or not at all).

What does a string do efficiently?

- Holds a sequence of characters efficiently in memory
- Maintains information about the size of the string
- Allows quick access to any individual element

What does a string *not* do efficiently (or not do at all)?

- Cannot modify a string element: strings are immutable, so you must make a copy to change anything
- Cannot efficiently manipulate elements for tasks like:
  - Find the largest element (have to look at all the elements)
  - Store elements other than characters
  - Other things (you will see shortly)

Other Example Data Structures

We can imagine some other data structures that might be handy to have around. In fact, the possibilities are endless. Here is a sampling:

- A *queue* is a sequence of data elements that "stand in a line," in which the data can only be removed from the front of the line and new elements can only be added to the back of the line (as in the British English: "queue up for the bus"). Elements enter the queue and wait, typically in order, until they come to the front of the queue for removal. Queues are useful for modeling how cars move through intersections or data flows through nodes on the Internet. Associated operations check to see if the queue is empty, add to the back, and remove from the front.
- A *dictionary* data structure, is one in which we can look up a key (like a word in the dictionary) and access some value (like the definition of the word). A phone book could

be implemented as a dictionary. Operations would include: look up a value associated with key, add key-value pairs, remove key-value pairs, etc.

- A *set* of unordered elements, which would allow us to access and modify individual elements. Operations would include: insertion, removal, union, intersection, etc.
- A *matrix* of numbers is a common mathematical data structure that is extensively used in science and engineering. Associated operations would include: multiplication, find determinant, invert, transpose, etc.

Some data structures are built into languages (Python has dictionaries and sets); others must be created by the programmer (Python does not have built-in matrix or queue data structures, though they are available in modules). Ideally, it will be good to define our own data structures to solve special problems. You will learn later how to combine the data structures provided by Python into structures tailored to our needs.

6.9 ALGORITHM EXAMPLE: U.S. EPA AUTOMOBILE MILEAGE DATA

The U.S. Environmental Protection Agency (EPA) gathers data on cars and trucks. It is best known for its mileage data, but they also gather information on car type (van, pickup, sports car, etc.), engine type, luggage capacity, seating, etc. This data is available online[1] in CSV-format (CSV = comma-separated values). We downloaded the data file and saved it under the file named "epaData.csv." If we are interested in mileage data, we must sift through a lot of other data to extract mileage. Take a look at the data to get a feel for what is there.

Here are some questions we might ask:

- What are the maximum and minimum mileage for cars?
- Which cars get the maximum mileage?
- Which cars get the minimum mileage?

As always when working with real data, we have to further define details to answer our question. Which year are we interested in? Let's take the year 2008. What is a car? Let's eliminate the van and pickup classes. There are different categories of mileage—which one do we use? Let's consider highway mileage.

Here is our algorithm:

1. Open the EPA data file.
2. Put the highway mileage data in a list.
3. Find the minimum and maximum values in the list.

---

[1] http://www.fueleconomy.gov/FEG/download.shtml

The EPA web site has a file describing how the data is arranged. For each vehicle, there are 31 different pieces of data.[2] Here are the first few column labels in the first line of the data file:

CLASS,MFR,CAR LINE,DISPLACEMENT,NUMB CYL,TRANS,DRIVE SYS,INDEX NUMB,CITY MPG,HWY MPG,...

The first thing to notice is that "HWY MPG" is the ninth element in the header (starting the count at zero). Also, the manufacturer ("MFR") is element 1 and type ("CAR LINE") is element 2. Finally, "CLASS" indicates the class of vehicle, e.g., "SUBCOMPACT", "VAN", which will be useful to eliminate "VAN" and "PICKUP" from consideration.

Now that we understand how the data in the file is structured, let's begin the process of developing a program. First, let's begin by opening the file and printing some information from it. Just to do something, let's print out every line that mentions "FERRARI." Because each line in the file is very long, we'll print out only the first characters. See Code Listing 6.8.

Code Listing 6.8

```
# highest mileage data
# from http://www.fueleconomy.gov/FEG/download.shtml

# 1. open EPA data file
epaFile = open("epaData.csv", "rU")

for line in epaFile:          # get each line one at a time from the file
    if 'FERRARI' in line:     # if 'FERRARI' is anywhere in the line print it
        print line[:75]       # only print the beginning of the line
```

```
>>>
TWO SEATERS,FERRARI,F430,4.3,8,Auto(A6),R,1,11,16,13,13.7498,22.4,16.6417,P
TWO SEATERS,FERRARI,F430,4.3,8,Manual(M6),R,1,11,16,13,13.8,22.2,16.6319,P,
TWO SEATERS,FERRARI,FERRARI 599 GTB FIORANO,5.9,12,Auto(A6),R,2,11,15,12,12
TWO SEATERS,FERRARI,FERRARI 599 GTB FIORANO,5.9,12,Manual(M6),R,2,11,15,12,
MIDSIZE CARS,FERRARI,FERRARI 612 SCAGLIETTI,5.7,12,Auto(A6),R,2,9,16,11,11.
MIDSIZE CARS,FERRARI,FERRARI 612 SCAGLIETTI,5.7,12,Manual(M6),R,2,10,15,12,
```

The output isn't elegant, but we demonstrated that we can open and read data from the data file we had downloaded.

The next step in the algorithm is to gather the highway mileage data into a list. Our first cut at the program read lines one at a time, so now we need to extract the highway data

---

[2] If you open the data file and name it epaFile, this command reads the first line—the header—and counts the entries: `len(epaFile.readline().split(','))`

from each line. Already we've noted that the highway mileage data is in column 9 (starting at 0). Since each line has its data separated by commas (remember the file is CSV, which stands for comma-separated values), we can make a list of data from each line using the `line.split(',')` method. Once the data is in a list, we can grab the ninth element using indexing. Finally, we need to put that highway mileage number into a list.

Here are those steps in algorithmic form. Note that this algorithmic segment expands the detail of step 2 in the previous algorithm:

1. initialize a mileage list to be empty
2. for each line in the file:
   (a) split the line at commas into a list
   (b) append list element 9 onto a list of mileage values

Let's place that algorithm in a function named `createMileageList`, and put that function in a program that opens the file, calls the function, and prints the list. We printed the `mileageList` so we could see what we have generated. In the following output, we cut out most of the output, since it is 1248 items long. For our discussion, we need to see only the beginning. See Code Listing 6.9.

Code Listing 6.9

```python
# highest mileage data
# from http://www.fueleconomy.gov/FEG/download.shtml

def createMileageList(epaFile):
    """Create a list of cars and mileage from epaFile."""
    # 2a create a mileage list and initialize it to empty
    mileageList = []

    for line in epaFile:                    # 2b. get each line from the file
        lineList = line.split(',')          # 2bI.  csv => split on comma
        mileageList.append(lineList[9])     # 2bII. append highway mileage
    return mileageList

################################

# 1. open EPA data file
epaFile = open("epaData.csv", "rU")
mileageList = createMileageList(epaFile)

print mileageList
```

```
>>>
['HWY MPG (GUIDE)', '20', '19', '19', '20', '29', '24', '24', '28', '28',...
```

The output looks odd because it is a long list of character strings (notice the quotes), and the first entry isn't a number. That first entry comes from the header line (first line of the file) that describes each column in the file. In this case we see that it is "HWY MPG," which is exactly the column we want. However, now that we see we have the right data, we don't need that header information. Also, since mileage data is numbers, we should convert each one to an integer. Let's clean up our code.

We want to clean up our code with the following:

- ignore the header line
- convert mileage data to integers before appending to `mileageList`

Converting the mileage data is easy by converting element 9 to an integer before appending:

```
mileageList.append(int(lineList[9]))
```

We can ignore a line using the **continue** control construct. In a **for** loop, the **continue** statement sends us back to get the next line—right now! By going back to the top of the loop, we skip the rest of the instructions in the loop. From our description of the header line, we know that the header line begins with "CLASS" so we can know that we are looking at the header line, if the first five characters are "CLASS": **if** line[0:5] == 'CLASS': **continue**

Let's add that code to our program and see what we have. Again, we show only the beginning of the `mileageList` output. See Code Listing 6.10.

Code Listing 6.10

```python
# highest mileage data
# from http://www.fueleconomy.gov/FEG/download.shtml

def createMileageList(epaFile):
    """Create a list of cars and mileage from epaFile."""
    # 2a create a mileage list and initialize it to empty
    mileageList = []

    for line in epaFile:                              # 2b. get each line from the file
        if line[0:5] == 'CLASS':
            continue                                  # skip header line
        lineList = line.split(',')                    # 2bI.  csv => split on comma
        mileageList.append(int(lineList[9]))          # 2bII. append highway mileage
    return mileageList

#################################

# 1. open EPA data file
epaFile = open("epaData.csv", "rU")
```

```
20  mileageList = createMileageList(epaFile)

    print mileageList
```

```
>>>
[20, 19, 19, 20, 29, 24, 24, 28, 28, 28, 28, 28, 28, 23,...
```

Now we have a list of integers from the highway mileage column. Let's find the minimum and maximum. Since those are built-in functions, that is easy: `max(mileageList)` and `min(mileageList)` (we leave writing your own `max` or `min` function as an exercise). If there is more than one maximum or minimum, the first will be selected. While we are at it, we specified that we didn't want to include vans and pickups, so lets ignore those lines. We can look at the raw data and see that vans and pickups are called just that so we can ignore lines with "VAN" and "PICKUP" by using the Boolean **or** operation. Let's see what we have (Code Listing 6.11).

Code Listing 6.11

```
    # highest mileage data
    # from http://www.fueleconomy.gov/FEG/download.shtml

    def createMileageList(epaFile):
5       """Create a list of cars and mileage from epaFile."""
        # 2a create a mileage list and initialize it to empty
        mileageList = []

        for line in epaFile:                    # 2b. get each line from the file
10          if line[0:5] == 'CLASS' or 'VAN' in line or 'PICKUP' in line:
                continue                        # skip header, vans and pickups
            lineList = line.split(',')          # 2bI.  csv => split on comma
            mileageList.append(int(lineList[9]))  # 2bII. append highway mileage
        return mileageList
15
    ################################

    # 1. open EPA data file
    epaFile = open("epaData.csv", "rU")
20  mileageList = createMileageList(epaFile)

    # 3. find max and min mileage
```

```
maxMileage = max(mileageList)
minMileage = min(mileageList)
25
print "Max and Min Mileage: ", maxMileage, minMileage
```

```
>>>
Max and Min Mileage:  45 12
```

We now have the maximum and minimum mileage for cars. That begs the question: which cars are those?

There are two algorithms (at least!) to find out which cars have maximum and minimum mileage. Currently, a single pass through the file finds that the maximum mileage is 45. To find the cars with that mileage, we would have to make a second pass through the file from the beginning. Let's take a different approach: each time we append mileage to `mileageList`, let's also append the name of the car, so we have a name with each data point. To keep names and mileage together, we could put each name and mileage in its own little list. Since such a list will never change, it would be better to use a tuple. Now our `mileageList` will no longer be a list of integers; instead, it will be a list of tuples. Each tuple will have a name and a mileage.

Here it is in algorithmic form:

1. get mileage data
2. get name (make and model, e.g., `'CHEVROLET' 'MALIBU'`)
3. put mileage and name in a tuple, e.g., `(30, 'CHEVROLET', 'MALIBU')`
4. append tuple to `mileageList`

From the description of the data, we can see that the make of the car is in element 1 and that the model is in element 2. We put the mileage first in the tuple because the max and min operations look at the first element in each tuple when there is a list of tuples. Let's see what this looks like in Code Listing 6.12.

Code Listing 6.12

```
# highest mileage data
# from http://www.fueleconomy.gov/FEG/download.shtml

def createMileageList(epaFile):
5       """Create a list of cars and mileage from epaFile."""
        # 2a create a mileage list and initialize it to empty
```

```
        mileageList = []

        for line in epaFile:                    # 2b. get each line from the file
10          if line[0:5] == 'CLASS' or 'VAN' in line or 'PICKUP' in line:
                continue                         # skip header, vans and pickups
            lineList = line.split(',')                # 2bI.  csv => split on comma
            # tuple (mileage, make, model)
            carTuple = (int(lineList[9]), lineList[1], lineList[2])
15          mileageList.append(carTuple)            # 2bII. append tuple
        return mileageList


##############################

20  # 1. open EPA data file
    epaFile = open("epaData.csv", "rU")
    mileageList = createMileageList(epaFile)

    # 3. find max and min mileage
25  maxMileage = max(mileageList)
    minMileage = min(mileageList)

    print "Max and Min Mileage: ", maxMileage, minMileage
```

```
>>>
Max and Min Mileage:  (45, 'TOYOTA', 'PRIUS') (12, 'CHRYSLER', 'ASPEN 2WD')
```

Our output is close to what we want, but there is only one name associated with the minimum and maximum mileage values. Also, the same code that previously only printed mileage, now prints the whole tuple with mileage and name. What we are observing is that min (and similarly max) returns the first minimum value, not all minimum values. In this case, we want all. How can we do that?

Observe that our mileageList has the information we want—all cars with maximum and minimum mileage values. That is, let's create a list of maximum mileage cars and a separate list of minimum mileage cars. Here is an algorithm which can create those lists:

1. create and initialize separate lists for minimum and maximum mileage cars
2. find the min and max mileage
3. for each car in mileageList:
   (a) if a car has maximum mileage, append it to the maximum mileage list
   (b) if a car has minimum mileage, append it to the minimum mileage list

In step 2, let's return to having maxMileage and minMileage only be the integer for mileage, not the car tuple. We can do that by extracting the mileage from the tuple that min(mileageList) returns. Since mileage is the first item in the tuple we can use the following: min(mileageList)[0]. This expression works because min(mileageList) is a tuple, and we can directly index that tuple with [0]. In the example, above we saw that min(mileageList) was the tuple (12, 'CHRYSLER', 'ASPEN 2WD') so using the index min(mileageList)[0] yields the integer 12. Here are the two lines to find the max and min:

```
maxMileage = max(mileageList)[0]
minMileage = min(mileageList)[0]
```

Steps 1 and 3 can be placed in a function named findMaxMinMileage that returns lists of all the maximum and minimum mileage cars. Let's add that code to our program. Code Listing 6.13 shows the function and the program output:

Code Listing 6.13

```
def findMaxMinMileage(mileageList, maxMileage, minMileage):
    """Make a list of cars with max and min mileage: list of car tuples."""
    maxMileageList = []
    minMileageList = []

    # 5. find max and min mileage cars; append them to the appropriate list
    #    carTuple[0] is item 0 of the tuple which is the mileage
    for carTuple in mileageList:
        if carTuple[0] == maxMileage:
            maxMileageList.append(carTuple)
        if carTuple[0] == minMileage:
            minMileageList.append(carTuple)

    return maxMileageList, minMileageList
```

```
>>>
Max and Min Mileage:  45 12

Maximum Mileage Cars:[(45, 'HONDA', 'CIVIC HYBRID'), (45, 'TOYOTA', 'PRIUS')]
Minimum Mileage Cars:[(12, 'CHRYSLER', 'ASPEN 2WD'), (12, 'DODGE', 'DURANGO 2WD'),
(12, 'CHRYSLER', 'ASPEN 4WD'), (12, 'DODGE', 'DURANGO 4WD'), (12, 'JEEP', '
COMMANDER 4WD'), (12, 'JEEP', 'GRAND CHEROKEE 4WD')]
```

The output is not pretty, so let's walk through the list of tuples and print only the make and model. With that modification and a few more comments, Code Listing 6.14 shows the final program and output:

Code Listing 6.14

```
# highest mileage data
# from http://www.fueleconomy.gov/FEG/download.shtml

def createMileageList(epaFile):
    """Create a list of cars and mileage from epaFile."""
    # 2a create a mileage list and initialize it to empty
    mileageList = []

    for line in epaFile:               # 2b. get each line from the file
        if line[0:5] == 'CLASS' or\
                if 'VAN' in line or\
                if 'PICKUP' in line:
            continue          #    skip pickups, vans and the header line
        lineList = line.split(',')           # 2bI. csv => split on comma
        # create tuple: (mileage, make, model)
        carTuple = (int(lineList[9]), lineList[1], lineList[2])
        mileageList.append(carTuple)          # 2bII. append tuple
    return mileageList

def findMaxMinMileage(mileageList, maxMileage, minMileage):
    """Make a list of cars with max and min mileage: list of car tuples."""
    maxMileageList = []
    minMileageList = []

    # 5. find max and min mileage cars; append them to the appropriate list
    #    carTuple[0] is item 0 of the tuple which is the mileage
    for carTuple in mileageList:
        if carTuple[0] == maxMileage:
            maxMileageList.append(carTuple)
        if carTuple[0] == minMileage:
            minMileageList.append(carTuple)

    return maxMileageList, minMileageList

###############################################
# 1. open EPA data file
epaFile = open("epaData.csv", "rU")

print "EPA Car Mileage"
print # blank line

# 2a create a mileage list
mileageList = createMileageList(epaFile)
```

```
45  # 3. find max and min mileage
    #    mileageList is a list of tuples (mileage, make, model)
    #    max(mileageList)[0] finds the max mileage tuple and extracts the mileage
    maxMileage = max(mileageList)[0]
    minMileage = min(mileageList)[0]
50
    print "Max and Min Mileage: ", maxMileage, minMileage
    print  # print blank line

    #4. create a list of all cars with max and min mileage: list of car tuples
55  maxMileageList, minMileageList = \
                findMaxMinMileage(mileageList,maxMileage,minMileage)


    print "Maximum Mileage Cars:"
    for carTuple in maxMileageList:
60      print "  ", carTuple[1], carTuple[2]
    print "Minimum Mileage Cars: "
    for carTuple in minMileageList:
        print "  ", carTuple[1], carTuple[2]
```

```
>>>
EPA Car Mileage

Max and Min Mileage:  45 12

Maximum Mileage Cars:
   HONDA CIVIC HYBRID
   TOYOTA PRIUS
Minimum Mileage Cars:
   CHRYSLER ASPEN 2WD
   DODGE DURANGO 2WD
   CHRYSLER ASPEN 4WD
   DODGE DURANGO 4WD
   JEEP COMMANDER 4WD
   JEEP GRAND CHEROKEE 4WD
```

Notice how we developed this program incrementally, especially, that we tested the code as we developed it. Also, notice how we developed the algorithm in stages.

One final step: does the output make sense? We see that two small, hybrid cars had the highest mileage and sport-utility vehicles (SUVs) had the lowest mileage. However, what happened to those high-performance Ferraris? If you look at where we printed out the Ferrari values earlier, you can count over nine elements and see that their highway mileage is 15 or greater. Why? At highway speeds, aerodynamic design has a dramatic impact on mileage. Therefore, our results look reasonable.

6.10 PYTHON DIVERSION: LIST COMPREHENSION

Let's take a diversion into an interesting Python operation: list comprehension. List comprehension is a compact way to construct lists. Its origins lie in mathematical set notation. There are at least two parts to a list comprehension, but three parts is more common:

[expression *for*-clause condition]

For example, to create a list of the even numbers from zero to twenty you can use *range* to generate the numbers from zero to twenty and then check remainders when dividing by two (i%2==0) to check whether numbers are even. Every element that satisfies the condition is collected into the list.

```
>>> [i for i in range(20) if i%2 == 0]
[0, 2, 4, 6, 8, 10, 12, 14, 16, 18]
```

Of course, the technique isn't limited to numbers. Let's create a list of vowels that are in a word.

```
>>> word = "solidarity"
>>> vowels = "aeiou"
>>> [v for v in word if v in vowels]
['o', 'i', 'a', 'i']
```

One can work from multiple sequences and can have complicated conditionals. For example, suppose you wanted to generate pairs of numbers (think of Cartesian coordinate pairs) with x in the range from zero up to three and y in the range from zero up to four, but only if x>y. One could further limit the pairs by requiring x to be even.

```
>>> [(x,y) for x in range(3) for y in range(4) if x > y]
[(1, 0), (2, 0), (2, 1)]
>>> [(x,y) for x in range(3) for y in range(4) if x > y and x%2 == 0]
[(2, 0), (2, 1)]
```

List comprehension is also useful for doing conversions. For example, consider a string of letters and digits, and we want a list of the numbers as int's converted from the digits—letters are ignored.

```
>>> someString="John Doe, 874 Main St., East Lansing, MI, 48823"
>>> [int(c) for c in someString if c.isdigit()]
[8, 7, 4, 4, 8, 8, 2, 3]
```

The complete rule for list comprehension is an expression followed by a *for* clause, then followed by zero or more *for* or *if* clauses.

For those who enjoy puzzles, list comprehension can be addicting. Once you get a feel for them, you will frequently use them for creating readable, compact code. Fortunately, they often execute quickly, so they are efficient to use.

VISUAL VIGNETTE

6.11 MORE PLOTTING

You saw in Section 2.3 that most of the plotting done with `matplotlib` is done using lists. You were not familiar with lists then, but you are now. Let's do some more plotting now that you know about lists.

As we said, the `plot` command imported from the `pylab` module takes a minimum of a single list, the list of y-values to be plotted. If two lists are provided, the first is assumed to be a list of x-values, the second the list of y-values. It is *required* that the length of the two lists be the same: one x-value for each y-value and vice versa.

Numpy Arrays

We mentioned briefly during the install process that `matplotlib` relies on another Python module called `numpy`, short for "numeric Python." The `numpy` module provides, in a single module, the following capabilities:

- A new data type, the *array* object
- Support for floating point data types
- Support functions for floating point values

The array datatype and its associated methods and functions is particularly useful. In fact, `matplotlib` works not with lists, but `numpy` arrays. If you provide a list as an argument, `matplotlib` converts it to an array.

Arrays and Arange

An array is similar to a list. It is a sequence data structure with indexing and slicing. It is also a mutable data structure and responds to index assignment. The big difference is that a `numpy` array can contain only the same data type, by default a floating-point number. It is type-restricted so that floating-point operations can be done more efficiently on the array. There are a number of ways to make an array. The `array` constructor can take a list object and converts it to an array. The elements of the list must consist only of numbers. The resulting array object will consist of numbers all of the same type. If mixed types exist (floats and ints), then all numbers will be converted to floats. When printed, an array has the string "array" printed as part of the object. One can append onto the end of an existing array using the `numpy` function `append`.

Very much like the *range* function, the `numpy` `arange` function generates a range of values. The differences are that the values are floating-point values instead of integers and the returned object is an array, not a list. The `arange` takes three arguments: the begin value (float), the end value (float), and an increment (float). The following session demonstrates the use of numpy arrays and `arange`.

```
>>> import numpy
>>> myArray = numpy.array([1,2,3,4])
>>> myArray
array([1, 2, 3, 4])                      # all integers
>>> numpy.append(myArray,50.0)
array([ 1.,    2.,    3.,    4.,    50.])    # append a float, now all floats
>>> newArray = numpy.arange(0,2,0.1)         # new array using arange
>>> newArray
array([ 0. ,   0.1,   0.2,   0.3,   0.4,   0.5,   0.6,   0.7,   0.8,   0.9,   1. ,
        1.1,   1.2,   1.3,   1.4,   1.5,   1.6,   1.7,   1.8,   1.9])
>>>
```

Broadcasting

One of the best aspects of using arrays is the ability to perform operations between two arrays using standard arithmetic operators. This means that the operators are overloaded for arrays. For example, if you were to multiply an array by a floating-point number, then *every* element of the array will be multiplied by that number, yielding a new array. The same will occur if you apply a function to an array. *Every* element of the array has the function applied, yielding a new array.

```
>>> import numpy
>>> myArray = numpy.arange(0,6.3,0.1)
>>> myArray
array([ 0. ,   0.1,   0.2,   0.3,   0.4,   0.5,   0.6,   0.7,   0.8,   0.9,   1. ,
        1.1,   1.2,   1.3,   1.4,   1.5,   1.6,   1.7,   1.8,   1.9,   2. ,   2.1,
        2.2,   2.3,   2.4,   2.5,   2.6,   2.7,   2.8,   2.9,   3. ,   3.1,   3.2,
        3.3,   3.4,   3.5,   3.6,   3.7,   3.8,   3.9,   4. ,   4.1,   4.2,   4.3,
        4.4,   4.5,   4.6,   4.7,   4.8,   4.9,   5. ,   5.1,   5.2,   5.3,   5.4,
        5.5,   5.6,   5.7,   5.8,   5.9,   6. ,   6.1,   6.2])
>>> newArray = myArray * 2
>>> newArray
array([ 0. ,   0.2,   0.4,   0.6,   0.8,   1. ,   1.2,   1.4,   1.6,
        1.8,   2. ,   2.2,   2.4,   2.6,   2.8,   3. ,   3.2,   3.4,
        3.6,   3.8,   4. ,   4.2,   4.4,   4.6,   4.8,   5. ,   5.2,
        5.4,   5.6,   5.8,   6. ,   6.2,   6.4,   6.6,   6.8,   7. ,
        7.2,   7.4,   7.6,   7.8,   8. ,   8.2,   8.4,   8.6,   8.8,
        9. ,   9.2,   9.4,   9.6,   9.8,   10. ,  10.2,  10.4,  10.6,
        10.8,  11. ,  11.2,  11.4,  11.6,  11.8,  12. ,  12.2,  12.4])
>>> newArray = numpy.sin(myArray)
>>> newArray
array([ 0.        ,  0.09983342,  0.19866933,  0.29552021,  0.38941834,
        0.47942554,  0.56464247,  0.64421769,  0.71735609,  0.78332691,
```

```
 0.84147098,  0.89120736,  0.93203909,  0.96355819,  0.98544973,
 0.99749499,  0.9995736 ,  0.99166481,  0.97384763,  0.94630009,
 0.90929743,  0.86320937,  0.8084964 ,  0.74570521,  0.67546318,
 0.59847214,  0.51550137,  0.42737988,  0.33498815,  0.23924933,
 0.14112001,  0.04158066, -0.05837414, -0.15774569, -0.2555411 ,
-0.35078323, -0.44252044, -0.52983614, -0.61185789, -0.68776616,
-0.7568025 , -0.81827711, -0.87157577, -0.91616594, -0.95160207,
-0.97753012, -0.993691  , -0.99992326, -0.99616461, -0.98245261,
-0.95892427, -0.92581468, -0.88345466, -0.83226744, -0.77276449,
-0.70554033, -0.63126664, -0.55068554, -0.46460218, -0.37387666,
-0.2794155 , -0.1821625 , -0.0830894 ])
>>>
```

Plotting Trigonometric Functions

Knowing about numpy arrays makes it a lot easier to create graphs. Consider Code Listing 6.15, which generates sine and cosine curves in the same graph; the plot is shown in Figure 6.11.

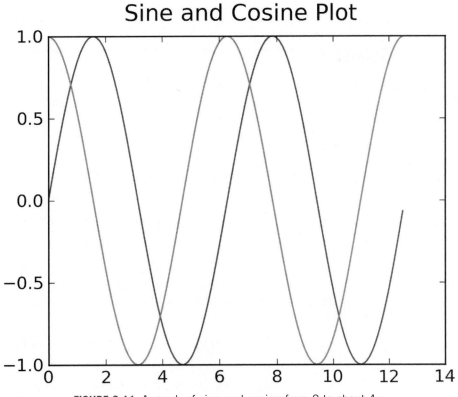

FIGURE 6.11 A graph of sine and cosine from 0 to about 4π.

Code Listing 6.15

```
import numpy
import pylab

# Generate lists of points for both sine and cosine
xVals = numpy.arange(0, 4*numpy.pi, 0.1)
y1Vals = numpy.sin(xVals)
y2Vals = numpy.cos(xVals)

# Plot two curves on the same graph
pylab.title('Sine and Cosine Plot')
pylab.plot(xVals,y1Vals,'b')
pylab.plot(xVals,y2Vals, 'r')
pylab.show()
```

Notice that we can place as many plots as we like in the figure before we show it.

Summary

In this chapter, we developed the list data structure in detail and introduced tuples. Our final example showed the incremental development of a program—an important problem-solving technique.

Exercises

1. Compare and contrast strings, lists, and tuples. For example, consider what they can hold and what operations can be done on the data structures.

2. Create a list containing 100 zeros. Can you find at least three different ways to do it?

3. Create a list of 100 integers whose value and index are the same, e.g., L[5]=5.

4. Given a list of integers, write Python code to create a new list with same number of elements as the original list such that each integer in the new list is the sum of its neighbors and itself in the original list. For example, if listA = [10,20,30,40,50], listB = [30,60,90,120,90].

5. Given the list L = [1,3,5,7,9] use slicing to create a new list without the value 3. That is, L2 = [1,5,7,9].

6. Make a list of the words in a sentence. No punctuation should be attached to a "word" in your list, e.g., "end." is not a correct word, but "end" is.

(a) Use a *while* loop.

(b) Use a *for* loop.

7. Make a list of the unique letters used in a sentence. That is, if the letter "x" is used twice in a sentence, it should only appear once in your list. No punctuation should appear in your list. For the purpose of simplicity consider the following characters as punctuation: . , ; ? ! -

(a) Use a *while* loop.

(b) Use a *for* loop.

8. Create a list of 20 even numbers without using *if*.

(a) Use a loop.

(b) Use list comprehension.

9. Modify the EPA mileage example to list the cars with the maximum and minimum city mileage.

10. Write your own versions of the Python built-in functions min and max. They should take a list as an argument and return the minimum or maximum element. Hint: pick the first element as the minimum (maximum) and then loop through the elements to find a smaller (larger) element. Each time you find a smaller (larger) element, update your minimum (maximum).

11. Program: Work with Census Data
Use this file: http://www.census.gov/population/www/censusdata/files/urpop0090.txt
The census file is a text file with data for the 10-year census from 1900 to 1990 (e.g., 1900, 1910, 1920, . . .). It has population data for each state as well as regional and overall data. Each state is on its own line, but the data are grouped so that only three decades of data is on each line—complicating the task of extracting the data. In addition, the data is further broken down into total, urban, rural, and percentages.

Write a program that for any census year input (e.g., 1970) the program will print the state and its total population with the minimum and maximum. For example:

```
Enter census year 1900 to 1990: 1970
Minimum: (302853, 'Alaska')
Maximum: (19971069, 'California')
```

We had the output display a tuple as a hint to assist with solving the problem rather than illustrating readable output. Some points to consider:

(a) Begin by generating clean data: there are footnotes that need to be eliminated, numbers contain commas, some rows (lines) have data you are not interested in (e.g., region data), you are not interested in all columns (e.g., percentages), and so on. Simply printing the lines with extraneous data removed is a good start.

(b) You will likely want to combine multiple state name strings into one, e.g., "New" "York" becomes "New York."

(c) A tuple (population, state) provides a way to tag population data with a state in a way that allows a list of tuples to be sorted (remember that by default, sorting uses the first value).

12. Refactor the following functions from the Gettysburg Address analysis using `enumerate`:

    (a) `printCommonestWords`
    (b) `printInterestingWords`

13. Print the interesting words in the Gettysburg Address in order from most used to least used.

14. Given the code:

```
myList = ['1','2','3','4','5']
for z in range(0,len(myList)):
    text = ' '.join(myList[z])
    text.center(10)
```

    (a) If this code is run in the shell, what is the output?
    (b) If this code is a program that is then run in the shell, what is the output?
    (c) Why is the output different?
    (d) Fix the program to run the same in both environments.

15. Given a list of items, write a program that generates a list of lists of the following form:
    `[a,b,c,...,z]` ⇒ `[[z], [y,z], [x,y,z], ... , [a,b, ... ,y,z]]`
    Hint: slicing is your friend.

16. Indexable and iterable:

    (a) Give two examples of types that are indexable.
    (b) Give two examples of types that are iterable.
    (c) Does membership in one category imply membership in the other? Explain.

17. A list shares characteristics with string, but there are some things that can be done with a list that cannot be done with a string. Describe them.

18. What is the result of this expression: `sorted(['7','q','e','3','m','n'])`? Explain.

19. Consider two lists, A and B, such that A returns `[1,2,3]` and B returns `[1,2,3]`.

    (a) Create A and B so A *is* B returns *True*.
    (b) Create A and B so A *is* B returns *False*.

20. What does the `strip` method do? What are its limitations?

21. Write a function that takes a string as an argument, converts the string to a list of characters, sorts the list, converts the list back to a string, and returns the resulting string.

22. Write a function that takes a string as an argument and returns a list of the words in the string.

23. Sort vs. Sorted:

(a) What is the difference between `sort` and `sorted`?

(b) Which built-in data types of Python can use each?

24. What does the command `len` do to the following inputs? Try counting it by hand, and then input it into your Python shell. It is important to understand how the `len` function deals with different inputs.

(a) `List1 = ["this", "is", "just", "an", "example",1,2,3,4]`

(b) `X = "I know that sometimes things look difficult, but don't worry you'll get it"`

(c) `Y = "I", "know", "that", "sometimes", "things", "look", "difficult", "but", "don't", "worry", "you'll", "get", "it"`

(d) `Z = "I know you can do it!"`

25. Write a function using a ***for*** loop that takes a string S as an argument and returns S in reversed order. For example, if S="stressed", it should return "desserts".

26. Write a function using a ***for*** loop that takes a sentence S as an argument and returns the words in S in reversed order. For example, if S="What is your quest", it should return "quest your is What".

27. Consider the following code:

```
list1=[1,2,99]
list2=list1
list3=list2
list1=list1.remove(1)
print list3
```

(a) What is printed?

(b) How can you change the code so list3 is unchanged?

28. In the following program replace the ***for*** with a ***while*** loop.

```
S="I had a cat named amanda when I was little"
count = 0
for i in S:
    if i == "a":
        count += 1
print count
```

29. Given a list L of words such as the following and assignment to List1:

```
L = ['Always', 'look', 'on', 'the', 'bright', 'side', 'of', 'life.']
List1=[[i.upper(), i.lower(), len(i)] for i in L ]
```

(a) What is the value of List1?

(b) Write a list comprehension that uses List1 to create a list of words of length 4.

30. Using list comprehension create an expression that sums up all the factors of a number that you input. (Hint: if you input 6, it should print 12 (i.e., 1 + 2 + 3 + 6 = 12).)

31. Given a list of integers L, use list comprehension to:

(a) find the sum of the even integers in list L

(b) find the sum of the odd integers in list L.

32. Given a = [1,2,3] and b = [1,2,3], what is the result of:

(a) a == b

(b) a *is* b

33. Given x = [1,2,3], write the Python code to:

(a) create a list y such that changing x also changes y.

(b) create a list y such that changing x does not change y.

34. Given the following program what will be printed?

```
numList = [1,2,3]
x = 'Hello There!'

for i in x
    print numList
    x.append(numList)
```

35. Transform the string 'abcde' into the list [1,'b','hello',15,'e',2]. (Note that there are many possible different answers.)

36. Tuples and Lists (try this in the Python shell).

(a) Is is possible to have a tuple in a list? Why or why not?

(b) Is it possible to have a list in a tuple? Why or why not?

37. What differentiates a tuple from a list? Be specific.

38. Create examples to illustrate three different methods to combine two lists. The resulting lists need not be the same.

39. Create a program that uses the Gettysburg Address as input and outputs a list of tuples for every two words. For example: [('Four', 'score'),('and', 'seven'), ...].

40. If a tuple is immutable, why are we able to modify x=[1, (2,3),4] into x=[1,(5,6),4]? Are we changing the tuple or changing the list?

41. Write a function that takes a tuple as an argument and returns the tuple sorted?

42. What will the following list return?

```
[ (n*n) for n in range(13) if (n*n)%2==0 ]
```

43. Given x='*January 1, 2000*':

(a) Using list comprehension, create a list of all the letters used in x.

(b) In one line, add to your list comprehension so the resulting list is sorted.

44. Given a list [4,8,9,6,5,4,8,7,8] and using the len and sum functions, determine the average value of the integers in the list.

45. Given a list L = [1,2,3,4], we want to convert the list to the string '*1234*'. We tried ''.join([i *for* i *in* L]), but it doesn't work. Fix it.

46. Come up with three different ways to create a list of 25 1's without simply typing the 25 1's.

47. Fractions:

You can express a fraction as a tuple: (numerator, denominator).

(a) Write a function that adds two fractions that are passed as tuples.

(b) Write a function that multiplies two fractions that are passed as tuples.

48. How will these lists be sorted by the sorted(L) function? Hint: consider their ASCII values.

(a) L = ['1','2','3','h','E','l','L','o','W','o','R','l','d']

(b) L = ['A','a','B','b','1','2','3']

49. It is often times advantageous to be able to transfer data between multiple lists while re-arranging their order. For instance, say that list1 = [1,2,3,4,5,6,7,8,9] and you wish to add the numbers in the index range 4:7 of list1 to another list, list2, in reverse order while simultaneously removing them from list1. If list2 = [100,200], the result will be list2 = [100,200,7,6,5]. Write a function named transform that takes as arguments list1, list2, r1, and r2, that removes items from list1 in the slice r1:r2, appends them onto list2 in reverse order, and returns the resulting list. For example, in this case, the function call will be transform(list1, list2, 4,70).

50. Tuples resemble lists in many ways. However, as an immutable type, the ways in which they can be interacted with are limited. Take the following statements. What will happen if you try to add to the tuple in the manner shown? How can you rewrite the code to achieve the intended result?

```
Tuple = ()
for i in range (10):
    Tuple += i
```

51. Consider:

```
ListA = [1,2,3,4,5]
ListB = ListA
ListA[2] = 10
```

What is the value of ListB[2]?

52. Consider:

```
ListA = [1,2,3,4,5]
ListB = []
for num in ListA:
    ListB.append(num)
ListA[2] = 10
```

(a) What is the value of ListB[2]?
(b) What is the value of ListB?

53. Given a list of numbers, create a new list of numbers such that the first and last numbers are added and stored as the first number, the second and second-to-last numbers are stored as the second number, and so on. Note that you need to check for even and odd length of lists. In case of an odd number of integers, leave the central integer in the original list as it is.

54. Given a list of N numbers, write a function to shift the numbers circularly by some integer k (where $k < N$). The function should take a list and k as a arguments and return the shifted list.

(a) Write a function that assumes shifting is to the left.
(b) Write a function that takes a third argument that specifies shifting left or right.

55. The letters a, b, d, e, g, o, p, and q all have something in common: a hole. If you imagine that the letters were made of stretchy material such as rubber, you could transform one letter into another while preserving the hole. If tearing or gluing are not allowed, no other letter (without a hole) could be transformed by stretching into one of these letters with holes. Mathemeticans say that these letters are topologically similar: one set has a hole, the rest do not.

(a) Write a function that takes as an argument a lowercase string and finds the counts of letters in the string with holes and and a count of letters without holes.
(b) Write a function that searches a word list and prints all the words that have two or more letters with holes.
(c) The set of upper-case letters with holes is different than the set of lowercase letters, e.g., lowercase "e" belongs to the set of letters with a hole, but its capital "E" does not. Refactor your functions to consider upper case letters.

56. Sally invited 17 guests to a dance party. She assigned each guest a number from 2 to 18, keeping 1 for herself. The sum of each couple's numbers was a perfect square. Write a program to find the number of Sally's partner.

57. Using the Python int operators +, -, *, /, ** (not %), and the numbers, 2, 3, 4, and 5, find an expression using all four numbers exactly once and any three of the operators exactly once that evaluates to 26. Hint: build strings and then use the Python `eval` function, which takes a string as an argument, evaluates the string, and returns its value, e.g., `eval('2*3+4')` returns the integer 10.

58. 123456789 = 100. Of course, it doesn't, but:

(a) Using only the addition operator +, can you insert some addition operators between those successive digits so that it does sum to 100?

(b) Similarly, but more complicated: using the four standard integer arithmetic operators +, -, *, and / (not %), how many different solutions can you find (there are more than 100)?

59. Jim Loy (http://www.jimloy.com) poses this puzzle: I have before me three numeric palindromes (numbers that read the same backwards and forwards, like 838). The first is two digits long, the second is three digits long, and when we add those two numbers together, we get the third number, which is four digits long. What are the three numbers? (Hint 1: numeric palidromes can be easily created by making strings of digits first. Hint 2: there is a reason that this exercise is in the lists chapter.)

Programming Projects

1. **Word Puzzles.**

Will Shortz is a noted puzzlemaster for the *New York Times* and National Public Radio who frequently posts challenging word puzzles. Many word puzzles can be solved by iterating through a list of words while checking for characteristics specified by the puzzle. Many word lists exist on the web and we provide one on the text's web site— any sufficiently large one will suffice. We have not covered file reading in detail yet, so here we provide a function that reads a file named "wordList.txt" and returns a list of words in lowercase. The file has one word per line. For each puzzle, copy this program and write your solution as the `puzzle` function. Note that the `puzzle` function has one parameter—the `wordList`.

Code Listing 6.16

```
# Word puzzle driver
# Assumes wordList.txt file of one word per line

def getWordList():
    """Return a list of words from a wordList.txt file."""
    dataFile = open("wordList.txt","r")
    wordList = []              # start with an empty word list
```

```
        for word in dataFile:  # for every word (line) in the file
            # strip off end-of-line characters and make each word lowercase
            # then append the word to the wordList
            wordList.append(word.strip().lower())
        return wordList

def puzzle(wordList):
    """Puzzle solution goes here."""
    pass     # filler that does nothing except put something in the suite

wordList = getWordList()
puzzle(wordList)
```

(a) The comparative form of the adjective "big" is *bigger*, and the superlative form is *biggest*. All three forms (big, bigger, and biggest) are related. However, there exists a root word that is not an adjective that when "er" is appended and "est" is appended, the result is a set of three words whose meanings are unrelated. Write a puzzle function that prints out all such triples (root, root + "er", root + "est"). Scan through your list to find a set of triples that are unrelated to each other.

(b) Find an uncapitalized, unhyphenated word that contains all but one of the letters of the alphabet from "l" to "v" ("lmnopqrstuv").

(c) What word consists of two consecutive pronouns? This list of pronouns will be helpful.
```
pronouns = ['thou', 'thee', 'thine', 'thy', 'i', 'me',
'mine', 'my', 'we', 'us', 'ours', 'our', 'you', 'yours',
'your','he','him','his', 'she', 'her', 'hers', 'it',
'its', 'they', 'them', 'theirs', 'their']
```

(d) What six-letter word has its meaning reversed when its first letter is changed from "c" to "h"? Print out the candidates and then select by hand.

(e) Find an uncapitalized, seven-letter word, containing just a single vowel that does not have the letter "s" anywhere within it.

(f) The word "mimeographs" contains all the letters of "memphis" at least once. Find other words that also contain all the letters of "memphis".

(g) Find a word that contains the string "tantan."

(h) The word "marine" consists of five consecutive, overlapping state postal abbreviations: Massachusetts (MA), Arkansas (AR), Rhode Island (RI), Indiana (IN), and Nebraska (NE). Find a seven-letter word that thas the same property.

(i) When you are writing in script, there are four letters of the alphabet that cannot be completed in one stroke: "i" and "j" (which require dots) and "t" and "x" (which require crosses). Find a word that uses each of these letters exactly once.

(j) There are four words that contain the consecutive letters "nacl". Find them.

(k) Find a word that contains the vowels "a", "e", "i", "o", and "u" in that order.

(l) Consider the word "sure". If we asked you to add two pairs of doubled letters to it to make an eight-letter word, you would add p's and s's to make "suppress". Find an eight-letter word resulting from adding two pairs of doubled letters to "rate".

(m) Find three words that are spelled the same except for their first two letters, which can be "sw", "tw", or "wh".

(n) Two U.S. state capitals have a prefix that is the name of a month. Find them.

2. **Pascal's Triangle:**

Pascal's triangle is a geometric arrangement of sums that have interesting mathematical properties—most famously, the binomial coefficients.

The rows of Pascal's triangle are conventionally enumerated starting with row 0, and the numbers in each row are usually staggered relative to the numbers in the adjacent rows. A simple construction of the triangle proceeds in the following manner. On row 0, write only the number 1. Then, to construct the elements of following rows, add the number directly above and to the left with the number directly above and to the right to find the new value. If either the number to the right or left is not present, substitute a zero in its place. For example, the first number in the first row is 0 + 1 = 1, whereas the numbers 1 and 3 in the third row are added to produce the number 4 in the fourth row. Here are the first six rows of Pascal's triangle:

```
           1
         1   1
       1   2   1
     1   3   3   1
   1   4   6   4   1
 1   5  10  10   5   1
```

Write a program that prompts for the height of Pascal's triangle, and then generates the triangle in the same style as above example.

Hint: use a list for each row, and use a list of row lists to hold the whole triangle.

3. **Scrambled English:**

Read the following paragraph as quickly as you can and see if you encounter any difficulties.

Aoccdrnig to rscheearch at an Elingsh uinervtisy, it deosn't mttaer in waht oredr the ltteers in a wrod are, the olny iprmoetnt tihng is taht the frist and lsat ltteer is at the rghit pclae. The rset can be a toatl mses and you can sitll raed it wouthit a porbelm. Tihs is bcuseae we do not raed ervey lteter by itslef but the wrod as a wlohe.

This paragraph was published as an example of a principle of human reading comprehension. If you keep the first letter and the last letter of a word in their correct positions and scramble the letters in between, the word is still quite readable in the context of a surrounding paragraph. However, it seems that this is a bit of a myth and not truly based on solid research. It turns out that for longer words, the task is much more difficult. Nonetheless, we are going to imitate the process on some English text.

Handling punctuation is tricky. You need to deal with punctuation that comes at the end of a word: comma, period, question mark, exclamation, etc. For example, in the previous sample, the word "university" ends with a comma, so you need to ensure that you do not treat the comma as the "last letter of the word" when you scramble all but the first and last letters.

Hints:

- Don't bother trying to scramble words fewer than four characters long.
- The string `split` method is useful to create a list of words from a string of words.
- The string `strip` method is useful to remove end-of-line characters and other whitespace.
- To scramble a string, convert it to a list, use `random.shuffle` from the `random` module to scramble the string, and then use the `join` string method to convert back to a string: `"".join(list)`

(a) A simple way to get some text to work with is to simply put it in a long string. (Note the backslash continuation character: \)

```
text =  "Four score and seven years ago \
         our fathers brought forth \
         on this continent a new nation,"
```

(b) Alternatively, you could use a modification of the wordlist driver from the word puzzle programming project above to read a file. To read a file named "someFile.txt" into one long string:

```
def getWordString():
    dataFile = open("someFile.txt","r")
    wordString =''                  # start with an empty string of words
    for line in dataFile:
        wordString += line          # add each line of words to the word string
    return wordString
```

(c) Optionally, add the capability to handle punctuation in the middle of words, e.g., a hyphen in a word. Scramble on either side of the hyphen.

4. **Code Breaking:**
   In this exercise we will break the code of an encrypted message using the technique of frequency analysis. If a substitution cipher such as the well-known Caesar cipher is used, it can be broken using that technique. First, you need to make a program that can encrypt and decrypt Caesar ciphers. Then we'll see how to break them.

(a) The Caesar cipher is named after Julius Caesar, who used this type of encryption to keep his military communications secret. A Caesar cipher replaces each plain-text letter with one that is a fixed number of places down the alphabet. The plain text is your original message; the cipher text is the encrypted message. The following example employs a shift of three so that "B" in the plain-text becomes "E" in the cipher-text, a "C" becomes "F" and so on. The mapping wraps around so that "X" maps to "A" and so on.

Here is the complete mapping for a shift of three:

```
Plain: ABCDEFGHIJKLMNOPQRSTUVWXYZ
Cipher: DEFGHIJKLMNOPQRSTUVWXYZABC
```

To encrypt a message, substitute the plain-text letters with the corresponding cipher-text letter. For example, here is an encryption of "the quick brown fox jumps over the lazy dog" using our shift-three cipher (case is ignored):

```
Plain text: the quick brown fox jumps over the lazy dog
Cipher text: WKH TXLFN EURZQ IRA MXPSV RYHU WKH ODCB GRJ
```

To decrypt the message, reverse the process.

Write a program that prompts for a shift value (such as the 3 in our example) and then prompts for plain text to encode. Output the encrypted cipher text, and then decrypt the cipher text and output that. If your program is correct, the decrypted ciper text should match the original plain text.

Hints:

i. Create the cipher by starting with an alphabet string. Use slicing and concatenating to accomplish the shift.

ii. If you plan to allow spaces in your plain text, you need to add a space character into your "Plain" alphabet string.

iii. If you have two strings like the "Plain" and "Cipher" shown earlier, notice that the letter to substitute is at the same index in both strings. You can use that fact for both encryption and decryption.

iv. Use pencil and paper to encrypt and decrypt before designing your algorithm.

v. Optional: one way to find indices is with modular arithmetic:

```
cipherTextIndex = (plainTextIndex + 3) % 26
```

(b) Now the fun part—code breaking. If we know that we are breaking a Caesar cipher, our goal is to find the shift. From the program in the previous exercise, we can see that if we know the shift, we can decrypt the message. One fact is important: to make code breaking more difficult, neither spaces nor capitalization is used. Frequency analysis is based on the concept that some letters are used more often than others. For example, in English the most common letter is "e", which occurs nearly 13% of the time. Knowing that we are dealing with a simple Caesar cipher, we need to find only the most common letter, guess that it encodes to "e", and figure out the appropriate shift. However, we need a large message to have confidence that we have actually found the most frequent letter. Note that, in general, if spaces are allowed, that will always be the most frequent character, by a lot—allowing spaces makes code breaking too easy.

Write a program that takes in a cipher text, determines the shift, decodes it, and outputs the decoded message.

Hints:

i. Make a list of counters, one for each letter.

ii. There is a maximum function for lists: max(someList).

iii. An easy way to input a large cipher text is to use the getWordString function from the previous exercise.

iv. You can create a cipher text by using the encrpytion program you created.

v. Remember, no spaces.

CHAPTER 7

More on Functions

WE INTRODUCED FUNCTIONS IN CHAPTER 5 AND SHOWED YOU HOW THEY ARE important for the divide-and-conquer problem solving introduced in Chapter 3. In this chapter, we introduce more capabilities of functions and some subtleties involved in their use. For example, now that you know the difference between mutable and immutable objects, we can observe how they behave differently when passed as arguments to functions.

7.1 FUNCTIONS CALLING FUNCTIONS

In Chapter 5, we mentioned that functions can call functions, but did not elaborate. There is no limitation to when a function can be called or even how often a function can be called. It is often the case that a function will call another function. This extension does not change the process described previously, though it does make it slightly more complicated for us to follow the control flow.

Let's revisit the checking of input that we did with the Babylonian square root problem of Section 3.5. In that section we used the string `isdigit` method to validate integer input, but did not have the tools for validating floating-point input. We will leave handling of scientific notation as an exercise and only consider here the validation of decimal entry. A decimal notation is composed of digits with at most one decimal point: 0.01, 2.7, 5, and so on. We can check for that input pattern by removing one decimal point, if any exist, and check whether the remaining characters are all digits. We will keep asking for input until we get valid input.

The string `replace` function can replace one string with another, and we can specify how many replacements to make. In our case, we will replace a decimal point (`'.'`) with an empty string (`''`) and perform replacement once. The call on string `'s'` is:

```
s.replace('.','',1)
```

Our input validation breaks down into two distinct tasks: a loop asking for valid input, and checking the validity of the input. This division suggests two functions, one called by the other:

- isfloat(s) returns *True*, if s is a valid floating-point string.
- readFloat(prompt) repeatedly prompts for input until a valid floating-point number is entered.

Let's look at the implementation using functions. To help us observe the sequence of function calls, we've inserted a print statement in each function. See Code Listing 7.1.

Code Listing 7.1

```
# Functions for valid input of floats
def isFloat(aStr):
    """True if aStr is a float: digits and at most one decimal point"""
    print "*** In the isFloat function."     # to observe function operation
    stripped = aStr.replace('.','',1)   # remove 1 decimal point, if it exists
    return stripped.isdigit()           # return Boolean, are there only digits?


def readFloat(prompt):
    """Keep reading until a valid float is entered"""
    print " *** In the readFloat function." # to observe function operation
    num_str = raw_input(prompt)
    while not isFloat(num_str): # keep asking until input is a valid float
        print 'Not a valid float, try again'
        num_str = raw_input(prompt)
    return float(num_str)               # convert to float and return
```

Two functions are defined:

isfloat(s): A float is a sequence of digits with at most one decimal point, so remove one decimal point from the string aStr using replace, and check whether the remainder is all digits using isdigits.

readFloat(prompt): Repeatedly prompt for a float using a call to isfloat to check whether the input is a valid floating-point string.

Now we have a float-checking input function that can be used in any future program—after removing or commenting out the print statements. In Chapter 14 you will learn a better way to check input.

The flow of control can be seen in the accompanying session. When the file is run (F5 in IDLE), both functions are defined so they are available for use in the shell. A call to readFloat generates successive calls to isfloat until the input is valid.

```
>>> ================================ RESTART ================================
>>>                       # F5 in IDLE loaded functions
>>> readFloat('Please enter a floating point number:')
```

```
 *** In the readFloat function.
Please enter a floating point number:a
*** In the isFloat function.                # call to isFloat
Not a valid float, try again               # bad float, try again
Please enter a floating point number:1.2.3
*** In the isFloat function.
Not a valid float, try again
Please enter a floating point number:3.14159 #successful float
*** In the isFloat function.
3.1415899999999999
>>>
```

Check Yourself: Functions Calling Functions Check

1. Given the following program, indicate what output would result for the given input:

```
import string

def func1 (str1):
    resultStr = ''
    for char in str1:
        if char in string.digits:
            resultStr = resultStr + char
    if resultStr:
        return resultStr
    else:
        return -1

def func2 (str1):
    if len(str1) > 0:
        str1 = str1.strip()
        resultInt = func1(str1)
    else:
        resultInt = 0
    return resultInt

# main program
responseStr = raw_input("Input a string:")
print func2(responseStr)    # Line 1
```

   (a) Given an input of abc123, what output results from Line 1?
   (b) Given an input of a1b2c3, what output results from Line 1?
   (c) Given an input of abc, what output results from Line 1?
   (d) Given an input of (the empty string), what output results from Line 1?

7.2 SCOPE: A FIRST CUT

The details of how arguments' values are passed to function parameters can be confusing, so we will examine the process in more detail here. An important concept in programming languages is *scope*. We will examine the concept of scope in more detail in Section 8.6 below, but for now, know that scope means:

The set of program statements over which a variable exists, i.e., can be referred to.

We bring up scope here because a function is the first place where we see the effect of different scopes. As we noted earlier, when a function is executed, it creates its own namespace. Any variable that comes into existence (for example, when a variable gets assigned a value) within the suite of that function gets entered in the function's namespace. We say that a function's variables are *local* to the scope of the *function*. Local scope means that the variable can only be referenced, its associated object accessed, within the suite of the function, because that is the active namespace. Variables defined locally within a function (within the scope of the function) are not accessible outside of the function, because when a call to a function ends, its namespace is hidden.

Every program and function has a namespace that defines a scope within which variables are defined and are available for use. Only variables within the current, active namespaces (note the plural), can be referred to during execution. Consider Code Listing 7.2.

Code Listing 7.2

```
# a function with a local variable
def scopeFunction (anInt):
    newInt = anInt     # local variable created
    print 'newInt value (in function) is: ',newInt

# main program
scopeFunction(27)
print 'newInt value is:',newInt   # ERROR! (scope)
```

```
>>>
newInt value (in function) is:  27
newInt value is:
Traceback (most recent call last):
  File "scopeFn1.py", line 8, in <module>
    print 'newInt value is:',newInt   # ERROR! (scope)
NameError: name 'newInt' is not defined
>>>
```

This program generates an error, because `newInt` is defined in the local scope of `scopeFunction` so it cannot be referenced outside of the suite of the function.

The scope determined by `scopeFunction` is the function's suite (indented under the **def** statement). Besides the suite, the namespace also includes the function's parameters as part of the function's local scope. The function's namespace becomes active when function execution begins and ends when function execution ends. The function's namespace doesn't exist outside of the function's execution of the suite, so the request in the main program for the object associated with `newInt` cannot be found. The the resulting error is that the variable cannot be found. Literally, the variable does not exist, as the namespace that defines it is not presently active.

PROGRAMMING TIP

A function name is just another name in the namespace. As we have mentioned, the **def** statement creates an entry in the namespace, associating the function name with the executable code of the function. You can reassign a function name to be associated with a different value. For example, the predefined `len` is initially associated with a function object. However, we are free to reassign it and associate it with anything we like, for example `len = 12`. At this point, `len` can no longer be called as a function. The name `len` is now associated with the integer 12.

Don't worry. If you restart Python, everything will go back to normal. However, be careful with your variable names! Don't step on existing names or odd things can happen.

Arguments, Parameters, and Namespaces

Let's take a closer look at passing information from arguments to parameters and the role of namespaces.

Before we begin, remember that a namespace contains a set of pairs: a name and a Python object associated with that name. The association is called a *reference* and we can say that the name *references* the object. Also, from the scope discussion earlier, remember that the main program and function each have their own separate namespaces.

Here's the big question. When we call a function, what gets copied between the argument and its corresponding parameter? The answer, is the association, the reference, is what gets copied, not a new copy of the object itself. That is worth saying again. The association (reference) is copied, not the object itself. This means that, after passing the argument to the parameter, both the parameter and argument will now be associated with the *same* object, as shown in Figure 7.1. The argument name in the calling namespace is `arg`, the parameter

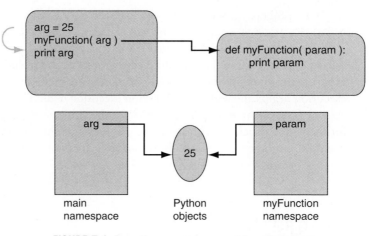

FIGURE 7.1 Function namespace: at function start.

name in the function namespace is `param`, and they both are associated with the same object, 25. Figure 7.1 shows the situation as the function begins execution.

Following is the example from Figure 7.1 in the Python shell. We begin by defining the function. Within the function, we print `param` and its `id`. Remember, the `id` function prints a unique identification number for each object. No two objects have the same ID. When we executed the **_def_** statement, the function is created and made available for invocation. We create the variable `arg` by assigning it the value 25. We also print the ID of the integer 25. We then use `arg` as an argument in a function call. Within the function we print the value and id of the parameter `param`. Both `arg` and `param` have an association with the same object.

```
>>> def myFunction(param):              # print value and id
        print 'parameter value is:%d, its id is:%d'%(param,id(param))

>>> arg = 25
>>> id(arg)                             # python id for object associated with arg
16790632
>>> myFunction(arg)
parameter value is:25, its id is:16790632   # arg and param objects the same
>>>
```

What if `myFunction` now changes the value associated with `param`? Let's add a line to `myFunction`: `param = 32`. The change is diagrammed in Figure 7.2.

With the addition of `param = 32`, the `param` reference is updated in the `myFunction` namespace to reference 32, a different object. Notice that `arg` is unaffected in the main program so now `arg` and `param` reference different values. The results of the `id` calls reflect that. While `param` initially references the same object as `arg` as

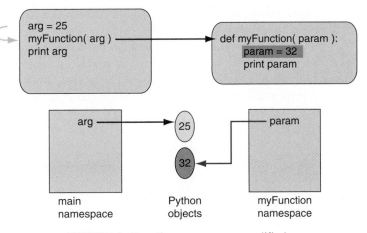

FIGURE 7.2 Function namespace modified.

shown in Figure 7.1, the assignment *changes the reference to a different object*, namely the integer 32, as shown in Figure 7.2. This change is illustrated in the following session.

```
>>> def myFunction(param):
...     param = 32
...     print 'parameter value is:%d, its id is:%d'%(param,id(param))
...
>>> arg = 25
>>> id(arg)
16790632
>>> myFunction(arg)
parameter value is:32, its id is:16790548
>>> arg
25
>>> id(arg)
16790632
>>>
```

Passing Mutable Objects

We discussed the concept of a shallow copy of mutable objects in Section 6.6. A similar problem arises when passing mutable arguments.

Though the argument and parameter start out with a reference to the same object, re-assigning the parameter to a new object changes the parameter reference. No change is made to the argument as a result. It keeps its reference.

If the object being referenced is immutable, such as a number, string, or tuple, it is not possible to change anything about that object. Whenever we assign a new object to a parameter, we *break* the association of both argument and parameter to the same object.

What about mutable objects? We can change the value(s) of a mutable object. How does that affect parameter passing?

In Figure 7.3 we pass a list—a mutable object. As with the previous example an argument *reference* (`argList` in this example) is passed to the parameter name (`paramList`) and both are associated with that object. The figure shows the state of the namespaces before the statement `paramList[0] = 100` is executed. Note the similarity to Figure 7.1.

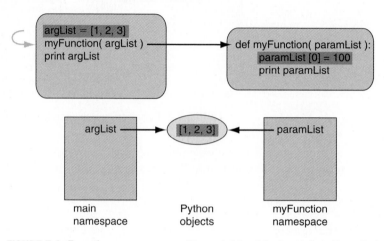

FIGURE 7.3 Function namespace with mutable objects: at function start.

The assignment statement `paramList[0] = 100` in the function does not assign a new object to `paramList`; it *changes the object* itself. Because `paramList` is associated with a list, we change the list object, not the reference. The variable `paramList` remains associated with the same list object, but that object's contents are changed to `[100,2,3]` as shown in Figure 7.4. Because `argList` references the same object, `argList` also reflects the modification. Such a change to the object would not be possible with an immutable object!

Here is the example from Figures 7.3 and 7.4 shown in the Python shell. An additional **_print_** statement is added to the function so we can see the object associated with `paramList` before and after it is modified. Note how `argList`, associated with the same object, reflects the change to that object.

```
>>> def myFunction(paramList):
        # print object as passed in
        print "paramList before modification:", paramList
        # modify paramList
        paramList[0] = 100
        # print modified object
        print "paramList after modification:", paramList
```

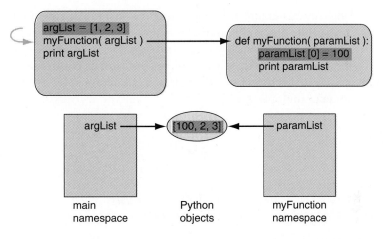

FIGURE 7.4 Function namespace with mutable objects after `paramList[0]=100`.

```
>>> argList = [1,2,3]
>>> myFunction(argList)
paramList before modification: [1, 2, 3]
paramList after modification: [100, 2, 3]
>>> argList                          # argList is changed too!
[100, 2, 3]
```

PROGRAMMING TIP

Passing mutable objects allows a function to change values in the calling program.

Handling mutable vs. immutable parameters is complicated by the fact that Python doesn't specify parameter *types*. Remember that we cannot tell the type of a variable unless we examine what has been assigned to it. Python allows flexibility on this point, but the flexibility affects readability. Having the type as part of the name improves that readability.

Returning a Complex Object

As we mentioned previously, a function returns one object. However, having worked with collections, we can now return a single object that has multiple parts. The following is an example of returning a list. The session defines a function `evens`. The function takes a single integer argument n, indicating the quantity of even numbers to generate, constructs a list of the first n even numbers and then returns those numbers as a list. In the first part of the main program, we invoke `evens` and the returned value is printed by Python. In the second part of the main program, we invoked `evens` and assigned the returned value it to a variable `numLst`. A single object is returned by `evens`, but that single list object contains multiple objects.

```
>>> def evens(n):
        evensLst = []                  # initialize list to empty
     # to get "n" numbers starting at 1, range must go to "n+1"
        for i in range(1,n+1):
            evensLst.append(2*i) # 2*i is always even; add it to the list
        return evensLst                # return the list of evens
>>> evens(5) # executing the function without assignment (return is printed)
[2, 4, 6, 8, 10]
>>> numLst = evens(3)     # executing the function with assignment to numList
>>> numLst                # let's see the value of numList
[2, 4, 6]
```

If you return a series of results separated by commas, Python will build a single tuple containing those values (in order) and return the tuple. Consider the function `mirror` in the following session. The function takes a single collection argument with at least two elements and returns the first two elements as a tuple in reverse order. In the first invocation of `mirror`, we pass a tuple of two integers and a tuple of those two integers is returned and printed by Python. In the second invocation, we do multiple assignment on the returned value and the elements of the returned tuple are assigned in order to x and y. If single assignment is used, then the assigned object is a tuple as shown associated with the variable z.

```
>>> def mirror(pair):
       # we assume that "pair" was passed as a tuple (or list)
          return pair[1], pair[0]
>>> mirror((2,3))  # values get reversed
(3, 2)       # the return was comma separated: implicitly handled as a tuple
>>> x,y = mirror((2,3))  # comma separated works on the left-hand-side also
>>> x
3
>>> y
2
>>> x,y                      # here "x,y" is again considered as a tuple
(3, 2)
```

Check Yourself: Passing Mutables Check

1. Give the output indicated for the following program. It will be helpful to draw diagrams to indicate the relationships among arguments, parameters, and their objects. Think about which arguments are mutable and which are immutable.

```python
def func1 (lst1, lst2, str1):
    if len(lst1) > 3:
        lst1 = lst1[:3]
    lst2[0] = 'goodbye'
    str1 = ''.join(lst2)

argList1 = ['a','b','c','d']
argList2 = ['hello','mother','and','father']
argStr = 'sister'

func1(argList1, argList2, argStr)
print argList1          # Line 1
print argList2          # Line 2
print argStr            # Line 3
```

(a) What output is produced by Line 1 when the program is executed?

(b) What output is produced by Line 2 when the program is executed?

(c) What output is produced by Line 3 when the program is executed?

```python
>>> z = mirror((2,3)) # if we return and assign to one name, we get a tuple!
>>> z
(3, 2)
```

An astute reader will notice that the `mirror` function is not very robust. That is, one can pass it a variety of values that will cause an error. Enter the function into a Python shell and try to break it (cause errors) in multiple ways.

Refactoring `evens`

The `evens` function offers an opportunity to illustrate refactoring. In Section 6.10 we introduced list comprehension as a way to build lists. Because `evens` builds a list, let's refactor the function using a list comprehension. In fact, the whole suite of the function can be replaced with one line:

```python
return [2*i for i in range(1, n+1)]
```

Note how the ***for*** header is the same, and that the expression from the append appears just after the left bracket. The exercises ask for yet another refactoring of the function by using the step argument of *range*.

When refactoring you should ask yourself two questions: (1) is the code "better"— usually more efficient? and (2) is the code more readable? It turns out that list comprehension is very efficient, so this version is certainly more efficient. Whether list comprehension is more readable is in the eyes of the reader.

7.3 DEFAULT VALUES AND PARAMETERS AS KEYWORDS

Two additional characteristics of parameter passing are the ability to have *default values* and the ability to *pass parameters by name*.

A default parameter value is pretty much just that: a value assigned to a function parameter by default because the user did not provide a value. We have seen defaults before, for example, in slicing. There is a default for each of the three values in a slice, if the user does not provide one. However, when the user does provide a value it *always* overrides the default value.

A default parameter is created in the parameter list of a function definition. A default parameter looks like an assignment statement in the parameter list, something like `paramName = value`. The `value` on the right-hand-side of the assignment is the default value for parameter `paramName`. If a parameter is simply listed without the assignment, it is a *required* parameter. The user must provide an argument for the parameter or Python will signal an error.

Arguments are mapped to parameters as before in a left-to-right positional matching. That is, the leftmost argument maps to the leftmost parameter, then the next leftmost argument is mapped to the next leftmost parameter, and so on. If there are more parameters then arguments, any unmatched parameters get their default values. Therefore, default values can only be used on the rightmost parameters.

Consider an example function `func1`, shown as follows, where the rightmost parameter, `paramDefault`, is assigned a default value. When the function is called with two arguments, the arguments are matched to parameters, from left to right as before, and the default value is ignored. However, when only one argument is used, `func1(5)`, the 5 is mapped to the leftmost parameter, `paramRequired`, and as there is no second argument, the parameter `paramDefault` gets its default value of 2.

```
>>> def func1(paramRequied, paramDefault = 2):  # note default value
        print paramRequired, paramDefault

>>> func1(5,6)    # both specified so default is ignored
5 6
>>> f(5)          # only paramRequired, default used for paramDefault
5 2
```

Python also allows you to use the names of the parameters as keywords in the function invocation. That is, in the invocation you may also use an assignment statement of the form `paramName = value`. This feature means that you wish to provide `value` as the argument value for the parameter named `paramName`. In this way you can, with some care, ignore the standard order of argument-to-parameter names by specifically indicating which argument-to-parameter match you wish. For example, using the same simple function `func1` from the session above, we change the function invocation to indicate which argument value should go with which parameter name using the invocation `func1(paramDefault=4,paramRequired=3)`.

```
>>> def func1(paramRequired, paramDefault = 2):
        print paramRequired, paramDefault

    # order doesn't matter: passing by name
>>> func1(paramDefault = 4, paramRequired = 3)
3 4
```

Use of parameter names as keywords in a function invocation is particularly useful when there are many parameters and many have default values. The programmer can then easily specify a few desired arguments they wish to change, without regard to order, and take the default values for the rest.

Example: Default Values and Parameter Keywords

Let's create a simple function that uses default values and parameter names as keywords. The `rhyme` function prints variations of the classic "Roses are red" poem. Let's parameterize the flower and color from the first two lines and leave the closing lines unchanged. We will assign each parameter a default so that if no parameters are specified, the original poem is printed. In the second call, we specify the first two arguments, and leave the remaining two to the default values. In the final call, we name the parameters so that the second flower and color are specified leaving the first two to their default values. Here is the session:

```
>>> def rhyme(flower1="Roses",color1="red",flower2="Violets",color2="blue"):
        print flower1, "are", color1
        print flower2, "are", color2
        print "Sugar is sweet"
        print "And so are you"

>>> rhyme()    # use all defaults
Roses are red
Violets are blue
Sugar is sweet
And so are you
>>> rhyme("Daises", "white")    # use default values for right-most parameters
```

```
Daises are white
Violets are blue
Sugar is sweet
And so are you
>>> rhyme(flower2="Irises")      # pass 1 parameter by name, the rest by default
Roses are red
Irises are blue
Sugar is sweet
And so are you
```

☞ PROGRAMMING TIP

Because any parameter name can be used as a keyword for function invocation, you should name your parameters in a meaningful way.

Issues with Default Values

Argument-to-parameter order can be a bit tricky when mixing standard invocation (i.e., without parameter keyword names) and parameter keywords. In general, you should stick with one style or the other (either invoke with all the parameters named or no parameters named), but if you do mix, make sure that:

- No argument is provided twice, for example once as just an argument and once as a parameter named argument.
- All the required arguments are provided.

A nastier problem can arise, if you use a parameter default value that is mutable, such as a list. Default parameter values are only evaluated once, when **def** is evaluated, and that association is preserved between invocations. This persistence means that changes to the default object associated with the parameter name persists between calls. We illustrate this phenomenon in the following example. We create a function func2 whose parameter listParam has a default value of the empty list. The default value is evaluated when the function is defined and the association between listParam and its object is preserved in the function namespace. The first call func2(1) uses the default for listParam and appends a 1 onto the default list: [1] is returned. When we make a second call using a default argument for listParam, func2(2), the 2 gets appended on to the default object as well. However, that object was modified in the previous call. Any change to the default object, if that object is mutable and modified, will be preserved across invocations. At the end of the session we make a final call that doesn't use defaults and see that the 4 is appended to the end of the list argument [7,8,9] as expected.

```
>>> def func2(element, listParam=[]):
        listParam.append(element)
        return listParam
```

```
>>> func2(1)    # uses the default for listParam
[1]
>>> func2(2)    # again uses default, but that object was modified previously
[1, 2]
>>> func2(3)    # again, the default object associated with listParam persists
[1, 2, 3]
>>> func2(4,[7,8,9])  # no defaults, works as required
[7, 8, 9, 4]
>>> func2(5)    # a final call using a default gets the previous L
[1, 2, 3, 5]
```

Such problems do not occur with immutable defaults, because those objects cannot be modified.

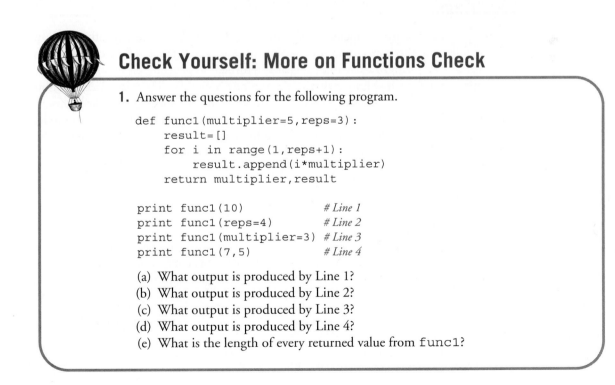

PROGRAMMING TIP

You should never use a default value that is a mutable. If a default mutable is required, it is better to provide a value such as None as the default value in the function definition, and then check for that default value in the function code itself. At that point in the code, you can make a new object and perform the required task.

Check Yourself: More on Functions Check

1. Answer the questions for the following program.

```
def func1(multiplier=5,reps=3):
    result=[]
    for i in range(1,reps+1):
        result.append(i*multiplier)
    return multiplier,result

print func1(10)            # Line 1
print func1(reps=4)        # Line 2
print func1(multiplier=3)  # Line 3
print func1(7,5)           # Line 4
```

(a) What output is produced by Line 1?
(b) What output is produced by Line 2?
(c) What output is produced by Line 3?
(d) What output is produced by Line 4?
(e) What is the length of every returned value from func1?

7.4 FUNCTIONS AS OBJECTS

As we observed earlier, defining a function creates an object in Python. As with any other object, there are methods and variables associated with function objects. To see what those methods and variables are, you can type in a known function name, followed by a dot (.) and the Tab character in IDLE to see what the associated methods and variables are.

Of particular interest are those properties that begin and end with double underscores (_). These are names reserved by Python and serve special purposes. Some of the values associated with functions include:

___name___ The name associated with the function.

___str___ The function used to construct a string from the function. This is the function that **print** uses to represent a function.

___dict___ The namespace of the function (it is a dictionary—Chapter 8).

___doc___ The docstring, which contains information about the function provided by the programmer.

We will cover some of these (and other) methods and properties when we investigate objects, but docstrings are particularly interesting, so we cover them in more detail next.

Docstrings

Python has a nice feature for documenting functions that can be accessed by other Python tools. By following this convention it is possible for a user to retrieve information about a function, for example, how to invoke it, what is returned, its general purpose, and so on.

Suppose you wanted to know what was in the `math` module. There is a `dir` function that lists the names in the module. If you want to know more about a particular function, you can use `__doc__` with double underscores to inquire about a function. For example, after using `dir` to get the names in the math module, you might wonder what the `ceil` and `pow` functions do. Here is a session in the Python shell illustrating these concepts:

```
>>> import math
>>> dir(math)
['__doc__', '__file__', '__name__', 'acos', 'asin', 'atan', 'atan2', 'ceil', 'cos',
 'cosh', 'degrees', 'e', 'exp', 'fabs', 'floor', 'fmod', 'frexp', 'hypot', 'ldexp',
 'log', 'log10', 'modf', 'pi', 'pow', 'radians', 'sin', 'sinh', 'sqrt', 'tan', '
tanh']
>>> math.ceil.__doc__
'ceil(x) \n\nReturn the ceiling of x as a float.\nThis is the smallest integral
value >= x.'
>>> math.pow.__doc__
'pow(x,y) \n\nReturn x**y (x to the power of y).'
```

Minimal information about each function is returned in the docstring, but if the protocol is followed, something useful can always be found.

A docstring is included in a function using triple quotes to delimit the string. It must appear after the header line (just after the **def**). A docstring should either be one brief line or a brief line followed by a blank line, followed by a lengthier description. We include one-line docstrings in most of our function examples. It is good practice.

7.5 EXAMPLE: DETERMINING A FINAL GRADE

For this example, we want to process a file that contains a list of grades and the owner of those grades, and determine the final grade. The grades will be weighted: that is, some grades are worth more to the overall final grade than others. In the end, our program will nicely print out the name, in order: first name, last name, and the final grade.

The Data

We make some assumptions about the file of grades:

- Each line of the file contains five comma-separated fields.
  - The first field is the last name.
  - The second field is the first name.
  - The last three fields are the exam1, exam2, and final exam grade.
- Each grade is an integer between 0 and 100.
- There are no empty fields.

Those are very specific assumptions, and it would take some work to ensure that the code we write enforces those assumptions. For this example, we will assume all files are in the correct format.

The Design

Our overall design will be something like the following:

- Read each line of the file.
- For the line, extract the name, then calculate that grade based on provided weights.
- Create a nice printout of the form: `firstName lastName finalGrade`.

The design suggests that we need at least one function and a main program. The main program should be:

- Prompt for a file to open.
- Read the file, one line at a time.
- Call the function `grade` to calculate the grade.
- Print out each grade in a nice format.

The `grade` function should receive a line of the file and process it. Remember that each function should "do one thing." This function seems to have three responsibilities:

- Parse the line into names and grades.
- Convert the grades (strings from the file) into integers.
- Do the weighted grade calculation.

That is too much for one function. Let's take the final item, the weighted grade calculation, and make that a function as well. We will call it `weightedGrade`. Now there are three functions with clearly identified responsibilities: the `main` program, the `grade` function and the `weightedGrade` function. Let's tackle them one at a time.

Function: `weightedGrade`

This function needs two parameters. The first is a list of three integers between 0 and 100, and the second is a list of weights to apply to each of those grades. Because the weights are usually fixed by the course, we will make them defaults. To avoid issues with mutable data structures as defaults, we will use a tuple as a default with three weights. See, tuples really are handy!

The processing then is to multiply each grade by its weight and to sum those products together into a final grade. We then return that value. The code is in Code Listing 7.3.

Code Listing 7.3

```
def weightedGrade(gradeLst, weights=(0.3,0.3,0.4)):
    '''Expects 3 elements in gradeLst. Multiples each grade
    by its weight. Returns the sum.'''
    result = \
        (gradeLst[0]*weights[0]) +\
        (gradeLst[1]*weights[1]) +\
        (gradeLst[2]*weights[2])
    return result
```

The continuations on lines 5–7, as well as the parentheses, are not necessary but make the process more readable. Note that there is a docstring for the function on lines 2–3.

Function: `grade`

The `grade` function receives a single parameter, a line from the file of grades. It should extract the two name parts, reverse the order of the names, and then call the `weightedGrade` function described earlier with a list of the integer grades. The re-ordered name and the final grade are returned as a tuple. The code is in Code Listing 7.4.

Code Listing 7.4

```
def grade(fileLine):
    '''Expects a line of form last, first, exam1, exam2, final.
    returns first+last and a final grade.'''
    fieldLst = fileLine.split(',')
5   name = fieldLst[1] + ' ' + fieldLst[0]
    grades = []
    for element in fieldLst[2:]:
        grades.append(int(element))
    theGrade = weightedGrade(grades)
10  return name,theGrade
```

Lines 2–3: Docstring description of the function.

Line 4: Extracts the five fields by splitting on the comma, creating a list of five strings.

Line 5: Takes the first two fields (lastName is field 0, firstName is field 1), and concatenates them together into firstName lastName with a space in-between.

Lines 7–8: Create a list of integers from the remaining three fields.

Lines 9–10: Calls the weightedGrade function on the list of integers, then returns the new name and final grade as a tuple. Note that the comma is enough to create a tuple on the return.

Function: main

The main program itself can be made into a function as well. This has some advantages. When the program is loaded, it does not begin running until the user invokes the function directly. It is also useful for creating stand-alone scripts in Python. In any event, we will create the function main to process the file. The code is in Code Listing 7-5.

Code Listing 7.5

```
def main ():
    '''Get a line from the file, print the final grade nicely.'''
    fileName = raw_input('Open what file:')
    fileObj = open(fileName, 'r')
5   print '% -15s %-15s' %('Name','Grade')
    print '-'*25
    for line in fileObj:
        line = line.strip()
        print '%-15s %7.2f'%grade(line)
```

Line 2: Docstring.

Lines 3–4: Prompt for a file name and open the file for reading.

Lines 5–6: Print a header for our output. Note the use of the replication operator on line 6.

Lines 7–9: For each line, strip it of extra characters and print the result of the grade function in a nice way. In particular, note that the value returned in the function call on line 9 is a tuple, and that the elements of the tuple are mapped to the two string format elements.

Example Use

Given a file such as:

```
Smith, John,      100,0,0
CableGuy, Larry,  0,100,0
Harder, Try,      0,0,100
Python, Monty,    100,100,100
Frost, Jack,      50,50,50
Jones, Terry,     75,75,75
```

An example of using our program on that file is shown in the session below.

```
>>> main()
Open what file:grades.txt
Name               Grade
-----------------------
 John Smith         30.00
 Larry CableGuy     30.00
 Try Harder         40.00
 Monty Python      100.00
 Jack Frost         50.00
 Terry Jones        75.00
>>>
```

7.6 ESOTERICA: ''BY VALUE'' OR ''BY REFERENCE''

Languages that trace their roots to procedural languages such as C++, Java, and C#, differentiate between parameters that are passed "by value" vs. "by reference." A common question is: which does Python use? The useful answer for novice programmers is "neither," in the sense the concept applies to those languages. It would take too long to both define those concepts precisely, and to explain why "neither" is the useful answer, but if you go on to study one of those languages, it is useful to know that Python programmers do not need to think in those terms.

The best answer is to say that Python passes *object references*. Everything in Python is an object, so every value passed is a reference to an object. Therefore, an object is not copied in this process. Python passes a reference to that object as illustrated in Figures 7.1–7.4. If the object is mutable, then a change made in the function is reflected in the outer scope of the object. If it is not mutable, a new object is referenced when the reference is updated.

Summary

In this chapter, we further developed the concept of functions in a programming language and showed how functions work in Python. As you will see in later chapters, functions aid us in the divide-and-conquer approach to problem solving. Finally, we examined the role of refactoring with respect to functions.

Exercises

1. In Section 7.2.3, we defined a function called `evens(n)` that generated a list of "n" even numbers. The `range()` function takes a third argument that is the "step"—the step between numbers in the range. Rewrite the function using the third argument in the range. Note that you will also need to change the second argument so that the correct number of even numbers is generated.

2. Refactor the Gettysburg Address Analysis program from Section 6.5 using at least four functions.

3. In Section 7.1 we created a `isFloat()` function. Modify that function so that exponential notation is accepted as valid. That is, floats in the form of "3.5e7" are also be accepted. Note that exponents (after the "e") can only be integers.

4. Modify the `isFloat()` function so that it has only one line by removing the **print** statement and combine the `replace()` and `isdigit()` into one statement.

5. In Section 7.1 we created a `readFloat()` function. Create a similar `readInt()` function and write a small program that uses your function.

6. The `mirror()` function example is not robust.
   (a) Determine function arguments that will generate errors.
   (b) Rewrite the function so those errors will be checked and avoided.

7. Anagrams. In an earlier chapter we created a program that tested whether two strings were anagrams. (We sorted the strings and then compared them.)
   (a) Write a function that returns True, if two strings are anagrams, and False otherwise. (Starting hint: how many parameters do you need?)

(b) Write a program that uses your function. The program should prompt for the two strings, call the function, and then print results (something other than "True" or "False").

8. Palindromes. A palindrome is a word that is the same backwards as forwards. The word "rotor" is an example of a palindrome.

(a) Write a function which returns True, if two strings are palindromes. (Hints: you can create a list from a string using the `list()` function. Lists are handy, because there is a `reverse()` method for strings.)

(b) Write a program that uses your function. The program should prompt for the two strings, call the function, and then print results (something other than "True" or "False").

(c) Some palindrome rules ignore spaces and capitalization so "Never odd or even" is an acceptable palindrome. Improve your function to ignore spaces and capitalization. (Hints: lists have a `remove()` method, and strings have a `lower()` method.)

9. Write a function that takes a list as an argument and verifies whether the list is sorted. Return True if sorted; False if not.

10. Remove Odds or Evens:

(a) Write a function that takes a list of integers as an argument, removes even numbers from the list, and returns the modified list.

(b) Write a function that takes a list of integers as an argument, removes odd numbers from the list, and returns the modified list.

(c) Write a function that takes a list of integers and a Boolean as arguments. If the Boolean is true the function removes odd numbers from the list; otherwise, evens are removed. The function returns the modified list.

11. What does the following code print? Explain.

```
def myFunction(bList):
    bList[0] = 100
    aList = [1,2,3]

aList = [5,6,7]
myFunction(aList)
print aList
```

12. What does the following code print? Explain.

```
def f(a, b=2):
    pass
f( a = 3, b = 4)
print a,b
```

13. Consider the following code. The "print x" statement generates an error. Provide two different ways to print "x" properly. You will need to make assumptions about what is reasonable to print.

```
def addOne(number):
    x=1
    number = number + x
    print number

addOne(3)
    print x
```

14. What is the difference between an argument and a parameter?

15. Create a function that takes as an argument a string and returns the string in reverse order (i.e., if the string is "stressed", your function should return "desserts").

16. Understanding scope is important when working with functions. The value of x was defined to be 1 (below), so why do we get an error when we inquired about its value?

```
def addOne(number):
    x=1
    number=number+x
    print number

>>> addOne(5)
6

>>> x
NameError: name 'x' not defined
```

17. Starting in 1999 the U.S. Government Mint released state-specific quarters at a rate of five states per year. Find the release year for each state's quarters online, e.g. www.usmint.gov. Copy that information into a Python program (as a string, or a list, or tuples, or list of lists, etc.) Write functions that do the following:

    (a) Print the names of the states in the order of release of their quarters. Also, print the years, along with the names.
    (b) Print the names of the states in increasing order of the length of their names. Also print the years along with the names.
    (c) Print the names of states whose quarters were released in the last year.

18. In the earlier chapter on functions there was an exercise based on DNA searching to make a multiFind() function. That function had two constraints that we can now remove: (i) it returned the indices in a string, and (ii) it couldn't handle default arguments. In this exercise we will fix both.

(a) Write a string function `multiFind(someString, subString [,start][,end])` where *start* and *end* are optional arguments with default values for the start and end of *someString*. The *start* and *end* are interpreted as they are in slicing, that is:

$$0 = \text{start} \leq \text{index} < \text{end} = \text{len(someString)}$$

The function should return a list of indices of occurrences of *subString* in *someString*. If the substring is not found, return an empty list.

(b) Demonstrate that your string function works and that you can use it in a Boolean expression.

19. In the chapter on strings there was an example that counted poker hands. Refactor that program with two goals: (i) break the program down into functions and (ii) use a list of counters rather than individual counter variables.

Programming Projects

1. **Data mining stock prices**

Data mining is the process of sorting through large amounts of data and picking out relevant information. It is usually used by business intelligence organizations, and financial analysts, but is increasingly being used in the sciences to extract information from the enormous data sets generated by modern experimental and observational methods.

In this project, we want to do some preliminary data mining to the prices of some company's stock. So that we can speak in specifics, let's look at Google. Your program will calculate the monthly average prices of Google stock from 2004 to 2008, and tell us the 6 best and 6 worst months for Google. We provide the data reading function; you write the next two and a main that calls the functions.

(a) First you need a history of stock prices. Go to finance.yahoo.com, enter Google in the search field, select "Historical Prices" (currently on the left of the page), and find the "download to spreadsheet" option. Choose to save the file in the folder where your Python program will be saved. The default name is "table.csv" so we will use that name. The file format is indicated by the first few lines:

```
Date,Open,High,Low,Close,Volume,Adj Close
2008-09-19,461.00,462.07,443.28,449.15,10006000,449.15
2008-09-18,422.64,439.18,410.50,439.08,8589400,439.08
```

(b) `getDataList(fileName)`

The "csv" file is a "comma-separated file", so we can split the data on commas. The following function will read a file, split the lines in the file on commas, and put the data in to a list that is returned. The result is a list of lists where each line is a list. Also, every item is a string. To read our file, call it using our file name: getDataList('*table.csv*'). Experiment with this function in the shell to get a sense of what is returned.

```
def getDataList(fileName):
    dataFile = open(fileName,"r")
    dataList = [ ]              # start with an empty list
    for line in dataFile:
        # strip end-of-line, split on commas, and append items
        to list dataList.append(line.strip().split(','))
    return dataList
```

(c) getMonthlyAverages(dataList)

In this function, you will use the dataList generated by the getDataList function as the parameter. Use the Date, Volume, and Adj Close fields to calculate the average monthly prices. Here is a formula for the average price for a month, where Vi is the volume and Ci is the day i's adjusted close price (Adj Close).

$$averagePrice = (V1 * C1 + V2 * C2 + \dots + Vn * Cn)/(V1 + V2 + \dots + Vn)$$

For each month create a tuple with two items: the average for that month, and the date (you need only the month and year). Append the tuple for each month to a list (e.g. monthlyAveragesList), and after calculating all the monthly averages, return this list. We use tuples here because once these values are calculated we don't want to accidentally change them!

(d) printInfo(monthlyAveragesList)

In this function, you need to use the list of monthly averages calculated in the getMonthlyAverages function. Here you will need to find and print the 6 best (highest average price) and 6 worst (lowest average price) months for Google's stock. Print them in order from highest to lowest and print to 2 decimal places. Format the output so that it looks good and include informative headers. This function does not return anything.

(e) If you don't call these functions, they are useless. Thus, you should write code to call them.

Hints:

(a) The list sort() and reverse() methods will be useful. Experiment with how they sort a list of tuples—notice how they sort on the first item.

(b) To create a tuple, put items in a comma-separated list with parentheses: (x,y).

(c) When working with a list-of-lists (or a list-of-tuples), the first item in the first list is someList[0][0] and the second item in that same first list is someList[0][1].

2. **Who was the Best NBA Basketball Player?**

The National Basketball Association (NBA) is the North America's professional men's basketball league. You are going to write a program to find the best players in NBA history. You are to get the raw NBA stats from the Web, compute the efficiency of nearly 4000 players, and output the 50 most efficient players, as well as some other interesting statistics.

Efficiency

How do many NBA coaches quickly evaluate a player's game performance? They check his efficiency. NBA.com evaluates all players based on the efficiency formula indicated below (and shown on the aboutstats.htm page) In this project, we will use this efficiency formula. Since we are not evaluating a player based on one game, we need to divide the total efficiency by the number of games the player played. So the formula is:

$$Efficiency = \frac{(pts + reb + asts + stl + blk) - ((fga - fgm) + (fta - ftm) + turnover)}{gp}$$

The abbreviations are described as below:

Other Stats Besides efficiency, also collect:

- The player who played the most minutes.
- The player who played the most games.
- The player who scored the most points.
- The player who got the most rebounds.
- The player who got the most penalties.
- The player who made the most free throws.

(a) `Get Data`

Go to `http://www.databasebasketball.com/stats_download.htm` and download the database (currently named databaseBasketball2.1.zip). Double-click on the file to unpack the zip file. We will use the file "player_regular_season_career.txt" so move that file into the folder where you will be writing your Python program. The first line of the file has headers for the columns, but they are abbreviated. At the bottom of the stats page is a link to a page describing the abbreviations (`http://www.databasebasketball.com/about/aboutstats.htm`).

(b) `Read Data`

To read the data we can use the `getDataList()` function from the previous problem, but we need to make one important modification. Since the basketball data file separates the fields using vertical bars (`'/'`), we must replace the comma in the split function with a vertical bar: `split('/')`. The function will return a list-of-lists that has one list for each player.

(c) Process Data

Calculate the statistics mentioned above, and then output them. For the efficiency, find the top 50 and then order them from best to worst. For calculating the "other" statistics, you could write one function for each, but you should notice a pattern after writing one or two that will indicate how to write one function that you can call for each statistic.

(d) Output

Format your output to make it readable and good-looking. Remember to print the 50 top in efficiency in order from best to worst. Printing should be a function.

CHAPTER 8

Dictionaries and Sets

WHEN WE INTRODUCED LISTS, WE ALSO INTRODUCED THE CONCEPT OF A DATA structure and the important role that data structures play in computer science. Understanding data structures means understanding how data is organized and the kind of algorithms that can work on data organized in that fashion. Lists and strings were examples of data structures that come with Python. In this chapter, we will add *dictionaries* and *sets*, data structures also included in Python. Dictionaries in particular are a very powerful data structure that are useful for solving many problems. In fact, Python relies heavily on dictionaries in its underlying organization.

8.1 DICTIONARIES

What is the dictionary data structure? A dictionary is a collection, but it is *not* a sequence. A dictionary is often referred to as a *map* collection, also sometimes as an *associative array*. You can think of a dictionary as a list of pairs, where the first element of each pair is the *key* and the second element of each pair is the *value*. A dictionary is designed so that a search for a key, and subsequently its associated value, is very efficient. The word "map" comes from this association: the key maps to the value.

All operations on dictionaries are built to work through keys. The data structure is called a dictionary because of its similarity to a real dictionary, such as Webster's dictionary. Think of the keys as the words in Webster's dictionary. It is easy to look up a word (the key) because of the organization of Webster's dictionary (alphabetical). Once the key is found, the associated value, the definition, is clearly indicated. Note that the opposite search, a search for the the value (i.e., the definition), is not easily done. Imagine trying to find a definition without the associated word (key) in Webster's dictionary. It is only possible by by examining every definition in the whole dictionary from beginning to end—not very efficient![1] Dictionaries, both the data structure and Webster's, are optimized to work with keys. However, the dictionary data structure and Webster's are different in one important way: Webster's key organization is based on an alphabetical (sequential) ordering of the keys. In a Python dictionary, instead of arranging keys sequentially, they are arranged for fast searching. Furthermore, the arrangement is hidden from the user. As a result, you cannot print a dictionary collection and count on a particular order. As key-value pairs are added, the dictionary is modified to make key searching efficient for Python.

Dictionary Example

A contact list such as is found in a cell phone could be implemented as a dictionary. Imagine that we have three people in our phone contact list, "bill," "rich," and "jane," and assume that we have a phone number for each one. Figure 8.1 diagrams the data structure. Each name is a *key* and for each key there is an associated *value*, a phone number as a string. If you want the phone number for "bill," you simply look up his name (the *key*) in the contacts and get the associated phone number (the *value*). Note that order of the names (keys) does not matter; only the association between a key and its value matters.

FIGURE 8.1 Phone contact list: names and phone numbers.

You will notice that the figure for the dictionary looks just like the figures for namespaces. That is not by accident: namespaces are implemented as dictionaries in Python. When Python wants the value of a variable it refers to the namespace dictionary using the variable name as the key and retrieves the associated object.

---

[1] Such an approach is often called a *brute force* approach, as it requires examining all possibilities.

Python Dictionaries

Let's implement the dictionary of "contacts" shown in Figure 8.1. Lists were created by the constructor *list* and a shortcut, the square brackets ([ ]). Dictionaries also have a constructor, called *dict* and have a shortcut, curly braces: { }. Like lists, curly braces are often used, although, as with lists, there are applications for the *dict* constructor. When designating the contents of a dictionary, the individual key-value pairs are separated by a colon (:). Values may be anything, but *keys can only be immutable objects* such as integers, strings, or tuples. In this session, we create a contacts dictionary, display it, get a number for "bill," and add a contact for "barb." Note the unordered nature of a dictionary when printed: it is not kept in any apparent order—not even the order of the key-value pair's creation.

```
# create contacts
>>> contacts={'bill': '353-1234', 'rich': '269-1234', 'jane':'352-1234'}
>>> contacts                          # display contacts: note order
{'jane': '352-1234', 'bill': '353-1234', 'rich': '269-1234'}
>>> contacts['bill']                  # get contact info for "bill"
'353-1234'
>>> contacts['barb']='271-1234'       # add contact info for "barb"
>>> contacts                          # observe change in contacts
{'jane':'352-1234', 'bill':'353-1234', 'barb':'271-1234', 'rich':'269-1234'}
>>>
```

Dictionary Indexing and Assignment

Dictionaries are collections that respond to the index operator: [ ]. However, we do not use a sequence number (0 for the first element, −1 for the last, etc) as the index, rather we use the *key as the index value*. Thus, contacts['bill'] is an index into the dictionary, using the key 'bill' to retrieve its associated value '353-1234'. If no such key presently exists in the dictionary, Python throws an error. To add a key-value pair to a dictionary, we can do so by index assignment. That is, contacts['barb']='271-1234' is an assignment of '271-1234' to the key 'barb'. If the key does not yet exist, it is created and then associated with the value. If the key already exists, the new value is associated with the key.

Dictionaries Are Mutable

Because we can do index assignment in a dictionary, a dictionary is our second example of a mutable data structure (the first was a list). In addition to index assignment, dictionaries have a number of methods that change the dictionary in place. As with lists, there are potential consequences to passing a mutable object to functions. If the dictionary is modified in a function, it is modified in the calling program. You will see examples of mutable methods later in this chapter.

Dictionaries with Different Key Types

The power of dictionaries is a combination of its indexing speed and the fact that the value can be any data structure, even another dictionary. Furthermore, the keys can be any immutable object and different types of keys can be used in the same dictionary. In the next session, we create a dictionary with keys that are an integer, a tuple, and a string. Of particular note is that the values are a list, an integer, and a dictionary. We then show access using each key, followed at the end by accessing an element of the dictionary within the dictionary. As with previous chained expressions, they proceed from left to right.

```
# values as list, int, dict
>>> demo = {2:['a','b','c'], (2,4): 27, 'x':{1:2.5, 'a':3}}
·>>> demo                          # kept in "arbitrary" order
{'x': {'a': 3, 1: 2.5}, 2: ['a', 'b', 'c'], (2, 4): 27}
>>> demo[2]                        # access dictionary with each key
['a', 'b', 'c']
>>> demo[(2,4)]                    # key is a tuple!
27
>>> demo['x']                      # value is a dictionary
{'a': 3, 1: 2.5}
>>> demo['x'][1]                   # access item "1" in the dictionary value
2.5
```

The expression demo['x'] yields a dictionary, and that yielded dictionary is further referenced by the index [1], yielding the value 2.5.

As with other data structures we have used, such as strings and lists, we often want to initialize a dictionary to be empty. A pair of curly brackets creates an empty dictionary. Alternately, one can use *dict* with no argument.

```
someDict = {}
anotherDict = dict()
```

Operators

Familiar Collection Operations

Most of the collection operations you have become familiar with work with dictionaries. However, keep in mind that dictionaries are focused on the key of the key-value pair and that dictionaries are mutable.

[ ]: indexing using key in square brackets.
len(): the "length" is the number of key-value pairs in the dictionary.

in: Boolean test of membership, is the key in the dictionary (not the value)?
for: iteration through keys in the dictionary.

In the following session, we illustrate the use of the standard operations. Again, note how they work on the keys of the dictionary, not the values. Also, length only measures the number of key-value pairs. Finally, notice how *for* iterates through all of the dictionary's keys. To discover the values associated with the keys, we must index the dictionary with that key (or use one of the iterators in the next section).

```
>>> myDict = {'a':2, 3:['x','y'], 'joe': 'smith'}   # create a dictionary
>>> myDict                                           # display it
{'a': 2, 3: ['x', 'y'], 'joe': 'smith'}
>>> myDict['a']                    # use square brackets to index
2
>>> len(myDict)                    # lenth is the number of key:value pairs
3
>>> 'a' in myDict                  # membership test
True
>>> 2 in myDict                    # "in" only looks at keys, not values
False
>>> for key in myDict:             # iteration is through the keys, not the values
        print key

a
3
joe
>>> for key in myDict:             # if you want values, include indexing []
        print key, myDict[key]

a 2
3 ['x', 'y']
joe smith
```

Some Dictionary Methods

Four methods for dictionaries are particularly useful, especially for iterating through dictionaries:

items(): all the key-value pairs as a list of tuples
keys(): all the keys as a list
values(): all the values as a list
copy(): a shallow copy of the dictionary

Check out their use in a session:

```
>>> myDict = {'a':2, 3:['x','y'], 'joe': 'smith'}
>>> myDict.items()                # keys and values
[('a', 2), (3, ['x', 'y']), ('joe', 'smith')]
>>> myDict.keys()                 # only keys
['a', 3, 'joe']
>>> myDict.values()               # only values
[2, ['x', 'y'], 'smith']
>>> for key,val in myDict.items(): # iterate yielding keys and values
        print key,val

a 2
3 ['x', 'y']
joe smith
>>> for key in myDict.keys(): # iterate over keys; like "for key in myDict:"
        print key

a
3
joe
>>> for val in myDict.values():    # iterate over values
        print val

2
['x', 'y']
smith
>>> newDict = myDict.copy()
>>> newDict['a']=7
>>> newDict[3][0]='z'
>>> myDict
{'a': 2, 3: ['z', 'y'], 'joe': 'smith'}
>>> myDict = {'a':2, 3:['x','y'], 'joe': 'smith'}
>>> newDict = myDict.copy()
>>> newDict['a']=7
>>> newDict
{'a': 7, 3: ['x', 'y'], 'joe': 'smith'}
>>> myDict
{'a': 2, 3: ['x', 'y'], 'joe': 'smith'}
>>> newDict[3][0]='z' # changes both dict's, index assignment of mutable!
>>> myDict
{'a': 2, 3: ['z', 'y'], 'joe': 'smith'}
>>>
```

The first three methods allow us to iterate through the dictionary yielding keys: value pairs (each as a separate item), only keys, or only values. Because the `items` method returns a list of tuples, we can assign two values for every iteration of the *for* loop: the first element is the key of the pair and the second is the value. The `copy` method makes a shallow copy of the dictionary values. This means that keys are copied properly (as they must be immutable), but if the values are mutable, problems such as we have seen before can arise. When a copy of `myDict` is created and assigned to `newDict`, copies of all the references are made, a shallow copy (see Section 6.6). If index assignment is made to the list value in `newDict`, the change is also shown in `myDict`.

Check Yourself: Dictionary Check

1. Indicate the requested output for the following program:

```
def f1 (myDict):
    temp = 0
    for value in myDict.values():
        temp = temp + value
    return temp

def f2 (myDict):
    temp = ''
    for key in myDict:
        if temp < key:
            temp = key
    return temp

def f3 (myDict,k,v):
    if k in myDict:
        myDict[k]=v

aDict={'bill':1,'rich':2,'fred':10,'walter':20}
print f1(aDict)                     # Line 1
print f2(aDict)                     # Line 2
print None == f3(aDict,'bill',-1)   # Line 3
print aDict                         # Line 4
```

(a) What output is produced by Line 1 of the program?
(b) What output is produced by Line 2 of the program?
(c) What output is produced by Line 3 of the program?
(d) What output is produced by Line 4 of the program?

8.2 WORD COUNT EXAMPLE

In Section 6.5, we introduced file analysis using the Gettysburg Address. In that section, we showed how to count the number of words in a file and how to count the number of unique words in a file.

With dictionaries, we can now do more analysis. In particular, we can determine the frequency of word use in a file using a dictionary. Dictionaries are well suited to such a task. For a word count, we use the word as a key and use as a value the number of occurrences of that word. For every word in the file, we check to see whether that word is already in the dictionary. If the word is in fact already there, we increase its associated count (value) by 1. If the word is not yet in the dictionary, we insert it with a count (value) of 1.

Count Words in a String

Let's warm up by first counting the frequency of words in a string. Our algorithm will be:

- Initialize our `wordCountDict` dictionary to be empty.
- Split the string `speech` into a list `speechList`.
- For every word in a `speechList`:
  - If the word is *in* `wordCountDict`:
    - Add 1 to its value.
  - Else:
    - Insert the word into `wordCountDict` with a value of 1.

We can check whether a word (the key) is in the dictionary using the *in* operator. If a word is already in the dictionary, we can access its value using the word (key) as an index and increment its associated value. If the word (key) is not present, we can use index assignment to create the key and set its associated value to 1. Code Listing 8.1 is the Python code followed by a session. The output is simply the dictionary. Using the words in the famous Shakespearean quote "to be or not to be," the result is "be" and "to" with counts of 2 and the other words with counts of 1.

Code Listing 8.1

```
# Count words in string

speech = "to be or not to be"
speechList = speech.split()

wordCountDict = {}
```

```
for word in speechList:
    if word in wordCountDict:
        wordCountDict[word] += 1
    else:
        wordCountDict[word] = 1

print wordCountDict
```

```
>>>
{'not': 1, 'to': 2, 'or': 1, 'be': 2}
```

Word Frequency for Gettysburg Address

Now that we have an understanding of how to use dictionaries to get word frequencies, let's apply them to the original problem: word frequency in a file, which in this case is the Gettysburg Address. As always, let's break the problem down:

- Open the file and process each line.
- Add each word to the dictionary or update its count.
- Nicely print the output, in this case from high to low frequency.

Again, we want to achieve each major goal with a function. In keeping with our "one function, one action" approach, we can find four functions in the goals stated:

addWord: Add each word to the dictionary. Parameters are the word and a dictionary. No return value.

processLine: There is some work to be done to process the line: strip off various characters, split out the words, and so on. Parameters are a line and the dictionary. It calls `addWord` with each processed word. No return value.

prettyPrint: Because formatted printing can be messy and often particular to each situation (meaning that we might need to modify it later), we separated out the printing function. The parameter is a dictionary. No return value.

main: We will use a main function as the main program. As usual, it will open the file and call `processLine` on each line. When finished, it will call `prettyPrint` to print the dictionary.

Now let's examine each function in detail.

addWord

This function is fairly straightforward and follows from the previous example on word counting. For each word, we check to see whether the word (key) is in the dictionary using the ***in*** operator. If it is, we increment the associated value count. If not, we add the new word to the dictionary as a key with an associated value of 1. The code is shown in Code Listing 8.2.

Code Listing 8.2

```
def addWord(w, wcDict):
    '''Update the word frequency: word is the key, frequency is the value.'''
    if w in wcDict:
        wcDict[w] += 1
    else:
        wcDict[w] = 1
```

Note that there is no return value. Because a dictionary is mutable and because the operations use index assignment, we modify the existing object and that change is reflected in the calling function (processLine in this case).

processLine

We get both the line and the dictionary as parameters. We need the dictionary because we need to pass that to the addWord function. From the line, we need to extract each word. The code is shown in Code Listing 8.3.

Code Listing 8.3

```
import string
def processLine(line, wcDict):
    '''Process the line to get lowercase words to add to the dictionary.'''
    line = line.strip()
    wordList = line.split()
    for word in wordList:
        # ignore the '--' that is in the file
        if word != '--':
            word = word.lower()
            word = word.strip()
            # get commas, periods and other punctuation out as well
            word = word.strip(string.punctuation)
            addWord(word, wcDict)
```

We've seen much of this code before in Code Listing 6.7, but briefly:

Lines 4–5: Strip whitespace from the front and back of the line, then split the line to get a list of words. Remember that the default argument to `split` splits at any whitespace character. These lines could be chained together as:

```
wordList = line.strip().split()
```

Lines 6–8: Iterate through each word in `wordList`. Skip the special string `'--'` that we found in the file (see Section 6.5).

Lines 9–10: Make each word all lowercase and strip off whitespace characters from either end. Lowercase allows us to get a better count so that `'Nation'` is not different from `'nation'`. If case matters, we need to fix that here. Also, these lines could be chained together as we showed earlier.

Line 12: This is the only really "different" line of code. Why do we strip the word twice? The first time stripped out whitespace, what `strip` uses when the default is provided. However, there are situations in the word where a punctuation mark follows a word. For example, if you look at the file, you will see `'nation,'` and `'nation'`. The default `strip` does not remove punctuation, but it seems reasonable that the two strings above should be equivalent. So we strip each line again using the variable `string.punctuation` as an argument to `strip`. That variable contains a string with all the normal punctuation characters. Using it as an argument to `strip` will remove punctuation marks at the beginning or end of a word (but not the middle!). To do so, we must first import the `string` module, which we do in line 1.

Line 13: Call `addWord` with the processed word and the dictionary that was provided as a parameter.

Again, the function does not return a value. All modifications made are made to a mutable data structure (a dictionary) using index assignments. Any change will be reflected in the calling function (`main` in this case).

prettyPrint

Printing the dictionary is a little more complicated than one might think at first. What we would like to do is print the dictionary in sorted order, sorting on the values (the frequencies) from largest to smallest. However, dictionaries are by definition un-ordered. The only way around this is to turn the dictionary into a list and sort that list (a tuple would work, too). The question is, how to do that? The code is shown in Code Listing 8.4.

Code Listing 8.4

```
def prettyPrint(wcDict):
    '''Print nicely from highest to lowest frequency.'''
    # create a list of tuples, (value, key)
```

```
    # valKeyList = [(val,key) for key,val in d.items()]
5   valKeyList=[]
    for key,val in wcDict.items():
        valKeyList.append((val,key))
    # sort method sorts on list's first element, here the frequency.
    # Reverse to get biggest first
10  valKeyList.sort(reverse=True)
    print '%-10s%10s'%('Word', 'Count')
    print '_'*21
    for val,key in valKeyList:
        print '%-12s   %3d'%(key,val)
```

Lines 5–7: do the hard work. We iterate through the dictionary using the `items` method. Remember that `items` returns a tuple in the form of (`key`, `value`) for each dictionary entry. We do multiple assignment to assign the key and value from the returned tuple, and then append them onto the list as a new tuple in (`value`, `key`) order, the reverse of what `items` provides. Why? The `sort` method compares list elements on their first value if the element is a compound object. Because we want to sort on the frequencies, we need them to be first in the tuple.

Line 4: is commented out: it is a list comprehension that performs all the tasks of Lines 5–7. We show it as an example of alternative ways you can accomplish a task as you become more familiar with Python.

Line 10: then sorts the list using the keyword argument `reverse = True` (note the lower-case first letter `'r'` of reverse). The remaining code prints out the frequency-word pairs in columns.

main

After all that, `main` is pretty straight forward. It initializes the dictionary `wcDict`, which gets passed to all the other functions. It opens the predetermined filename, grabs each line, and processes that line. It then prints the dictionary. The code is shown in Code Listing 8.5.

Code Listing 8.5

```
def main ():
    wcDict={}
    fObj = open('gettysburg.txt','r')
    for line in fObj:
        processLine(line, wcDict)
5   print 'Length of the dictionary:',len(wcDict)
    prettyPrint(wcDict)
```

Output and Comments

An abbreviated output of our code on the Gettysburg Address follows. It has 138 entries, as we discovered in Section 6.5, most of which have frequencies of 1. To again reflect the number of unique words, `main` prints the length of the dictionary, which is, in fact, the number of unique words.

```
>>> main()
Length of the dictionary: 138
Word            Count

_____
that            13
the             11
we              10
to               8
here             8
a                7
and              6
of               5
not              5
nation           5
it               5
have             5
...
altogether       1
all              1
ago              1
advanced         1
add              1
above            1
>>>
```

A few things are worth noting:

- The `sort` method will use other elements of a compound object to order objects when the first element is equivalent. Thus all the words with a frequency of 1 are listed in reverse alphabetical order.
- We can easily exclude any word with a frequency of 2 or less in our output. If we do so, the number of words is reduced to only 27. Where would this change be made?
- We could also exclude from the list common, non-meaningful words such as articles (and, the, in, it, etc.). These are often called *stop words* and lists of stop words can be found online. More easily, one can exclude any word with three or fewer letters (which are typically stop words). Where would this change be made?

If we print under the conditions we just listed, frequency greater than 2 and key length greater than 3, we get the following 11 entries:

```
>>> main()
Length of the dictionary: 138
Word          Count
--------------------
that          13
here           8
nation         5
have           5
this           4
dedicated      4
they           3
shall          3
people         3
great          3
dead           3
>>>
```

The results here are more interesting. We see that "nation" is used five times, "dedicated" is used four times, and "great", "dead", and "people" are each used three times. Because the Gettysburg Address was given at a dedication of a cemetery for the historic Battle of Gettysburg the words "dedicated", "great", "dead," and "people" would be expected. The frequent use of "nation" is interesting, and indicates that the speech was about more than dedicating the cemetery. Look what our analysis revealed!

8.3 PERIODIC TABLE EXAMPLE

Using a dictionary requires that you first identify the key and value elements to be used. Consider the example of the periodic table of the elements. We can use an element's symbol as a key and store any interesting data as another data structure associated with that key. For example, the symbol for silicon is "Si" and if our dictionary is named "periodicTable," we can access the data on silicon using `periodicTable["Si"]`.

Working with CSV Files

We'll need a periodic table for our data. There are many online, but the particular one we are using here was found as a spreadsheet.[2] Spreadsheets and other application formats often store data in a proprietary format, one developed by the company. However, many can also save the data in the "comma-separated values" (CSV) format that we saw earlier. CSV files are text files and more portable than an application's proprietary format. Typically a CSV file has a single line for each row (in this case, the row with data about a particular element)

---

[2] http://www.jeffbigler.org/documents/Periodic-Table.xls

where each value in the row is separated from the other values by a comma (hence the name). The row information for the periodic table is listed in Figure 8.2. We are particularly interested in the fields that contain the atomic symbol and the atomic mass (rounded).

```
'atomic #', 'symbol', 'New Group', 'Old Group', 'Period', 'name', 'atomic
mass', etc.'1', 'H', '1', 'I A', '1', 'hydrogen', '1.008', '\xb11', ...
```

FIGURE 8.2 Periodic table CSV file showing column headers and one row.

Many programs can generate a text CSV file for portability (database programs, spreadsheets, etc.), but there is no one standard for CSV file format. Small differences in the actual CSV format used can make reading such a file difficult. Python to the rescue! As we have said many times, one of the strengths of Python is the existence of modules to deal with common problems. Dealing with CSV files is common, so there is a useful Python module named csv that cuts through the mess of the small differences in CSV formats generated by various programs. The module is simple to use. We import the csv module and then open a file in the normal way, creating a file object. We then create a special csv-reader object by calling the function csv.reader with an argument of the file object. The csv-reader object can be used with **for** to iterate through the CSV file. Each iteration yields a row of the file as a list of strings where each element of the list is one of the comma-separated fields in that row.

```
>>> import csv
>>> fileObj = open('Periodic-Table.csv','rU')
>>> reader = csv.reader(fileObj)
>>> for row in reader:
...     print row
...
# some of the output data
['2', 'He', '18', 'VIII A', '1', 'helium', '4.003', '0', '', '', '', '', '', '', ''
, '']
['3', 'Li', '1', 'I A', '2', 'lithium', '6.941', '+1', '', '', '', '', '', '', '',
'']
['4', 'Be', '2', 'II A', '2', 'beryllium', '9.012', '+2', '', '', '', '', '', '', '
', '']
['5', 'B', '13', 'III A', '2', 'boron', '10.81', '+3', '', '', '', '', '', '', '',
'']
# etc. etc.
```

Note a couple of things. We opened the file for reading in universal new line mode ('rU') to avoid the problems of operating system conventions on new lines. It is possible to read the file without the csv reader, but the format of the csv reader is much friendlier. Each value is separated in a list (which we can index), and each row is a separate list. Again, very handy!

Algorithm Overview

For this example we will store some general data about each element (extracted from the CSV periodic table) in our dictionary and use the atomic mass of each element to determine a chemical compound's atomic weight. That is, if someone enters the formula for sulfuric acid (H_2SO_4) as "H2-S-O4" we can look up the mass of each element, multiply by how many atoms of each element there are (e.g., H2 means two hydrogen atoms), and add all the masses together. One challenge will be to parse the compound formula, e.g., to split "H2" into "H" and 2.

Let's begin with an algorithm:

1. Read in the contents of the periodic table CSV file.
2. Create a dictionary of the periodic table using each element symbol as a key and the CSV file information (shown in Figure 8.2) as the value.
3. Prompt for a compound and convert it into a list of elements.
4. Parse the compound into symbol-quantity pairs, e.g., "H2" becomes ("H", 2).
5. Print the name of each element in the compound.
6. Add each component's atomic mass to the total mass using the information in the dictionary.

Functions for Divide and Conquer

Let's take the top two actions listed previously and create two functions to achieve those goals:

readTable(fileObject) takes a file object as input and returns a dictionary where the key is the atomic symbol and the values are the remaining information for each element found in the CSV file.

parseElement(elementString) takes a string of the form '*SymbolCount*' in, such as '*H2*', and return a pair of the form (Symbol, count) such as ('H', 2).

readTable

The readTable(dataFile) function takes a regular file object as its single argument. Its processing should:

1. Create a csv.reader (from the csv module) to read the file.
2. Go through every row of the file and extract the atomic symbol (to use as the key) and the remaining values.
3. Place them in a dictionary.
4. Return the constructed dictionary.

Shown in Code Listing 8.6.

Code Listing 8.6

```
def readTable(dataFile):
    """Read Periodic Table file into a dict. with element symbol as key."""
    dataFile = csv.reader(fileObj)
    periodicTable = {}

5
    for row in dataFile:
        # ignore header rows: elements begin with a number
        if row[0].isdigit():
            symbol = row[1]
10          periodicTable[symbol] = row[:8]    # ignore end of row

    return periodicTable
```

Some things to note:

Line 4: We begin with an empty dictionary: `periodicTable = {}`.

Lines 6–10: The **for** loop processes each data row. We get the element's symbol: `symbol =row[1]`, and then add the element to the dictionary using the symbol as the key. For the dictionary's value, only the first seven fields of the row are used, because the rest of the row happens to have extraneous data (the fields are not filled in). The file has quite a few header rows that we wish to discard (they are descriptive of the data that follows). Because every data row begins with a number (the element's atomic number), we can discard any line that does not begin with a number (line 5). Grabbing the first seven fields includes the symbol in the dictionary's value, but it is neither a problem nor an advantage.

parseElement(elementStr)

The function `parseElement(elementStr)` takes a single string, such as `'H2'`, and converts it to a tuple of symbol and quantity, `('H',2)`. Note a couple of tricky issues:

- `'H2'` should return `('H',2)`
- A singleton, such as `'H'`, should have a quantity 1
- Some symbols have two letters, so `'Si4'` should return `('Si',4)`

The pattern is one or more letters followed by zero or more digits.
The function should:

- Gather all the characters at the beginning of the string. This is the symbol.
- Gather all the digit characters (which we assume to be digits) after the last character. This is the quantity.
- Create the tuple of (symbol, quantity) and return.

The function is shown in Code Listing 8.7.

Code Listing 8.7

```
def parseElement(elementStr):
    """Parse element string into symbol and quantity,
       e.g. Si2 returns ('Si',2)"""
    symbol=""
5   quantity = ""
    for ch in elementStr:
        if ch.isalpha():
            symbol = symbol + ch
        else:
10          quantity = quantity + ch
    if quantity == "":  # if no number, default is 1
        quantity = 1
    return symbol, int(quantity)
```

Some things to note:

Lines 7–10: The *if* statement is used to separate characters from numbers using the `isalpha` method.

Lines 11–12: This *if* statement sets the quantity to 1, if no quantity is found.

assumption: Note that this code assumes a well-formed string of the format indicated. A string with the wrong format will not return the proper value. We'll leave input checking as an exercise for the reader.

With those two functions in hand, we can now write the complete program. We open the file, and then call the function to create the periodic table dictionary. We prompt for a hyphen-separated compound, split the compound into a list using `split("-")` to split on hyphens. Then we walk through that list, and call our `parseElement` function on each item in the list. Now we have a symbol that we can use to access the row values stored in `periodicTable[symbol]`. We access the name (at index 5), and print it. Then we use the atomic mass (at index 6), convert it to a float, and multiply by the `quantity` to calculate the mass that we add onto our total. Here is the program and output using sulphuric acid, H2-S-O4. See Code Listing 8.8.

Code Listing 8.8

```python
import csv

def readTable(fileObj):
    """Read Periodic Table file into a dict. with element symbol as key."""
    dataFile = csv.reader(fileObj)
    periodicTable = {}

    for row in dataFile:
        # ignore header rows: elements begin with a number
        if row[0].isdigit():
            symbol = row[1]
            periodicTable[symbol] = row[:8]   # ignore end of row

    return periodicTable

def parseElement(elementStr):
    """Parse element string into symbol and quantity,
       e.g. Si2 returns ('Si',2)"""
    symbol=""
    quantity = ""
    for ch in elementStr:
        if ch.isalpha():
            symbol = symbol + ch
        else:
            quantity = quantity + ch
    if quantity == "":   # if no number, default is 1
        quantity = 1
    return symbol, int(quantity)

# 1. Read File
fileHandle = open("Periodic-Table.csv", "rUb")

# 2. Create Dictionary of Periodic Table using element symbols as keys
periodicTable = readTable(dataFile)

# 3. Prompt for input and convert compound into a list of elements
compoundString = \
            raw_input("Input a chemical compound, hyphenated, e.g. C-O2: ")
compoundList = compoundString.split("-")

# 4. Initialize atomic mass
mass = 0
print "The compound is composed of: ",
```

```
45 # 5. Parse compound list into symbol-quantity pairs, print name, and add mass
   for c in compoundList:
       symbol, quantity = parseElement(c)
       print periodicTable[symbol][5],    # print element name
       mass = mass + quantity*float(periodicTable[symbol][6]) # add atomic mass
50
   print "\n\nThe atomic mass of the compound is", mass

   fileHandle.close()
```

```
>>>
Input a chemical compound, hyphenated, e.g. C-O2: H2-S-O4
The compound is composed of:  hydrogen sulfur oxygen

The atomic weight of the compound is 98.086
```

Notice how convenient it was in this example to access the periodic table using the element's symbol. That is the power of the dictionary data structure.

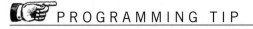 PROGRAMMING TIP

Sometimes you will want to reverse the mapping of a dictionary so that the keys become values and vice-versa. For a dictionary d the d.items() function generates all the key-value pairs. Starting with a new empty dictionary, say d2, you can reverse the mapping with d2[v]=k.

Here is a session illustrating the swapping of key-value pairs in a dictionary.

```
>>> d = {'blue': 500, 'white': 300, 'red': 100}
>>> d2 = {}
>>> for (k,v) in d.items():
        d2[v]=k

>>> d2
{300: 'white', 500: 'blue', 100: 'red'}
```

See Section 8.7, for an alternative way of swapping key-value pairs.

8.4 SETS

The next built-in data structure we consider is the *set*. Sets should be familiar to you from either elementary or middle school mathematics. Python sets work exactly the same way.

History

Sets were invented by Georg Cantor, a German mathematician, in the late 1800's. Though not old by the standards of math, sets have become an integral part of mathematical theory and used to revolutionize many aspects of mathematics. In spite of their power, the main concepts are so simple that they can be taught at an early age.

Let's review the set theory we all learned in elementary and middle school as we learn about Python's sets.

What's in a Set?

A *set* is a collection of objects, regardless of the objects' types. These are the *elements* or *members* of the set. Only *one copy* of any element may exist in the set—a useful characteristic. There is no order to the elements in the set, thus it is, like a dictionary, not a sequence. A set with no elements is the "empty set," also known as the "null set."

Python Sets

A set is created by calling the set constructor. Unlike many of the other data structures we have studied, there is no shortcut for set construction. Thus, to create a set we use the `set` constructor. The set constructor can take zero arguments or one argument. If it has zero arguments, it creates a null set. If it has one argument, then the argument must be iterable such as a string or a list, and every element of the iterable object will be made a member of the set. Here's a session that illustrates these concepts:

```
>>> nullSet = set()        # null set is the empty set
>>> nullSet
set([])
>>> aSet = set("abcd")     # set constructor with iterable argument: a string
>>> aSet
set(['a', 'c', 'b', 'd'])
>>> aSet = set([1,2,3,4])  # set constructor with iterable argument: a list
>>> aSet
set([1, 2, 3, 4])
>>> bSet = set([1,1,2,2,2]) # if list has multiple elements, set will not
>>> bSet
```

```
set([1, 2])
>>> cSet = set(['a', 1, 2.5, (5,6)])  # set of different types is OK
>>> cSet
set(['a', 1, (5, 6), 2.5])
```

When printing a set object, the word "set" is printed to avoid confusing them with lists—it appears that the language designers ran out of unique delimiters. Note that a Python set can contain a mixture of types, just like a list.

If duplicate values are added to a Python set, only one such element is actually placed in the set. This means that you can add an element as many times as you wish to a set and only one example of the element will appear.

Python Sets are Mutable

Like lists and dictionaries, sets are a mutable data structure. Though index assignment is not possible on a set, various methods of the set (such as add or remove) change the elements of a set.

Methods, Operators, and Functions for Python Sets
Typical Operations

len() Like all collections, you can determine the number of elements in a set using the len function.

in Is an element in the set? The *in* operator returns a Boolean, *True* or *False*, depending on whether the element is in the set.

for Like all collections, you can iterate through the elements of a set using the *for* statement.

These operations are shown in the following session.

```
>>> mySet = set('abc123')
>>> print mySet
set(['a', 'c', 'b', '1', '3', '2'])
>>> len(mySet)
6
>>> 'a' in mySet
True
>>> 'z' in mySet
False
>>> for element in mySet:
...     print element
...
```

```
a
c
b
1
3
2
>>>
```

Set Methods

Python provides methods that implement the typical mathematical set operations. Each operation is a method. It is called using the dot notation, with a set as the calling data structure, taking a single argument, another set. For some methods, the order matters (that is, which set is the argument and which set is the method caller); for others order does not matter.

Intersection

The *intersection* method creates a new set of the elements that are common to both sets (Figure 8.3). The order of the sets does not matter.

```
>>> aSet
set(['a', 'c', 'b', 'd'])
>>> bSet                              # notice that sets are not ordered
set(['c', 'e', 'd', 'f'])
>>> aSet.intersection(bSet)           # elements in both aSet and bSet
set(['c', 'd'])
>>> bSet.intersection(aSet)
set(['c', 'd'])                       # order of caller and argument not important
```

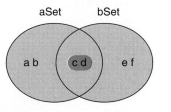

FIGURE 8.3 Intersection of *set*(['a', 'b', 'c', 'd']) and *set*(['c', 'd', 'e', 'f']).

Union

The *union* operator creates a set that contains all the elements in both sets (Figure 8.4). The order of the sets does not matter.

```
>>> aSet
set(['a', 'c', 'b', 'd'])
>>> bSet
set(['c', 'e', 'd', 'f'])
>>> aSet.union(bSet)        # union contains everything in both sets
set(['a', 'c', 'b', 'e', 'd', 'f'])
>>> bSet.uniion(aSet)
set(['a', 'c', 'b', 'e', 'd', 'f'])   # order doesn't matter
```

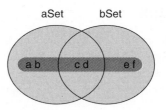

FIGURE 8.4 Union of `set(['a', 'b', 'c', 'd'])` and `set(['c', 'd', 'e', 'f'])`.

Difference

The *difference* operator collects those elements that are in the invoking set and not in the argument set (Figure 8.5). Unlike the other set operators, the difference operator is *not commutative* (much in the same way that integer subtraction is not commutative: $5 - 2$ is not the same as $2 - 5$). That is, `aSet.difference(bSet)` is different than `bSet.difference(aSet)`.

```
>>> aSet
set(['a', 'c', 'b', 'd'])
>>> bSet
set(['c', 'e', 'd', 'f'])
>>> aSet.difference(bSet) # elements of aSet that are not in bSet
set(['a', 'b'])
>>> bSet.difference(aSet) # change order: elements of bSet not in aSet
set(['e', 'f'])
```

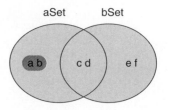

FIGURE 8.5 Difference of `set(['a', 'b', 'c', 'd'])` and `set(['c', 'd', 'e', 'f'])`.

Symmetric Difference

The *symmetric difference* is the opposite of intersection: it collects those elements that are not shared in the two sets (Figure 8.6). The order of the sets does not matter.

```
>>> aSet
set(['a', 'c', 'b', 'd'])
>>> bSet
set(['c', 'e', 'd', 'f'])
>>> aSet.intersection(bSet)
set(['c', 'd'])
>>> aSet.symmetric_difference(bSet)    # everything not in the intersection
set(['a', 'b', 'e', 'f'])
>>> bSet.symmetric_difference(aSet)
set(['a', 'b', 'e', 'f'])              # order does not matter
```

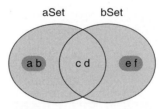

FIGURE 8.6 Symmetric difference of `set(['a', 'b', 'c', 'd'])` and `set(['c', 'd', 'e', 'f'])`.

Subset and Superset

The concept of *subset* and *superset* should be familiar. A set is a subset of another set only if *every* element of the first set is an element of the second set. Superset is the reversed concept: set A is a superset of set B only if set B is a subset of set A. Clearly, the order of set operation matters in these operations; i.e., it is not commutative. See Figure 8.7.

```
>>> smallSet
set(['a', 'c', 'b'])
>>> bigSet
set(['a', 'c', 'b', 'e', 'd', 'f'])
>>> smallSet.issubset(bigSet)      # is smallSet a subset of bigSet?
True
>>> bigSet.issubset(smallSet)      # reversed: is bigSet a subset of smallSet?
False
>>> smallSet.issuperset(bigSet)    # superset?
False
>>> bigSet.issuperset(smallSet)
True
>>> smallSet.issubset(smallSet)    # is a set a subset of itself?
```

```
True
>>> smallSet.issuperset(smallSet) # how about superset?
True
```

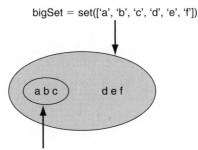

bigSet = set(['a', 'b', 'c', 'd', 'e', 'f'])

a b c   d e f

samllSet = set(['a', 'b', 'c'])

FIGURE 8.7 `set(['a', 'b', 'c'])` is a subset of `set(['a', 'b', 'c', 'd', 'e', 'f'])`.

Check Yourself: Set Check

1. Indicate the requested output for the following program.

```
def f1 (s1,s2,op=4):
    if op == 1:
        temp = s1.intersection(s2)
    elif op == 2:
        temp = s1.difference(s2)
    else:
        temp = s1.union(s2)
    return temp

set1 = set('ab')
set2 = set('cd')

print f1(set1,set2)          # Line 1
print f1(set1,set2,1)        # Line 2
print f1(set1,set2,2)        # Line 3
```

(a) What output is produced by Line 1 of the program?

(b) What output is produced by Line 2 of the program?

(c) What output is produced by Line 3 of the program?

Other Set methods

There are a few other set methods that you might find useful;

add(element) adds the element to the set. There is no effect if the element is already
   in the set (remember, only one copy of an element in a set). It modifies the set, so there
   is no return value.

clear() Removes all the elements of the set (making it empty).

remove(element) and discard(element) Both methods remove the element
   if it exists. The difference is that remove will cause an error if the element being
   removed is not part of the set. In contrast, discard will not give an error even if the
   argument being removed does not exist in the set. There is no value returned.

copy() Returns a shallow copy of the set (see Section 6.6).

8.5 SET APPLICATIONS

There are many applications that can make use of sets. However, two general categories are
worth mentioning:

- Finding the unique elements (of a list, file, etc.). It is relatively simple to do: just add
  each element to the set and let the set deal with multiples copies.
- Finding various combinations of elements using the set operators.

Relationship between Words of Different Documents

Earlier in this chapter (Section 8.2), we counted the frequency of words in a file using the
Gettysburg Address as an example. Let's build on this work to do even more file analysis,
by comparing the words used in two different files to see what that might tell us about the
documents. We will use sets to discover properties such as: the common words, the number
of unique words used by both, and the number of unique words used in each document.
For this example, we will continue to use the Gettysburg Address and compare its contents
to the Declaration of Independence.

The good news is that the outline of work from Section 8.2—even some of the code
itself—can be reused or only slightly modified to solve this new problem. Code reuse is one
of the advantages of good, modular design. Functions that solve a problem well can be used
in other contexts with little or no change required.

Here is a list of functions we will reuse. Modifications are described as well.

addWord: Add each word to the set. Parameters are the word and a set. No return value.
   This function must be modified from its previous definition to use the appropriate set
   methods.

processLine: There is some work to be done to process the line: strip off various characters,
   split out the words, and so on. Parameters are a line and the set. It calls addWord with

each processed word. No return value. Happily, this function can be used as is! Though the parameter names are inappropriate for this context, the code functions perfectly.

prettyPrint: The parameters are the two file sets. No return value. *As the output required is quite different, this function will have to be re-written.*

main: We will use a main function as the main program. As before it will open each file and call `processLine` on each line. When finished, it will call `prettyPrint` and print the results for the two sets. *This function requires some slight modifications.*

Let's take a look at the functions in detail.

addWord

We are working with sets, so we must use different methods—in particular the `add` method. Again, it is useful to note that this change is isolated in this function. We need not change other parts of the code to deal with changing the set. The code is shown in Code Listing 8.9.

Code Listing 8.9

```
def addWord(w, theSet):
    '''Add the word to the set. No word smaller than length 3.'''
    if len(w) > 3:
        theSet.add(w)
```

As we hinted at in Section 8.2, it is useful to treat any word of length 3 or less as a stopword. The *if* statement on line 3 does this.

processLine

This code is untouched from the previous version except to use an appropriate parameter name for this context. The code is shown in Code Listing 8.10.

Code Listing 8.10

```
  def processLine(line, theSet):
      '''Process the line to get lowercase words to be added to the set.'''
      line = line.strip()
      wordList = line.split()
5     for word in wordList:
          # ignore the '--' that is in the file
          if word != '--':
              word = word.strip()
              # get commas, periods and other punctuation out as well
```

```
10      word = word.strip(string.punctuation)
        word = word.lower()
        addWord(word, theSet)
```

main

The main program is modified slightly. We must now open two files to do the comparison, and for each we must create a set for processing and then process all the lines of the file using `processLine`. After both sets are created, we call `prettyPrint` with the two sets to print out the information. The code is shown in Code Listing 8.11.

Code Listing 8.11

```
def main ():
    '''Compare the Gettysburg Address and the Declaration of Independence.'''
    GASet = set()
    DoISet = set()
5   GAFileObj = open('gettysburg.txt')
    DoIFileObj = open('declOfInd.txt')
    for line in GAFileObj:
        processLine(line, GASet)
    for line in DoIFileObj:
10      processLine(line,DoISet)
    prettyPrint(GASet, DoISet)
```

prettyPrint

The main differences of the program are here. The function takes the two sets as parameters and then prints out various pieces of information about the documents. At the end, we print out the common words in a nice format as well. As is often the case with print-oriented code, it appears complicated, but each element is straight forward. The code is shown in Code Listing 8.12.

Code Listing 8.12

```
def prettyPrint(gaSet, doiSet):
    # print some stats about the two sets
    print 'Count of unique words of length 4 or greater'
```

```
 5    print 'Gettysburg Addr: %d, Decl of Ind: %d\n'%(len(gaSet),len(doiSet))
      print '%15s %15s'%('Operation', 'Count')
      print '-'*35
      print '%15s %15d'%('Union', len(gaSet.union(doiSet)))
      print '%15s %15d'%('Intersection', len(gaSet.intersection(doiSet)))
10    print '%15s %15d'%('Sym Diff', len(gaSet.symmetric_difference(doiSet)))
      print '%15s %15d'%('GA-DoI', len(gaSet.difference(doiSet)))
      print '%15s %15d'%('DoI-GA', len(doiSet.difference(gaSet)))

      # list the intersection words, 5 to a line, alphabetical order
15    intersectionSet = gaSet.intersection(doiSet)
      wordList = list(intersectionSet)
      wordList.sort()
      print '\n Common words to both'
      print '-'*20
20    cnt = 0
      for w in wordList:
          if cnt % 5 == 0:
              print
          print '%13s'% (w),
25        cnt += 1
```

Some comments.

Line 4: We print the lengths of the two sets. These lengths represent the number of unique words (no duplicates in a set, remember) for each document. Because of the change we made to addWord, these are only the words of length four or greater.

Lines 8–13: Here we print out the lengths, not the contents, of the sets that result from various set operations. We format the results in two columns.

Lines 15–17: The only contents we'll print are the intersection result, as it is the smallest. We create the intersection set, then turn the contents into a list. We do this because it would be nice to list the common words in alphabetical order and sets are unordered. Once converted to a list, we sort the list.

Line 20–25: All of this code is to print the list of sorted words in a five-column format. We iterate through the list and print each word one at a time. That print statement on line 24 has a comma at the end indicating that no new line character is printed. All the words will print to the same line. However, we keep a variable cnt to track how many words are printed. Every fifth word triggers the *if* statement on line 23, which prints a blank line. The result is that the code prints five columns of words.

Output and Comments

The session below show the output of the program on the two files.

```
>>> main()
Count of unique words of length 4 or greater
Gettysburg Addr: 100, Decl of Ind: 487

        Operation           Result
---------------------------------
            Union             556
     Intersection              31
         Sym Diff             525
           GA-DoI              69
           DoI-GA             456


Common words to both
--------------------

        cause       civil       created        earth       equal
         from        full    government        great        have
         here     liberty         lives         long      nation
       people       power     remaining        shall      should
         that       their         these         they        this
        those        thus         under        which        will
        world

>>>
```

We can confirm that these numbers make sense. The sum of the two sets is 587, but the intersection has 31 words, meaning that the union should have a count of 587 − 31 = 556. Good so far. The GettysburgAddr - DeclOfIndependence should be the difference of the first set size minus the common set size, 100 − 31 = 69. Also good. The symmetric difference should be the difference between the union size and the intersection size, 556 − 31 = 525. All good.

As for the common (intersection) words, they are interesting to see. Words appear that you would expect such as "nation", "liberty", "government," "people," and so on.

8.6 SCOPE: THE FULL STORY

In Section 7.2, we defined the term "scope," mostly as it applies to functions. Now that we have dictionaries, we can provide a more complete explanation. A novice programmer can get by without a complete understanding of scope, but a greater understanding is useful as you advance in Python (or another programming language). Also, a better understanding of scope can help interpret some error messages.

Namespaces and Scope

Remember, a namespace is a relation between names and objects. It is easy to think of a namespace as a dictionary, where the keys are the names and the values are the objects.[3] Namespaces do not share names. A name in one namespace can have as a value any Python object, and the same name in different namespaces can be associated with a different object. However, multiple namespaces can work together to resolve a name if a name-resolution protocol exists. That is, if there are multiple namespaces (and there always are), we can define an order of search to look through different namespaces to find a name (or find that the name does not exist in any recognized namespace). That process defines scope in Python.

In Python we resolve names by defining a search rule that defines the order that Python looks through multiple namespaces to find a name (or find that the name is not yet defined).

Search Rule for Scope

In the book *Learning Python*[4], the authors define a lovely acronym that summarizes the Python rule for scope. They call it the *LEGB* rule, where the letters stand for:

- **L**ocal
- **E**nclosing
- **G**lobal
- **B**uilt-in

This *LEGB* rule defines the sequence of namespaces examined when looking for a name (variable name, function name, etc.). If the entire sequence is examined and the name is not found, then Python returns an error. Let's take a look at each of the namespaces searched.

Local

The local namespace is the namespace that we discussed in Section 7.2 in the context of a function. It is the namespace within a function that comes into being when the function is invoked, and disappears when the function invocation ends. While the local namespace is active, it is the first namespace that is checked for the existence of a name. If the name is found in the local namespace, then the associated object (or an error if the name exists but no value is yet associated) is returned. Look at Code Listing 8.13 and session.

---

[3] The Python documentation notes that, although namespaces are currently implemented as dictionaries, it would be dangerous to count on that fact, as the implementation might change!

[4] *Learning Python,* 3rd Edition, by: Mark Lutz, Published by O'Reilly Media, Inc., ©2007 Mark Lutz, All rights reserved. Used with Permission, ISBN #0596513984.

Code Listing 8.13

```
globalX = 27

def myFunction(param1=123, param2='hi mom'):
    localX = 654.321
    print '\n=== local namespace ==='
    for key,val in locals().items():
        print 'key:%s, object:%s' % (key, str(val))
    print 'localX:',localX
    print 'globalX:',globalX

myFunction()
```

```
=== local namespace ===
key:localX, object:654.321
key:param1, object:123
key:param2, object:hi mom
localX: 654.321
globalX: 27
>>>
```

The special function `locals` takes no arguments and returns a dictionary of the local namespace—in this case, the namespace found in the function `myFunction` while it is running. Notice that there are three entries: the two parameters `param1` and `param2` and the variable created by assignment in the function suite, `localX`. Further, notice that the variable `globalX` assigned outside of the function is not found in the local namespace of the function. Yet, as evidenced by the print statement, it is available and can be printed in the function.

Python is able to resolve `globalX` because `globalX` is in the global namespace. The search rule, LEGB, says to look first in the local space, (then in the Enclosing space—described later), and then in the global space. Let's look at the global namespace.

Global

One place where a namespace is maintained is in a module. Modules are Python files, and they contain objects such as functions that can be imported and used by other programs. The `math` module is the one we've discussed the most. When a module like `math` is imported, that module brings with it a namespace that relates all the names of the module to objects. This namespace can be observed by looking at the dictionary stored in `__dict__` in each module. This dictionary is the namespace for the module.

If we want to reference one of the objects in a module such as math, we precede the associated name with the module name using dot notation. When we do so, we are asking for the object associated with a name in that module. For example, math.pi is a request for the object (in this case, a floating-point number) associated with the name pi in the math module.

When the Python interpreter starts up, it loads two default modules without requiring an import: the module __main__ and the module __builtins__. The __main__ is the default, global module in which all new objects are stored. The dictionary of that namespace can be accessed by using the function globals. When we type interactively to the Python interpreter, globals is the active namespace.

Look at Code Listing 8.14 and resulting session. The function is identical to the function in the previous example.

Code Listing 8.14

```python
import math
globalX = 27

def myFunction(param1=123, param2='hi mom'):
    localX = 654.321
    print '\n=== local namespace ==='
    for key,val in locals().items():
        print 'key: %s, object: %s' % (key, str(val))
    print 'localX:',localX
    print 'globalX:',globalX

myFunction()

print '\n--- global namespace ---'
for key,val in globals().items():
    print 'key: %-15s object: %s' % (key, str(val))

print '\n----------------------'
#print 'LocalX:', localX
print 'GlobalX:', globalX
print 'Math.pi:',math.pi
print 'Pi:',pi
```

```
=== local namespace ===
key: localX, object: 654.321
key: param1, object: 123
```

```
key: param2, object: hi mom
localX: 654.321
globalX: 27

--- global namespace ---
key: myFunction        object: <function myFunction at 0xe15a30>
key: __builtins__      object: <module '__builtin__' (built-in)>
key: __package__       object: None
key: globalX           object: 27
key: __name__          object: __main__
key: __doc__           object: None
key: math              object: <module 'math' from '/Library/Frameworks/Python.
framework/Versions/2.6/lib/python2.6/lib-dynload/math.so'>

----------------------
GlobalX: 27
Math.pi: 3.14159265359
Pi:

Traceback (most recent call last):
  File "/Volumes/Admin/Book/chapterDictionaries/localsAndGlobals.py", line 22, in
<module>
    print 'Pi:',pi
NameError: name 'pi' is not defined
```

The local function results are exactly as in the previous example, but we now also print the global values. Notice a few things. First, `globalX` is indeed in the global namespace, which is why the print statement in `myFunction` does work. Python first looks in the local namespace, fails, and moves on to look in the global namespace.

Second, `myFunction` is itself a name in the global namespace! Finally, the variable `localX` is not in the global namespace. If we try to print its value, we get an error. There is an error, because at that point in the program, outside of the running function, the function's namespace is unavailable. The function's namespace is active only while the suite of the function is actually executing.

Third, `math` is now a name in the global namespace due to the import of the math module, so we can use `math` as a prefix to names in that module. When we print `math.pi`, we get a value, but when we print `pi` by itself, we get an error. That name `pi` is not in the global namespace!

The Local Assignment Rule

One interesting effect of Python's approach is something we call the "local assignment" rule. If anywhere in a function a local assignment is made, then that assignment is assumed to create a name *only in the presently active namespace*. This has the sometimes painful side effect shown in Code Listing 8.15.

Code Listing 8.15

```
myVar = 27

def myFunction(param1=123, param2='Python'):
    for key,val in locals().items():
        print 'key %s: %s' % (key, str(val))
    myVar = myVar + 1      # causes an error!

myFunction(123456, 765432.0)
```

```
key param2: 765432.0
key param1: 123456
Traceback (most recent call last):
  File "localAssignment1.py", line 9, in <module>
    myFunction(123456, 765432.0)
  File "localAssignment1.py", line 7, in myFunction
    myVar = myVar + 1      # causes an error!
UnboundLocalError: local variable 'myVar' referenced before assignment
>>>
```

We first create the variable myVar by assignment in the global namespace. The natural expectation is that, when we try to add 1 to that value within the function, the function looks in the local namespace, cannot find it, and moves on to the name in the global namespace. Sadly, that is not how it works.

Python makes the following assumption. If an assignment of a variable takes place *anywhere* in the suite of a function, Python adds the name to the local namespace. The statement myVar = myVar + 1 has an assignment of the name myVar. Python assumes, no matter where the assignment occurs, that myVar is part of the local namespace of the function myFunction. When Python tries to add 1 to myVar, the name is in the local namespace but has no value (yet), so Python generates an error.

The problem is *when* Python decides to make myVar local. It does so *before* the code is run, i.e., when Python encounters the function definition. As the local namespace is created (before the code actually runs), Python examines the code and populates its local namespace. Before it runs the offending line, it sees the assignment to myVar and adds it to the local namespace. When the function is executed, the Python interpreter finds that myVar is in the local namespace but has no value yet—generating an error.

The global Statement

There is a way around this conundrum. If, within a function suite, a variable is declared to be a global variable using the ***global*** statement, then Python will not create a local name in the namespace for that variable. The following session shows the change in the new function `betterFunction` while keeping the old code around for comparison.

Code Listing 8.16

```python
myVar = 27

def myFunction(param1=123, param2='Python'):
    for key,val in locals().items():
        print 'key %s: %s' % (key, str(val))
    myVar = myVar + 1        # causes an error!

def betterFunction(param1=123, param2='Python'):
    global myVar
    for key,val in locals().items():
        print 'key %s: %s' % (key, str(val))
    myVar = myVar + 1
    print 'myVar:',myVar


# myFunction(123456, 765432.0)
betterFunction()
```

```
key param2: Python
key param1: 123
myVar: 28
>>>
```

Built-Ins

As we mentioned earlier, there are two namespaces that are created when Python starts: `__main__` and `__builtins__`. The latter is a link to all the regular Python programs and data types that are provided by default. Following the LEGB search rule, if Python cannot find a name in first the local namespace, then the global namespace, it looks for a Python built-in name.

The `builtin` module, like other modules, has a `__dict__` attribute, which is the module's namespace. The following code will print out the key-value pairs in that namespace. The output from Code Listing 8.17 is too long to include here.

Code Listing 8.17

```
builtinDict = __builtins__.__dict__
print 'Builtin dictionary has %d entries\n'%(len(builtinDict))

for key,val in builtinDict.items():
    print 'key:: %-20s val:: %s'%(key,str(val))
```

Enclosed

An astute reader will note that we skipped one letter: what about the "E" in the LEGB rule, the "Enclosed" namespace? A beginning programmer may not encounter this situation, but we include it for completeness.

The "Enclosed" scope rule applies when a function defines a function; that is, within a function's suite, a new function is defined. Take a look at the code and output in Code Listing 8.18.

Code Listing 8.18

```
globalVar = 27

def outerFunction(paramOuter = 123):
    outerVar = globalVar + paramOuter

    def innerFunction(paramInner = 0):
        # get inner, enclosed and global
        innerVar = paramInner + outerVar + globalVar
        # print inner namespace
        print '\n--- inner local namespace ---'
        for key,val in locals().items():
            print '%s:%s'%(key,str(val))
        return innerVar

    result = innerFunction(outerVar)
    # print outer namespace
    print '\n--- outer local namespace ---'
    for key,val in locals().items():
```

```
        print '%s:%s'%(key,str(val))
    return result

result  = outerFunction(7)
print '\n--- result ---'
print 'Result:',result
```

```
--- inner local namespace ---
outerVar:34
innerVar:95
paramInner:34

--- outer local namespace ---
outerVar:34
paramOuter:7
result:95
innerFunction:<function innerFunction at 0xe2ba30>

--- result ---
Result: 95
>>>
```

The innerFunction is defined within the suite of outerFunction. In the session output, you can see that innerFunction is part of the local namespace of outerFunction, meaning that *only* outerFunction can call it. The innerFunction is available for execution only during the execution of outerFunction. The full LEGB rule is to check the local namespace, then any functions that enclose our local namespace, as outerFunction encloses innerFunction, then the global namespace, and ending with the built-ins. The output shows the dependencies of the various pieces.

For the beginning programmer, this kind of "nested" function is uncommon. Still, it does show fairly clearly how the scope search rule of Python works.

8.7 PYTHON POINTER: USING ZIP TO CREATE DICTIONARIES

An interesting and very useful operator is zip, which creates pairs from two parallel sequences. The zip operator works like a zipper to merge multiple sequences into a list of tuples. It is not special to dictionaries, but when combined with the *dict* constructor, it provides a useful way to create dictionaries from sequences.

```
>>> keys = ["red","white","blue"]
>>> values = [100, 300, 500]
>>> d = dict(zip(keys,values))
>>> d
{'blue': 500, 'white': 300, 'red': 100}
```

The `zip` function provides another way to reverse key-value pairs, but it is possible only if values are immutable so that they are allowable as keys. Here is a session that reverses the key-value pairs of the previous session:

```
>>> d
{'blue': 500, 'white': 300, 'red': 100}
>>> d2 = dict(zip(d.values(), d.keys()))
>>> d2
{300: 'white', 500: 'blue', 100: 'red'}
```

VISUAL VIGNETTE

8.8 BAR GRAPH OF WORD FREQUENCY

Having constructed the dictionary of word-frequency pairs, it would be interesting to plot the words versus their frequency to visualize the results. Matplotlib provides a `bar` command to plot bar charts, so that is a natural choice.

There are three general steps to make the bar chart in this case. The first is to set up the x-axis to use the words as the labels. The second is to get the dictionary data gathered together in the appropriate format for plotting. The third is to actually make the plot. Let's see some code, then go through these issues one at a time. We add a new function, the `barGraph` function, that takes as a parameter our `wcDict` from Section 8.2 and plots a bar graph of word versus frequency. The code is shown in Code Listing 8.19.

Code Listing 8.19

```
def barGraph(wcDict):
    '''bar graph of word–frequency, xaxis labeled with words'''
    # collect key and value list for plotting
    wordList = []
```

```
5    for key,val in wcDict.items():
         if val>2 and len(key)>3:
             wordList.append((key,val))
     wordList.sort()
     keyList = [key for key,val in wordList]
10   valList = [val for key,val in wordList]
     # get ticks as the keys/words
     barWidth=0.5
     xVals = numpy.arange(len(keyList))
     pylab.xticks(xVals+barWidth/2.0,keyList,rotation=45)
15   # create the bar graph
     pylab.bar(xVals,valList,width=barWidth,color='r')
     pylab.show()
```

Getting the Data Right

Ultimately, what we want are two lists: a list of the keys in alphabetical order and another corresponding list of values. "Corresponding" means that we want the index of the key list to "line up" with its associated value in the value list. Let's take a look:

Lines 4–7: We make a list wordList and append onto it all the key-value pairs as tuples from wcDict. As we did in Section 8.2, we take only those words that appear to be important: frequencies greater than 2 and word length greater than 3. We order the tuples in (key,value) order because we want to then sort the list into alphabetical order on the words. Thus we need the key to be first in each tuple.

Lines 9–10: We then create the two lists, keyList and valueList, that contain the keys and the values, respectively. The index of the keys and values are aligned, that is, the key at index 0 corresponds to the value at index 0 and so forth. We use a list comprehension in both cases.

Labels and the xticks Command

Matplotlib provides a command to orient and label each x-axis entry. These entries are often called "ticks," so the commands to label them are called xticks and yticks. If you do not provide such a command, matplotlib will label the ticks with the appropriate number. However, you have the option to say what each tick label should be and where it should be located. Let's look.

Line 12: We set a width barWidth for the width of our bars in the graph.

Line 13: We create a list with numbers from 0 to the size of our keyList. We use the NumPy function arange, similar to range, to generate the list (see Appendix C). This will be the number of xticks on our graph.

Line 14: This is the `xticks` command. It takes three arguments here. The first is the location of the tick being placed. We are using a NumPy array to indicate the position of each tick, and to each of those ticks we add the tick position and the `barWidth` and divide by 2. Because it is a NumPy array, the addition-division is done to each element of the `xVals` array (see Appendix C for more details). The second argument is the list of labels, the `keyList`. The third is an option, asking to rotate each label 45 degrees.

Plotting

Lines 16–17 do the plotting. The `bar` command takes four arguments here. The first is the xtick locations. The labels were set previously by the `xticks` command. The second is the list of values to plot, the `valList`. The last two are plot options, the bar width and the bar color. The `show` command then draws the plot.

The plot is shown in Figure 8.8.

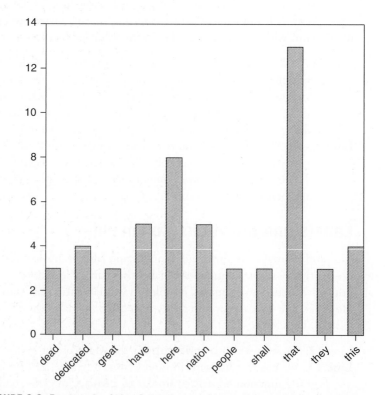

FIGURE 8.8 Bar graph of the Gettysburg Address "important" word frequencies.

Summary

In this chapter, we introduced the powerful and useful dictionary and set data structures.

Exercises

1. Revisit the Gettysburg analysis of Chapter 6 and rewrite the word-counting part of the program using dictionaries.

2. A Caesar cipher encrypts a message by shifting letters in the alphabet. For example, a shift of 4 maps 'a' to 'e' and maps 'p' to 't' Here is a famous line from Shakespeare encrypted with a shift of 4: 'vq dg qt pqv vq dg: vjcv ku vjg swguvkqp.'

   (a) Write a program that takes as input a string to be encrypted and an integer encrpytion shift (such as 4 mentioned above), and prints the encrypted string. Hint: `zip()` is helpful in building a dictionary.

   (b) Extend your program to take an additional input that indicates if your program is to encrypt or decrypt the string.

3. Texting on portable devices has developed a set of abbreviations due to the necessary brevity of text messages. Create a dictionary of texting abbreviations, and use it to write functions that can translate to and from English. Of course, your dictionary cannot be complete. For example: "y r u l8?" translates to "Why are you late?"

4. Given the following sets, predict the outputs and then check them in your shell. (Hint: remember which is independent of the order, i.e., when it matters that aset is first versus bset being first.)

```
aset=set(["the", "coat", "had", "many", "colors", "red", "blue", "yellow"])
bset=set(["my", "coat", "had", "two", "main", "colors", "red", "blue"])
x= aset.intersection(bset)
y= bset.intersection(aset)
print x
print y
w= aset.union(bset)
v= aset.union(aset)
print w
print v
t= aset.difference(bset)
u= bset.difference(aset)
print t
print u
r= aset.symmetric_difference(bset)
s= bset.symmetric_difference(aset)
print r
print s
```

5. What are the characteristics and limitations of sets?

6. What does the set operator "in" return? Give an example.

7. Why is it important for a *key* of a dictionary to be immutable, even though the dictionary itself is mutable?

8. Refactor the program from Chapter 6 to determine the number of unique words in the Gettysburgs Address. This time use sets. Be sure to strip the words of their punctuation and make all the letters lowercase.

9. Letter Counts Using Dictionaries

   (a) Write a function that takes as input a string and returns the most common letter in the string.

   (b) Write a function that takes as input a string and returns a dictionary of letter counts.

   (c) Write a function that takes as input a string and prints a histogram of letter counts.

10. Write a function that takes a person's first and last names as input and

    (a) uses lists to return a list of the common letters in the first and last names (the intersection).

    (b) uses sets to return a set that is the intersection of the characters in the first and last names.

    (c) uses sets to return the set that is the symmetric difference between the first and last names.

11. Given D = {'a':3, 'x':7, 'r':5}:

    (a) Write Python code that returns the value at key 'x'.
    (b) Write Python code that returns the key given value '7'.

12. A dictionary that Refers to Itself.
    Consider this code:

```
otherHash = {}
otherHash[2] = 10

selfHash = {}
selfHash[2] = otherHash
selfHash[3] = 4
selfHash["2"] = selfHash
```

Whats the output of selfHash["2"]["2"]["2"]["2"][2][2]?
Try it!

13. If you had 2 lists, one of first names and one of last names [Jane, John, Jack] and [Doe, Deer, Black], use zip to create a dictionary with the keys as the first names and the values as the last names.

14. If `mySet = set('bcd')` and `yourSet = set('abcde')`

(a) What is the value of `mySet.issubset(yourSet)`?

(b) What is the value of `yourSet.issubset(mySet)`?

15. If `myDict = {'a':15 , 'c':35, 'b':20}`, write Python code

(a) to print all the keys.

(b) to print all the values.

(c) to print all the keys and values pairs.

(d) to print all the keys and values pairs in order of key.

(e) to print all the keys and values pairs in order of value.

16. Create a dictionary that maps countries to their capitals. You may start with an empty dictionary. Ask the user to input the name of the country and its capital and add them to the dictionary.

E.g. Capitals = { 'Argentina':'Buenos Aires', 'France':'Paris', 'US':'Washington D.C.'}

Once the dictionary is created, print the capitals in alphabetical order.

17. Consider a file in which every line is of the format: City, Country. Read the file, record the information in a dictionary, and report the number of cities in each country. For example, if the file contains

```
London, UK
Chicago, US
Detroit, US
```

The output will be:

```
UK : 1
US : 2
```

18. A book could be written by a single author or multiple authors. Consider the organization of a dictionary, e.g., what should be used as the key in the dictionary?

(a) What should the organization of the dictionary be, if we want to find the names of all the books written by a given author?

(b) What should the organization of the dictionary be, if we want to find the names of all the authors of a given book?

(c) Find a list of books and authors on the Internet (there are many). Put the list in a file. Write a program to read the books and authors in the file and put them in a dictionary. Output the books organized by author.

19. A person can have more than one credit card, but a credit card can belong to only person. Create a hypothetical file that contains the name and credit card number of a person on each line. Read the file and organize a dictionary to return all the credit cards associated with a person. Your program should behave as follows:

```
Input : Name of person
Output : List of credit cards.
```

20. The table of ASCII values is included in Appendix E. It also can be found online. Read the ASCII characters and corresponding codes from a file and store them in a dictionary. Ask the user to input an ASCII character and then display its ASCII code. (Note that Python provides the ord() function for that purpose as well as its inverse chr(), but we wish you to not use those functions in this exercise except to check your work.)

21. In an earlier set of exercises, we provided a code framework for solving word puzzles. Using that framework, solve this puzzle: find an uncapitalized seven-letter word in which six of the seven letters use the same number on a telephone key pad. For example, the word "cabbala" on a telephone would be 222-2252.

22. Morse Code uses a series of short and long pulses called dots and dashes respectively to encode letters and digits. For example, the letter "A" is "dot-dash", "B" is "dash-dot-dot-dot". Find a table of Morse Code on the Internet to create a dictionary for mapping characters and digits to Morse Code. Use the dictionary to create a program that can translate between Morse Code and characters and digits.

23. Use a dictionary to create a program that prompts for an integer and prints out the integer using words. For example: 138 will print "one three eight."

24. Say the last letter in a word is missing. For example, let the word be "fantasti." Could you find out the original word ("fantastic") from a word list? Write a function to retrieve the original word and print it. In some cases, a set of words might have to be returned, e.g., if the word is "bas", the original word could have been "bask" or "bass". So far in this problem, you have not needed to use a Python dictionary. Rather than linearly scanning through the input word list and checking for the original word, how could you store the words so you can search faster?

25. Write a program that reads a word list and prints out all the anagrams in the word list. In earlier exercises you saw how to read a word list. Also, in earlier examples we saw how the sorted characters of a word are a useful canonical representation of an anagram (hint: therefore, useful as a key).

26. Find two historic documents to compare—similar to the example in this chapter. For example, use the preamble to the U.S. Constitution and compare it to the Declaration of Independence. Find the most common, meaningful words, and output them in alphabetical order.

27. In Chapter 10 we mentioned the Machine Learning Repository `http://archive.ics.uci.edu/ml`. One of their most popular databases is the Iris database. Iris' come in three different species: setosa, virginica, and versicolor. Each entry in the data set has five values: sepal length, sepal width, petal length, petal width, and the species name (setosa, virginica, and versicolor). Read in the data and create a dictionary with the key as the species name and the values as the averages of each of the four characteristic values: sepal length, sepal width, petal length, petal width. That is, the size of the dictionary will be three. Write functions to create the dictionary and display the contents of the dictionary.

28. According to *Time* magazine[5] here is a list of 50 Worst Cars:

```
1899 Horsey Horseless
1909 Ford Model T
1911 Overland OctoAuto
1913 Scripps-Booth Bi-Autogo
1920 Briggs&Stratton Flyer
1933 Fuller Dymaxion
1934 Chrysler/Desoto Airflow
1949 Crosley Hotshot
1956 Renault Dauphine
1957 King-Midget Model III
1957 Waterman Aerobile
1958 Ford Edsel
1958 Lotus Elite
1958 MGA Twin Cam
1958 Zunndapp Janus
1961 Amphicar
1961 Corvair
1966 Peel Trident
1970 AMC Gremlin
1970 Triumph Stag
1971 Chrysler Imperial LeBaron Two-Door Hardtop
1971 Ford Pinto
1974 Jaguar XK-E V12 Series III
1975 Bricklin SV1
1975 Morgan Plus 8 Propane
1975 Triumph TR7
1975 Trabant
1976 Aston-Martin Lagonda
1976 Chevy Chevette
1978 AMC Pacer
1980 Corvette-305 "California"
1980 Ferrari Mondial 8
```

---

[5] http://www.time.com/time/specials/2007/completelist/0,,1658545,00.html

```
1981 Cadillac Fleetwood V-8-6-4
1981 De-Lorean DMC-12
1982 Cadillac Cimarron
1982 Camaro Iron Duke
1984 Maserati Biturbo
1985 Mosler Consulier GTP
1985 Yugo GV
1986 Lamborghini LM002
1995 Ford Explorer
1997 GM EV1
1997 Plymouth Prowler
1998 Fiat Multipla
2000 Ford Excursion
2001 Jaguar X-Type
2001 Pontiac Aztek
2002 BMW 7-series
2003 Hummer H2
2004 Chevy SSR
```

Create a dictionary with keys as the car manufacturer with values a tuple for the (year, model). Note that in some cases, the model might be absent. Then, write a function to find the company that has made the maximum number of worst cars.

Programming Projects

1. **Data mining the Internet Movie Data Base**
   Websites like the Internet Movie DataBase (www.imdb.com) maintain extensive information about movies and actors. If you search for a movie on the web site, a web page showing information about the movie is displayed. It also shows all the actors in the movie. If you click on the link for an actor, you are taken to an actor's page, where you can find information about him or her, including the movies they are in. This assignment should give you some insight into the working of such web sites. Here is what we'd like to do with the data:

   (a) Given two titles of a movie, each representing the set of actors in that movie:
       i. Find all the actors in those movies: i.e. A union B (A & B).
       ii. Find the common actors in the two movies: i.e. A intersection B (A | B).
       iii. Find the actors who are in either of the movies but not both: symmetric difference (A - B).

   (b) Given an actor's name, find all the actors with whom he or she has acted.
   The data is available as a huge, compressed text file (at www.imdb.com/interfaces) that lists each actor followed by their movies and the year the movie was made. Here is a small sample (also available on the text website) that you can work with for this exercise:

Brad Pitt, Meet Joe Black (1998), Oceans Eleven (2001), Se7en (1995), Mr &
Mrs Smith (2005) Tom Hanks, Sleepless in Seattle (1993), Catch Me If You Can (2002),
You've got mail (1998) Meg Ryan, You've got mail (1998), Sleepless in Seattle (1993),
When Harry Met Sally (1989) Anthony Hopkins, Hannibal (2001), The Edge (1997), Meet
Joe Black (1998), Proof (2005) Alec Baldwin, The Edge (1997), Pearl Harbor (2001)
Angelina Jolie, Bone Collector (1999), Lara Croft Tomb Raider (2001), Mr &
Mrs Smith (2005) Denzel Washington, Bone Collector (1999), American Gangster (2007)
Julia Roberts, Pretty Woman (1990), Oceans Eleven (2001), Runaway Bride (1999)
Gwyneth Paltrow, Shakespeare in Love (1998), Bounce (2000), Proof (2005)
Russell Crowe, Gladiator (2000), Cinderella Man (2005), American Gangster (2007)
Leonardo Di Caprio, Titanic (1997), The Departed (2006), Catch Me If You Can (2002)
Tom Cruise, Mission Impossible (1996), Jerry Maguire (1996), A Few Good Men (1992)
George Clooney, Oceans Eleven (2001), Intolerable Cruelty (2003)
Matt Damon, Good Will Hunting (1997), The Departed (2006), Oceans Eleven (2001)
Ben Affleck, Bounce (2000), Good Will Hunting (1997), Pearl Harbor (2001)
Morgan Freeman, Bone Collector (1999), Se7en (1995), Million Dollar Baby (2004)
Julianne Moore, Assassins (1995), Hannibal (2001)
Salma Hayek, Desperado (1995), Wild Wild West (1999)
Will Smith, Wild Wild West (1999), Hitch (2005), Men in Black (1997)
Renee Zellweger, Me-Myself & Irene (2000), Jerry Maguire (1996), Cinderella Man
(2005)

What is an appropriate data structure? A dictionary is suggested, as we want to access the movies and actors efficiently, but what should be the key? A key needs to be unique, which rules out actors' names—they are unique in our sample, but not in the whole database. On the other hand, movie titles and production dates form a unique identity that suggests an immutable tuple—perfect as keys. We can arrange our dictionary with (title, year) pairs as keys, and have a collection of actors in each movie as the dictionary values. As we will be looking at the intersection and union of actor combinations, that suggests using sets for the collection of actor's names in each movie. Read in the data and add the data to a dictionary that is structured as described.

Repeatedly prompt the user until some sentinel is entered. If two movies are entered, they should be separated by the appropriate operator: &, |, - to indicate the appropriate set operation to be performed (union, intersection, symmetric difference). If an actor is entered, find all the actors that he or she has been in movies with.

2. **Metadata: Organizing your iTunes.**
   Digitized music such as that managed by iTunes has metadata such as the name, artist, and so on. Internally, iTunes uses the XML format to manage its metadata, and Python has modules to work with XML, but XML has more complexity than we can deal with in a problem (or even a few chapters). However, using copy-and-paste you can copy your iTunes metadata from the text "list" view of your playlist into your favorite text editor such as TextEdit or WordPad. The result is a file that is tab-separated, i.e., fields are separated by the tab character. Because the `split()` method can take an argument

of what to split on, we can split the lines of your text file using `line.split("\t")`. Remember that we can specify the tab character with `"\t"`.

What is an appropriate data structure? It is natural to organize music around the artist and an artist's name is immutable, so a dictionary is suggested with the artist as the key. The remaining metadata becomes the value of each record. You can read in your metatdata and place it in a dictionary.

Write a program that does the following:

(a) Reads the metadata from a file into a dictionary.

(b) Loops to repeatedly prompt for:
  i. Name: list all tunes by the specified artist.
  ii. Album: list all tunes on the specified album.
  iii. Genre: list all tunes in a specified genre.
  iv. Add: add a tune.
  v. Delete: delete a specified tune (specify its name).
  vi. Popular: finds the artist with the most tunes in your collection.
  vii. Longest: finds the longest tune in your collection and prints its metadata.

Hint: to sort to find the most popular or longest, you need to convert your dictionary into a data structure that you can sort, such as a list or tuple. Remember that the Python sort will sort on the first item in each list (or tuple), so you will need to arrange your lists appropriately.

CHAPTER 9

Files

WE HAVE BEEN WORKING WITH FILES THROUGHOUT THE BOOK WITHOUT TAKING THE time to explain either what a file is or some of the nuances of file input and output. Here we take a closer look at handling files.

9.1 WHAT IS A FILE?

A file is a collection of bytes of information that usually resides permanently on a disk. Files fall into two broad categories: text files and binary files. Text files were originally organized as ASCII data (and still often are in English-speaking countries; Appendix E), but now include Unicode data that can handle a greater variety of characters that are required by many languages. In either case, text files are human-readable (when displayed in a text editor or browser, they will be readable). Binary files are all other files—they use some other coding scheme. A classic example is the format that Microsoft uses for Word documents. If you open a Word document in a text editor, it appears as random stuff—not human-readable characters. For the rest of this chapter, we will focus on text files.

9.2 ACCESSING FILES: READING TEXT FILES

To access a file from Python you must open a connection between the Python shell and the file residing on a disk. Thus, we are creating a kind of "pipe" between the information on the disk and the program that will use it. This "pipe" will be the conduit for the file contents to pass back and forth between the disk where the file resides and the program. The pipe in Python is a *file object* that is created when the connection is established. The file object uses the main memory of the computer to store data as they are moved between the disk and program. The Python *open* command sets up that connection, and returns the file object that represents the connection. All subsequent actions we perform on a file are done through this file object, also sometimes called a *file descriptor* or *stream*. A file can be opened for reading or writing (or both).

Let's assume that a text file named `temp.txt` exists and is in the same folder as the program we are coding resides (see Section 9.9 for a discussion of where the file needs to be). Here are the contents of the file `temp.txt`:

```
First line
Second line
Third line
```

Let's examine a Python shell session that opens the file for reading, reads the contents of the file, and then closes the file. The first line calls the *open* function with arguments specifying the file name and whether it is being opened for reading ("r") or writing ("w"). The connection to the file is created as a file object named `testFile`. Using `testFile` we can iterate through the file contents line by line using a ***for*** statement, as we have done before. Remember, when iterating through a file object we are iterating one *line* at a time. At the end we *close* the file with `testFile.close()`, tearing down the connection between the shell and the file. If we forget to close the file, the Python shell will close it when the shell exits or is restarted.

```
>>> testFile = open("temp.txt","r")    # open the file for reading
>>> for line in testFile:   # using the name we can iterate through the file
        print line


First line

Second line

Third line

>>> testFile.close()         # close the file when done
```

Other File Access Methods

In the previous session, lines are extracted from the file one at a time using iteration. There are also methods available to access file contents. For example, the `read` method reads the *entire* contents of a file in one call, returning the contents as a single string. Depending on the size of the file, performance of this all-at-once approach can be a good or bad idea (bad idea to read in gigabytes of data at one time). Furthermore, because the returned value is a single string, iteration through the result iterates through the string one *character* at a time. In other words, the programmer is responsible for parsing out the file contents from the string. An example session is shown here. To save space in displaying the session, we cut out many lines of output.

```
>>> testFile = open("temp.txt","r")    # open file for reading
>>> wholeFile = testFile.read()         # read whole file
>>> for line in wholeFile:
        print line

F
i
r
s
t

l
i
n
e

# many lines of output omitted here

>>> testFile.close()
```

Another method is `readline`, which, as it says, reads a single line. However, notice what happens when it is followed by a *for* statement. The *for* picks up where the `readline` left off in the file. Notice how the line stored in `aline` contains a "carriage return" at the end of the string represented by the backslash-n character sequence (\n).

```
>>> testFile = open("temp.txt","r")    # open file for reading
>>> aLine = testFile.readline()          # read exactly one line
>>> aLine
'First line\n'
>>> for line in testFile:
        print line

Second line                            # "for" picks up where readline() left off

Third line

>>> testFile.close()
```

The `readline` command is useful to "remove" header lines from the beginning of a file. You can use `readline` to skip past them so your *for* loop logic is simpler and possibly easier to read.

What's Really Happening?

When you set up a connection between your Python program and a file, you are creating what is called a "stream" of data. Data flows from the file (on disk) to your program, as in Figure 9.1. An important part of the stream is the *buffer* that is in main memory where the data is stored on its way between the file on the disk and your program. The stream is managed by the operating system which tries to ensure that when your **for** loop needs the next line, that line will already be in the buffer in memory. A buffer is needed because disk access is slow, so the computer, when it isn't busy, stores a lot of the file's contents in memory. If everything is working well, the whole process will be invisible to the programmer.

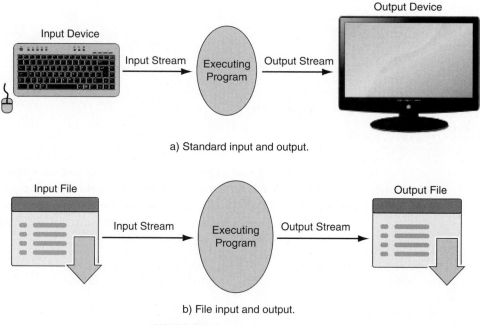

a) Standard input and output.

b) File input and output.

FIGURE 9.1 Input-output streams.

9.3 ACCESSING FILES: WRITING TEXT FILES

Writing files requires first creating a file object connection as we did for reading a file. The only difference is that one specifies "w" rather than "r" in the *open* command. Also, if the file doesn't exist, it will be created.

Once a file is open, you can just write a string to the file using the `write` method. This method writes *only* strings to the file (so conversion from other types might be necessary).

If you want multiple lines output to the file, you must insert the carriage-return character sequence (\n) between the lines. A common approach in Python is to assemble a string from various pieces and then write the final string to a file. Not surprisingly, it can be difficult to keep track of very long strings, so there is good reason to have multiple writes, often writing a single line on each iteration of the algorithm. Every `write` appends to the end of the file's present contents, making the file longer with each write. Let's look at a sample.

```
# open file for writing: creates file if it doesn't exist
>>> dataFile = open("temp2.txt", "w")
>>> s = "first line \n second line"    # some string: two lines
>>> dataFile.write(s)                   # write the string to the file
>>> dataFile.close()
```

Here we open a file for writing, create a string, write the string and then close the file. This is what the file looks like when we finish:

```
first line
 second line
```

Note how the string that appeared in the Python shell as one line, was written as two lines because of the insertion of a carriage return character sequence (\n). Also, notice how the second line begins with a blank character—exactly as it appeared in the string s in the Python shell.

PROGRAMMING TIP

It is common to write other types than strings to files (or to expect values from a file other than strings). All interaction with text files is done only with strings. Any other type must be converted to a string before it can be written to a text file. If not, you will get a `TypeError`, indicating that the value you are trying to write needs to be converted to a string.

9.4 READING AND WRITING TEXT FILES IN A PROGRAM

Let's put these concepts together into a program. This program opens two files: one for reading, the other for writing. The program reads the first line from the input file and writes that string to the shell. The remaining lines are read one at a time and immediately written one at a time to the output file named `output.txt`. See Code Listing 9.1.

First, we use an editor to create an input file that we will name input.txt. Here is what input.txt looks like:

```
First Line
Second Line
Third Line
```

When we run the program, we can observe the first line from the file being printed in the shell. The output in the shell contains an extra carriage return, because the **print** command adds a carriage return to the string it prints, as well as the carriage return that was already in the line (as you saw earlier).

Code Listing 9.1

```python
# File reading and writing

inFile = open("input.txt", "r")
outFile = open("output.txt", "w")

oneLine = inFile.readline()
print oneLine    # this gets printed in the Python shell

for line in inFile:
    outFile.write(line)    # this gets written to the output file

inFile.close()
outFile.close()
```

```
>>>
First Line

>>>
```

Here is the file output.txt after the program finishes. It contains everything from the input.txt except the first line, which was printed to the shell:

```
Second Line
Third Line
```

9.5 FILE CREATION AND OVERWRITING

When one opens a file for reading and the file doesn't exist on the disk (or the operating system cannot find the file), an error is generated. If the file exists, the file object connection is created and we can read values from the file.

When one opens a file for writing and the file doesn't exist, a file will be created in the folder where the program is running (see Section 9.9 on how to change that behavior). If the file already exists, its contents will cleared; that is the file contents will be lost, and any new material is added to the now-empty file by default. The program looks for the file in the folder that the program is running in.

The modes in which you can open a file and the effects they have on existing (or nonexisting) files are shown in Table 9.1.

Mode	How opened	File Exists	File Does Not Exist
'r'	read-only	Opens that file	Error
'w'	write-only	Clears the file contents	Creates and opens a new file
'a'	write-only	File contents left intact and new data appended at file's end	Creates and opens a new file
'r+'	read and write	Reads and overwrites from the file's beginning	Error
'w+'	read and write	Clears the file contents	Creates and opens a new file
'a+'	read and write	File contents left intact and read and write at file's end	Creates and opens a new file

TABLE 9.1 File modes.

Universal New Line Format

There is one modifier for file input and output, the U modifier, that is particularly useful. Depending on the operating system, there is a particular character, or set of characters, that change when writing to a file. That special character is the newline character: the character placed at the end of a string to indicate that the next character goes on the following line of text. There have been a number of ways to indicate a new line through the history of computer operating systems,[1] but two characters are used most commonly: ' $\backslash n$ ' and ' $\backslash r$ '. Though not strictly true, they are usually referred to as the "newline" character and the "carriage-return" character, respectively. Commonly used combinations are shown in Table 9.2.

What an inconvenience! To avoid having to worry about this issue, Python provides the ' U ' modifier to open a file that allows Python to sort out the issue. Thus,

---

[1] http://en.wikipedia.org/wiki/Newline

Operating System	Character Combination
Unix & Mac OS X	'\n'
MS Windows	'\r\n'
Mac (pre-OS X)	'\r'

TABLE 9.2 End-of-line characters.

`fd = open('file.txt','rU')` will open a file for reading and Python will sort out the details of the particular new line sequence used in the file. Very handy!

Moving Around in a File

Table 9.1 indicates where reads and writes will begin in a file by default. However, Python provides a way to control where we are in a file when we read or write, and to change the position of where a read or write occurs.

Remember how the file object gains access to the contents of a disk file: the `open` function creates a buffer—a location in memory—where the disk contents are copied. Once the contents are read into the file object buffer, the file object treats the buffer as a very large list in which each element of the list has an index. A file object counts each byte (roughly each character) as an index into the file object buffer. Furthermore, the file object maintains a *current file position*, which is the present index where reads (or writes) are to occur. See Figure 9.2.

FIGURE 9.2 Current file position.

Many of the file methods implicitly use the current file position. For example, after a `readline` occurs, the current file position moves to the position after the next carriage return. The `write` method writes at the current file position.

Python provides methods to work with the current file position. The first is the `tell` method. The `tell` method reports the position of the current file position relative to the beginning of the file in bytes. The second is the `seek` method. This methods shifts the current file position to a new position in the file object buffer.

There are two arguments to the seek method. The first is a byte count; the second is the reference point. The idea is that the current file pointer is moved the number of bytes indicated from the provided reference point. If no reference point is provided, then the byte count is assumed to be from the beginning of the file. The reference point is a little confusing, but it takes on one of three values:

- 0   reference to the *beginning* of the file. This is the default if not specified.
- 1   reference to the *current* file position.
- 2   reference to the *end*-of-file position.

A typical use is fd.seek(0), resetting the current file position to the beginning of the file object fd (literally, 0 bytes away from the beginning of the file). Again, the second argument defaults to 0 if not provided. To illustrate these concepts let's use "arthur.txt", a quote from the movie *Monty Python and the Holy Grail*:

```
King Arthur: I am your king.
Woman: Well I didn't vote for you.
King Arthur: You don't vote for kings.
Woman: Well how'd you become king then?
King Arthur: The Lady of the Lake, her arm clad in the purest shimmering
samite held aloft Excalibur from the bosom of the water, signifying by
divine providence that I, Arthur, was to carry Excalibur. THAT is why I am your
king.
Dennis: [interrupting] Listen, strange women lyin' in ponds distributin'
swords is no basis for a system of government. Supreme executive power derives
from a mandate from the masses, not from some farcical aquatic ceremony.
```

```
>>> fd = open('arthur.txt')
>>> fd.tell()           # where is the current file position?
0L
>>> for line in fd:
...     pass            # read all the lines, do nothing with them
...
>>> fd.tell()           # where is the current file position now (end of file)
604L
>>> fd.readline()       # try reading past the end of the file
''
>>> fd.seek(0)          # seek to the beginning
>>> fd.tell()           # where is the current file position now?
0L
>>> fd.seek(-30,2)      # seek to 30 bytes from the end
>>> fd.tell()
574L
>>> fd.readline()       # read from current file position to end of line
'e farcical aquatic ceremony. \n'
```

```
>>> fd.close()
>>> fd.tell()
Traceback (most recent call last):
  File "<stdin>", line 1, in <module>
ValueError: I/O operation on closed file
>>>
```

There are a few things to note about this session:

- `fd.tell()` reports its byte position as a long integer (hence the "L").
- When you try to read information from a file and the current file position is at the end of the file, the read returns an empty string.
- You can seek to a negative offset from some position. Thus, `fd.seek(-30,2)` seeks to 30 bytes *backwards* from the end-of-file.
- Trying to read a file after closing it generates an error.

The most common operation is probably to seek to the beginning of the file. Remember `fd.seek(0)`!

9.6 CLOSING A FILE

Closing a file is the process of tearing down the connection between the program and a file. In particular, everything in the buffer that is in memory is written back to the disk. Closing a file ensures that no information is lost.

PROGRAMMING TIP

Not closing a file, especially a file that is being written, risks losing the contents of the file. Because the program writes data to the file object in memory (not directly to the file on disk), the operating system will occasionally "synchronize" the contents of the file object and disk file contents, to make sure that everything that was written to the file object gets written to the disk file. Closing the file ensures this synchronization. Although Python is very good about closing files if you forget, it is always best to close your files once opened.

9.7 CSV FILES

We have shown the use of CSV files in a couple of examples. Here we will discuss those files in a little more detail.

A CSV is not a different kind of file, but rather a different kind of file *format*. A CSV is actually a text file and can be used in conjunction with the functions and methods we have just discussed. However, the arrangement of data in the file is special, and we can take advantage of that.

The wikipedia page on CSV files describes them as follows:

> A file format is a particular way to encode information for storage in a computer file. Particularly, files encoded using the CSV format are used to store tabular data. The format dates back to the early days of business computing and is widely used to pass data between computers with different internal word sizes, data formatting needs, and so forth. For this reason, CSV files are common on all computer platforms.

The problem with this file format, as we have mentioned previously, is that the standards for reading and writing do not really exist, especially given the age of the format. Nonetheless, it is a very useful way to exchange data between applications and therefore an important format for us to understand.

CSV Module

As we have mentioned many times, one of the great advantages of Python is the community that supports its use. When common problems arise, the Python community provides powerful, free solutions. Such is the case with CSV files. To help alleviate the difficulties of dealing with multiple variations in CSV files, Python provides the `csv` module. The `csv` module allows us to read and write CSV files in a way that is compatible with multiple sources and is less difficult.

To work with CSV-formatted files, we need some new objects: a `csv.reader` object to read the file and a `csv.writer` object to write a CSV file. We will use the following example to show reading and writing to such a file. We created a simple spreadsheet using Microsoft Excel 2008, shown in Figure 9.3. The values in bold are calculated values using

Name	Exam1	Exam2	Final Exam	Overall Grade
Bill	75.00	100.00	50.00	**75.00**
Fred	50.00	50.00	50.00	**50.00**
Irving	0.00	0.00	0.00	**0.00**
Monty	100.00	100.00	100.00	**100.00**
Average				**56.25**

FIGURE 9.3 A simple spreadsheet from Microsoft Excel 2008.

simple Excel formulas to average the four rows for a grade, then average grades for an overall grade average. The corresponding CSV file is also shown here:

```
Name,Exam1,Exam2,Final Exam,Overall Grade
Bill,75.00,100.00,50.00,75.00
Fred,50.00,50.00,50.00,50.00
Irving,0.00,0.00,0.00,0.00
Monty,100.00,100.00,100.00,100.00

Average,,,,56.25
```

First, it is important to note that some information from the original Excel file is lost. The CSV format preserves only values. For example, the four grades and the grade average are no longer formulas. Changes to one of the row values will *not* update the corresponding averages. Second, series of commas in the last line of the CSV file indicate empty values for that field.

CSV Reader

To create a `csv.reader` object, we use the constructor method `reader`. Interestingly, the `reader` method takes as an argument a file object, meaning that you must have already opened a file for reading and created a file object. The `reader` constructor returns a reader object that can be used to iterate through the file, much like a file object can be used to iterate the contents of a text file.

The difference, however, is that the `csv.reader` returns a single *row* of the file for each iteration (not necessarily a line). Further, the returned value from the iteration is not a string but a *list of strings*, where each element of the list represents one of the fields of the row. The code and its results are shown here in Code Listing 9.2.

Code Listing 9.2

```python
import csv
fObj = open('Workbook1.csv','rU')
csvReader = csv.reader(fObj)

for row in csvReader:
    print row

fObj.close()
```

```
>>>
['Name', 'Exam1', 'Exam2', 'Final Exam', 'Overall Grade']
['Bill', '75.00', '100.00', '50.00', '75.00']
```

```
['Fred', '50.00', '50.00', '50.00', '50.00']
['Irving', '0.00', '0.00', '0.00', '0.00']
['Monty', '100.00', '100.00', '100.00', '100.00']
[]
['Average', '', '', '', '56.25']
>>>
```

A few things to note:

- It is recommended that the created file object be opened in universal new line format. This increases the number of CSV variations that can be accommodated. For this particular Excel spreadsheet, it was required—otherwise, an error is generated. The error is even very helpful, suggesting you use that mode.[2] Isn't Python nice?
- The blank line of the CSV file between the "Monty" row and the "Average" row does appear in the output as an empty list. Every row, even blank rows, are returned by the `reader` object.
- If a field in a row is not filled in, the row is still marked with an empty string, as shown in the last row.

CSV Writer

Like the `reader`, we create a `csv.writer` object using the `writer` constructor. As with the reader, the required argument is a file object, but in this case that file must have been opened for writing.

The `csv.writer` object has a method `writerow` that will write a row of data to the file the writer object was constructed with.

Example: Update Some Grades

As an example, let us update Irving's final grade to 100.00. In so doing, we have a lot of work that must be done, as all the formulas for updating the spreadsheet are missing. We must update Irving's average as well as the grade average. The code is shown in Code Listing 9.3.

Code Listing 9.3

```
import csv
readFileObj = open('Workbook1.csv','rU')
csvReader = csv.reader(readFileObj)

5 sheet = []
```

---

[2] _csv.Error: new-line character seen in unquoted field – do you need to open the file in universal-newline mode?

```
   for row in csvReader:
       sheet.append(row)
   readFileObj.close()

10 sheet[3][3] = '100.00'    # give Irving a break, 100 on the final

   # update Irving's average
   #sheet[3][4]='%.2f'%(sum([float(fieldStr) for fieldStr in sheet[3][1:-1]])/3)
   theSum = 0
15 for fieldStr in sheet[3][1:-1]:    # fields 1, 2 and 3: the grades
       theSum += float(fieldStr)
   avg = theSum/3
   # we have to write a string, convert to two decimal places using str
   formatting
   sheet[3][4] = '%.2f'%avg
20
   # update the overall grade average
   # sheet[-1][-1] = '%.2f'%(sum([float(row[-1]) for row in sheet[1:-2]])/4)
   theSum = 0
   for row in sheet[1:-2]:         # rows 1,2,3,4: the student rows
25     theSum += float(row[-1])    # the average of that row
   gradeAverage = theSum/4
   # we have to write a string, convert to two decimal places using str
   formatting
   sheet[-1][-1] = '%.2f'%gradeAverage

30 writeFileObj = open('NewWorkbook1.csv','w')
   writer = csv.writer(writeFileObj)
   for row in sheet:
       writer.writerow(row)
   writeFileObj.close()
```

There is a lot of slicing going on here, which is a good exercise for us. Let's take a look.

Lines 2–5: We do the normal opening and reading of the CSV file. However, we create a variable sheet as an empty list to hold all the rows.

Lines 6–8: Iterate through the rows and append them to the sheet. At the end, sheet contains a list of lists (the inner lists are the rows).

Line 10: Give Irving a break; update his final exam grade to 100.00 as a string. Remember, CSV files are text files!

Lines 12–19: This code updates Irving's average based on the new grade. Check to make sure you understand the slicing there! Look at the CSV file contents in the example. The comments give some hints (as they should). Line 19 is interesting. We need to write a string for the final average (a floating-point number). We want to write it with only two decimal places, so we use string formatting to do the work. By the way, the commented line Line 13 does all the work of Lines 14–19. Is it readable? Readability depends on the reader, but this code is more dense and therefore more likely to have a mistake.

Lines 21–28: Now we must update the overall average based on the new averages. Again, lots of slicing going on—make sure you can follow it. As we did earlier, the commented-out Line 22 does all the work of Line 23–28.

Lines 30–33: Having updated `sheet`, we now write it out to a new file using the `writerow` method, one row a a time.

The updated CSV file is shown here. The Excel spreadsheet created from reading in that file is shown in Figure 9.4.

```
Name,Exam1,Exam2,Final Exam,Overall Grade
Bill,75.00,100.00,50.00,75.00
Fred,50.00,50.00,50.00,50.00
Irving,0.00,0.00,100.00,33.33
Monty,100.00,100.00,100.00,100.00

Average,,,,64.58
```

Some of the formatting is lost in the spreadsheet, but the values are correct. Again, no formulas are preserved.

Name	Exam1	Exam2	Final Exam	Overall Grade
Bill	75	100	50	75
Fred	50	50	50	50
Irving	0	0	100	33.33
Monty	100	100	100	100
Average				64.58

FIGURE 9.4 The updated Excel spreadsheet created from the new CSV file.

9.8 EXAMPLE: REPROMPTING FOR A "GOOD" FILE NAME

In this example, we will extend the simple input/output program by allowing the user to specify the file names. Because the value returned by *raw_input* is a string, we can use that string directly as an argument for the *open* command.

Anytime we ask users for input, there is the possibility that they will provide bad, or even malicious, data. We have to protect the program from such occurrences, that is, to make sure it does not fail under erroneous input. Let's use *exceptions* to handle that possibility. We will cover exceptions in more detail in Chapter 14, but we provide a preview here, because using exceptions is the right way to open a file.

The *try ... except* code works as follows (see Code Listing 9.4). We *try* the code in the *try* suite. If the lines in the *try* suite complete without error, we ignore the *except* suite and continue with code after the *try ... except*. However, if during the execution of the line(s) in the *try* suite an error occurs, execution stops on the error in the *try* suite and control is passed to the *except* suite. If an appropriate *except* suite is found (one that deals with the error that was raised), then the *except* suite begins execution. The idea is that the code in the *except* suite can be used to repair the error, or to at least deal with the error and provide feedback to the user. Note that there can be multiple *except* clauses to any *try* statement, each catching a particular error. Each *except* clause indicates what error it can catch (such as an IOError when you try to open a file that does not exist).

In our example, if the user incorrectly inputs a file name, the exception handler will direct control to the *except* suite, in particular to the IOError suite, where it will print an error message. By encasing the exception handler within a *while* loop, we repeatedly prompt until a file is correctly opened.

Note how the Boolean openedFile is used to control the loop. If the *open* (fileName, "r") on Line 9 fails, then execution in the *try* suite stops, and execution passes to the *except* suite. Because of that error, the second line of the *try* suite, openedFile = *True* on Line 10 fails to execute—we don't get that far. Thus, the variable openedFile remains *False* if the file cannot be opened.

On the error, control passes to the *except* suite on Line 11, which prints a message and then continues. Continuing here means continuing with the code after the *try ... except*, which is the *while* loop and re-evaluation of its condition on line 6. As long as an error occurs on *open*(fileName, "r"), the *while* loop will continue looping. If a file opens successfully (without error), the openedFile = *True* on Line 10 does execute, the *except* suite is skipped, and the *while* loop conditional is re-evaluated. At that point the *while* loop ends and the rest of the program is run.

The remainder of the program will reverse the words in each line before writing to the output file—just to do something. In the output, we see both a successful opening of files as well as the error that is generated where we are unsuccessful at opening a file. Here is the output file that was created:

```
Line Second
Line Third
```

Code Listing 9.4

```
# simple file example
#little snippet to repeatedly ask for a file to open for read
```

```
    #continues to prompt until a file opens successfully
 5  openedFile = False
    while (not openedFile):
        fileName = raw_input("Open what file: ")
        try:
            inFile = open(fileName,"r")
10          openedFile = True  # line skipped, if file doesn't open
        except IOError:
            print "File opening failed, try again "

    # first let's mess with the file names:
15  # make a new file, keep the extension but change the name
    # so that it ends in "Rev". Thus textFile.txt => textFileRev.txt
    fileParts = fileName.split(".")
    outFile = open(fileParts[0]+"Rev."+fileParts[1],"w")

20  # now do something with the files:
    # write each line in reverse word order
    for line in inFile:
        words = line.split()     # split out individual words
        words.reverse()          # reverse the list of words
25      for w in words:
            outFile.write(w)
            outFile.write(" ")   # put back space between words
        outFile.write("\n")      # tack carriage return onto end of line

30
    inFile.close()
    outFile.close()
```

```
>>>
Open what file: dummy
File opening failed, try again
Open what file: input.txt
>>>
```

9.9 MODULE: os

Let's take a look at the os module("os" is an abbreviation for "operating system"). It is a module included with the Python distribution—like the math module. The os module has many capabilities, but we will look at the file-related ones here. You can find the full list of functions in the documentation that comes with Python, or you can simply search online for "Python os module." To appreciate some of the capabilities we have at hand, let's begin with a look at how files are organized on your disk.

Directory/Folder Structure

Part of the role of an operating system is to keep files organized. The currently popular operating systems such as Microsoft Windows, Linux, and Apple's OS X maintain files in a *directory structure*. This assumes the existence of a special container called a *directory* in Linux and OS-X, or a *folder* in Windows.[3] Each directory can hold three things:

- A list of files that are in the directory.
- A list of other directories, also contained in the directory.
- A link to the directory's parent in the directory structure.

Directories are organized by the last two items: directories they contain and the parent directory they are connected to. The organization is typically referred to as a *hierarchy*, or often by computer scientists as a *tree*. The tree contains the relationship of each directory to its "parent" and "children." The "children" of a directory are those directories that it contains. The parent of a directory is the directory that contains it. Overall, we can draw the *tree structure* of the directories as shown in Figure 9.5. However, it is an odd tree. It has a root, branches, and leaves, but it is upside down: the root is at the top and the leaves are at the bottom. Each circle in the tree is a directory (more generally a *node*) and each line connecting nodes is the relationship between directories (more generally called an *edge*). The root is a special directory, alone at the top, whereas leaves are special nodes at the bottom: nodes with no children (files).

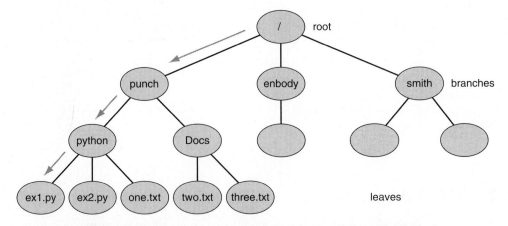

FIGURE 9.5 Directory tree with path /punch/python/ex1.py highlighted.

---

[3] We'll continue to just use the word "directory" from now on, but be aware that in Windows it would be called a "folder."

The operating system finds files by beginning at the root, represented by "/" (spoken as "slash"). The operating system moves down the tree structure by following edges and directories until it finds the desired file (contained in a directory) or a directory itself. The path taken through the tree structure is called just that: a *path*. The path represents an ordered list of directories traversed to get to the desired directory. For example, in Figure 9.5 the file "ex1.py" is found in the directory "python", which is a child of the directory "punch", which is a child of the directory "/". The full path is indicated by separating each directory with a "/", thus "/punch/python/ex1.py" is the *fully qualified name* of the file. That path is highlighted with arrows in Figure 9.5. Every leaf node (usually a file) can be represented by a fully qualified name, indicating a path from the root. Of importance to us is that a path can be represented as a string in Python: `"/punch/python/ex1.py"`.

Paths are represented slightly differently by different operating systems. The path shown in the example is the Unix style used in Linux and OS X (underneath OS X is a flavor of Unix). Microsoft Windows uses backslashes (\) instead of forward slashes, and starts its paths with the device name, e.g., C:\punch\python\ex1.py. Fortunately, Python understands which operating system it is working on, so it automatically converts whichever style you use to the appropriate one.

There are two special directory (folder) names: "." (spoken as "dot") and ".." (spoken as "dot-dot"). The single dot represents the directory you are currently working in. For example, if you are working in punch's python directory, the "." is synonymous with the path "/punch/python/" so whenever you use ".", the operating system will fill in the current path "/punch/python". The double-dot is synonymous with the parent directory (folder), that is, the node "above" where you are currently working. For example, if your current directory (folder) is "punch/python" then ".." is "/punch/".

PROGRAMMING TIP

In Python, if you type a file name without a full path, the assumption is that the file is in the directory where the program currently running resides. Thus, if you run your program from a directory, you can open any file in that directory without qualifying the full path. Otherwise, Python requires that the full path be provided.

os Module Functions

Let's look at a few sessions illustrating a small subset of the many functions available in the os module. The directory tree we use in this example is shown in Figure 9.5.

The first session illustrates functions that allows one to move about the directory tree, and list the contents of any directory:

- The `os.getcwd` function. Here getcwd stands for "get cwd" and "cwd" stands for "current working directory"—the directory or folder that you are currently working in.

By default, the current working directory is set to the directory from where the program started (see the previous programming tip).

- The os.chdir function. Here the "chdir" stands for "change directory," so it changes the current working directory to the path that was used as an argument. All paths are strings in Python, where the directories are separated by "/" as mentioned earlier.

- In the os.listdir function. Here "listdir" stands for "list directory" that lists the files and directories in the node specified by the path argument. These functions return values that can be named.

```
>>> import os                   # load the os package
>>> os.chdir("/punch/python")   # change to the example starting point
>>> os.getcwd()                 # check that we are there
'/punch/python'
>>> os.listdir(".")  # list contents of current directory, indicated by "."
['ex1.py', 'ex2.py', 'one.txt']
>>> dir = os.listdir(".")       # we can give that list a name
>>> dir
['ex1.py', 'ex2.py', 'one.txt']
>>> os.listdir("/punch")        # list the contents at some path
['Docs', 'python']
```

The second session illustrates functions that manipulate path and file names. Notice how this group begins with os.path, indicating the "path" subset of the os module. The first functions are Booleans returning *True* or *False* to indicate whether the path "is a file" (isfile), "is a directory" (isdir) or generically if such an item "exists" (exists). The final functions manipulate path names. They can extract a file name from a path (basename) or extract the directory part of the path from the whole path (dirname). Some can create a list by splitting off the file name from a path (split) or splitting off only the file extension from a path (splitext). Finally, there is a join function to combine partial paths into a complete path—note how it inserts a slash (/) character as needed.

```
>>> import os                              # load the os package
>>> os.path.isfile("/punch/python/ex1.py")  # check if a file exists
True
>>> os.path.isfile("/punch/python/ex3.py")
False
>>> os.path.isdir("/punch/python")         # check if a directory exists
True
>>> os.path.exists("/punch/python")        # check if file or directory exists
True
>>> os.path.basename("/punch/python/ex1.py")# split a file name off a path
'ex1.py'
>>> os.path.dirname("/punch/python/ex1.py") # split the directory from a path
'/punch/python'
>>> os.path.split("/punch/python/ex1.py")   # split path to [directory, file]
```

```
('/punch/python', 'ex1.py')
>>> os.path.splitext("/punch/python/ex1.py") # split off extension (after ".")
('/punch/python/ex1', '.py')
>>> os.path.join("/punch/python", "ex1.py")  # join a path to a file name
'/punch/python/ex1.py'
>>> p = os.getcwd()                          # name a path "p"
>>> p
'/punch/python'
>>> os.path.join(os.path.split(p)[0], "dummy.py") # join directory in "p" to
filename
'/punch/dummy.py'
>>> os.path.join("/punch/python/", "ex1.py")
'/punch/python/ex1.py'
>>>
```

The final session illustrates the os.walk(pathString) function. This is a particularly useful function for moving through the contents of a directory tree. It takes a pathString argument (a valid path string), and yields three values: the name of the current directory, a list of subdirectories in the directory, and a list of files in the directory, for *every directory* on the tree under the directory argument provided. If you put os.walk in a *for* loop, it will visit every node in the directory tree under the pathString directory. In the following session, we walk through the directory tree of Figure 9.5, starting in /punch.

```
>>> os.getcwd()                              # check our starting point
'/punch'
>>> for dirName, dirs, files in os.walk("."): # "walk" in the current directory
        print dirName, dirs, files  # directory, subdirectory list, file list

. ['Docs', 'python'] []    # current directory, list of 2 subdirectories, no files
./Docs [] ['three.txt', 'two.txt']       # Does directory, no subdirectories, 3 files
./python [] ['ex1.py', 'ex2.py', 'one.txt'] # directory, no subdirectories, 3 files
>>>
```

os Module Example

Here is an example that shows something you can do with the os module functions. The task is to write a Python program that searches a directory tree for any text file that contains a particular string. We'll walk down the directory tree, starting in the current working directory. In addition, we will make a list of text files that contain the string and a list of directories those files are in.

The basic idea is this. In each directory, we look at each file in the directory to see if it is a text file (extension ".txt"). If it is a text file, we open it, read it in and then check to see if our search string is in the file. If so, we add the file to our list of files, and add the directory to the list of directories. Once we finish with the files in the directory, we output what we found.

We begin with a function that does most of the work:

I. Walk the directory tree, starting at the current directory.
   1. For each `file` in the directory:
     (a) If `file` is a text file:
        i. Add to the count of text files examined.
        ii. Open the file and read its contents into a string.
        iii. If `searchString` is in the `file` string:
            A. Create path for file.
            B. Add file to list of files containing `searchString`.
            C. Add directory to list of directories.

The program prompts for a search string, initializes the count and lists, and then calls the function. After the function call, the information is output.

When looking at Figure 9.5, assume that files "one.text" and "two.txt" contain the string "red." Code Listing 9.5 is the program and the output.

Code Listing 9.5

```
# search for a string:
#    starting from the current directory, walk a directory tree
#    look in all text files (extension ".txt") for the string

import os

# walk the directory subtree starting at the current directory
# search for searchStr, count files examined,
# keep lists of files found and directories
def check(searchStr,count,fileList,dirList):
    for dirName,dirs,files in os.walk("."):      # walk the subtree
        for f in files:                          # for files at the node
            if os.path.splitext(f)[1] == ".txt":  # if it is a text file
                count = count + 1                 # add to count of files examined
                aFile = open(os.path.join(dirName,f),'r')  # open text file
                fileStr = aFile.read()            # read whole file into string
                if searchStr in fileStr:          # is searchStr in file?
                    fileName = os.path.join(dirName,f)  # is so, create path for
file
                    fileList.append(fileName)     # and add to file list
                    if dirName not in dirList:    # if directory is not
                                                  # already in the list
                        dirList.append(dirName)   # and directory list
    aFile.close()
```

```
        return count

theStr = raw_input('What string to look for: ')
fileList = []      # list of files containing string
dirList = []       # list of directories of files containing string
count = 0          # count of text files examined

# call our function that examines directory tree for string
count = check(theStr,count,fileList,dirList)

print 'Looked at %d text files'%(count)
print 'Found %d directories containing files \with ".txt" suffix and target
string:%s'\
        %(len(dirList),theStr)
print 'Found %d files with ".txt" suffix containing the target string: %s'\
        %(len(fileList),theStr)
print '\n****Directory List*****'
for d in dirList:
    print d

print '\n-----File List-----'
for f in fileList:
    print f
```

```
What string to look for: red
Looked at 3 text files
Found 2 directories containing files with ".txt" suffix and target string:red
Found 2 files with ".txt" suffix containing the target string: red
****Directory List*****
./Docs
./python

-----File List-----
./Docs/two.txt
./python/one.txt
```

Summary

Although we have been using files in earlier chapters, in this chapter, we explained file input and output in greater detail. We also looked at handling CSV-formatted files in more detail. Finally, we showed more complex file handling using the os module.

Exercises

1. Why is closing a file important? Be specific.

2. File manipulations:

    (a) Write a Python program that will open a file named "thisFile.txt" and write every other line into the file "thatFile.txt."

    (b) Extend your program using the `os` module to save your file to a different directory (folder).

3. Create a file "words.txt" that contains a paragraph of random words (approximately 100 words long). Next, create a program that prompts for the file name then iterates through each word in this file and counts the frequency of each letter (a through z) and stores the values in a dictionary. Make each letter lower-cased and ignore punctuation. Print a histogram of the word counts.

4. Create a test file with a single sentence of 20 words. Read the file, then insert carriage-return characters (\n) and write the test to a new text file that will be composed of four lines of five words.

5. In the exercises for Chapters 1, 2, and 5, the football quarterback pass rating was developed into a program. Go to `http://nfl.com`, find the quarterback data, and copy that data into a file. It is easiest to grab the data of the "qualified" quarterbacks, as they fit on only one web page. Write a program that reads your file, uses your pass rating function to calculate the pass ratings of the quarterbacks, and prints the players from best to worst.

6. Assume that a file has opened as "somefile," such as `somefile = open('test.txt','r')`. Try the following (note the "s" in the second method name).

    (a) What will `somefile.readline()` return?

    (b) What will `somefile.readlines()` return?

7. Given a test file named "test.txt" containing the following three lines:

```
Line One
Line Two
Line Three
```

Consider the following code:

```
someFile = open('test.txt','r')
for line in someFile:  # Loop 1
    print line
for line in someFile:  # Loop 2
    print line
```

(a) What will be printed by Loop 1?

(b) What will be printed by Loop 2?

(c) How can you modify the code so that both Loop 1 and Loop 2 print the same thing (other than having them both print nothing)?

8. Suppose that a text file contains student records on each line and each record is of the format:

`Name of Student, Student Id, GPA.`

Write code to read the file line by line and store all the records in lists or tuples. Hint: you need to create a list of lists or list of tuples.

9. Write a function that takes one argument: a string file name. The function should return a list of lists such that each list is a list of the words in the file. In addition

(a) Remove all whitespace from each word and remove all punctuation. The string module constants will be useful for the last task.

(b) Clean the words before placing them in the list. Specifically, convert all words to lower case and throw out any "words" that contain anything other than letters.

Programming Projects

1. **Spreadsheets.**

   Spreadsheet programs such as Microsoft Excel or OpenOffice Calc have an option to export data into CSV files). In this exercise, you will create a program that will read in a spreadsheet (in CSV format), and manipulate it. Provide the following capabilities:

   • Print the data
   • Delete a row or column
   • Insert a row or column
   • Change a value in a cell
   • Output the data in csv format

   Issues to consider:

   • Use Python's `csv` module to read in a spreadsheet. Choose an appropriate data structure to store the data. Should you use lists, tuples, or dictionaries?
   • Construct a driving loop in your program that will prompt for the operations specified previously. A useful interface is to allow choices to be specified with a single letter related to the operation, e.g., "d" for delete.

2. **File copy.**

   All operating systems have commands that will create a copy of a file. In this exercise, you are to create a program that will make an *exact* copy of a file. Provide the following capabilities:

- Copy only files that end with a ".txt" extension. Generate an appropriate error if something else is specified.
- Using the os module, check whether the source file exists.
- Using the os module, check whether the destination file exists. If so, ask the user if he or she wants to overwrite it.
- If no paths are specified, assume that the file is in the current folder (directory). Otherwise, use the os module to separate the path from the file name. If a path is specified for the destination file, check whether the path exists—otherwise, generate an error.

CHAPTER 10

More Program Development

10.1 INTRODUCTION

In Chapter 3, we covered designing algorithms and subsequently building programs. We introduced strategies to help with that task.

Now that you have functions and new data structures such as lists and dictionaries in your repertoire, we can do an even better job of breaking larger problems into smaller, more manageable, pieces.

10.2 DIVIDE AND CONQUER

> *The ability to simplify means to eliminate the unnecessary so that the necessary may speak.*
>
> Hans Hofmann

We have developed a number of programs, but these programs tended to be relatively small. As programs get bigger, designing those programs so they can be easily implemented and tested becomes more important. We described simplification as one strategy available for writing programs in Chapter 3, especially *divide and conquer*. Divide and conquer is a general strategy for problem solving: breaking a problem down into smaller, interacting pieces that can be addressed more easily individually than the problem as a whole. Functions can be particularly useful in a divide-and-conquer approach as parts of the program can be broken off into functions that can be refined later.

Top-Down Refinement

As we have done with previous development, we will use divide and conquer and the principle of *top-down refinement* to guide our development of a program.

Approaching design from the top down begins with a description of a solution at a very high level—not in Python. Having done so, we then refine that description into more detail. Where we identify an appropriate piece of the solution description, we create a function to fulfill the role identified.

In the initial (top-level) design, we worry about the "big picture" approach to solving the problem. We describe what data structures we need and what "big" processing steps we might take along the way.

To make this process concrete, we will use a complicated example that will require more development on our part.

10.3 THE BREAST CANCER CLASSIFIER

Scientists make data sets available for use by other researchers in the hopes that the data itself will be helpful in solving important problems. Various repositories exist around the world that distribute such data sets, made freely available to everyone. One such repository is the University of California-Irvine Machine Learning Repository (`http://archive.ics.uci.edu/ml`). As of this writing, this repository houses 177 datasets on topics from character recognition to flower identification. One of the datasets describes tumors removed from breast cancer patients. The data was provided by Dr. William H. Wolberg at the University of Wisconsin Hospitals in Madison. Each of the patients had a tumor *biopsy*—a small needle was inserted into the tumor to remove some tissue. That tissue was examined by oncologists (physicians who specialize in cancer) to describe various features of the tissue. Subsequent to that examination, they determine if the tumor was *benign* or *malignant*. A malignant cancer is the bad one: that means that the cancer is spreading. Benign means that the cancer is isolated to the tumor itself so it is much less of a threat to the woman.

The Problem

The problem is to determine, based on the the tumor attributes, whether the tumor is malignant or benign. We do so by examining the data provided by Dr. Wolberg. The data lists 699 patients, each with nine tumor attributes, as well as whether that patient was ultimately diagnosed as having a benign or malignant cancer. That is, the "solution" (malignant or benign) is included in the data set. Therefore, every patient has a set of eleven values: a patient ID, the nine tumor attribute values, and the ultimate diagnosis. By examining this data, we hope to discover patterns that *predict* based on the tumor attributes alone whether the tumor is malignant or benign. That is, for a patient we have not yet seen (and do not yet know her diagnosis), we wish to predict whether the tumor is malignant or benign based on the tumor attributes.

How are we going to do that?

The Approach: Classification

It turns out that there are a number of approaches we could take to solve this problem. In fact, there is an entire research area, "data mining," that works on ways to solve such problems. Most of those approaches share some high-level concepts that we will use to solve our problem. The approach we will use is to create a *classifier*, a program that takes in a new example (patient, in our case) and determines, based on previous examples it has observed, what "class" the new example belongs to.

For this problem we consider patients, along with their associated tumor attributes, as our examples and separate each into one of two classes: benign or malignant.

Now that we have identified a broad approach to solving this problem, how do we create a classifier? We begin with a look at training and testing.

Training and Testing the Classifier

A classifier begins by *training* on examples with known solutions. In training, the classifier looks for patterns that indicate classifications (e.g., malignant or benign). After patterns have been identified, they are *tested* against "new" examples with known solutions. By testing with known solutions, we can determine the accuracy of the classifier.

In our case, we provide patients' tumor attributes to the classifier that have a known result (benign or malignant). Each patient contributes towards building an *internal model* of what patterns are used to distinguish between our two classes. Once we have trained the classifier, we must test the effectiveness of our classifier. We do this by providing "new" patients, or patients who were not used as data for the training process, to see what class the classifier predicts each new patient belongs to.

We have to take our data and split it into two parts: data we will use to "train" the classifier, and data we will use to "test" the classifier. In practice, we will create two separate files with most of the data in the training file and the remainder in the testing file.

Now the issue is this: how do we write a program that can find patterns in the training data?

Building the Classifier

There are many interesting internal models that a classifier could use to predict the class label of a new example. We will use a simple one, but as you will see, it can be quite effective.

The model we choose is itself a result of divide and conquer and problem solving. The approach is as follows. Look at each tumor attribute of the individual one at a time, and then combine the observations into a decision as to the class the individual belongs to. For example, one attribute is tumor thickness on a scale of 1–10. A thick tumor (e.g., greater than 7) may predict malignancy; i.e., most malignant tumors in the data have thickness greater than 7. In the end, we evaluate the decision for each attribute and let the majority decide the final classification result.

How do we do that? For each of the nine tumor attributes, let us develop two averages. The first average for each attribute will represent the average value over all the training data for women with *benign* tumors. The second average for that attribute will represent that average value over all the training data for women with *malignant* tumors. After training on the nine attributes, we should end up with eighteen averages: nine averages for benign tumors and nine averages for malignant tumors.

Our classifier will be constructed as follows: for each attribute average, we will find the midpoint between the benign average and the malignant average. This midpoint of averages will be our *class separation value*. Our classifier will consist of nine separation values, one for each attribute. If a new sample comes along with a value less than the midpoint on an attribute, we will predict that this patient is benign, at least on that attribute. If the sample is greater than the midpoint, we predict that it is malignant.

To select which overall class that we predict the patient belongs to, we compare each of the nine patient attributes with respect to each attribute's classifier separation value. We label that attribute based on whether it is larger or smaller than the separator value. Remember, in this case, smaller indicates benign and greater indicates malignant. For the overall patient, we let the majority rule. Whichever class label predominates over the nine attributes, we use that label for the patient overall.

Figure 10.1 shows an overview of the process.

10.4 DESIGNING THE CLASSIFIER ALGORITHM

That's a lot of description for what we have to do. Let's see if we can use our top-down refinement to get started. Here is our first cut of an algorithm in English:

1. Create a training set from a training file.
2. Create a classifier by using the training set to determine separator values for each attribute.
3. Create a test set from a test file.
4. Use the classifier (separator values) to classify data in the test set while keeping score of the accuracy of those decisions.

Code Listing 10.1 is a Python version. It simply creates a function for each algorithm step, but it provides a starting point.

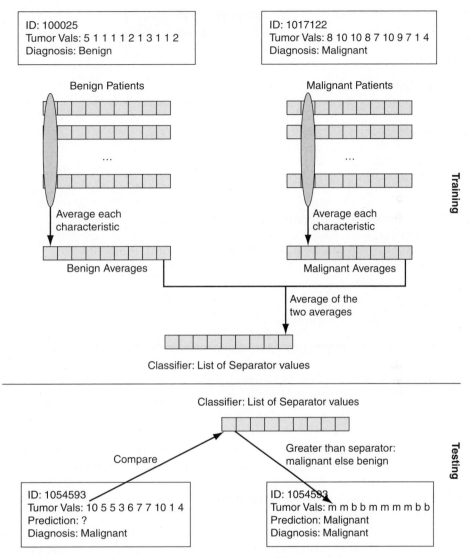

FIGURE 10.1 Overview of classifier approach.

Code Listing 10.1

```
def main():

    print "Reading in training data..."
    trainingFile = "breast-cancer-training.data"
5   trainingSet = makeTrainingSet(trainingFile)
    print "Done reading training data.\n"

    print "Training classifier..."
    classifier = trainClassifier(trainingSet)
10  print "Done training classifier.\n"

    print "Reading in test data..."
    testFile = "breast-cancer-test.data"
    testSet = makeTestSet(testFile)
15  print "Done reading test data.\n"

    print "Classifying records..."
    resultSet = classifyTestSet(testSet, classifier)
    print "Done classifying."

20
    reportResults(resultSet)

    print "Program finished.\n"
```

Notice that the code listing has all the essential elements of the algorithm we described earlier, even though it lacks most of the details. For example:

- **Line 1** defines a main function, a function to be called by the user to run the rest of the program.
- **Line 5** calls a function called makeTrainingSet that takes the name of a file (training data) and returns a trainingSet data structure (not yet defined).
- **Line 9** calls a function called trainClassifier that takes the trainingSet as an argument and returns a classifier data structure (not yet defined).
- **Line 14** calls a function called makeTestSet that takes the name of a file (test data) and returns a testSet data structure (not yet defined).
- **Line 18** returns a resultSet data structure from the function classifyTestSet, which take both the testSet and classifier as arguments.
- **Line 21** calls the reportResults function, which takes the resultSet as an argument.

This is not code that will presently run, as there are five undefined functions. However, it does show us a couple of things we need to do:

- Define the four data structures: `testSet`, `trainingSet`, `classifier`, `resultSet`
- Define five functions: `makeTrainingSet`, `trainClassifier`, `makeTestSet`, `classifyTestSet`, `reportResults`

We can fix up our main program to run by defining skeleton versions of all the functions. Again, by "skeleton," we mean that the function is defined, the argument numbers are correct, and the function returns a value. Otherwise, the function definitions are empty. By doing so, we create a running program with all the requisite parts. Sadly, it doesn't *do* anything, but that is something we can work on. Code Listing 10.2 is a second version with skeleton functions. Remember that the functions *must* be defined before they are called.

Code Listing 10.2

```python
def makeTrainingSet(trainFile):
    return []

def trainClassifier(trainSet):
    return []

def makeTestSet(testFile):
    return []

def classifyTestRecords(testSet,classifier):
    return []

def reportAccuracy(results):
    print "Reported the results"

def main():

    print "Reading in training data..."
    trainingFile = "breast-cancer-training.data"
    trainingSet = makeTrainingSet(trainingFile)
    print "Done reading training data.\n"

    print "Training classifier..."
    classifier = trainClassifier(trainingSet)
    print "Done training classifier.\n"
```

```
         print "Reading in test data..."
         testFile = "breast-cancer-test.data"
         testSet = makeTestSet(testFile)
30       print "Done reading test data.\n"

         print "Classifying records..."
         resultList = classifyTestSet(testSet, classifier)
         print "Done classifying."
35
         reportResults(resultList)

         print "Program finished.\n"
```

Following is a test of that code. The important thing to notice is that it works! Of course, it doesn't do anything useful, but it is a working program that we can continue to develop. Most importantly though, it gives an outline for the entire program.

```
>>> import secondCut
>>> secondCut.main()
Reading in training data...
Done reading training data.

Training classifier...
Done training classifier.

Reading in test data...
Done reading test data.

Classifying records...
Done classifying.
Reported the results
Program finished.

>>>
```

Divided, now Conquer

By designing the program as we did, we have in fact divided the program into smaller pieces, tied together by the overall design. Of course, there are many ways we could have divided up the program. Our job now is to decide about the required data structures and further apply our divide-and-conquer strategy to each of the functions.

Data Structures

We need to make some decisions about our data structures—this is what design is all about. Again, there are many valid possibilities—we show only one.

- `trainingSet, testSet`: The data structures `trainingSet` and `testSet` contain information about each individual patient. Because the data on each patient is never modified, each patient's data could be stored as a tuple of values. A list of tuples would then hold all patient data. Therefore, a list of tuples will serve for the training and test data structures. The tuple format will be:
  - First position: patient ID. String.
  - Second position: patient diagnosis. String (single letter, `'m'` or `'b'`).
  - Positions 3–12: tumor attributes 1–9 in order. Integer.
- `classifier`: The classifier is simply a sequence of nine values, the separation values. A tuple of values will suffice, as these values also do not change. It will consist of nine floating-point values: the average of each benign and malignant attribute average (the midpoint between each of the two averages).
- `results`: For the results, we need a list of tuples again, but what to put in each tuple? The classifier provides the number of attributes for each patient that indicate malignant and benign. We also need the actual diagnosis for the patient. Therefore, we need to store:
  - The patient ID: String
  - The number of attributes which indicate malignant: Integer
  - The number of attributes which indicate benign: Integer
  - The actual diagnosis: String (either `'m'` or `'b'`).

File Format

We have not yet discussed the actual data. The file format as provided by Dr. Wolberg through the ML Repository is shown in Table 10.1:

The "id number" can be interpreted as a string; the "Class" at the end of the file line is the known diagnosis: 2 for benign, 4 for the malignant. The values in between are the attributes as integers between 1 and 10. Figure 10.2 is an example of the first few file lines.

Note that on a file line, each attribute is separated by a comma. We could either use the `csv` module discussed previously in Section 9.7 or do the parsing by hand. In this case, we can do the parsing by hand, because parsing the file happens to be well behaved—most likely because it didn't come from a spreadsheet.

Function: makeTrainingSet

With our main program defined, we must now work on the functions. Which one should we do first?

#	Attribute	Domain
1	Sample code number	id number
2	Clump Thickness	1 - 10
3	Uniformity of Cell Size	1 - 10
4	Uniformity of Cell Shape	1 - 10
5	Marginal Adhesion	1 - 10
6	Single Epithelial Cell Size	1 - 10
7	Bare Nuclei	1 - 10
8	Bland Chromatin	1 - 10
9	Normal Nucleoli	1 - 10
10	Mitoses	1 - 10
11	Class	(2 for benign, 4 for malignant)

TABLE 10.1 File format.

```
1000025,5,1,1,1,2,1,3,1,1,2
1002945,5,4,4,5,7,10,3,2,1,2
1015425,3,1,1,1,2,2,3,1,1,2
1016277,6,8,8,1,3,4,3,7,1,2
1017023,4,1,1,3,2,1,3,1,1,2
1017122,8,10,10,8,7,10,9,7,1,4
```

FIGURE 10.2 A small part of the data file.

One way to choose is by doing the easiest, or at least the most obvious, first. We have a working program, so by filling in an existing empty function with a working function, we maintain a working program, but the program does more of what it is supposed to do.

The input and output are often easy and the input will be needed by other functions. Therefore, let's begin with the `makeTrainingSet` function. According to our main function, `makeTrainingSet` takes as an argument the name of the file that has the patient data for training. It returns the filled-in data structure `trainingSet` whose format was described earlier. We need to further refine what the function will accomplish—more divide and conquer. Here are some of the things the function must do:

- Open the file. Optionally, we should also have some tests to make sure the file exists, and help the user if the file name does not exist. We will focus on just the opening for now, and refine it to have error checking later.
- Initialize the training set list to be empty.
- For each line in the file.

      - Parse the line into its constituent parts as described earlier.
      - Create a tuple for the patient.
      - Append the tuple to the training set list.
- Return the training set list.

We can write the function as a series of comments, reflecting what we need to do in the function, and then fill each one in. Remember, if any piece gets too complex, we should think about breaking that piece out as a function. Code Listing 10.3 is that first cut.

Code Listing 10.3

```
def makeTrainingSet(fileName):
# open file

# initialize trainingSet list

# for each line in the file

    # parse the line into its 11 parts

    # create a tuple for the patient

    # append to the end of the trainingSet list

# return the training set
```

As expected, some of those elements are fairly easy to fill in.

- **Line 2**: *open* the file (no error checking, something we need to fix later).
- **Line 4**: We need to make an empty list to hold the training set (called tSet).
- **Line 6**: Get each line from the fileDescriptor using a *for* iterator.
- **Line 8**: Extract each of the fields with a split method on the fileLine using the comma (,) as the separation element. We can do multiple assignment to create 11 new variables: id, diag, and attributes a1–a9. Remember, they are all strings initially! We could have used a list, but decided this was more readable.
- **Line 14**: When we are all done, we return the resulting tSet. Note the nesting: the indentation of the return is at the same level as the statements of the function, *not* at the level of the *for* iterator.

Our second cut is shown in Code Listing 10.4. Note that at some point the comments start to interfere with the readability of the program. We can clean up the comments as we fill in the code.

> ### Code Listing 10.4
>
> ```python
> def makeTrainingSet(fileName):
>     tSet = []
> # open file
>     trainingFile = open(fileName)
> 5 # read in a line of the file
>     for line in trainingFile:
> # parse the line into its 11 parts
>         id,a1,a2,a3,a4,a5,a6,a7,a8,a9,diag = line.split(',')
>
> 10 # create a new trainingSet element
>
> # append to the end of the trainingSet
>
> # return the training set
> 15     return tSet
> ```

We did the easy and obvious coding. Now let's finish it. The next pass is shown in Code Listing 10.5.

> ### Code Listing 10.5
>
> ```python
> def makeTrainingSet(fileName):
>     tSet = []
>
> # open file. Fix the error checking
> 5     trainingFile = open(fileName)
>
>     for line in trainingFile:
>         id,a1,a2,a3,a4,a5,a6,a7,a8,a9,diag = line.split(',')
>         patientTuple=(id,diag,int(a1),int(a2),int(a3),int(a4),\
> 10         int(a5),int(a6),int(a7),int(a8),int(a9) )
>         tSet.append(patientTuple)
>     return tSet
> ```

In this version, we did the following:

- We removed comments that were no longer really needed. However, we did keep some, including a note that we need to clean up the error checking on file opening.
- **Line 9**: Created the newly formatted patient as a tuple, called `patientTuple`, We need to take those 11 new variables, re-arrange them to go with our specified data

structure format (id, diag, a1, ..., a9). We specified that the attributes would be integers, and everything we brought in from the file is a string, so the attributes have to be converted to integers using the *int* constructor. The comma operator (,) is used to make a tuple. Note the use of the line continuation character (\), because the line is so long.

- **Line 11**: Once patientTuple is created, we simply use the append method to append it to the end of the tSet list and return it.

How did we do? We should test this little piece of code to make sure that it works. We need to do it now while we are freshly working on it. Once it's tested, we can set it aside and move on to the other parts of the program. How do we go about testing it? We *could* open the training data set, but that is a pretty big file making the results hard to visualize easily. Instead, let's create a small file in the same format. We'll call the file "testData.txt," and use the data shown in Figure 10.2—just has a few lines from the original file.

Here is a test session using the function and the small input file. We'll be honest: we did find a few typing bugs at this point (not shown above, of course!). Testing at this level is a good idea!

```
>>> import fileInputThirdCut
>>> fileInputThirdCut.makeTrainingSet('testData.txt')
[('1000025', '2\n', 5, 1, 1, 1, 2, 1, 3, 1, 1), ('1002945', '2\n', 5, 4, 4, 5, 7,
10, 3, 2, 1), ('1015425', '2\n', 3, 1, 1, 1, 2, 2, 3, 1, 1), ('1016277', '2\n', 6,
8, 8, 1, 3, 4, 3, 7, 1), ('1017023', '2\n', 4, 1, 1, 3, 2, 1, 3, 1, 1), ('1017122',
'4\n', 8, 10, 10, 8, 7, 10, 9, 7, 1)]
>>>
```

How well did we do? Well, it is close to what we want. We did get a list of tuples, and the tuples have the correct information in the correct order. The attributes are all integers and the id is a string. However, there are a couple of problems. Look at the the first tuple and its second element. It has the value '2\n'. According to the earlier specifications, it should be a string, either 'm' or 'b'. Furthermore, where did that '\n' come from?

What we did to fix these issues:

- **Line 8**: '\n' is the linefeed or end-of-line character. It exists on every line. Remember in our line format that the diagnosis was originally the last character on every line. We can use the strip method to remove them.
- **Lines 11–14**: Convert the '2' and '4' to 'm' or 'b', respectively. A simple *if*-statement will do, with the creation of a new variable diagMorN.

The final cut is shown in Code Listing 10.6, along with the session output.

Code Listing 10.6

```
def makeTrainingSet(fileName):
    """Reads a training set from the specified file."""
    tSet = []

5   # open file. Fix the error checking
    trainingFile = open(fileName)

    for line in trainingFile:
        line = line.strip()  # strip off end-of-line character " \n"
10      id,a1,a2,a3,a4,a5,a6,a7,a8,a9,diag = line.split(',')
        if diag == '4':  # diagnosis is "malignant"
            diagMorB = 'm'
        else:            # diagnosis is "benign"
            diagMorB = 'b'
15      patientTuple=(id,diagMorB,int(a1),int(a2),int(a3),int(a4),\
            int(a5),int(a6),int(a7),int(a8),int(a9))
        tSet.append(patientTuple)
    return tSet
```

```
>>> import fileInputFourthCut
>>> fileInputFourthCut.makeTrainingSet('testData.txt')
[('1000025', 'b', 5, 1, 1, 1, 2, 1, 3, 1, 1), ('1002945', 'b', 5, 4, 4, 5, 7, 10,
3, 2, 1), ('1015425', 'b', 3, 1, 1, 1, 2, 2, 3, 1, 1), ('1016277', 'b', 6, 8, 8, 1,
3, 4, 3, 7, 1), ('1017023', 'b', 4, 1, 1, 3, 2, 1, 3, 1, 1), ('1017122', 'm', 8,
10, 10, 8, 7, 10, 9, 7, 1)]
>>>
```

We hope you get the idea of how to slowly break the problem down, first as functions, then as pieces within the functions, to solve the problem. Remember that testing each piece is important to make sure they do what they are required! Testing each function as you write it allows you to fix problems while your design is fresh in your head. Let's take a look at the remaining functions.

The makeTestSet Function

There is good news with the makeTestSet function. If you look closely, the makeTrainingSet and makeTestSet functions perform similar tasks. They take in a file name and return the same data structure format. The only real difference is that they read from two different files: the test data and the training data, both of which have the same file format.

Thus, we can *reuse* our code from `makeTrainingSet` to accomplish the same task in the `makeTestSet` function. To reflect this, we will rename the function to `makeDataSet` and use it in for both operations in the `main` function.

The trainClassifier Function

The `trainClassifier` function is the heart of the program. Based on Figure 10.1, let's outline what this function needs to do:

- The function takes the training set as an argument. The training set is a list of patient tuples where the tuples are in the format described earlier.
- For each patient tuple in the training set:
  - If the tuple represents a benign tumor, add each patient attribute to the running sum of benign attributes. Keep a count of the number of benign patients as well.
  - If the tuple represents a malignant tumor, do the same as the above but find a sum of all malignant patient tumor attributes.
  - In the end we have 18 sums, the sum of every benign patient's attributes and the sum of every malignant patient's attributes. We also end up with two counts, the number of benign patients and the number of malignant patients.
- Find the average attribute value (sum/count) for the nine benign attributes and the nine malignant attributes.
- Find the nine averages of each of the benign and malignant average attributes (the average of the average). These nine separator values specify the midpoint, the separation value, between a malignant diagnosis and a benign diagnosis for that attribute. These nine values are the classifier
- Return the classifier: a list of 9 separator values.

As before, let's implement the function, beginning with comments and obvious structure. We can fill in the details later. Code Listing 10.7 is the first cut.

Code Listing 10.7

```
def trainClassifier(trainingSet):

    for patientTup in trainingSet:
#       if patientTup is benign:
#           add attributes from patientTup to corresponding benignSum attribute
#           increase the benignCount by 1
#       else:
#           add attributes from patientTup to corresponding malignantSum attribute
#           increase the malignantCount by 1
```

```
10  #   create benignAvgs by dividing each benignSum by the benignCount
    #   create malignantAvgs by dividing each malignantSum by the malignantCount

    #   create classifier by dividing the sum of each attribute from benignAvg
    #   and malignantAvg by 2
15
        return classifier
```

Some Utility Functions for Manipulating Lists

In looking at the first cut for `trainClassifier`, it seems we have to keep track of a lot of individual sums and averages. The 18 sums and averages are a lot of variables, so let's organize the variables into lists. For example, a list of the benignSums, a list of the benignAverages, etc. If we use lists instead of individual variables, we have to write code to add two lists. Because we have to find this sum multiple times, a function will make this task easier. We also need to turn a list of sums into a list of averages. As we have to find averages multiple times, it makes sense to break this out as a function, too.

Let us call these two functions `sumLists` and `makeAverages`. These functions are *utility functions*—general-purpose functions that help with the work to be done.

The sumLists Function

The `sumLists` function takes two arguments, two lists of the same size, and returns a new list that contains the sums of the elements from the two argument lists. That is, we take the first element from the first argument list and add it to the first element from the second argument list, and store that sum as the first element in the sum list. The code for this function is shown in Code Listing 10.8.

Code Listing 10.8

```
def sumLists(list1,list2):
    """Element—by—element sums of two lists of 9 items."""
    listOfSums=[0.0]*9
    for index in range(9):
5        listOfSums[index]=list1[index]+list2[index]
    return listOfSums
```

Some things to note:

- **Line 3**: We create a new list called listOfSums that will hold the sums. We create it as a list of nine zeros using the multiplication operator. Remember, for lists, multiplication is a repetition operator.
- **Lines 4–5**: We create a variable called index, that can be used as an index into the three lists. We iterate through the indices, adding the two argument list elements at index into the corresponding listOfSums at index.
- **Line 6**: Return listOfSums.

Note that the size of the lists are all fixed at 9. This fixed size is fine for our present application, but is limiting if this function is to be used in other applications. How could you make the function more general? (See the exercises.)

The makeAverages Function

The function makeAverages is not much different than the sumLists function earlier. It takes in a list and a total, and divides each element in the list by the total, collecting the results in a list to be returned. The code for this function is shown in Code Listing 10.9.

Code Listing 10.9

```
def makeAverages(listOfSums,total):
    """Convert each list element into an average by dividing by the total."""
    averageList=[0.0]*9
    for index in range(9):
        averageList[index]=listOfSums[index]/float(total)
    return averageList
```

Some things to note:

- **Line 3**: Initialize averageList as a list of nine values at 0.0
- **Lines 4–5**: As before, iterate through the list, dividing each element in the list and placing the result in averageList. Note that we convert the total variable to a float to ensure that we do not lose precision in our result.
- **Line 6**: Return averageList.

trainClassifer, Round 2

Using our utility functions and the trainClassifier function outline, we can fill in the details for the trainClassifier function. See Code Listing 10.10.

Code Listing 10.10

```python
    def sumLists(list1,list2):
        """Element—by—element sums of two lists of 9 items."""
        listOfSums=[0.0]*9
        for index in range(9):
5           listOfSums[index]=list1[index]+list2[index]
        return listOfSums

    def makeAverages(listOfSums,total):
        """Convert each list element into an average by dividing by the total."""
10      averageList=[0.0]*9
        for index in range(9):
            averageList[index]=listOfSums[index]/float(total)
        return averageList


15
    def trainClassifier(trainingSet):
        """Build a classifier using the training set."""
        benignSums=[0]*9      # list of sums of benign attributes
        benignCount=0         # count of benign patients
20      malignantSums=[0]*9   # list of sums of malignant attributes
        malignantCount=0      # count of malignant patients

        for patientTup in trainingSet:
            if patientTup[1]=='b':    # if benign
25              # add benign attributes to benign total
                benignSums=sumLists(benignSums,patientTup[2:])
                benignCount += 1
            else:                     # else malignant
                # add malignant attributes to malignant total
30              malignantSums=sumLists(malignantSums,patientTup[2:])
                malignantCount += 1

    #   print benignSums,benignCount,malignantSums,malignantCount

35      # find averages of each set of benign or malignant attributes
        benignAvgs=makeAverages(benignSums,benignCount)
        malignantAvgs=makeAverages(malignantSums,malignantCount)

    #   print benignAvgs,malignantAvgs
40
        # separator values for each attribute averages benign and malignant
        classifier=makeAverages(sumLists(benignAvgs,malignantAvgs),2)

        return classifier
```

Some things to note:

- **Lines 18–21**: These lines establish and initialize the two nine-value lists: `benignSums` and `malignantSums` and the two count variables, `benignCount` and `malignantCount`.
- **Line 24**: We can determine if the patient tuple represents either a malignant or benign tumor based on the diagnosis at position 2 (index 1).
- **Lines 26 and 30**: Calls the `sumLists` function to add the patient tuple to the appropriate sum list.
- **Lines 27 and 31**: When the tuple is added to the sum, the appropriate count is incremented by 1.
- **Line 36 and 37**: Once the sums and counts are calculated, we can calculate the benign and malignant averages by calling the `makeAverages` function with the appropriate sum list and count.
- **Line 42**: Finally, we create the classifier. We use *both* of the utility functions we wrote. We use the `sumLists` function to add the two averages and then pass the resulting list to the `makeAverages` function to divide each sum by 2.
- **Lines 33 and 39**: These two ***print*** statements were useful during development, but are commented out once the code is working correctly.

A Little Testing
We need to test to ensure that we are on the right track. We can load the code we have written so far and test how well the classifier works on the simple data file we created, which was shown in Figure 10.2. Following is that session:

```
>>> import makeDataSet
>>> import trainClassifier
>>> dSet = makeDataSet.makeDataSet('testData.txt')
>>> for pat in dSet:
...     print pat
...
('1000025', 'b', 5, 1, 1, 1, 2, 1, 3, 1, 1)
('1002945', 'b', 5, 4, 4, 5, 7, 10, 3, 2, 1)
('1015425', 'b', 3, 1, 1, 1, 2, 2, 3, 1, 1)
('1016277', 'b', 6, 8, 8, 1, 3, 4, 3, 7, 1)
('1017023', 'b', 4, 1, 1, 3, 2, 1, 3, 1, 1)
('1017122', 'm', 8, 10, 10, 8, 7, 10, 9, 7, 1)
>>> classifier = trainClassifier.trainClassifier(dSet)
>>> for avg in classifier:
...     print "%.3f"%avg
...
6.300
6.500
6.500
```

```
5.100
5.100
6.800
6.000
4.700
1.000
>>>
```

In the session, we first imported the `makeDataSet` file, then the "trainClassifier" file. The "trainClassifier" file has both the two utility functions and the `trainClassifier` function. We read in the test set to create a test set. We then printed out the data set in a nice format so we could verify that the file was read correctly. We then used the created data set to create a classifier, and printed out the classifier values. To make the classifier values easier to read, we used string formatting.

Using a calculator, we can check the averages of the data set and verify that they match the classifier.

Testing the Classifier on New Data

Now we need to see whether the classifier we have created will properly predict the patient diagnosis based only on the patient's tumor attributes. This testing is done with the `classifyTestSet` function.

Let's remember what this function has to do. It takes in a set of test data, consisting of patient tumor data along with the determined diagnosis. We compare each attribute in the patient with the corresponding classifier average. If the attribute is larger than the classifier average, that attribute is considered to be evidence of malignancy. If it is smaller, then that attribute indicates benignity. For each of those patients, we count the number of benign and malignant attributes, and the majority rules. That is, whichever type of attribute is in the majority, that is the classifier's predicted diagnosis.

Code Listing 10.11 is an outline of our code in our typical way, listing comments and obvious pieces of code.

Code Listing 10.11

```python
def classifyTestSet(testSet,classifier):

    # for each patient in the set
    for patient in testSet:
        # for each attribute of the patient
            # if attribute is greater than the classifier corresponding attribute
                # increase the count of attributes indicating malignancy, otherwise
```

```
          # increase the count of attributes indicating benignity
          # create result tuple: (id, benignCount, malignantCout, diagnosis)
10        # add the result tuple to the list of result tuples
      # return the list of result tuples
```

Some notes about this example code:

- **Line 5**: A loop to go through each tuple in the `testSet` list, i.e., each patient.
- **Line 6**: This is a loop nested within the outer, patient loop. This inner loop iterates through each attribute in the patient tuple.
- **Line 10**: Once the two counts are set, we create a result tuple in the format indicated earlier, that is: (`patientID`, `benignCount`, `malignantCount`, `actualDiagnosis`).

The nested loop is an important concept. There are two parts: an outer loop and an inner loop. Nested loops work as follows: for every iteration of the outer loop, the inner loop runs through a complete loop (all iterations). Thus, if the outer loop runs five iterations and the inner loop runs four iterations, a total of 20 iterations are run.

Code Listing 10.12 is a final version of the `classifyTestSet` function.

Code Listing 10.12

```python
def classifyTestSet(testSet, classifier):
    """Run classifier on the test set."""
    results = []
    # for each patient
5   for patient in testSet:
        benignCount = 0
        malignantCount = 0
        # for each attribute of the patient
        for index in range(9):
10          # if actual patient attribute is greater than separator value
            if patient[index] > classifier[index]:
                # predict malignant for that attribute
                malignantCount += 1
            else:
15              # predict benign for that attribute
                benignCount += 1
        # record patient id, both counts, and actual diganosis
        resultTuple = (patient[0], benignCount, malignantCount, patient[1])
```

```
        # add patient to list of results
20      results.append(resultTuple)
    return results
```

Notes about this code:

- **Line 6 and 7**: We need to reset the two counts, `benignCount` and `malignant Count`, at the beginning of the inner loop. After the inner loop runs, the two counts will be set to the respective counts for that patient. When the outer loop runs again, it has moved on to the next patient, and we need to reset those counts to 0 so we can get an accurate count for the next patient.
- **Line 9**: Again, we need to use an index so we can access the same element in the two lists.
- **Line 18**: Create the result tuple by using the patient ID (from the first element of the patient), the two counts, and then the actual diagnosis (from the second element of the patient list).
- **Line 20**: Append the tuple to the end of the complete set of results.

Testing the classifyTestSet Function

We continue by testing using our small "testData" set. Following is the session.

```
>>> import makeDataSet
>>> import trainClassifier
>>> import classifyTestSet
>>> dSet = makeDataSet.makeDataSet('testData.txt')
>>> classifier = trainClassifier.trainClassifier(dSet)
>>> results = classifyTestSet.classifyTestSet(dSet,classifier)
>>> for p in dSet:
...     print p
...
('1000025', 'b', 5, 1, 1, 1, 2, 1, 3, 1, 1)
('1002945', 'b', 5, 4, 4, 5, 7, 10, 3, 2, 1)
('1015425', 'b', 3, 1, 1, 1, 2, 2, 3, 1, 1)
('1016277', 'b', 6, 8, 8, 1, 3, 4, 3, 7, 1)
('1017023', 'b', 4, 1, 1, 3, 2, 1, 3, 1, 1)
('1017122', 'm', 8, 10, 10, 8, 7, 10, 9, 7, 1)
>>> for avg in classifier:
...     print "%.3f"%avg,
...
6.300 6.500 6.500 5.100 5.100 6.800 6.000 4.700 1.000
>>> for p in results:
...     print p
...
```

```
('1000025', 6, 3, 'b')
('1002945', 4, 5, 'b')
('1015425', 6, 3, 'b')
('1016277', 4, 5, 'b')
('1017023', 6, 3, 'b')
('1017122', 0, 9, 'm')
>>>
```

How are we doing? Something is wrong. Look at the first patient, the counts are wrong. From our earlier testing, the classifier appeared to be working (though that isn't a guarantee; it is an indication), so something we did with the `classifyTestSet` function is wrong. Let's look at the first patient (ID 1000025), their attributes, and the classifier values. We'll print them again so they are easier to examine:

```
patient tuple:        ('1000025', 'b', 5, 1, 1, 1, 2, 1, 3, 1, 1)
classifier averages: 6.300 6.500 6.500 5.100 5.100 6.800 6.000 4.700 1.000
resultTuple:          ('1000025', 6, 3, 'b')
```

Looking at the patient attributes and the classifier cutoffs, the counts are indeed wrong. For example, by examining the values from the first patient number 1000025 and the classifier, we should have come out with all nine predictions benign. That is, count values of "9, 0" instead of the "6, 3" in the output. What did we do wrong?

The indexing is off. The problem is in Line 10. We compared the first element (index 0) of `patient` against the first element (index 0) of `classifier`. But what is the format of the patient tuple? The first two values are the ID and the diagnosis, respectively. In fact, we want to compare the *third* element of `patient` with the first of `classifier`. We can solve this issue by adding 2 to each index for the patient tuple (line 13), so we skip over the first two values.

Code Listing 10.13 shows the working version and session.

Code Listing 10.13

```
    def classifyTestSet(testSet, classifier):
        """Run classifier on the test set."""
        results = []
        # for each patient
5       for patient in testSet:
            benignCount = 0
            malignantCount = 0
            # for each attribute of the patient
            for index in range(9):
10              # if actual patient attribute is greater than separator value
                # Note: the patient tuple has two extra elements at the beginning
```

```
              # so we add 2 to each patient index to only index attributes.
              if patient[index+2] > classifier[index]:
                  # predict malignant for that attribute
15                malignantCount += 1
              else:
                  # predict benign for that attribute
                  benignCount += 1
          # record patient id, both counts, and actual diganosis
20        resultTuple = (patient[0], benignCount, malignantCount, patient[1])
          # add patient to list of results
          results.append(resultTuple)
      return results
```

```
>>> import makeDataSet
>>> import trainClassifier
>>> import classifyTestSet
>>> dSet = makeDataSet.makeDataSet('testData.txt')
>>> classifier = trainClassifier.trainClassifier(dSet)
>>> results = classifyTestSet.classifyTestSet(dSet,classifier)
>>> for p in dSet:
...     print p
...
('1000025', 'b', 5, 1, 1, 1, 2, 1, 3, 1, 1)
('1002945', 'b', 5, 4, 4, 5, 7, 10, 3, 2, 1)
('1015425', 'b', 3, 1, 1, 1, 2, 2, 3, 1, 1)
('1016277', 'b', 6, 8, 8, 1, 3, 4, 3, 7, 1)
('1017023', 'b', 4, 1, 1, 3, 2, 1, 3, 1, 1)
('1017122', 'm', 8, 10, 10, 8, 7, 10, 9, 7, 1)
>>> for avg in classifier:
...     print "%.3f"%avg,
...
6.300 6.500 6.500 5.100 5.100 6.800 6.000 4.700 1.000
>>> for p in results:
...     print p
...
('1000025', 9, 0, 'b')
('1002945', 7, 2, 'b')
('1015425', 9, 0, 'b')
('1016277', 6, 3, 'b')
('1017023', 9, 0, 'b')
('1017122', 1, 8, 'm')
>>>
```

The reportResults Function

Finally, we need to report the results. You might think that this would be pretty straightforward and not really require a function, but what should be reported? The accuracy would be nice, but one could imagine reporting how many 9/0 votes, how many close votes, and so on. Therefore, we write a function because we want to isolate potential future changes.

For now, we'll just report the accuracy. Remember that the results data structure is a list with four elements, in order: `id`, `benignCount`, `malignantCount`, `diagnosis`. Also, remember that the diagnosis in the results is the actual patient's diagnosis, not our classifier prediction.

What do we mean by accuracy? "Majority Rules" means that if the `benignCount > malignantCount`, our prediction is benign ("b"), and similarly for malignant. Does our predictor correctly predict the actual diagnosis?

The function is shown in Code Listing 10.14:

Code Listing 10.14

```python
def reportResults(results):
    """Determine accuracy of classifier and report."""
    totalCount=0           # count of the total number of results
    inaccurateCount = 0    # count of incorrect results

    for r in results:
        totalCount += 1
        # if benignCount > malignantCount, we should predict 'b'
        if r[1] > r[2]:
            if r[3] == 'm':   # oops! we were wrong...
                inaccurateCount += 1
        # if malignantCount > benignCount, we should predict 'm'
        elif r[3] == 'b':     # oops! we were wrong...
            inaccurateCount += 1

    print "Of ",totalCount," patients, there were ",\
        inaccurateCount," inaccuracies"
```

Notes on this function:

- **Line 2** and **3**: Initialize the total and inaccurate counts.
- **Line 7–9**: If the benign count > malignant count, then we must check if the diagnosis is "b" for benign. In that case, there is an inaccuracy.
- **Line 11–12**: Similar logic for the malignant count.
- **Line 13**: Print the results.

The following session shows a test of the code.

```
>>> import makeDataSet
>>> import trainClassifier
>>> import classifyTestSet
>>> import reportResults
>>> dSet=makeDataSet.makeDataSet('testData.txt')
>>> classifier=trainClassifier.trainClassifier(dSet)
>>> results=classifyTestSet.classifyTestSet(dSet,classifier)
>>> for r in results:
...     print r
...
('1000025', 9, 0, 'b')
('1002945', 7, 2, 'b')
('1015425', 9, 0, 'b')
('1016277', 6, 3, 'b')
('1017023', 9, 0, 'b')
('1017122', 1, 8, 'm')
>>> reportResults.reportResults(results)
Of  6  patients, there were  0 inaccuracies
>>>
```

10.5 RUNNING THE CLASSIFIER ON FULL DATA

Now comes the real test. We have assembled all the functions and tested them in parts. Now, we need to put the full code together and test it on the entire breast cancer data set.

Training versus Testing

We need to take the full 699 patients and divide them into two files: one file to train the classifier and one file for testing. There are many strategies for testing the accuracy of a classifier. The goal is to train the classifier on as many examples as possible while still testing many patient values. We will take a simple approach and just divide the original file in half: 349 for training, 350 for testing. We put all our code together and run it as indicated in this example getting the following result.

```
>>> import bcancerClassifier
>>> bcancerClassifier.main()
Reading in training data...
Traceback (most recent call last):
  File "<stdin>", line 1, in <module>
  File "bcancerClassifier.py", line 74, in main
    trainingSet = makeDataSet(trainingFile)
  File "bcancerClassifier.py", line 14, in makeDataSet
    int(a5),int(a6),int(a7),int(a8),int(a9)
ValueError: invalid literal for int() with base 10: '?'
```

What happened? The error message says that we have the error in the fourteenth line of the makeDataSet function. Apparently, Python tried to convert a "?" into an integer. Why?

A look at the data files shows the problem. There are a number of patients out of the 699 that have an unknown value as part of their data, indicated by a "?" instead of an integer. That is the source of our problem. We missed that in testing because we looked at only a small portion of the data.

We have a few choices. We can throw out the "bad" data (there are 16 patients that have a "?" instead of an integer), or we can fix the problem in the makeDataSet function. It may be a bad idea to throw away the 16 patients with a "?" for an attribute. However, it may also be a bad idea to "make up" a substitute value for the missing data.

We chose to modify makeDataSet to ignore any patient with a "?." We do that at Line 10–11, providing a test to see whether there is a "?" in the line. If so, we **continue**, meaning that we skip the rest of the loop and go on to the next patient. That probably deserves a comment, so we place one in.

The final code and session output are shown in Code Listing 10.15.

Code Listing 10.15

```
    def makeDataSet(fileName):
        tSet = []

    # open file. Fix the error checking
5       fileDescriptor = open(fileName)

        for fLine in fileDescriptor:
            fLine = fLine.strip()
            # if a '?' in the patient data, skip that patient
10          if '?' in fLine:
                continue
            id,a1,a2,a3,a4,a5,a6,a7,a8,a9,diag = fLine.split(',')
            if diag == '4':
                diagMorB = 'm'
15          else:
                diagMorB = 'b'
            patientTuple=id,diagMorB,int(a1),int(a2),int(a3),int(a4),\
                int(a5),int(a6),int(a7),int(a8),int(a9)
            tSet.append(patientTuple)
20      return tSet
```

```
   def sumLists(list1,list2):
       sumList=[0.0]*9
25     for indx in range(0,9):
           sumList[indx]=list1[indx]+list2[indx]
       return sumList

   def makeAverages(sumList,total):
30     averageList=[0.0]*9
       for indx in range(9):
           averageList[indx]=sumList[indx]/float(total)
       return averageList


35
   def trainClassifier(trainingSet):
       benignSums=[0]*9
       benignCount=0
       malignantSums=[0]*9
40     malignantCount=0

       for patientTup in trainingSet:
           if patientTup[1]=='b':
               benignSums=sumLists(benignSums,patientTup[2:])
45             benignCount += 1
           else:
               malignantSums=sumLists(malignantSums,patientTup[2:])
               malignantCount += 1

50     benignAvgs=makeAverages(benignSums,benignCount)
       malignantAvgs=makeAverages(malignantSums,malignantCount)

       classifier=makeAverages(sumLists(benignAvgs,malignantAvgs),float(2))

55     return classifier

   def classifyTestSet(testSet, classifier):
       results = []
       # for each patient
60     for patient in testSet:
           benignCount = 0
           malignantCount = 0
           # for each attribute of the patient
           for index in range(0,9):
65             if patient[index+2] > classifier[index]:
                   malignantCount += 1
```

```
            else:
                benignCount += 1
        resultTuple = patient[0],benignCount,malignantCount,patient[1]
70      results.append(resultTuple)
    return results

def reportResults(results):
    totalCount=0
75  inaccurateCount = 0
    for r in results:
        totalCount += 1
# if benignCount > malignantCount
        if r[1] > r[2]:
80          if r[3] == 'm':
                inaccurateCount += 1
# if malignantCount > benignCount
        elif r[3] == 'b':
            inaccurateCount += 1
85  print "Of ",totalCount," patients, there were ",\
        inaccurateCount," inaccuracies"

def main():

90  print "Reading in training data..."
    trainingFile = "fullTrainData.txt"
    trainingSet = makeDataSet(trainingFile)
    print "Done reading training data.\n"

95  print "Training classifier..."
    classifier = trainClassifier(trainingSet)
    print "Done training classifier.\n"

    print "Reading in test data..."
100 testFile = "fullTestData.txt"
    testSet = makeDataSet(testFile)
    print "Done reading test data.\n"

    print "Classifying records..."
105 resultList = classifyTestSet(testSet, classifier)
    print "Done classifying."

    reportResults(resultList)

110 print "Program finished.\n"
```

```
>>> import bcancerClassifier
>>> bcancerClassifier.main()
Reading in training data...
Done reading training data.

Training classifier...
Done training classifier.

Reading in test data...
Done reading test data.

Classifying records...
Done classifying.
Of  348  patients, there were  7 inaccuracies
Program finished.

>>>
```

10.6 OTHER INTERESTING PROBLEMS

Here are some other, interesting problems. We don't solve them fully, but we provide you the background information for you to solve them yourself.

Tag Clouds

Tag clouds are a useful way to provide a visual description of the word content of a document. In a tag cloud, words that are used more frequently have a larger font—less frequently used words have a smaller font. For example, Figure 10.3 shows a tag cloud for the Declaration of Independence. Common words, called *stop words*, such as "a," "and," "the," and so on, are usually removed before the analysis, because their frequency isn't usually of interest. As this tag cloud illustrates, one can quickly see the words emphasized in the declaration.

Most of the work with a tag cloud is similar to what we did for the Gettysburg Address earlier in Section 8.2: get a count of each word in the document. As with every problem, there are many details to be handled: "stop words" need to be removed from consideration, punctuation needs to be eliminated, non-ASCII characters need to be removed, and so on. Also, it isn't interesting to display all words, so, as we did with the Declaration of Independence we display only words that occur three or more times are shown. Finally, one must come up with a way to translate word counts into font sizes for display.

A common way to display tag clouds is on the Web. The language of the Web is HTML. You create a document with HTML tags, and then point your web browser to it. Two tasks are needed to to create the HTML document: first, you need to create words with different font sizes in HTML, and second, you need to pack those words into a box. Code Listing 10.16 shows two functions which accomplish those two tasks.

abolishing absolute assent colonies consent
free government hold independent
justice large laws long mankind new
pass peace people power powers
refused repeated right rights seas states
time usurpations war world

FIGURE 10.3 Tag cloud for the U.S. Declaration of Independence.

Code Listing 10.16

```
# Functions adapted from ProgrammingHistorian
# http://niche.uwo.ca/programming-historian/index.php/Tag_clouds

# Take one long string of words and put them in an HTML box.
# If desired, width, background color & border can be changed in the function
# This function stuffs the "body" string into the the HTML formatting string.
def makeHTMLbox(body):
    boxStr = """<div style=\"
    width: 560px;
    background-color: rgb(250,250,250);
    border: 1px grey solid;
    text-align: center\">%s</div>
    """

    return boxStr % (body)


# Take word(str) and fontsize(int), and create an HTML word in that fontsize.
# These words can be strung together and sent to the make HTMLbox() function.
# This function stuffs the body and fontsize into an HTML word format string.
def makeHTMLword(body, fontsize):
    wordStr = '<span style=\"font-size:%spx;\">%s</span>'
    return wordStr % (str(fontsize), body)
```

S&P 500 Predictions

The S&P 500 is a stock market index containing the stocks of 500 large corporations. It is one of a number of important bellwethers of the stock market—showing trends in overall market performance. A number of sites on the Web collect stock market data and make it available. One such site is Yahoo! Finance.[1] The site provides a download in CSV format—the first few lines are shown in Figure 10.4. We selected to download weekly values.

```
Date,Open,High,Low,Close,Volume,Adj Close
2008-07-21,1261.82,1267.74,1255.70,1260.00,4630640000,1260.00
2008-07-18,1258.22,1262.23,1251.81,1260.68,5653280000,1260.68
2008-07-17,1246.31,1262.31,1241.49,1260.32,7365209600,1260.32
2008-07-16,1214.65,1245.52,1211.39,1245.36,6738630400,1245.36
```

FIGURE 10.4 CSV file downloaded from Yahoo!® Finance.

The first line of the file is a header line that labels each of the comma-separated fields in each line. Let's consider the "Date" and "Adj Close" values—the latter is the final, adjusted value for the index at the end of the week. To smooth out the data, let's consider 13 weeks at a time—13 weeks is one-quarter of a year. Finally, let's consider data over the last 20 years—roughly the lifetime so far of a college student. Here are some questions we might ask:

- What is the greatest difference between the max and min values in any 13-week interval?
- What is the smallest difference between the max and min values in any 13-week interval?
- What is the greatest change between the first and last values in any 13-week interval?
- What is the smallest change between the first and last values in any 13-week interval?
- If we fit a line to a 13-week interval of data, what is the slope of the line?
- What are the difference, change, and slope for last week?

Note that as we phrased the questions, the first two values will always be positive, and the next three could be negative. That is, the last value may be less than the first value. Also, a line fit to the data may be sloping downward (negative slope).

How might we approach this problem? We can go through the data line by line and split on commas yielding date as the first value and close as the last value in the resulting list. We can gather 13 values together into a list and find the differences and changes over that 13-week interval. Using the max and min functions we can find the difference as max - min on each 13-week list. We can find the change by subtracting the first week

---

[1] S&P 500 data: http://finance.yahoo.com/q/hp?s=GSPC, ©YAHOO! and the YAHOO! logo are registered trademarks of Yahoo! Inc.

from the last week: `thirteenWeekList[-1]` - `thirteenWeekList[0]`. We can then put the differences into one list and changes into another list. The `max` and `min` of those latter lists provide the answers to the first four questions.

The slope of a line made from the data is a bit trickier. Fitting a line to data is called a linear least squares fit; a search on the Web provides the following formula, which can be put in a function. The x values will be 0 to 12 representing the 13 weeks, and the `range(13)` function will be useful for generating those values. The y values will be the 13 closing values in the `thirteenWeekList`. The formulas for p, q, r, and s look intimidating, but the Python `sum` function does that summation calculation for us. For example, to calculate q you simply sum over the list: `q = sum(thirteenWeekList)`.

$$slope = \frac{ns - pq}{nr - p^2}$$

where

$$p = \sum_{k=1}^{n} x_k$$

$$q = \sum_{k=1}^{n} y_k$$

$$r = \sum_{k=1}^{n} x_k^2$$

$$s = \sum_{k=1}^{n} x_k y_k$$

We formatted our output as follows:

```
>>>
Twenty years of S&P 500 in 13-week intervals.

max and min difference between high and low values in 13 weeks: 191.33, 11.47
max and min change from first week to 13th week: 191.33, -171.73
max and min slope of line fit to data over 13 weeks: 15.33, -14.36
latest week difference, change, slope,  2008-07-02 : 58.79 , 1.52 , 0.87
```

From that output we can observe that over 20 years:

- The biggest difference between the `max` and `min` in any 13-week interval was 191.
- The smallest difference between the `max` and `min` in any 13-week interval was 11.

- The biggest increase from the first to last week in any 13-week interval was 191.
- The biggest decrease from the first to last week in any 13-week interval was -171.
- The biggest trend increase over any 13-week interval (slope) was 15.
- The biggest trend decrease over any 13-week interval (slope) was -14.
- The 13-week trend was nearly flat, but going up a little.
- The index has gone up as much as it has gone down in any 13-week interval.

Finally, we can see that in the last week, the index has been volatile—that it ended slightly better than it started and that overall the trend is positive.

With some real data and a little Python programming, we were able to do some real analysis of stock market data. One could easily substitute another index or individual stock performance to do the same or similar analysis.

Predicting Religion with Flags

The design of a flag is influenced by the political and cultural roots of a country. Is it possible to determine the predominate religion of a country simply by looking at its flag?

Characteristics of flags were collected from a book of flags and are available online.[2] Twenty-eight different characteristics of flags were collected, such as number of vertical bars, horizontal stripes, colors, circles, crosses, or stars. Some characteristics were Boolean—that is, they exist or do not—such as crescent, triangle, some icon, some animate object, or some text. Finally, some non-numeric data was collected: dominate color, color in upper-left corner, and color in the bottom-right corner. The data set was augmented with the predominate religion of the country. Roughly half the 194 countries in the data set were Christian, so using the techniques we used for the breast cancer study, we created a flag classifier to predict whether the predominate religion of a country is Christian or not.

The simple classifier correctly predicted the predominate religion from flag characteristics 70% of the time. It was better at predicting that a country was *not* Christian (88% correct), than it was a predicting that a country was Christian (52% correct).

Here is a sample of the data set:

```
Andorra,3,1,0,0,6,0,3,0,3,1,0,1,1,0,0,0,gold,0,0,0,0,0,0,0,1,1,1,blue,red
Angola,4,2,1247,7,10,5,0,2,3,1,0,0,1,0,1,0,red,0,0,0,0,1,0,0,1,0,0,red,black
Anguilla,1,4,0,0,1,1,0,1,3,0,0,1,0,1,0,1,white,0,0,0,0,0,0,0,0,1,0,white,blue
```

[2] Richard Forsyth (1990). UCI Machine Learning Repository http://archive.ics.uci.edu/ml/machine-learning-databases/flags/flag.names. Irvine, CA: University of California, School of Information and Computer Science.

Fields 1–6 are country characteristics such as location, size, population, and language, so they are ignored for this exercise. Consider the flag of Andorra in Figure 10.5. Using brackets to note indices in the data line above: it has 3 vertical bars[7], 0 stripes[8], 3 colors[9], red[10], blue[12], gold[13], gold dominates[17], an icon[25], an animate object[26], text[27], blue in the top left[28], and red in the bottom right[29].

FIGURE 10.5 Flag of Andorra.

As with the breast-cancer data, averages were calculated for each field and then a midpoint was found. If a country's data fell on the correct side of the midpoint for a field, the score was increased by 1. A high score was considered to be a match, i.e., a predominately Christian country. The non-numeric color fields were handled by determining the dominant color for Christian flags—listing, counting, sorting, and selecting the dominant color. If a field matched the Christian-dominate color, the score was increased. As the dominant color for the bottom right was red for both Christian and non-Christian, it was not used as a discriminator.

Because the overall accuracy is barely 70%, it is easy to find countries that are identified incorrectly by our simple predictor. In the following output, we illustrate with two correct and two incorrect input:

```
Flags

Enter a country: UK
UK is Christian
Enter a country: China
China is not Christian
Enter a country: Spain
Spain is not Christian
Enter a country: Qatar
Qatar is Christian
Enter a country: done
```

Summary

In this chapter, we showed how Python could be applied in a variety of domains. We walked through one problem in detail, and outlined approaches to a few very different problems. One interesting observation about this chapter is the complexity of problems that you now have the tools to solve.

Exercises

1. The function `sumLists` works only with two lists of exactly nine elements.

   (a) Fix the function to work with lists of any size.
   (b) Fix the function to work even if the lists are of different sizes.
   (c) Rewrite the function using list comprehension. Can you reduce the function to one line, yet have it still be readable?

2. The function `makeAverages` works only with lists of exactly nine elements.

   (a) Fix the function to work with lists of any size.
   (b) Rewrite the function using list comprehension. Can you reduce the function to one line, yet have it still be readable?

3. Find an online transcription of a political debate online, and download the file.

   (a) Generate separate tag clouds for each participant.
   (b) Analyze the tag clouds and write a one-page essay on what the tag clouds tell about the debate.

4. Find online stock transactions, and download the data. Pick an interesting and volatile period, such as the second half of 2008.

   (a) Choose a feature of the market that you find interesting and write a program that analyzes the data.
   (b) Write a one-page analysis of your output.

5. Choice of appropriate data structure is an important step in designing algorithms. Suppose a text file contains student records on each line and each record is of the format: Name of Student, Student ID, GPA. Now consider reading that file to create a list of lists, a list of tuples, or a tuple of tuples.

   (a) If you just want to create a report using the data, would you choose a list or a tuple as the underlying data structure for the record?
   (b) If you want to modify the name or student ID or GPA, would you choose a list or a tuple as the underlying data structure for the record?

6. A major holiday is coming, and you need to keep track of all the things to do to prepare for the relatives coming to your place to celebrate. What data structure do you use to keep track?

Programming Projects

1. **Classifier: Income predictor**

   An alternative classifier assignment can be constructed from another data set out of the UCI Machine-Learning Repository. The "Adult Data Set" can be used to predict whether someone's income will be greater than $50,000 or not. The process is the same as for classifying cancer as benign or malignant.

   In this case, there are three information fields that can be ignored. They are labeled "Fnlwgt" (field 3), "Native-country" (field 14), and "Education" (field 4). The last one is ignored, because that value is captured in the adjacent field "Education-num."

   The other difference in this data set is that some fields have discrete attributes. Calculating averages for attributes such as "Hours per week" is simple: just add up all the values and divide by the count of values. The discrete attributes are a little more interesting. Imagine that we have 10 records, all of which are examples of the >50K examples. If the "Relationship" attribute for 2 of these 10 records is "Wife," 3 is "Own-child," 2 is "Husband," 1 is "Not-in-family," 1 is "Other-relative," and 1 is "Unmarried," then the "Relationship" attribute in the >50K model would be as follows:

Relationship		
	Wife:	0.2
	Own-child:	0.3
	Husband:	0.2
	Not-in-family:	0.1
	Other-relative:	0.1
	Unmarried:	0.1

   Follow the six steps outlined for the cancer classifier.

2. **Tag Cloud**

   Choose a document to analyze and use the tag cloud function of Section 10.6 to create a tag cloud web page. An interesting alternative is to use a transcript of a political debate for analysis.

3. **Stock Analysis**

   Using the formulas of Section 10.6 gather and analyze stock trends. An interesting alternative is to analyze a particular stock.

4. **Flag Analysis**

   Using the outline of Section 10.6 and the URL provided, recreate the flag analysis.

## PART 4

Classes: Making Your Own Data Structures & Algorithms

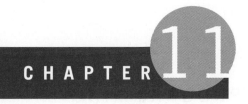

CHAPTER 11

Introduction to Classes

WE HAVE DISCUSSED AT LENGTH THE USE OF BUILT-IN DATA STRUCTURES AND methods for problem solving. What we have not addressed is how to build our *own* data structures. What if our problem requires a data structure and/or methods of our own design? In this chapter, we will introduce *classes* and how they can help us do exactly that.

Simple Student Class

To get a flavor of classes let's define a simple Student class. The class definition and a session using it are shown in Code Listing 11.1. Our class has a few attributes such as a first name, last name, and ID. Once the class is defined, we can create an instance object named `stu1` and then print its attributes in the accompanying session. You will notice a number of unusual features such as names beginning and ending with underscores, and the name *self* appearing in many places. We will explain these and many other interesting aspects of classes in this chapter.

Code Listing 11.1

```
class Student(object):
    """Simple Student class."""
    def __init__(self,first='', last='', id=0): # initializer
        self.firstNameStr = first
        self.lastNameStr = last
        self.idInt = id

    def __str__(self): # string representation, e.g. for printing
        return "%s %s, ID:%s" % \
                (self.firstNameStr, self.lastNameStr, self.idInt)
```

```
>>> stu1 = Student('Terry', 'Jones', 12345)
>>> print stu1
Terry Jones, ID:12345
```

11.1 OBJECT-ORIENTED PROGRAMMING

A common concept in modern programming languages design is the *object-oriented* programming paradigm. Object-oriented programming, or OOP for short, is a general approach to programming that grew out of a need to handle the increasing complexity of programming. It is not the only approach, and hopefully you will be exposed to others, but it is common and has a number of advantages.

OOP is really a point of view. That point of view is that a program is a series of *objects*, where each object can interact with other program objects to accomplish the programmer's goal. Each object can potentially:

- Group together some values that represent the object.
- Perform some action on the object.

OOP takes the view that elements in a program are objects. These objects will have two characteristics:

- the object has *attributes* (e.g., color, make).
- the object responds to some *commands* that are particular for that kind of object (e.g., move-forward, print).

Python Is Object-Oriented!

The good news is that we have been working with the OOP paradigm all along, because Python is fundamentally an OOP language. We have spoken often of Python objects and their associated methods. When we call a constructor such as *list* or *str* (or their shortcuts [ ] or ' '), we are making a new object. Those objects have attributes. Both a list and string object are collections with multiple parts. Those objects respond to commands called methods. We can sort a list with the statement myList.sort(), change a string to lower case with the method myString.lower(). We know how to work with objects, now we are moving on to making our own.

In Python, there is a strong similarity between a type and a class. We have previously seen that items of type *int* differ from items of type *float* in both their attributes and the operations that can be performed on them. For example, the "%" operator is not available to floats, and the "/" operator behaves differently.

Object-oriented programming compels the programmer to think of the items in a program as objects. We have a lot of experience with this point of view in the programs we have written to date!

Characteristics of OOP

There are three characteristics typically associated with the OOP paradigm. They are:

- Encapsulation
- Polymorphism
- Inheritance

It is difficult to define these characteristics exactly at this point, so we will return to them after we get a better understanding of OOP. Keep them in mind as we lead you through the concepts of OOP.

We will begin with a discussion of OOP in general, and then examine the implementation of those concepts in Python.

11.2 WORKING WITH OBJECT-ORIENTED PROGRAMMING

There are some terms commonly associated with OOP that we introduce here. We acknowledge that OOP terminology is not universally accepted, but there are some general things we can discuss that will span most OOP approaches. We will begin with a generic view of OOP and then consider Python's view.

Class and Instance

The terms *class* and *instance* are important for understanding OOP. They can be surprisingly tricky to understand at first, so we will approach the concepts slowly.

The viewpoint we take in this book is that a *class* is a *template* for making a new object, and that an object made by a class template is called an *instance* of that class. Using a simple analogy, class and instance have a relationship similar to that between a cookie cutter and a cookie. A cookie cutter is a template for stamping out cookies. Once the template is made, we can stamp out any number (an infinite number, in fact) of cookies, each one formed in the likeness defined by the cutter (template).

OOP works similarly. A class is a template for making an instance, and the instance reflects the structure provided by the template, the class. The class can "stamp out" any number (in fact, an infinite number) of instances, each in the likeness of the class.

As we said earlier, a class operates in much the same way as a type. The type `int` is in fact a template; a general model of the attributes of an integer and the operations that can be performed on an integer. In contrast, the specific integers 1, 2, 3, 145, 8857485, etc., are each instances of the `int` type. Because they are of the same type, each integer instance shares the operations that can be performed on *all* integers, but each integer instance has local, individual characteristics, i.e., their individual value.

The class template defines the two major aspects of an instance: the attributes that might be contained in each instance and the operations that can be performed on each instance. It is important to remember that the class defines the structure and operations of an instance, but that those operations are operations for class instances, not the class itself.[1] If we stay with the cookie analogy, the operations to be performed on the instance (cookie), such as eat a cookie, or dunk it in milk, are not operations that can be performed on the cookie cutter (at least, we hope not!). We can again look to the integers. We can add two integers, 1 + 2, but what does it mean to perform the same operation on the type *int* itself, *int + int*?

The traditional view is that class defines the instance, the potential attributes (though not the values) of the instance, and the operations that can be performed on that instance. In this first take, the most important operation that a class can do is the "instance-making" operation. All other operations are associated with the instance.

11.3 WORKING WITH CLASSES AND INSTANCES

Let's take a look at some real classes and instances in Python, and see what we can do with them.

Built-In Class and Instance

We can apply our new terminology, class and instance, to the programming we have been doing. Any of the built-in data structures are defined as a class: a list is a class, as is a string, set, tuple, or dictionary. These classes can be used to make individual instances using either the constructor (respectively *list, str, set, tuple, dict*) or their short cuts where available. The constructor creates a new object, which is an instance of the class. These instances have internal attributes and associated methods that may be applied to those instances.

The *type* function helps us understand this detail. Look at the following session:

```
>>> myList = [1,2,3]
>>> type(myList)
<type 'list'>
>>> myStr = 'abc'
>>> type(myStr)
<type 'str'>
>>> myDict = {1:'a',2:'b',3:'c'}
>>> type(myDict)
```

---

[1] Note that it is possible to make new classes as instances of other classes with associated methods, so—called *metaprogrammng*. We leave this for more involved discussions of OOP, but Python does support metaprogramming; see http://www.onlamp.com/pub/a/python/2003/04/17/metaclasses.html

```
<type 'dict'>
>>> myList
[1, 2, 3]
>>> myList.sort(reverse=True)
>>> myList
[3, 2, 1]
>>> myStr.upper()
'ABC'
>>> myDict.values()
['a', 'b', 'c']
>>> myStr.sort()
Traceback (most recent call last):
  File "<stdin>", line 1, in <module>
AttributeError: 'str' object has no attribute 'sort'
>>> myList.values()
Traceback (most recent call last):
  File "<stdin>", line 1, in <module>
AttributeError: 'list' object has no attribute 'values'
>>>
```

When an instance is made of any of the built-in data structures, the new instance has a type: the type of the class it was created from. As a result, certain methods defined by the class are available to those instances. However, when an instance attempts to use a method *not* defined as part of the class, an error results. The error message is also very telling—for example: `AttributeError: 'str' object has no attribute 'sort'`. It clearly states that the attribute being sought is not part of an element of this type (of this class).

Our First Class

Take a look at the following Python session. In the session, we create a class named `myClass` and create an instance of that class that we name `myInstance`.

```
>>> class myClass (object):
        pass

>>> dir(myClass)
['__class__', '__delattr__', '__dict__', '__doc__', '__getattribute__', '__hash__',
'__init__', '__module__', '__new__', '__reduce__', '__reduce_ex__', '__repr__', '
__setattr__', '__str__', '__weakref__']

>>> myInstance = myClass()
>>> dir(myInstance)
```

```
['__class__', '__delattr__', '__dict__', '__doc__', '__getattribute__', '__hash__',
'__init__', '__module__', '__new__', '__reduce__', '__reduce_ex__', '__repr__', '
__setattr__', '__str__', '__weakref__']

>>> type(myInstance)
<class '__main__.myClass'>
>>>
```

Figure 11.1 shows the basic components of a class definition.

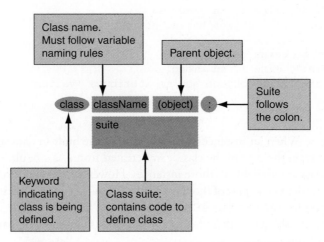

FIGURE 11.1 The basic format of a class definition.

A class definition starts with the **class** keyword, followed by the class name. As with all names, the class name must adhere to normal Python naming rules (see Section 1.4). After assignment and **def**, the keyword **class** is our third example of making a new association in a namespace. The name that follows the keyword is the name of the class and that name becomes associated with a class object. After the class name we include, in parentheses, the name of the parent class of our class. In Section 12.6, we will cover more on parent and base classes, but for now we always include the class object in parentheses followed by a colon.

What follows the colon, as in previous Python statements, is a suite that defines the class. The suite can contain any relevant Python code, typically methods or variable assignments. This particular class has what is essentially an empty suite, except, Python will not allow a truly empty suite. We use the Python keyword **pass** to indicate that the suite is indeed empty. The keyword **pass** is an indication of intent. We, the class designers, did not forget to add content; we intended to have no content.

Once the class is defined, we can inspect what we have made with the Python function `dir`. The function `dir` lists all of the *attributes* of the class. Python uses the word "attribute" to indicate both the methods of an object and the names of any values stored in an object. An attribute is a name associated with another object.

You may have noticed something strange about the previous paragraph. We said that `dir` lists all the attributes of an object, and used it on our class `myClass`. Yes, a class is also an object. We will talk more about a class as an object later, but every class, every instance—in fact, nearly everything *in* Python is an object!

The function `dir` with the argument `myClass` produced a long list attributes. Most of these were provided, by default, by Python through the special object named `object`. Even though we provided no attributes to `myClass`, that class does indeed have a set of attributes, most of which begin and end with double underscore characters (__). Python reserves a number of special methods and variables that begin with with a pair of underscore characters. These have predefined meaning to Python in its OOP class system. We will be seeing more of these special names shortly.

A Simple Instance

Even though we have included nothing in our class definition, `myClass` comes with one very important, built-in ability. It has the ability to *make* an instance. We, as class designers, are given the opportunity to affect the instance-creation process, but even if we choose not to avail ourselves of it, our class can make an instance.

We invoke any class's instance-making function by using the *name* of the class as a function. In our case, the name of our class is `myClass`, so the name of the instance creation function is `myClass()`. This is the normal approach in Python. Every constructor we have seen is named the same as the class name it is associated with. We can see this action in the previous session. Because our class is empty, we use the default instance-making ability of Python.

What is created is an instance of the class. We can use the `dir` function to see what attributes the instance contains. Not surprisingly, the instance attributes look like the class attributes, because the instance was made from the class as a template. More importantly, what type is the instance? It is an instance of the class `myClass` as indicated by the result from the `type` function. An instance is made from a class and carries that class as its type. We have created a new type by creating a class and can make instances of that type!

Changing Attributes

Now we have a class and an instance. How can we change them?

In general, you can reference any object using the standard "dot notation" we have been using. Also, as in any other assignment, we need only assign a value to a variable for a variable to be created. However, in this case, we assign the variable internally to the object when we use the dot notation. That is, as with other objects, a class and instance have a namespace, and when we make a new assignment we add the name to the namespace. Look at the following session.

```
>>> class myClass (object):
        pass

>>> myInstance = myClass()
>>> dir(myClass)
['__class__', '__delattr__', '__dict__', '__doc__', '__getattribute__', '__hash__',
'__init__', '__module__', '__new__', '__reduce__', '__reduce_ex__', '__repr__',
'__setattr__', '__str__', '__weakref__']
>>> dir(myInstance)
['__class__', '__delattr__', '__dict__', '__doc__', '__getattribute__', '__hash__',
'__init__', '__module__', '__new__', '__reduce__', '__reduce_ex__', '__repr__',
'__setattr__', '__str__', '__weakref__']
>>> myClass.classAttribute = 'hello'
>>> print myClass.classAttribute
hello
>>> dir(myClass)
['__class__', '__delattr__', '__dict__', '__doc__', '__getattribute__', '__hash__',
'__init__', '__module__', '__new__', '__reduce__', '__reduce_ex__', '__repr__',
'__setattr__', '__str__', '__weakref__', 'classAttribute']
>>> myInstance.instanceAttribute = 'world'
>>> print myInstance.instanceAttribute
world
>>> dir(myInstance)
['__class__', '__delattr__', '__dict__', '__doc__', '__getattribute__', '__hash__',
'__init__', '__module__', '__new__', '__reduce__', '__reduce_ex__', '__repr__',
'__setattr__', '__str__', '__weakref__', 'classAttribute', 'instanceAttribute']
>>> print myInstance.classAttribute
hello
>>>
```

To create a new attribute in a class, one can simply assign a value to an object, that is, to objectName.attributeName using dot notation. In the previous session, we make the assignment myClass.classAttribute = 'hello', resulting in the attribute classAttribute being added to myClass with the value 'hello'. We can print that value back using a normal *print* statement and the full name, i.e., *print* myClass.classAttribute. Furthermore, we can see that using the dir function on myClass clearly shows that classAttribute is now part of myClass.

As we have mentioned, a namespace is actually a dictionary that establishes a relationship between names and objects. The namespace for a class is named __dict__ and that name can be seen in the previous session.

We can also add an attribute to the instance, `myInstance`, again using dot notation and assignment. As before, we can view the attribute's value by printing it. However, look closely at the result of the `dir` function on `myInstance`. See anything odd?

The Special Relationship Between an Instance and Class: instance-of

The oddity is the fact that the attribute `classAttribute`, set to be part of `myClass`, shows up as an attribute of `myInstance` even though we never assigned `classAttribute` to the instance. How can that be?

Look at the following session.

```
>>> class myClass (object):
        pass

>>> myInstance = myClass()
>>> myClass.classAttribute = 'hello'
>>> myInstance.instanceAttribute = 'world'
>>> dir(myInstance)
['__class__', '__delattr__', '__dict__', '__doc__', '__getattribute__', '__hash__',
'__init__', '__module__', '__new__', '__reduce__', '__reduce_ex__', '__repr__', '
__setattr__', '__str__', '__weakref__', 'classAttribute', 'instanceAttribute']
>>> print myInstance.__class__
<class '__main__.myClass'>
>>> type(myInstance)
<class '__main__.myClass'>
>>> print myInstance.instanceAttribute
world
>>> print myInstance.classAttribute
hello
>>> print myClass.instanceAttribute

Traceback (most recent call last):
  File "<pyshell#11>", line 1, in <module>
    print myClass.instanceAttribute
AttributeError: type object 'myClass' has no attribute 'instanceAttribute'
>>>
```

A special relationship holds between a class and its instance. This relationship is often called an *instance-of* relationship. That is, every instance is related to its respective class by the instance-of relationship: the instance is an instance-of its template class. In fact, we can even see how that relationship is established. In the previous session we printed the value of `myInstance.__class__`, an attribute of `myInstance`. When an instance is created, the class from which it was created is recorded in the special attribute name `__class__` in the instance. In this way, an instance always "remembers" its class, the

template from which it was created. When we ***print*** myInstance.__class__, we
see that it is an instance of the class myClass. This is shown in Figure 11.2.

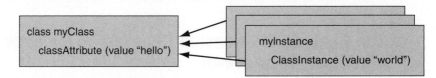

FIGURE 11.2 The instance-of relationship.

Again, if we ask Python to indicate the type of myInstance using the type function,
it reports that myInstance is of type myClass.

Part of the Python Scope Rules for Objects: Instance, then Class

You saw in Section 7.2 that the scope of a variable is related to the namespace that defines
where a variable is referenced. The previous rule was called the LEGB rule, that is, we look
for a variable: first in the local namespace (L), second in the enclosing (function) namespace
(E), third in the global namespace (G), and then finally in the built-in namespace (B). If it
cannot be found in that search process, then the variable is undefined.

A similar rule applies to objects. We can search through different namespaces to find
the value associated with a name. The instance-of relationship provides half of the object
rule (Section 12.6 reveals the full rule). If the name cannot be found in the *instance* itself,
Python will look up the instance-of relation to see whether the name can be found in
the associated *class* namespace. In this way, OOP provides an economy of definition. A
name defined in the class namespace is available to *all* instances of that class. The class
acts as a kind of global repository for attributes to be used and shared by all its instances.
This is how classAttribute becomes available to myInstance; it is not found
in the instance itself, but is found in the class, myClass, that formed myInstance.
Note that the relationship does not hold both ways. Python throws an error if we ask to
print myClass.instanceAttribute. The direction of the arrows in Figure 11.2
illustrates that one-way relation.

Interestingly, a programmer is free to "override" the class-global definition. Because the
rule is to first look in the instance, *then* the class, defining any attribute in the instance
over-rides the definition in the class.

What happens if the class resets the attribute classAttribute, as in
myInstance.classAttribute='*goodbye*'? That invocation is perfectly legal
Python, but now *every instance* of myClass will be affected by the change *unless* they have
changed the attribute locally. Look at the following session.

```
>>> class myClass (object):
        pass

>>> inst1 = myClass()
```

```
>>> inst2 = myClass()
>>> inst3 = myClass()
>>> myClass.classAttribute = 27
>>> inst1.classAttribute = 72
>>> print inst1.classAttribute
72
>>> print inst2.classAttribute
27
>>> print inst3.classAttribute
27
>>> myClass.classAttribute = 999
>>> print inst1.classAttribute
72
>>> print inst2.classAttribute
999
>>> print inst3.classAttribute
999
>>>
```

The instance `inst1` set the attribute locally. It is not affected by the class change, and it does not affect the value of the attribute as seen by `inst2` and `inst3`. However, when the class changes the attribute value, both `inst2` and `inst3` reflect the change, as they are using the instance-of link to find the value. This situation is shown in Figure 11.3.

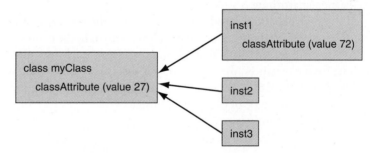

FIGURE 11.3 A mixture of local and instance-of attribute relationships.

11.4 OBJECT METHODS

We added attributes to objects, but not methods. How do we add methods to an object? In fact, exactly what is a method? How do we use methods?

Using Object Methods

We alluded earlier to the fact that a method and a function are different. In Chapter 5, we discussed functions and what they can do. A function is a small program—an encapsulation of an operation. It takes in parameters and returns a value. By providing encapsulation of a task, we can write more readable code.

Functions that define the operations that can be done on a class object are called *methods*.

We know a lot about calling methods. We first discussed how a method is called in Chapter 4 but here's a refresher. Consider a string and the string's `count` method. The `count` method takes a single argument, a string, and counts the number of occurrences of the argument string in the calling string. For example, to count the number of times the "m" character occurs in the `aStr` string:

```
>>> aStr = "hi mom"
>>> print aStr.count("m")
2
>>> print aStr.count
<built-in method count of str object at 0xcb0f20>
>>>
```

The variable `aStr` is associated with an instance of the string class, the string "hi mom". If we want to call a method on `aStr`, we use the the same "dot notation" that we used for attributes. The notation works because a method *is* just another attribute of an object. It just so happens that a method is a callable, or invokable, attribute. Just to make that clear, when we ***print*** `aStr.count`, we get a value back indicating that this particular attribute is a method of the str object.

To invoke the method, we must do so in the context of a string object, in this case the object associated with `aStr`. We can call `count` in the context of a string instance, because `count` works only with string instances. There might be other `count` methods (there is one for list instances, for example), but this particular method works only for strings while the other `count` works only for lists. The names may be the same, but their operation depends on the type of object being used.

The invocation is:

$$aStr.count('m')$$

which can be read as "Call the string `count` method using the string `aStr` along with the argument `'m'`." The result is how many times `'m'` shows up in the calling string, `aStr`.

The important thing to note is that `aStr` is the object that is used in the calling of `count`. This observation points out two important issues:

- We know which method to call. Both the type of the object (type *str* for `aStr`, in this case) and the method name (`count` in this case) are used to find the correct method. Using both names directs Python to the correct method even if it is overloaded (Section 1.7).
- The calling object (`aStr`, in this case) is *part* of the invocation. In a very real sense, it is another argument to the method.

The method, written specifically for a particular type of object, is specialized for working with just that type.

Writing Methods

Now we need to define our own methods. When defining a method there, are really only a few differences between it and a function:

- Where a method is defined
- An extra argument that is added to every method

Methods are added to a class by defining functions in the suite of a class. By providing these specialized functions in the class, those functions become available to every instance made from the class using the class-instance scope rules we discussed previously.

The code in Code Listing 11.2 adds a method to our simple class.

Code Listing 11.2

```
class myClass (object):
    classAttribute = 'world'

    def myMethod (self, param1):
        print '\nhello %s' % (param1)
        print 'The object that called this method is: %s' % str(self)
        self.instanceAttribute = param1


myInstance = myClass()
print "output of dir(myInstance):"
print dir(myInstance)
myInstance.myMethod('world')
print "Instance has new attribute with value: %s" % \
        myInstance.instanceAttribute
```

```
output of dir(myInstance):
['__class__', '__delattr__', '__dict__', '__doc__', '__format__', '__getattribute__
', '__hash__', '__init__', '__module__', '__new__', '__reduce__', '__reduce_ex__',
'__repr__', '__setattr__', '__sizeof__', '__str__', '__subclasshook__', '
__weakref__', 'classAttribute', 'myMethod']

hello world
The object that called this method is: <__main__.myClass object at 0xe010d0>
Instance has new attribute with value: world
```

The method is called myMethod and takes a single argument, as evidenced by the invocation—one can also see the parameter param1 in the method definition. We invoke it as we described, calling the method in the context of an instance of the class. The scope search process looks first in the instance and, not finding the method there, looks next in the class and, finding the method in the class, runs that method.

The dir command shows that the method myMethod and the attribute classAttribute, both defined in the class, are available to the instance myInstance.

The Special Argument `self`

There is an oddity about the definition of our method that you may have noticed. We noted in the invocation that only one argument was passed, but in fact two parameters show up in the definition of the method: *self*, and param1. Our argument mapped to param1, but what is *self*?

Python automatically maps the first parameter in a method definition to the object that called the method. This mapping is shown in Figure 11.4.

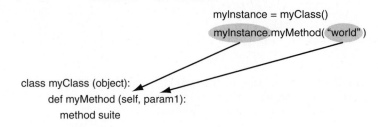

FIGURE 11.4 How the calling object maps to **self**.

Traditionally, this first parameter is called *self*, indicating that the object we are calling this method on is the object "itself." The variable can be called anything, but *self* is the expected name. Any other name would be confusing to other programmers who have to read the code.

The name *self* allows us to always have a way to reference the object that called the method. Anywhere in the method where the code references *self*, we are referencing the object that called the method. In this way, we can perform the method's operation on the object that called it.

Look again at the previous code example. In the class definition, myMethod prints the value of *self* and also performs the following operation *self*.instanceAttribute = param1. This means that the object that called the method (in this case myInstance) is associated with *self*, and *self* has a new attribute added to it called instanceAttribute. In the code following the class definition of Code Listing 11.2, we see that we can **print** myInstance.instanceAttribute to see that myMethod really assigns param1 to the instanceAttribute.

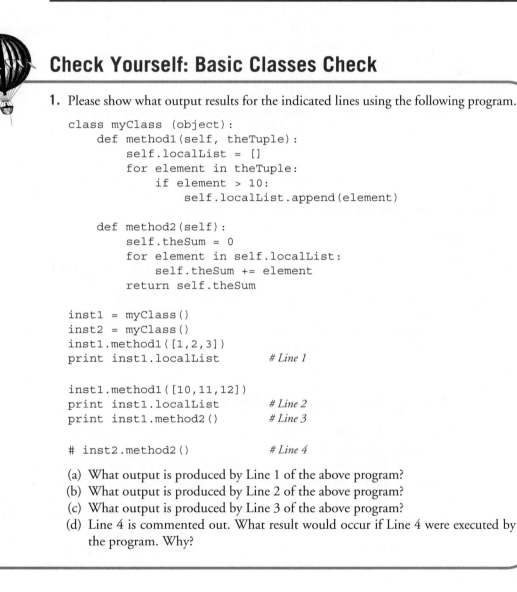

PROGRAMMING TIP

The method parameter *self* must *always* be placed as the first parameter in any method definition. Further, any reference to the calling object must be made *through* *self*. That is, when we refer to a part of the calling object, we use dot referencing as in *self.* instanceAttribute. This is a reference to the attribute instanceAttribute in *self*, where *self* is associated with the calling object.

Check Yourself: Basic Classes Check

1. Please show what output results for the indicated lines using the following program.

```
class myClass (object):
    def method1(self, theTuple):
        self.localList = []
        for element in theTuple:
            if element > 10:
                self.localList.append(element)

    def method2(self):
        self.theSum = 0
        for element in self.localList:
            self.theSum += element
        return self.theSum

inst1 = myClass()
inst2 = myClass()
inst1.method1([1,2,3])
print inst1.localList         # Line 1

inst1.method1([10,11,12])
print inst1.localList         # Line 2
print inst1.method2()         # Line 3

# inst2.method2()             # Line 4
```

(a) What output is produced by Line 1 of the above program?
(b) What output is produced by Line 2 of the above program?
(c) What output is produced by Line 3 of the above program?
(d) Line 4 is commented out. What result would occur if Line 4 were executed by the program. Why?

Methods are the Interface to a Class Instance

The methods of a class object define what the object can do and, at the same time, define the interface to the object. That is, a user's interaction with an instance of a class is defined by the methods the class has to offer.

Consider the interface to an MP3 player such as an iPod. The only interaction you can have with the iPod is through the functions (for us, methods) available in the interface. Those functions define what you can do with the iPod. You could perform other actions: open up the case and modify the electronics, but that is outside the design of the object itself. If the interface provided is sufficient, then the object is, in a very real sense, defined by that interface for the normal user.

The class designer, in designing the class, provides an interface by defining a set of methods. The expectation is that a well-designed class need not be modified, only accessed through the provided methods. If the class is well written, then all the user of the class should ever need to use are those methods. How those methods accomplish their job should not be that user's concern. Should we be required to understand the underlying electronics of our iPod? No, the interface provided should be "good enough".

Whatever the underlying structure of an instance, its methods (which come from the class it was created from) define everything the user needs to know about that instance. In particular, manipulation of the internal structure of an instance should be defined by and limited to the available methods.

11.5 FITTING INTO THE PYTHON CLASS MODEL

Every OOP approach provides an underlying class model that the class designer uses. Python does as well, and if we are to effectively use classes, we must understand a little more about Python's class model. We have seen an introduction in the previous pages; now we will delve a little more deeply into the model. To do so, we must first build a class.

Making Programmer-Defined Classes

How do we decide what should or should not be a class in our program? What counts as an object depends on the context of the program. It should be something recognizable to someone familiar with the problem, regardless of their ability to write a program. For example, if the program is a racing game, an object might be a car. A car's actions might include move-forward, turn-right, and report-position. The car object might have attributes such as color, make, or top-speed. By making objects that interact in the program that *make sense* in the context of the program, it is easier to design the program.

The other components of the car game should also be recognizable objects. You will have other cars as well as a racetrack—all objects. Obstacles that appear in the track will also be objects. People will be objects. By designing the objects and how they interact, an overall design unfolds.

A Student Class

Let's make a new class that we can use to represent a Python student. The Student class will have three attributes: idInt, lastNameStr, and firstNameStr. It will also have three methods described in detail next. One method initializes the class, the second allows updates, and the third defines how information about the class is organized for printing. We will explain this class over the next few sections. See Code Listing 11.3.

Code Listing 11.3

```python
class Student(object):
    def __init__(self,first='', last='', id=0):
        # print 'In the __init__ method'
        self.firstNameStr = first
        self.lastNameStr = last
        self.idInt = id

    def update(self,first='',last='',id=0):
        if first:
            self.firsNameStr = first
        if last:
            self.lastNameStr = last
        if id:
            self.idInt = id

    def __str__(self):
        # print "In __str__ method"
        return "%s %s, ID:%s" % \
            (self.firstNameStr, self.lastNameStr, self.idInt)
```

Python Standard Methods

We mentioned earlier in Section 11.3 that Python reserves some special methods that begin and end with the underscore characters (__). The first method in our Student class is one of those special Python methods, the constructor __init__. We call the __init__ method a *constructor*, because it is part of the sequence of constructing a new instance of a class.[2] When an instance is made of the class by using the name of the class as a function,

---

[2] Strictly speaking, __init__ is not a constructor in the strictest sense of OOP terminology; rather, it is an *initializer*.

the user can affect the creation of that instance through `__init__`. How that happens is shown in Figure 11.5.

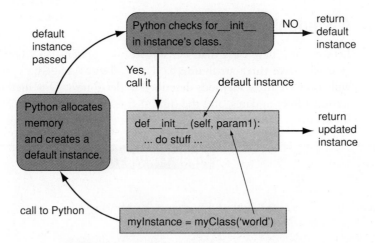

FIGURE 11.5 How an instance is made in Python.

Beginning at the bottom of Figure 11.5, Python creates a default instance when a constructor is called (that is, when the name of a class is used as a function, e.g., `myClass` (`'world'`)). After the default instance is made, Python searches for an `__init__` method in the class. If it is found, then the newly created default instance is passed to the parameter *self* of `__init__`, the remaining arguments are passed to the method's parameters (e.g., `'world'` passed to `param1`). The instance is modified according to the method ("do stuff"). The updated instance is then returned from `__init__`. If no such `__init__` method exists, then the default instance is returned. In this example, the instance returned is assigned to `myInstance`.

It is very important to note that `__init__` does not have an explicit `return` statement. Because `__init__` is part of the instance creation cycle, Python handles the return automatically.

Initializing the instance

By providing an `__init__` method, the class designer can add attributes to any instance made of that class. Because dot-notation assignment creates attributes, the designer must make an assignment to *self*.`newAttribute`, creating the attribute as part of the instance (remember, *self* is associated with the instance being made). It is also important to assign some value to each attribute, as assignment is how a value attribute is created. For example, in the `Student` class `__init__`, we have `self.firstNameStr = first`.

Following is a session using our `Student` class of Code Listing 11.3..

```
>>> s1 = Student()
>>> print s1.lastNameStr

>>> dir(s1)
['__class__', '__delattr__', '__dict__', '__doc__', '__getattribute__', '__hash__',
'__init__', '__module__', '__new__', '__reduce__', '__reduce_ex__', '__repr__', '
__setattr__', '__str__', '__weakref__', 'firstNameStr', 'idInt', 'lastNameStr', '
update']
>>> s2 = Student(last='Python', first='Monty')
>>> print s2.lastNameStr
Python
>>> dir(s2)
['__class__', '__delattr__', '__dict__', '__doc__', '__getattribute__', '__hash__',
'__init__', '__module__', '__new__', '__reduce__', '__reduce_ex__', '__repr__', '
__setattr__', '__str__', '__weakref__', 'firstNameStr', 'idInt', 'lastNameStr', '
update']
>>>
```

Two instances of Student are created, s1, s2. The first instance, s1, is created without any arguments to the constructor call: Student(). The second instance, s2, is made with two of the three arguments Student(last='Python', first ='Monty'). A dir of the s1 instance shows that all three attributes were created: firstNameStr, lastNameStr, and idInt. Each instance and its attributes are now available to be updated, printed, or otherwise acted upon. Remember, each instance carries its own copies of the three attributes, since they were created by assignment in the __init__ method. They are part of the instance's namespace. The dir also shows the three methods we defined in the class: __init__, update, __str__ which are also available to the instance.

Printing the Instance

The next special Python method in Code Listing 11.3 is the __str__ method. As you might guess from the name, it is a method to provide a string that represents the instance. This method is most useful in calls to the **print** statement, as the **print** statement attempts to convert any object it is provided into a string. By providing a __str__ method, we can print a representation of our object.

For the Student class, the __str__ method creates a single string that brings together the three attributes and returns that string. When a **print** function is called, the object is "converted" to a string and printed. Converted may not necessarily be the best word—clearly there is more to our object than the string we produce, but that is essentially what Python tries to do.

Following is a session that utilizes the __str__ method.

```
>>> s1 = Student()
>>> s2 = Student(first='Monty', last='Python')
```

```
>>> print s1
, ID:0
>>> print s2
Monty Python, ID:0
>>>
```

You may notice some commented print statements in the definition of our methods. Sometimes it is useful to print out when a method is invoked so that you can track more clearly *when* Python calls your methods. Here is the same session with the comments removed:

```
>>> s1 = Student()
In __init__ method
>>> s2 = Student(last='Punch', first='Bill')
In __init__ method
>>> print s1
In __str__ method
, ID:0
>>> print s2
In __str__ method
Bill Punch, ID:0
>>>
```

By turning these print statements on and off, you can better trace the interplay between Python's class model and your methods.

 PROGRAMMING TIP

Make *sure* that the __str__ returns a value and that the value is a *string*. Odd things can happen otherwise.

Changing an instance

In Python, the initialization of each instance by __init__ ensures that every instance of the class is created in the same way. Each instance will contain the same number of attributes (though the values of the attributes may be different) and has access to the the same number of methods from the class. However, Python does not restrict the programmer from changing an instance once it is made. One may add a new attribute to an instance, and even add a method directly to the instance's namespace (not easy to do, but it can be done). This ability differs from some other OOP languages such as Java and C++ in that those languages can prevent a user from changing an instance once it is created.

However, no matter the language, most OOP models agree that the *interface* to the object should be through its methods. In this way, the class designer can ensure that the instance is only modified in class designer-approved ways. The user may be free to "mess with" an instance, but they do so at hir or her own risk. If the class designer provides an interface to the instance, then that is what the user should use.

In that spirit, we provide the `update` method to our `Student` class of Code Listing 11.3. This method is the class designer's interface for modifying the three attributes of a `Student` instance. Very similar to the `__init__` method, it provides the user with access to the instance's internal attributes.

Check Yourself: Defining Special Methods

1. Show the output that results for the indicated lines using the following program.

```
class newClass(object):
    def __init__(self,intVal=1):
        self.theInt = intVal
        if intVal%2==0:
            self.parity='even'
        else:
            self.parity='odd'
    def process(self,instance):
        theSum = self.theInt + instance.theInt
        if theSum < 0:
            return 'negative'
        elif theSum % 2==0:
            return 'even'
        else:
            return 'odd'
    def __str__(self):
        return 'Value %d is %s'%(self.theInt,self.parity)

inst1=newClass(4)
inst2=newClass(-5)
inst3=newClass()
print inst1                         # Line 1
print inst1.parity                  # Line 2
print inst1.process(inst2)          # Line 3
print inst3.process(inst1)          # Line 4
```

(a) What output is produced by Line 1 of the example program?
(b) What output is produced by Line 2 of the example program?
(c) What output is produced by Line 3 of the example program?
(d) What output is produced by Line 4 of the example program?

Now There Are Three: Class Designer, Programmer, and User

So far, we have discussed two kinds of players in our programming world: the programmers that make the programs and the users who use those programs. With the introduction of classes, we introduce a third player, the *class designer*.

The class designer is *also* a programmer, but this programmer provides code for *other programmers* to use. In designing a class, the class designer provides a tool that, ideally, is intended to only be used and not modified by other programmers. Therefore, the class designer creates the class with other programmers in mind, and the programmer creates the program with the user in mind.

The programmer has a different view of the class than the class designer. The programmer sees the class only through the interface that the class designer provides. The programmer is shielded from the details of "how" the class does its job and is only aware of the interface—in particular, the operations, that the class designer provides. This is the promise of encapsulation. By designing the class well, the class stands as a library to be used by other programmers, providing those programmers with a more abstract, functional unit to solve their problems.

The class designer provides the class; the programmer uses it. When we design a class, we are designing it to be used by other programmers. Our job is to provide a reasonable interface to the class so that it:

- Does its job
- Can be updated or modified with minimal impact on the users

11.6 EXAMPLE: POINT CLASS

Let's tackle an example using Cartesian coordinates: dealing with points in a graph—something you should be familiar with from middle-school mathematics. We want to represent the two-dimensional points on the Cartesian coordinate plane. Each point is completely described by its coordinate pair: (x, y). We will choose two instance attributes, x and y, to represent the pair of values.

Once we have the instance attributes in place, we can consider what operations we wish to perform on these objects and write methods to take those actions. For illustration, we will choose finding the distance between two points and the sum of two points (also known as a vector sum).

More specifically we will implement these methods:

- distance: returns a distance (a floating-point number) between two points using the standard distance formula: The distance between (x_1, y_1) and (x_2, y_2) is:

$$distance = \sqrt{(x_1 - x_2)^2 + (y_1 - y_2)^2}$$

- sum:, returns a *new point* that is the vector sum of two points. First, the new point must be created. Then for points (x_1, y_1) and (x_2, y_2), the new point's coordinates are updated to be:

$$(x_1 + x_2, y_1 + y_2)$$

We'll show the code and output, and then describe it. To "run" this class code you simply "run" the program as normal (e.g., F5 from IDLE), which loads the class into the Python shell so that it can then be used as shown in the following Python shell session. At this point, the output isn't interesting, because the points are simply (0, 0) and (0, 0). See Code Listing 11.4.

Code Listing 11.4

```
import math  # need sqrt (square root)

# a Point is a Cartesion point (x,y)
class Point(object):
    def __init__(self):  # create and initialize
        self.x = 0.0
        self.y = 0.0

    def distance (self,pt):  # standard distance formula
        """Distance between self and a Point"""
        xDiff = self.x - pt.x  # (x1 — x2)
        yDiff = self.y - pt.y  # (y1 — y2)
        # square differences, sum, and take sqrt
        return math.sqrt(xDiff**2 + yDiff**2)

    def sum (self,pt):  # new point from vector sum
        """Vector Sum of self and a Point"""
        newPt = Point()           # create a new point
        newPt.x = self.x + pt.x   # calculate x value sum from self and pt
        newPt.y = self.y + pt.y
        return newPt
```

```
>>> p1 = Point()     # create a Point named "p1"
>>> p2 = Point()
>>> print p1.x, p1.y # print the Point's x and y values
0.0 0.0
>>> print p2.x, p2.y
0.0 0.0
>>> print p1.distance(p2) # find distance from p1 to p2
0.0
```

```
>>> p3 = p1.sum(p2)   # find sum of p1 and p2
>>> print p3.x, p3.y
0.0 0.0
```

Construction

The `__init__` method creates two attributes: the coordinates `x` and `y` in each instance. We can show this by printing the two attributes of each of the `Point` instances: `p1` and `p2`. Note that the coordinates are each set to 0 in all instances.

Distance

To find the distance from `p1` to `p2`, we can call the `distance` method using `p1.distance(p2)`. This means that during that method invocation `self` resolves to `p1` and the second parameter `pt` resolves to `p2`.

Within the method, we apply our distance formula. We must first find the difference as indicated in the formula $(x_1 - x_2)$. This is implemented as `xDiff = self.x - pt.x`. Be careful that you understand that particular statement! The `self.x` is the calling object's attribute `x` and `pt.x` is the x attribute of the second object, the argument object. The formula then states that we must square that difference: $(x_1 - x_2)^2$, implemented as `xDiff **2`. The same algorithm is applied to the y values. The formula adds the differences and then take the square root. $distance = \sqrt{(x_1 - x_2)^2 + (y_1 - y_2)^2}$. We implement this as `math.sqrt(xDiff**2 + yDiff**2)`. The resulting distance floating-point value is then returned.

Because distance is symmetric, we could have found the distance from `p2` to `p1` with the call `p2.distance(p1)`. In that invocation, `self` would resolve to `p2` and `pt` would resolve to the parameter `p1`.

Summing Two Points

To sum `p1` and `p2` the invocation would be `p3 = p1.sum(p2)`. As we are calling the sum using `p1` as the calling object, `self` resolves to `p1` and the second parameter `pt` resolves to `p2`.

Within that method we must first create a new `Point` for the sum: `newPt = Point()`. The summation process creates a new point, so `newPt` will be the return object. We have constructed it, but the method must set its attributes before it is returned. To do so is straightforward. We add the x values as `newPt.x = p1.x + p2.x` and y values as `newPt.y = p1.y + p2.y`, and then return the new `Point` as **return** `newPt`. The new point `newPt` is returned and then assigned to `p3`.

Similar to distance, because the sum is symmetric, we could have found the sum of `p2` and `p1` with the call `p3 = p2.sum(p1)`, and in this case `self` would resolve to `p2` and `pt` would resolve to `p1`.

The output isn't interesting because the points we are creating are simply (0, 0) and (0, 0) so the both the distance and sum are zero. We start the session by "running" the program which is only the class—that loads the class into the Python shell so we can use it.

Improving the Point Class

Default Initialization

The __init__ method is like any other method, in that it too can take parameters. These parameters are used to set the attribute values of each instance.

Often in __init__ we use default parameter values (see Section 7.3). In this way, if the user does not specify all the attributes, every attribute is still created in the instance. Remember, only by assignment is a variable (attribute) created! The following example has parameters x and y each initialized to 0.0. If the user's method call has arguments, those will be used. If not, the default values of 0.0 will be used.

Code Listing 11.5 is the improved __init__ method—the rest of the class is unchanged.

Code Listing 11.5

```
def __init__(self, xParam = 0.0, yParam = 0.0):    # include defaults
    self.x = xParam
    self.y = yParam
```

Let's use the improved version in a session. This time the point p1 will have some non-zero values for x and y.

```
>>> p1 = Point(2.0,4.0)      # create a point with x and y values specified
>>> p2 = Point()             # create a point with default values
>>> print p1.distance(p2)    # find and print the distance
4.472135955
>>> p3 = p1.sum(p2)          # calculate the sum and then print it
>>> print p3.x, p3.y
2.0 4.0
>>>
```

When the instance is made, you can now pass arguments to set up the instance. We see that in the creation of p1 = Point(2.0,4.0) which passes x an initial value of 2.0 and passes y an initial value of 4.0.

You do not have to explicitly set the values for x and y: you can use default arguments. We see that with the creation of p2 = Point(), no arguments are passed to __init__ so the specified default values of 0.0 are used.

As we saw earlier, the call p1 = Point(2.0,4.0) resolves *self* to be p1, so in the __init__ function, *self*.x resolves to p1.x and *self*.y resolves to p1.y.

Printing the Values

It is painful to have to print each value of a class instance, especially if it is a complex object with many instance variables. As we have seen, we can provide a __str__ method that will get called by **print**. Code Listing 11.6 is that method for the Point class.

Code Listing 11.6

```
def __str__(self):
    """Print as a coordinate pair."""
    return "(%.2f, %.2f)"% (self.x,self.y)
```

Let's look a a session using our improved Point class with the ability to print:

```
>>> p1 = Point(2.0, 4.0)
>>> print p1
(2.00, 4.00)
```

In this example, we create a p1 instance as before with initial values for x as 2.0 and y as 4.0. However, we have added the __str__ method, so when we call the **print** function, as in **print** p1, the __str__ method is implicitly called with *self* being set to p1 in the method. Therefore, *self*.x yields the same value as p1.x and *self*.y yields the same value as p1.y. Now the string is formatted using those values, and the formatted string is returned to the **print** function for printing.

Updated Point Class

Now let's take a final look at the whole class with these two special methods in Code Listing 11.7. We can also take an opportunity to refactor the sum method. Notice that we can simplify the sum method a little because Point creation can take arguments, in this case xNew and yNew. Also, this change allows us to combine Point with the **return** statement (we could have created a newPt separately as newPt = Point(xNew, yNew) and left **return** newPt).

Code Listing 11.7

```
import math  # need sqrt (square root)

# a Point is a Cartesion point (x,y)
```

```
class Point(object):
    # create and initialize with defaults
    def __init__(self, xParam = 0.0, yParam = 0.0):
        self.x = xParam
        self.y = yParam


    def __str__(self):
        """Print as a coordinate pair."""
        return "(%.2f, %.2f)"% (self.x,self.y)



    def distance (self,pt):   # standard distance formula
        """Distance between self and a Point"""
        xDiff = self.x - pt.x  # (x1 − x2)
        yDiff = self.y - pt.y  # (y1 − y2)
        # square differences, sum, and take sqrt
        return math.sqrt(xDiff**2 + yDiff**2)

    def sum (self,pt):  # new point from vector sum
        """Vector Sum of self and a Point"""
        xNew = self.x + pt.x         # calculate x value from self and pt
        yNew = self.y + pt.y
        return Point(xNew, yNew)     # create and return a new point
```

11.7 PYTHON AND OOP

In the introduction, we noted that Object-Oriented Programming (OOP) had three concepts:

- Encapsulation
- Inheritance
- Polymorphism

Python provides these concepts, but differs from other OOP languages in significant ways.

Encapsulation

Python, and really all languages with OOP support, provide *encapsulation*. That is, details of underlying class structure such as the instance variables are hidden and the method interface provides all necessary access to those instance variables.

In addition, Python steps beyond simple function encapsulation, as it allows the encapsulation of both data and methods in a class.

Inheritance

Inheritance allows one to create a class that is built upon the characteristics of another class. We do so by using a two-step process. First, we impose a relationship on our *classes*, much like the relationship found between instance and class. Second, this relationship allows us to "inherit" attributes found in a class that is "above" it in the relationship scheme. By inheriting those attributes, we can share common code. We can pursue the car analogy used earlier: imagine there exits a `Vehicle` class with attributes such as `numberOfWheels`, `motorSize`, `fuelSource`, etc. A specialization of `Vehicle` could be a particular vehicle, a `Truck` class. `Truck` inherits the common attributes listed above and adds others specific to trucks (i.e., `carryingCapacity`, `trailerSize`, etc.). A different specialization might be a `Sedan` class that also inherits the same common attributes of `Vehicle` but adds a different set of special attributes (i.e., `trunkSize`). The next chapter (Chapter 12 will cover inheritance in more detail, but this gives you the general idea.

Polymorphism

Polymorphism is the process of using an operator (such as plus +) or method (such as `count`) to perform different operations depending on the types that invoke them. We have shown that with the plus (+) operator we get addition with integers but concatenation with strings. In the next chapter, you will see how to write class methods with that characteristic.

11.8 AN ASIDE: PYTHON AND OTHER OOP LANGUAGES

Although Python does provide a class and OOP support, it differs from some other OOP languages in some of the details. We review those here.

Public versus Private

Given the nature of the two groups using a class (class designer and programmer), one can differentiate the access that a member of each group can have. That is, the class designer may want to control and protect internal class structure from access other than that provided by methods. In so doing, the designer guarantees (or attempts to guarantee) that the provided interface remains constant, but the designer can still modify the internal structure otherwise to meet changing demand. This demarcation of roles, designer and programmer, makes changes to code more manageable.

In OOP terminology, this protection is often discussed in terms of *public* versus *private* attributes:

- Public attributes (variables, methods) are available to everyone (designer and programmer).
- Private attributes (variables, methods) are available only to the designer.

The impetus for separation is to help with large software development. Guarantees of public access to an object, while providing flexibility on private aspects of the object, allows code to be written that can be more easily adapted to changing demands and requirements. Note that large can be quite large indeed. For example, an operating system such as Microsoft Windows 7 will have tens of *millions* of lines of code. Partitioning responsibility is critical for containing potential chaos.

Indicating Privacy Using Double Underscores (__)

Python does not enforce this separation between the designer and programmer. All methods and instance variables are public, so both designers and programmers have access. Python *does* provide support for the designer to indicate attributes that the programmer *should not* modify directly.

Whenever a class designer names an attribute with two leading underscores, Python "mangles" the name of the attribute for outside use (outside of the class). The verb "mangle" here means that the attribute name is actually changed. The change is that an attribute named __myAttribute is changed to be _className__myAttribute for outside use. Look at the code and session in Code Listing 11.8.

Code Listing 11.8

```python
class newClass (object):
    def __init__(self, attribute='default', name='Instance'):
        self.name = name               # public attribute
        self.__attribute = attribute   # a "private" attribute
    def __str__(self):
        return '%s has attribute %s' % (self.name, self.__attribute)
```

```
>>> inst1 = newClass(name='Monty', attribute='Python')
>>> print inst1
Monty has attribute Python
>>> print inst1.name
Monty
>>> print inst1.__attribute

Traceback (most recent call last):
  File "<pyshell#3>", line 1, in <module>
    print inst1.__attribute
AttributeError: 'newClass' object has no attribute '__attribute'
>>> dir(inst1)
['__class__', '__delattr__', '__dict__', '__doc__', '__getattribute__', '__hash__',
'__init__', '__module__', '__new__', '__reduce__', '__reduce_ex__', '__repr__', '
__setattr__', '__str__', '__weakref__', '_newClass__attribute', 'name']
```

```
>>> print inst1._newClass__attribute
Python
>>>
```

In the `__init__` method, we assign two attributes: `name` and `__attribute`. By preceding the second with two underscores, we indicate to Python to change the name for outside use, that is, outside of the class. Look at the `__str__` method. It makes reference to the name directly as *self.__attribute*. The `__str__` method is permitted this access, as it is within the class. However, in the session we see that if we try to print `inst1.__attribute`, we get an error. The print is a use of the attribute outside the class and the name is no longer correct. Interestingly, if we do `dir(inst1)` we see that, indeed, the name has been changed to `_newClass__attribute`.

This change of name *does not* prevent the programmer from accessing the attribute value. It only provides a layer of obfuscation. By obfuscation, we mean a layer of difficulty. The programmer can "get around" the class designer if they choose, but they do so in violation of the designer's intent. Perhaps in the future the class will change and the programmer's code will no longer work because of their disregard for the "rules." When an attribute is marked with the double-underscore prefix, it means leave it alone!

Python's Philosophy

The philosphy that Python promotes is best summarized by the phrase "We are all adults here." If the designer indicates something should be private, then a programmer violates privacy at their own peril. By reducing the overhead of indicating what is and what is not private, the code is simpler and, using some simple rules, what *should* be private can be easily indicated.

Modifying an Instance

Many OOP languages use the class to define the state of the instance: what methods are defined that the instance can use and what attributes are parts of the instance. Their class model supports this view. Once the instance is made, it cannot be modified. Attributes cannot be added or removed.

Python, on the other hand, takes a less restrictive stance. A Python class, like the other OOP languages, provides the template for the initial state (variables and methods). However, after the instance is created, that instance can be modified as the programmer sees fit. Again, the phrase "We are all adults here" applies. Why restrict what the programmer might do? As class designers we indicated what we think a programmer *should* do, but trying to *prevent* a programmer from doing something clutters the language. Besides, if a programmer really does want to do something, even if the designer does not, there is always a way.

11.9 CONCLUSION

The concept of Object-Oriented Programming is a powerful development tool. It is particularly supportive of the divide-and-conquer style of problem solving. If you can organize your design thoughts around OOP, you can design large programs around basic objects.

The concept of *self* is important in understanding how class objects work, especially in the creation and use of instances. Reread this chapter, if you feel that you have not yet grasped the concept of self in Python classes.

Exercises

1. In your own words, describe the purpose of the `__init__` method.

2. Write a Shopping Cart class to implement a shopping cart that you often find on web sites where you could purchase some goods. Think about what things you could store in a cart and also what operations you could perform on the cart.

   To simplify matters, you could consider the web site to be an electronics e-store that has goods like flat—panel TVs, boomboxes, iPods, camcorders, and so on.

3. Consider a table fan. Write a Table Fan class. What would be the attributes of this class? Examples of attributes could be speed levels of fan, side-to-side movement (on/off, and degrees of movement), manufacturer name, cost, used/new and so on. Think about it this way. You want to be able to *get* information about the fan; e.g., if you want to buy or sell a fan from some web site such as Craigslist, what features would you be interested in? Also, consider control (operations) you might want to have over the fan such as setting the fan speed or having it pan from side to side.

4. There are many web sites where you could listen to music, e.g., rhapsody.com. A music album contains many soundtracks and each soundtrack has a name, time duration, name of artist, year and other data.

   Design classes for the album and soundtrack. Think about the methods appropriate for the classes. For soundtrack, some methods could be play, pause, stop etc.

5. Design a class for an airline ticket. Some of the fields of an airline ticket are start, destination, date of travel, class (economy, first class, business class), price of ticket, number of people traveling, and name of the primary person. Think about the methods appropriate for the class.

6. Design a class for a book such as an online retailer (such as Amazon.com) might use to keep track of the book. Fields might include: name of the book, publisher, price, author, ISBN. Think about the methods appropriate for the class that an online retailer might use.

7. Consider a hospital scenario. Design classes for:

   • Patients. The class might have fields like unique ID for the patient, name, male or female, age, address, phone number, date of birth, height, and weight.
   • Doctor. Fields might include the doctor's name, unique registration number, qualification (DO or MD), specialization (surgeon, pediatrician, etc.), phone number, office hours, and office location.
   • Patients' records in a hospital. The record might have fields like last date of check-up, doctor's unique ID, patient's unique ID, list of health problems in the patient, list of medicines prescribed, cost of the checkup, final report, and so on.

   Methods of these classes would be mostly get and *set* methods for the corresponding fields.

8. Consider the design of a class for managing the Olympics—to simplify things, consider management of Olympic medal awards. Design a medal class.

   • Fields: Name of the athlete, country, event, medal type (gold, silver, bronze)
   • Methods: get, *set*, and so on.

9. Design a schedule class for classes that a student (you!) take during a semester.

10. In a supermarket, all vegetables have a product code, name, some description, and price per unit. Design a class called "Vegetable" to represent the vegetables. Provide get and set methods for the class.

11. Design a class called Sentence that has a constructor that takes a string representing the sentence as input. The class should have the following methods:

    • `getFirstWord`
    • `getAllWords`
    • `replace(index, newWord)`—Change a word at a particular index to "newWord". e.g. If sentence is "I'm going back." and `setWordAtIndex(2, "home")`, then sentence becomes "I'm going home."

Programming Projects

1. **Solitaire: Using Classes**
   Writing a program to play the popular card game of solitaire offers an opportunity to work with classes while developing problem solving skills. A large number of variations of solitaire exist—the web site `http://worldofsolitaire.com` alone has over 50 variations. In this exercise your program will enforce the rules of the game—the user will be playing the game.

   We provide a module `cards.py` that contains two classes: `Card` and `Deck`. A `Deck` is a collection of `Cards`. We also provide a sample piece of code that demonstrates how to use the cards module. The Card and Deck classes are general-purpose for developing card games, so they contain many methods that may not be used in any particular implementation.

Each `Card` has two primary attributes: `rank` and `suit`. In an English deck, there are four suits—spades, diamonds, hearts, and clubs—that we represent by their first letters: `'S'`, `'D'`, `'H'`, `'C'`. Each suit has thirteen cards—Ace, 2–10, Jack, Queen, and King—with ranks 1-13 in that order. Each card has a **value** that for most cards is the same as its rank, but for face cards (Jack, Queen, King), the value is 10.

Some card games such as poker have an Ace with a rank greater than a King; other games such as Blackjack allow the Ace to have a value of 1 or 11. The Card class does not incorporate those alternative ranks and values, so those differences need to be added to the class for those games or incorporated into the game program itself.

The primary methods for the Card class are:

- `get_rank` returns the rank of a Card (*int*).
- `get_suit` returns the suit of a Card (*string*).
- `get_value` returns the value of a Card (*int*).

There are other methods that are explained in the module, but two are worth mentioning because they are useful when debugging: `set_rank` and `set_suit`. They allow you as the programmer to set up particular scenarios when testing your code.

A `Deck` is a collection of cards; in fact it is a sequence, because we expect a deck to be ordered.

Although there are many methods in the class, the primary methods for the `Deck` class are:

- `shuffle` randomly rearranges the cards in the deck (returns nothing).
- `deal` returns one card and removes the card from the deck (`Card`).
- `empty` returns *True* if there are no cards in the deck (`bool`).

Both classes have `__str__` and `__repr__` defined to make printing easy.

Here is a sample session illustrating a few `Card` and `Deck` methods:

```
>>> import cards
>>> aDeck = cards.Deck()
>>> aDeck.shuffle()
>>> c = aDeck.deal()
>>> print c
 8D
>>> c.get_suit()
'D'
>>> c.get_rank()
8
>>> JackClubs = cards.Card('J','C')
>>> print JackClubs
 JC
>>> print aDeck
```

```
5C   QS   6S   2D   4D   10C  8H   6D   4C   AH   9S   AD   8C
9H   4H   7S   3H   10H  QD   7C   6C   2H   5S   3S   AS   QC
KC   3C   8S   7H   JH   KD   KH   JD   7D   AC   9C   2C   JS
2S   KS   10S  5H   9D   3D   5D   10D  QH   6H   JC   4S
```

Every solitaire game has three main components: the stock, the tableau, and the foundation. The *stock* is the source of new cards, i.e. the deck of cards. The *foundation* is where the cards get stacked in four stacks (one for each suit) in order from Ace to King—four complete stacks in the foundation indicate winning the game. The `tableau` is where the main part of solitaire is played and varies significantly from game to game. A losing game is when no more moves can be made in the tableau and the stock is empty.

Write a program to play the *Easthaven* version of solitaire—complete rules and versions to play with to learn the game can be found online (e.g., `http://worldofsolitaire.com`).

Easthaven solitaire (tableau rules):

- The tableau begins with seven columns with three cards in each column. In each column, initially, only the top card is visible.
- Build down by rank and by alternating color. For example, you can play a two of Hearts on a three of Spades (the column goes down by rank, and alternates colors) .
- Either the top card may be moved or complete or partial correctly ranked piles may be moved as a pile. If a pile is moved, the top card of the pile must follow the rules (down rank and alternating color) and all the rest of cards in the pile must also follow the rules.
- An exposed face-down card may be turned face up.
- An empty spot may be filled with any card or correctly ranked pile.
- If you cannot make any moves on the tableau, or any moves from the tableau to the foundation, you can take cards from the stock.
- **Different!** When the stock is used, a card is added to the end of *each* tableau column.
- Any fully exposed card can be moved to the foundation as long as the foundation rules are adhered to: placement in the foundation must follow both suit and rank (Ace up to King).

Create a main program that is a loop that drives the game. Repeatedly prompt for commands such as move_within_tableau, move_to_foundation, and deal_from_stock. Each command suggests its own method, but you are likely to want many more helping methods.

Note: This set-up can be used for any of the solitaire games so this exercise provides a framework for many, many exercises: simply adjust the tableau rules appropriately. The `cards.py` module can be also used for any card game, but the single-player solitaire is an excellent exercise.

2. **GPS Unit for Hikers**

GPS has been built into a wide variety of consumer devices. They share many features, but differ in details. Here we consider the GPS unit used by hikers and back-country explorers. An important feature of such units is the ability to mark *waypoints*, including the ability to collect them into a path that can be retrieved later. Another important feature is distance and bearing to a waypoint: you have a target waypoint and you want to know what direction it is in and the distance to that target. This last feature is particularly useful in geocaching or locating your starting point, if you are lost.

When queried the GPS hardware generates the current longitude and latitude: a pair of floating-point values. The range of longitude is −180 degrees to +180 degrees (the reference point (0) is the meridian through Greenwich, England). The range of latitude is −90 degrees to +90 degrees (the reference point (0) is the equator with positive values in the northern hemisphere). For example, according to the "Farmer's Almanac" the "middle" of the United States is at latitude 39.83333 degrees, longitude −98.5833 degrees. That is near the town of Lebanon, in Smith County, Kansas. We need to simulate that capability in this exercise. Write a method named `gpsGetLongLat` that returns a longitude and latitude pair. The method uses the Python `random` module to generate the pair.

A waypoint will be a position, a longitude—latitude pair, with a name.

Implement the following capabilities:

- Your GPS unit should be able to save the current waypoint; i.e., save the current position as a waypoint, and associate a name with the position.
- Your GPS unit should be able to save and retrieve named paths consisting of a sequence of waypoints.
- It should also be able to find the length of a given path—assuming a straight line between each waypoint.
- Your GPS unit should be able to calculate the distance to a waypoint (from the current location).

Write a main program that loops and prompts the user for functionality provided by the GPS unit. Create a session that tests all methods.

Optional: add a method to calculate a bearing between the current position and a waypoint. Hint use the math inverse tangent (`atan`) function, but the `atan2` function may be slightly easier to work with.

CHAPTER **12**

More on Classes

CLASSES NOT ONLY HELP YOU CREATE AND ORGANIZE NEW DATA STRUCTURES, BUT also affect how you think about problem solving. In this chapter, we take a look at more capabilities provided by object-oriented thinking.

12.1 MORE ABOUT CLASS PROPERTIES

As mentioned in Chapter 11, there are three major object-oriented programming (OOP) characteristics: encapsulation, inheritance, and polymorphism.

We have focused so far on encapsulation, which:

- *Hides details* of implementation to aid reading and understanding.
- Provides *modularity* that makes it easier to use a class in other contexts.
- Provides an *interface* in the form of methods to access and manipulate a class instance.

We add a new concept to encapsulation: *consistency*. There are two characteristics to consider with respect to consistency:

- A new class should be consistent with the rules and syntax of the language.
- A new class should respond to "standard methods" (such as construction, printing, iteration, etc.) that are appropriate for the object.

A class you create should behave like any other object so that it can be used in a natural way—just like they have used other objects. In a similar vein, one would expect familiar methods to work in familiar ways. For example, the "+" operator sums integers and concatenates strings. The operations are quite different, but each operation is appropriate for its specific type.

In this section, you will see how to make the classes we create behave in a way that is consistent with built-in objects.

Rational Number (Fraction) Class Example

Python, like most computer languages, has built-in objects for integers and "decimals" (floating points). However, only with the release of Python 2.6 did Python provide support for rational numbers with the `fractions` module and the `Fraction` class. We implement here a rational numbers class of our own design which, when it is completed, you can compare to Python's built-in class.

Rational numbers have two parts, a numerator and a denominator, that our class implementation must represent. Furthermore, the class should behave in a way that is consistent with other number objects we have become familiar with such as *int* and *float*. In particular, the following kinds of operations should be applicable to a rational number:

- Construction
- Printing
- Arithmetic operators (+, -, *, /)
- Comparison operators (<, >, ==, etc.)

Assuming that we have written the class (or are using the built-in `Fraction` class), a rational number should have the kinds of behavior shown in the following session. Later in this chapter we will see how you can build the class to achieve this consistency.

```
>>> from fracClass1 import *   # get our rational number class named fracClass1
>>> r1 = Rational(1,2)         # create the fraction 1/2
>>> r2 = Rational(3,2)         # create the fraction 3/2
>>> r3 = Rational(3)           # default denominator is 1, so really creating 3/1
>>> rSum = r1 + r2             # use "+" in a familiar way
>>> print rSum                # use "print" in a familiar way
4/2
>>> rSum                       # display value in session in a familiar way
4/2
>>> if r1 == r1:              # use equality check "==" in a familiar way
...     print 'equal'
... else:
...     print 'not equal'
...
equal
>>> print r3 - r2             # combine arithmetic and printing in a familiar way
3/2
```

In this session, the rational number instance looks like any other number. It responds syntactically to methods as we expect, and uses operators as we expect. It is consistent.

There are a couple of things to point out about this session. The first line uses *from* . . . *import* *. This import syntax allows us to use the class methods without using the class name. That is, we can use the shortened `Rational(1,2)` instead of the longer `fracClass1.Rational(1,2)`. Also, you will note that when a rational number is printed, it has not been reduced, e.g., 4/2 is printed instead of the reduced value 2. Not reducing the value is a design decision made by the designer of the class (the text authors, in this case). It would be equally reasonable to have decided that all values should be reduced before printing.

12.2 HOW DOES PYTHON KNOW?

How can Python "know" what operators and methods can apply to a new class we create?

- Python can distinguish operators and methods to apply based on the *type* of the objects being used.
- Python provides some special method names that represent typical operators (binary operators, standard functions, etc.) in the language.

Classes, Types, and Introspection

When we first introduced classes we stated that *a class is just a type*. When we create a new class, we are effectively creating a new type. With numbers we had *int* as a type, and now we have created our own class, `Rational`, that can be used as a type. Remember that type does not go with a variable name, but instead with the object with which the name is associated.

Because the type associated with any variable name can change, it is useful to be able to inquire about an object's type. This process is called *introspection*. That is, while the program is running, we can ask an object (or a variable associated with an object) what type the object is.

Python provides two different introspection functions:

- `type(someVariable)` returns the type of the object associated with `someVariable`. We have seen this in previous chapters, but have not used it programmatically. We will here!
- `isinstance(someVariable,someType)` returns a Boolean indicating whether `someVariable` is of type `someType`.

Here is a session showing these functions in action:

```
>>> import math             # get some objects to play with
>>> float                   # what is the "value" of "float"?
<type 'float'>
>>> list                    # list?
<type 'list'>
>>> type(math.pi)           # try the introspection functions
```

```
<type 'float'>
>>> isinstance(math.pi,float)
True
>>> isinstance(math.pi,list)
False
>>> type(float)            # ask what the type of float is? it is a "type"!
<type 'type'>
>>> type(list)
<type 'type'>
>>> class myClass(object):  # create a new class with nothing in it
...     pass                #      ("pass" does that)
...
>>> myInstance=myClass()    # create an instance of our new class
>>> type(myInstance)        # check the type of our new instance
<class '__main__.myClass'>
>>> type(myClass)           # a class is a type!
<type 'type'>
>>> isinstance(myInstance,myClass)
True
```

Things to note from the session:

- Every type is represented by its name as a variable. For example, *float* and *list* are associated with their respective types. When comparison is required—e.g., "is this object of some type"—these names can be used.
- The type of both *float* and *list* is of type "type." A bit confusing, but the object associated with those variable is a type.
- The type of math.pi is *float*, because the object associated with that variable is the value of π, a floating-point number.
- We make an empty class called myClass. It is empty because it has no structure or any associated methods—only the filler statement **pass**. It is still a class.
- Even though we don't define a constructor for myClass, one is provided by default and we can make an instance, called myInstance using the class name as a constructor.
- *Very Important:* what is the type of myInstance? It is of type myClass.
- Finally, myClass is of type type, just like *float* and *list*.

We can write code that takes advantage of the types of variables to produce different results. Code Listing 12.1 is a function that does division, but does it differently for floats and integers.

Code Listing 12.1

```
def specialDivide(a,b):
    if type(a)==int and type(b)==int:
```

```
         return a/b,a%b
     else:
5        return a/b,None
```

Notes on the `specialDivide` function:

- **Lines 2–3**: The function checks the types of the two parameters. If they are both integer, it does integer division and integer remainder.
- **Line 4**: If one or both of the numbers is *not* an integer, floating division occurs. Note the function returns a tuple of the form (quotient,remainder). However, the remainder operator (`%`) does not apply to floats, so the special value `None` is used as the returned remainder to preserve consistency with respect to the number of returned values.

We have seen the special variable `None` before. It is a represents "nothing." As such it resolves a conundrum: something is needed to represent the intention of using nothing in the code where something (a value, an expression) is required.

Remember Operator Overloading

We first mentioned the topic of overloading in Section 1.7 and further showed its effects on strings in Section 4.2. Remember the concept:

- 4 + 3 is integer addition, producing an integer result.
- `'four'` + `'three'` is string concatenation, producing a string result.
- `'four'` + 3 is undefined—no "+" operation is defined for those mixed types.

How can Python tell which operation to use when presented with the "+" operator? It works similar to our `specialDivide` function: it examines the types of the arguments, using introspection. By examining the types, it can "look up" the appropriate operation. If no such operation is found (no operation exists for that particular combination of values), an error is raised.

12.3 CREATING YOUR OWN OPERATOR OVERLOADING

You can create your own operator overloads for the new class you have created—the new "type."

Python provides a special set of operators that you can overload. You cannot overload just any operator—only the ones that Python allows.

When Python examines an expression such as 3 + 4, it checks the types of the operands and then searches for that operation (method) on those types. For each allowed overloading operation, Python has a specially named method.

The special method names come in three general classes:

- math-like operators, such as +, -, *, /
- collection operators, such as [ ], len
- general class operators, such as methods for printing, construction, etc.

Table 12.1 lists some of the more commonly overloaded operators.[1]

Math-like Operators		
Expression	**Method name**	**Description**
x + y	__add__()	Addition
x − y	__sub__()	Subtraction
x * y	__mul__()	Multiplication
x / y	__div__()	Division
x == y	__eq__()	Equality
x > y	__gt__()	Greater Than
x >= y	__ge__()	Greater Than or Equal
x < y	__lt__()	Less Than
x <= y	__le__()	Less Than or Equal
x != y	__ne__()	Not Equal
Sequence Operators		
len(x)	__len__()	length of the sequence
x in y	__contains__()	does the sequence y contain x
print x[key]	__getitem__()	access element *key* of sequence x
x[key]=y	__setitem__()	set element *key* of sequence x to value y
General Class Operations		
x=myClass()	__init__()	constructor
print (x)		
str(x)	__str__()	convert to a readable string
	__repr__()	print a representation of x
	__del__()	finalizer, called when x is garbage collected

TABLE 12.1 Python special method names.

---

[1] For a full list see http://docs.python.org/ref/specialnames.html

Mapping Operators to Special Methods

How does "+" get mapped to add? Python has a special built-in mechanism to map binary operations to methods. We, as class designers, have to fit into the Python mold for this mapping by providing the appropriate methods. An example mapping:

$$\text{var1} + \text{var2} \Rightarrow \text{var1.\_\_add\_\_(var2)}$$

These are equivalent expressions. Either one does exactly the same thing, but the first is more familiar.

The first variable in a binary operation (in this case, var1) becomes the variable that calls the associated method (in this case, __add__) and the second variable becomes the argument (in parentheses). For example, if we reverse the operands:

$$\text{var2} + \text{var1} \Rightarrow \text{var2.\_\_add\_\_(var1)}$$

Order matters, so we will have to pay attention to it!

Let's examine a simple example that illustrates how the special methods can be defined. In Code Listing 12.2, there is one "math-like" method that performs addition (__add__), and one general method that performs conversion to a string (__str__). A few *print* statements have been added to the methods to illustrate when these functions are called. Such print statements can help when developing and debugging functions, but should be removed once the code is working correctly.

Code Listing 12.2

```python
class myClass(object):
    def __init__(self,val):
        print 'in constructor'   # shows when function is called
        self.value = val
5
    def __str__(self):
        """ Convert 'value' to string."""
        print 'in str'
        return 'Val is: %s'%(str(self.value))
10
    def __add__(self,param2):
        """ Perform addition with param2."""
        print 'in add'
        sum = self.value + param2.value
15      return myClass(sum)
```

Let's examine a few lines in the example:

- **Line 4**: The constructor sets a local instance variable named `value`. We will assume it is a number (not safe, but this is a simple example).
- **Line 9**: The string conversion method must return a string! Note that we need to convert the integer to a string using string formatting.
- **Line 11**: The add method. The name *self* is bound to the variable that calls the method (the first operand in the binary expression), and `param2` is bound to the second operand in the binary expression. That is, x + y binds x to *self* and binds y to `param2`.
- **Line 15**: After calculating the sum, we create a new myClass instance and return it, initialized with the sum. If an operation, such as addition, should return an object of the same type, we must make sure we create such an object.

Here is a session that exercises the little class:

```
>>> from simpleAddClass import * # myClass is in the simpleAddClass.py file
>>> inst1 = myClass(27) # create an instance with value = 27
in constructor   # "print" from inside constructor: we see that it was called
>>> type(inst1)
<class 'simpleAddClass.myClass'>
>>> type(myClass) # it is a type, just like float or list
<type 'type'>
>>> print inst1   # "print" calls the __str__ function
in str            # here we see the result of "print" from inside __str___
Val is:27
>>> sum = inst1 + inst1 # this "+" expression calls the __add__ method
in add            # here is the "print" within __add__
in constructor    # __add__ calls a constructor so we see constructor's print
>>> print sum
in str
Val is:54
>>> type(sum)       # __add__ returned a result that was of type myClass
<class 'simpleAddClass.myClass'>
>>>
```

Here are a few observations about the session:

- When we created `inst1`, the constructor (via the `__init__` method) was called and we see the associated print statement "in constructor" printed in the session.
- The name `inst1` is of type `myClass`, and `myClass` is of type `type`. We have made a new type!
- The statement **print** inst1 calls `__str__` to convert the instance to a string. We see the "in str" line in the session as a result. Note the associated **print** statement "in str".
- When we invoke the line sum = `inst1` + `inst1`, we see that we get a call to the add method (Python translates "+" to `__add__` as described above) as well as

a call to the constructor when we make a new instance in `__add__` (in line 15 of the code).
- The variable `sum` is assigned to an object of type `myClass` since `__add__` returned a new `myClass` instance.

Again, the `print` statements showing "in constructor," "in add," and "in str" help see where these functions are called.

12.4 BUILDING THE RATIONAL NUMBER CLASS

At the beginning of this chapter, we showed a session in which rational numbers were used in a standard way, responding to standard operations. In that session, we explicitly used the "+", "-", and "==" operators. Therefore, to implement the class used in that session, we need:

- `__init__()` which we always need
- `__str__()` which we also always need
- `__add__()` for the "+" operator
- `__sub__()` for the "-" operator
- `__eq__()` for the "==" operator
- and, any other supporting function

Making the Class

Usually the first step in designing a class is to define the structure of the class and define the `__init__` method to establish the attributes that will be available in each instance. For the rational number class, we need to store a numerator and a denominator, both integers. We also need to print a rational number instance in a nice way. We must implement `__init__` and `__str__` to accomplish both of those tasks. Let's take a first cut at our rational number class implementing those methods. As before, we include some *print* statements to help us recognize when these methods are called.

Within the interpreter, we also expect to be able to type the name of a variable and have its associated object displayed. The method that Python calls to accomplish this is named `__repr__` (short for representation). If we do not have the `__repr__` method, then Python types a default value. For clarity, it is good to include it in our basic class. Our implementation simply calls the `__str__` method, which is sufficient for most cases when you are first learning to construct classes. Note the dot notation and the use of `self` in the call to the `__str__` method in Code Listing 12.3.

Code Listing 12.3

```
class Rational(object):
    """ Implements a Rational number"""
    def __init__(self,numer,denom=1):    # note the default for "denom"
```

```
        print 'in constructor'  # a "print" for illustration
5       self.numer = numer
        self.denom = denom

    def __str__(self):
        """ String representation for printing"""
10      print 'in str'
        return str(self.numer)+'/'+str(self.denom) # print as a fraction

    def __repr__(self):
        print 'in repr'
15      return self.__str__()  # simply call __str__
```

Things to note in our first pass at a rational number class:

- `__init__` assigns the two attributes to each instance, `numer` and `denom`.
- `__init__` also takes a default argument on parameter two, `denom`. If only the numerator is provided, the denominator will be 1, meaning that the fractional value will be the value of the numerator (essentially an integer, which will be very useful later on).
- `__str__` creates a new string by concatenation. It converts the numerator and denominator to strings and places a slash (/) between them. It then returns that combined string.
- Note the `__repr__` method, which just calls the `__str__` method.
- We add debugging print calls at lines 4, 10, and 14, so we may see when the methods are called.

Let's exercise these methods in a session. As before, the embedded print statements help illustrate when each method is called.

```
>>> from rationalNumber1 import *  # get class from rationalNumber1.py file
>>> rationalInst1 = Rational(1,2)  # create the Rational number 1/2
in constructor             # indicates that the constructor __init__ was called
>>> print rationalInst1            # print calls __str__
in str
1/2
>>> rationalInst1                  # this calls __repr__ which calls __str__
in repr
in str
1/2
>>> rationalInst2 = Rational(2)    # create the Rational number 2/1
in constructor
```

```
>>> rationalInst2
in repr
in str
2/1
>>> type(rationalInst2)
<class 'rationalNumber1.Rational'>
```

This session reinforces what we have seen before, namely:

- When a new `Rational` instance is created, the constructor (`__init__`) is automatically called, indicated by the ***print*** statement "in constructor."
- When a `Rational` instance is printed, the `__str__` is automatically called.
- When we type a variable name in the shell containing a `Rational` instance, Python looks for and calls `__repr__` which we have programmed to call `__str__`.
- If only one value is provided to the `Rational` constructor, it is assumed to be the numerator, so the denominator is set to 1 by default.
- The type of a `Rational` instance is the `Rational` class.

Now that we have the basics of a class, let's include addition.

Review Fraction Addition

Do you remember how to add fractions? An important component was the common denominator. We'll review the elementary arithmetic, and then use what we remember to create an algorithm for adding fractions.

How do you add 1/5 + 2/5? How about 1/5 + 1/3?

- The first case is easy, because both fractions have a common (same) denominator. If the denominators are the same, we simply add the numerators and keep the common denominator: 1/5 + 2/5 = 3/5.
- The second case does not have a common denominator, so we have to manipulate the fractions so that they have a common denominator. Once accomplished, addition is simple like the first case. One common denominator is the *least common multiple* (a.k.a. *lcm*) of the two denominators. The *lcm* is the smallest number that each of the denominators divides into evenly, i.e., *without* a remainder. By inspection, we know that in this case that number is 15, but what algorithm can we use to find it in general?

The *lcm* is most easily computed in terms of another value, the *greatest common divisor* (a.k.a. *gcd*). The *gcd* is the largest value that divides two values without a remainder. The relation between *lcm* and *gcd* is shown in Equation 12.1.

$$lcm(a, b) = \frac{a * b}{gcd(a, b)}$$

(12.1)

Just to be clear, here are some examples:

- By inspection, the lowest common multiple (lcm) of 6 and 15 is 30, and is expressed as $lcm(6, 15) = 30$. Let's see if the lcm Equation 12.1 is also 30. To begin with, the greatest common divisor (gcd) of 6 and 15 is 3; represented as $gcd(6, 15) = 3$. Plugging $a = 6$ and $b = 15$ into the lcm Equation 12.1, we get $lcm(6, 15) = (6 * 15)/gcd(6, 15) = (90)/3 = 30$, the expected value.
- Similarly, by inspection, the lowest common multiple (lcm) of 8 and 20 is 40, and is expressed as $lcm(8, 20) = 40$. Let's check those values in the lcm Equation 12.1. Beginning again with the greatest common divisor (gcd), the gcd of 8 and 20 is 4, and is expressed as $gcd(8, 20) = 4$. Again, using the lcm Equation 12.1, we plug in $a = 8$ and $b = 20$ to get $lcm(8, 20) = (8 * 20)/gcd(8, 20) = (160)/4 = 40$, the expected value.

Our task has been reduced to finding an algorithm for the *gcd*. Once we have that algorithm, we can use Equation 12.1 to find the *lcm*, which we can use as a common denominator.

Euclid and the gcd

It turns out that one of the oldest known algorithms is a method to calculate the *gcd* of two numbers. It was first recorded by Euclid in his book titled *Elements*, written approximately 300 B.C.E., but it was likely known earlier than that.

Euclid happened to have used geometry to derive it, but the algorithm is the same. Euclid's algorithm uses two positive integers, where both are not 0.

Euclid's GCD algorithm (on two positive integers):

1. If one of the numbers is 0, return the other number and halt.
2. Find the integer remainder of the larger number divided by the smaller number.
3. Reapply the algorithm to the smaller number from the previous iteration and the remainder.

Using the values from the previous example, let's apply Euclid's algorithm to find gcd(8,20).

Step 1 Neither number is 0; proceed.
Step 2 The integer remainder of 20/8 is 4 (i.e., 20%8 = 4).
Step 3 Reapply the algorithm, finding the gcd(8,4).
Step 4 Neither number is 0; proceed.
Step 5 Remainder of 8/4 is 0 (i.e., 8%4 = 0).
Step 6 Reapply the algorithm, finding the gcd(4,0).
Step 7 One number is 0; return the other (4) and halt.

The final result is that gcd(8,20) is 4 as expected.

This algorithm can easily be implemented in a *recursive* function, but we aren't quite there yet (see Chapter 16).

Let's rewrite our GCD algorithm so that it is easier to implement in Python. We'll begin by naming the two positive integers a and b so we can be more explicit. Also, because the algorithm refers to one number as the "smaller" number, let's arbitrarily assume that a > b (if a < b, we can swap their values). Here is an updated version of the algorithm:

Euclid's GCD algorithm (on two positive integers, a and b, such that a > b):

1. If b == 0, return a and halt.
2. Find the remainder of a divided by b: a%b.
3. Reapply the algorithm using b and the remainder.

Notice that the algorithm continues until b == 0, which is equivalent to continuing while b != 0. A *while* loop fits that description: *while* b!=0:.

After we find a remainder in step 2, we reapply the algorithm using b and the remainder. That is, we must set a and b to be respectively b and remainder for the previous iteration. To accomplish this, we use multiple assignment (Section 2.2). We include a *print* statement in line 7 so we can observe how the function is working—it can be removed later. The code is shown in Code Listing 12.4.

Code Listing 12.4

```
def gcd(a,b):
    """Calculate the greatest common divisor of two positive integers."""
    if not a>b:     # swap a and b if necessary so a > b
        a,b=b,a
    while b!=0:              # 1. if b == 0, halt
        remainder = a%b     # 2. find remainder
        print a,":",b,":",remainder  # while developing, let's watch values
        a,b = b,remainder   # 3. reapply the algorithm using b and remainder
    return a
```

Let's observe our gcd function in operation:

```
>>> from gcd import *
>>> gcd(8,20)
20 : 8 : 4    # output is in the form of a : b : remainder
8 : 4 : 0
4
>>> gcd(22,8)
22 : 8 : 6    # each step the last 2 values become the next first 2
8 : 6 : 2
6 : 2 : 0
2
```

Once we have a gcd function, we can use our *lcm* relation from Equation 12.1 to write an lcm function. Remember that we need to have the gcd function loaded before we can call the lcm function because gcd is used in lcm. Note that in Code Listing 12.5 we commented out the print in gcd because we have completed development of the gcd function and no longer need to debug it—at least not now!

PROGRAMMING TIP

If you write *print* statements in your code for debugging purposes, you can comment or uncomment them as needed. Commenting them reduces the "print load" you get when your algorithm runs, but they are always good to have around, if you want to uncomment them and test something out again.

Code Listing 12.5

```
def lcm (a,b):
    """Calculate the lowest common multiple of two positive integers."""
    return (a*b)/gcd(a,b)   # Equation 12.1
```

Here is a session using the same values from the previous exercise:

```
>>> from lcm import *
>>> lcm(8,20)
40
>>> lcm(22,8)
88
```

Back to Adding Fractions

Armed with some basic arithmetic, we can return to the original problem of adding two fractions. In the __add__ method, we need to do the following:

1. Find the *lcm* of the two fraction objects' denominators.
2. Modify the existing fractions to have the *lcm* as the denominator. That means that for each fraction, we must:
   • Find the multiple needed to raise the existing denominator to the *lcm* denominator.
   • Multiply the numerator by that multiple to keep the fraction the same.
3. Now we can add the modified numerators to find their sum.
4. Create a new fraction, with the sum as the numerator and the *lcm* as the denominator, and return it.

Subtraction is basically the same. We show the next version of the class in Code Listing 12.6.

Code Listing 12.6

```python
# simple Rational number class
# assumes both gcd and lcm are already imported

class Rational(object):
    """ Implements a Rational number"""
    def __init__(self,numer,denom=1):  # note the default for "denom"
        print 'in constructor'  # a "print" for illustration
        self.numer = numer
        self.denom = denom

    def __str__(self):
        """ String representation for printing"""
        print 'in str'
        return str(self.numer)+'/'+str(self.denom) # print as a fraction

    def __repr__(self):
        """ Representation of Rational number"""
        print 'in repr'
        return self.__str__()

    def __add__(self,f):
        """ Add two Rationals"""
        print 'in add'
        # find a common denominator (lcm)
        theLcm = lcm(self.denom,f.denom)
        # multiply each numerator by the lcm to get, then add numerators
        numeratorSum = (theLcm/self.denom * self.numer) + \
                       (theLcm/f.denom * f.numer)
        return Rational(numeratorSum,theLcm)

    def __sub__(self,f):
        """ Subtract two Rationals"""
        print 'in sub'
        # subtraction is the same as addition with "+" changed to "−"
        theLcm = lcm(self.denom,f.denom)
        numeratorDiff = (theLcm/self.denom * self.numer) - \
                        (theLcm/f.denom * f.numer)
        return Rational(numeratorDiff,theLcm)
```

Comments on the `Rational` class so far:

- For brevity's sake, we assume that both the `gcd` and `lcm` have already been imported, even though they are not shown.
- Line 25 calculates the `lcm` and Line 27 both modifies each numerator and then sums them together as the new numerator.
- Line 28 returns a new instance of a `Rational`, because the sum of two rational numbers is a rational number. The new instance is created by calling the `Rational` constructor with the two new values for numerator and denominator.
- In our example code, every method and function prints out a line when it is called. Tracking code is easier, but it must be commented out when done debugging.

Let's look at an output session to see how this expanded example works:

```
>>> from rationalNumber2 import *
>>> oneHalf = Rational(1,2)    # build 1/2 using the constructor __init__
in constructor
>>> twoFifths = Rational(2,5) # built 2/5
in constructor
>>> theSum = oneHalf + twoFifths # call oneHalf.__add__(twoFifths)
in add
in lcm                   # __add__ calls lcm which calls gcd
in gcd
in constructor # __add__ calls the Rational constructor to return a Rational
>>> print theSum
in str                   # "print" calls __str__
9/10
>>> two = Rational(2)     # build 2/1 using the default denominator 1
in constructor
>>> theSum = oneHalf + two # test that our Rational using a default works
in add
in lcm
in gcd
in constructor
>>> print theSum
in str
5/2
>>> theDiff = twoFifths - oneHalf  # test subtraction for a negative result
in sub
in lcm
in gcd
in constructor
>>> print theDiff
in str
-1/10
```

Here are some observations on that session:

- We begin by creating two fractions, oneHalf=1/2 and twoFifths=2/5.
- When we add oneHalf and twoFifths, note how many functions and methods get called. First, the system converts the binary operation into a method call by calling __add__ with oneHalf bound to *self* and twoFifths as the parameter. The __add__ calls lcm, (Line 25, which calls gcd). The lcm value is returned to the __add__ method. Because we need to return a Rational, a call is made to the Rational constructor to construct the result.

Check Yourself: Check Defining Your Own Operators

1. Provide the indicated output for the following code:

```
class testClass(object):
    def __init__(self,aStr=''):
        self.theStr=''
        for c in aStr:
            if c.isalpha():
                self.theStr += c
    def __add__(self,param):
        if type(param)==testClass:
            theStr = self.theStr + param.theStr
            return testClass(theStr)
        else:
            return self

    def __str__(self):
        return 'Value: %s'%(self.theStr)

inst1 = testClass('abc')
inst2 = testClass('123ijk')
sumInst1 = inst1 + inst2
sumInst2 = inst1 + 'xyz'
print inst1                             # Line 1
print sumInst1                          # Line 2
print sumInst2                          # Line 3
print isinstance(sumInst2,testClass)    # Line 4
```

(a) What output is produced by Line 1 when executing the indicated code?
(b) What output is produced by Line 2 when executing the indicated code?
(c) What output is produced by Line 3 when executing the indicated code?
(d) What output is produced by Line 4 when executing the indicated code?

- We test the default in the constructor by creating a rational number object 2/1 using the constructor call `Rational(2)`. To that number we add 1/2, correctly yielding 5/2.
- Finally, we test that subtraction correctly produces a negative result: −1/10.

The overall process is a bit complicated, but each step is fairly simple and the organization of the whole process is accomplished by us, the class designers, fitting in with the Python class structure.

Assignment

You likely noticed that we used assignment (=) with rational numbers in the sessions without defining an assignment operator within the `Rational` class. Assignment is different than the other operators, because it is simply a manipulation of the namespace. Assignment only associates an object with a name, so, no matter the object, assignment establish that association. No special operator is needed for assignment based on an object type. Assignment works, as is, with all objects.

Equality and Reducing Fractions

In this section, we consider the tasks of comparing two rational numbers to see whether they are equal.

The simple case is to compare the two numerators and two denominators. If both are the same, then the fractions are the same. So is 1/2 == 1/2? Sure.

However, checking equality is complicated by the fact that two different rational numbers can be equal, because their reduced values are equal, e.g., 12/16 == 6/8 because they both reduce to 3/4.

Therefore, to check for equality we need to reduce the fractions. That begs for a reduction function. To check for equality, we can reduce both fractions and then compare.

Fortunately, we already have the tools (functions) to accomplish this task. The first step in reducing a fraction is to find the greatest number that will divide into both the numerator and denominator. That is, the *gcd* and we already have that function. Having found that divisor, we divide both the numerator and denominator by that value, creating a new `Rational` instance that is reduced.

Once we can reduce a fraction, we can then compare the numerators and denominators. The methods in question are shown in Code Listing 12.7.

Code Listing 12.7

```
def reduceRational(self):
    """ Return the reduced fractional value. """
    print 'in reduce'
```

```
      # find the gcd and then divide numerator and denominator by gcd
5     thegcd = gcd(self.numer,self.denom)
      return Rational(self.numer/thegcd,self.denom/thegcd)

  def __eq__(self,f):
      """ Compare two Rationals for equality"""
10    print 'in eq'
      # reduce both; then check that numerators and denominators are equal
      f1 = self.reduceRational()
      f2 = f.reduceRational()
      return f1.numer == f2.numer and f1.denom == f2.denom
```

Comments on our Rational class:

Line 5: reduceRational finds the gcd of the provided Rational object now associated with self.

Line 6: A new Rational object is created and returned in reduced form. The numerator and denominator of this new object are made by dividing self.numer and self. denom by the gcd.

Lines 12–13: Note how reduceRational is called in both cases. It is a method of the class, so we call it using f.reduceRational and self.reduceRational without arguments. Both return new Rational objects, which are assigned to f1 and f2, respectively. Neither f nor self is modified! That makes sense. The result of testing two rational numbers should not modify those numbers.

For the reduceRational method, if the fraction is already in its reduced form, then the gcd is 1. We still divide, even if it is 1, as that is simpler to do than to check for that special case.

We expect __eq__ to return a Boolean. After reducing, we compare both the numerator and the denominator and then logically **and** the results, returning a Boolean.

An alternate way to design a rational number class would be to *always* keep fractions in reduced form. That is, if you create a fraction 12/16, it will be reduced to 3/4 when the fraction is created. Arithmetic operations would operate similarly. It is not obvious that one design is "better" than the other: both have merits. If you work with the Fraction class in Python 2.6 fractions module, you will see that they always reduce their fractions.

The session that exercises Code Listing 12.7 is interesting:

```
>>> from rationalNumber3 import *
>>> oneHalf = Rational(1,2)     # create 1/2
in constructor
>>> fiveTenths = Rational(5,10) # create 5/10
in constructor
>>> fiveTenths.reduceRational() # call reducing function using dot notation
```

```
in reduce                       # notice all the methods and functions visited!
in gcd
in constructor
in repr
in str
1/2
>>> fiveTenths
in repr
in str
5/10
>>> oneHalf == fiveTenths        # check the equality comparison operator
in eq
in reduce
in gcd
in constructor
in reduce
in gcd
in constructor
True
>>> (oneHalf + oneHalf) == (fiveTenths + fiveTenths)
in add
in lcm
in gcd
in constructor
in add
in lcm
in gcd
in constructor
in eq
in reduce
in gcd
in constructor
in reduce
in gcd
in constructor
True
```

- The method `fiveTenths.reduceRational` returns the appropriate result, 1/2. The value in `fiveTenths` is not modified.
- Can you follow the sequence of invocations of functions and methods for `fiveTenths.reduceRational()`?
  - `reduceRational` method is called.
  - `gcd` is called in `reduceRational`.
  - Once reduced, a new `Rational` is created by calling the constructor.
  - The results is to be displayed by the shell, which calls `__repr__` to do that.
  - `__repr__` calls `__str__`.

- oneHalf == fiveTenths converts to oneHalf.__eq__(fiveTenths), which produces True. Neither value is modified. Note that reduceRational is called twice, once for each fraction.
- Complicated expressions can now be created that exercise the class, e.g., (oneHalf + oneHalf) == (fiveTenths + fiveTenths)

Divide and Conquer at Work

Notice again how we applied a divide-and-conquer approach to solving this problem. We broke the problem of performing operations on rational numbers into smaller pieces, each of which was easily testable, e.g., lcm, lcd, and reduceRational. We then combined the parts to solve the problem at hand. Re-emphasizing this approach is important, especially when building your own classes. Many small functions are easier to develop and debug than a few large ones. The interactive nature of Python makes testing of small functions and methods easy. It is a hallmark of object-oriented code to build in this way.

12.5 WHAT DOESN'T WORK (YET)

Our testing sessions seem to indicate that our class is sufficient, but look at the following session. Why don't these expressions work?

```
>>> from rationalNumber3 import *
>>> oneHalf = Rational(1,2)
in constructor
>>> oneHalf + 1
in add
Traceback (most recent call last):
  File "<stdin>", line 1, in <module>
  File "rationalNumber3.py", line 35, in __add__
    theLcm = lcm(self.denom,f.denom)
AttributeError: 'int' object has no attribute 'denom'
>>>
>>> 1 + oneHalf
Traceback (most recent call last):
  File "<stdin>", line 1, in <module>
TypeError: unsupported operand type(s) for +: 'int' and 'Rational'
```

First, it is reasonable to expect that we should be able to mix other numeric types with our new Rational class, but so far we cannot. Second, we get two different error messages for the the expressions:

- oneHalf + 1: error is trying to find 'denom' in 1.
- 1 + oneHalf: error is unsupported types for '+'.

It is useful to try to interpret what these error messages are telling us. Let's begin by reviewing how these expressions get translated.

$$\text{oneHalf + 1} \Rightarrow \text{oneHalf.\_\_add\_\_(1)}.$$

However, in our `__add__` method, we assume that the argument being passed is of type `Rational`. In this case, it isn't: 1 is of type *int*.

In the second example, `1 + oneHalf` doesn't get fully translated. Because the first argument is an *int*, the system looks for defined operations on *int*'s, and there is no "+" operation for an *int* and a `Rational`.

We need to fix both errors, but they will each require their own solution.

Introspection

To fix the first problem, namely `oneHalf + 1`, we need to fix our assumptions about the `__add__` method. Take a look at that code. When we designed the method, we assumed that the type of the passed parameter is `Rational`. We try to access the `numer` and `denom` attributes of the parameter. What if that is not a `Rational`? We, the class designers, need to check the type first and then take appropriate action. We need to utilize introspection. Remember, we discussed introspection in Section 12.2. Introspection allows us to query the type of a variable while the program is running, and take appropriate action.

Our `__add__` method presently works correctly with type `Rational` parameters. What other types might it work with? Clearly it could work with integers. We might do other types as well, but let's work with *int* for now.

We need to check the type of the parameter as it comes in. If the parameter is an *int*, then convert the *int* to a `Rational` so we can continue as before. Conveniently, if we call the `Rational` constructor with only an integer, it does create a `Rational` (with a denominator of 1)—good design!

To save space, we show only relevant parts of the class in Code Listing 12.8.

Code Listing 12.8

```
    def __add__(self,f):
        """ Add two Rationals """
        print 'in add'
        if type(f) == int:   # convert ints to Rationals
5           f = Rational(f)
        if type(f) == Rational:
            # find a common denominator (lcm)
            theLcm = lcm(self.denom,f.denom)
            # multiply to make denominators the same, then add numerators
```

```
10          theSum = (theLcm/self.denom * self.numer) + \
                     (theLcm/f.denom * f.numer)
            return Rational(theSum,theLcm)
       else:
            print 'wrong type'  # problem: some type we cannot handle
15          raise(TypeError)
```

Line 4: of __add__ checks the parameter's type with the type function. If it is of type *int*, then the parameter is converted to a Rational by calling the Rational constructor, passing the single argument.

Line 6: We have either converted an *int* to a Rational or had received a Rational initially to get past this *if* statement. If so, we then do what we did previously to add the two fractions.

Line 13: If we get to this line, then we did not end up with a Rational type for the passed parameter. We print an error message then *raise* an error. The command *raise* is a way to signal to Python that an error has occurred that will be dealt with if possible. Such an error is called an exception. We will deal with exceptions more in Chapter 14, but for now, it will stop the program and indicate that a TypeError has occurred.

Let's test it!

```
>>> from introspectAdd import *
>>> oneHalf = Rational(1,2)  # create 1/2
in constructor
>>> oneHalf + oneHalf  # check that addition of two rationals still works
in add
in lcm
in gcd
in constructor
in repr
in str
2/2
>>> oneHalf + 1   # try adding a rational and an int
in add
in constructor
in lcm
in gcd
in constructor
in repr
in str
3/2
>>> oneHalf + 3.2 # try adding a type we haven't included: error is generated
in add
wrong type
```

```
Traceback (most recent call last):
  File "<stdin>", line 1, in <module>
  File "introspectAdd.py", line 42, in __add__
    raise(TypeError)
TypeError
>>> 1 + oneHalf    # try reversing to add int and rational: still a problem
Traceback (most recent call last):
  File "<stdin>", line 1, in <module>
TypeError: unsupported operand type(s) for +: 'int' and 'Rational'
```

In our session, testing indicates that regular `Rational` addition still works (we didn't break it!), as does `Rational` + *int*. `Rational` + anythingElse raises the TypeError exception—correctly, as that's how we designed it. However, *int* + `Rational` still does not work, so we have more to do.

Repairing int + Rational Errors

Introspection allows us to examine the type of the parameter(s) passed into a method, but we still cannot address the problem of an expression such as `1 + oneHalf`. The problem is that, because the first element of the binary operation is an *int*, there is no way for us to automatically route the addition (+) operation to the `__add__` method of `Rational`. This is because our translation of binary operator to method depends on the type of the *first* operand. The first operand is an *int*, and we cannot (and likely wouldn't want to) change the underlying functionality of *int*'s for every new type (class) we define.

Python provides a way around this problem. For each math-like method predefined by the system, a "reversed" method exists: `__radd__`, `__rsub__`, `__rmul__`, `__rdiv__`, `__rand__`, `__ror__`.[2] The Python process here is a little complicated, so follow carefully for the expression `1 + Rational(1,2)`.

1. Python tries to find an appropriate `__add__` method for *int*'s. However, no such method exists that had a parameter of type `Rational`.
2. Given the error, Python looks for the existence of an `__radd__` method in the *second* operand. If this exists, then Python *automatically* reverses the expression and calls `__radd__`. In this case, that expression will be `Rational(1,2).__radd__(1)`.
3. If neither of these work, Python indicates an error.

In our case of *int* + `Rational`, the `__radd__` maps the `Rational` to *self* and the *int* to the parameter. For addition, because addition is commutative (order doesn't matter), we just call the non-reversed `__add__` with the now properly ordered expression. Because introspection allows us to have *int*'s as a parameter, all should be well. Let's take a look at just that method in Code Listing 12.9.

---

[2] Others exist for mod, shift, etc., but *not* for comparison operations.

Code Listing 12.9

```
def __radd__(self,f):
    """ Add two Rationals (reversed)"""
    # mapping is reversed: if "1 + x", x maps to self, and 1 maps to f
    print "in radd"
5   # mapping is already reversed so self will be Rational; call __add__
    return self.__add__(f)
```

Take a look at a session to see that it works:

```
>>> from rationalNumber4 import *
>>> x = Rational(1,2)    # create 1/2
in constructor
>>> print x
in str
1/2
>>> z = 1 + x            # mixed "int + Rational"
in radd                  # calls __radd__ which
in add                   # calls __add__ which
in constructor           # calls __init__ constructor to make int a Rational
in constructor           # at end calls __init__ constructor for return type
>>> print z
in str
3/2
```

Make sure you can follow along. The 1 + x begins with a call to __radd__ because an "int + Rational" method doesn't exist. Once we are within the __radd__, Python remaps *self* and f is in reverse order of the original expression. Because addition is commutative, we call *self*.__add__(f). That is, 1 + x through __radd__ will map x to *self* and 1 to f, which our __add__ can handle. We see "in add" printed followed by the first "in constructor," where the *int* 1 is converted to a Rational. The final "in constructor" is when we construct a Rational to return. Phew!

Mixed-Type Comparisons

What about handling mixed-type comparisons? Unfortunately, comparisons do not have "reversed" versions of methods, so something that does a comparison between an *int* and a Rational cannot be solved so easily. That is, 1 == oneHalf, which compares an *int* with a Rational will fail, and a reversed equality operator does not exist to help us out. A solution exists, but it is messy and beyond the scope of this introductory text. The complexity comes from the fact that comparisons behave quite different than arithmetic, and the concept of "equality" or "greater-than" can get messy at the language implementation level. Therefore, at this stage, mixed-type comparisons such as "equal," "greater-than," "less-than," "not-equal," and so on are left for a more-advanced text.

Collection Operators and Iteration

If the class we are constructing is a collection, we can also define operators such as indexing ([ ]), and iteration. Please see the Python manual for details.

12.6 INHERITANCE

As we have mentioned, one of the hallmarks of a OOP system is inheritance. Let us finally get down to details and examine what inheritance means. We'll first see *what* it is and then get into *why* it is a good idea.

The "Find the Attribute" Game

In Section 11.3, we discussed how information is shared between instances and classes. Remember:

- A single class can have many instances, where each instance is initialized by the class's constructor method, `__init__`.
- When constructed, one of the instance's attributes is the `__class__` attribute, indicating the class the instance was created from. This establishes the *instance-of* relationship. Every instance remembers what class it is an instance of.
- When referencing a value in an attribute (e.g., `myInstance.attributeName`), Python first looks in the instance for the attribute and, if not found there, it then looks in the class the instance was derived from. In this way, methods stored in the class are available to every instance derived from that class.

We want to extend the "find the attribute" search algorithm from Section 11.3 to include other classes besides the one the instance is derived from. But how? As it turns out, classes can also have a relationship with other classes, a relationship independent of the class-instance relationship. Let's explore that a bit.

Class "is-a" Relationship and the Class Hierarchy

Remember when we wrote our first class, shown in Figure 11.1? In every definition of a Python class, the final element is a parenthetical list of classes that we called the "parent object." We noted at that time that, until we got to inheritance, this list was always to contain the special class `object`. Now that we are at inheritance, we can explain this argument in more detail.

Every class maintains at least one *parent* class. The two classes are said to have a "parent-child," "superclass-subclass," or "base-derived class" relationship depending on who is doing the describing. However you describe the two classes, the relationship is meant to represent the specialization of an object. It is often called an *is-a* relationship. For example, if you create a `Car` class, then a `Ford` class "is-a" `Car`, but a more particular kind of `Car`. Subsequently, a `Mustang` class "is-a" `Ford` class, but a more particular kind of `Ford`. Remember, these are still classes, not instances! A `Mustang` is a general class of `Car`, not a single, particular car, such as "Bill's 1967 Green Shelby Cobra Mustang" (don't I wish!), which is an individual car, an instance. `Car`, `Ford` and `Mustang` are still classes of vehicles—templates from which individual instances are derived.

The "is-a" relationship is "one-way," much as the "instance-of" relationship is "one way." The instance remembers who its class is, but the class does not track its instances. A class remembers who its parent class is, but the parent class does not track its child classes.

Each Python class indicates specifically in its class definition who its parent class is. This relationship gets recorded in the `__bases__` attribute of each class.

Taken together, all the classes and their parent relationships form a *hierarchy* of classes. The Oxford English Dictionary includes as one of the definitions of "hierarchy" the following:

> hierarchy: A body of persons or things ranked in grades, orders, or classes, one above another.

A hierarchy of Python classes is an organization, through the parent class of each class, indicating how classes are related to one another via an "is-a" relation. Figure 12.1 shows the situation.

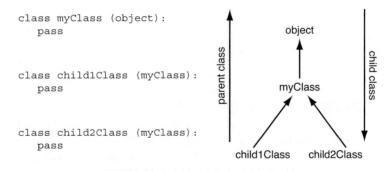

FIGURE 12.1 A simple class hierarchy

The figure shows three, rather empty, classes. The important point is that this figure shows that the parent class value in each class establishes an "is-a" relationship, and how, taken together, the "is-a" relationships establish a hierarchy. One class that is shown in the hierarchy but never defined is object (note the lowercase!). Python provides the object named object as the "top object" in the Python class hierarchy. *Every* class defined in Python ultimately ends up at object by following the parent class links. All of the built-in objects (list, set, tuple, dictionary, etc.) are objects whose parent is object. Code Listing 12.10 shows this. Note who the parent class of object is.

Code Listing 12.10

```
class myClass (object):
    pass

class myChildClass (myClass):
5   pass

myChildInstance = myChildClass()
myClassInstance = myClass()

10  print myChildClass.__bases__          # the parent class
    print myClass.__bases__               # ditto
    print object.__bases__                # ditto

    print myChildInstance.__class__       # class from which the instance came
15  print type(myChildInstance)           # same question, asked via function
```

```
(<class 'myClass'>,)    # Line 10 print statement
(<type 'object'>,)      # Line 11
()                      # Line 12
<class 'myChildClass'>  # Line 14
<class 'myChildClass'>  # Line 15
```

Back to the Game

Now we know of two relationships: "is-a" between classes and "instance-of" between an instance and the class it was created from. We can now update the "instance-of" relationship of Figure 11.2 by including the "is-a" relationship as shown in Figure 12.2. We call the illustrated process of determining relationships, the "find the attribute" game.

The order of search is now:

1. Look in the instance; if not found there, go on.
2. Look in the class of the instance (up the "instance-of" relation); if not there, go on.

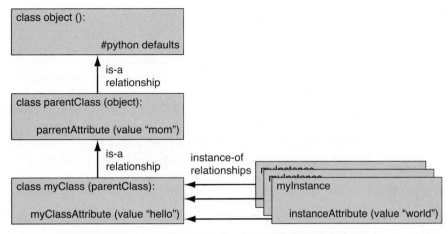

FIGURE 12.2 The players in the "Find the Attribute" game.

3. Look up the class parent link, the "is-a" relation, and look in the parent class. Continue looking up the "is-a" relation until the attribute is found or there are no more "is-a" relation links to follow (meaning that ultimately you arrived at object and the attribute was not found).

Using Figure 12.2, how does Python find myInstance.parentAttribute? Following the rules:

- Python first looks in the instance itself. The attribute is not in the instance, so on to rule 2.
- Python then looks in the class from which it was instantiated, via the "instance-of" link, myClass. The attribute is not in the class, so on to rule 3.
- Python moves up the class hierarchy via the "is-a" link to parentClass. It finds the attribute there and returns it.

If the process gets to the class object and it doesn't find the attribute, the search fails and Python generates an error.

Using Inheritance

Let's review. We can now impose a structure on a set of classes using the "is-a" ("parent-of") relationship. This organization fits into the already existing "instance-of" relationship, and extends the search process for finding attributes of an instance (and remember, attributes include methods). So what?

The promise of inheritance as an aspect of OOP relates to the ability to share common code:

- If a new class is created as part of an existing class hierarchy, then the new class can reuse existing code from the hierarchy, specializing only those aspects or attributes that are unique to the new class.
- By sharing code from the class hierarchy, the coding of classes can be somewhat standardized. If a group of developers must work together, they can establish "standard code" to accomplish common tasks and a framework in which to develop new tasks. This means that the group works together by sharing as much as possible, preventing errors and incompatibilities in their code.

Group Development and OOP

The last of the previous points is important, because it emphasizes a need that OOP often fills: group development. One of the main reasons that OOP has been successful is that it helps in coordinating group development of software. It is a drawback of an introductory course that group development is often not emphasized (students can only do so much in a single course!), but OOP works best in a group environment.

More importantly, a group environment is really how modern software is developed. It is rare that a single programmer (or even a small group of programmers) does an entire development cycle. It requires too much work and takes too much time. Developers need to work together to create software, and OOP is a tool to help in that regard. That is why the term *software engineering* is so often used in regards to development. Software engineering is concerned with developing tools to make development, especially group development, easier to accomplish. OOP is one of those tools.

How does OOP help in a group setting? Let's look at the various aspects we have used. Encapsulation means that a class designer can write code for another programmer to solve a problem. The details of the class are hidden from the programmer; only the interface is made available. If the class must be modified in some way (to be faster, to use less memory, to interact with a new device, etc.), then the class designer can modify the class as long as he can maintain the interface, the methods made available to the programmer. This division of duty—class design and class use—makes it easier to share code.

Inheritance does much the same thing. By providing standard methods via a class hierarchy, the group can make decisions as to how their code should be developed and shared.

Example: The Standard Model

Physicists who investigate the nature of the atom have worked for many years to develop a model of matter and the forces that act on that matter. The results of this research are currently termed the *Standard Model*. The Standard Model is a description of all the fundamental "pieces" from which matter is constructed and three of the fundamental forces of nature (gravity not yet being incorporated). It is a crowning achievement of an enormous amount of work, but its description is relatively easy to provide. Figure 12.3 shows a summary of the model.[3]

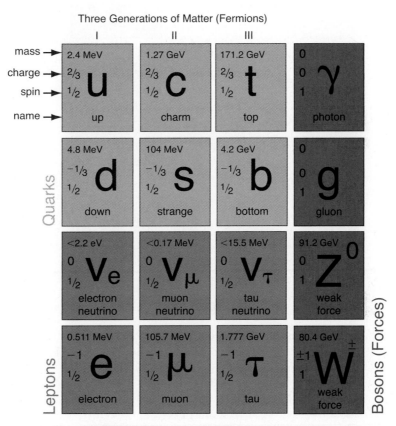

FIGURE 12.3 The Standard Model of physics.

Each of the 12 particles shown in the model have a number of attributes including: mass, spin, charge, and name. They also have intrinsic attributes, such as location (in three-dimensional space) and velocity (direction of movement in three-dimensional space). This classification of particles is perfect for a class hierarchy. Let's try and develop at least part of it.

Every particle has both a *name* and the quantity called *spin* as well as a position in 3D space and a velocity. Our base class then will be called particle and the __init__ and __str__ methods will manipulate those values. A second class, called massParticle will be a child class of particle. It will add the quantity mass to any instance.

---

[3] It should be noted that the Standard Model is a working hypothesis, well-established, but not fully proven. This version of the model ignores some particles, such as anti-particles.

FIGURE 12.4 The particle class hierarchy.

The final class will be called `chargedParticle`. It will add the quantity `charge` to any instance. An example of this hierarchy is shown in Figure 12.4. An implementation is shown in Code Listing 12.11.

Using Parent Class Methods

Code Listing 12.11

```
class particle (object):
    def __init__ (self, name='', position=(0.0,0.0,0.0), \
                  velocity=(0.0,0.0,0.0), spin=0.0):
        self.position = position
        self.velocity = velocity
        self.name = name
        self.spin = spin

    def __str__ (self):
        print 'in particle str'
```

```
        pos = '(%f:%f:%f)'% \
            (self.position[0],self.position[1],self.position[2])
        vel = '(%f:%f:%f)'% \
            (self.velocity[0],self.velocity[1],self.velocity[2])
        theStr = "%s at %s with velocity %s and spin %f"% \
            (self.name, pos, vel, self.spin)
        return theStr

class massParticle (particle):
    def __init__ (self, name='',position=(0.0,0.0,0.0), \
                velocity=(0.0,0.0,0.0), spin=0.0, mass=0.0):
        particle.__init__(self, name, position, velocity, spin)
        self.mass = mass

    def __str__(self):
        print 'in mass str'
        tempStr = particle.__str__(self)
        tempStr = tempStr + ' and mass %f' % (self.mass)
        return tempStr

class chargedParticle(massParticle):
    def __init__(self, name='', position=(0.0,0.0,0.0), \
                velocity=(0.0,0.0,0.0), spin=0.0,mass=0.0, charge=0.0):
        massParticle.__init__(self,name,position,velocity,spin,mass)
        self.charge = charge

    def __str__(self):
        print 'in charged str'
        tempStr = massParticle.__str__(self)
        tempStr = tempStr + ' and charge %f'%(self.charge)
        return tempStr
```

```
>>> photon = particle(name='photon', spin=1.0)
>>> tau = chargedParticle (name='tau', spin=0.5, charge=-1.0, mass=1.777)
>>> print photon
in particle str
photon at (0.000000:0.000000:0.000000) with velocity (0.000000:0.000000:0.000000)
and spin 1.000000
>>> print tau
in charged str
in mass str
in particle str
tau at (0.000000:0.000000:0.000000) with velocity (0.000000:0.000000:0.000000) and
spin 0.500000 and mass 1.777000 and charge -1.000000
>>>
```

As you have seen, Code Listing 12.11 implements our class hierarchy. For simplicity, we implement only the `__init__` and `__str__` methods.

If you look carefully at the `__init__` and `__str__` methods of the two child classes, you will see something odd. An example would be the `__init__` of `massParticle`. It contains the line: `particle.__init__(self, name, position, velocity, spin)`. What is that? All of our previous work used instances to call methods. Here, we are calling the method with a *class* and passing `self` in the argument list.

The problem is this. When we make a child class, we want it to have an `__init__` method just like every other class. However, if it is a child class, we *also* want to make sure we call its parent class's `__init__` as well. In this way, we do locally to any instance what needs to be done for our class, but we also must do what the *parent* class requires.

We cannot do this initialization with something like `self.__init__` in the local class's `__init__`. That just calls the same method again! We need a way to call the parent class `__init__` (and any other inherited method).

Python provides a way to do this. When called in the context of a method, such as `s1.update`, it is called a "bound method." This usage means that the first argument `s1` is bound automatically to the instance `s1`. On the other hand, the method can be called without an (automatic) instance, but the user must then provide the instance explicitly. This latter case is called an "unbound method." With an unbound method, we specifically indicate the method (what class, what method) using dot notation and then explicitly pass `self` as the first argument.

In Code Listing 12.11, there are some print statements in each of the `__str__` methods to indicate which method is being called to show which methods are in fact being used.

Changing Code Using Class Inheritance

The print output of the `__str__` method is not very well formatted. The good news is that we can fix most of the problems by changing the `__str__` in `particle`. Fixing the code in `particle` updates the formatted output that occurs for *all* particles (remember the "find the attribute" rules). An updated version and session output are shown in Code Listing 12.12.

Code Listing 12.12

```
# simple hierarchy for the standard model

class particle (object):
    def __init__ (self, name='', position=(0.0,0.0,0.0), \
                  velocity=(0.0,0.0,0.0), spin=0.0):
```

```
        self.position = position
        self.velocity = velocity
        self.name = name
        self.spin = spin

    def __str__ (self):
        # print 'in particle str'
        pos = '(%.2f:.2%f:.2%f)'% \
              (self.position[0],self.position[1],self.position[2])
        vel = '(%.2f:.2%f:.2%f)'% \
              (self.velocity[0],self.velocity[1],self.velocity[2])
        theStr = "%s\n at %s\n with velocity %s\n and spin %f\n"% \
                 (self.name, pos, vel, self.spin)
        return theStr

class massParticle (particle):
    def __init__ (self, name='',position=(0.0,0.0,0.0), \
                  velocity=(0.0,0.0,0.0), spin=0.0, mass=0.0):
        particle.__init__(self, name, position, velocity, spin)
        self.mass = mass

    def __str__(self):
        # print 'in mass str'
        tempStr = particle.__str__(self)
        tempStr = tempStr + ' and mass %f\n' % (self.mass)
        return tempStr

class chargedParticle(massParticle):
    def __init__(self, name='', position=(0.0,0.0,0.0), \
                 velocity=(0.0,0.0,0.0), spin=0.0,mass=0.0, charge=0.0):
        massParticle.__init__(self,name,position,velocity,spin,mass)
        self.charge = charge

    def __str__(self):
        # print 'in charged str'
        tempStr = massParticle.__str__(self)
        tempStr = tempStr + ' and charge %f'%(self.charge)
        return tempStr
```

```
>>> photon = particle(name='photon', spin=1.0)
>>> tau = chargedParticle(name='tau', spin=0.5, charge = -1.0, mass= 1.777)
>>> print photon
photon
 at (0.00:.20.000000:.20.000000)
```

```
with velocity (0.00:.20.000000:.20.000000)
and spin 1.000000

>>> print tau
tau
 at (0.00:.20.000000:.20.000000)
 with velocity (0.00:.20.000000:.20.000000)
 and spin 0.500000
 and mass 1.777000
 and charge -1.000000
>>>
```

This is the beauty of inheritance. If the parent class is doing work, we just call the parent class method and then, in our local method, add on whatever we need. If we need to modify any common functionality, we do it in the class where it resides and all inheriting classes "see" the effect.

In this session, we can see that even though we did not change the `__str__` method of the `chargedParticle` we inherited the changes made in `particle` so the print of the `chargedParticle` is also nicely formatted.

Summary

In this chapter, you learned how to increase the capabilities of classes that we design. You learned the value of consistency, the use of introspection, and how to overload some operators.

Exercises

1. Describe what the `isinstance` function does, and give an example of its use.

2. Augment the Rational number class to include multiplication and division. Include the ability to accommodate operands of type *int*.

3. The human body has many organs (heart, lungs, brain, and kidneys, to name a few). We could think of the human body as a complex object made up of simpler objects (organs).

   (a) Create classes for heart and brain. Think about what the functions of the heart and brain are in our body and map these functions into methods.

   (b) Create an Organ class as the base class for the organs and derive the classes created earlier from the base class.

4. There are Web sites such as `http://www.vehix.com` that provide information about second-hand vehicles. Design a base class for vehicle with fields such as model year, total mileage, Vehicle Identification Number (VIN), EPA class, EPA mileage, engine, transmission, and options.

   Design subclasses for car, truck, SUV, and minivan. Think about the specific fields and methods required for the subclasses.

5. Design a class called Bill that has fields to store the list of items, their prices per unit, quantity of each item in the bill, and the grand total of the items. Create an overloaded add operator so that when you add two bills, you get a new bill with all the items in the two bills (there may be duplicates in the final bill) and a new grand total.

   Would you have multiply and divide overloaded operators in this case? Think!

   For example, a McDonald's bill might include: 2 burgers @ $4.00 each, 4 strawberry milkshakes @ $2.50 each.

6. In Newtonian physics, we know that two velocities in the same direction add to each other; in the opposite direction, they subtract from each other to give a net result in the direction of the bigger velocity.

   Design a simple class called Velocity that has a field for the speed in meters per second. (Forget about the direction for now).

   The default constructor would work with meters/sec metric.

   Write a constructor that takes three parameters: a) distance, b) time, c) whether the velocity is in meters/sec or feet/sec.

   This constructor should accordingly convert the feet/sec into meters/sec. Create overloaded unary, addition, and subtraction operators for velocity.

   A more advanced version of this class would consider the directions other than same or opposite directions.

7. Every semester, students take a number of courses, and at the end of the semester, they get their final grades. Design a SemTranscript class that stores the name of the student, list of courses taken by the student and the corresponding grades, and the average grade for that semester. Also, create a overloaded addition operator so that you can add two semester grades to get courses taken in two semesters and calculate the final grade for a year.

   Note: in the overloaded operator, you cannot just directly take an average of the grades of the two SemTranscript objects to get the average final grade of the year.

8. File Concatenation: Many operating systems allow one to concatenate files. Design a class called TextDocument that reads the contents of a text file only. Create a constructor that takes the path of a text file. Create an overloaded addition operator for this class that adds (concatenates) two TextDocument objects (appends the second one at the end of the first one) and creates a new text file. Handle all possible error cases, such as for file existence.

9. Consider a specific type of chemical reaction that takes in two compounds and returns a new compound. Design a class called Compound with fields for the name of the compound (such as hydrochloric acid), chemical formula of the compound (HCl). Create an addition operator for the compound class so that when you add two compounds, you get a new one. In the operator function, just print a string indicating the two compounds being added.

10. Design a class called Color. The fields of the class are three decimals for Red, Green, and Blue components in the range 0 to 1, inclusive (0 indicates Black and 1 indicates White). Add checks to ensure that the values are always in the given range. Provide addition and subtraction operators for the color class. Include saturation in the addition and subtraction: if any component goes less than 0 or greater than 1, assign them 0 or 1, respectively.

11. Design a Sound class with a field for decibels. Provide addition and subtraction operators as well as `get` and *set* methods.

12. Design a Logarithm class. Fields should be the base and number. Provide addition and subtraction operators—remember to adjust bases appropriately. Hint: use base 2 or 10 as a canonical base for operations.

13. Write a wholeNumber class. The whole numbers are the non-negative integers: $0, 1, 2, \ldots$ Your class must handle addition, subtraction, and multiplication of whole numbers— no division or mixed-type (whole number and integer) operations need be handled. Your class must also handle printing, e.g., if x is an instance of the wholeNumber class, you must be able to write: ***print*** x.

Two cases must not be allowed: (1) you must not be able to create a wholeNumber that has a negative value; (2) an arithmetic operation cannot be allowed to have a negative result. In both cases, an error message must be printed.

Remember that arithmetic must return a whole number. That is, if x and y are whole numbers, the result of $x + y$ must be a whole number.

Include sample code that uses your class and demonstrates the use of all methods as well as error handling.

14. Write a class for linear equations. A generic linear equation is of the form $y = mx + b$ where m and b are constants. Include the following methods:

(a) `__init__`, `__str__`, `__repr__`.
(b) `value(x)`, which returns the value of the equation given x.
(c) `compose(linearEquation)` that composes two linear equations. That is, if $y = x + 1$ and $z = 2a + 5$, then $y(z) = 2x + 6$ and will be called as `y.compose(z)`. Note that the `compose` operation is not commutative.
(d) `__add__` returns the sum of two linear equations. That is, if $y = ax + b$ and $z = cx + d$, then $y + z = (a + c)x + (b + d)$.

Include sample code that uses your class and demonstrates the use of all methods as well as error handling.

15. Write an Odometer class. An odometer is the gauge on your car that measures distance traveled. In the U.S. an odometer measures miles; elsewhere, it measures kilometers. Many vehicles with electronic odometer interfaces have the ability to switch between miles and kilometers. The accuracy is 1/10 of a mile (kilometer).

     Something to consider: if an odometer gets replaced, a new one must be able to be set to some specified mileage.

     Include the following methods:

     (a) `__init__`, `__str__`, `__repr__`.
     (b) The constructor must take two arguments that both have default values: one is mileage, and the other specifies units.
     (c) Addition and subtraction both have one odometer operand and one numeric operand, where the numeric operand represents the miles being added/subtracted (not two odometer operands).
     (d) Addition should be commutative (but not subtraction).
     (e) Output should always be rounded to a 1/10 of a mile (kilometer), but the odometer itself should maintain full floating-point accuracy.

     Include sample code that uses your class and demonstrates the use of all methods as well as demonstrating error handling.

16. Write a Clock class that measures hours, minutes, and seconds.
     Include the following methods:

     (a) `__init__`, `__str__`, `__repr__`.
     (b) Addition allows for both clock-to-clock operations and clock-to-integer operations. If one argument is an integer, the integer is assumed to represent hours. Addition should be commutative!
     (c) Output should always be rounded to the second.
     (d) If inappropriate values are passed to the constructor, the created clock instance should get a value of 0 hours, 0 minutes, and 0 seconds.

     Include sample code that uses your class and demonstrates the use of all methods as well as error handling.

17. Write a Compass class. A compass provides bearings. A bearing is a measure of direction as indicated by clockwise rotation around a circle. There are 360 degrees in a bearing and within each degree are 60 minutes. Thus a legal bearing would be 270 degrees, 36 minutes (approximately due west). There are never more than 359 degrees in a bearing, or more than 59 minutes in a bearing. Both degrees and minutes are integer values.
     Include the following methods:

     (a) `__init__`, `__str__`, `__repr__`.

(b) Addition allows for both bearing-to-bearing operations and bearing-to-integer operations. If one argument is an integer, the integer is assumed to represent degrees. Addition should be commutative!

(c) Output should always be rounded to the minute.

(d) If inappropriate values are passed to the constructor, the created bearing instance should get a value of 0 degrees, 0 minutes.

Include sample code that uses your class and demonstrates the use of all methods as well as error handling.

CHAPTER 13

Program Development with Classes

IN THIS CHAPTER, WE WILL DEVELOP A MORE IN-DEPTH EXAMPLE USING CLASSES SO you can see how problem-solving design can be accomplished using classes (objects).

13.1 PREDATOR–PREY PROBLEM

For this problem, we will consider a simulation of a natural habitat: a predator–prey problem. Predator–prey problems are a study of the varying sizes of populations as two groups of animals interact. One group constitutes the prey, a population of animals that are the food source for the other population of animals, the predators. The simulation shows the dynamic interaction of these two populations. It represents a kind of habitat war as the two populations struggle to survive or thrive.

Typically, both groups have a fixed birthrate. The prey usually procreate faster than the predators, allowing for a growing prey population. However, as the population of prey increases, the habitat can support a higher number of predators. This in turn leads to an increasing predator population and, after some time, a decreasing prey population. Around that time the population of predator grows so large as to reach a critical point, the point where the number of prey can no longer support the present predator population and the predator population begins to wane. As the predator population declines, the prey population recovers and the two populations continue this interesting interaction of growth and decay. Though predator–prey relationships have been modeled with equations[1] it is interesting to simulate the relationship on a computer and observe how they interact. A number of such simulations have become are common simulation problems. The classic may be the WAT-OR game,

---
[1] Lotka–Volterra equations.

based on a "Scientific American" article by A.K. Dewdney.[2] We choose a slightly different model here.

As with any simulation, the programmer gets to choose what is represented, as no reasonably sized computer program could encompass the complexity of a full habitat (at least not for what we need to do here). Within such a simulation, the user can adjust the identified parameters, such as birth and death rates of each population, and observe the impact on each cycle, and each population.

An actual example of studying predator-prey relationships in their habitat is the one between wolves and moose on Isle Royale in Lake Superior, as shown at the website `http://www.isleroyalewolf.org`. Isle Royale is located in the northwest of Lake Superior and its population of wolves and moose are isolated to the island (occasionally, Lake Superior does freeze enough for walking to land). Its isolation is a perfect laboratory for studying the effects of predator–prey interaction. A graph of the varying population sizes as actually has occurred since 1959 can be found at: `http://www.isleroyalewolf.org/data/data/womoabund.html`.

The Rules

These are the rules we will use for our simulation:

- The habitat updates itself in units of time called clock *ticks*. During one tick of our habitat clock, every animal in the island gets an opportunity to do something.
- All animals are given an opportunity to move into an adjacent space, if an empty adjacent space can be found. One move per clock tick is allowed.
- Both the Predators and Prey can reproduce. Each animal is assigned a fixed *breed time*. If the animal is still alive after breed-time ticks of the clock, it will reproduce. The animal does so by finding an unoccupied, adjacent space and fills that space with the new animal—its offspring. The animal's breed time is then reset to zero. An animal can breed at most once in a clock tick.
- The Predators must eat. They have a fixed *starve time*. If they cannot find a Prey to eat before starve-time ticks of the clock, they die.
- When a Predator eats, it moves into an adjacent space that is occupied by Prey (its meal). The Prey is removed and the Predator's starve time is reset to zero. Eating counts as the Predator's move during that clock tick.
- At the end of every clock tick, each animal's local event clocks is updated. All animals' breed times are decremented and all Predators' starve times are decremented.

This is the model we will need to support. It doesn't perfectly model the actual environment, but it does sufficiently well to provide insight into predator–prey interactions.

---

[2] *Scientific American*, December Issue, 1984.

Simulation Using Object-Oriented Programming

Simulation is perfectly suited for object-oriented programming. In OOP, we need to identify objects and define their interactions to create a program. Simulations naturally require these kind of identifications. It is for this reason that OOP evolved out of the programming language Simula, a programming language for writing simulations.[3]

What objects do we need for our simulation? We need an island, some moose (the prey), and a few wolves (the predators). We also need all the methods that govern how they interact with each other, as well as a main program. Let's focus on the classes we need for the moment. We need:

- `Island` Class
- `Prey` Class
- `Predator` Class

Having a single `Prey` class and a single `Predator` class, we can create many instances of these classes and have the instances interact. Very efficient!

We now need to identify for each class:

- *What* we need to have represented in each class instance.
- *How* these instances can be manipulated, i.e., what methods are needed.

Next, look at each class and try to sketch out what is required.

13.2 CLASSES

Island Class

Isle Royale is shaped like an elongated rectangle, but to keep our example simple, we choose to model an `Island` instance as a square, an $n \times n$ grid. Every element in the grid could potentially have *one* of three values. Either it contains nothing, a predator or a prey.

To begin with, the grid is initialized to be empty at every grid position. The value 0 will be used to represent an empty grid position. Every class needs a constructor (`__init__`) and it is generally useful to have an `__str__` method so that we can easily display an `Island` instance. When we create an instance, we need to specify only its size—in our case, we'll specify the length of a side since the island is square. This will be an argument to our constructor. See Code Listing 13.1.

Code Listing 13.1

```
class Island():
    """Island
```

---
[3] http://en.wikipedia.org/wiki/Simula

```
            n X n grid where zero value indicates an unoccupied cell."""
        def __init__(self, n):
            '''Initialize cell to all 0's, then fill with animals
            '''

            self.gridSize = n
            self.grid = []
            for i in range(n):
                row = [0]*n      # row is a list of n zeros
                self.grid.append(row)


        def __str__(self):
            '''String representation for printing.
               (0,0) will be in the lower-left corner.
            '''

            s = ""
            for j in range(self.gridSize-1,-1,-1):  # print row size-1 first
                for i in range(self.gridSize):         # each row starts at 0
                    if not self.grid[i][j]:
                        # print a '.' for an empty space
                        s+= "%-2s" % '.' + "  "
                    else:
                        s+= "%-2s" % (str(self.grid[i][j])) + "  "
                s+="\n"
            return s
```

```
>>> from island1 import *
>>> royale = Island(10)
>>> print royale
.   .   .   .   .   .   .   .   .   .
.   .   .   .   .   .   .   .   .   .
.   .   .   .   .   .   .   .   .   .
.   .   .   .   .   .   .   .   .   .
.   .   .   .   .   .   .   .   .   .
.   .   .   .   .   .   .   .   .   .
.   .   .   .   .   .   .   .   .   .
.   .   .   .   .   .   .   .   .   .
.   .   .   .   .   .   .   .   .   .
.   .   .   .   .   .   .   .   .   .

>>>
```

In the __init__ constructor, we save the size of the instance and the grid that represents the instance. Those two items are sufficient to represent the present state of the Island instance—essentially, the location in the grid of all the predators and prey.

A grid of *n* rows and *n* columns can be thought of as a list of *n* rows—each of length *n*. We create a row that is a list of *n* items of value 0 using the repeat (*) operator. We then add *n* rows to our instance grid, making the *n* × *n* grid.

The `__str__` method prints the contents of each grid element. To keep with standard Cartesian coordinates, we have the method print in such a way that (0,0) is in the lower-left corner. This means we have x increasing to the right and y increasing to the top. However, because printing occurs from the top down, we must print the highest-numbered row first.

The output in the previous session shows the creation of a 10 × 10 `Island` instance named "royale" followed by printing of the current state of the instance: empty.

Predator and Prey, Kinds of Animals

At this point, it is worth our time to think a little about the rest of our simulation design. If we look at the requirements for the two kinds of animals in our simulation, predator and prey, we can see that they share some important characteristics. They occupy locations on the `Island` instance, and they must be able to move and breed. Because they share these characteristics, it makes sense that they *inherit* those characteristics from a common parent, the `Animal` object.

Animal Object

What state does each prey instance need? Each instance needs to know where it is on the `Island` instance. The question is: where do we keep that location information—with the `Animal` instance, with the `Island` instance, or with both? Each `Animal` instance needs to know where it is, its local information, but it also needs to be aware of what else is in its surroundings, the global information. In addition, we will probably want to control how many animals can be at the same place at the same time. For those reasons, an `Animal` instance will have as *local* state its location on the island grid, its *x* and *y* coordinates. We let the `Island` instance keep *global* state information on all the inhabitants by marking in each grid location what is presently there, including nothing.

Therefore, our `Animal` object will need the following:

- Its name (string representation).
- Its location: (x,y) coordinates on the island.
- The `Island` instance, i.e., the island the animal is on.

The `__init__` constructor will need to take in each of these values as parameters. The *x* and *y* values indicate where on the island the animal will be placed. The `Animal` instance will also need to know the island it is located on. Finally, the instance will need its name: moose and wolf.

We need to inform the `Island` instance when a new `Animal` instance is added to the island. For that purpose we create the `register` method in the `Island` class. This method will "place" (register) the `Animal` instance in the `Island` grid at the *x* and *y* coordinates stored in the instance. In this way, we coordinate the local information (*x* and *y* coordinates stored in the `Animal` instance) with the global information (location of each instance in the `Island` instance grid) for the simulation.

Also, each `Animal` instance will need to know how big the `Island` instance is so that it can move around without falling into the surrounding water. For that purpose, we will also create a `size` method in the `Island` class.

Our communication between the animal and the island will be:

- `n = island.size()`   `# get the size from the island instance`
- `island.register(self)`   `# register an animal (self) location with the island instance`

Let's add those two methods to the `Island` class. Also, let's create the bare bones of the `Animal` class so that we can begin to work with the interaction between animals and the island. This is shown in Code Listing 13.2.

Code Listing 13.2

```python
class Island (object):
    """Island
    n X n grid where zero value indicates not occupied."""
    def __init__(self, n, preyCnt=0, predatorCnt=0):
        '''Initialize grid to all 0's, then fill with animals
        '''

        print n,preyCnt,predatorCnt
        self.gridSize = n
        self.grid = []
        for i in range(n):
            row = [0]*n     # row is a list of n zeros
            self.grid.append(row)
        self.initAnimals(preyCnt,predatorCnt)


    def size(self):
        '''Return size of the island: one dimension.
        '''

        return self.gridSize

    def register(self,animal):
        '''Register animal with island, i.e. put it at the
        animal's coordinates
        '''

        x = animal.x
        y = animal.y
```

```
            self.grid[x][y] = animal

    def __str__(self):
        '''String representation for printing.
           (0,0) will be in the lower left corner.
        '''

        s = ""
        for j in range(self.gridSize-1,-1,-1):   # print row size-1 first
            for i in range(self.gridSize):        # each row starts at 0
                if not self.grid[i][j]:
                    # print a '.' for an empty space
                    s+= "%-2s" % '.' + "  "
                else:
                    s+= "%-2s" % (str(self.grid[i][j])) + "  "
            s+="\n"
        return s

class Animal(object):
    def __init__(self, island, x=0, y=0, s="A"):
        '''Initialize the animal's and their positions
        '''

        self.island = island
        self.name = s
        self.x = x
        self.y = y

    def __str__(self):
        return self.name
```

```
>>> royale = Island(10)
>>> animal1 = Animal(island=royale,x=4,y=8,s='a1')
>>> animal2 = Animal(island=royale,x=6,y=4,s='a2')
>>> royale.register(animal1)
>>> royale.register(animal2)
>>> print royale
.    .    .    .    .    .    .    .    .    .
.    .    .    .    a1   .    .    .    .    .
.    .    .    .    .    .    .    .    .    .
.    .    .    .    .    .    .    .    .    .
.    .    .    .    .    .    .    .    .    .
.    .    .    .    .    .    a2   .    .    .
.    .    .    .    .    .    .    .    .    .
.    .    .    .    .    .    .    .    .    .
.    .    .    .    .    .    .    .    .    .
.    .    .    .    .    .    .    .    .    .
```

```
>>> print animal1
a1
>>>
```

Notice how the printing of an Island is accomplished in its __str__ method. We access the grid with self.island[i][j], but what is located there? Examine the Island register method. It is passed an Animal instance as a parameter. It is this instance value that is stored in the grid. Thus self.island[i][j] is a reference to that Animal instance, and because that call is within __str__, it is asking for the string representation of that particular animal. That is found in the Animal's __str__ method. At the end of the session, we show an explicit call to the Animal's __str__ method by way of a *print* statement.

For debugging purposes, it would be nice to confirm that the Animal instance grid coordinates agree with the island grid location. Printing the Island instance indicates the location that instance is maintaining for each Animal instance. The opposite, accessing position information for an Animal instance, requires a new Animal method. Let's call it position, and we will have it simply return the Animal instance's (x, y) coordinate pair. Code Listing 13.3 shows the method (without the rest of the Animal class). We can see in the accompanying session that both the Island instance and the Animal instance have the same location coordinates for that Animal instance.

Code Listing 13.3

```
def position(self):
    """Return coordinates of current position."""
    return self.x, self.y
```

```
>>> royale = Island(10)
>>> animal1 = Animal(island=royale,x=0,y=8,s='a1')
>>> animal1.position()
(0, 8)
>>> print royale
.  .  .  .  .  .  .  .  .  .
a1 .  .  .  .  .  .  .  .  .
.  .  .  .  .  .  .  .  .  .
.  .  .  .  .  .  .  .  .  .
.  .  .  .  .  .  .  .  .  .
.  .  .  .  .  .  .  .  .  .
.  .  .  .  .  .  .  .  .  .
.  .  .  .  .  .  .  .  .  .
.  .  .  .  .  .  .  .  .  .
.  .  .  .  .  .  .  .  .  .
```

Predator and Prey Classes

The Predator and Prey classes share many characteristics, which are collected in the Animal class. We can take advantage of this sharing by having each be a subclass of Animal. Each Predator and Prey class will require particular methods, but they can also share many methods and variables by being subclasses of the Animal class.

In particular, remember that the `__init__` method of the subclass must call the `__init__` of the parent class to fully initialize the instance. Code Listing 13.4 shows the two new classes with just their respective `__init__` methods. Note that we do not need to define a `__str__` method for either subclass, as this method already exists in the Animal class.

Code Listing 13.4

```python
class Animal(object):
    def __init__(self, island, x=0, y=0, s="A"):
        '''Initialize the animals and their positions
        '''
        self.island = island
        self.name = s
        self.x = x
        self.y = y

    def __str__(self):
        return self.name

class Prey(Animal):
    def __init__(self, island, x=0,y=0,s="O"):
        Animal.__init__(self,island,x,y,s)

class Predator(Animal):
    def __init__(self, island, x=0,y=0,s="X"):
        Animal.__init__(self,island,x,y,s)
```

Object Diagram

It is useful to create a diagram of the objects we have created to help understand the relationships among them. See Figure 13.1.

Filling the Island

Now that we have the Prey, Predator and Island classes, we need a way to fill an Island instance with instances of both Predator and Prey. We could leave this as

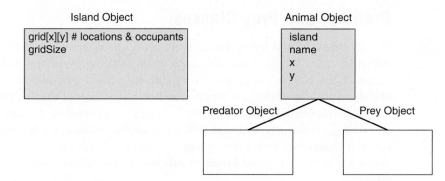

FIGURE 13.1 Objects: Island, Animals, Predators, and Prey.

a separate function to be written as part of the main program, but it makes sense that the Island instance should be able to fill itself given some counts for each class.

To accomplish this we add the initAnimals method of Island. It takes two parameters, the predator and prey counts, and fills the island with the correct number of instances of these two classes.

We would like to place the animal instances at random spots on the Island instance. That means that we will need to import the random module and use the randint method to get the x and y coordinates to place an animal. The value generated will be between 0 and the island's size, inclusive.

The generated values must place the new instance at an unoccupied grid location. If the present (x, y) is occupied, another pair must be generated.

Querying a Grid Location

We need some way to query an Island instance to see if an Animal instance is at a location. To do that, the island needs a method to respond to that query. Let's call that method animal(). It will take the x and y coordinates as arguments:

```
def animal(self,x,y):
    if 0 <= x < self.size   and   0 <= y < self.size:
        return   self.island[x][y]
    else:
        return   -1 # outside island boundary
```

The method returns either an instance (if one occupies the position) or 0 (if the position is empty).

Repeat Until Full

With these pieces in hand we can do the following to fill the island:

- Generate an (x, y) pair using random.randint(0,gridSize)
- Check to see whether that position is empty or has an animal instance using the animal method

- If the position is empty:
  - Create the new instance, record the *x* and *y* values in the instance, then register the instance.
  - Increment the count of created instances. Initialization of that animal (predator or prey) ends when the count reaches the goal count for the animal (passed as an argument to the constructor).
- If the position is occupied:
  - The **while** loop continues, but the count of created instances is not incremented.

If the Island instance is very full, this process could be rather inefficient. Perhaps you could improve it? (See the exercises.)

The remaining detail of this section is to make two small changes to the Island __init__ method. First, two more parameters are passed to Island: the counts for the Predator and Prey instances. They default to 0, if not specified. Second, a line is added to the end of the constructor to call the initAnimals method. The Island class with these additions is shown in Code Listing 13.5, but to avoid clutter we have omitted the unmodified methods: size, register, and __str__.

Code Listing 13.5

```
class Island (object):
    def __init__(self, n, preyCnt=0, predatorCnt=0):
        '''Initialize grid to all 0s, then fill with animals
        '''
        # print n, preyCnt, predatorCnt
        self.gridSize = n
        self.grid = []
        for i in range(n):
            row = [0]*n     # row is a list of n zeros
            self.grid.append(row)
        self.initAnimals(preyCnt, predatorCnt)

    def animal(self, x, y):
        '''Return animal at location (x,y)'''
        if 0 <= x < self.gridSize and 0 <= y < self.gridSize:
            return self.grid[x][y]
        else:
            return -1 # outside island boundary

    def initAnimals(self, preyCnt, predatorCnt):
        ''' Put some initial animals on the island
        '''
        cnt = 0
```

```
    # while loop continues until preyCnt unoccupied positions are found
    while cnt < preyCnt:
        x = random.randint(0,self.gridSize-1)
        y = random.randint(0,self.gridSize-1)
        if not self.animal(x,y):
            newPrey=Prey(island=self,x=x,y=y)
            cnt += 1
            self.register(newPrey)
    cnt = 0
    # same while loop but for predatorCnt
    while cnt < predatorCnt:
        x = random.randint(0,self.gridSize-1)
        y = random.randint(0,self.gridSize-1)
        if not self.animal(x,y):
            newPred=Predator(island=self,x=x,y=y)
            cnt += 1
            self.register(newPred)

## Unmodified methods not shown: size, register, __str__
```

13.3 ADDING BEHAVIOR

We have a start with our simulation. We have an `Island` instance on which we can place `Predator` and `Prey` instances. Now we need to have these animals do something—let's begin with movement.

Refinement: Add Movement

Neither the `Predators` nor `Prey` instances should stay still, so let's add movement. Immense complexity of movement can be modeled, but we will begin with simple "random" movement (truly random movement will added later). Because both kinds of instance needs to move, we will add a new method to `Animal`.

The movement we allow is to move to a neighboring region, if it is empty. If no neighboring locations are empty, the animal instance cannot move and remains at its present location.

Our algorithm to find a location to move to is as follows:

1. for each neighboring location:
   (a) if neighboring location is empty:
       i. move to neighboring location
       ii. break (stop looking for a place to move to)

What is a "neighboring region"? Any square shares edges with four neighbors, but also shares a corner with another four neighbors. See Figure 13.2. A reasonable argument can be made for moving only to the four neighboring regions sharing edges. However, let's allow these animals more freedom of movement and let them jump to any of the eight neighboring regions.

(2,8)	(3,8)	(4,8)
(2,7)	(3,7)	(4,7)
(2,6)	(3,6)	(4,6)

(−1,1)	(0,1)	(1,1)
(−1,0)	(x,y)	(1,0)
(−1,−1)	(0,−1)	(1,−1)

(a) Example centered on (3,7)   (b) Offset values from location x,y

FIGURE 13.2 Eight neighbors.

If an animal is at a particular location (particular coordinates), what are the coordinates of the eight neighboring locations that it might move to? Figure 13.2(b) shows the offsets of the eight neighbors. We can add the offset to an animal's current coordinates to find the coordinates of a neighbor. For example, if an animal is at (3,7), the location immediately below it has offset (0,−1) so the neighboring coordinates are (3+0,7−1) = (3,6). See Figure 13.2(a).

To implement movement, we can loop through the neighbors, but what is the best way to represent neighbors for looping? The offsets provide regularity that can be worked into a loop. Let's make a list of offsets, and then refer to the offset list each time we want to determine coordinates for a neighbor. Examining each neighbor becomes a walk through the offset list, applying each offset to an animal's current location. A refinement of our algorithm now looks like this:

1. for each offset:
   (a) neighbor_x = current_x + offset_x
   (b) neighbor_y = current_y + offset_y
   (c) if neighboring location is empty:
       i. move to neighboring location
       ii. break (stop looking for a place to move to)

We now have two new actions to consider. First, how do we know if a neighbor is empty? We can use the `animal` method previously defined for the `Island` class. That method returns an `Predator` or `Prey` instance, if it exists at the specified location.

Second, how do we move to a neighboring location? We can update the local location, the *x* and *y* coordinates in the animal instance, but we also need to update the island to keep the global information in synch. We also need to remove the animal from its current location and then register it in its new location. Therefore, the Island class needs a method to remove an animal from a given location. Removal simply sets the grid location to 0.

```
def remove(self,x,y):
    self.grid[x][y] = 0
```

With those two island methods in hand, we can write the Prey's move method and test it. This is shown in Code Listing 13.6.

Code Listing 13.6

```
def move(self):
    """Move to an open, neighboring position."""
    # neighbor offsets
    offset = [(-1,1),(0,1),(1,1),(-1,0),(1,0),(-1,-1),(0,-1),(1,-1)]
    for i in range(len(offset)):
        x = self.x + offset[i][0]   # neighboring coordinates
        y = self.y + offset[i][1]
        if self.island.animal(x,y) == 0: # neighboring spot is open
            self.island.remove(self)  # remove from current spot
            self.x = x   # new coordinates
            self.y = y
            self.island.register(self) # register new coordinates
            break   # finished with move
```

```
>>> royale = Island(5)          # create island
>>> moose1 = Prey(royale,"m1")  # create two moose
>>> moose2 = Prey(royale,"m2")
>>> print royale      # print initial state of island
.    .    .    .    .
.    .    .    .    .
.    .    m1   .    .
.    m2   .    .    .
.    .    .    .    .

>>> moose1.move()     # move each moose
>>> moose2.move()
>>> print royale      # observe island after moves
```

```
.    .    .    .    .
.   m1    .    .    .
m2   .    .    .    .
.    .    .    .    .
.    .    .    .    .
```

Note how each neighboring coordinate is calculated using offset. Each item in the offset list is a tuple: (x,y). To get the x value of offset "i" we use offset[i][0], that is, the first item of the pair. The y value is similar. Also, note how the first offset is up-and-left so each animal in the test moves up one and left one position.

Falling Off the Island?

Some of you may be asking, "How do we keep from falling off the island?" It is a good question. Some models of a "world" allow the world to "wrap" at the edges. That is, if you walk off the island going left (an x value less that 0), you reset yourself to the right (to an x value of 9, or whatever the size of the island is). Other approaches simply prevent you from making a "bad" move.

Our particular approach is the latter: we prevent a bad move. This prevention is done in the animal method of Island. If the passed arguments are out of range, the method returns a −1 indicating the problem.

Is this a good approach? See the exercises for other options.

Refinement: Time Simulation Loop

Let's add a main function to initialize our world and a loop to drive our simulation. We add a number of each of the Predator and Prey instances to an Island instance. Then, in the main loop, each trip through the loop constitutes one unit of time. In that unit of time, we give each instance the opportunity to move. We do this by moving through each grid element in the Island instance and, if the element holds an animal, allow it to move.

Here is an outline of our driving loop:

1. Create Island instance with a set number of Predator and Prey instances.
2. Loop for a specified number of time ticks:
   (a) Move each instance.

Let's take a look in Code Listing 13.7 at how that driving loop might be implemented in Python. We included a ***print*** statement so we can observe the movement in each time step. However, we only print the first two time steps here.

Code Listing 13.7

```
def main ():
    # initialization of the simulation
    royale = Island(5,1,1) # 5x5 island, 1 predator, 1 prey
    timeSteps = 20

    # run the event loop
    islandSize = royale.size()
    cnt = 0
    while cnt < timeSteps:
        print royale # print the island
        for x in range(islandSize):
            for y in range(islandSize):
                animal = royale.animal(x,y)
                if animal:
                    animal.move()
        cnt += 1
```

```
.   m   .   .   .
.   .   .   w   .
.   .   .   .   .
.   .   .   .   .
.   .   .   .   .

m   .   .   w   .
.   .   .   .   .
.   .   .   .   .
.   .   .   .   .
.   .   .   .   .
< rest of simulation not shown >
```

Notice again how animals tend to move up and to the left. That is because our move method always works through the offsets in the same order. Improving on that movement is left as an exercise.

13.4 REFINEMENT: EATING, BREEDING, AND KEEPING TIME

The next refinements introduce a number of complications that require close attention. First, we need to add breeding to the Animal class, allowing both Predator and Prey instances to breed. Second, we differentiate Prey and Predator classes by introducing the eating behavior to the `Predator` class. In our simple model only predators eat and, if they cannot eat, they starve. Third, the time span in which prey and predators breed must be different. For the simulation to work, prey must breed at a faster rate than predators—otherwise, predators quickly starve. Finally, yet another time span must be introduced in which predators must eat or, if they cannot, starve.

The ability to set these time spans is important as their values are critical for the simulation. If `Prey` instances cannot breed quickly enough, then they will *all* be consumed, ending the simulation. If not enough `Prey` instances are provided, the `Predator` instances will *all* starve and the simulation will end. Part of the interest in the simulation is examining what values will work and how they affect the simulation. We must therefore find a way for the user to easily changes these values.

Improved Time Loop

We can start by improving the main function, both for initialization of values and for introducing the new (yet unwritten) behaviors into the main loop. The new main function will now take seven parameters to establish the various aspects of the simulation. Those parameters are:

predBreed: the time span that must pass before a `Predator` instance can breed.
predStarve: the time span that a `Predator` instance must eat within, otherwise it will starve.
predInit: the number of `Predator` instances that will initially be placed on the Island.
preyBreed: the time span that must pass before a `Prey` instance can breed.
preyInit: the number of `Prey` instances that will initially be placed on the island.
size: the size of a single side of the `Island` instance (which, you remember, is a square).
ticks: the number of time "ticks" that will pass before the simulation ends.

We can also provide default values for these parameters that constitute a runnable version of the simulation. However, the user is now free to change them by simply indicating which ones to override when calling the new main function.

Remembering the Breed and Starve time spans

Where can we place the breeding and starving time spans (`predBreed`, `preyBreed`, `predStarve`)? They are set as variables in the main function (as parameters), but this does not make them available to each individual Prey and Predator instance. One option would be to set the values outside of the main function as global variables, but global variables are undesirable, for a number of reasons. Another option would be to pass them as arguments when we create `Predator` and `Prey` instances—adding another parameter to the classes. That is a good option, but let's choose yet another option that shows off some of Python's object-oriented capabilities.

Remember how a variable is searched for in a class hierarchy (see Section 12.6). First Python looks in the instance, then in the class, then up the class hierarchy through the class's parent class. If we place a variable in both the Predator and Prey *classes* (not the instance, the class), that value will be globally available to all instances of the two classes. A potential issue is that if we later change the value of that variable, it is changed for all instances, so we must be careful! That issue may be desirable or undesirable, depending on our needs. In our case, we will use these values only in the constructor (`__init__`) so any changes to the values will impact instances as they are created. We create three variables in the main function with the initial parameter values: `Predator.breedTime`, `Predator.starveTime` and `Prey.breedTime`. Because each specifies a class name (`Predator` or `Prey`), these assignments augment the respective class definitions; that is, these names are added to the class namespace. These values will now be available for all the instances of those classes when we create them.

We then extend the event loop to include eating and breeding (for `Predator` instances only in the listing). We also include at the end of the event loop a new method, `clockTick`. This method will "change" each instance based on its type. Anything that must happen every time tick for an instance is handled here. The updated driver is shown in Code Listing 13.8.

Code Listing 13.8

```python
def main(predBreed=6, predStarve=3, predInit=10, \
        preyBreed=3, preyInit=50, size=10, ticks=300):
    ''' main simulation; sets defaults, runs event loop, plots at the end
    '''
    # initialization values
    Predator.breedTime = predBreed
    Predator.starveTime = predStarve
    Prey.breedTime = preyBreed

    # make an island
    isle = Island(size,preyInit, predInit)
    print isle

    # event loop.
    # For all the ticks, for every x,y location.
    # If there is an animal there, try eat, move, breed and clockTick
    for i in range(ticks):
        for x in range(size):
            for y in range(size):
                animal = isle.animal(x,y)
                if animal:
                    if isinstance(animal,Predator):
                        animal.eat()
```

```
animal.move()
animal.breed()
animal.clockTick()
```

Updating the __init__ Methods

We need to include these new time spans in the instance. Each instance will have its own clock to keep track of its breeding time. The `Predator` instance will have a second clock to keep track of its starvation time. That is, when an instance is created its internal "clocks" need to be initialized. Both `Predator` and `Prey` instances should be initialized with a `breedClock` whose value is set to the respective class `breedTime` value. Each instance will then update its clock during every clock tick via that `clockTick` method. When their individual breeding clocks hit 0, they may breed. Similarly, `Predator` instances should be initialized with a `starveClock`, initialized to the value in `Predator.starveTime`.

The updated methods are shown Code Listing 13.9.

Code Listing 13.9

```
class Prey(Animal):
    def __init__(self, island, x=0,y=0,s="O"):
        Animal.__init__(self,island,x,y,s)
        self.breedClock = self.breedTime

class Predator(Animal):
    def __init__(self, island, x=0,y=0,s="X"):
        Animal.__init__(self,island,x,y,s)
        self.starveClock = self.starveTime
        self.breedClock = self.breedTime
```

Where did `self.breedTime` and `self.starveTime` get set? They are not assigned in the `Predator` or `Prey` class definitions. As mentioned earlier, they were added to the class namespace in the `main` function where we assigned `Predator.breedTime`, `Predator.starveTime` and `Prey.breedTime`. When we assigned those values, they were added to the respective classes' namespace, so they were available when the constructors were called. Notice how in the `Predator` and `Prey` classes the `self` in `self.breedTime` was resolved to the respective class name (`Predator` or `Prey`) when in the `main` function we assigned values to `Predator.breedTime` and `Prey.breedTime`. The starve time worked similarly.

Taking this approach with the `breedTime` and `starveTime` shows how class definitions can be dynamically augmented in Python—a powerful capability, but one that must be used carefully to ensure that readability is maintained.

Breeding

The breeding method is common to both subclasses (except for their time spans, as described in the previous section) so we place the `breed` method in `Animal`.

The rules described for the simulation said that when an animal breeds, the local neighborhood is examined for the first unoccupied location. If such a location is found, the new instance (the offspring) is placed at that location. It is unspecified what to do if an unoccupied location cannot be found—something we will have to resolve.

The "Neighbor" Method and Updating Move

Again, a little introspection is useful here. The process of looking for an unoccupied space used for breeding looks quite like the `move` method already described, which also requires an unoccupied neighbor. In fact, when we get to the `eat` method we will need to do something similar again, though in the eating case it will be to look for a neighbor that is `Prey`, not an unoccupied neighbor. It seems that we might be able to abstract out the "check neighbors" function and use it in many places.

We separate the "check neighbors" method from the existing `move` method so we can abstract the neighbor-checking aspect. That is, we *refactor* the move code! We call the new method `checkGrid`, also part of the `Animal` class. It checks the eight neighbors for a location and returns either the location or 0.

One change is that we add a new parameter to `checkGrid`, the "typeLookingFor" parameter. Instead of looking only for empty grid locations, we look for a location that contains the "typeLookingFor" type. If we want an unoccupied location, we are looking for a grid location with type *int* since an unoccupied location has a 0 value. However, we could also look for a location that has a `Prey` instance (for eating).

The updated move code and added checkGrid are shown in Code Listing 13.10.

Code Listing 13.10

```
def checkGrid(self,typeLookingFor=int):
    ''' Look in the 8 directions from the animal's location
    and return the first location that presently has an object
    of the specified type. Return 0 if no such location exists
    '''
    # neighbor offsets
```

```
        offset = [(-1,1),(0,1),(1,1),(-1,0),(1,0),(-1,-1),(0,-1),(1,-1)]
        result = 0
        for i in range(len(offset)):
            x = self.x + offset[i][0]    # neighboring coordinates
            y = self.y + offset[i][1]
            if not 0 <= x < self.island.size() or \
               not 0 <= y < self.island.size():
                continue
            if type(self.island.animal(x,y))==typeLookingFor:
                result=(x,y)
                break
        return result

def move(self):
    '''Move to an open, neighboring position '''
    location = self.checkGrid(int)
    if location:
        # print 'Move, % s, from % d,% d to % d,% d ' % \
        #        (type(self),self.x,self.y,location[0],location[1])
        self.island.remove(self)    # remove from current spot
        self.x = location[0]    # new coordinates
        self.y = location[1]
        self.island.register(self)  # register new coordinates
```

Back to Breeding

Now we have a method that can check the eight neighbors for a location of a particular type. If our instance's local `breedClock` hits 0, we will look for an open neighbor. Using the `checkGrid` method, we will look for a location that contains an *int*. If one is found, we can initialize the breed process. That requires the following steps:

- We must reset the instance's `breedClock` to the standard `breedTime` contained in the class so it may breed again.
- We must create a new instance with the proper *x* and *y* values—from the open neighboring location.
- We must register the new instance with the `Island` instance.

Interestingly, if this is an `Animal` method, how do we know which kind of instance to make, a `Predator` or a `Prey`? We want the method to be flexible so it will make either under the correct circumstances. Usefully, every instance knows the class to which it belongs, stored in the special variable `__class__`. We capture that class in the `theClass` variable, then call the constructor on that class. The `breed` method is shown in Code Listing 13.11.

Code Listing 13.11

```
def breed(self):
    ''' Breed a new Animal.  If there is room in one of the 8 locations,
    place the new Prey there.  Otherwise, you have to wait.
    '''
    if self.breedClock <= 0:
        location = self.checkGrid(int)
        if location:
            self.breedClock = self.breedTime
            theClass = self.__class__
            newAnimal = theClass(self.island,x=location[0],y=location[1])
            self.island.register(newAnimal)
```

Eating

Interestingly, the eat method has much in common with both the move and breed method given the existence of the checkGrid method. There are some differences, though. This eating method *must* be in the Predator class, as Prey instances are not allowed to eat. Further, there is a little more manipulation that must be done to deal with eating.

Remember the rules. A Predator instance can look in the local neighborhood for a Prey instance. If one is found, the Predator instance moves to that location and removes the Prey instance from the Island instance. In particular, the eating method must do the following:

- Call the checkGrid method passing the Prey class as the "typeLookingFor" argument.
- If a location is found with a Prey instance:
  - Remove the Prey instance from the island.
  - Remove the Predator instance—the instance indicated by the *self* variable, from the Island instance.
  - Update the Predator instance to the new *x* and *y* coordinates, the coordinates of the Prey that was just removed.
  - Re-register the Predator instance, now at the new location.
  - Set the starveClock of the Predator instance to the original Predator. starveTime value (so it will not starve and will continue to operate).
- If no Prey instance is found, the method does nothing.

The code for eating is shown in Code Listing 13.12.

Code Listing 13.12

```python
def eat(self):
    ''' Predator looks for one of the eight locations with Prey. If found,
    moves to that location, updates the starve clock, removes the Prey.
    '''
    location = self.checkGrid(Prey)
    if location:
        self.island.remove(self.island.animal(location[0],location[1]))
        self.island.remove(self)
        self.x=location[0]
        self.y=location[1]
        self.island.register(self)
        self.starveClock=self.starveTime
```

The Tick of the Clock

Every pass through the event loop should update each instance's present status. In particular, the individual clocks that were initialized to their class values (breed and starve times) must be decremented. Therefore, we need a method for each class that updates the internal instance clocks on each tick of the clock. We create two methods in each subclass, called clockTick.

The Prey clockTick decrements the instance's breedClock. The Predator clockTick method decrements its breedClock, but it also checks to see whether the starveClock has hit 0. If so, then the instance has starved and must be removed.

The two methods are shown in the following code:

Code Listing 13.13

```python
class Prey(Animal):
    # ...
    def clockTick(self):
        '''Prey updates only its local breed clock
        '''
        self.breedClock -= 1

class Predator(Animal):
    # ...
```

```
def clockTick(self):
    ''' Predator updates both breeding and starving
    '''
    self.breedClock -= 1
    self.starveClock -= 1
    if self.starveClock <= 0:
        self.island.remove(self)
```

13.5 REFINEMENTS

We have sketched out a fairly good solution to the predator–prey simulation, but the astute reader may have noticed some problems. We examine some issues in the following sections.

Refinement: How Many Times to Move?

Remember our picture of the eight neighbors available for a local move? (Figure 13.2)
Our present event loop does the following:

- It moves through the Island instance a row a time, through each y value.
- If there is an animal instance in that row (the x value) and y value, it gives that animal an opportunity to:
  - Potentially eat, if it is a Predator instance.
  - Move if it can
  - Breed if it can
  - Do whatever must be done to the instance every clock tick

If our animal moves up or to the left, things seem to work fine. But what happens if our animal moves down or to the right? In those cases, either x is incremented (moving down) or y is incremented (moving right). Lets look at the "moving down" case. From wherever the instance starts, it moves to a new location with an x value one greater. The event loop processes x and y values by incrementing first all the y values in a row, then incrementing the x value to begin a new row. This ordering means that the instance we just moved will be given the opportunity to move again because it moved into the next row. If it moves down again, it will get yet another chance to move. Thus, a single instance may move multiple times during the same clock tick. A Predator instance could similarly eat multiple times, if—every time it eats—it eats going down or to the right.

The result may or may not be the behavior we wanted, but in truth it makes sense to have one move (eat) per clock tick per instance. Each instance should move (eat) at most one time-event clock tick. The problem is really one of isolating the global state, the grid of Predator and Prey instances, in time. Each clock tick should have its own global state, but in the implementation we present, we have a common global state across all ticks of the clock.

How can we repair this? There are a number of approaches we might take. We could:

- Have *two* grids, one for the present clock tick and one for the next. Moves would be from the location in the present grid to the future grid of the next clock tick, as would eating. When the present clock tick ends the new grid becomes the present grid and a fresh empty grid, created for the next clock tick.
- Create a list of instances from the global state and move only instances from the list. Once moved, they are removed from the list and not moved again during this clock tick.
- Mark each instance with a flag, indicating movement. During the present clock tick, if an instance is moved, its flag is changed. All of the movement methods pay attention to the flag and will not move it again if the flag is set. All the movement flags must be cleared on every instance after the present clock tick.

Each approach has its advantages and disadvantages. The multiple-grid approach is more realistic, and more in tune with having multiple global states for different time periods. However, the changes to the present code to include multiple grids would be extensive. Moreover, instances that cannot move must still be copied into the new grid. The list approach is easy for movement, but complicated for eating. If a `Predator` instance eats a `Prey` instance, we have to search through the list to make sure it is also removed. Marking is conceptually simple and requires minimal code updates, but it is time consuming. We have to manipulate all the instances on every cycle to clear their move flags.

Ultimately, we chose the marking approach because it fit best with our existing design. To implement it, we need to make changes in the following locations:

- The `Animal __init__` method must add a new variable `moved` to every instance and initialize it to *False* (the instance has not been moved).
- The `move` and `eat` methods must be modified to check whether the instance has its moved flag set to *True*. If so, it should not be moved again. If the flag is not set, the instance can be moved and its `moved` flag should be set to *True* (so it cannot move again during this clock tick).
- The `Island` class gains a new method, `clearAllMovedFlags`. This method clears the `moved` flag of every instance on the island to *False*.
- The main loop must call the `clearAllMovedFlags` at the beginning of every clock tick.

Refinement: Graphing Population Size

One of the original ideas of predator–prey simulations is to follow the change in population size during the course of the simulation. Watching the print outs of the `Island` instance does not convey that well. It would be useful to add graphing to observe the changes. Matplotlib to the rescue!

In this situation, it would be useful to plot both the `Predator` and `Prey` population counts during the course of the run. Matplotlib works best by collecting the *y* values of each clock tick. We do so for both `Predator` and `Prey` by creating two lists, `predCounts` and `preyCounts`. These lists will contain the counts of each population at a particular clock tick: index 0 will have the value for clock tick 0, and so on.

We need methods to actually find the counts for both Predator and Prey on the Island. We add two methods, `predatorCount()` and `preyCount()`. Each will count the number of each type of instance and return the value. At the end of every clock tick we query the island for the counts and append them to the appropriate list.

Once the counts are collected and the simulation ends, we plot each list individually and then display the results.

FIGURE 13.3 Graph of population sizes using our simulation

A typical graph is shown in Figure 13.3 for the following parameter settings (the defaults for the main function): `predBreed=6`, `predStarve=3`, `predInit=10`, `preyBreed=3`, `preyInit=50`, `size=10`, `ticks=300`. The population swings are more pronounced for the `Prey` instances than the `Predator` instances, which is typical of the real situation. Note that when the `Predator` population rises (around tick 160), the `Prey` population falls dramatically. This results in `Predator` loss and `Prey` recovery, just as predicted!

The final code is available online.

13.6 CONCLUSION

In this chapter, we developed a predator–prey simulation simulator to illustrate the use of classes in problem solving.

Exercises

1. Add randomness to the direction chosen in `move`.

2. Have `Prey` move away from neighboring `Predators`.

3. Add the ability to look two "hops" away to see `Predators` or `Prey`, and move toward or away from them as appropriate.

4. Adjust survival rules so `Predators` starve quickly.

5. Adjust survival rules so `Prey` reproduce quickly.

6. `initAnimals` can be inefficient, especially if the island is quite full. Improve it.

7. Test the code to determine situations in which multiple moves can occur.

8. Implement one of the `move` improvements:
   - Multiple grids
   - List
   - Marking

PART 5

Becoming a Better Programmer

CHAPTER 14

Exceptions and Exception Handling

All input is evil, until proven otherwise.

Michael Howard & David LeBlanc, *Writing Secure Code*[1]

Most security failures in software come from failing to abide by the Howard and LeBlanc observation that: all input is evil until proven otherwise. Secure programs protect themselves from evil, bad, and erroneous input. It is through "holes" provided via input routines, or passages directly into your code, that most security break-ins occur. Protecting your code's input points protects your code from being used in ways you did not intend!

The consistency of Python's input handling helps to some extent with this problem. The fact that all input is a string requires the developer to manipulate that input after receiving it rather than having the system do it by default. For example, if the string must be converted to some other type, the developer can protect their code using tools like *exception handling*. By using these tools, the developer can confirm that manipulation of the provided input, such as conversion, worked correctly. If not, the developer can either indicate corrective action (reprompting the user for input, recontacting the server for a connection) or even ignore the input.

14.1 INTRODUCTION

Up to this point, the constructs we have used to modify normal sequential control flow are statements such as **if**, **for**, and **while**. These statements execute their associated suites either conditionally or repetitively. A slightly different form of control modification can

---

[1] Michael Howard and David LeBlanc, *Writing Secure Code* (Washington: Microsoft Press, 2003).

occur with exception handlers. An *exception* is basically a runtime error, a request by the code to perform an operation that simply cannot be done. For example, if we try to execute the statement *int*('abc'), Python can run the statement; it is syntactically correct, but the result requested cannot be calculated. What is an integer representation of the string 'abc'? Python does not know either. Here is a session showing this result:

```
>>> someStr = raw_input("Enter a number: ")
Enter a number: abc    # oops! when asked for a number we entered a string
>>> int(someStr)       # a programmer expecting a number might try this
                       # and get an error
Traceback (most recent call last):
  File "<pyshell#1>", line 1, in <module>
    int(someStr)
ValueError: invalid literal for int() with base 10: 'abc'
```

At this point, you have seen these errors enough to know what happens when they occur. Python stops executing the code at the point of the error, prints the line where the problem occurred, then prints something about the error it encountered. Control then returns to the Python shell, waiting for us to fix the problem!

What Python and many other modern programming languages provide is a way for the developer to *handle* the error. This means that the developer is given the opportunity to provide code that is invoked when the error occurs. When the programmer provides handlers for errors, Python does *not* simply stop running code whenever an error occurs; rather, Python searches for programmer handlers and, if found, lets that code handle that error. If the developer provided such code, Python passes control to the developer's error-handling code. If no such handler exists, Python stops, as we have seen so many times before.

One thing to notice in the previous example session is that every error has a name: ValueError in this case. The spelling is particular and case is important! Noticing the error name in an error report is useful for distinguishing the kind of error that occurred so that we may choose to handle it. For example, if one wants to handle the error that occurs when trying to convert a string to an integer, you now know that Python labels such errors as "ValueError."

Events

Besides input and related errors, another major type of exception that occurs in programs comes from *events* that need to be handled. These are not errors, but "things that happened" and that need to be addressed. Handling events as they occur is an important task. For example, in an operating system an event occurs every time someone clicks a mouse button. The operating system, also a program (and typically a very large one), may be working on something else such as processing information coming from a network when the mouse-click event happens. However, the mouse-click event needs attention right now! The operating system needs to divert its "attention" to that mouse-click event now (waiting a long time to deal with a mouse click would not be good for the user). Once it's finished handling that mouse click, it can go back to deal with other events (keyboard clicks, network information arrival, video updates, etc.). Exception handling is a way for the developer to handle such an event. In this chapter, we will focus on exceptions with respect to errors. However, the topic of *event-driven* programming is very important in computer science.

14.2 BASIC EXCEPTION HANDLING

The basic flow of exception handing is as follows:

1. Keep "watch" on a particular suite of code.
2. If an error or exception occurs within the "watched" suite, stop executing the code at the error line and abandon the rest of the suite. If unexecuted lines of watched code remain, they will be ignored.
3. *Raise* (let it be known that) the particular exception that was encountered.
4. Look for a "catcher" that can catch (handle) that exception.
5. If a handler is found, jump to that code that handles the exception; otherwise, let Python handle it (which means print the typical error message, stop the program, and go back to the interpreter).

The basic syntax of Python exception handling is called a **try-except** suite:

```
try:
    # code to watch here
except aParticularErrorName:
    # some code to handle the named error, if it occurs
```

There are two parts to the handling of exceptions:

try suite: the suite of code after **try**. It contains the code we want to watch to see whether any exception occurs. If an exception occurs anywhere in the **try** suite, Python will halt execution of the suite at the error line and look for some exception code to handle the particular error that occurred. If no handler is found, Python will halt the entire program and print the exception.

exception suite: the suite of code associated with an exception—almost always a particular exception as indicated by Python's standard error names, e.g., ValueError, KeyError, etc. There may be multiple exception suites, with each one written to handle a particular kind of error that might have happened in the **try** suite.

If no error occurs, the **try** suite finishes normally; all exception suites are ignored (not executed) and control passes to whatever code follows the **try-except** group. The flow is illustrated in Figure 14.1.

FIGURE 14.1 Exception flow.

A Simple Example

Let's take a look at an example that shows the flow of control. Code Listing 14.1 prompts for two integers where the first (the dividend) is to be divided by the second (the divisor). Two errors are possible here. The first occurs if the provided input cannot be converted to a floating-point number: a `ValueError`. The second occurs if the divisor value is a 0, Python raises a `ZeroDivisionError` exception. The ***print*** statements at the beginning and the end of the ***try*** suite help indicate what parts of the ***try*** suite are executed. The code also provides two `except` suites—one for each of those specific errors. In this simple example, the handling code simply prints that the error occurs. The code ends with a ***print*** statement, something to illustrate what gets executed **after** the ***try-except*** group is finished.

Code Listing 14.1

```
try:
    print 'Entering the try suite'
    dividend = float(raw_input("Provide a dividend to divide:"))
    divisor = float(raw_input("Provide a divisor to divide by:"))
    result = dividend/divisor
    print '%2.2f divided by %2.2f yields %2.2f'%(dividend,divisor,result)
except ZeroDivisionError:
    print "Divide by 0 error"
except ValueError:
    print "Value error, couldn't convert to a float"

print 'Continuing on with the rest of the program'
```

```
>>>
Entering the try suite
Provide a dividend to divide:10
Provide a divisor to divide by:2
10.00 divided by 2.00 yields 5.00
Continuing on with the rest of the program
>>> ================================ RESTART =================================
>>>
Entering the try suite
Provide a dividend to divide:10
Provide a divisor to divide by:a
Value error, couldn't convert to a float
Continuing on with the rest of the program
>>> ================================ RESTART =================================
>>>
Entering the try suite
Provide a dividend to divide:10
Provide a divisor to divide by:0
Divide by 0 error
Continuing on with the rest of the program
>>> ================================ RESTART =================================
>>>
Entering the try suite
Provide a dividend to divide:

Traceback (most recent call last):
  File "/Users/bill/book/v3.5/chapterExceptions/divide.py", line 3, in <module>
    dividend = float(raw_input("Provide a dividend to divide:"))
KeyboardInterrupt
>>>
```

Four examples of input are provided for this code, shown in the previous session. It is useful to go through the four examples and follow the control of the program:

No Error: The input values are 10 and 2. This session has no errors. The entire **try** suite is executed (Lines 2-6), the two exception suites are skipped, and the code finishes by executing Line 12.

Value Error: The input values are 10 and 'a'. In this case the conversion of the second value to a float will generate an exception. The flow of control gets through lines 1–4. Line 4 ends in an exception, meaning that lines 5–6 of the **try** suite are skipped. Control then skips to Line 9, the ValueError handler, and executes Line 10, the exception suite. The **try-except** group ends and the program finishes by executing Line 12.

Zero Division Error: The input values are 10 and 0. The **try** suite executes lines 2–5. Line 5 results in an exception, meaning that line 6 of the **try** suite is skipped. Control skips to Line 7, the ZeroDivisionError handler, which then executes Line 8,

```
+– Exception
    +– GeneratorExit                        |  |   +– IndexError
    +– StopIteration                        |  |   +– KeyError
    +– StandardError                        |  +– MemoryError
    |   +– ArithmeticError                  |  +– NameError
    |   |   +– FloatingPointError           |  |   +– UnboundLocalError
    |   |   +– OverflowError                |  +– ReferenceError
    |   |   +– ZeroDivisionError            |  +– RuntimeError
    |   +– AssertionError                   |  |   +– NotImplementedError
    |   +– AttributeError                   |  +– SyntaxError
    |   +– EnvironmentError                 |  |   +– IndentationError
    |   |   +– IOError                      |  |       +– TabError
    |   |   +– OSError                      |  +– SystemError
    |   |       +– WindowsError             |  +– TypeError
    |   |       +– VMSError                 |  +– ValueError
    |   +– EOFError                         |  |   +– UnicodeError
    |   +– ImportError                      |  |       +– UnicodeDecodeError
    |   +– LookupError                      |  |       +– UnicodeEncodeError
                                            |  |       +– UnicodeTranslateError
```

FIGURE 14.2 Python exceptions.

the exception suite. The **try-except** group ends and the program finishes by executing line 12.

Keyboard Interrupt: Lines 1–3 are executed. At the first prompt for input, the user enters a Control-C (holding down the Ctrl key and then typing C). This is an event sent to the program to indicate "stop processing," resulting in an exception, the KeyInterrupt exception. The lines 3–6 of the **try** suite are skipped. Python finds no handler for this exception, so Python halts the program with an error and prints the error message shown.

An obvious question concerns the error names. Specifically, where do we find that ZeroDivisionError is the specific exception name for dividing by zero? Figure 14.2 lists the Python exceptions.[2] However, the easiest way to find the error is to simply cause the error and see what Python prints. For example, here is a Python shell generating a couple of errors:

```
>>> 1/0

Traceback (most recent call last):
  File "<pyshell#9>", line 1, in <module>
    1/0
```

_____

[2] http://www.python.org/doc/current/lib/module-exceptions.html

```
ZeroDivisionError: integer division or modulo by zero
>>> open('junk')

Traceback (most recent call last):
  File "<pyshell#10>", line 1, in <module>
    open('junk')
IOError: [Errno 2] No such file or directory: 'junk'
```

Notice that the beginning of the last line of the error message states the error name. In fact, this session indicates unhandled exceptions: the exception was raised, but no handler was provided, so Python eventually raises the error to the shell and halts the program.

It is legal to have an exception handler with no particular exception name specified. Such a handler will catch *all* exceptions, but that is generally not a good idea. Consider what that handler must do. Any error that occurs it must handle. That is as general a problem as just passing control to Python and the shell. Specific exception handlers can be created with strategies to handle specific exceptions. A general exception handler can do very little, as it does not have enough specific information about the error.

14.3 A PHILOSOPHY CONCERNING EXCEPTIONS

There are really two ways to look at dealing with errors, both of which can be summarized with pithy expressions: "Easier to Ask Forgiveness than Permission," EAFP, or "Look Before You Leap," LBYL. First-time programmers, when they think of dealing with errors at all, tend to take the LBYL approach. In this approach, the programmer will provide conditional expressions that test for all the possible error conditions that might occur and, if none are found, then the associated code is run. However, as you gain more experience with programming, you might find EAFP to be easier to work with and, subsequently, to read: try to do something, whatever it is, but catch any potential errors that occur and handle them. It is a kind of "clean up any messes" approach. It focuses on creating good code to solve the problem and then, in a separate construct, deal with any errors. This means that EAFP better separates the main intent of the code from the error conditions that might arise.

Take a look at two examples in Code Listing 14.2 that convert a string value to an int using the two different philosophies.[3]

Code Listing 14.2

```
# check whether int conversion will raise an error, two examples.
# Python Idioms, http://jaynes.colorado.edu/PythonIdioms.html
```

---

[3] Taken from the *Python idioms page*, http://jaynes.colorado.edu/PythonIdioms.html. This information is now part of the PyCogent Paper: PyCogent: a toolkit for making sense from sequence. <http://www.ncbi.nlm.nih.gov/pubmed/17708774?ordinalpos=2&itool= EntrezSystem2.PEntrez.Pubmed.Pubmed_ResultsPanel.Pubmed_DefaultReportPanel.Pubmed_RVDocSum>

```
#LBYL, test for the problematic conditions
if not isinstance(s, str) or not s.isdigit:
    return None
elif len(s) > 10:     #too many digits for int conversion
    return None
else:
    return int(str)

#EAFP, just try it, clean up any mess with handlers
try:
    return int(str)
except (TypeError, ValueError, OverflowError): #int conversion failed
    return None
```

Which approach seems more readable? The EAFP is more succinct and the list of errors being caught is clearly labeled. We can certainly understand the other, LBYL, approach, but EAFP seems clearer.

In general, if you are adding code to test for possible error conditions, it makes sense to just *try* what you intend and then *handle* the errors you are concerned about. That is what **try-except** groups are for.

14.4 EXCEPTION: ELSE AND FINALLY

Another clause that can be added to a **try-except** group is the **finally** clause. The finally suite is run as you exit the **try-except** group *no matter whether an error occurred or not*. If something absolutely, positively has to be done, whether an error occurs not, this is the place for that code. For example, if you are working with files, the file should be closed at the end of processing, regardless of whether an error occurred. The finally clause gives you an opportunity to clean up as the **try-except** group ends.

The **try-except** group also can have an **else** clause. The else suite is executed only if the try suite does *not* encounter an error. One can think of the try as a kind of conditional execution: if an exception occurs, you jump to the exception handler, otherwise (else) you jump to the else suite and perform a "normal" exit from the group.

Example: Refactoring the Reprompting of a File Name

In Section 9.8, we provided a glimpse of how you might use exceptions to reprompt for a file name when the user-provided name does not exist. Here we refactor that code to be more complete and show how the **else** and **finally** clauses can be used. Assume that a file named "test.txt" exists with the following content:

> This is a test.
> It is only a test.

As before, the goal of this code is to repeatedly ask the user for a file name until the name provided can be opened. Once opened, the file is processed and subsequently the file is closed.

We create a **while** loop that loops forever, **while True:**, requiring that a **break** statement occur somewhere in the subsequent code so that the loop can end. In the loop, we prompt for a file name to open.

The **try** suite monitors the *open* function. Either the file opening succeeds or it does not. That is, there are two possible cases: the error case or the success case.

ERROR CASE: If the *open* fails, it raises an IOError. Control jumps to the **except** suite, which prints an error message, finishes, and control moves to the **finally** clause (finally is *always* executed) where the finally suite is executed. What we would like to do here is close the file that was opened, but in this case (the error case), no file was opened and the variable dataFile has not been assigned a value. Nonetheless, in EAFP tradition, we close it anyway, but monitor *that* closure in a **try** suite. If the closure fails, as it does here, we catch the error, in this case a NameError because the variable dataFile has not yet been assigned a value (because of the opening error). The **except** suite prints a message and the loop continues, reprompting for a file to open.

SUCCESS CASE: If the *open* succeeds, dataFile is assigned the file descriptor and no exception is raised. Therefore, control moves to the **else** clause and executes the **else** suite. The **else** suite executes the processFile function, which prepends the line number to each line of the file and prints the new line. When processFile ends, control flows back to the **else** clause of the **try-except** group, which executes a **break**. The **break** will end the loop, but as always, the finally suite must be executed before the **try-except** group can end. The **finally** suite executes dataFile.*close*(), which now succeeds, because dataFile was defined by the assignment in the open process earlier. The **finally** suite finishes, the **break** leaves the loop, and the last **print** line of the code is executed.

Code Listing 14.3

```
# all aspects of exceptions

def processFile(dataFile):
    """Print each line of a file with its line number."""
    count = 1
```

```
    for line in dataFile:
        print 'Line ' + str(count) + ': ' + line.strip()
        count = count + 1

while True:        # loop forever: until "break" is encountered
    fileName = raw_input('Input a file to open: ')
    try:
        dataFile = open(fileName)
    except IOError:                        # we get here if file open failed
        print 'Bad file name; try again'
    else:
        # no exception so let's process the file
        print 'Processing file',fileName
        processFile(dataFile)
        break        # exit "while" loop (but do "finally" block first)
    finally:                # we get here whether there was an exception or not
        try:
            dataFile.close()
        except NameError:
            print 'Going around again'

print 'Line after the try-except group'
```

```
>>>
Input a file to open: aaaa            # bad input raises exception
Bad file name, try again             # line from except block
Going around again...                # line from finally block
Input a file to open: test.txt       # good file name this time
Processing the file test.txt         # in else block we call function to process file
Line 1: This is a test.
Line 2: It is only a test.
Line after the try/except block.   # line after try/except block
```

14.5 EXCEPTION USAGE

Check Input

We began this section with the Howard and LeBlanc observation that "all input is evil until proven otherwise." Therefore, all input should be checked before usage. We have shown that exceptions are useful for checking that input data is of a known type, but they can be further used to check that data is in an acceptable range (e.g., greater than zero, lowercase), have the correct file suffix, etc. Up to this point, the code in this book did not typically check input in order to keep the code short and readable, but this choice does not mean that such checks are not important. They are!

PROGRAMMING TIP

Check all input.
All converted input should be checked using *try-except* blocks. It generally works best within a *while* loop so that you can keep asking until the user gets it right as shown in Code Listing 14.4.

Code Listing 14.4

```
while True:      # loop until input is good
    try:
        valueStr = raw_input("Input integer: ")
        valueInt = int(valueStr)  # convert to int (possible exception)
        break    # success! so break out of while loop
    except ValueError:
        print "Bad input."
```

```
>>>
Input integer: x
Bad input.
Input integer: 2.4
Bad input.
Input integer: 5
```

Check File Opening

Using *try-except* blocks for correct opening of files is another good programming practice. In this case, it is the easiest way to ensure that a file has been properly opened before proceeding. If you do not check, an attempt to access a file that hasn't been opened will result in an error that halts the program.

PROGRAMMING TIP

Check all file openings.
Put all file openings into a *try-except* block within a *while* loop so that you can keep asking until the user gets it right as shown in Code Listing 14.5.

Code Listing 14.5

```
while True:     # loop until file is correctly opened
    try:
        fileName = raw_input("Open file: ")
        dataFile = open(fileName,"r") # open a file (possible exception)
        break     # break out of while loop
    except IOError:
        print "Bad file name."
```

```
>>>
Open file: xxx
Bad file name.
Open file: test.txt
```

14.6 MORE ON EXCEPTIONS

Raise

It is possible for you to *raise* an exception anytime you wish, instead of having Python raise it for you. Simply use the keyword ***raise*** followed by the exception name:

$$\textit{raise}\ \text{exceptionName}$$

Raising an exception allows you to also pass a particular value to the exception handler. In Code Listing 14.6, we use an ***if*** statement to identify the problem and then use the ***raise*** command to pass the offending value. This example is not compelling, because in this case a simple ***if-else*** would suffice. However, in a very large program, the except block may be in a distant calling function.

Code Listing 14.6

```
valueStr = raw_input("Input an integer: ")
try:
    if valueStr.isdigit():
        valueInt = int(valueStr)
    else:
        raise ValueError, valueStr     # raise an exception here!
```

```
except ValueError:
    print "Conversion to int Error: ", valueStr
```

Check Yourself: Basic Exception Control

1. Answer the questions regarding the following program:

```
myDict = {'bill':100, 'zach':'hi mom', 'laurie':'bye mom'}

try:
    result = ''
    theKey = raw_input("Give me a key:")
    val = myDict[theKey]
    result = result + val
except KeyError:
    result = 'hi mom'
except TypeError:
    result = '100'
else:
    result = result+" "+'all done'
finally:
    if result.isdigit():
        result = int(result) + 10

print result                # Line 1
```

(a) What output does Line 1 produce with the input 'bill'?
(b) What output does Line 1 produce with the input 'zach'?
(c) What output does Line 1 produce with the input 'fred'?
(d) What output does Line 1 produce with the input 0?

Create Your Own

It is also possible to create your own exceptions. In Python, exceptions are classes. To make your own exception, you must create a subclass of one of the existing exception classes shown in Figure 14.2. By using inheritance, all the essential features of exceptions are preserved. However, the new exception provides a way for you to communicate unique errors for user-built classes. Though this can be done in more detail, all that is really required is to make a subclass of an existing exception class. No body is required of this new class. Thus the expression **class** NewException (Exception): **pass** is sufficient to make a new exception. The class definition is empty (hence the keyword **pass**), but the characteristics of base Exception class are inherited by NewException.

14.7 EXAMPLE: PASSWORD MANAGER

The following example creates a new class that is a password manager. It can be used to validate a user's name and password or to add a new user to the password database. For simplicity's sake, in this example we do not securely manage our password database. It is just a dictionary. However, it would not be too much work to import an encryption module and securely manage the dictionary data. We leave that as an exercise for those interested.

The code for the passManager class is shown in Code Listing 14.7.

Code Listing 14.7

```
import string

# define our own exceptions
class NameException (Exception):
    ''' For malformed names '''
    pass
class PasswordException (Exception):
    ''' For bad password '''
    pass
class UserException (Exception):
    ''' Raised for existing or missing user '''
    pass


def checkPass(passStr, targetStr):
    """Return True, if password contains characters from target."""
    for char in passStr:
        if char in targetStr:
            return True
    return False


class passManager(object):
    """A class to manage a dictionary of passwords with error checking."""
    def __init__(self, initDict=None):
        if initDict==None:
            self.passDict={}
```

```
        else:
            self.passDict = initDict.copy()

    def dumpPasswords(self):
30      return self.passDict.copy()

    def addUser(self,user):
        """Add good user name and strong password to password dictionary."""
        if not isinstance(user,str) or not user.isalnum():
35          raise NameException
        if user in self.passDict:
            raise UserException
        passStr = raw_input('New password:')
        # ensure strong password
40      if not (checkPass(passStr, string.digits) and\
                    checkPass(passStr, string.uppercase) and\
                    checkPass(passStr, string.punctuation)):
            raise PasswordException

45  def validate(self,user):
        """Return True, if valid user and password."""
        if not isinstance(user,str) or not user.isalnum():
            raise NameException
        if user not in self.passDict:
50          raise UserException
        passWd = raw_input('Passwd:')
        return self.passDict[user]==passWd
```

Here are some notes about this class:

Lines 4–12: Define three new exceptions. The doc strings indicate their purpose.

Lines 14–19: The function checkPass looks to see whether parameter passStr contains any character of the parameter targetStr.

Lines 23–27: The __init__ method takes a default argument for the password dictionary, None, which can then be checked for in the code (see the programming tip in Section 7.3). Using None and then checking for its use avoids the issues of modifying a mutable default value. If a parameter value is provided, it should be a dictionary and we make a shallow copy of it. Given that all the values should be strings, this approach should be sufficient.

Lines 32–43: The addUser method ensures three conditions. First, the user parameter should be a string and consist only of letters or digits. Second, the user being added should not already be in the dictionary. Third, the password provided should have at least one uppercase letter, at least one punctuation mark and at least one digit.

The second and third conditions are checked using checkPass and the appropriate string from the string module. Any violation of these conditions raises one of our user-defined errors.

Lines 45–52: The validate method does most of the checks done in addUser. It makes sure that the name is a valid name (only letters and digits), and it makes sure the user *is* in the dictionary. Finally, it returns a Boolean indicating whether the dictionary password matches the provided password.

Code Listing 14.8 utilizes passManager for validating a user. Notice that, except for the return value from validate, most of the interaction between the main program and the module is via monitoring of exceptions. The comments should be fairly helpful, so we point out only the most interesting points.

Code Listing 14.8

```python
from pmModule import *

def main ():
    pm = passManager({'bill':'$4Donuts', 'rich':'123ABC!'})

    maxTries = 3  # three tries allowed
    cnt = maxTries
    result = False
    while cnt > 0 and not result:
        userStr = raw_input('User name:')
        try:
            result = pm.validate(userStr) # validate prompts for password
        except NameException:
            print 'Bad name!'
        except UserException:
            if raw_input('No such name, add as new user (Y or y)? ') in 'Yy':
                try:
                    pm.addUser(userStr)
                    # only get here if no exceptions raised in addUser
                    result = True
                except NameException:
                    print 'Bad name!'
                except UserException:
                    print 'User already exists!'
                except PasswordException:
                    print 'Bad password!'
        finally:
```

```
            cnt -=1
      if not result:
30          print 'Session timed out.'
      else:
          print 'Welcome user',userStr
```

Line 1: We import, using the ***from*** statement, the new exception classes, and the
passManager class.

Lines 4–8: We establish some variables. We instantiate a passManager and pass a
dictionary as a initial value. Again, this is not a secure password approach, but it is
simple and useful for this example. The maximum times a password can be guessed is
three times (stored in cnt). The result is what is returned from validate.

Lines 9–12: As long as the number of tries is greater than 0 and result is *False*
(validation has not yet succeeded), we will try to validate the user. Note that if
validate raises an exception, result will not be set to *True*.

Lines 15–26: This userException occurs if no such user exists in the passManager
as determined by the validate call of Line 12. In this case, we provide the option to add
a new user. We add a new ***try-except*** block to add the new user. If addUser
does not raise an exception, then result will be set to *True*.

Line 27: The ***finally*** statement goes with the outer ***try-except*** block. No matter
what finally ensues, every time through the loop cnt is decremented, so that only three
tries are allowed.

The following session shows a basic interaction of the two modules:

```
>>> import pmMain
>>> pmMain.main()
User name:bill
Passwd:$4Donuts
Welcome user bill
>>> pmMain.main()
User name:fred
No such name, add as new user (Y or y)? y
New password:abc123
Bad password!
User name:fred
No such name, add as new user (Y or y)? y
New password:Good4You!
Welcome user fred
>>>
```

Summary

In this chapter, we introduced a new flow of control: exceptions. It is particularly useful for ensuring that input is valid. We provided a couple of code snippets for checking input and checking file openings.

Exercises

1. A `KeyError` exception exists if you attempt to access a dictionary with an invalid key. Write a small program that illustrates using a ***try-except*** block to handle a `KeyError` exception. Create a small dictionary and write a special error message if an attempt is made to access the dictionary with an invalid key.

2. Given dictionary D, rewrite this code using exceptions:

```
if x in D:
    D[x] += 1
else:
    D[x] = 1
```

3. Write a function that takes a string of words and integers as an argument and returns two lists: one a list of the words, the other a list of the integers. Use exceptions to distribute words and integers to their respective lists.

4. Write a program that prompts for three numbers. Divide the first number by the second number and add that result to the third number. Using exceptions check for the following errors: IOError, ValueError, and ZeroDivisionError.

5. Write a function named `safe_input(prompt,type)` that works like the Python *raw_input* function, except that it only accepts the specified type of input. The function takes two arguments:

   • prompt: *str*
   • type: *int, float, str*

   The function will keep prompting for input until correct input of the specified type is entered.

   The function returns the input. If the input was specified to be a number (*float* or *int*), the value returned will be of the correct type; that is, the function will perform the conversion.

   The default for a prompt is the empty string. The default for the type is string.

6. Write a function named `promptOpen` that prompts for a filename and repeatedly attempts to read the specified file until a correctly specified file has been entered. The function takes one mode argument, `'r'` or `'w'`, and returns the file handle that *open* returns.

7. Phone Records.

Telecom operators such as AT&T or Verizon maintain records of all the calls made using their network (named "call detail records" or CDRs). Usually, the CDRs are collected at the routers within the telecom networks, and millions of CDRs are stored in a single file. Although most of the records are in correct format, some records (a handful) either do not contain all the requisite fields or contain garbled data; these records cause problems during any data processing.

Consider a simplified version of a CDR that has only four fields: date and time of the call, source number, destination number, and duration of the call. Create a comma-separated file containing multiple CDRs. In that file include some erroneous or incomplete records that:

- Do not have duration of the call (no duration, no billing!).
- Have garbled phone numbers like 12-345-6789 or 123-45?-6789.

Also, create some records in which the source or destination number is recorded as null (this happens sometimes if it was an international call). It's a valid record. Create some records in which the comma is missing between the source and destination numbers, e.g., 123-456-7890 987-654-3210.

Note: if a comma is missing between the source and destination or they have null values, you can still get the required information and it should not be counted as an erroneous record.

Also, create another file containing all the North American area codes (see http://www.bennetyee.org/ucsd-pages/area.html).

(a) Find the call that had the longest duration and find its source and destination regions.

(b) Find the number of garbled or incomplete CDRs.

(c) How many international calls were made?

(d) List of all calls made on a particular date.

(e) List of all calls made during a particular hour.

(f) Optional: plot a distribution of the arrival times of the calls. This plot could help in identifying busy and idle periods of the network.

Use exceptions (IndexError, ValueError, TypeError) to handle erroneous CDRs rather than checking individual cases using if-else constructs.

CHAPTER 15

Testing

15.1 WHY TESTING?

Why should a book on introductory computer programming be interested in talking about testing? In Chapter 14 we, talked about the need to protect ourselves from "evil" input. We could not count on users providing the "correct" input requested for our programs (wrong type, wrong length, wrong number of elements, etc.), so we have to check to make sure their potentially incorrect input does not crash our program. But what other sources of error must we protect our programs from? How about ourselves—the programmers!

Programmers make mistakes when writing programs. These mistakes come in many different forms: assumptions about the data, misunderstanding of the algorithm, incorrect calculations, poorly designed data structures, and—best of all—just plain blunders. Testing is a way to protect us from ourselves. If we make a mistake, it would be most useful to be informed *before* we release code for use. Without some form of testing, how will we ever really know how well our program works?

Kinds of Errors

There are at least three classes of errors:

- Syntactic errors
- Runtime errors
- Design errors

Syntactic errors are the easiest to detect and are detected for us by the interpreter. They are errors in the use of the programming language. Examples of syntactic errors include forgetting a colon (:) at the beginning of a suite, a misplaced parenthesis, and a misspelling of a Python command—the list is long. When a program is run that contains a syntax error, Python reports the error, and (as best it can) identifies where the error occurred.

Runtime errors are errors of intent. They are legal language statements; they are syntactically correct, but they ask Python to do something that cannot be done. Their incorrectness cannot be detected by the Python interpreter syntactically, but occur when Python attempts to run code that cannot be completed. The classic example is to make a list of length 10 (indices 0–9) and then at some point during processing ask for the list element at index 10. There is no syntactic error; requesting a value at some index is a reasonable request. Furthermore, requests of values at index 0–9 provide results. Only when the tenth index value is requested does Python encounter the problem. Python cannot provide that value at index 10 because it doesn't exist; hence the runtime error. Runtime errors can be hard to find, even with testing. They may occur intermittently: we may only occasionally ask for the index 10 element, depending on our calculations. Runtime errors may occur only under special circumstances. For example, if the name of the file we open has a suffix ".txt" and an error is triggered, any other suffix might be fine. Whatever the cause, just because you haven't seen the error doesn't mean it isn't there!

Design errors are a broad class of errors that basically cover everything else that is neither a syntactic nor a runtime error. The program is syntactically correct and we do not ask Python to do something that it inherently cannot do. However, the results we get are simply wrong. Design errors are just that: errors. We didn't write our averaging equation correctly, we skipped a value in the list, we multiplied instead of dividing, we didn't reset a default value in our function call, and so on. We made a mistake and, through no fault of the language, we got the wrong answer.

Testing for Runtime and Semantic Errors

Testing is about minimizing our errors as we program. We will make errors—that's a given. Can we recover from them, find them early, and minimize their effect? These are important questions.

"Bugs" and Debugging

Programmers often talk about bugs in their programs. The source of the term "bug" is something much discussed in computer science. The source of the term is not clear, but it is clear that it pre-dates computers. There are a number of documented letters of Thomas Edison using the term "bug" to indicate defects in his inventions. There is some evidence that the term dates back to telegraphy equipment and the use of semi-automatic telegraph keys that were called "bugs" and, though efficient, were difficult to work with. One of the most famous computer examples is traced to Admiral Grace Hopper. See Figure 15.1.

Removing bugs from a program has been called "debugging," likely from this incident.

To call these errors "bugs" is a bit self-forgiving of us. It implies that these errors were not our fault. Rather, they slipped into our program without our knowing. We may not have known it at the time, but they are our errors. Edsger Dijkstra, a famous professor of computer science, said the following about the word "bug":

In 1946, when Hopper was released from active duty, she joined the Harvard Faculty at the Computation Laboratory where she continued her work on the Mark II and Mark III. Operators traced an error in the Mark II to a moth trapped in a relay, coining the term *bug*. This bug was carefully removed and taped to the log book. Stemming from the first bug, today we call errors or glitch's [sic] in a program a *bug*. [a]

[a] http://ei.cs.vt.edu/~history/Hopper.Danis.html

FIGURE 15.1 A real hardware bug!

> We could, for instance, begin with cleaning up our language by no longer calling a bug "a bug" but by calling it an error. It is much more honest because it squarely puts the blame where it belongs, viz., with the programmer who made the error. The animistic metaphor of the bug that maliciously sneaked in while the programmer was not looking is intellectually dishonest as it is a disguise that the error is the programmer's own creation. The nice thing of this simple change of vocabulary is that it has such a profound effect. While, before, a program with only one bug used to be "almost correct," afterwards a program with an error is just "wrong."[1]

15.2 KINDS OF TESTING

Testing is a very broad category; it would be difficult to cover it in sufficient depth in an introductory programming book. However, it is an interesting topic and one often ignored in introductory books. We think it is important enough to take a quick look. Let's get started.

There are various philosophies on how, when and why testing should be done. Some of these include:

• Planning versus code testing. This might be better phrased as *static* versus *dynamic* testing. Static testing is work done without running the code. You might think of it as the various stages of understanding the requirements of the code and then planning to achieve those goals. Dynamic testing is the kind of testing done with the code,

[1] http://www.cs.utexas.edu/users/EWD/ewd10xx/EWD1036.PDF

during execution of the code. It should be noted that in good software development, developing static tests is an important part of the overall software development process. However, this chapter will focus on dynamic testing, that is, testing with code.

- When to test: *post-coding* versus *pre-coding* testing. Traditionally, code is developed and then handed off to an independent testing group. The testing group develops the tests and, when errors are found, passes that information back to the developers, all in a cycle. However, more modern testing approaches, including *agile* and *extreme* programming, focus on developing the tests to be applied to code *before* the code is written. As the code is written and updated, these tests are used as the standard for gauging progress and success.

- Levels of testing. *Unit* testing is focused on the individual pieces (modules, functions, classes) of code as they are developed. *Integration* testing focuses on bringing tested modules together to see whether they work as intended. *System* testing focuses on the entire system to see whether it meets the goals of the project.

- What to test? This is probably a category all unto itself, as there are many goals one might focus on for testing. They would include:
  - **Correctness**. Are the results produced correct? What counts as correct? Do we know all the cases?
  - **Completeness**. Are all the potential cases covered: all user entries, all file formats, all data types, and so on?
  - **Security**. Is the program safe from being "broken into" by another user, through the Internet, or otherwise?
  - **Interface**. Is the interface "usable"? Are its features complete? Does the user get what he or she expects when using the program?
  - **Load**. Does the program respond well if it is presented with a heavy load: many users, large data sets, heavy Internet traffic, and so on?
  - **Resources**. Does the program use "appropriate" amounts of memory, CPU, network?
  - **Responsiveness**. Does the program respond in a "reasonable" amount of time? If there are time limits, does it meet those limits?

And on and on. Testing is a complicated business!

Testing is Hard!

One of things we want to convey is that testing is hard—at least as hard as writing the program in the first place. That is one of the reasons we have left testing to the end. You have had enough on your hands, learning to design programs, implement them in code, and then fix them.

Correctness

How hard is is testing? Let's just pick one of the examples mentioned earlier: correctness. How does one determine whether a program is correct? One type of correctness would be a *proof.* There is a branch of software engineering that focuses on that very topic: taking a program, turning it into a mathematical expression, and proving its correctness. However, that is a very difficult task. In fact, at this time it is not possible to take an arbitrary program and prove it correct. So correctness is often practically measured against a specification of behavior provided by the user. But even that measurement can be difficult.

In 1993, Intel released its first Pentium^{TM} desktop CPU. It was a new architecture and required many years of development, including new software to make the chip run. In 1994, it was discovered that the floating-point division instruction had a small flaw, due to an error in tables that the algorithm used for its calculations (these tables were stored on the chip). It resulted in a rare error in some divisions. *Byte* magazine in 1994 estimated that about 1 in 9×10^9 divisions of random numbers would show the defect. How many cases should Intel have tested to see whether it was correct? Yet a professor at Lynchburg college performing some mathematical calculations *did* hit the error in his work, rare or not.[2] To further illustrate the insidiousness of this example, Intel *had* developed both the correct algorithm and table, but when the table was loaded into the chip, a portion was inadvertently set to zeros!

Importance of Testing

Testing is important. In fact, many modern software developers put testing as the first problem to be solved! As we mentioned earlier, *agile* software development focuses on writing the tests before the code is written. In so doing, a developer accomplishes two very important tasks:

- Focus on what the code *should* do before actually coding the implementation. It relates to our old maxim: think before you program. By writing the tests first, you focus on what the code should do.
- Once tests have been set up, every new piece of code or change to existing code has a test-base in place to assure the developer that their code is "correct", at least as far as the measures provided.

Even beginning programmers should try to integrate testing into their development process. Python embeds tools to make this process easier. We will introduce some examples here and hope that you will be exposed to more in your programming career.

15.3 EXAMPLE PROBLEM

We will use a fairly simple example to show the kinds of testing that a developer might use and some of the tools that Python provides to support the developer in this activity.

---

[2] See more information at the wikipedia page on the FDIV error, http://en.wikipedia.org/wiki/Pentium_FDIV_bug.

NBA Efficiency

The National Basketball Association (NBA) has collected various statistics throughout its history. These statistics are freely available at sites such as `http://basketballreference.com/stats_download.htm` and include information on coaches, players, and teams. You can use this information to do a variety of interesting analysis of your team, similar to the "safe lead" heuristic we presented in Section 2.1. One of the statistics used to rate players is called a player's *efficiency*.[3] The basic efficiency formula for a player has the following form:

$$efficiency = ((points + rebounds + assists + steals + blocks) - ((shotAttempts - shotsMade)$$
$$+ (freeThrowsAttempts - freeThrowsMade) + turnOvers))/gamesPlayed$$

Those players who are most efficient by this measure are often the best players. If we take a look at all the players who have ever played in the NBA, which players were the most efficient?

Basic Algorithm

The data we will use is the player_career.csv file provided by the NBA. It contains all the player statistics for every player of the NBA. It is a CSV file, which we have worked with before. The file is simply formatted, so we chose to not use the `csv` module.

Figure 15.2 shows the first five lines of the file. The first line of the file describes the file format, though the abbreviations are terse. Table 15.1 describes the format a little more clearly.

ilkid,firstname,lastname,leag,gp,minutes,pts,oreb,dreb,reb,asts,stl,blk,turnover,pf,fga,fgm,fta,ftm,tpa,tpm

ABDELAL01 ,Alaa,Abdelnaby,N,256,3200,1465,283,563,846,85,71,69,247,484,1236,620,321,225,3,0

ABDULKA01 ,Kareem,Abdul-jabbar,N,1560,57446,38387,2975,9394,17440,5660,1160,3189,2527,4657,28307,15837,9304,6712,18,1

ABDULMA01 ,Mahmo,Abdul-rauf,N,586,15633,8553,219,868,1087,2079,487,46,963,1107,7943,3514,1161,1051,1339,474

ABDULTA01 ,Tariq,Abdul-wahad,N,236,4808,1830,286,490,776,266,184,82,309,485,1726,720,529,372,76,18

FIGURE 15.2 The NBA player career statistics file, first five lines.

Our goal is to read in this information, calculate the player efficiency for each player, and report the top *x* players, where *x* is something like the top 10, top 50, top 100. Our first pass at an algorithm is:

---

[3] http://www.nba.com/statistics/efficiency.html There is also a more complicated evaluation called the Performance Efficiency Rating.

```
for every line in the player file:
    gather the player information
    calculate the efficiency for each player

find the top X players
print the top players in a nice format
```

field	abbreviation	meaning	field	abbreviation	meaning
1	ilkid	unique ID	2	firstName	player's first name
3	lastName	player's last name	4	leag	league (NBA or ABA)
5	gp	games played	6	minutes	minutes played
7	pts	points scored	8	oreb	offensive rebounds
9	dreb	defensive rebounds	10	reb	total rebounds
11	asts	total assists	12	stl	total steals
13	blk	total blocks	14	to	total turn overs
15	pf	personal fouls	16	fga	2-pt shots attempted
17	ftm	2-pt shots made	18	fta	free throws attempted
19	ftm	free throws made	20	tpa	3-pt shots attempted
21	tpm	3-pt shots made			

TABLE 15.1 NBA player fields.

By now, you know that divide and conquer is the right design approach for this problem. There are three functions we need:

calcEfficiency: Gather the information from the file, calculate that player's efficiency, and store it in a dictionary. The function takes as arguments a file line (string) and a dictionary. The key is the concatenation of the player's last name and first name. The value will be another dictionary of *all* the gathered player stats as well as the just-calculated efficiency.

findMostEfficient: Takes as arguments the player dictionary and how many of the top players we wish to identify. It returns a sorted list of tuples, where the first element is the efficiency and the second element is the player name.

printResults: Takes the list of tuples results and nicely prints the top X players.

A first cut at the main program and the function calcEfficiency is shown in Code Listing 15.1.

Code Listing 15.1

```python
def calcEfficiency (line, theDict):
    """Calculate player efficiency."""
    fields = line.split(',')
    firstName = fields[1]
    lastName = fields[2]

    # mapping fields in a line to their particular variable.
    # league is a str, everything else an int
    leag,gp,mins,pts,oreb,dreb,reb,asts, \
        stl,blk,to,pf,fga,fgm,fta,ftm,tpa,tpm = \
        fields[3],int(fields[4]),int(fields[5]),int(fields[6]),int(fields[7]),\
        int(fields[8]),int(fields[9]),int(fields[10]),int(fields[11]),\
        int(fields[12]),int(fields[13]),int(fields[14]),int(fields[15]),\
        int(fields[16]),int(fields[17]),int(fields[18]), int(fields[19]),\
        int(fields[20])

    # calculate the player's efficiency
    efficiency = ((pts+reb+asts+stl+blk)-((fga-fgm)+(fta-ftm)+to))/float(gp)

    theDict[lastName+firstName] = {'first':firstName, 'last':lastName, \
                        'league':leag,'mins':mins,'gp':gp,'pts':pts,\
                        'oreb':oreb,'dreb':dreb,'reb':reb,'asts':asts,\
                        'stl':stl,'blk':blk,'to':to,'fga':fga,'fgm':fgm,\
                        'fta':fta,'ftm':ftm,'tpa':tpa,'tpm':tpm,\
                        'efficiency':efficiency}

def findMostEfficient(theDict,howMany):
    '''return list of tuples(efficiency, name) from dictionary
    hoMany is number of tuples to gather'''
    # user must implement
    return []

def printResults(lst):
    ''' pretty print the results '''
    print 'The top %d players in effency are'%len(lst)
    print '*'*20

# main program as a function
def main (fName):
    fd = open(fName)
    nbaDict={}
    for line in fd:
        calcEfficiency(line,nbaDict)
```

```
       results = findMostEfficient(nbaDict,20)
45     printResults(results)
       fd.close()
```

Though the function code is a bit long, it really doesn't do much. It seems long because of all the data we are gathering. In summary, the code does the following:

Line 3: Split the line into fields based on comma separation.
Lines 4–5: Extract the first and last name.
Lines 9–16: A large multiple assignment and conversion of each field value.
Line 18: Calculate the efficiency.
Line 20: Fill the dictionary. Each key is a string consisting of `lastName+firstName`. The associated value is another dictionary containing all the player statistics including the efficiency.

Now, let's add some testing and error checking to both the `main` function and `calcEfficiency`.

15.4 INCORPORATING TESTING

In Chapter 14, we introduced exceptions to catch user errors. By "user errors", we mean to catch the misuse of the program by the user as we have defined it and to try, if possible, to keep the program running. For example, if a user mistypes the file he or she wishes to open, we catch the error and re-prompt. We, the developers, are protecting ourselves from the users. These are, in a sense, expected errors. We know where the user provides input, and at that point, we check to see whether they have provided what we requested. If not, we do what we can to help.

Catching User Errors

What errors should we catch in the example code? As we have discussed, this is often a hard question to answer. In looking at our example code, where does the user touch the program, and how can we catch any potential errors? It would be most useful if you were to look at the code and think about it before you go further.

A couple of things come to mind:

- The user might enter a nonexistent file.
- The user might enter an existing file but not a file with the format we expect (could be the wrong file, could be the correct file but the format changed).

To catch the nonexistent file case, we use an exception to the *open* clause on line 40. If it can open the file, then there is no error (an ***else*** situation) and we continue processing, otherwise we catch the resulting `IOError`, print a useful error message, and quit the program. The following snippet shows this approach.

Code Listing 15.2

```python
def main ():
    fName = raw_input('NBA player file name:')
    try:
        fd = open(fName)
    except IOError:
        print 'File named %s not found'%fName
    else:   # file opened correctly
        nbaDict={}
        for line in fd:
            if 'ilkid' in line:
                continue
            calcEfficiency(line,nbaDict)
        results = findMostEfficient(nbaDict,20)
        printResults(results)
        fd.close()
```

To catch that the file is correctly formatted, we need to do a little more work. First, it would be good to notice that the first line of the file is different from all the others! The fields on the first line are all strings, and the remaining lines have integers in fields from index 4 on. We need to ignore that first line (header line) for our regular processing, but, at the same time, we can use that line to check whether this is a correctly formatted file. The first field of the first line should have the string 'ilkid'. If not, it isn't the correct file. We grab the first line using the `readline` method and check the first field (the first five characters). If it has the right value, we keep going otherwise, we raise an `IOError`. Code Listing 15.3 shows the approach.

Code Listing 15.3

```python
def main ():
    fName = raw_input('NBA player file name:')
    try:
        fd = open(fName)
    except IOError:
        print 'File named %s not found'%fName
    else:
        nbaDict={}
```

```
# check the first line
line = fd.readline()
if line[0:5]!='ilkid':
    print 'Bad File Format, first line was:',line
    raise IOError
# process the rest of the lines
for line in fd:
    calcEfficiency(line,nbaDict)
results = findMostEfficient(nbaDict,20)
printResults(results)
fd.close()
```

What about checking the format of each line? You could look at that in two ways. On the one hand, we remember that all input is evil and this is indeed input. One the other, this is a file specifically provided with the correct format. To be safe you could check each line: for number of fields, and for format of each field, before it gets processed. We leave that as an exercise.

Catching Developer Errors

In testing, we must also ask the question of, who is protecting us, the developers, from ourselves? How do we check for situations that should *never happen* if the program we designed is used correctly? This is the job of the assert statement. We use assert to check for programming errors, things that should never happen. We use exceptions to check for events that, although unpredictable (they may or may not happen), can occur. The best description is perhaps that assert tells the *programmer* when he or she has made a mistake while exceptions tell the *users* when they have made a mistake. We insert assert into our code to guard against mistakes that the programmer should never make. If they do, the assert catches the programming error forcing the developer to fix it.

The Python function assert takes two arguments. The first is a Boolean that is checked by assert. If the Boolean check is *True*, the code continues. If the Boolean check is *False*, assert will raise an error, AssertionError. If a second expression, separated by a comma, also exists, it is printed at the time of the error. These arguments allow the developer to print out information about the error when it occurs.

The calcEfficiency Function

What could we assert in the calcEfficiency function? We know the following:

- The first argument, the line being processed, should never be empty. That would be a misuse of the function.

- The second argument should be a dictionary. That is what the function requires.
- The value gp (standing for "games played") should never be 0 (only players that have played games should be in the file). This is an issue because our efficiency formula divides by gp.

These are all issues that should *never happen*. If they do, then there is something wrong from the point of view of the programmer and it should be repaired.

The snippet in Code Listing 15.4 inserts that assert calls in the calcEfficiency function.

Code Listing 15.4

```
def calcEfficiency (line, theDict):
    # asserts on the parameters
    assert isinstance(theDict,dict),\
           'bad parameter, expected a dictionary, got %s'%theDict
    assert isinstance(line,str) and line != '', \
           'bad parameter, expected string, got %s'%line

    line = line.strip()
    fields = line.split(',')
    firstName = fields[1]
    lastName = fields[2]

    # mapping fields in a line to their particular variable.
    # league is a str, everything else an int
    leag,gp,mins,pts,oreb,dreb,reb,asts,\
       stl,blk,to,pf,fga,fgm,fta,ftm,tpa,tpm = \
       fields[3],int(fields[4]),int(fields[5]),int(fields[6]),int(fields[7]),\
       int(fields[8]),int(fields[9]),int(fields[10]),int(fields[11]),\
       int(fields[12]),int(fields[13]),int(fields[14]),int(fields[15]),\
       int(fields[16]),int(fields[17]),int(fields[18]), int(fields[19]),\
       int(fields[20])

    # gp can't be 0
    assert gp!= 0, '%s %s has no games played'%(firstName, lastName)

    # need to address this problem!
    # assert lastName+firstName not in theDict,
    #      'duplicate on name %s'%firstName + lastName

    # calculate the player's efficiency
    efficiency = ((pts+reb+asts+stl+blk)-((fga-fgm)+(fta-ftm)+to))/float(gp)
```

```
theDict[lastName+firstName] = {'first':firstName, 'last':lastName,\
                   'league':leag,'mins':mins,'gp':gp,'pts':pts,\
                   'oreb':oreb,'dreb':dreb,'reb':reb,'asts':asts,\
                   'stl':stl,'blk':blk,'to':to,'fga':fga,'fgm':fgm,\
                   'fta':fta,'ftm':ftm,'tpa':tpa,'tpm':tpm,\
                   'efficiency':efficiency}
```

We can also `assert` that a player's name should not be duplicated in the file, and as part of the testing add that to the function. Interestingly, when we tried that, our assert *was* triggered. Upon inspection of the file, it turns out that player names *are* duplicated. Some players played in the old ABA league and then transfered to the NBA. Some players moved back and forth and have many entries! You will note that our program does not deal with this problem, but by thinking of what to test we discovered that issue and noticed that we should fix it. That is what testing is about!

15.5 AUTOMATION OF TESTING

Now that we have placed tests in our code, it would be good to try different examples against our code to make sure that we have covered all our important cases. In fact, we should recheck our examples every time we make a change to the code. It is always possible that, by making some code change, some test example will no longer run properly.

Let's also be honest. If it were left up to the individual developer to manually run tests after every code change, those tests would not get done. No developer believes that his or her changes have caused any problem! Thus, Python has provided some tools to help automatically run test code.

doctest

The `doctest` module provides a way to test individual elements of your code to make sure that they perform as you expect. As such, `doctest` is an example of a unit-test approach, a way to test each piece (function/method/class) of your program. How `doctest` does this is interesting.

The `doctest` module operates by placing examples of code use, or misuse, as a part of the docstring of a piece of code—in this case, a function. Each example provides the code invocation, as well as the results that are expected to be returned as a result of the invocation. In this way, the docstring serves as documentation, as good examples of code use and misuse, and as an automatic test system since we can ask doctest to run all the examples and make sure the desired output is provided.

Each doctest example is provided by prefacing the example with the characters '>>>'. These are the standard prompt characters by the Python shell. What follows the '>>>' on the same line is the invocation. The next lines are the expected output that the invocation should generate. You can easily collect the examples by simply running your example in the Python shell, and then cut and paste the example invocation and output into the function. How easy is that!

Code Listing 15.5 example of placing doctest examples in the code is listed in the Code Listing 15.5 for the main function.

Code Listing 15.5

```
def main (fName):
    '''
    >>> main('')
    File named  not found
    >>> main('x')
    Traceback (most recent call last):
        ...
    IOError: bad file format, line was: this is a bad file
    >>> main('player_career.csv')
    The top 10 players in efficency are
    *******************
        Wilt Chamberlain : 41.50
            Bill Russell : 31.71
        Oscar Robertson : 31.61
            Bob Pettit : 31.11
    Kareem Abdul-jabbar : 30.93
            Larry Bird : 29.77
            Elgin Baylor : 29.74
        Michael Jordan : 29.19
        Magic Johnson : 29.10
        Charles Barkley : 28.16
    '''
    try:
        fd = open(fName)
    except IOError:
        print 'File named %s not found'%fName
    else:
        nbaDict={}
        line = fd.readline()
        if line[0:5]!='ilkid':
            raise IOError('bad file format, line was: %s'%line)
        for line in fd:
            calcEfficiency(line,nbaDict)
```

```
        results = findMostEfficient(nbaDict,10)
        printResults(results)
        fd.close()

if __name__ == '__main__':
    import doctest
    doctest.testmod()
```

This code lists three example invocations: the first two check error conditions (missing file and file of the wrong format) and the last checks a successful run. Each invocation begins with the '>>>' and is followed by the expected output. Note the special code listed at the bottom:

```
if __name__ == '__main__':
    import doctest
    doctest.testmod()
```

This code is a short-cut to invoke `doctest`. Remember that the special variable `__name__` is the name of the current module. If that module is named `'__main__'`, then this means that the code was invoked from the command line, i.e. `python nbaEfficiency.py`. In this case, the `doctest` module is run and every element that has `doctest` examples is invoked.

Interestingly, if you were to invoke that code from the command line as listed, you would get no output. The `doctest` code is run, but only provides output, if the test fails. However, if you want to see all the tests run in detail, you can invoke the command line code with the special `'-v'` switch at the end of the line. This switch setting will provide detailed information of the `doctest` run. The session below lists a run of our `main` function.

```
>python nbaEfficiency.py -v
Trying:
    main('')
Expecting:
    File named  not found
ok
Trying:
    main('x')
Expecting:
    Traceback (most recent call last):
        ...
    IOError: bad file format, line was: this is a bad file
ok
Trying:
    main('player_career.csv')
```

```
Expecting:
    The top 10 players in efficency are
    ********************
                Wilt Chamberlain : 41.50
                    Bill Russell : 31.71
                Oscar Robertson : 31.61
                     Bob Pettit : 31.11
          Kareem Abdul-jabbar : 30.93
                     Larry Bird : 29.77
                   Elgin Baylor : 29.74
                 Michael Jordan : 29.19
                  Magic Johnson : 29.10
                Charles Barkley : 28.16
ok
4 items had no tests:
    __main__
    __main__.calcEfficiency
    __main__.findMostEfficient
    __main__.printResults
1 items passed all tests:
    3 tests in __main__.main
3 tests in 5 items.
3 passed and 0 failed.
Test passed.
```

Note that by running with the `'-v'` switch at the end of the line, you not only get information on the tests run, but also information on which elements had tests available and which did not.

Once the example tests are in place, you can run all the tests by simply running the code. This feature makes test creation at the unit level very easy. The only drawback can be the length of the docstring now associated with the code.

Other Kinds of Testing

Python provides a number of support modules for testing. The `unittest` module provides a much greater level of control to run testing. The module `nose`[4] also provides a greater level of control, and both can do some system testing. In-depth coverage of that module is beyond the scope of an introductory book and is left to the reader.

15.6 CONCLUSION

In this chapter, we introduced the built-in testing capabilities of Python. These techniques assist in developing better code.

---

[4] http://code.google.com/p/python-nose.

Exercises

1. The `findMostEfficient` function is not implemented. Implement it as indicated in the comments.

2. Having written the `findMostEfficient` function, add tests for that function using the `doctest` approach discussed in the chapter.

3. In Chapter 6 an anagram function was developed. Add tests using the `doctest` approach of this chapter.

4. Multiple exercises developed a `multiFind` function. Add tests using the `doctest` approach of this chapter.

5. In Chapter 8, the example counted words in the Gettysburg Address. Add tests using the `doctest` approach of this chapter.

6. Choose a function that you have written and add tests using the `doctest` approach of this chapter.

CHAPTER 16

Recursion: Another
Control Mechanism

"A journey of a thousand miles begins with a single step."

Lao-Tzu, *The Way of Lao-Tzu*

Earlier you learned about looping and selection as control techniques. In this chapter you learn about another control mechanism: recursion. Recursion does not add any power to our programming, as looping and selection are sufficient for all programs, but there are some solutions that are easier to both understand and implement with recursion. In fact, there is a class of languages called *functional programming languages*, such as Haskell, Scheme, and Lisp, that feature recursion as their primary control mechanism. Once understood, recursion can be a natural way to express a solution to a problem, so we need it in our problem-solving tool box.

16.1 WHAT IS RECURSION?

Syntactically, recursion is simple: it is a function that calls itself. For example:

```
def f(n):
    ...
    f(n-1)
```

At first blush, however, it looks rather odd. Take a look ahead at the recursive function `factorial` in Section 16.2. It seems that there is nothing there. It looks quite "circular," defining something in terms of itself. How could that work?

The key is to understand that recursion is not circular, if there is a condition under which the circularity ends: it "bottoms out" at some point. That is the key. Understanding recursion implies understanding two parts of your problem:

- How to break your problem into smaller pieces, each of which can be addressed by your function and then "put back together."
- Determining when the recursive invocation of a function ends, when the recursion "bottoms out."

Recursion ends up being an algorithm that, in itself, uses a form of divide and conquer, our frequently applied approach for designing algorithms. Recursion breaks a problem down into pieces, down to the "smallest" piece, solves that smallest piece and then reassembles the smaller solutions into an overall answer.

Correctly controlling recursion requires dealing with two different cases. The first case terminates a recursive sequence and is known as the *base case*. If the base case is missing, the recursive function calls go on forever. Such a program never halts with an answer—known as *infinite recursion*. The second case is the *recursive step*. It both breaks the problem down and reassembles the partial solutions.

Recursion can occur in many situations. The English language allows for recursion and a classic (and humorous) case of infinite recursion is a recursive definition that simply refers to itself. Here is an actual, and useless, definition of a "recursive definition" from the Jargon File:[1]

> **Recursion:**
> *see Recursion*

Another example of a recursive definition of an English word is a definition of one's *ancestors*:

> ***def*** ancestors:
> One's parents are one's ancestors (base case).
> The parents of one's ancestors are also one's ancestors (recursive step).

We can think of Lao-Tzu's quote at the beginning of this chapter as a recursive description of how to make a long journey. For the purpose of illustrating recursion, let's rewrite the quote as: "a journey of a thousand *steps* begins with single step." If you have taken nine-hundred-and-ninety-nine steps, you can easily take that thousandth step. If you have taken nine-hundred-and-ninety-*eight* steps, you can easily take the nine-hundred-and-ninety-ninth step. The process continues recursively until you get to that first step (the base case), and you know how to take that first step.

---

[1] A glossary of so called "computer hacker" slang, see: http://www.catb.org/~esr/jargon

Written recursively, our modified version of Lao-Tzu's quote becomes:

def journey:

 The first step is easy (base case).

 The nth step is easy after already completing the previous $n-1$ steps (recursive step).

We can express this journey of a thousand steps as a Python function that expresses each step as a string—the first step is the string "Easy." All other steps are strings in the form of step(n). A call to `takeStep(4)` results in the string `'step(4) + step(3) + step(2) + Easy'`. Recursively, the `takeStep` function begins with n = 4, then calls itself with n = 3, and so on until it is called with n = 1. At that point, the calling sequence reaches its end, and we return from the calls backwards from n = 1 with string "Easy". See Code Listing 16.1.

Code Listing 16.1

```python
def takeStep(n):
    if n == 1:     # base case
        return "Easy"
    else:
        thisStep = "step(" + str(n) + ")"
        previousSteps = takeStep(n-1)          # recursive call
        return thisStep + " + " + previousSteps
```

```
>>> takeStep(4)
'step(4) + step(3) + step(2) + Easy'
```

We'll look at how the control is managed a little later. An astute reader will notice that the ***else*** is not necessary, because if n != 1, the first ***return*** will not happen, and the program will proceed to the ***else*** clause anyway.

16.2 MATHEMATICS AND RABBITS

Let's consider a recursive definition from mathematics. The factorial function may be familiar to you. The factorial function is so frequently used in mathematics and statistics that the shorthand expression uses an exclamation point. That is, `factorial(4)` is written as 4! and its value is 4! = 4 × 3 × 2 × 1. Because 1! is defined to have a value of 1, we can define the factorial function recursively as follows:

```
factorial(n):
    factorial(1) = 1                         # base case
    factorial(n) = n * factorial(n - 1)   # recursive step
```

Our base case, where we "bottom out," is when the factorial function gets an argument of 1. At that point, we know the answer (no calculation is required), and we return the value 1.

The recursive step both breaks the problem down and reassembles the partial answer. At every step, we divide the problem into two parts:

- The value n
- The value of `factorial(n-1)`

Once those two parts are calculated, we combine them (the conquer step) by multiplying the two values and returning that product.

That is, to find `factorial(4)` recursively:

$$4! = 4 * 3!$$
but we know $\quad 3! = 3 * 2!$
but we know $\quad 2! = 2 * 1!$
but we know $\quad 1! = 1 \quad$ *base case*
so $\quad\quad\quad\quad 2! = 2 * 1 = 2$
so $\quad\quad\quad\quad 3! = 3 * 2 = 6$
so $\quad\quad\quad\quad 4! = 4 * 6 = 24$

Written to look more like Python, we can write the function as:

```
factorial(n):
    if n == 1, return 1                      # base case
    if n > 1, return n * factorial(n - 1)  # recursive case
```

Code Listing 16.2

```python
def factorial(n):
    """Recursive factorial."""
    if n == 1:
        return 1
    else:
        return n * factorial(n-1)
```

```
>>> factorial(4)
24
```

Another classic example of recursion is the Fibonacci sequence, which first appeared in print almost a thousand years ago. The author, Fibonacci, presented the sequence as an artificial example of how rabbits might breed. If you start with two rabbits, they will breed, to created a third rabbit. The three rabbits will produce two more offspring, to yield a total of five. Fibonacci's pattern to find the number of rabbits in the next generation was to add the totals from the two previous generations:

```
1               # first rabbit
1               # second rabbit
2 = 1 + 1       # two rabbits (summing the first and second rabbits)
3 = 1 + 2       # three rabbits (summing the previous two generations)
5 = 2 + 3       # five rabbits (summing the previous two generations)
8 = 3 + 5       # eight rabbits (summing the previous two generations)
...
```

What is our base case? In the case of the Fibonacci sequence, there are two base cases, because we are summing the previous *two* generations in our recursive step. That is, our first base case is the "first rabbit" and the second base case is the "second rabbit."

For the recursive step, we divide the data into two parts:

- The value for `fibonacci(n-1)`
- The value for `fibonacci(n-2)`

The conquer stage is to sum those two values together, once calculated, and return that sum as the function value.

The resulting recursive definition is (in English first):

```
fibonacci(n):
        For the first two cases (n=0 or n=1): there is 1 rabbit   # base case
        if n > 1: sum the previous two generations               # recursive case
```

The definition translated into Python is shown in Code Listing 16.3.

Code Listing 16.3

```python
def fibonacci(n):
    """Recursive Fibonacci sequence."""
    if n == 0 or n == 1:      # base case
        return 1
    else:
        return fibonacci(n-1) + fibonacci(n-2)   # recursive case
```

```
>>> fibonacci(4)
5
>>> fibonacci(6)
13
```

fibonacci(4) = fibonacci(3) + fibonacci(2)
so we next determine fibonacci(3) = fibonacci(2) + fibonacci(1)
and fibonacci(2) = fibonacci(1) + fibonacci(0) *base case*
the base case yields fibonacci(2) = 1 + 1 = 2
so fibonacci(3) = 2 + fibonacci(1) = 2 + 1 = 3
and fibonacci(4) = fibonacci(3) + fibonacci(2) = 3 + 2 = 5

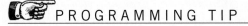 PROGRAMMING TIP

Recursion must have a base case, and it must appear *first* in the function.

16.3 LET'S WRITE OUR OWN: REVERSING A STRING

You've seen some examples—now let's write our own recursive function. Let's reverse a string. You already know an easy way to reverse a string (what is it? remember the slicing with a negative step in Section 4.1), but let's write a recursive function that does the same job.

As always, we need to define the base case and the recursive step. In the recursive step we need to define the divide process and the conquer process. A skeleton function would then look like Code Listing 16.4:

Code Listing 16.4

```
# recursive function to reverse a string

def reverser (aStr):
    # base case
    # recursive step
        # divide into parts
        # conquer/reassemble

theStr = raw_input("Reverse what string:")
result = reverser(theStr)
print "The reverse of %s is %s\n" % (theStr, result)
```

What is the base case for a string reversal? Well, what string is easy to reverse? Certainly a string with a length of 1 is trivial to reverse—it is just the string itself! We put that in as the base case as shown in Code Listing 16.5.

Code Listing 16.5

```
# recursive function to reverse a string

def reverser (aStr):
    # base case
    if len(aStr) == 1:
        return aStr
    # recursive step
        # divide into parts
        # conquer/reassemble

theStr = raw_input("Reverse what string: ")
result = reverser(theStr)
print "The reverse of %s is %s\n" % (theStr,result)
```

Now let's consider the divide-and-conquer step. We need to answer the two questions: how to divide the data up and how to reassemble (conquer) that data once the parts are calculated. As you have seen previously, these two steps are often done together.

What to do? Let's assume that `reverser` does what it is supposed to do: reverse a string. If that is true, how can we take advantage of that? If we were to break a string into two pieces: one sent to the reverser function recursively and one not, what data should we send?

Consider the string `'abcde'`. If the reverser function works as advertised, we could just take the first letter, in this case, `'a'`, and append that to the *end* of the rest of the string if that string was reversed. That is,

beginning with: first-character + rest-of-string
the reverse is: reverse of rest-of-string + first-character

or, in Python,

```
reverser(aStr[1:]) + aStr[0].
```

This approach reverses the position of the first letter and leaves the work of reversing the rest of the string to a recursive call. In typical recursive fashion, we continue with the process until we hit a string of length 1, and then we can begin reassembly.

Code Listing 16.6 shows the final product. We add some **print** statements just to show the "divide" steps as they happen, the "bottoming out" of the base case, and then finally the reassembly.

Code Listing 16.6

```
# Reverse a string using a recursive function.

def reverse (aStr):
    """Recursive function to reverse a string."""
    print "Got as an argument:",aStr
    # base case
    if len(aStr) == 1:
        print "Base Case!"
        return aStr
    # recursive step
    else:
        newStr =reverse(aStr[1:]) + aStr[0]
        print "Reassembling %s and %s into %s"%(aStr[1:],aStr[0],newStr)
        return newStr

theStr = raw_input("What string: ")
print
resultStr = reverse(theStr)
print "\nThe reverse of %s is %s\n"%(theStr,resultStr)
```

```
>python reverser.py
What string:abcde

Got as an argument: abcde
Got as an argument: bcde
Got as an argument: cde
Got as an argument: de
Got as an argument: e
Base Case!
Reassembling e and d into ed
Reassembling de and c into edc
Reassembling cde and b into edcb
Reassembling bcde and a into edcba

The reverse of abcde is edcba
```

16.4 HOW DOES RECURSION ACTUALLY WORK?

How is it possible for a function to call itself, and how does the computer keep track of all the function calls that result?

Stack Data Structure

The computer keeps track of function calls on a data structure known as a *stack*. A stack is a data structure that grows and shrinks only at one end. Imagine a stack of plates, as you might find in a cafeteria (see Figure 16.1).

FIGURE 16.1 A stack of plates, cafeteria-style. [Photos.com.]

The stack of plates is spring-loaded. You may add more plates to the stack, but only the top plate is available. If you remove a plate from the top, the stack of plates lifts up, presenting the next user with a new "top" plate. The process can continue until the stack fills up or the stack runs out. One can imagine a data structure with much the same behavior. You can add and remove new data to and from the stack. The order of availability is often called *LIFO*, meaning **L**ast **I**n, **F**irst **O**ut. The last data item you add to the stack is the first item you can retrieve. Such a stack might fill to capacity or run out of data items to provide. A data structure stack is shown in Figure 16.2. A stack has three standard operations: pop, push, and top. The names are really quite descriptive of our "stack of plates":

pop: Pop removes the item at the top of the stack and returns it. The stack is one element smaller as a result. In our plate analogy, this action removes the top plate from the stack of plates.

push: Push takes a parameter and adds that parameter as an element to the top of the stack. The stack is one element larger as a result. The item just pushed becomes the top

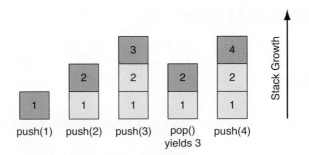

FIGURE 16.2 The operation of a stack data structure.

element of the stack. In our plate analogy, this action puts a plate on top of the stack of plates.

top: Top returns, but does not remove, the top element of the stack. The stack is not modified. In our plate analogy, in this action we simply look at the top plate.

We can implement a stack data structure using a Python list. Remember, `append` adds an element to the end of the list (the *top*), and `pop` removes an element from the end of a list (the *top*). The `top` method corresponds the last element of the list. The correspondence is shown in Table 16.1.

Stack Terminology	Python Terminology	Action
top()	List[-1]	Return the value of top of stack
push(x)	List.append(x)	Push x onto top of stack
y = pop()	y = List.pop()	Pop top off of stack and assign to y

TABLE 16.1 Stack terminology translated to Python.

Here is a Python session illustrating stack behavior using Python list methods. We name the stack "stackList", and illustrate pop, push (Python append), and top:

```
>>> stackList = [1,2,3]        # create a stack
>>> x = stackList.pop()        # pop an item off the stack
>>> x                          # the poped item was assigned to x
3
>>> stackList                  # pop removed the item
[1, 2]
>>> stackList.append(7)        # push 7 onto the stack (using append)
>>> stackList
[1, 2, 7]
>>> stackList[-1]              # top ()
```

```
7
>>> stackList              # top() doesn't change the stack
[1, 2, 7]
```

Stacks and Function Calls

Python keeps track of function calls by pushing the namespace for each function call onto a stack. Examining the stack during recursive calls illustrates how Python keeps track of the many calls to the same function.

Remember the recursive factorial function of the previous section:

```
factorial(n):
    if n == 1, return 1              # base case
    if n > 1, return n * factorial(n - 1) # recursive case
```

Let's examine the stack when we execute `factorial(4)`. First, let's adjust our factorial function to print information about the state of each recursive function call. An `indent` variable was added so that deeper recursion gets more indentation so that it is easier to visualize the recursion. Printed statements with the same indentation are made within the same function instance. Also, the recursive function call is moved to a separate line to allow us to print a line right after the recursive call returns. Included in that line is the value returned by the recursive call. See Code Listing 16.7.

Code Listing 16.7

```
def factorial(n):
    """Recursive Factorial with print to show operation."""
    indent = 4*(6-n)*" "   # more indent on deeper recursion
    print indent + "Enter factorial n = ", n
    if n == 1:             # base case
        print indent + "Base case."
        return 1
    else:                  # recursive case
        print indent + "Before recursive call f(" + str(n-1) + ")"
        # separate recursive call allows print after call
        rest = factorial(n-1)
        print indent + "After recursive call f(" + str(n-1) + ") = ", rest
        return n * rest
```

```
>>> factorial(4)
        Enter factorial n =  4
        Before recursive call f(3)
            Enter factorial n =  3
```

```
Before recursive call f(2)
    Enter factorial n =  2
    Before recursive call f(1)
        Enter factorial n =  1
        Base case.
    After recursive call f(1) =  1
After recursive call f(2) =  2
After recursive call f(3) =  6
```
24

Notice the the pattern of calls. First, is a series of "Enter-Before" pairs that reflect entering each function call ("Enter . . . ") followed by a recursive call ("Before . . . "). This series of "Enter-Before" pairs reflects the ever deeper recursive calls until we finally reach the base case. Each is indented as we go deeper. The base case is followed by a series of "After . . . " lines, one after each return from a recursive call. Notice how each "After . . . " line matches up with a corresponding "Before . . . " line—identical indentation indicates that the lines are being printed in the same function instance.

The overall pattern is a series of recursive calls that go deeper and deeper until the base case is reached. This is followed by an unwinding of the sequence of calls each completing and returning a value until the original factorial value is computed.

To see how Python actually keeps track of the values and recursive function calls, see Figure 16.3. The figure shows the call stack for `factorial(4)`. As time moves from left to right we see the stack grow until the base case is reached and then shrink until we get back to the original call. To fit the notation into the figure, we abbreviated "factorial(n)" to "f(n)".

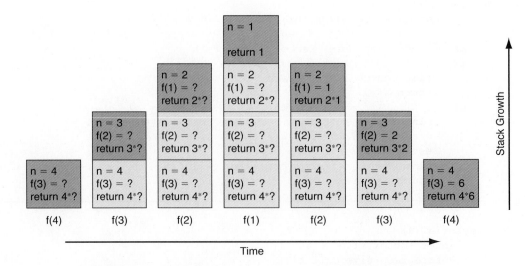

FIGURE 16.3 Call stack for `factorial(4)`. Note the question marks.

Values that are yet to be determined are labeled with a question mark (?). For example, in the first call to `factorial(4)`, we see that $n = 4$, $f(3) = ?$ (the recursive call hasn't been completed), and we will eventually execute **return** 4 * ? once "?" is resolved by the recursive call. The second stack shows a frame added for the recursive `factorial(3)` call. Note the question marks that remain in the bottom frame as well as in this new frame, because we have not yet determined what those values are. In fact, no question marks are resolved until we reach the base case at `factorial(1)`. At that point, we finally have a value (1) to return. After that point, the rightmost stacks successively shrink as the recursive function calls return and the question mark values are resolved. Eventually, we see a final **return** 6*4 that yields our final value of 24.

Compare Figure 16.3 to the output we printed above for the same `factorial(4)` call earlier. There is a direct correspondence between the height of the stack in the figure and the amount of indentation in the output. Also, observe the values of n and the recursive calls $f(n - 1)$ in both the output and in the figure. It is important to be able to see the correspondence between the stack and the values output by the program.

16.5 RECURSION IN FIGURES

Recursive Tree

Recursion is used to describe fractals—mathematical figures that can be used to describe many, highly irregular, real-world objects in nature. Figures drawn recursively can also help illustrate how recursion works. Consider a recursively drawn "tree" in Figure 16.4(a). Branches are drawn recursively by first drawing a straight line, then turning left, drawing

FIGURE 16.4 Recursive tree: (a) Python-drawn on left; (b) order-of-drawing on right.

a (recursive) branch, turning right, drawing a (recursive) branch, and then returning back along the original line. Figure 16.4(b) shows the order in which the branches were drawn.

The recursive algorithm follows. The "edge" labels refer to the numbered edges in Figure 16.4(b). Notice how when we draw edge 2, we recursively draw that whole left branch before returning to this instance and drawing edge 17 and its recursively drawn right branch. Each time we encounter the first recursive branch, we draw a left branch. For example, edges 2, 3, 4, and 5 are all drawn first as we successively call on drawing a left branch. When we eventually reach the base case after drawing edge 5, we finally return from a (left) branch call, turn right 90°, and draw a right branch (edge 6). We then move backward along edge 4, which completes that recursive branch instance, so we can turn right and recursively execute a right branch starting with edge 7. And so on.

At the highest level, our drawing looks like this:

```
draw edge 1
turn left
draw edge 2 and left branch        # recursive case
turn right
draw edge 17 and right branch   # recursive case
turn left
move back
```

Figure 16.4(a) was drawn using the following Python program with Turtle Graphics. Notice how the `level` parameter is reduced on each call, so it provides a way to work down to the base case. We added a length parameter to our program so that branches become shorter as we progress to lower levels. Since Turtle Graphics draws relatively slowly, it is instructive to watch as the branches are drawn. Notice the pattern: forward, turn left, recursive call, turn right, recursive call, move back. See Code Listing 16.8.

Code Listing 16.8

```python
# Breadth—first tree

from turtle import *

def branch(length, level):
    if level <= 0:           # base case
        return
    forward(length)
    left(45)
    branch(0.6*length, level-1) # recursive case
    right(90)
```

```
    branch(0.6*length, level-1) # recursive case
    left(45)
    backward(length)
    return

# turn to get started
left(90)
branch(100,5)
```

Sierpinski Triangles

Drawing fractal patterns is a fun way to experiment with recursion. Here is another fractal figure, the Sierpinski triangle (Figure 16.5). Like the tree we drew previously, it has a simple pattern: forward, recursive call, backward, turn left 120°. It must also keep track of levels, so we can define a base case to stop, and there is a length parameter, so the edges get smaller with each recursive call. When it reaches the base case, it stamps a triangle shape at that spot.

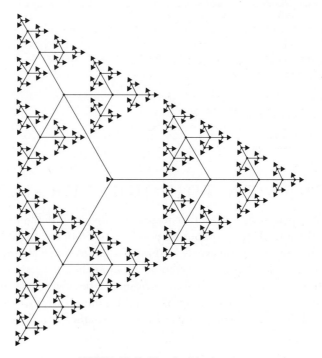

FIGURE 16.5 Sierpinski triangle.

Finally, a dot marks the start of each recursive call to help us observe the calls. As with the tree example, it is instructive to watch the Turtle Graphics slowly draw the triangle so that you can observe the recursive calls in action. See Code Listing 16.9.

Code Listing 16.9

```
# Draw Sierpinski figure

from turtle import *

def sierpinski(length, depth):
    if depth > 1: dot()   # mark position to better see recursion
    if depth == 0:        # base case
        stamp() # stamp a triangular shape
    else:
        forward(length)
        sierpinski(length/2, depth-1)   # recursive call
        backward(length)
        left(120)
        forward(length)
        sierpinski(length/2, depth-1)   # recursive call
        backward(length)
        left(120)
        forward(length)
        sierpinski(length/2, depth-1)   # recursive call
        backward(length)
        left(120)

sierpinski(200,6)
```

16.6 RECURSION TO NONRECURSION

We mentioned earlier that recursion provides a different way to view a problem, but it does not add any computing power to our tool kit. In fact, there exists an algorithm that can convert a recursive algorithm to a nonrecursive algorithm. Such an algorithm can be found in an algorithms textbook.[2] Because there is overhead in calling functions, the many function calls in a recursive algorithm can be slower than the non-recursive version. When that is the case, one can think of a solution recursively, write and test a recursive solution, and then convert the solution into a more efficient nonrecursive one.

---

[2] For example, Sedgewick, R., *Algorithms*, Addison-Wesley, 1988.

16.7 CONCLUSION

In this chapter, we introduced the concept of recursion. Some problems are naturally recursive, and this technique can be particularly effective for crafting a solution to such problems. For example, we show that fractals can be very complex, but many can be expressed with relatively simply recursive algorithms.

The recursive function syntax is simple: a function simply calls itself. However, a base case is needed at the beginning of the function so that the series of recursive calls will eventually terminate.

Exercises

1. A common task in an editor application, such as WordPad or TextEdit, is parentheses matching. For example, "(()())" is a valid string of parentheses, because each opening bracket has a corresponding closing bracket. On the other hand, "(()" is not a valid string. Another invalid example would be ")(", as the opening bracket should precede the closing bracket.

   Write a recursive function that takes a string as input and returns True if the string is valid with respect to matched parentheses. To simplify matters, begin by considering that the input string has only "(" or ")" and no other characters.

2. An XML file has entries of the type:

```
<abc>
    <xyz> Mother </xyz>
    <pqr> Father </pqr>
    <lmn> Brothers </lmn>
    <def> Sisters </def>
</abc>
```

   In this example, <abc> is a start tag and </abc> is the corresponding end tag, and so on for the others. Your task is to write a recursive function to check whether each start tag has a corresponding end tag in the correct order. Return *True* if the XML file is valid; otherwise, return *False*.

   The order is important here—the end tag for any tag cannot occur before its corresponding start tag.

3. When developing the Rational class, we created a function to calculate the greatest common denominator: gcd. Refactor the function to be recursive.

4. A recursive function to calculate the Fibonacci numbers was presented in this chapter. However, each time a number was calculated, it recalculated previous Fibonacci numbers. Refactor your recursive function to retain previous, already calculated

Fibonacci numbers and reference them instead of recalculating them. A list could be used, but a dictionary works better. The name for this technique is "memoization."

5. A formula exists for calculating the amount of money in a savings account that begins with an initial value (the initial principal, P), and earns interest with an annual interest rate i, for n years: $P(1 + i)^n$.

    Write a recursive function that calculates that same value, and check your result against the formula.

6. Converting decimal numbers to binary numbers can be done recursively. Write a function that takes a positive int argument and returns the corresponding binary number as an int composed of only ones and zeros. For example, `convert(5)` returns the int: 101.

    The insight for this problem comes from the fact that the rightmost digit of a decimal n is easy to calculate. It is the remainder when dividing by the base 2: $n\%2$. To get the next rightmost digit, you take the resulting quotient, i.e. $n_2 = n/2$, and find its remainder, $n_2\%2$, which is the next digit. Unfortunately, that generates the digits from right to left and we want them from left to right. We could easily do that non-recursively using string concatenation or string reversal, but in this exercise you are to use recursion to recursively calculate the digits. Effectively, you are letting recursion reverse the ordering: think in terms of calculating the rightmost digit as described previously, but then let recursion reverse the digits.

7. The United States still uses the traditional English system of measurement. Each inch on a ruler is marked off as fractions, using tick marks that look like this:

    The tallest tick mark falls at the center dividing into halves, two shorter tick marks indicate the quarter divisions, and even shorter ones are used to mark the eighths and sixteenths, and so on. Write the following recursive function:

    ```
    drawRuler(x, y, width, height)
    ```

    where (`x,y`) represents the lower-left corner of a rectangle that has dimensions `width` × `height`. The ruler will be drawn within that rectangle. The function draws a line along the rectangle's bottom edge, and then recursively draws vertical tick marks. The rectangle itself is not drawn. The middle-most tick mark is centered in the rectangle, and is as tall as the rectangle height. Each smaller tick mark is half the height of the next larger one. Once the tick marks become sufficiently small, the recursion terminates. The recursive insight to this problem is to recognize that the middle-most tick mark subdivides the rectangle into two smaller rectangles, each of which is a smaller ruler of its own. Use Turtle Graphics to draw the figure.

Getting and Using Python

A.1 ABOUT PYTHON

History

Python was conceived in the 1980s by Guido van Rossum, and the first version was published in 1991. Python was designed around a philosophy that emphasized the importance of programmer effort over computer effort, so it prioritized readability. Python is often characterized as minimalist, but only with respect to the core language's syntax and semantics. Both of these characteristics make it appropriate for a first language. The large number of modules developed to support Python allows it to be used in a wide variety of environments which greatly enhances its utility beyond a first language. That is, it offers the best of both worlds: it's readable and powerful to use.

An important goal of the Python developers was to make Python fun to use. This goal is reflected in the origin of the name (after the television series *Monty Python's Flying Circus*), in the common practice of using Monty Python references in example code, and in an occasionally playful approach to tutorials and reference materials. For example, although many programming languages choose the nonsense words *foo* or *bar* for arbitrary variable names in examples, one is more likely to find *nit* and *spam* in Python literature. We will hold to Python tradition.

Python is Free and Portable

It is important to note that the Python language and many of its components are *free*. It is also important to note that Python is *mostly* agnostic[1] when it comes to operating

---

[1] There are some aspects of Python that depend on the particular operating system being used, but for the most part Python works the same anywhere.

systems. You can run Python on a Windows machine, a Macintosh machine, or under any of the Unix variants out there, especially Linux. Even more useful is that fact that a Python program written on one kind of machine should run exactly the same on another without any changes being required.[2] This portability means that you can work in *your* favorite environment. You can also move to a new environment, and your Python program should run there as well. Very convenient!

You can download Python for the operating system of your choice from the Web at `http://www.python.org`. Go to the download section (currently on the left-hand side of the web page) and select the Python version that is right for you (actually, right for your computer, depending on the operating system that you are using). Download that package and install Python. You are now all set to begin experimenting!

Included in your Python download are hundreds of packages. If you are feeling adventurous, you can also browse the list of more packages (at the time of this writing, over 8667 supporting packages) at `http://pypi.python.org/pypi`.

What you get

When you install Python for your computer, you get a number of features:

- A Python "shell," a window into which you can directly type Python commands and where interaction between you and programs you write typically occurs.
- A simple editor called IDLE[3], in which you can type programs, update them, save them to disk ,and run them. IDLE's interface is essentially the same on any machine you run it, because it is a Python program!
- You get access to all the Python documentation on your local computer, including:
  - A tutorial to get you started
  - A language reference for any details you might want to investigate
  - A library reference for modules you might wish to import and use
  - Other nifty items

Starting Python Up

Let's get started with Python. To start the Python/IDLE combination on Windows, go to Start Menu $\Longrightarrow$ All Programs $\Longrightarrow$ Python 2.6 $\Longrightarrow$ IDLE (Python GUI), as shown in Figure A.1.

For the Mac (OS X), go to the Finder and Select Applications $\Longrightarrow$ Mac Python 2.6 $\Longrightarrow$ Idle.app, as shown in Figure A.2:

For Linux, it depends on the distribution you are using and even the window manager. If you just start a terminal session, you should be able to start the system by just typing

---

[2] The exceptions being when you use operating-system-specific code.
[3] Named after Monty Python actor Eric Idle.

FIGURE A.1 Starting Python in Windows XP.

FIGURE A.2 Starting Python in Mac OS X.

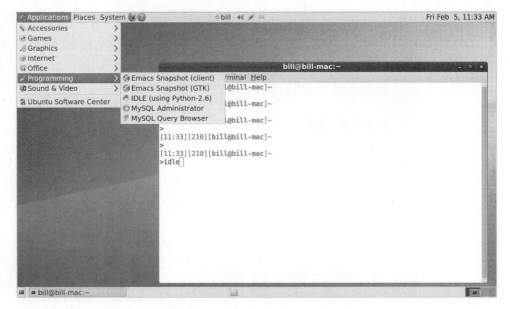

FIGURE A.3 Starting Python in Linux.

"idle." The window in Figure A.3 shows an Ubuntu Linux install in GNOME, with the two ways to start IDLE.

Working with Python

The good news is that no matter how you start it, you should get a window that looks like pretty much like Figure A.4 (this one is from XP).

What you type shows up after the $>>>$ prompt. When you type something and hit the Enter key, the result shows up on the next line(s). For example, go to the Python shell and type in the following:

```
1 + 1 <Enter Key>
print 'Hi Mom' <Enter Key>
```

The output you get should look like Figure A.5.

```
Python Shell                                                              _ □ X
File  Edit  Shell  Debug  Options  Windows  Help
Python 2.6.4 (r264:75708, Oct 26 2009, 08:23:19) [MSC v.1500 32 bit (Intel)] on
win32
Type "copyright", "credits" or "license()" for more information.

    ***************************************************************
    Personal firewall software may warn about the connection IDLE
    makes to its subprocess using this computer's internal loopback
    interface.  This connection is not visible on any external
    interface and no data is sent to or received from the Internet.
    ***************************************************************

IDLE 2.6.4
>>> |




                                                                    Ln: 12 Col: 4
```

FIGURE A.4 The Python interactive "shell."

```
Python Shell                                                              _ □ X
File  Edit  Shell  Debug  Options  Windows  Help
Python 2.6.4 (r264:75708, Oct 26 2009, 08:23:19) [MSC v.1500 32 bit (Intel)] on
win32
Type "copyright", "credits" or "license()" for more information.

    ***************************************************************
    Personal firewall software may warn about the connection IDLE
    makes to its subprocess using this computer's internal loopback
    interface.  This connection is not visible on any external
    interface and no data is sent to or received from the Internet.
    ***************************************************************

IDLE 2.6.4
>>> 1 + 1
2
>>> print 'Hi Mom'
Hi Mom
>>> |




                                                                    Ln: 16 Col: 4
```

FIGURE A.5 Typing your first Python commands.

Sometimes you can get some surprising results; sometimes an error. For example, try entering:

```
1 + 1.2 <Enter Key>
print hello <Enter Key>
```

The results would look like Figure A.6:

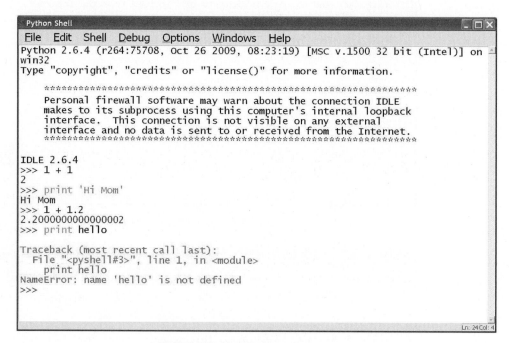

FIGURE A.6 How Python shows errors.

The last output shows that an error occurred. Because `hello` was not a variable and did not have quotes around it, ***print*** failed to perform.

Making a Program

Typing into the shell is useful, but the commands that you write there are not saved as a file and therefore cannot be reused. We need to save our commands in a file so we can run the program again and again, and more importantly, turn programs in as assignments!

To open a file, go to the shell window, and left-click on File $\implies$ New Window as shown in Figure A.7:

A second window will appear, into which you can type Python commands. This window is an editor window, into which you can type your first programs.

FIGURE A.7 Opening an editing session in IDLE to make a Python program.

There is a tradition in computer science: the first program you run in a new language is the Hello World program. This program does nothing put print the words *Hello World*. It is a tradition, because it does very little except focus on the mechanics of writing your first program and running it. There is a wikibooks.org page with more than 200 programming language examples of "Hello World" programs.[4] In Python, the Hello World program is very easy. Type the following in the Untitled window:

```
print 'Hello World'
```

The phrase after **print** should be in quotes. Having done that, we should save our first program so that we can use it again. How and where you save a file differs depending on your operating system. For XP, in the Untitled Window select the menu File ⟹ SaveAs. Your system will look something like Figure A.8:

This figure shows part of the way to save a file—not quite completed. It shows the file dialog, and there are a few things to note. First, we type the name of the file at the bottom of the dialog. The name I have chosen is helloWorld.py. The .py file extension is important to add. If you do not, then all the nice coloring and formatting you get in the IDLE editing window will be lost. Second, once saved, you will notice that the title of the editing window changes to the file name you used to save your program.

You can then run your module to see what your program produces. To run the program in the editing window menu, select Run ⟹ Run Module (see Figure A.9).

---

[4] http://en.wikibooks.org/wiki/List_of_hello_world_programs

FIGURE A.8 Saving your Python program.

FIGURE A.9 Running your Python program.

Congratulations—you wrote your first Python program. Celebrate with a Spam sandwich!

A Couple of Early Tips

Every time you make a change to a file, IDLE asks you to save the file before you run it. If you try to run it before you save, it will display the following dialog to remind you (Figure A.10).

FIGURE A.10 Python reminds you to save a file before you run it.

After saving the program, you will then be able to run the program.

After some time, you will come to find two keyboard shortcuts very useful. After you save the file for the first time, the keyboard combination Ctrl-S will re-save the file under the present file name (Command-S on a Mac). The key F5 will then run the program. So the combination Ctrl-S followed by F5 will help you try things out quickly and clean up errors as you go.

A.2 SOME CONVENTIONS FOR THIS BOOK

Looking at screen shots can be a bit tedious as the fonts can be small and hard to read. We have adopted the following conventions for both interactive and edited code in this book.

Interactive Code

When we type code that is interactive—that is, typing directly into the Python shell—we will frame the interaction as follows:

```
>>> print "Something"
Something
>>> 3 + 4 * 7
31
>>> 4/7    # watch out
0
>>> 7/4    # weird!
1
>>> 4.0/7.0
0.5714285714285714
>>> 7.0/4.0
1.75
```

Program: Written Code

When we display a program (written in IDLE), we will use code listings, as shown here:

```
Code Listing A.1

# calculate area of a triangle

base = 4
height = 3

area = 1.0/2.0 * base * height

print "Area is: ", area
```

Combined Program and Output

Sometimes we will display both a program and its output (after it was "run"), so we will use this type of code listing:

Code Listing A.2

```
# calculate area of a triangle

base = 4
height = 3

area = 1.0/2.0 * base * height

print "Area is: ", area
```

```
Area is:   6.0
>>>
```

A.3 SUMMARY

Now you have Python. You can begin to learn to program!

APPENDIX B

Simple Drawing with Turtle Graphics

TURTLE GRAPHICS IS A SIMPLE WAY TO DO GRAPHICS THAT DATES BACK TO THE 1960S. A `turtle` module has been included with standard distributions of Python, starting with version 2.X. The "turtle" is a cursor that you can control to draw on a palette. The last half-century of experience indicates that it is relatively easy for novice programmers to control a turtle by imagining that they are the turtle as it moves around.

A turtle has three attributes:

- A position
- An orientation
- A pen, with attributes such as color, width, and up versus down

Commands move a turtle relative to its current position, e.g., "move forward 10 spaces" or "turn right 45 degrees." The pen is carried by the turtle, and the pen can be up or down. If the pen is up, the turtle moves without drawing. If the pen is down, the turtle draws a line as it moves.

Let's begin by drawing a simple square. By default, the pen begins in the down (drawing) position. We loop four times: each time, we move forward and turn right 90 degrees. Figure B.1 shows a square drawn by the code in Code Listing B.1. Notice how the turtle starts in the middle of the screen pointing right.

Code Listing B.1

```
# draw a square
import turtle
```

631

```
for i in range(4):
    turtle.forward(50)
    turtle.right(90)
```

FIGURE B.1 Turtle square.

There are a large number of available commands. We will list some here—the remainder can be found in the documentation. There are two main groupings of commands: turtle movement and pen control. Table B.1 shows turtle movement commands; Table B.2 shows pen control commands. Many commands have abbreviations. Angle units default to degrees, but can be changed to radians.

forward(*distance*)	Move forward *distance* in current direction.
backward(*distance*)	Move backward *distance* in the opposite direction.
right(*angle*)	Turn right by *angle* units.
left(*angle*)	Turn left by *angle* units.
goto(*x,y*)	Move turtle to absolute position (*x,y*).
stamp()	Stamp a copy of the turtle shape at current position.
speed(*speed*)	Set turtle drawing *speed* as int in range 0.10.

TABLE B.1 Turtle movement commands.

Next we provide a small piece of code that calls a variety of commands to illustrate their use. The resulting random drawing is shown in Figure B.2.

pendown()	Put the pen down—drawing when moving.
penup()	Pull the pen up—no drawing when moving.
pensize(*width*)	Set the line thickness to *width*, a positive int.
pencolor(*colorstring*)	Set pen color, e.g., "red", "blue", . . .
pencolor(*r, g, b*)	Set pen color by specifying RGB values.
colormode(255)	Allows one to specify RGB values between 0 and 255.
fillcolor(*colorstring*)	Set fill color, e.g., "red", "blue", . . .
fillcolor(*r, g, b*)	Set fill color by specifying RGB values.
fill(True)	Call before drawing the shape you want to fill.
fill(False)	Call after the shape you want to fill.

TABLE B.2 Turtle pen commands.

FIGURE B.2 Turtle demo.

Code Listing B.2

```
# illustrate a variety of turtle commands
import turtle

turtle.forward(50)
turtle.stamp()
turtle.backward(90)
turtle.right(45)
```

```
turtle.penup()
turtle.forward(50)
turtle.pendown()
turtle.pensize(10)
turtle.forward(20)
turtle.colormode(255)
turtle.pencolor(240,160,80)
turtle.forward(20)
turtle.goto(-10,20)
turtle.left(90)
turtle.penup()
turtle.forward(50)
turtle.pendown()
turtle.right(90)
turtle.forward(50)
```

B.1 TIDBITS

Keeping the Window Open

The drawing window has a tendency to disappear very quickly. One way to "hold" the window is to use the `sleep` function in the time module, as follows:

```
import time
time.sleep(seconds)
```

The program will wait the number of seconds indicated before it ends.

Working Nicely With IDLE

IDLE does not tend to work well with other graphics windows. Subsequently, after you open a program in IDLE that does graphics (such as Turtle), some of the windows may hang, or not close. To get around this, you can use the `os._exit(1)` function from the `os` module. Note the underline in the name. Make the `os._exit(1)` function the last line in the program. Using the `time.sleep` call right before the `os._exit(1)` call works well so that the window will stay open for some number of seconds and then close.

```
import os
os._exit(1)
```

APPENDIX C

Plotting and Numeric
Tools: A Quick Survey

None of us is as smart as all of us.

Ken Blanchard

As we have said previously, one of the strengths of Python is its fantastic user base—in particular, the many useful modules that those users provide. In fact, this is exactly what open source software is about—the sharing of effort for the good of all users.

In this chapter, we will take a brief look at the `numpy` and `matplotlib` modules. Note that examples of their use are sprinkled throughout the book, so this appendix stands as a jumping-off point for more details.

C.1 MATPLOTLIB

Matplotlib is a software package provided for creating figures. As matplotlib itself puts it:

matplotlib is a python 2D plotting library (and soon some 3D) which produces publication quality figures in a variety of hard copy formats and interactive environments across platforms. . . . matplotlib tries to make easy things easy and hard things possible.

As you have seen in some of the examples (see Figure 2.10 or Figure 2.11 and their associated code), it is relatively easy to do simple 2D plotting. However, matplotlib is *not* part of the standard Python distribution. It requires that you download some extra packages into your existing Python environment. Once downloaded and installed, matplotlib can be used in your Python code.

Getting matplotlib

As is true for many open software projects, matplotlib is hosted by SourceForge. SourceForge (`http://sourceforge.net`) is the largest open source collection on the Internet. As of February 2009, SourceForge reported it was hosting more 230,000 projects, with more than 2 million registered users.

The matplotlib web site is `http://matplotlib.sourceforge.net`

The Simplest Way

The simplest way to get matplotlib, and a lot of other tools not packaged with the standard Python distribution, is to get an *augmented* Python distribution that comes with all the extra tools preinstalled! In this way, you can not only get all of the standard Python distribution, and not only matplotlib, but also a host of other tools that you can explore as you wish. Two such distributions exist that can be downloaded off the Internet:

- **Enthought Python Distribution (EPD)**. The EPD (`http://www.enthought.com/products/epd.php`) distribution contains approximately 100 extra modules in its distribution. The download is free for educational use and requires a nominal fee otherwise. It is available for multiple platforms, including Windows, Macintosh, and Linux.
- **Python(x,y)**. Python(x,y) (`http://www.pythonxy.com/foreword.php`) is a Python distribution focused on scientific and numeric computation, data visualization, and data analysis. It is specific to the Windows platform only.

If you have not yet installed Python, take a look at these distributions as a possible alternatives. Installing one of these might save you a bit of time when it comes to adding modules later.

The Standard Way

The standard way to install any Python module is to begin with the standard Python distribution, then add modules as you need them by downloading the module from the Internet. There are even a couple of ways to do the downloading.[1] The simplest way is to go to the appropriate web site, download the package, then install it.

Dependencies

One problem with this approach is called a *dependency*. A dependency occurs when a module that you download requires another module to function. A dependency necessitates

---

[1] If you are interested, take a look the easy_install package (http://peak.telecommunity.com/DevCenter/EasyInstall) in setuptools, which will do a pretty good job of downloading a module, as well as any module it depends on.

downloading the dependency module *before* you download the module you are interested in. Sometimes tracking dependencies can be complicated, which is why we bring it up here.

Matplotlib has one dependency. It requires that you download the Numeric Python (always shortened to numpy, great name!) package first. We will discuss Numeric Python in the next section, but for now you just need to have it before we can do plotting.

Platform and Python version.

One other thing to worry about when downloading a Python module off the Web is getting the right one which means two things:

- You need to get the correct version for your platform. Depending on what kind of computer you have, you need to get the correct distribution. Windows distributions come with an installer, typically with a suffix of .exe or .msi. Macintosh distributions come as a disk image, usually with a suffix of .dmg. Linux distributions often come as tar files with a suffix of .tar.gz or .tar.zip.[2] Make sure to select the distribution that is correct for your platform. It is not hard to do, but it does require that you pay attention.
- You need to get the correct Python version for the Python on your machine. There are different versions of Python, each with its own unique numeric identifiers. Because Python is a language that is under constant development, these numeric identifiers are useful for developers to identify the particular characteristics of any Python distribution.

  Consider the current 2.x Python version (as of the writing of this book), Python 2.6.2. The first number is referred to as the *major* number, the second the *minor* number and the third the *maintenance* number. Python versions with different major numbers are very different. Python 3.0, which is discussed in Appendix D, is significantly different from any Python whose version number is 2 or 1. Differences in minor numbers on a Python distribution indicate more subtle differences between versions. Thus Python 2.6 is similar to, but not the same as, Python 2.5 . The maintenance number indicates the level of bug fixes that have been applied. There is no difference in Python 2.6.1 and 2.6.2 except that more bug fixes have been applied to the latter.

  When you download a module, you must download it such that the module matches the major and minor number of your Python distribution. The maintenance number is not relevant for compatibility.

Thus, for my local machine (a Macintosh) running Python 2.6.2, I would be sure to select a Mac distribution for Python 2.6 of any module I download.

Download numpy

Go to the numpy web site (`http://numpy.scipy.org`), select the Download link and download the correct platform and version number for your computer.

---

[2] Most Linux distributions would use some type of package manager to load a new Python module.

How you start the actual install depends on your computer type. For Windows, double-clicking the downloaded file should start the installation. For the Mac, the disk image should open up and allow you to start the install. For Linux, again, a package manager should get the process going.

Test that numpy works.

Before you go any farther, it would be good to make sure that numpy was installed properly. Open up Python (through IDLE or however you typically do it), and type the following into the shell:

```
>>> import numpy
>>> numpy.__version__
'1.2.1'
>>>
```

Numpy has a version as well, and its version number should be greater than 1.1 to work properly with matplotlib.

Now matplotlib

If numpy worked, then next install matplotlib. Go the matplotlib web site (`http://matplotlib.sourceforge.net`) and, as with numpy, download the proper matplotlib for your platform and Python version. As with numpy, install matplotlib.

Test that matplotlib works.

Try the following to see if your matplotlib installed properly:

```
>>> import pylab
>>> pylab.plot([5,4,3,2,1])
[<matplotlib.lines.Line2D object at 0x1fed8b0>]
>>> pylab.show()
>>>
```

You should get a new window with a plot, titled Figure 1, as in Figure C.1.

Warning About IDLE Shell and matplotlib

IDLE and matplotlib do not always "play well" with each other. They are essentially sharing the graphics routines that draw to your screen and they sometimes get confused. It may

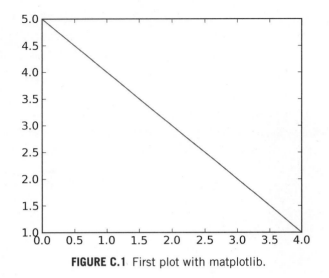

FIGURE C.1 First plot with matplotlib.

require that you stop Python and restart. If this is a problem, you can always run your programs from a command line—covered next.

Working from the Command Line

Although IDLE is a great way to get started with Python, you may find that other editors are more to your liking. That is fine—Python is not restricted to working with IDLE. In fact, many people develop Python code using a variety of editors.

There are many Integrated Development Environments (or IDEs) that work well with Python. The Python wiki page (`http://wiki.python.org/moin`) is a good place to find out information about current IDEs for Python.

Whatever your editor (including IDLE), a common way to execute Python code is to use what is variously called a *terminal* or *command line*. All current operating systems provide access to a command line window.

The name "command line" or "terminal" is pretty descriptive of these applications' functioning. They are windows into which you can type commands to perform various tasks. It turns out that the list of commands is quite long and, occasionally complicated, but a command line is a useful way to interact with your computer, one that does not involve a mouse or a graphic user interface (GUI). More importantly, it is also a way to run a Python program!

Both Linux and Mac come with a terminal. The Mac Terminal.app can be found in Applications $\Longrightarrow$ Utilities. Both allow you to either start a Python interactive session by typing `python`, or to run a Python program you have edited by typing `python yourProgram.py`. Most Python programs are stored with the suffix ".py".

FIGURE C.2 (a) the Control Panel search. (b) the System Properties panel.

Setting Up the Windows Command Line.

Windows makes things a little harder. You can launch the command line by either clicking on the Start button, and typing in cmd and clicking Run, or by going to Computer ⟹ Local Disk (C:) ⟹ Windows ⟹ System32 and clicking on the "cmd" application. However, once up, if you type python in the window, you will get an error. What to do?

We need to inform Windows where Python is stored so the command line can run it. There are various methods, but here is the quickest (yes, there are longer ways):

1. Go to the Start Menu, and select the Control Panel on the right-hand side.
2. In the Control Panel, type "system path" (no quotes) in the top right-hand corner. Select "Edit the system environment variables," as shown in Figure C.2.
3. In the System Properties window that pops up, select the Environment Variables Button at the bottom right.
4. In the Environment Variables window that pops up, look at the lower pane, named System Variables. Scroll down until you see a variable named "Path." Select that line and click Edit (see Figure C.3).
5. In the Edit System Variable window that pops up, we have to edit the values listed in Path, listed in the pane called Variable Value. Select the pane and use the arrow keys to reach the end of the line. Add the following to the end of the line, exactly as typed: ;C:\Python26;C:\Python26\Lib\idlelib. This assumes that you installed Python 2.6 in the "standard" or default location. Change the names (Python25 or Python30) to suit your distribution.

FIGURE C.3 (a) the Environment Variables. (b) editing the Path value.

Once you complete this, you should be able to open a command line and type in Python commands or start IDLE.

C.2 WORKING WITH MATPLOTLIB

Examples of working matplotlib code will be sprinkled throughout the book, but there are some wonderful repositories of more complicated examples at the matplotlib web site. In particular, the gallery (`http://matplotlib.sourceforge.net/gallery.html`) provides a number of beautiful examples of what you can do with matplotlib!

Let's quickly review some of the basic plotting commands. Remember, the online documentation is very good and provides a great deal of detail as well as examples.

Plot Command

The `plot` command allows you to make two-dimensional line drawings. We first *import* `pylab`, then we can do plots of the following kinds:

- `pylab.plot(xVals,yVals)`: Assumes two lists of numeric values of equal length. Plot with default properties.

- `pylab.plot(yVals)`: Creates *x* values in range of 0 to `len(yVals)-1`. Plot with default properties.
- `pylab.plot(xVals, yVals, 'bo')`: Plot the *x* and *y* values, modify the line type to blue circles.
- `pylab.plot(xVals,yVals, 'gx', xVals2, yVals2, 'y+')`: Plot with two graphs in the same window. First plot is xVals vs. yVals with green x's, second plot is xVals2 vs. yVals2 with yellow +'s.

See the online documentation for all the variations on color and line styles.

Plot Properties

There are a number of properties you can attach to a plot. Here are some simple examples:

- The x-axis can be labeled in your plot using the `pylab.xlabel('aString')` command. The provided string will be used as an x-axis label.
- The y-axis can also be labeled in your plot using the `pylab.ylabel('aString')` command. Again the string will be used and printed vertically along the y-axis.
- The figure can be given a title (which shows up just above the plot) using the command `pylab.title('aString')`.
- The figure can have a grid superimposed on the plot area. The command is `pylab.grid(True)`.

The program in Code Listing C.1 shows the sine plot from earlier with labels, as shown in Figure C.4.

Code Listing C.1

```python
import math
import pylab
import numpy

# use numpy arange to get an array of float values.
x_values = numpy.arange(0,math.pi*4,0.1)
y_values = [math.sin(x) for x in x_values]
pylab.plot(x_values,y_values)
pylab.xlabel('x values')
pylab.ylabel('sine of x')
pylab.title('Plot of sine from 0 to 4pi')
pylab.grid(True)
pylab.show()
```

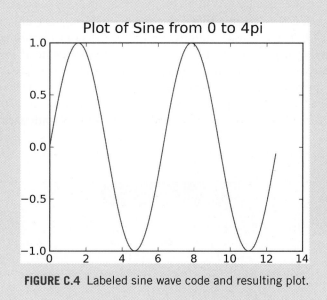

FIGURE C.4 Labeled sine wave code and resulting plot.

Tick Labels

Matplotlib provides a command to orient and label each x-axis entry. These entries are often called "ticks," so the commands to label them are called xticks and yticks. If you do not provide such a command, matplotlib will label the ticks with the appropriate number. However, you have the option to say what each tick label should be and where it should be located.

The xticks command can take a number of arguments. The first is the location of the tick being placed. A *range* can be used by numpy to center the label in the middle of the tick. This means we can add a bar width to each element and divide by 2 to center, such as numpy.arange(5)+barWidth/2.0. The second argument is the list of labels. The remaining arguments are optional; for example, the rotation argument to describe label orientation. See Section 6.9 for an example.

Bar Graphs

The bar command also takes a number of arguments. The first is the xtick locations, typically a numpy *arange*. The second is the list of values to plot. The remaining arguments are optional, such as the width and the color arguments. See Section 6.9 for an example.

Histograms

A histogram is a graph that shows the number of elements within a range of values. The range, called a *bin*, is used uniformly for all the data in the histogram. Thus, the x-axis indicates the various bins, and the y-axis the number of elements in each bin.

The command for a histogram is `pylab.hist`. There are a number of arguments that can be provided, but the two most important are the list of values and the number of bins. For example, the program in Code Listing C.2 generates 10,000 values, randomly distributed between 0 and 1000. We allow for 100 bins (thus each bin is of size 10, 100 bins for a range from 0–1000). Note that the distribution is fairly, but not exactly, equal in all bins. See Code Listing C.2 with the associated Figure C.5.

Code Listing C.2

```python
import pylab
import random

x_values = [random.randint(0,1000) for x in range(10000)]

pylab.hist(x_values,100)
pylab.xlabel('bins of size 10')
pylab.ylabel('frequency')
pylab.title('plot of 10,000 random ints 0-1000, bins of size 10')
pylab.show()
```

FIGURE C.5 Histogram code and its associated plot.

Pie Charts

Pie charts show the percentage of the whole that each value in the list occupies. The command is `pylab.pie(values,...)` and provides for each element in the given value the percentage (oneValue/sum(values)) that each value occupies in a list. It takes a number of optional arguments, but two very useful ones are:

- `colors=(...)`, a list of strings, each a single letter indicating a color. This is the progression of colors in the pie chart. The length of this list must be the same as the number of values in the chart.
- `labels=(...)`, a list of strings, each one a label for its corresponding pie value. It also must have the same number of entries as the number of values being plotted.

An example pie chart is provided in Figure C.6 for Code Listing C.3.

Code Listing C.3

```
import pylab

values = [10,20, 50,100,200,1000]
pieLabels = ['first','second','third','fourth','fifth','sixth']

# these are the default colors. You get these if you do not provide any
colorLst = ('b', 'g', 'r', 'c', 'm', 'y', 'k', 'w')

pylab.pie(values,labels=pieLabels,colors=colorLst)
pylab.title('Pie chart of 6 values')
pylab.show()
```

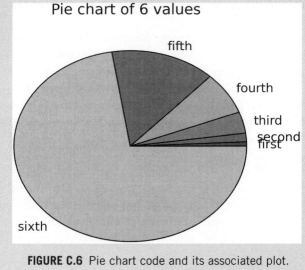

FIGURE C.6 Pie chart code and its associated plot.

C.3 NUMERIC PYTHON (NUMPY)

Numeric Python—or, as it is called, "numpy"—is the base module for scientific, mathematical, and engineering computing in Python. It implements a special *array* data type that is efficient, can be manipulated easily, and interfaces with other programming languages (C, C++, Fortran, and others).

As with plotting, a full discussion of numpy is out of the scope of this book, but we can take a quick tour and show you how useful numpy is.

Arrays Are Not Lists

The basic unit of numpy is the `array`. An array is a sequence, similar to a list, but differs in two important ways:

- Arrays can consist only of numbers.
- The type of the numbers must be the same throughout the entire array.

Arrays can be indexed, sliced, and iterated through, just like lists, but only with numbers and only with the same type of number (integer or floats) throughout the entire array.

Creating a numpy Array

An array is created by one of two general methods:

- Using the `array` constructor. The array constructor takes a *single* sequence of same-type, numeric elements and creates an array, for example `aray=numpy.array ([10,20,30])`.
- Numpy provides a separate range function called `arange()`. Like *range*, it takes three potential arguments (the begin value, the end value, and the increment value), but it differs in that it can also work with floats. For example: `aray=arange(0, math.pi*4, 0.1)`, generates the sequence from 0 to 4*π by increments of 0.1.
- Two special array constructors are `zeros` and `ones`. They create arrays of all 0's or all 1's. The argument can be a type of *n* values, and an *n*-dimensional array will be created.

Manipulating Arrays

Arrays can be manipulated in ways that lists cannot. Because the type of an array is fixed at its creation (a float or integer array), you can perform mathematical operations on the entire array using an approach called *broadcasting*. By broadcasting, numpy means that a single operation is "broadcast" across the entire array. For example:

- `aray * 4` multiplies each element of the numpy array `aray` by 4. The other operations of +, -, / would produce similar results.

- `aray + aray` adds each element of `aray` together, creating a third array of values. The two numpy arrays must be of the same "shape," which for us really means of the same dimension (length).

The following code (Code Listing C.4) will generate a normal distribution of 10,000 values with a $\mu = 100$ and $\sigma = 15$, which is then plotted as a histogram (see Figure C.7).

Code Listing C.4

```python
import numpy
import pylab

vals = numpy.ones((10000))
vals = vals * 100
# standard distribution, 10,000 elements, mu = 0, std = 1
sigma = numpy.random.standard_normal(10000)
sigma = sigma*15
# generate a standard distribution, mu = 100, std = 15
vals = vals + sigma
pylab.hist(vals,100)
pylab.show()
```

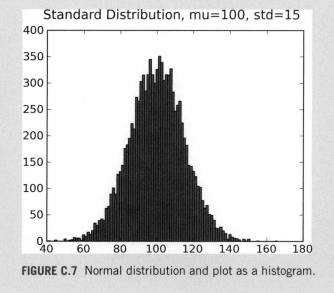

FIGURE C.7 Normal distribution and plot as a histogram.

Python 3.0

IN THE FALL OF 2008, A NEW VERSION OF PYTHON, NAMED PYTHON 3.0, WAS introduced, which is not completely backward-compatible with previous versions of Python, referred to as Python 2.x. In this appendix, we take a brief look at the differences as they relate to this text. Because the Python 3.0 specification was available when this text was written, we had it in mind, so that the students who learn Python 2.x from this text will have an easier time transitioning to Python 3.0.

Why didn't we simply write the text for Python 3.x (for whatever x represents the present version number)? There are three reasons:

1. Python 2.x will dominate for many years.
2. The Python community will take years to get modules rewritten to 3.x.
3. Once the transition is complete, the changes for an introductory course are small.

Details can be found at `http://docs.python.org/3.0/`, but here we point out the changes that affect the subset of Python covered in this introductory text. There are many differences beyond the subset covered here.

D.1 SIMPLER BUILT-IN TYPES

In Python 3.x, the type *str* expands to be able to handle Unicode—a representation that is supposed to handle all international languages, not just English. More precisely, Unicode existed in Python 2.x (known as the type `unicode`), but in 3.X is now the default. Our use of the string built-in type is unaffected in Python 3.x.

D.2 UNSURPRISING ARITHMETIC

Python 3.x has changed the division operator: 1/2 now returns 0.5. More precisely, the division symbol "/" now returns a `float`. To get the quotient of two integers, one now doubles the symbol, "//", so that 1//2 returns 0. That is, with the `int` type, one must use "//" in Python 3.x to get the behavior of "/" in Python 2.x. The double-slash operator ("//") exists in Python 2.x, but it was rarely used. The behavior of the modulo (remainder) operator "%" is unchanged.

This change will likely make Python 3.x arithmetic more familiar to novices. However, it will complicate the transition to C-based languages such as C, C++, C#, and Java, which use the Python 2.x interpretation of the integer operator "/". In addition, the change affects many examples in this text—albeit in a trivial way: simply replace integer "/" with "//".

D.3 CLEANER COMPARISONS

Comparisons between incompatible types is now an error. That is, the nonsensical 3 < `'cat'` is an error, specifically a `TypeError` exception.

Python 2.x returned a seemingly random Boolean from such mismatched comparisons. A consequence of this change is that the sorting of incompatible types will now fail—likely a good thing.

We avoided comparisons of incompatible types in this text.

D.4 CONSISTENT I/O

An inconsistency exists in that input uses a function (*raw_input*), whereas output used the ***print*** statement. You likely didn't notice, but inconsistency is generally a bad idea so Python 3.x has resolved this one by making ***print*** a function. Most of the difference is that you will need to use parentheses around the arguments—a small change. For example,

```
print "Hello World!"
```
becomes
```
print("Hello World!")
```

The new ***print*** function includes the option of specifying the character that separates output (`sep`) as well as the character that terminates the output (`end`).

The C-style output formatting that we covered (using "%") is still accepted, but a new style of formatting has been introduced. If you have become comfortable with the C-style output, you can still use it, but if it didn't appeal to you, try the new style.

For input, we always used *raw_input*, but a function named `input` existed. In Python 3.x, the `input` function has replaced the *raw_input* functions used in this text. You only need to change the name. For example:

```
someStr = input("Enter a string: ")
print(someStr)
```

D.5 ITERATOR CHANGES

The consistency and performance of some frequently used functions and methods have been improved. This is the case for *range* and the dictionary methods, *dict*.keys, *dict*.items, and *dict*.values. They no longer return lists. However, we used them almost exclusively as iterators in **for** statements, and in that context they perform the same. We seldom used zip, but it also no longer returns a list. If you need a list, you can easily get a list in Python 3.x by coercing one, e.g., x = *list(dict*.keys()).

D.6 STRING MODULE

We used the string module in several examples. To be consistent with the change for strings to handle Unicode by default, the string module changes string.letters to string.ascii_letters. The string.lowercase and string. uppercase are similarly changed.

D.7 CONVERSION

To assist in conversion, the default Python 2.x installation comes with code to implement conversion from Python 2.x. The program is named 2to3.py, and will likely successfully convert the code that most novices create.

D.8 TEXT EXAMPLES IN PYTHON 3.X

The examples used in the text will be converted to Python 3.x, and made available online.

D.9 CONCLUSION

This brief appendix only touches on only a small part of the many significant changes in Python 3.x. Our goal was not to present Python 3.x, but to show the small difference between what is covered in this text and what is needed for these concepts in Python 3.x.

Table of ASCII Values

THE FIRST STANDARDIZED SET OF COMPUTER CHARACTERS WAS THE ASCII (AMERICAN Standard Code for Information Interchange) set developed in 1963 and reproduced in Table E.1.

653

Char	Dec	Char	Dec	Char	Dec	Char	Dec
NUL	0	SP	32	@	64	`	96
SOH	1	!	33	A	65	a	97
STX	2	"	34	B	66	b	98
ETX	3	#	35	C	67	c	99
EOT	4	$	36	D	68	d	100
ENQ	5	%	37	E	69	e	101
ACK	6	&	38	F	70	f	102
BEL	7	'	39	G	71	g	103
BS	8	(	40	H	72	h	104
HT	9	)	41	I	73	i	105
LF	10	*	42	J	74	j	106
VT	11	+	43	K	75	k	107
FF	12	,	44	L	76	l	108
CR	13	-	45	M	77	m	109
SO	14	.	46	N	78	n	110
SI	15	/	47	O	79	o	111
DLE	16	0	48	P	80	p	112
DC1	17	1	49	Q	81	q	113
DC2	18	2	50	R	82	r	114
DC3	19	3	51	S	83	s	115
DC4	20	4	52	T	84	t	116
NAK	21	5	53	U	85	u	117
SYN	22	6	54	V	86	v	118
ETB	23	7	55	W	87	w	119
CAN	24	8	56	X	88	x	120
EM	25	9	57	Y	89	y	121
SUB	26	:	58	Z	90	z	122
ESC	27	;	59	[	91	{	123
FS	28	<	60	\	92	|	124
GS	29	=	61	]	93	}	125
RS	30	>	62	∧	94	~	126
US	31	?	63	_	95	DEL	127

TABLE E.1 Table of ASCII characters.

Precedence

Operator	Description
()	Parentheses (grouping)
f(args. . .), x[i:i], x[i], x.attr	Fuction call, slicing, subscript, dot
**	Exponentiation
+x, -x, ~x	Positive, negative, bitwise NOT
*, /, %	Multiplication, division, remainder
+, -	Addition, subtraction
<<, >>	Shifts
&	Bitwise AND
^	Bitwise XOR
|	Bitwise OR
<, <=, >, >=, !=, ==, is, is not, in, not in	Comparisons, identity, membership
not x	Boolean NOT
and	Boolean AND
or	Boolean OR
lambda	Lambda expression

TABLE F.1 Precedence of Python operators: highest to lowest.

INDEX

Symbols

' (apostrophe) in strings, 206
* (asterisk)
  ** (exponentiation) operator, 64, 107
  *= (multiplication and assignment) operator
  multiplication operator, 62, 64, 107,
    254, 498
  repetition in strings, 184
  repetition in tuples, 281
\ (backslash)
  line continuation, 45, 208, 217
  Windows directory paths, 409
: (colon)
  :: (double colon) in index operator, 181
  denoting range in index operator, 179
  separating key/value pairs, 57
, (comma)
  separating list items, 57
  in tuples, 281
{ } (curly braces), indicating dictionaries, 57
. (dot) notation, 463
= (equal) sign
  = = (equal to) operator, 81, 102–104, 107
    list comparisons, 255
    special method equivalent
      to, 498
    string comparisons, 186
  assignment operator, 50
  confusing = and = = in programming, 101
> > > prompt in Python shell, 596

> (greater than) operator, 81, 107, 498
  list comparisons, 255
  string comparisons, 186
>= (greater than or equal to) operator, 81,
    107, 498
  list comparisons, 255
< (less than) operator, 81, 107, 498
  list comparisons, 255
  string comparisons, 186
<= (less than or equal to) operator, 81, 107, 255, 498
– (minus sign)
– = (subtraction and assignment) operator, 64
  subtraction operator, 62, 63, 107, 498
  unary minus operator, 107
! = (not equal to) operator, 81, 107, 255, 498
( ) (parentheses)
  delimiting tuples, 281
  grouping operator, 107
  operator precedence and, 63
+ (plus sign)
  += (addition and assignment) operator, 64
  addition operator, 59, 62, 63, 107, 498
  concatenating lists, 254
  concatenating strings, 59, 184
  concatenating tuples, 281
  deciding if addition or concatenation, 185
  overloading, 498
  unary operator, 107
' (quotation marks, single) in strings, 57
" (quotation marks, double) in strings, 57
""" (quotation marks, triple) in strings, 176, 230

657